Scale 1:250,000
or 3.95 miles to 1 inch
(2.5km to 1cm)

35th edition June 2012

Revised version of the atlas formerly known as *Complete Atlas of Britain*. Original edition printed 1979.

Cartography:
All cartography in this atlas edited, designed and produced by the Mapping Services Department of AA Publishing (A04866).

Publisher's Notes:
Published by AA Publishing (a trading name of AA Media Limited, whose registered office is Fanum House, Basing View, Basingstoke, Hampshire RG21 4EA, UK. Registered number 06112600).

ISBN: 978 0 7495 7352 2

A CIP catalogue record for this book is available from The British Library.

Disclaimer:
The contents of this atlas are believed to be correct at the time of the latest revision, it will not contain any subsequent amended, new or temporary information including diversions and traffic control or enforcement systems. The publishers cannot be held responsible or liable for any loss or damage occasioned to any person acting or refraining from action as a result of any use or reliance on material in this atlas, nor for any errors, omissions or changes in such material. This does not affect your statutory rights.

The publishers would welcome information to correct any errors or omissions and to keep this atlas up to date. Please write to the Atlas Editor, AA Publishing, The Automobile Association, Fanum House, Basing View, Basingstoke, Hampshire RG21 4EA, UK.
E-mail: *roadatlasfeedback@theaa.com*

Acknowledgements:
AA Publishing would like to thank the following for their assistance in producing this atlas:
RoadPilot® Information on fixed speed camera locations provided by and © 2012 RoadPilot® Driving Technology.
Crematoria data provided by the Cremation Society of Great Britain. Cadw, English Heritage, Forestry Commission, Historic Scotland, Johnsons, National Trust and National Trust for Scotland, RSPB, The Wildlife Trust, Scottish Natural Heritage, Natural England, The Countryside Council for Wales (road maps).

Transport for London (Central London Map), Nexus (Newcastle district map).

Printer:
Printed in Italy by Canale & C S.p.A.
Paper: 90gsm Matt.

Atlas contents

UBLIN
Dún Laoghaire
(Apr-Sept)
EPUBLIC
OF
RELAND
(July-Sept)
Holyhead
Anglesey
Llandudno
Colwyn Bay
Rhyl
Bangor
Conwy
Abergele
Bethesda
Denbigh
Caernarfon
SNOWDONIA
Betws-y-coed
Birkenhead
Widnes
Warrington
John Lennon
Runcorn
Knuts
Holywell
Ellesmere Port
Northwich
Queensferry
Mold
Chester
Ruthin
Crewe
Kids
Nantwich
Wrexham
Newcastle-under-Lyme
Llangollen
Whitchurch
46
Pwllheli
Porthmadog
Bala
Abersoch
Oswestry
Market Drayton
Barmouth
Dolgellau
Newport
Shrewsbury
Welshpool
Telford
38
Machynlleth
Church Stretton
WOLVERHAMPTO
Bridgnorth
36
Cardigan Bay
Newtown
Stourbrid
Hale
Aberystwyth
WALES
Llangurig
Kidderminster
Ludlow
Broms
Rhayader
Knighton
Aberaeron
Tregaron
Llandrindod Wells
Leominster
Worceste
Kington
Cardigan
Lampeter
Builth Wells
Great Malvern
24
Fishguard
Newcastle Emlyn
26
Llandovery
Hay-on-Wye
28
Hereford
Ledbury
St David's
Brecon
Carmarthen
Llandeilo
BRECON BEACONS
Ross-on-Wye
PEMBROKESHIRE COAST
Haverfordwest
St Clears
Abergavenny
Gloucester
Monmouth
Milford Haven
Merthyr Tydfil
Pembroke Dock
Pembroke
Tenby
Llanelli
Neath
Cwmbran
Chepstow
Swansea
Pontypridd
Port Talbot
Newport
Avonmouth
Bridgend
CARDIFF
16
Cardiff
Clevedon
BRISTOL
Bath
Weston-super-Mare
Bristol
Bristol Channel
Cheddar
Frome
Motorway
Toll motorway
Primary route dual carriageway
Primary route single carriageway
Other A road
Vehicle ferry
Fast vehicle ferry or catamaran
National Park
36
Atlas page number
14
Lundy
Ilfracombe
Lynton
Minehead
Wells
Shepton Mallet
EXMOOR
Glastonbury
Bridgwater
Barnstaple
Wincanton
Bideford
Great Torrington
South Molton
Taunton
Yeovil
Ilminster
Sherborne
Tiverton
Chard
Crewkerne
Bude
Hatherleigh
6
Crediton
Holsworthy
Exeter
Honiton
Axminster
Bridport
Okehampton
Dorche
Exeter
Lyme Regis
4
Launceston
DARTMOOR
Exmouth
Weymo
Dawlish
Wadebridge
Tavistock
Teignmouth
Fortuneswell
2
Newquay
Bodmin
Buckfastleigh
Newton Abbot
Newquay
Liskeard
Plymouth
Torquay
Isles of Scilly inset
Lostwithiel
Saltash
PLYMOUTH
Totnes
Paignton
Torpoint
St Austell
Channel Islands inset
Dartmouth
Guernsey
Jersey
St-Malo
Redruth
Truro
Kingsbridge
Camborne
Penzance
Falmouth
Land's End
Helston
Santander (Mar-Oct)
Roscoff
Lizard

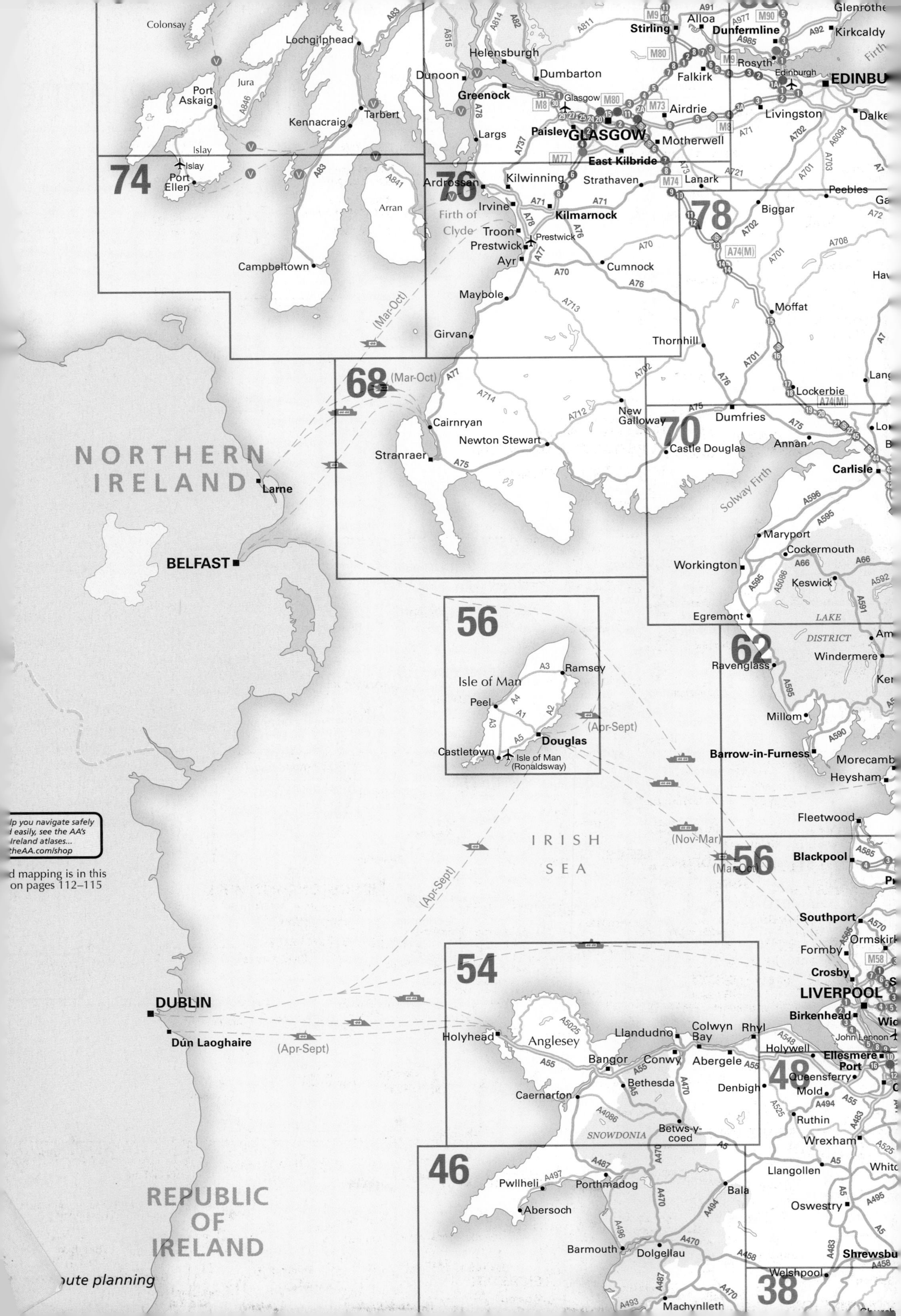

74
76
78
68
70
56
62
56
54
48
46
38
NORTHERN IRELAND
REPUBLIC OF IRELAND
IRISH SEA
BELFAST
Larne
DUBLIN
Dún Laoghaire
(Apr-Sept)
(Mar-Oct)
(Nov-Mar)
Colonsay
Lochgilphead
Jura
Port Askaig
Islay
Port Ellen
Kennacraig
Tarbert
Campbeltown
Arran
Firth of Clyde
Dunoon
Greenock
Helensburgh
Dumbarton
Largs
Paisley
GLASGOW
Motherwell
East Kilbride
Airdrie
Stirling
Alloa
Dunfermline
Kirkcaldy
Glenrothes
Rosyth
Falkirk
Livingston
EDINBU
Ardrossan
Kilwinning
Strathaven
Lanark
Irvine
Kilmarnock
Troon
Prestwick
Ayr
Cumnock
Maybole
Girvan
Thornhill
Biggar
Peebles
Moffat
Lockerbie
Cairnryan
Stranraer
Newton Stewart
New Galloway
Castle Douglas
Dumfries
Annan
Carlisle
Solway Firth
Maryport
Cockermouth
Workington
Keswick
Egremont
LAKE DISTRICT
Ravenglass
Windermere
Millom
Barrow-in-Furness
Morecamb
Heysham
Fleetwood
Blackpool
Southport
Ormskirk
Formby
Crosby
LIVERPOOL
Birkenhead
Isle of Man
Ramsey
Peel
Douglas
Castletown
Isle of Man (Ronaldsway)
Holyhead
Anglesey
Llandudno
Colwyn Bay
Rhyl
Bangor
Conwy
Abergele
Holywell
Ellesmere Port
Queensferry
Mold
Denbigh
Bethesda
Caernarfon
Ruthin
SNOWDONIA
Betws-y-coed
Wrexham
Llangollen
Pwllheli
Porthmadog
Bala
Abersoch
Oswestry
Barmouth
Dolgellau
Shrewsbu
Welshpool
Machynlleth
lp you navigate safely
d easily, see the AA's
Ireland atlases...
theAA.com/shop
d mapping is in this
on pages 112–115
oute planning

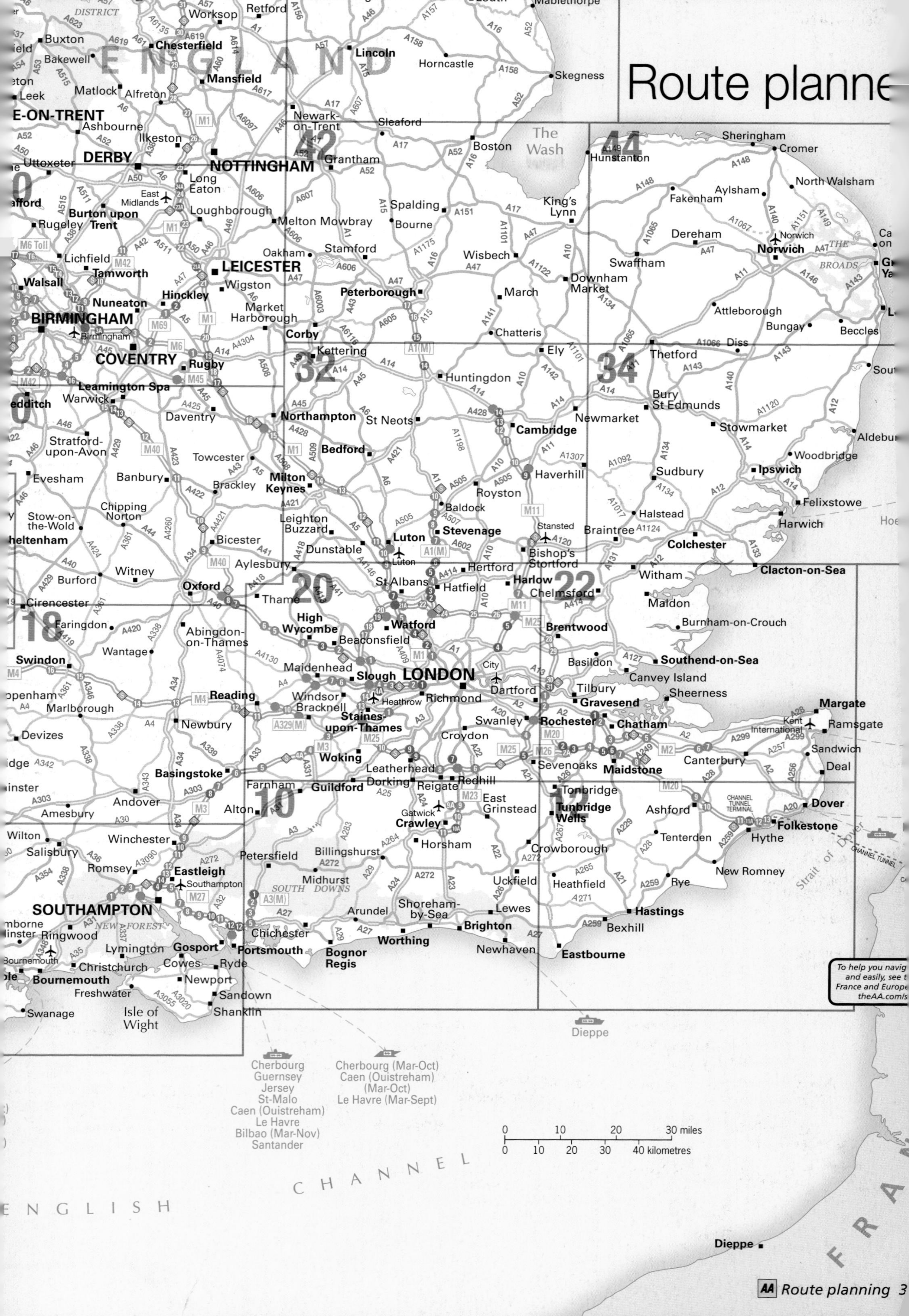
Route planne
ENGLAND
LONDON
BIRMINGHAM
COVENTRY
LEICESTER
NOTTINGHAM
DERBY
SOUTHAMPTON
Norwich
Cambridge
Oxford
Reading
Brighton
Dover
Folkestone
Margate
Ramsgate
Canterbury
Maidstone
Chatham
Rochester
Gravesend
Southend-on-Sea
Colchester
Ipswich
Chelmsford
Luton
Watford
Slough
Guildford
Portsmouth
Eastleigh
Bournemouth
Isle of Wight
Peterborough
Northampton
Milton Keynes
Bedford
Lincoln
Mansfield
Chesterfield
The Wash
Strait of Dover
CHANNEL TUNNEL
Dieppe
Cherbourg
Guernsey
Jersey
St-Malo
Caen (Ouistreham)
Le Havre
Bilbao (Mar-Nov)
Santander
Cherbourg (Mar-Oct)
Caen (Ouistreham) (Mar-Oct)
Le Havre (Mar-Sept)
ENGLISH CHANNEL
0 10 20 30 miles
0 10 20 30 40 kilometres
To help you navig and easily, see t France and Europe theAA.com/s
10
12
18
20
22
32
34
42
44

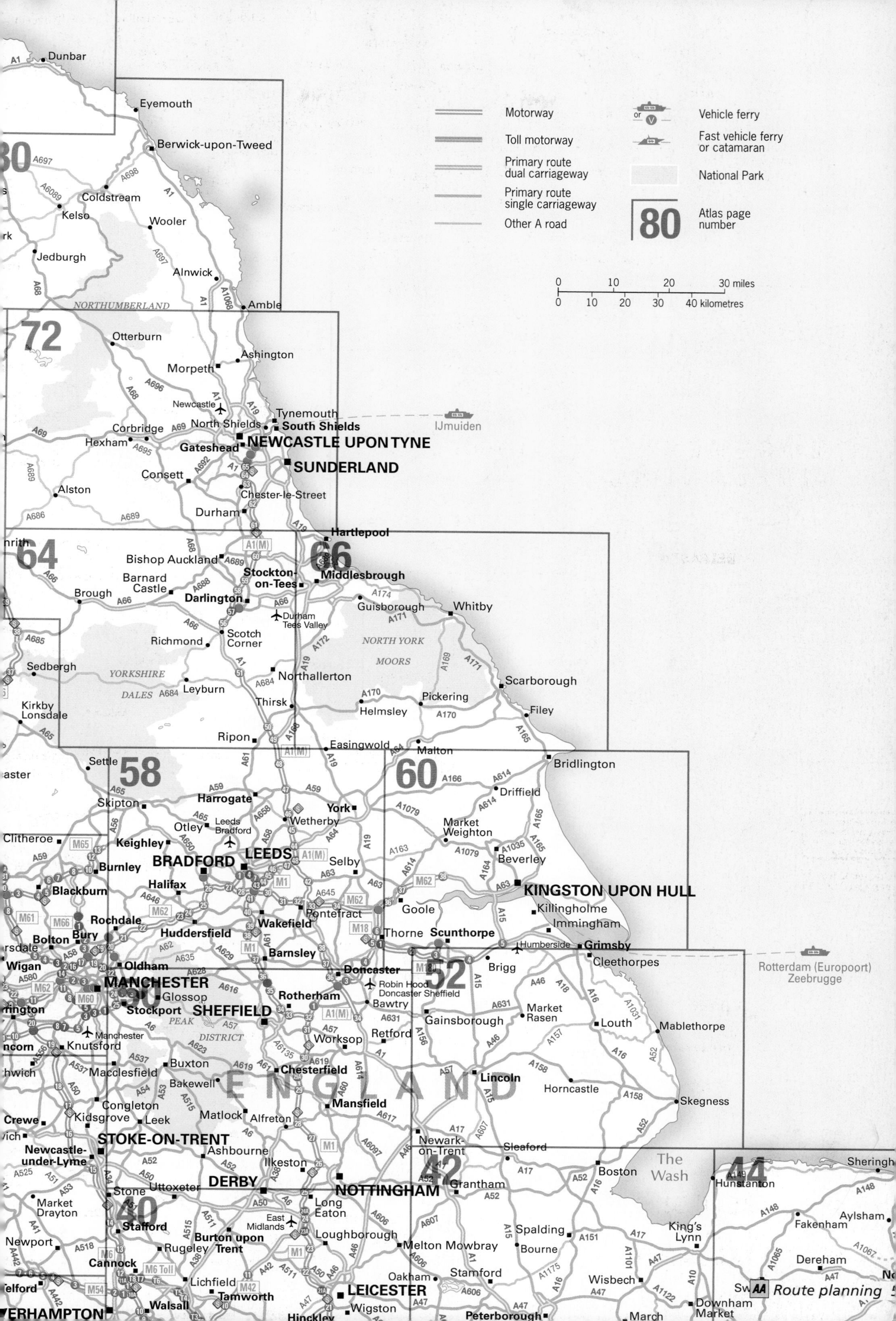

Motorway
Toll motorway
Primary route dual carriageway
Primary route single carriageway
Other A road
Vehicle ferry
Fast vehicle ferry or catamaran
National Park
Atlas page number
80
0 10 20 30 miles
0 10 20 30 40 kilometres
Dunbar
Eyemouth
Berwick-upon-Tweed
Coldstream
Kelso
Wooler
Jedburgh
Alnwick
Amble
NORTHUMBERLAND
72
Otterburn
Ashington
Morpeth
Newcastle
Tynemouth
North Shields
South Shields
IJmuiden
Corbridge
Hexham
Gateshead
NEWCASTLE UPON TYNE
SUNDERLAND
Consett
Alston
Chester-le-Street
Durham
Hartlepool
64
66
Bishop Auckland
Stockton-on-Tees
Middlesbrough
Barnard Castle
Brough
Darlington
Guisborough
Whitby
Durham Tees Valley
Scotch Corner
Richmond
NORTH YORK MOORS
Sedbergh
YORKSHIRE DALES
Leyburn
Northallerton
Scarborough
Kirkby Lonsdale
Thirsk
Helmsley
Pickering
Filey
Ripon
Easingwold
Malton
Bridlington
Settle
58
60
Driffield
Skipton
Harrogate
York
Wetherby
Otley
Leeds Bradford
Market Weighton
Clitheroe
Keighley
Beverley
BRADFORD
LEEDS
Selby
Burnley
Halifax
KINGSTON UPON HULL
Blackburn
Goole
Killingholme
Rochdale
Pontefract
Immingham
Wakefield
Thorne
Scunthorpe
Bolton
Bury
Huddersfield
Humberside
Grimsby
Barnsley
Cleethorpes
Wigan
Oldham
Brigg
Doncaster
Rotterdam (Europoort)
Zeebrugge
MANCHESTER
52
50
Glossop
Robin Hood Doncaster Sheffield
Rotherham
Stockport
SHEFFIELD
Bawtry
Market Rasen
Gainsborough
PEAK DISTRICT
Louth
Mablethorpe
Manchester
Knutsford
Worksop
Retford
Buxton
Chesterfield
Macclesfield
Bakewell
ENGLAND
Lincoln
Horncastle
Mansfield
Skegness
Congleton
Kidsgrove
Leek
Matlock
Alfreton
Crewe
Newark-on-Trent
STOKE-ON-TRENT
Sleaford
Newcastle-under-Lyme
Ashbourne
The Wash
Ilkeston
Boston
Sheringham
42
44
Hunstanton
DERBY
NOTTINGHAM
Grantham
Stone
Uttoxeter
Market Drayton
40
Long Eaton
East Midlands
Aylsham
Fakenham
Stafford
Burton upon Trent
Spalding
King's Lynn
Newport
Rugeley
Loughborough
Melton Mowbray
Bourne
Cannock
Dereham
Oakham
Stamford
Lichfield
Wisbech
Telford
Tamworth
LEICESTER
Walsall
Wigston
Downham Market
Hinckley
Peterborough
March

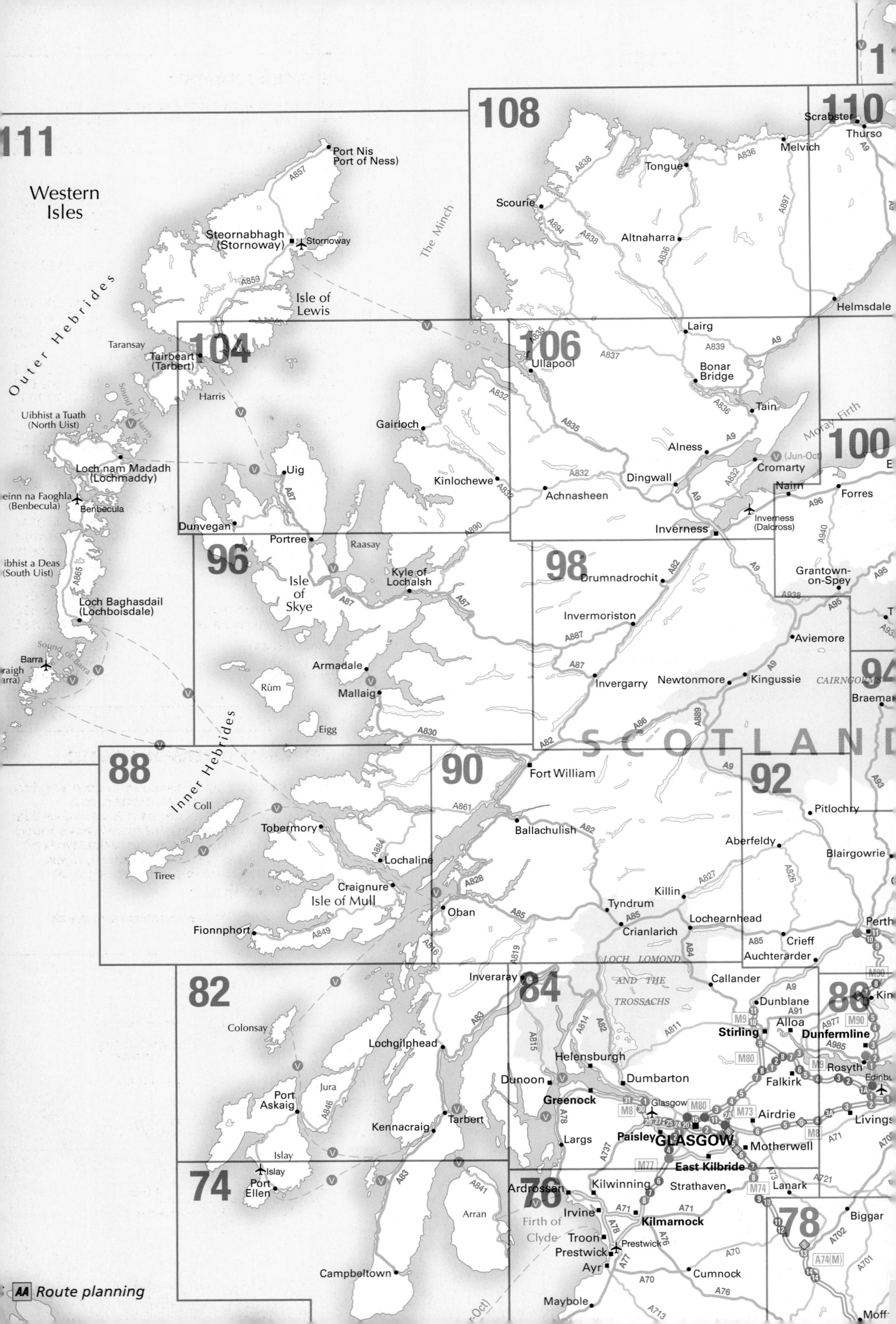

111
Western Isles
Outer Hebrides
Port Nis (Port of Ness)
A857
Steornabhagh (Stornoway)
Stornoway
The Minch
A859
Isle of Lewis
Taransay
Tairbeart (Tarbert)
Harris
Sound of Harris
Uibhist a Tuath (North Uist)
Loch nam Madadh (Lochmaddy)
einn na Faoghla (Benbecula)
Benbecula
ibhist a Deas (South Uist)
A865
Loch Baghasdail (Lochboisdale)
Sound of Barra
Barra
raigh
arra)

108
A838
Scourie
A894
A838
Tongue
A836
Melvich
A897
Altnaharra
A836
110
Scrabster
Thurso
A9
Helmsdale

104
Uig
A87
Dunvegan
Gairloch
Kinlochewe
A832
A832
106
A835
Ullapool
A837
A835
A832
Achnasheen
Lairg
A839
A9
Bonar Bridge
A836
Tain
Alness
A9
Dingwall
A832
Cromarty
(Jun-Oct)
Moray Firth
100
Nairn
A96
Forres
A9
Inverness
Inverness (Dalcross)
A940

96
Portree
Raasay
A890
Isle of Skye
Kyle of Lochalsh
A87
A87
Armadale
Mallaig
Rùm
Eigg
A830
98
Drumnadrochit
A82
Invermoriston
A887
A87
Invergarry
Newtonmore
Kingussie
A9
A889
A86
A82
Aviemore
A95
A938
Grantown-on-Spey
A95
CAIRNGORMS
94
Braemar
SCOTLAND

Inner Hebrides
88
Coll
Tiree
Tobermory
A884
Lochaline
Craignure
Isle of Mull
Fionnphort
A849
A816
Oban
A828
90
A861
Fort William
Ballachulish
A82
A85
Tyndrum
A85
Crianlarich
Killin
A827
Lochearnhead
A84
A819
LOCH LOMOND AND THE TROSSACHS
92
A9
Pitlochry
A93
Aberfeldy
A826
Blairgowrie
A85
Crieff
Auchterarder
Perth

82
Colonsay
Inveraray
84
A83
Lochgilphead
A815
A814
A82
Callander
A9
Dunblane
A91
M9
A811
Stirling
Alloa
A977
M90
Dunfermline
86
Kin
A985
M80
Rosyth
M9
Falkirk
Edinbu
Jura
Port Askaig
A846
Kennacraig
Tarbert
Helensburgh
Dunoon
Dumbarton
Greenock
A78
Glasgow
M8
M80
M73
Airdrie
Livings
M8
Largs
Paisley
GLASGOW
Motherwell
A71
A70
Islay
M77
East Kilbride
A737
A73

74
Islay
Port Ellen
A83
A841
Arran
Campbeltown
Oct)
76
Ardrossan
Kilwinning
Strathaven
M74
Lanark
A721
Irvine
A71
A71
Kilmarnock
Firth of Clyde
A78
A76
Troon
Prestwick
Prestwick
Ayr
A77
A70
Cumnock
A70
A76
Maybole
A713
78
Biggar
A702
A74(M)
A701
Moff

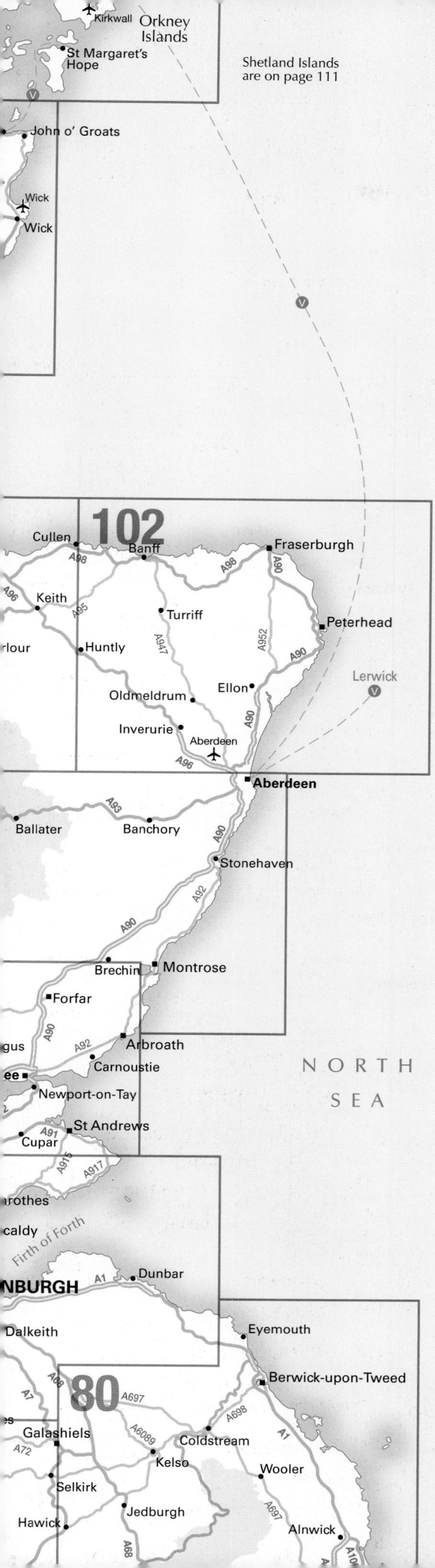

Shetland Islands are on page 111

FERRY INFORMATION

Route / website	Telephone
Hebrides and west coast Scotland	
calmac.co.uk	0800 066 5000
skyeferry.co.uk	01599 522 756
western-ferries.co.uk	01369 704 452
Orkney and Shetland	
northlinkferries.co.uk	0845 6000 449
pentlandferries.co.uk	01856 831 226
orkneyferries.co.uk	01856 872 044
shetland.gov.uk/ferries	01595 693 535
Isle of Man	
steam-packet.com	08722 992 992
Ireland	
irishferries.com	08717 300 400
poferries.com	08716 642 020
stenaline.co.uk	08447 70 70 70
North Sea (Scandinavia and Benelux)	
dfdsseaways.co.uk	08715 229 955
poferries.com	08716 642 020
stenaline.co.uk	08447 70 70 70
Isle of Wight	
wightlink.co.uk	0871 376 1000
redfunnel.co.uk	0844 844 9988
Channel Islands	
condorferries.co.uk	0845 609 1024
Channel hopping (France and Belgium)	
brittany-ferries.co.uk	0871 244 0744
condorferries.co.uk	0845 609 1024
eurotunnel.com	08443 35 35 35
ldlines.co.uk	0844 576 8836
dfdsseaways.co.uk	08715 229 955
poferries.com	08716 642 020
transeuropaferries.com	01843 595 522
transmancheferries.co.uk	0844 576 8836
Northern Spain	
brittany-ferries.co.uk	0871 244 0744
poferries.com	08716 642 020

EMERGENCY DIVERSION ROUTES

In an emergency it may be necessary to close a section of motorway or other main road to traffic, so a temporary sign may advise drivers to follow a diversion route. To help drivers navigate the route, black symbols on yellow patches may be permanently displayed on existing direction signs, including motorway signs. Symbols may also be used on separate signs with yellow backgrounds.

For further information see www.highways.gov.uk

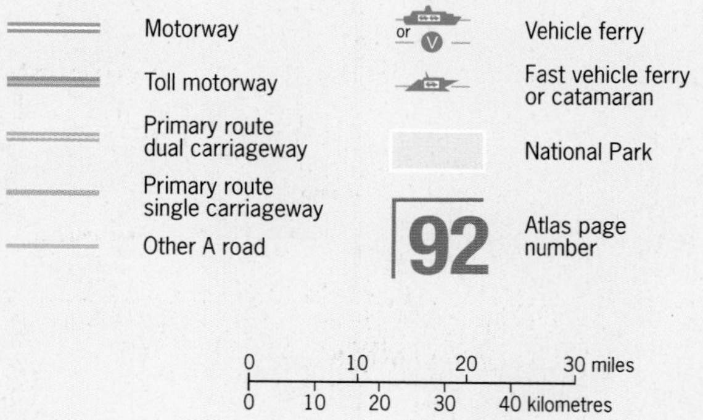

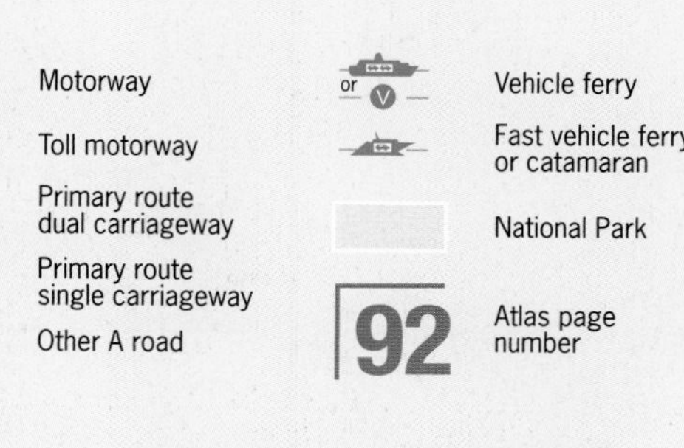

Map pages

Orkney Islands
111
Kirkwall
Shetland Islands
111
Lerwick
Western Isles
Steornabhagh (Stornoway)
111
Thurso
Wick
108
109
110
Ullapool
104
105
106
107
Uig
Gairloch
Tain
Dingwall
Inverness
Banff
Elgin
Peterhead
100
101
102
103
Portree
Kyle of Lochalsh
96
97
98
99
Aviemore
Aberdeen
Mallaig
94
95
Montrose
Fort William
Pitlochry
88
89
90
91
92
93
Oban
Crianlarich
Perth
Dundee
Stirling
82
83
84
85
86
87
Largs
Glasgow
138
139
Edinburgh
Kilmarnock
Berwick-upon-Tweed
74
75
76
77
Peebles
80
81
Ayr
78
79
Campbeltown
Alnwick
Moffat
Londonderry Derry
72
73
Newcastle upon Tyne
142
143
68
69
Dumfries
Larne
114
115
Stranraer
70
Carlisle
71
Belfast
Penrith
Workington
Middlesbrough
64
65
66
67
Sligo
Kendal
Scarborough
56
Douglas
Isle of Man
62
63
Thirsk
Westport
Cavan
Newry
Lancaster
Settle
York
58
59
60
61
Leeds
Kingston upon Hull
Blackpool
140
56
57
Galway
Athlone
DUBLIN
Liverpool
Manchester
Sheffield
Grimsby
Holyhead
Colwyn Bay
141
54
55
52
53
Chester
50
51
Lincoln
Caernarfon
Newark-on-Trent
Stoke-on-Trent
48
49
Nottingham
Boston
Limerick
46
47
Stafford
42
43
44
Norwich
45
Shrewsbury
King's Lynn
Dolgellau
Leicester
Great Yarmouth
41
Tralee
Newtown
Birmingham
40
Peterborough
112
113
136
137
Coventry
Bury St Edmunds
Aberystwyth
38
39
Rosslare Harbour
Waterford
Ludlow
Northampton
Cambridge
Killarney
36
37
34
35
Bedford
Cardigan
Worcester
Stratford-upon-Avon
32
33
Ipswich
Hereford
30
31
Cork
Fishguard
Brecon
Luton
Carmarthen
Abergavenny
Gloucester
To help you navigate safely and easily, see the AA's Ireland atlases... theAA.com/shop
24
25
26
27
28
29
Oxford
Watford
Chelmsford
Pembroke
Swansea
Swindon
20
21
22
23
Cardiff
Bristol
Reading
LONDON
18
19
144 - 147
Bath
Basingstoke
Sevenoaks
Maidstone
Barnstaple
Andover
Guildford
16
17
Dover
Folkestone
14
15
Salisbury
10
11
12
13
Taunton
Yeovil
Southampton
Chichester
Brighton
Bude
8
9
Hastings
Newhaven
Exeter
Lyme Regis
Bournemouth
6
7
Weymouth
Bodmin
4
5
Torquay
2
3
Truro
Plymouth
Isles of Scilly
2
6 - 7
Channel Islands
To help you navigate safely and easily, see the AA's France and Europe atlases... theAA.com/shop

Road map symbols

Motoring information

M4	Motorway with number
Toll, T4, Toll	Toll motorway with toll station
1	Motorway junction with and without number
3	Restricted motorway junctions
S, Fleet	Motorway service area
	Motorway and junction under construction
A3	Primary route single/dual carriageway
1	Primary route junction with and without number
3	Restricted primary route junctions
S	Primary route service area
BATH	Primary route destination
A1123	Other A road single/dual carriageway
B2070	B road single/dual carriageway
	Minor road more than 4 metres wide, less than 4 metres wide
	Roundabout
	Interchange/junction
	Narrow primary/other A/B road with passing places (Scotland)
	Road under construction/ approved
	Road tunnel
Toll	Road toll, steep gradient (arrows point downhill)
5	Distance in miles between symbols
or V	Vehicle ferry
	Fast vehicle ferry or catamaran
	Railway line, in tunnel
	Railway station and level crossing
	Tourist railway
	Airport, heliport
F	International freight terminal
H H	24-hour Accident & Emergency hospital, other hospital
C	Crematorium
50	Speed camera site (fixed location) with speed limit in mph
60	Section of road with more fixed speed c with speed limit in r
50 50	Average speed (SP camera system with limit in mph
V	Fixed speed camer with variable speed
P+R	Park and Ride (at least 6 days per
	City, town, village o other built-up area
628, 637, Lecht Summit	Height in metres, m
	Sandy beach
	National boundary
	County, administrati boundary

Touring information

To avoid disappointment, check opening times before visiting.

	Scenic route
	Tourist Information Centre
	Tourist Information Centre (seasonal)
	Visitor or heritage centre
	Picnic site
	Caravan site (AA inspected)
	Camping site (AA inspected)
	Caravan & camping site (AA inspected)
	Abbey, cathedral or priory
	Ruined abbey, cathedral or priory
	Castle
	Historic house or building
	Museum or art gallery
	Industrial interest
	Aqueduct or viaduct
	Garden, arboretum
	Vineyard
	Country park
	Agricultural showground
	Theme park
	Farm or animal centre
	Zoological or wildlife collection
	Bird collection
	Aquarium
RSPB	RSPB site
	National Nature Reserve (England, Scotland, Wales)
	Local nature reserve
	Wildlife Trust reserve
	Forest drive
	National trail
	Viewpoint
	Hill-fort
	Roman antiquity
	Prehistoric monument
1066	Battle site with year
	Steam railway centre
	Cave
	Windmill, monument
	Golf course
	County cricket ground
	Rugby Union national stadium
	International athletics stadium
	Horse racing, show
	Air show venue, motor-racing circuit
	Ski slope (natural, artificial)
	National Trust proper (England & Wales, Scotland)
	English Heritage site
	Historic Scotland site
	Cadw (Welsh heritag
	Other place of intere
	Boxed symbols indic attractions within urb areas
	World Heritage Site (UNESCO)
	National Park and National Scenic Area (Scotland)
	Forest Park
	Heritage coast
	Major shopping centr

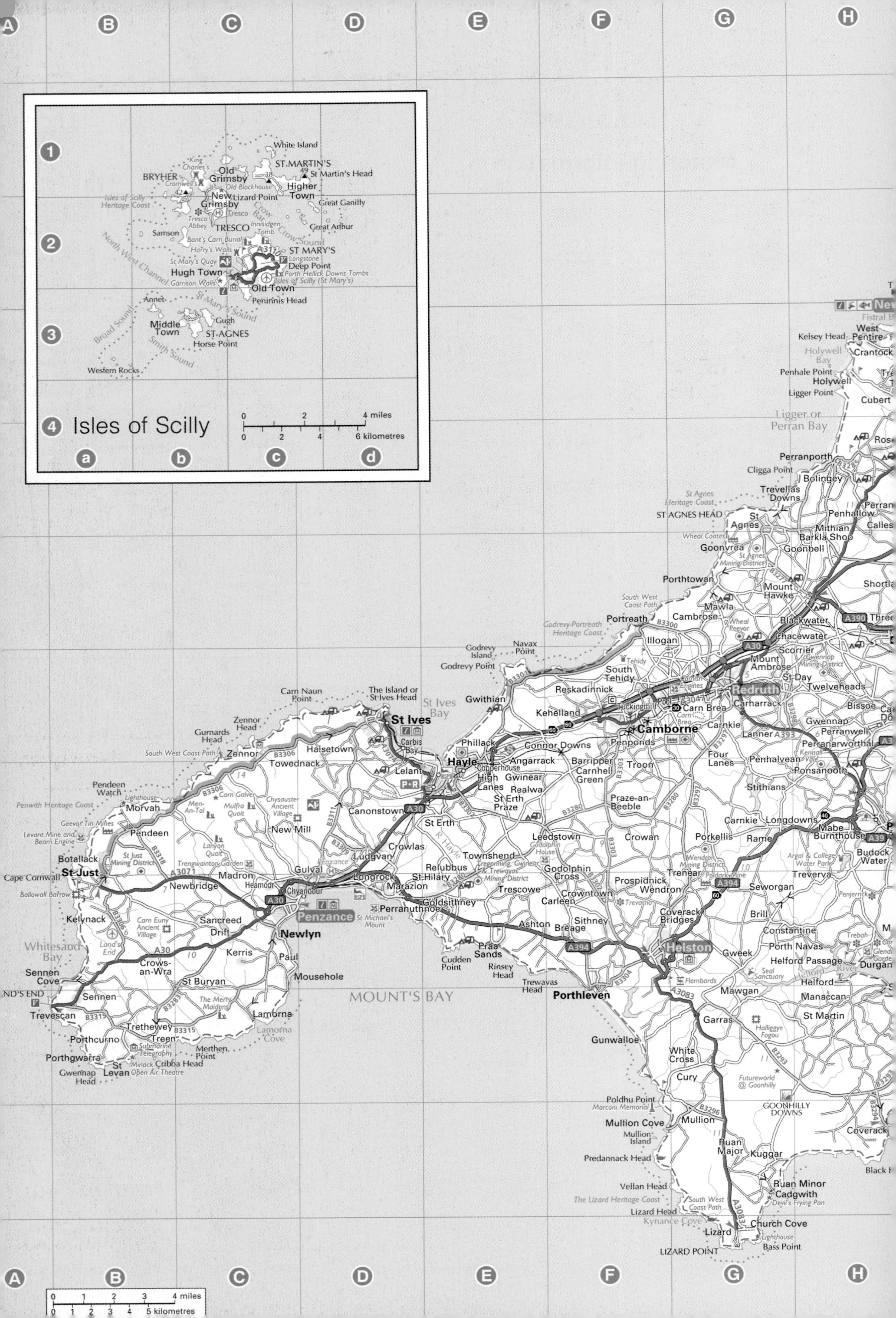
A
B
C
D
E
F
G
H
Isles of Scilly
White Island
ST MARTIN'S
St Martin's Head
Higher Town
King Charles's
Old Grimsby
BRYHER
Cromwell's
Old Blockhouse
New Grimsby
Lizard Point
Isles of Scilly Heritage Coast
Tresco Abbey
Tresco
TRESCO
Innisidgen Tomb
Crow Bar
Crow Sound
Great Ganilly
Great Arthur
Samson
Bant's Carn Burial
Harry's Walls
ST MARY'S
Longstone
Deep Point
St Mary's Quay
Hugh Town
Porth Hellick Downs Tombs
Isles of Scilly (St Mary's)
Garrison Walls
Old Town
Peninnis Head
North West Channel
Annet
St Mary's Sound
Gugh
Broad Sound
Middle Town
ST AGNES
Horse Point
Smith Sound
Western Rocks
4 miles
6 kilometres
St Ives
St Ives Bay
Carbis Bay
The Island or St Ives Head
Carn Naun Point
Zennor Head
Gurnards Head
Zennor
South West Coast Path
Halsetown
Towednack
Lelant
Hayle
Phillack
Gwithian
Godrevy Island
Godrevy Point
Navax Point
Godrevy-Portreath Heritage Coast
Portreath
Illogan
Tehidy
South Tehidy
Reskadinnick
Kehelland
Camborne
Carn Brea
Redruth
Tuckingmill
Pool
Penponds
Connor Downs
Angarrack
Barripper
Carnhell Green
Troon
Copperhouse
High Lanes
Gwinear
Realwa
St Erth Praze
St Erth
Canonstown
Pendeen Watch
Penwith Heritage Coast
Lighthouse
Morvah
Men-An-Tol
Carn Galver
Mulfra Quoit
Chysauster Ancient Village
Geevor Tin Mines
Levant Mine and Beam Engine
Pendeen
Botallack
St Just Mining District
St Just
Cape Cornwall
Ballowall Barrow
Lanyon Quoit
Trengwainton Garden
New Mill
Madron
Heamoor
Gulval
Ludgvan
Crowlas
Newbridge
Chyandour
Longrock
Marazion
St Michael's Mount
Penzance
Perranuthnoe
Goldsithney
St Hilary
Relubbus
Townshend
Leedstown
Godolphin House
Godolphin Cross
Trescowe
Tregonning, Gwinear & Trewavas Mining District
Praze-an-Beeble
Crowan
Carnkie
Four Lanes
Lanner
Carharrack
Kelynack
Carn Euny Ancient Village
Sancreed
Drift
Newlyn
Whitesand Bay
Land's End
Sennen Cove
Crows-an-Wra
Kerris
Paul
Mousehole
St Buryan
Sennen
Trevescan
The Merry Maidens
Lamorna
Lamorna Cove
Trethewey
Treen
Porthcurno
Submarine Telegraphy
Minack Open Air Theatre
Porthgwarra
Gwennap Head
St Levan
Cribba Head
Merthen Point
MOUNT'S BAY
Praa Sands
Cudden Point
Rinsey Head
Trewavas Head
Ashton
Breage
Sithney
Carleen
Crowntown
Prospidnick
Wendron
Trevarno
Coverack Bridges
Helston
Porthleven
Flambards
Gunwalloe
Garras
White Cross
Cury
Poldhu Point
Marconi Memorial
Mullion Cove
Mullion Island
Mullion
Predannack Head
Vellan Head
The Lizard Heritage Coast
South West Coast Path
Lizard Head
Kynance Cove
Lizard
LIZARD POINT
Church Cove
Lighthouse
Bass Point
Ruan Minor
Cadgwith
Devil's Frying Pan
Ruan Major
Kuggar
GOONHILLY DOWNS
Futureworld @ Goonhilly
Coverack
Black Head
Mawgan
Halliggye Fogou
Gweek
Seal Sanctuary
Helford River
Helford
Manaccan
St Martin
Porth Navas
Helford Passage
Durgan
Constantine
Brill
Seworgan
Treverva
Trenear
Porkellis
Wendron Mining District
Poldark Mine
Rame
Carnkie
Longdowns
Mabe Burnthouse
Budock Water
Argal & College Water Park
Penjerrick
Trebah
Stithians
Penhalvean
Ponsanooth
Kennall Vale
Perranarworthal
Perranwell
Gwennap
Bissoe
Twelveheads
St Day
Mount Ambrose
Gwennap Mining District
Scorrier
Chacewater
Blackwater
Threemilestone
Wheal Peevor
Cambrose
Mawla
Mount Hawke
Porthtowan
South West Coast Path
St Agnes Mining District
Goonvrea
Wheal Coates
St Agnes
ST AGNES HEAD
St Agnes Heritage Coast
Goonbell
Barkla Shop
Mithian
Penhallow
Trevellas Downs
Cligga Point
Bolingey
Perranporth
Ligger or Perran Bay
Cubert
Ligger Point
Holywell
Penhale Point
Holywell Bay
Crantock
Kelsey Head
West Pentire
Fistral Bay
Shortlanesend
Callestick
A30
A394
A3083
A390
A393
A3047
A3071
A3074
A311
B3306
B3318
B3315
B3283
B3311
B3309
B3302
B3280
B3303
B3297
B3300
B3301
B3296
B3293
B3304
B3285
B3277
0 1 2 3 4 miles
0 1 2 3 4 5 kilometres

J
K
L
M
N
P
Q
R
4
West Cornwall
Trevose Head Heritage Coast
Gunver Head
Polzeath
Trebetheric
St Minver
St Endellion
Trelill
A39
Michaelstown
Churchtown
BODMIN MOOR
TREVOSE HEAD
Mother Ivey's Bay
Harlyn Bay
Dinas Head
Constantine Bay
Prideaux Place
Trevone
Rock
Harlyn
Padstow
Chapel Amble
St Kew
Trequite
St Tudy
St Kew Highway
St Breward
De Lank River
Jamaica Inn
Bolventor
North Hill
Middlewood
SMALLACOMBE DOWNS
Henwood
Windmill
St Merryn
Constantine Bay
St Mabyn
Blisland
Colliford Lake
River Fowey
Porthcothan
B3276
A389
St Issey
Wadebridge
Egloshayle
Temple
Colliford Lake Park
Cheesewring
The Hurlers Stone Circle
BROWNGELLY DOWNS
Minions
Sterts Open-Air Theatre
Park Head
Penrose
Little Petherick
Royal Cornwall
St Breock
B3266
Pencarrow
St Ervan
Rumford
Trenance
Burlawn
Washaway
Helland
A30
Caradon Mining District
Darite
Bedruthan Steps
St Jidgey
St Breock Downs Monolith
Crealy Great Adventure Park
Warleggan
Common Moor
St Eval
Camel Valley
Cardinham
Mount
St Neot
Golitha
King Doniert's Stone
Trethevy Quoit
Tremar
St Cleer
Trenance
Nine Maidens
Ruthernbridge
Berryls Point
Griffins Point
Mawgan Porth
Trevarrian
B3276
B3274
A39
Nanstallon
Bodmin
St Mawgan
Vale of Mawgan
Talskiddy
Rosenannon
Bodmin & Wenford Railway
Carnglaze Caverns
Dobwalls
Liskeard
Watergate Bay
St Wenn
Withiel
A38
Newquay
Lanivet
West Taphouse
Moorswater
A3059
St Columb Minor
St Columb Major
Tregonetha
Lanhydrock
Trevelmond
Porth
Colan
A3058
Higher Town
Victoria
A391
Sweetshouse
A390
East Taphouse
St Pinnock
A38
Mountjoy
Ruthvoes
Lockengate
Restormel Castle
Paul Corin Music
Lane
Quintrell Downs
A392
St Columb Road
Goss Moor
Roche
Bodwen
Helman Tor
Herodsfoot
St Keyne
Kestle Mill
Dairyland
Fraddon
Indian Queens
B3279
Bugle
Lostwithiel
Porfell Animal Land
Trerice
Lanlivery
Duloe
Widegates
Newlyn East
St Enoder
A30
St Dennis
Whitemoor
Luxulyan
Luxulyan Valley
Lappa Valley
Summercourt
Treviscoe
Nanpean
Stenalees
Carthew
Penwithick
Lerryn
Lanreath
Muchlarnick
Sandplace
Wheal Martyn Heritage Centre
Trethurgy
Eden Project
A3076
Fiddlers Green
Mitchell
Scarcewater
Foxhole
St Blazey
Tywardreath
St Veep
Penpoll
Pelynt
St Martin
Monkey Sanctuary
A3058
High Street
St Stephen
St Austell
Trewoon
Holmbush
Par
A3082
Golant
Lanteglos Highway
Looe
Zelah
A39
Bodinnick
B3269
Polkerris
Fowey
Crumplehorn
Porthallow
Model Village
Looe Bay
St Allen
Trispen
Ladock
Coombe
Polgooth
Charlestown
Porthpean
Tregorrick
St Austell Bay
St Catherine's Castle
Polruan
Lansallos
Pencarrow Head
Lantivet Bay
Lantic Bay
Polperro
Talland Bay
South West Coast Path
Looe or St George's Island
Gribbin Head - Polperro Heritage Coast
Grampound Road
B3275
Sticker
Hewas Water
London Apprentice
GRIBBIN HEAD
St Erme
Idless
Probus
A390
Grampound
Creed
Black Head
Pentewan
Lost Gardens of Heligan
Mevagissey Bay
Kenwyn
Tresillian
B3287
St Ewe
Kestle
Truro
River Fal
Polmassick
Penare Point
Mevagissey
St Clement
Tregony
Portmellon
Malpas
A3078
Chapel Point
St Michael Penkevil
Ruan Lanihorne
St Michael Caerhays
Gorran Churchtown
Gorran Haven
Playing Place
Lamorran
Boswinger
Maenease Point
Trelissick Garden
Philleigh
Veryan Bay
Veryan
Portloe
DODMAN POINT
Trewithian
The Roseland Heritage Coast
Gerrans Bay
Nare Head
St Just-in-Roseland
Carrick Roads
Portscatho
Mylor
Gerrans
Flushing
Greeb Point
St Mawes
Pendennis Castle
Bohortha
Falmouth
Pendennis Point
ZONE POINT
South West Coast Path
Falmouth Bay
Newquay
0
200 m
Fistral Beach
Atlantic Hotel
Memorial
Newquay Bay
Fly Cove
Tithy Cove
Towan Beach
Tolcarne Beach
First Aid
Great Western Beach
Great Western Hotel
Lifeboat Station
The Island
Lifeguard Stn (high season only)
Newquay Golf Club
Superstore
Blue Reef
Travelodge
NEWQUAY STATION
Police Sta
The Royal British Legion
Hotel Victoria
Register Office
Christian Ctr
Jobcentre Plus
Newquay School
Salvation Army
Superstore
St John's Ambulance
Buccaneer Bay
St Michael's
Ambulance Sta
Trenance School
Surgery
Newquay
Newquay AFC
Recreation Ground
Fire Station
Trenance Gardens
Tregunnel Park Caravan Park
Gannel
GANNEL ROAD
TREVEMPER ROAD
A392
A3058
MELLANVRANE ROUNDABOUT
ST COLUMB MINOR
REDRUTH, BODMIN
LLA

Port of Plymouth
Bodmin Moor
Bodmin
Launceston
Wadebridge
Padstow
St Austell
Liskeard
Looe
Fowey
Camelford
Boscastle
Tintagel
Lostwithiel
Mevagissey
Polperro
St Austell Bay
Veryan Bay
Crackington Haven
Dockyard Station
Devonport Station
Plymouth Station
Torpoint Vehicle Ferry
Continental Ferry Terminal
River Tamar
The Sound
Cremyll
0 1 2 3 4 miles
0 1 2 3 4 5 kilometres

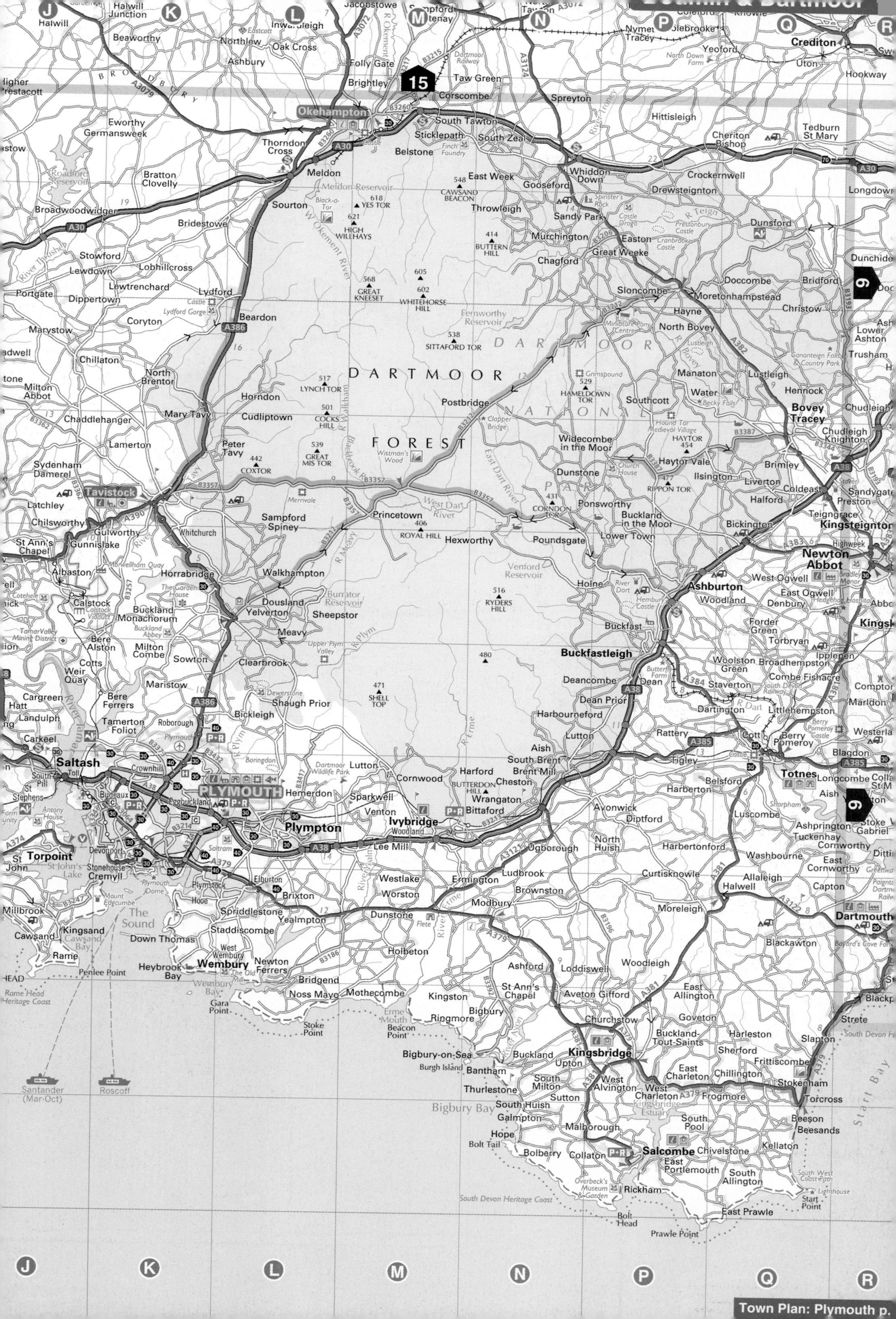

Town Plan: Plymouth p.

Town Plan: Exeter p.12

17
South Dorset & Devon Riviera
J
K
L
M
N
P
Q
R
Kingstone
Lopen
East Chinnock
West Coker
Thornford
Bishop's Caundle
Dinnington
Knowle St Giles
Dowlish Wake
Ludney
Hinton St George
Merriott
Middle Chinnock
Hardington Mandeville
Hardington Moor
East Coker
Stoford
Lillington
Longburton
Caundle Marsh
Holwell
Fifehead Neville
Chardleigh Green
Cudworth
Chillington
Higher Chillington
Crewkerne
Haselbury Plucknett
Beer Hackett
Pendomer
Ryme Intrinseca
Yetminster
Knighton
Crouch Hill
King's Stag
Kingston
Chaffcombe
Purtington
Roundham
North Perrott
Hardington Marsh
Closworth
Hazelbury Bryan
Cricket St Thomas
Hewish
Woolminstone
Misterton
South Perrott
BIRTS HILL
Halstock
Hamlet
Leigh
Glanvilles Wootton
Pulham
Forton
Whatley
Wayford
Clapton
Melbury Osmond
Chetnole
Middlemarsh
Wonston
Droop
Tatworth
Winsham
Seaborough
Mosterton
Corscombe
East Chelborough
Stockwood
Hermitage
Duntish
Netherhay
Drimpton
Chedington
Melbury Bubb
Lyon's Gate
Chard Junction
Laymore
River Axe
Forde Abbey
Mappowder
Evershot
Holywell
Minterne Magna
Buckland Newton
Tytherleigh
Hewood
Blackdown
Benville
Uphall
Batcombe
Henley
Higher Ansty
Lower Ansty
Holditch
Thorncombe
Burstock
Broadwindsor
Rampisham
Frome St Quintin
Alton Pancras
Melcombe Bingham
Plush
Birdsmoorgate
Pilsdon Pen
Stoke Abbott
Beaminster
Higher Wraxhall
Lower Wraxhall
The Giant
Cerne Abbas
Hawkchurch
Weycroft
Bettiscombe
Mapperton
Hooke
Marshwood
Pilsdon
Netherbury
Melplash
Cattistock
Sydling St Nicholas
Piddletrenthide
Cheselbourne
Chilfrome
Nether Cerne
White Lackington
Waytown
North Poorton
PUDDLETOWN DOWN
Monkton Wyld
Wootton Fitzpaine
Marshwood Vale
Broadoak
Salway Ash
Toller Porcorum
Maiden Newton
Godmanstone
Piddlehinton
Whitchurch Canonicorum
South Poorton
West Milton
Toller Fratrum
Powerstock
Hog Cliff
Harcombe Bottom
Catherston Leweston
Ryall
North Chideock
Nettlecombe
West Compton Abbas
Wynford Eagle
Frampton
Higher Waterston
Pymore
Bradpole
EGGARDON HILL
Loders
Uploders
Southover
Grimstone
Charlton Down
Puddletown
Uplyme
Charmouth
Morcombelake
Symondsbury
Stratton
Athelhampton
Chideock
St Andrews Well
Allington
Spyway
Compton Valence
Lyme Regis
Bridport
Walditch
Askerswell
Bradford Peverell
Charminster
YELLOWHAM HILL
Hardy's Cottage
GOLDEN CAP
Seatown
Eype
Watton
Bothenhampton
Kingston Russell
Winterbourne Abbas
Dorchester
Higher Bockhampton
Shipton Gorge
Chilcombe
Barrows
Stinsford
Woodsford
Jurassic Coast World Heritage Site
West Bay
Litton Cheney
Long Bredy
Nine Stones
Kingston Maurward
West Stafford
Burton Bradstock
R Bride
Winterbourne Steepleton
Martinstown
Winterborne Came
Maiden Castle
Swyre
Puncknowle
Littlebredy
Valley of Stones
Whitcombe
West Knighton
Winterborne Monkton
Hardy Monument
L Y M E   B A Y
West Bexington
Abbotsbury Castle
Kingston Russell
WHITE HILL
Portesham
Broadmayne
Warmwell
Abbotsbury
Abbey Remains
South West Coast Path
Rodden
Bincombe
White Horse
Poxwell
Chapel
Swannery
Osmington
Langton Herring
Overcombe
Upton
West Chaldon
Buckland Ripers
Preston
Jordan Hill
Osmington Mills
Chickerell
Weymouth Bay
Ringstead Bay
Chesil Beach
The Fleet
Fleet
Water Gardens
Chesil Bank & The Fleet
Westham
Weymouth
Deep Sea Adventure
Nothe Fort
Wyke Regis
Portland Harbour
Portland Castle
West Bay
Fortuneswell
PORTLAND
Easton
Portland Museum & Shipwreck Centre
Guernsey Jersey St-Malo
Portland Bill Lighthouse
PORTLAND BILL
0 10 mls
0 20 km
ALDERNEY
St Anne
FRANCE
St Peter Port
HERM
SARK
GUERNSEY
JERSEY
St Helier
0 1 2 miles
0 1 2 kilometres
Grosnez Point
Plemont Point
Sorel Point
Ronez Point
Belle Hougue Point
La Colombière
Vicard Point
St John's Bay
Fremont Point
La Grève de Lecq
Rouge Nez
La Mare
St John
Mourier Valley
Bouley Bay
Nez du Guet
Rozel Bay
La Coupe Point
L'Etacq
Grève de Lecq Valley
St Mary
Trinity
Rozel
Fliquet Bay
St Ouen
Carrefour
Hamptonne Country Life
Durrell Wildlife Conservation Trust
Verclut Point
St Martin
St Catherine's Bay
St Ouen's Bay
St Peter
St Lawrence
Jersey War Tunnels
Grand Chemins
Maufant
Faldouët
St Peter's Valley
Bellozanne Valley
Mont Orgueil
Les Quennevais
Millbrook
Five Oaks
Queen's Valley Reservoir
Gorey
St Brelade
Beaumont
St Saviour
Royal Bay of Grouville
St Aubin
Longueville
Corbière Point
St Brelade's Bay
St Aubin's Bay
St Helier
Grouville
Corbière
Swiss Valley
Samarès Manor
St Clement
Elizabeth Castle
Fort Regent
Point La Moye
Point La Fret
Portelet Bay
Noirmont Command Bunker
La Rocque
La Rocque Point
Jersey
Poole
Le Croc
Plat Rocque Point
St Clement's Bay
Weymouth via Guernsey
St Malo
Guernsey, Portsmouth
a
b
c
1
2
Weymouth Harbour
DORCHESTER
WAREHAM
ABBOTSBURY
GRANBY WAY
B3157
WEYMOUTH WAY
GOLDCROFT ROAD
RADIPOLE PARK DRIVE
DORCHESTER ROAD
GREENHILL
B3155
WEYMOUTH
WEYMOUTH STATION
RADIPOLE LANE
B3158
Westham
Weymouth Bay
COMMERCIAL ROAD
FERRY TERMINAL
ABBOTSBURY ROAD
NEWSTEAD ROAD
WESTWEY ROAD
CHICKERELL ROAD
B3154
Lanehouse
RODWELL AVENUE
RODWELL RD
LANEHOUSE ROCKS ROAD
B3156
WYKE ROAD
B3153
CROSS RD
Rodwell
BUXTON ROAD
A354
Southlands
OLD CASTLE ROAD
RYLANDS LANE
0 500 m
LLA
PORTLAND

Town Plans: Bournemouth p.124, Salisbury p.13

Town Plans: Portsmouth p.131, Southampton p.133, Winchester p.

20
19
9
A
B
C
D
E
F
G
H
Odiham
Farnham
Guildford
Shalford
Godalming
Alton
Whitehill & Bordon
Haslemere
Liphook
Liss
Petersfield
Midhurst
Petworth
Cranleigh
Billingshurst
Pulborough
Storrington
Arundel
Littlehampton
Rustington
East Preston
Angmering
Ferring
Chichester
Bognor Regis
Selsey
Selsey Bill
Havant
Emsworth
Southbourne
South Hayling
Southsea
Waterlooville
Horndean
Portsmouth
Bembridge
Middleton-on-Sea
Mapledurwell
North Warnborough
Crondall
Upton Grey
Long Sutton
South Warnborough
Weston Corbett
Weston Patrick
Well
Bentley
Southrope
Lower Froyle
Upper Froyle
Golden Pot
Lasham
Shalden
Holybourne
Binsted
Neatham
East Worldham
West Worldham
Chawton
Four Marks
Medstead
Beech
Upper Farringdon
Lower Farringdon
Selborne
Blackmoor
Oakhanger
Kingsley
Empshott
Greatham
East Tisted
Newton Valence
Charlwood
Colemore
Hawkley
Burgates
Privett
High Cross
Froxfield Green
Steep
Sheet
Stroud
Langrish
Ramsdean
Ripplington
East Meon
Weston
Buriton
Butser Hill
War Down
Chidden
Clanfield
Hambledon
Catherington
Blendworth
Chalton
Finchdean
Denmead
Lovedean
Anmore
Soake
Cowplain
Stakes
Purbrook
Bedhampton
Drayton
Farlington
Langstone
Brockhampton
Northney
North Hayling
Stoke
Hayling Island
Langstone Harbour
Chichester Harbour
Hayling Bay
Thorney Island
West Thorney
West Town
Eastney
Fort Cumberland
Rowland's Castle
Forestside
Westbourne
Hambrook
Nutbourne
Chidham
Bosham
Fishbourne
Woodmancote
West Ashling
East Ashling
Funtington
West Stoke
Mid Lavant
East Lavant
Summersdale
Woodend
Walderton
Stoughton
Bow Hill
Kingley Vale
Compton
West Marden
Up Marden
East Marden
North Marden
South Harting
East Harting
Uppark House & Garden
Treyford
Elsted
Didling
Bepton
Cocking
West Harting
Nyewood
Rogate
Fyning
Trotton
Chithurst
Iping
Woolbeding
Stedham
Minsted
Cocking Causeway
West Lavington
Easebourne
South Ambersham
Selham
Tillington
River
Lodsworth
Upperton
Byworth
Heyshott
Graffham
East Lavington
Upper Norwood
Duncton
Sutton
Bignor
Barlavington
Coates
Fittleworth
Little Bognor
Codmore Hill
Stopham
Marehill
West Chiltington
Hardham
Coldwaltham
Greatham
Watersfield
Bury
Amberley
Houghton
North Stoke
South Stoke
Offham
Burpham
Wepham
Warningcamp
Poling Corner
Poling
Patching
Clapham
Lyminster
Wick
Ford
Climping
Binsted
Walberton
Yapton
North End
Barnham
Eastergate
Westergate
Woodgate
Aldingbourne
Norton
Nyton
Fontwell
Slindon
Eartham
Halnaker Hill
Halnaker
Boxgrove
Tangmere
Westhampnett
Strettington
Waterbeach
Goodwood
East Dean
Charlton
Singleton
West Dean
Chilgrove
The Trundle
Weald & Downland Open Air Museum
Upwaltham
Oving
Colworth
Shripney
North Bersted
South Bersted
Flansham
Bilsham
Felpham
Aldwick
Rose Green
Nyetimber
Pagham
Pagham Harbour
Church Norton
Runcton
Merston
North Mundham
South Mundham
Hunston
Street End
Sidlesham
Highleigh
Earnley
Apuldram
Dell Quay
Donnington
Birdham
West Itchenor
Shipton Green
Somerley
West Wittering
East Wittering
Bracklesham
Bracklesham Bay
Walton
Broadbridge
Seale
Tongham
Runfold
Badshot Lea
Weybourne
Hale
Ewshot
Crookham
Wrecclesham
Lower Bourne
Tilford
Rowledge
Bucks Horn Oak
Millbridge
Frensham
Spreakley
Rushmoor
Frensham Great Pond
Churt
Thursley
Elstead
Puttenham
Compton
Shackleford
Wanborough
Flexford
Eashing
Upper Eashing
Milford
Mousehill
Witley
Wormley
Brook
Sandhills
Bowlhead Green
Beacon Hill
Hindhead
Devil's Punch Bowl
Grayshott
Headley
Headley Down
Arford
Lindford
Standford
Bramshott
Sleaford
Blacknest
Wheatley
Isington
Grayswood
Chiddingfold
Highstreet Green
Ramsnest Common
Hambledon
Hascombe
Loxhill
Dunsford
Alfold Crossways
Alfold
Ifold
Loxwood
Plaistow
Northchapel
Kirdford
Balls Cross
Wisborough Green
Lurgashall
Lickfold
Fernhurst
Kingsley Green
Linchmere
Longmoor Camp
Langley
Rake
Milland
Woodmansgreen
Redford
Henley
Blackdown Hill
Black Down 280
Hill Brow
Bramley
Wonersh
Farley Green
Shamley Green
Peaslake
Grafham
Rowly
Ewhurst
Ewhurst Green
Okewood
Ellen's Green
Rudgwick
Bucks Green
Adversane
Broadford Bridge
Nutbourne
Five Oaks
Chilworth
Blackheath
Albury
Albury Heath
Shere
Gomshall
Abinger Hammer
Holmbury Hill
Pitch Hill
Forest Green
Catteshall
Farncombe
Binscombe
Winkworth Arboretum
Loseley Park
Hollycombe Steam
South Downs Way
South Downs National Park
Harrow Hill
Kithurst Hill
Highdown Hill
Bignor Hill
Duncton Hill
Levin Down
Linch Down
Nore Hill
Portsmouth Harbour
Continental Ferry Terminal
500 m
Buckland
Landport
HM Naval Base
Portsea
Portsmouth & Southsea Sta
Portsmouth Harbour Sta
Spinnaker Tower
Isle of Wight Ferry Terminal
Somers Town
Old Portsmouth
Fratton
Queen Street
High Street
Lake Road
Holbrook Road
Kingston Rd
London Rd
Fratton Rd
Churchill Ave
M27, Southampton, Chichester
LLA
Cherbourg
Guernsey
Jersey
St-Malo
Caen (Ouistreham)
Bilbao (Mar-Nov)
Le Havre
Santander
Cherbourg
Caen (Ouistreham)
Le Havre (Mar-Sept)
(Mar-Oct)
Foreland
Whitecliff Bay
The Duver
0 1 2 3 4 miles
0 1 2 3 4 5 kilometres

Dorking
Reigate
Salfords
Horley
Gatwick
Smallfield
Lingfield
Edenbridge
Four Elms
Crowhurst
Sevenoaks Weald
Hildenborough
Chiddingstone Causeway
Leigh
Tonbridge
Bough Beech
Hever
Chiddingstone
Penshurst
Bidborough
Markbeech
Southborough
Speldhurst
Fordcombe
Ashurst
Dawesgreen
South Holmwood
North Holmwood
Norwood Hill
Parkgate
Beare Green
Newdigate
Charlwood
Povey Cross
Capel
Russ Hill
Lowfield Heath
Tinsley Green
Shipley Bridge
Burstow
Outwood
Horne
Blindley Heath
Newchapel
Felcourt
Felbridge
Dormans Land
Marsh Green
Cowden
Copthorne
Crawley Down
East Grinstead
Ashurstwood
Forest Row
Hartfield
Upper Hartfield
Balls Green
Groombridge
Eridge Green
Withyham
Frant
Ifield
Rusper
Lambs Green
Three Bridges
Pound Hill
CRAWLEY
Maidenbower
Kingsfold
Faygate
Tilgate
Turner's Hill
Colgate
Pease Pottage
St Leonards Forest
Horsham
Littlehaven
Roffey
West Hoathly
Highbrook
Birchgrove
Ardingly
Horsted Keynes
Danehill
Chelwood Gate
Coleman's Hatch
Ashdown Forest
Crowborough
Lye Green
Mark Cross
Rotherfield
Tidebrook
Balcombe
Handcross
Staplefield
Manning's Heath
Lower Beeding
Slaugham
Widening in progress
Southwater
Monk's Gate
Nuthurst
Warninglid
Copsale
Maplehurst
Crabtree
Cuckfield
Lindfield
Haywards Heath
Scayne's Hill
Fletching
Nutley
Maresfield
Sweethaws
Fairwarp
Five Ash Down
High Hurstwood
Pound Green
Hadlow Down
Five Ashes
Mayfield
Splayne's Green
Piltdown
Buxted
Ansty
Bolney
Cowfold
Shipley
West Grinstead
Newick
North Chailey
Chailey
Uckfield
Framfield
Blackboys
Cross in Hand
Heathfield
Broad Oak
Wineham
Twineham
Hickstead
Partridge Green
Sayers Common
Worlds End
Wivelsfield
Wivelsfield Green
Burgess Hill
South Chailey
Town Littleworth
New Town
Ridgewood
Isfield
Little Horsted
Waldron
Little London
Maynard's Green
Henfield
Hurstpierpoint
Blackstone
Albourne
Keymer
Plumpton Green
East Chiltington
Halland
East Hoathly
Horam
Ashurst
Woodmancote
Clayton
Hassocks
Ditchling
Streat
Plumpton
Westmeston
Barcombe
Barcombe Cross
Upper Wellingham
Shortgate
Chiddingly
Whitesmith
Gun Hill
Vines Cross
Cowbeech
Small Dole
Edburton
Poynings
Pyecombe
Ditchling Beacon
Offham
Hamsey
Laughton
Ringmer
Muddles Green
Hellingly
Steyning
Upper Beeding
Fulking
Saddlescombe
Pangdean
South Downs National Park
Mount Harry
Lewes
South Malling
Lower Dicker
Upper Dicker
Horsebridge
Hailsham
Bramber
Truleigh Hill
Devil's Dyke
Stanmer
Wallands Park
Glynde
Chalvington
Ripe
Botolphs
Coombes
Patcham
Coldean
Falmer
Kingston near Lewes
Iford
Firle
Selmeston
Arlington
Lancing College Chapel
Mile Oak
Hangleton
West Blatchington
Withdean
Hollingbury
Moulsecoomb
Preston
Rodmell
Beddingham
Alciston
Berwick
Polegate
Lancing
Old Shoreham
Shoreham-by-Sea
Portslade
Southwick
Portslade-by-Sea
HOVE
BRIGHTON
Kemp Town
Ovingdean
Woodingdean
Newmarket Hill
Southease
Telscombe
Tarring Neville
South Heighton
Denton
Firle Beacon
Wilmington
Folkington
Wannock
Willingdon
Lower Willingdon
Hampden Park
Ratton Village
WORTHING
Rottingdean
Saltdean
Piddinghoe
Peacehaven
Newhaven
Norton
Bishopstone
East Blatchington
Alfriston
Litlington
Jevington
Westdean
Friston
Old Town
Seaford
Seaford Bay
Seaford Head
Sutton
Seven Sisters
East Dean
Beachy Head
Sussex Heritage Coast
Dieppe
Newhaven Harbour
LEWES
THE DROVE
NORTH WAY
SOUTH WAY
BRIGHTON RD
NEWHAVEN TOWN STATION
FERRY TERMINAL
NEWHAVEN
NEWHAVEN HARBOUR STATION
RAILWAY ROAD
BEACH ROAD
Lifeboat Station
Newhaven Harbour
GIBBON ROAD
FORT ROAD
EAST QUAY COMMERCIAL TERMINAL
Newhaven Marina
Rec Ground
EASTBOURNE
500 m
21
12
Town Plan: Brighton p.

Town Plan: Tunbridge Wells p.1

Eastbourne to Dover
23
J
K
L
M
N
P
Q
R
Godmersham
Sole Street
Crundale
Waltham
Bossingham
Stelling Minnis
Barfrestone
Woolage Green
Lower Eythorne
Eythorne
Sutton
East Studdal
Ringwould
Walmer Castle
Kingsdown
Shepherdswell
Ashley
Sutton Downs
Martin
West Langdon
Coldred
Denton
Westwell Leacon
Boughton Aluph
Westwell
Wye
Wye Crown
North Downs Way
Bodsham
Hastingleigh
Elmsted
Brook
Kennington
Ashford
South Ashford
Singleton
Stanhope
Willesborough Lees
Willesborough
South Willesborough
Hinxhill
Sevington
Chart
Mersham
Park Farm
Kingsnorth
The Forstal
Smeeth
Brabourne
Brabourne Lees
Lymbridge Green
Rhodes Minnis
Elham
Swingfield Minnis
Stowting
Ottinge
Lyminge
Postling
Paddlesworth
Etchinghill
Channel Tunnel Terminal
Peene
Newington
Sellindge
Stanford
Stop 24
Shadoxhurst
Aldington Corner
Aldington
Folkestone
Brockhill
Saltwood
Lympne
Pedlinge
Port Lympne
Bonnington
Orlestone
Bilsington
Ruckinge
Hamstreet
Warehorne
Newchurch
Burmarsh
ROMNEY MARSH
Snave
Romney, Hythe & Dymchurch Railway
Dymchurch
Martello Tower
Brenzett Green
St Mary in the Marsh
Snargate
Aeronautical
Ivychurch
Brenzett
St Mary's Bay
Romney Marsh
Brookland
Old Romney
Littlestone-on-Sea
New Romney
Greatstone-on-Sea
WALLAND MARSH
Lydd
Rye Bay
Old Lighthouse
DUNGENESS
Wootton
Lydden
Selsted
Ewell Minnis
Kearsney
Swingfield Street
Butterfly Centre
Densole
Hawkinge
Upper Standen
Lower Standen
Alkham
South Alkham
Drellingore
St Radigund's
Maxton
West Hougham
Capel-le-Ferne
Battle of Britain
Cheriton
Morehall
Sandgate
Seabrook
West Hythe
Hythe
FOLKESTONE
East Wear Bay
Samphire Hoe
Dover - Folkestone Heritage Coast
Whitfield
Temple Ewell
River
Buckland
Guston
East Langdon
St Margaret's at Cliffe
St Margaret's Bay
West Cliffe
SOUTH FORELAND
South Foreland Heritage Coast
Lighthouse
Gateway to the White Cliffs
DOVER
Dunkerque
Calais
Channel Tunnel (Rail)
STRAIT OF DOVER
A2
A20
A256
A258
A259
A2070
B2011
B2061
B2071
B2075
M20
Folkestone Terminal
400 yards
500 metres
Ashley Wood
Peene
Terminal Building
Newington
Beachborough Crossroads
Check-in
Channel Tunnel Terminal
Police Station
Ashford Road
Cheriton Interchange
Cheriton
Superstore
Cheriton High Street
Church Road
ASHFORD, MAIDSTONE, M25 & LONDON
DOVER, FOLKESTONE, CANTERBURY
Departures to France follow
Arrivals from France follow
Calais / Coquelles Terminal
400 yards
500 metres
Coquelles
D243E
Ibis Hotel
Etap Hotel
Novotel
Cité de l'Europe
Passenger Terminal
Petrol Station
Check-in
Frontier Controls
Freight only
A16 (E402) Rocade Littorale
Boulevard de la Côte d'Opale
Boulevard de l'Europe
HGV Fuel Station
Freight Terminal
Eurotunnel Administration Headquarters
Parc d'activites les Terrasses
Arrivals Platforms
Departure Platforms
D304
BOULOGNE
CALAIS
DUNKERQUE, A26 (PARIS)
Departures to England follow
Arrivals from England follow

A
B
C
D
E
F
G
H
North West Point
Lundy Heritage Coast
LUNDY
142
Marisco
Surf Point
Shutter Point
Bull Point
Rockham Bay
Morte Point
Woolacombe
Morte Bay
Baggy Point
Georgeham
Croyde Bay
Croyde
B3231
Saunton
Braunton Burrows
North Devon Heritage Coast
BARNSTAPLE
OR
BIDEFORD BAY
Crow Point
Appledore
Westward Ho!
Northam
B3236
Abbotsham
Hartland Heritage Coast
Bideford
Fairy Cross
Ford
Horns Cross
Woodtown
Littleham
Saltrens
Goldworthy
Parkham
Buckland Brewer
Monkleigh
Frithelstock
Frithelstock Stone
HARTLAND POINT
Shipload Bay
Titchberry
Hartland Abbey & Garden
Damehole Point
Stoke
Hartland Quay
Hartland
B3248
Spekes Mill Mouth
Milford
Docton Mill Gardens
Philham
Clovelly
B3237
Buck's Mills
Milky Way
Buck's Cross
A39
Woolfardisworthy
Hardisworthy
Welcombe
Darracott
Meddon
Ashmansworthy
East Putford
Gnome Reserve
West Putford
Haytown
Langtree
B3227
Gooseham
Morwenstow
Dinworthy
Higher Sharpnose Point
South West Coast Path
Shop
Woodford
Bradworthy
Bulkworthy
Stibb Cross
Abbots Bickington
A388
Peters Marland
Lower Sharpnose Point
Tamar Lakes
Kilkhampton
Brocklands
Sutcombe
Newton St Petrock
Steeple Point
Stibb
Dinscott
Sutcombemill
Venngreen
Milton Damerel
Sandy Mouth
B3254
Thornbury
Shebbear
Northcott Mouth
Poughill
Dunsdon
Holsworthy Beacon
Woodacott
Bradford
Flexbury
Bude Bay
Bude
Stratton
Launcells
Grimscott
Chilsworthy
Cookbury
Pancrasweek
A3072
Holemoor
Holsworthy
Hollacombe
Marhamchurch
Bridgerule
Pyworthy
Chasty
Widemouth Bay
Titson
Winsford Walled Garden
Halwill Junction
Halwill
Dizzard Point
Poundstock
Bangors
Clawton
Beaworthy
St Gennys
Treskinnick Cross
Whitstone
Penhallam
Week St Mary
Crackington Haven
Cambeak
Coxford
North Tamerton
Tetcott
A388
Higher Prestacott
Sweets
Jacobstow
4
Southcott
Ashwater
Wainhouse Corner
Eworthy
Germansweek
B3263
A39
Maxworthy
Chapmans Well
Virginstow
Marshgate
Witchcroft
Pentire Point
Trespa...ett
...worthy Water
Boyt...
Northcott
Roadford Reservoir
Lesnewth
Otterham
Warbstow
Tamar Otter & Wildlife Centre
North Petherwin
St Giles-on-
Broadwoodwidger
0 1 2 3 4 miles
0 1 2 3 4 5 kilometres

North Devon & Exmoor
J
K
L
M
N
P
Q
R
Foreland Point
Lynmouth Bay
Countisbury Cove
Hurlstone Point
Porlock Bay
SELWORTHY BEACON 308
South West Coast Path
Water Mouth
Combe Martin Bay
Elwill Bay
Woody Bay
Hele Bay
racombe
Hele
Slade
Chambercombe Manor
The Old Corn Mill
Watermouth Castle
Berrynarbor
Combe Martin
Martinhoe
Trentishoe
Lynton
Brass Rubbing
Lynmouth
Countisbury
Brendon
Malmsmead
Toll
Dean
Barbrook
Rockford
Oare
Porlock Weir
West Porlock
Bossington
Allerford
Woodcombe
Porlock
Holnicote
Selworthy
Horner
Luccombe
Huntscott
Wootton Courtenay
Alcombe
Lynton & Barnstaple Railway
Watersmeet House
Paracombe
Wildlife & Dinosaur Park
Kentisbury
A399
A3123
A39
B3223
B3225
HOAROAK HILL 474
Dunkery & Horner Woods
EXMOOR FOREST
EXMOOR NATIONAL PARK
Wistlandpound Reservoir
West Down
Bittadon
Clifton
Arlington
Arlington Court
Exmoor Zoological Park
Challacombe
Barton Town
River Exe
444 DRY HILL
519 Dunkery Beacon DUNKERY HILL
Ranscombe
Knowle
Burrow
Timberscombe
Wheddon Cross
Cutcombe
Milltown
Loxhore
Higher Muddiford
Muddiford
Marwood
Guineaford
Marwood Hill
B3230
B3358
River Barle
Simonsbath
B3223
Edgcott
B3224
410 Newland
Exford
Luckwell Bridge
A396
Heanton
Shirwell
Lower Loxhore
Bratton Fleming
Prixford
R Bray
493 SPAN HEAD
Kinsford Water
Withypool
Winsford
Ashford
Bradiford
Pilton
Goodleigh
Stoke Rivers
Brayford
A399
High Bray
Bentwichen
WINSFORD HILL
B3223
Exton
Bridgetown
Derby
Barnstaple
Bickington
Gunn
Charles
Tarr Steps
Liscombe
Landkey
Swimbridge Newland
Stoodleigh
West Buckland
East Buckland
Heasley Mill
Hawkridge
Brompton Regis
Tawstock
North Molton
Twitchen
16
A39
A361
St John's Chapel
Bishop's Tawton
Hannaford
Swimbridge
Castle Hill
Upcott
Molland
West Anstey
Dulverton
HADDON 355
Bury
Newton Tracey
Harracott
East Stowford
Filleigh
B3226
South Molton
Battleton
B3222
Cobbaton
Quince Honey Farm
Aller
East Anstey
Hiscott
Chapelton
Chittlehampton
B3227
Bish Mill
Newtown
Bishop's Nympton
Brushford
Exbridge
A377
Umberleigh
Warkleigh
George Nympton
Crooked Oak
Knowstone
Yarnscombe
Atherington
B3232
Huntshaw
B3137
Ash Mill
Satterleigh
Alswear
River Mole
Mariansleigh
Rose Ash
A361
B3227
Chittlehamholt
Yard
Oakford
Great Torrington
High Bickington
Kings Nympton
Romansleigh
Meshaw
St Giles in the Wood
Kingscott
Creacombe
Rackenford
Stoodleigh
Exe Valley
Roborough
A3124
Burrington
B3217
Little Dart River
Loxbeare
Washfield
Beaford
Lurley
Bolham
Knightshayes Court
Ashreigney
Chulmleigh
Witheridge
Riddlecombe
Cheldon
B3096
B3137
Templeton
Calverleigh
Halsdon
Worlington
Chawleigh
Nomansland
Merton
Huish
Dolton
Hollocombe
Ashley
B3042
B3042
Washford Pyne
Withleigh
R Dart
Tiverton
Eggesford
Pennymoor
Dowland
B3217
Puddington
Way Village
R Dalch
River Exe
Wembworthy
Nymet Rowland
Eastington
Black Dog
Poughill
Upham
Devon Railway Centre
Butterleigh
Meeth
Iddesleigh
Ingleigh Green
Brushford
Lapford
Morchard Bishop
Woolfardisworthy
Cadeleigh
Bickleigh Mill
Bickleigh
Barwick
Winkleigh
Coldridge
Kennerleigh
Stockleigh English
Cheriton Fitzpaine
R Torridge
A3124
B3220
R Yeo
A377
East Village
6
Bickleigh Castle
Fursdon
Monkokehampton
Broadwood Kelly
Bondleigh
Hatherleigh
Splatt
Down St Mary
A3072
Cadbury
Zeal Monachorum
Newbuildings
Honeychurch
Copplestone
Upton Hellions
Stockleigh Pomeroy
Up Exe
Silverton
B3216
R Taw
Sandford
A386
Exbourne
West Sandford
Thorverton
Jacobstowe
Sampford Courtenay
North Tawton
A3072
Bow
Coleford
Knowle
Shobrooke
Inwardleigh
Eastcott
R Okement
A3072
Nymet Tracey
Colebrooke
Shute
Kille
Killerton
Northlew
Oak Cross
B3215
Dartmoor Railway
Yeoford
Crediton
Sweetham
Brampford Speke
Rewe
North Down Farm
Uton
Stoke Canon
Ashbury
Folly Gate
B3217
Taw Green
A3124
Hookway
Upton Pyne
Huxham
Brightley
Newton St Cyres
Poltimore
Corscombe
Spreyton
River Troney
Okehampton
B3260
South Tawton
5
Hittisleigh
Cowley
Pinhoe
Thorndon Cross
Sticklepath
South Zeal
Cheriton Bishop
Tedburn St Mary
Whitestone Cross
EXETER
Whipton
Blackho
B3260
A30
Castle
Belstone
Finch Foundry
A30
Exwick
Heavitree
Meldon
Whiddon Down
Crockernwell
Longdown
Wonford
Meldon Reservoir
548 CAWSAND BEACON
Gooseford
Drewsteignton
Sourton
Black-a-Tor
618 YES TOR
Throwleigh
Spinster's Rock
Sandy Park
Castle
R Teign
B3212
Ide

Bridgend
Coity
Laleston
Tythegston
Merthyr Mawr
Newton
Coychurch
Treoes
Llangan
Corntown
Ewenny
Ogmore
Ogmore-by-Sea
St Bride's Major
Colwinston
Pentre Meyrick
Llysworney
Southerndown
Llandow
Wick
Sigingstone
Broughton
Monknash
Marcross
St Donats
Nash Point
Llantwit Major
Glamorgan Heritage Coast
Gileston
St Athan
Llanmaes
Flemingston
Llancarfan
Llanbethery
Penmark
Llancadle
East Aberthaw
Limpert Bay
Breaksea Point
Rhoose
Porthkerry
Cold Knap Point
Barry
(Y Barri)
Barry Island
Sully
Sully Island
Flat Holm
Lavernock
Lavernock Point
Cosmeston Lakes & Medieval Village
Penarth
Lower Penarth
Penarth Head
Cogan
Llandough
Dinas Powys
Cadoxton
Moulton
St Andrew's Major
Wenvoe
Michaelston-le-Pit
St Lythans
Bonvilston
Llantrithyd
St Hilary
Old Beaupre Castle
St Mary Church
Llandough
Llanblethian
Cowbridge
Aberthin
Maendy
Welsh St Donats
Penllyn
Trerhyngyll
Ystradowen
Pendoylan
Clawdd-coch
St Brides super-Ely
Peterston-super-Ely
St George's
St Nicholas
Miskin
Llanilid
Llanharry
Brynsadler
Groes-faen
Radyr
Whitchurch
St Fagans
Fairwater
Llandaff
Canton
Ely
Caerau
Birchgrove
Rumney
Llanrumney
St Mellons
Roath
Pengam
Splottlands
CARDIFF
(CAERDYDD)
Peterstone Wentlooge
Steep Holm
WESTON-SUP
BRIDGWATER
BAY
Burnham-o
Hurlstone Point
Porlock Bay
Porlock Weir
West Porlock
Bossington
SELWORTHY BEACON
South West Coast Path
Exmoor Heritage Coast
Allerford
Woodcombe
Minehead
Porlock
Holnicote
Selworthy
Horner
Luccombe
Huntscott
Periton
Alcombe
Marsh Street
Blue Anchor Bay
Blue Anchor
Dunster
Dunster Castle
Wootton Courtenay
Ranscombe
Knowle
Timberscombe
Burrow
Dunkery Beacon
DUNKERY HILL
EXMOOR
NATIONAL PARK
Carhampton
Withycombe
Old Cleeve
Bilbrook
Hungerford
Washford
Cleeve Abbey
Watchet
St Audries Bay
West Somerset Railway
Doniford
Williton
Sampford Brett
East Quantoxhead
West Quantoxhead
Weacombe
Woolston
Bicknoller
Kilve
Lilstock
Knighton
Stolford
Steart
Stockland Bristol
Burton
Stogursey
Shurton
Otterhampton
Combwich
Stringston
Holford
Dodington
Coleridge Cottage
Nether Stowey
Fiddington
Over Stowey
Aley
Cannington
Charlinch
Spaxton
Adscombe
QUANTOCK HILLS
Bridgwater
Four Forks
Enmore
Lexworthy
Lower Aisholt
Aisholt
Lower Merridge
Goathurst
Courtway
Huntstile
North Petherton
Wheddon Cross
Cutcombe
Edgcott
Exford
Newland
Luckwell Bridge
Rodhuish
Luxborough
Lower Roadwater
Roadwater
Kingsbridge
Treborough
BRENDON HILLS
Monksilver
Stogumber
Preston
Kingswood
Lawford
Crowcombe
Triscombe
Flaxpool
Withypool
Winsford
WINSFORD HILL
Tarr Steps
Liscombe
Hawkridge
Exton
Bridgetown
Withiel Florey
Clatworthy Reservoir
Combe Sydenham
Elworthy
Brompton Ralph
Rooks Nest
Willett
Tolland
Lydeard St Lawrence
Combe Florey
West Bagborough
Fyne Court
Broomfield
Toulton
Shearston
Kingston St Mary
Thurloxton
Adsborough
Fulford
Hestercombe
Gotton
Cheddon Fitzpaine
West Monkton
Monkton Heathfield
Bathpool
Langaller
Ruishton
Henlade
Pickney
Nailsbourne
Bishops Lydeard
Ash Priors
Pyleigh
Gaulden Manor
Clatworthy
Whitefield
Wimbleball Lake
Brompton Regis
Huish Champflower
Langley Marsh
West Leigh
Chapel Leigh
Fitzhead
Ford
Halse
Langley
Wiveliscombe
Maundown
Upton
HADDON HILL
Bury
Dulverton
West Anstey
East Anstey
Battleton
Brushford
Skilgate
Chipstable
Vale of Taunton Deane
Preston Bowyer
Heathfield
Cotford St Luke
Norton Fitzwarren
Staplegrove
Milverton
Hillcommon
Oake
Hillfarrance
Bishops Hull
Taunton
Morebath
Shillingford
Petton
Waterrow
Bathealton
Langford Budville
Nynehead
Bradford-on-Tone
Exbridge
Clayhanger
Stawley
Runnington
Cider Farm
Dipford
Trull
Shoreditch
Stoke St Mary
Staplehay
Bampton
Kittisford
Ashbrittle
Appley
Thorne St Margaret
Wellington
West Buckland
Duddlestone
Orchard Portman
Thurlbear
Heale
Corfe
Staple Fitzpaine
Oakford
Huntsham
Cove
Greenham
Holywell Lake
Staple Cross
Hockworthy
Holcombe Rogus
White Ball
Sampford Arundel
Ford Street
Lowton
Pitminster
Blagdon
Sampford Moor
Wrangway
Wellington Monument
BLACKDOWN HILLS
Blagdon Hill
STAPLE HILL
Curland
Creacombe
Rackenford
Stoodleigh
Exe Valley
R Lowman
Westleigh
Red Ball
Knightshayes Court
Loxbeare
Washfield
Chevithorne
Uplowman
Burlescombe
Ayshford
Whitnage
Nicholashayne
Culm Davy
Rosemary Lane
Clayhidon
Burnworthy
Churchstanton
Birch Wood
Buckland St Mary
Lurley
Bolham
Templeton
Calverleigh
Sampford Peverell
Appledore
Woodgate
Prescott
Culmstock
Hemyock
Stapley
Nomansland
Withleigh
Tiverton
Uffculme
Craddock
Bolham Water
Churchinford
Bishopswood
Halberton
Ash Thomas
Willand
Ashill
0 1 2 3 4 miles
0 1 2 3 4 5 kilometres
27
15
6
Town Plans: Cardiff p.126, Taunton p.13

J
K
L
M
N
P
Q
R
SEVERN ESTUARY
28
18
8
7
Battery Point
Avonmouth
Portishead
Hallen
Kings Weston
Shirehampton
Filton
Stoke Gifford
Frenchay
Winterbourne
Westerleigh
Codrington
Hinton
Pucklechurch
Abson
Dyrham
Doynton
Wick
Cold Ashton
BRISTOL
Redland
Clifton
Fishponds
Soundwell
Eastville
Mangotsfield
Siston
Goose Green
Warmley
Kingswood
Hanham
Oldland
Bitton
Upton Cheyney
North Stoke
Langridge
Woolley
Swainswick
Weston-in-Gordano
Walton-in-Gordano
Walton Park
Clapton-in-Gordano
Portbury
Easton-in-Gordano
Abbots Leigh
Lower Failand
Failand
Leigh Woods
Tyntesfield
Clevedon
Tickenham
Wraxall
Nailsea
Long Ashton
Flax Bourton
Bedminster
Bedminster Down
Bishopsworth
Withywood
Knowle
Brislington
Stockwood
Keynsham
Saltford
Kelston
Queen Charlton
Whitchurch
Chewton Keynsham
Burnett
Corston
Newton St Loe
Twerton
BATH
Weston
Charlcombe
Batheaston
Claverton
Englishcombe
Combe Down
Odd Down
Kenn
West End
Chelvey
Farleigh
Backwell
West Town
Barrow Gurney
Kingston Seymour
Woodspring Bay
Wick St Lawrence
Claverham
Brockley
Cleeve
Lulsgate Bottom
Upper Town
Felton
Dundry
Maiden Head
East Dundry
Norton Malreward
Norton Hawkfield
Yatton
Congresbury
Kewstoke
West Hewish
St Georges
Worle
Milton
Ashcombe
Puxton
Wrington
Redhill
Regil
Winford
Chew Magna
Stanton Drew
Stanton Wick
Belluton
Publow
Pensford
Compton Dando
Hunstrete
Stanton Prior
Chelwood
Marksbury
Inglesbatch
Priston
South Stoke
Midford
Combe Hay
Stock
Blackmoor
Butcombe
Cowslip Green
Havyat
Chew Stoke
Nempnett Thrubwell
Bishop Sutton
Stowey
Clutton Hill
Clutton
Farmborough
Tunley
Timsbury
Dunkerton
Hinton Charterhouse
Locking
Hutton
Stonebridge
Sandford
Churchill
Lower Langford
Rickford
Blagdon Lake
Chew Valley Lake
Banwell
Oldmixon
Upper Langford
Star
Burrington
Blagdon
North Widcombe
Sutton Wick
Temple Cloud
High Littleton
Meadgate
Camerton
Carlingcott
Wellow
Bleadon Hills
Yarborough
Sidcot
Rowberrow
Winscombe
Christon
Bleadon
Shipham
Ubley
Compton Martin
West Harptree
South Widcombe
Cameley
Hallatrow
Hinton Blewett
Paulton
Peasedown St John
Shoscombe
Radstock
Foxcote
Loxton
Compton Bishop
King John's Hunting Lodge
Charterhouse
MENDIP HILLS
East Harptree
Sherborne
Coley
Litton
Farrington Gurney
Midsomer Norton
Westfield
Welton
Writhlington
Faulkland
Woolverton
Brean
Biddisham
Lower Weare
Cross
Axbridge
Cheddar Resr
Cheddar
Ubley Warren
Edingworth
East Brent
Tarnock
Rooks Bridge
Badgworth
Weare
Alston Sutton
Chewton Mendip
Bathway
Ston Easton
Clapton
Chilcompton
Charlton
Stratton-on-the-Fosse
Kilmersdon
Hemington
Hardington
Laverton
Lullington
Brent Knoll
Stone Allerton
Chapel Allerton
Draycott
Priddy
Ebbor Gorge
Green Ore
Emborough
Gurney Slade
Holcombe
Highbury
Newbury
Buckland Dinham
Mells
Great Elm
Clewer
Cocklake
Rodney Stoke
Westbury-sub-Mendip
Wookey Hole
Binegar
Nettlebridge
Vobster
Coleford
Whatley
Little Green
Mark
Blackford
Wedmore
Walcombe
West Horrington
East Horrington
Ashwick
Oakhill
Leigh upon Mendip
Frome
Chantry
Lower Whatley
Bason Bridge
Westham
Theale
Easton
Bagley
Henton
Wookey
Dulcote
Dinder
Stoke St Michael
East End
Downhead
Nunney
East Huntspill
Catcott Burtle
Westhay Moor
Bleadney
Yarley
Coxley Wick
Wells
Croscombe
Darshill
Shepton Mallet
Dean
Doulting
Edington Burtle
Lower Godney
Upper Godney
Coxley
West Compton
Cranmore
East Cranmore
Trudoxhill
Puriton
Woolavington
Westhay
Godney
North Town
North Wootton
Pilton
East Somerset Railway
Chesterblade
Chilton Polden
Oxenpill
Meare
Meare Fish House
Wanstrow
Witham Friary
Cossington
Edington
East Compton
Prestleigh
Horsey
Bawdrip
Catcott
POLDEN HILLS
Shapwick
Glastonbury
Glastonbury Tor
Street on the Fosse
Stoney Stratton
Westcombe
Batcombe
Upton Noble
Stawell
Moorlinch
Ashcott
Pylle
Evercreech
Milton Clevedon
North Brewham
West Pennard
West Bradley
East Pennard
Chedzoy
Sutton Mallet
Walton
Street
Parbrook
Lamyatt
Kilmington
Bussex
Greinton
Pedwell
Butleigh Wootton
Overleigh
Tilham Street
Ham Street
Wraxall
Ditcheat
Alhampton
South Brewham
Kilmington Common
Huntworth
Westonzoyland
Middlezoy
Baltonsborough
Hornblotton Green
Wyke Champflower
Bruton
Hardway
Compton Dundon
Butleigh
Clanville
Ansford
Cole
Stourhead
Henley
Dundon
Barton St David
West Lydford
East Lydford
Alford
Lovington
Castle Cary
Pitcombe
Redlynch
Stoney Stoke
Gasper
Othery
Burrow Bridge
Burrow Mump
Beer
High Ham
Bradley Hill
Littleton
Kingweston
Keinton Mandeville
Lydford on Fosse
Foddington
Galhampton
Bratton Seymour
Shepton Montague
Charlton Musgrove
Barrow
Penselwood
Lyng
Stathe
Aller
Low Ham
Bramwell
Pitney
Somerton
Charlton Mackrell
Babcary
North Barrow
South Barrow
Yarlington
Bayford
Stoke Trister
Athelney
Woodhill
Stoke St Gregory
Oath
Wearne
Langport
Huish Episcopi
Upton
Charlton Adam
Haynes Motor Museum
Brookhampton
Woolston
Wincanton
Meare Green
Huntham
Heale
Curry Rivel
North Curry
Pibsbury
Long Sutton
Catsgore
Lytes Cary Manor
Kingsdon
Downhead
West Camel
Sparkford
North Cadbury
Little Weston
Blackford
Holton
Compton Pauncefoot
South Cadbury
Lattiford
Maperton
Cucklington
North Cheriton
South Cheriton
Buckhorn Weston
Horsington
Greenway
Willtown
Drayton
Muchelney
Knole
Little Load
Long Load
Podimore
Queen Camel
Wales
Sutton Montis
Bridgehampton
RNAS Yeovilton
Fleet Air Arm
Yeovilton
Limington
Chilton Cantelo
Marston Magna
Corton Denham
Charlton Horethorne
Abbas Combe
Templecombe
Kington Magna
Curry Mallet
Fivehead
Isle Abbotts
Isle Brewers
Thorney
Muchelney Ham
Hambridge
Kingsbury Episcopi
Milton
Ilchester
Witcombe
Ashington
West Mudford
Rimpton
Adber
Sandford Orcas
Stowell
Milborne Wick
Yenston
Beercrocombe
Westport
Stapleton
Coat
Ash
Tintinhull Garden
Chilthorne Domer
Yeovil Marsh
Mudford Sock
Mudford
Up Mudford
Poyntington
Henstridge Ash
Henstridge
Milborne Port
West Lambrook
New Cross
Stembridge
Martock
Tintinhull
Trent
Oborne
Purse Caundle
Marnhull
Stalbridge
Puckington
Ilford
Ilton
Ashill
Barrington
East Lambrook
Compton Durville
Stocklinch
Shepton Beauchamp
South Petherton
Stoke sub Hamdon
Montacute
Odcombe
Yeovil
Over Compton
Nether Compton
Stallen
Goathill
Sherborne
Stalbridge Weston
Whitelackington
Ilminster
Seavington St Michael
Seavington St Mary
Kingstone
Donyatt
Norton sub Hamdon
Wigborough
Over Stratton
Lopen
Little Norton
Chiselborough
Preston Plucknett
Brympton
West Coker
Barwick
Bradford Abbas
Thornford
North Wootton
Allweston
Stourton Caundle
Bishop's Caundle
Lydlinch
Bagber
Sturminster Newton
Allowenshay
Dinnington
West Chinnock
Middle Chinnock
East Chinnock
Hardington Mandeville
East Coker
Stoford
Lillington
Folke
Caundle Marsh
Holwell
Fifehead Neville
Knowle St Giles
Dowlish Wake
Hinton St George
Merriott
Chillington
Cudworth
Higher Chillington
Chaffcombe
Crewkerne
Haselbury Plucknett
North Perrott
Hardington Marsh
Pendomer
Closworth
Beer Hackett
Ryme Intrinseca
Yetminster
Knighton
Longburton
Crouch
M5
M4
M32
M49
A38
A37
A39
A361
A371
A303
A368
A370
A4
A420
A46
A36
A367
A362
A3088
A30
A372
A357
A359
Town Plans: Bath p.123, Bristol

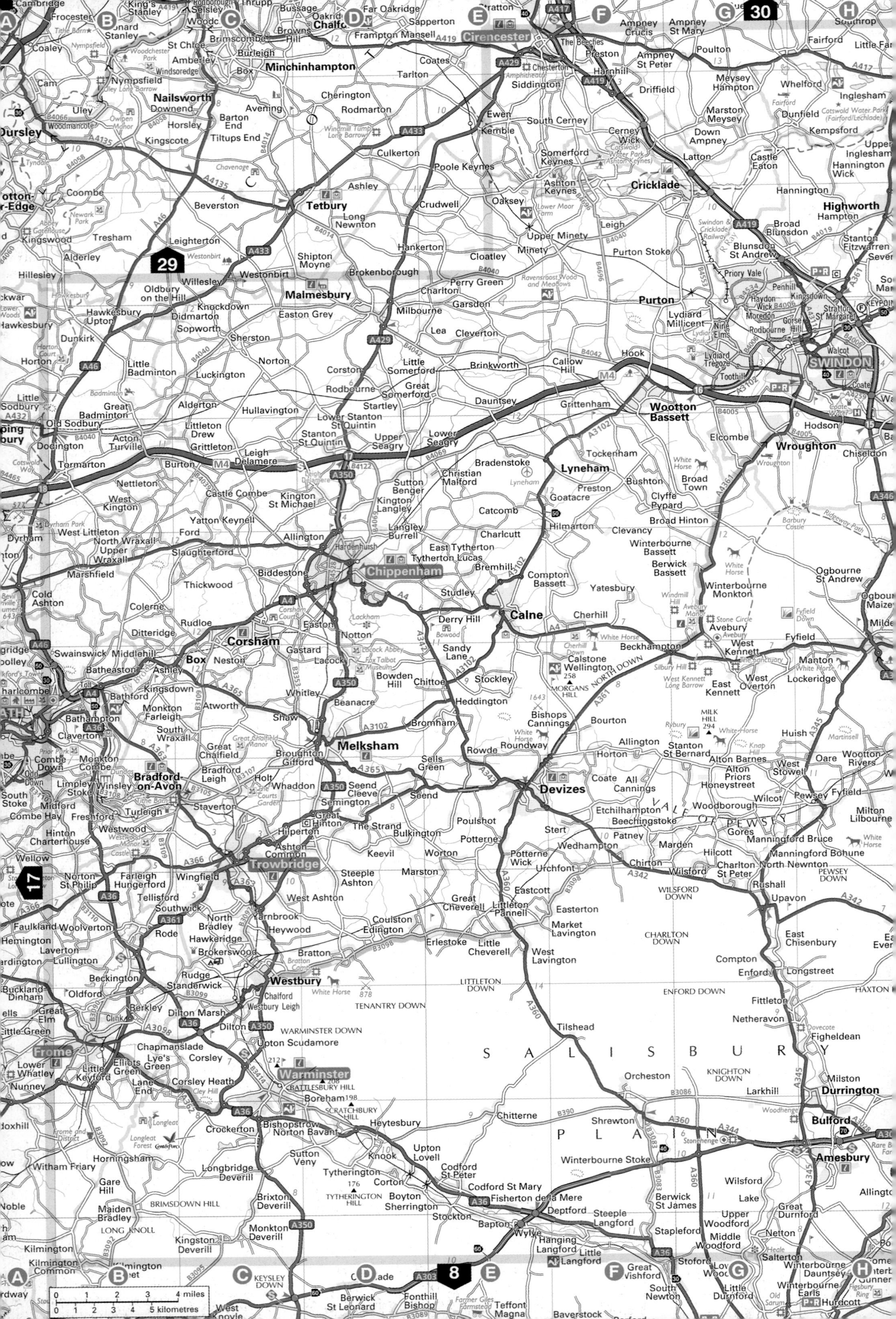

30
29
17
8
Cambridge
Frocester
Stanley
King's Stanley
Selsley
Woodchester
Thrupp
Bussage
Oakridge
Chalford
Far Oakridge
Sapperton
Frampton Mansell
Stratton
Cirencester
Ampney Crucis
Ampney St Mary
Southrop
Fairford
Little Faringdon
Coaley
Nympsfield
St Chloe
Brimscombe
Amberley
Burleigh
Minchinhampton
Box
Coates
Tarlton
The Beeches
Preston
Chesterton
Ampney St Peter
Poulton
Siddington
Harnhill
Driffield
Meysey Hampton
Whelford
Inglesham
Cam
Uley
Nailsworth
Downend
Horsley
Barton End
Avening
Cherington
Rodmarton
Ewen
South Cerney
Cerney Wick
Marston Meysey
Dunfield
Kempsford
Dursley
Woodmancote
Kingscote
Tiltups End
Kemble
Culkerton
Somerford Keynes
Down Ampney
Latton
Castle Eaton
Upper Inglesham
Hannington Wick
Poole Keynes
Ashton Keynes
Cricklade
Hannington
Ashley
Tetbury
Crudwell
Oaksey
Highworth
Coombe
Wotton-under-Edge
Beverston
Long Newnton
Upper Minety
Leigh
Broad Blunsdon
Hampton
Kingswood
Tresham
Leighterton
Hankerton
Minety
Purton Stoke
Blunsdon St Andrew
Stanton Fitzwarren
Sevenhampton
Alderley
Hillesley
Westonbirt
Shipton Moyne
Cloatley
Brokenborough
Perry Green
Priory Vale
Willesley
Oldbury on the Hill
Malmesbury
Charlton
Garsdon
Purton
Penhill
Haydon Wick
Stratton St Margaret
Hawkesbury
Hawkesbury Upton
Knockdown
Didmarton
Sopworth
Easton Grey
Milbourne
Lydiard Millicent
Moredon
Rodbourne
Gorse Hill
Nine Elms
Sherston
Lea
Cleverton
Dunkirk
Walcot
Horton
Little Badminton
Norton
Luckington
Corston
Little Somerford
Brinkworth
Callow Hill
Hook
Lydiard Tregoze
Toothill
SWINDON
Coate
Little Sodbury
Great Badminton
Alderton
Rodbourne
Great Somerford
Dauntsey
Grittenham
Wootton Bassett
Old Sodbury
Hullavington
Startley
Lower Stanton St Quintin
Stanton St Quintin
Littleton Drew
Upper Seagry
Lower Seagry
Hodson
Chiseldon
Elcombe
Wroughton
Dodington
Acton Turville
Grittleton
Leigh Delamere
Tormarton
Burton
Tockenham
Sutton Benger
Christian Malford
Bradenstoke
Lyneham
Broad Town
Nettleton
Castle Combe
Kington St Michael
Kington Langley
Preston
Bushton
Clyffe Pypard
West Kington
Goatacre
Catcomb
Broad Hinton
Yatton Keynell
Dyrham
West Littleton
Ford
Allington
Langley Burrell
Charlcutt
Hilmarton
Clevancy
North Wraxall
Upper Wraxall
Slaughterford
Hardenhuish
East Tytherton
Tytherton Lucas
Winterbourne Bassett
Berwick Bassett
Marshfield
Biddestone
Chippenham
Bremhill
Compton Bassett
Yatesbury
Ogbourne St Andrew
Thickwood
Studley
Winterbourne Monkton
Cold Ashton
Colerne
Rudloe
Derry Hill
Calne
Cherhill
Avebury
Easton
Notton
Ditteridge
Corsham
Gastard
Lacock
Sandy Lane
Beckhampton
West Kennett
Fyfield
Swainswick
Middlehill
Box
Neston
Calstone Wellington
Manton
Batheaston
Ashley
Stockley
Kingsdown
Bowden Hill
Chittoe
Whitley
Bathford
Atworth
East Kennett
West Overton
Lockeridge
Monkton Farleigh
Beanacre
Heddington
Bathampton
Shaw
Bishops Cannings
Bourton
Claverton
South Wraxall
Bromham
Roundway
Allington
Stanton St Bernard
Huish
Combe Down
Monkton Combe
Great Chalfield
Broughton Gifford
Melksham
Sells Green
Rowde
Horton
Alton Barnes
Oare
Wootton Rivers
Limpley Stoke
Winsley
Bradford-on-Avon
Bradford Leigh
Holt
Whaddon
Seend Cleeve
Semington
Seend
Devizes
Coate
All Cannings
Alton Priors
Honeystreet
West Stowell
Pewsey
Fyfield
South Stoke
Midford
Turleigh
Staverton
Great Hinton
The Strand
Poulshot
Etchilhampton
Beechingstoke
Woodborough
Wilcot
Milton Lilbourne
Combe Hay
Freshford
Westwood
Hilperton
Bulkington
Potterne
Stert
Patney
Gores
Manningford Bruce
Hinton Charterhouse
Ashton Common
Keevil
Worton
Potterne Wick
Wedhampton
Marden
Hilcott
Manningford Bohune
Wellow
Norton St Philip
Farleigh Hungerford
Wingfield
Trowbridge
Steeple Ashton
Marston
Urchfont
Chirton
Wilsford
Charlton St Peter
North Newnton
Tellisford
West Ashton
Eastcott
Rushall
Upavon
Southwick
North Bradley
Great Cheverell
Littleton Pannell
Easterton
Faulkland
Woolverton
Yarnbrook
Coulston
Edington
Market Lavington
Hemington
Rode
Hawkeridge
Heywood
Erlestoke
Little Cheverell
West Lavington
East Chisenbury
Laverton
Brokerswood
Bratton
Compton
Lullington
Enford
Longstreet
Beckington
Rudge
Standerwick
Westbury
Buckland Dinham
Oldford
Chalford
Westbury Leigh
Fittleton
Berkley
Dilton Marsh
Netheravon
Great Elm
Dilton
Upton Scudamore
Tilshead
Figheldean
Frome
Chapmanslade
Lye's Green
Corsley
Lower Whatley
Little Keyford
Elliots Green
Warminster
Nunney
Corsley Heath
Lane End
Boreham
Orcheston
Milston
Larkhill
Durrington
Crockerton
Bishopstrow
Heytesbury
Chitterne
Shrewton
Bulford
Norton Bavant
Upton Lovell
Stonehenge
Amesbury
Horningsham
Sutton Veny
Knook
Winterbourne Stoke
Witham Friary
Longbridge Deverill
Tytherington
Codford St Peter
Wilsford
Gare Hill
Corton
Boyton
Codford St Mary
Berwick St James
Lake
Allington
Maiden Bradley
Brixton Deverill
Sherrington
Fisherton de la Mere
Deptford
Steeple Langford
Upper Woodford
Great Durnford
Stockton
Bapton
Wylye
Netton
Monkton Deverill
Kingston Deverill
Hanging Langford
Stapleford
Middle Woodford
Kilmington
Little Langford
Salterton
Kilmington Common
Great Wishford
Stoford
Winterbourne Dauntsey
Winterbourne Gunner
Little Durnford
South Newnton
Winterbourne Earls
Berwick St Leonard
Fonthill Bishop
Teffont Magna
Baverstock
Hurdcott
SALISBURY PLAIN
VALE OF PEWSEY
NORTH DOWN
PEWSEY DOWN
WILSFORD DOWN
CHARLTON DOWN
ENFORD DOWN
LITTLETON DOWN
TENANTRY DOWN
WARMINSTER DOWN
KNIGHTON DOWN
HAXTON DOWN
BRIMSDOWN HILL
LONG KNOLL
KEYSLEY DOWN
BATTLESBURY HILL
SCRATCHBURY HILL
TYTHERINGTON HILL
MORGANS HILL
MILK HILL
0 1 2 3 4 miles
0 1 2 3 4 5 kilometres

31
Kennington
Sandford on-Thames
Abingdon-on-Thames
Faringdon
Wantage
Grove
Didcot
Wallingford
Cholsey
Goring
Theale
Hungerford
Newbury
Thatcham
Tadley
Kingsclere
Whitchurch
Overton
Oakley
BASINGSTOKE
Andover
Ludgershall
Stockbridge
Kings Worthy
Alresford
Broadwell
Bampton
Aston
Brighthampton
Standlake
Cote
Northmoor
Appleton
Wootton
Sandleigh
Sunningwell
Bayworth
Garsington
Great Milton
Great Haseley
Little Milton
Little Haseley
Toot Baldon
Marsh Baldon
Chiselhampton
Stadhampton
Stoke Talmage
Langford
Clanfield
Weald
Chimney
Duxford
Longworth
Kelmscott
Grafton
Hinton Waldrist
Buckland
Southmoor
Tubney
Cothill
Radley
Fyfield
Kingston Bagpuize
Frilford
Shippon
Eaton Hastings
Littleworth
Buscot
Pusey
Charney Bassett
Garford
Marcham
Sutton Wick
Drayton
Culham
Clifton Hampden
Long Wittenham
Berinsfield
Dorchester
Newington
Chalgrove
Drayton St Leonard
Berrick Prior
Berrick Salome
Brightwell Baldwin
Pyrton
Cuxham
Brightwell Upperton
Warborough
Shillingford
Roke
Benson
Ewelme
Hatford
Little Coxwell
Great Coxwell
Fernham
Shellingford
Stanford in the Vale
Lyford
East Hanney
West Hanney
Sutton Courtenay
Appleford
Little Wittenham
Vale of White Horse
Goosey
Baulking
Denchworth
Steventon
Milton
Milton Hill
Harwell
Brightwell-cum-Sotwell
Longcot
Watchfield
Uffington
Shrivenham
Woolstone
Kingston Lisle
Compton Beauchamp
West Challow
Sparsholt
East Challow
Charlton
Ardington
West Hendred
East Hendred
West Lockinge
East Lockinge
Childrey
Letcombe Regis
Letcombe Bassett
Upton
Chilton
Blewbury
East Hagbourne
West Hagbourne
South Moreton
North Moreton
Aston Upthorpe
Aston Tirrold
Crowmarsh Gifford
North Stoke
Nuffield
Ashbury
Idstone
Bishopstone
Hinton Parva
LAMBOURN DOWNS
Upper Lambourn
Lambourn
Fawley
West Ilsley
East Ilsley
Farnborough
Moulsford
South Stoke
Cleeve
Streatley
Ipsden
Checkendon
Woodcote
Stoke Row
Exlade Street
Catmore
Compton
Aldworth
Brightwalton
Chaddleworth
Beedon
Baydon
Aldbourne
Eastbury
East Garston
Great Shefford
Leckhampstead
Leckhampstead Thicket
Peasemore
East Shefford
Ashampstead
Hampstead Norreys
Yattendon
Lower Basildon
Upper Basildon
Pangbourne
Whitchurch Hill
Tidmarsh
Purley
Sulham
Tilehurst
READING
Ramsbury
Weston
Welford
Chieveley
Hermitage
Winterbourne
Westbrook
Boxford
Frilsham
Bradfield
Stanford Dingley
Englefield
Chilton Foliat
Hungerford Newtown
Wickham
Curridge
Cold Ash
Bucklebury
Upper Bucklebury
Chapel Row
Beenham
Sulhamstead
Froxfield
Avington
Kintbury
Stockcross
Speen
Donnington
Shaw
Ashmore Green
Midgham
Woolhampton
Ufton Nervet
Burghfield
Burghfield Common
Chisbury
Little Bedwyn
Great Bedwyn
Inkpen
Hamstead Marshall
Enborne
Enborne Row
Crookham
Brimpton
Aldermaston
Padworth
Mortimer
Shalbourne
Ham
Upper Green
West Woodhay
Broad Layings
Woolton Hill
Burghclere
Headley
Ashford Hill
Mortimer West End
Stratfield Mortimer
Pamber Heath
Silchester
Stratfield Saye
Eastcourt
Wilton
Marten
East Grafton
West Grafton
Combe
East Woodhay
East End
Pilot Hill
Highclere
Whitway
Old Burghclere
Ecchinswell
Browninghill Green
Baughurst
Pamber Green
West End Green
Bramley Corner
Fair Oak Green
Wexcombe
Oxenwood
Linkenholt
Faccombe
Ashmansworth
Sydmonton
Wolverton
Towns End
Charter Alley
Little London
Pamber End
Bramley
Sherfield on Loddon
Tidcombe
Fosbury
Vernham Street
Vernham Dean
Brunton
Collingbourne Kingston
Crux Easton
BEACON HILL
LADLE HILL
Ramsdell
Monk Sherborne
Sherborne St John
Hannington
Upton
Cadley
Collingbourne Ducis
Upper Chute
Lower Chute
Tangley
Hurstbourne Tarrant
Ibthorpe
Binley
Litchfield
Ibworth
Wootton St Lawrence
Chineham
Old Basing
Stoke
Hatherden
Clanville
Enham Alamein
Penton Mewsey
Appleshaw
Little London
Smannell
St Mary Bourne
Southington
Freefolk
Ashe
Deane
Kempshott
Mapledurwell
Cliddesden
Perham Down
Kimpton
Fyfield
Weyhill
Thruxton
Monxton
Anna Valley
Hurstbourne Priors
Tufton
Laverstoke
Steventon
North Waltham
Farleigh Wallop
Herriard
Weston Corbett
Dummer
Ellisfield
Quarley
Amport
Abbotts Ann
Upper Clatford
Longparish
Middleton
Forton
Southrope
Goodworth Clatford
Grateley
Bransbury
Bullington
Micheldever Station
Woodmancott
Preston Candover
Axford
Bradley
Lasham
Wherwell
Newton Stacey
Barton Stacey
Chilton Candover
Lower Wield
Fullerton
Chilbolton
Northbrook
East Stratton
Bentworth
Over Wallop
Middle Wallop
Nether Wallop
Longstock
Leckford
Sutton Scotney
Wonston
Stoke Charity
Micheldever
Brown Candover
Upper Wield
Wivelrod
Northington
Swarraton
Medstead
Crawley Down
East Winterslow
Whiteshoot Hill
Broughton
Little Somborne
Littleton
Abbots Worthy
Martyr Worthy
Itchen Abbas
Old Alresford
New Alresford
Bighton
Gundleton
Four Marks
20
10
9
Town Plan: Basingstoke

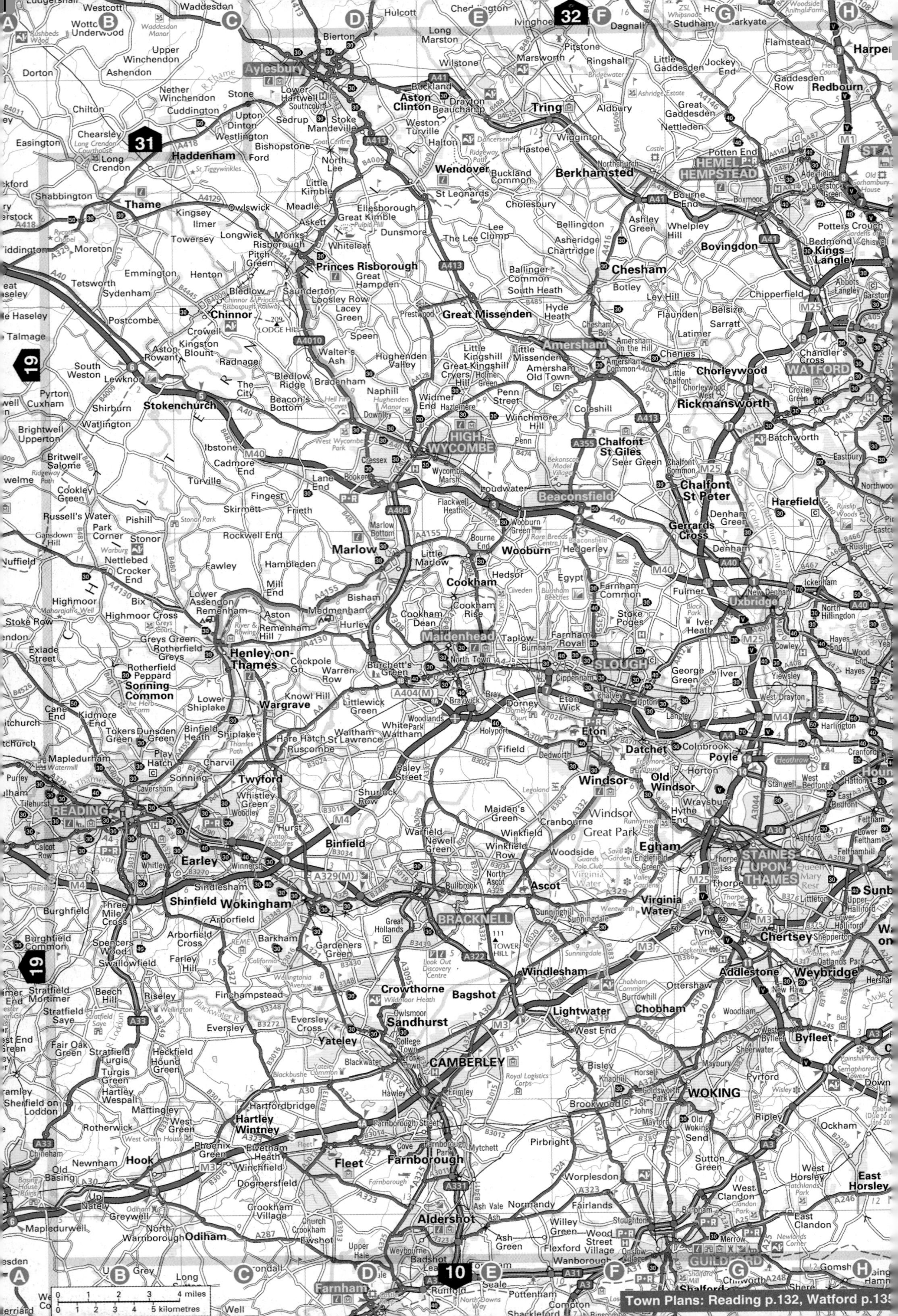

A
B
C
D
E
F
G
H
32
31
19
10
Westcott
Waddesdon
Wotton Underwood
Upper Winchendon
Ashendon
Dorton
Hulcott
Long Marston
Bierton
Aylesbury
Ivinghoe
Dagnall
Studham
Markyate
Flamstead
Harpenden
Pitstone
Ringshall
Marsworth
Little Gaddesden
Jockey End
Gaddesden Row
Redbourn
Wilstone
Nether Winchendon
Stone
Lower Hartwell
Aston Clinton
Buckland
Drayton Beauchamp
Tring
Aldbury
Great Gaddesden
Nettleden
Chilton
Cuddington
Upton
Dinton
Sedrup
Stoke Mandeville
Weston Turville
Halton
Wigginton
Chearsley
Long Crendon
Easington
Westlington
Bishopstone
Haddenham
Ford
North Lee
Hastoe
Wendover
Buckland Common
Berkhamsted
Northchurch
Potten End
Hemel Hempstead
Shabbington
Thame
Owlswick
Little Kimble
Meadle
St Leonards
Cholesbury
Bourne End
Boxmoor
Kingsey
Ilmer
Askett
Ellesborough
Great Kimble
Ashley Green
Whelpley Hill
Bellingdon
Potters Crouch
Bedmond
Kings Langley
Towersey
Longwick
Monks Risborough
Dunsmore
Lee Clump
The Lee
Asheridge
Chartridge
Bovingdon
Moreton
Pitch Green
Whiteleaf
Princes Risborough
Great Hampden
Ballinger Common
South Heath
Chesham
Botley
Ley Hill
Chipperfield
Abbots Langley
Tetsworth
Emmington
Henton
Bledlow
Saunderton
Loosley Row
Lacey Green
Prestwood
Great Missenden
Hyde Heath
Flaunden
Belsize
Sarratt
Latimer
Sydenham
Chinnor
Crowell
Postcombe
Speen
Little Kingshill
Little Missenden
Amersham
Amersham on the Hill
Amersham Common
Chenies
Chorleywood
Watford
Chandler's Cross
Aston Rowant
Kingston Blount
Radnage
Walter's Ash
Hughenden Valley
Great Kingshill
Cryers Hill
Holmer Green
Amersham Old Town
Little Chalfont
Croxley Green
South Weston
Lewknor
Bledlow Ridge
Bradenham
Naphill
Widmer End
Hazlemere
Penn Street
Coleshill
Rickmansworth
Pyrton
Cuxham
Shirburn
The City
Beacon's Bottom
Stokenchurch
Watlington
Downley
High Wycombe
Winchmore Hill
Penn
Chalfont St Giles
Batchworth
Brightwell Upperton
Ibstone
M40
Cadmore End
West Wycombe Park
Cressex
Booker
Wycombe Marsh
Seer Green
Chalfont Common
Eastbury
Britwell Salome
Turville
Lane End
Loudwater
Beaconsfield
Chalfont St Peter
Northwood
Cookley Green
Fingest
Skirmett
Frieth
Flackwell Heath
Wooburn Green
Gerrards Cross
Denham Green
Harefield
Russell's Water
Pishill
Stonor
Marlow Bottom
Bourne End
Wooburn
Hedgerley
Denham
Park Corner
Nettlebed
Crocker End
Rockwell End
Fawley
Hambleden
Marlow
Little Marlow
Cookham
Hedsor
Egypt
Farnham Common
Fulmer
Ickenham
Uxbridge
Nuffield
Highmoor
Bix
Highmoor Cross
Lower Assendon
Remenham
Mill End
Aston
Medmenham
Bisham
Hurley
Cookham Dean
Cookham Rise
Stoke Poges
Iver Heath
North Hillingdon
Stoke Row
Greys Green
Rotherfield Greys
Henley-on-Thames
Remenham Hill
Maidenhead
Taplow
Burnham
Farnham Royal
Cowley
Hayes
Exlade Street
Rotherfield Peppard
Sonning Common
Cockpole Green
Warren Row
Burchett's Green
North Town
Slough
Cippenham
George Green
Iver
Yiewsley
West Drayton
Lower Shiplake
Knowl Hill
Wargrave
Littlewick Green
Bray
Dorney
Eton Wick
Eton
Chalvey
Upton
Langley
Harlington
Cane End
Kidmore End
Tokers Green
Dunsden Green
Binfield Heath
Shiplake
Woodlands Park
White Waltham
Holyport
Datchet
Colnbrook
Poyle
Cranford
Mapledurham
Play Hatch
Charvil
Hare Hatch
Waltham St Lawrence
Ruscombe
Fifield
Dedworth
Windsor
Old Windsor
Horton
Heathrow
Stanwell
West Bedfont
Hatton
Purley
Caversham
Sonning
Twyford
Paley Street
Shurlock Row
Maiden's Green
Legoland
Wraysbury
East Bedfont
Reading
Tilehurst
Whistley Green
Woodley
Hurst
Warfield
Newell Green
Winkfield
Cranbourne
Windsor Great Park
Hythe End
Egham
Feltham
Ashford
Lower Feltham
Calcot
Binfield
Winkfield Row
Woodside
Englefield Green
Staines upon Thames
Feltham Hill
Whitley
Earley
Winnersh
Sindlesham
Bullbrook
North Ascot
Ascot
Virginia Water
Thorpe Lea
Thorpe
Sunbury
M4
Shinfield
Wokingham
Arborfield
Bracknell
Sunninghill
Sunningdale
Littleton
Upper Halliford
Lower Halliford
Three Mile Cross
Burghfield
Great Hollands
Lyne
Chertsey
Shepperton
Burghfield Common
Spencers Wood
Arborfield Cross
Barkham
Gardeners Green
Tower Hill
Walton-on-Thames
Swallowfield
Farley Hill
Crowthorne
Windlesham
Addlestone
Weybridge
Stratfield Mortimer
Beech Hill
Riseley
Finchampstead
Bagshot
Lightwater
Chobham
Ottershaw
Stratfield Saye
Eversley
Eversley Cross
Owlsmoor
Sandhurst
West End
Woodham
New Haw
Fair Oak Green
Stratfield Turgis
Heckfield
Hound Green
Yateley
College Town
Camberley
Blackwater
Bisley
Horsell
West Byfleet
Byfleet
Turgis Green
Hartley Wespall
Mattingley
Hawley
Frimley
Knaphill
Woking
Pyrford
Sherfield on Loddon
Hartfordbridge
Hartley Wintney
West Green
Rotherwick
Brookwood
St Johns
Mayford
Old Woking
Ripley
Ockham
Farnborough Street
Cove
Pirbright
Send
Chineham
Newnham
Hook
Phoenix Green
Elvetham Heath
Winchfield
Fleet
Farnborough
Mytchett
Sutton Green
Old Basing
Dogmersfield
Worplesdon
West Horsley
East Horsley
West Clandon
Crookham Village
Ash Vale
Normandy
Fairlands
Burpham
Nately
Up Nately
Greywell
Aldershot
Church Crookham
Ewshot
Willey Green
Wood Street Village
East Clandon
Mapledurwell
North Warnborough
Odiham
Ash
Ash Green
Flexford
Stoughton
Merrow
Upper Hale
Weybourne
Badshot Lea
Wanborough
Onslow Village
Guildford
Gomshall
Crondall
Farnham
Runfold
Seale
Puttenham
Compton
Shalford
Chilworth
Shere
Long Sutton
Well
0 1 2 3 4 miles
0 1 2 3 4 5 kilometres
Town Plans: Reading p.132, Watford p.13

33
Wheathampstead
Welwyn Garden City
Hertford
Ware
Sawbridgeworth
High Wych
Hatfield Heath
Sandridge
Hatfield
Hertingfordbury
Hoddesdon
Stanstead Abbotts
HARLOW
Matching Tye
London Colney
Brookmans Park
Cuffley
Cheshunt
Epping
North Weald Bassett
Chipping Ongar
Potters Bar
South Mimms
Waltham Abbey
Theydon Bois
Borehamwood
Barnet
Enfield
Loughton
Chigwell
Navestock
22
BRENTWOOD
Edgware
Hendon
Romford
Wembley
Camden Town
Islington
Hackney
Barking
Ealing
Hammersmith
LONDON
Greenwich
Woolwich
Rainham
South Ockendon
Aveley
Richmond
Lewisham
Dartford
Dartford Crossing
Kingston upon Thames
Bromley
Swanley
Orpington
Croydon
Sutton
Epsom
Banstead
Biggin Hill
Otford
West Kingsdown
Kemsing
Borough Green
Westerham
Caterham
Oxted
Limpsfield
Redhill
Reigate
Dorking
Sevenoaks
Hildenborough
Edenbridge
11
Town Plan: Central London pp.148-

33
34
21
12
THE RODINGS
Hatfield Broad Oak
Gaston Green
High Roding
Hatfield Heath
Roundbush Gn
White Roding
Leaden Roding
Pleshey
High Easter
Good Easter
Great Waltham
Broad's Green
Little Waltham
Chatham Green
Great Leighs
Fuller Street
Fairs
Terling
Witham
Little Braxted
Great Braxted
Great Totham
Tiptree Heath
Oxley Green
Tolleshunt Knights
Wickham Bishops
Hatfield Peverel
Tolleshunt Major
Langford
Goldhanger
Heybridge
Museum of Power
Boreham
Little Baddow
Sheering
Matching Tye
Old Harlow
Abbess Roding
Matching Green
Threshers Bush
Beauchamp Roding
Birds Green
Boyton Cross
Chignall St James
Chignall Smealy
Broomfield
Roxwell
Springfield
CHELMSFORD
Foster Street
Shellow Bowells
Newney Green
Hastingwood
Fyfield
Moreton
Willingale
Cooksmill Green
Radley Green
Great Oxney Green
Writtle
Woodham Walter
Maldon
Northey Is
Osea Is
Norton Heath
Loves Green
Widford
Great Baddow
Danbury
Sandon
Howe Green
Woodham Mortimer
Hazeleigh
Rudley Green
Mundon Hill
Maylandsea
North Weald Bassett
High Ongar
Chipping Ongar
Coopersale Common
Toot Hill
Hylands House & Park
Galleywood
Bicknacre
Cock Clarks
Purleigh
Blackmore
Margaretting
Margaretting Tye
East Hanningfield
Howegreen
Latchingdon
Stondon Massey
Mill Green
Fryerning
Heybridge
Ingatestone
Woodham Ferrers
Stow Maries
Cold Norton
Althorne
Doddinghurst
Nuclear Bunker
Kelvedon Hatch
West Hanningfield
Hanningfield Reservoir
Coalhill
Rettendon
South Woodham Ferrers
North Fambridge
Bridgemarsh Island
Navestock Side
Navestock
Mountnessing
Stock
Tropical Wings
South Hanningfield
Marsh Farm
Abridge
Lambourne End
Pilgrims Hatch
Coxtie Green
Shenfield
BRENTWOOD
Hutton
Billericay
Downham
Ramsden Bellhouse
Runwell
Battlesbridge
Hullbridge
South Fambridge
River Crouch
Canewdon
Stapleford Abbotts
Bournebridge
Chigwell Row
Havering-atte-Bower
South Weald
Brook Street
Harold Hill
Little Burstead
Great Burstead
Ingrave
Wickford
Shotgate
Crays Hill
Rawreth
Hockley
Hawkwell
Ashingdon
Rayleigh
Great Stambridge
Rochford
Collier Row
Gidea Park
Harold Wood
Great Warley
Thorndon
North Benfleet
BASILDON
Bowers Gifford
Thundersley
Southend
Little Wakering
Chadwell Heath
Romford
West Horndon
Laindon
Lee Chapel
Pitsea
Vange
Eastwood
Prittlewell
Bournes Green
Goodmayes
Rush Green
Hornchurch
Upminster
Corbets Tey
Westley Heights
Langdon
One Tree Hill
Hadleigh
Hadleigh Castle
Leigh-on-Sea
Westcliff-on-Sea
Southchurch
Thorpe Bay
Becontree
Elm Park
Dagenham
South Hornchurch
Bulphan
South Benfleet
Fobbing
Horndon on the Hill
Corringham
Leigh Beck
Canvey Point
SOUTHEND-ON-SEA
Rainham
Wennington
South Ockendon
Orsett
Stanford le Hope
Coryton
Canvey Island
THAMES ESTUARY
Thamesmead
Rainham Marshes
Aveley
North Stifford
Belvedere
Abbey Wood
Erith
Purfleet
West Thurrock
Lakeside
Chadwell St Mary
West Tilbury
Grays
Little Thurrock
East Tilbury
Tilbury
Tilbury Fort
Coalhouse Fort
Cliffe
Cooling
St Mary's Hoo
Allhallows
Isle of Grain
Lower Stoke
Grain
Slade Green
Dartford Crossing
Queen Elizabeth II Bridge
Greenhithe
Bexleyheath
Crayford
Dartford
Bexley
Swanscombe
Ebbsfleet International
Northfleet
Milton
Chalk
GRAVESEND
Higham
Church Street
High Halstow
Fenn Street
Middle Stoke
Cliffe Woods
Hoo St Werburgh
River Medway
West Minster
Mile Town
Queenborough
Joyden's Wood
Wilmington
Hextable
Darenth
South Darenth
Betsham
Southfleet
Green Street Green
Hook Green
Singlewell
Istead Rise
Shorne
Chattenden
Wainscott
Upnor Castle
Frindsbury
The Historic Dockyard Chatham
Rushenden
Swanley
Swanley Village
Sutton at Hone
Dean Bottom
Longfield
New Barn
Cobham
Strood
ROCHESTER
Rochester Castle
Brompton
GILLINGHAM
CHATHAM
Lower Halstow
Iwade
Upchurch
Crockenhill
Horton Kirby
Farningham
Hartley
Sole Street
Cuxton
Borstal
Rainham
Wigmore
Orpington
Eynsford
Fawkham Green
Meopham
Luddesdown
Newington
Bobbing
Milton Regis
Sittingbourne
Chelsfield
Lullingstone Roman Villa
Eynsford Castle
New Ash Green
North Downs Way
Wouldham
Hartlip
Chalkwell
Maplescombe
West Kingsdown
Ash
Hodsoll Street
Harvel
Halling
Buckmore Park
Walderslade
Lords Wood
Bredhurst
Hill Green
Borden
Bapchild
Tunstall
Pratt's Bottom
Shoreham
Stansted
Fairseat
Culverstone Green
Paddlesworth
Snodland
Burham
Blue Bell Hill
Stockbury
South Green
Oad St
Highsted
Halstead
Trottiscliffe
Vigo
Birling
Ryarsh
Eccles
Kit's Coty
Aylesford
Bredgar
Knockholt Pound
Knockholt
Otford
Kemsing
Wrotham
Heaverham
Addington
Leybourne
Lunsford
Larkfield
Ditton
Boxley
Detling
Bicknor
Milstead
Chevening
Dunton Green
Borough Green
Ightham
Platt
West Malling
Offham
British Legion Village
Thurnham
White Horse Wood
Hucking
Wormshill
Frinsted
Doddington
Seal
Chipstead
Riverhead
Sevenoaks
St Johns
Stone Street
Oldbury
East Malling
MAIDSTONE
Bearsted
Broad Street
Hollingbourne
Sundridge
Brasted Chart
Knole House
Ivy Hatch
Old Soar Manor
Kings Hill
Herne Pound
Mereworth
Wateringbury
Teston
East Barming
Tovil
Willington
Otham
Leeds
Leeds Castle
Eyhorne Street
Broomfield
Harrietsham
Lenham
Plaxtol
Dunk's Green
Under River
Shipbourne
West Peckham
Nettlestead
Nettlestead Green
East Farleigh
West Farleigh
Loose
Boughton Green
Langley
Sandway
Ide Hill
Sevenoaks Weald
Hadlow
Yalding
Coxheath
Linton
Boughton Monchelsea
Chart Sutton
Ulcombe
Grafty Green
Hildenborough
Parkers Green
Higham
East Peckham
Hale Street
Hunton
Sutton Valence
Golden Green
Barnes Street
Tonbridge
Laddingford
Mockbeggar
Fowlhall
Whetsted
Five Oak
Collier
Cross-at-Hand
Egerton
0 1 2 3 4 miles
0 1 2 3 4 5 kilometres

35
Peldon
Brightlingsea
Hurst Green
Great Holland
St Osyth
Holland-on-Sea
Great Wigborough
MERSEA ISLAND
Gudmore Grove
East Mersea
Rush Green
CLACTON-ON-SEA
West Mersea
Jaywick
Colne Point
Shinglehead Point
Sales Point
Bradwell Waterside
Bradwell-on-Sea
Tillingham
Dengie
Asheldham
Southminster
Holliwell Point
Foulness Point
Courtsend
Churchend
FOULNESS ISLAND
BROADSTAIRS
St Ethelbert's School
HERESON ROAD
Granville
Bandstand
Chatham House School
St George's
MARGATE
MARGATE RD
CHATHAM ST
Royal Victoria Pavilion
(under repair)
Maritime
Salvation Army
Kingdom Hall
Sports Centre
Police Sta
Priory School
Fire Sta
Clarendon House School
Royal Harbour
Marina
Lifeboat Station
Jobcentre Plus
The Old Priory School
St Augustine's Abbey
Christchurch School
LD Lines & Transeuropa Ferries
ROYAL PARADE
PARAGON
Ramsgate
200 m
LONDON, (M2), CANTERBURY
Warden Point
Leysdown-on-Sea
Eastchurch
SHEPPEY
Isle of Harty
Shell Ness
The Swale
Whitstable
Whitstable Bay
Herne Bay
Bishopstone
Reculver
Reculver Towers
Minnis Bay
MARGATE
Foreness Point
Westgate on Sea
Westbrook
Cliftonville
Northdown
Kingsgate
NORTH FORELAND
Lighthouse
Birchington
Garlinge
Salmestone Grange
Reading Street
St Peter's
Broadstairs
Tankerton
Swalecliffe
Greenhill
Beltinge
Broomfield
Hampton
Chestfield
South Street
Herne
St Nicholas at Wade
Acol
ISLE OF THANET
Lydden
RAF Manston
Manston
Westwood
Dumpton
Hereson
Boyden Gate
Sarre
Monkton
Kent International
St Lawrence
Ramsgate
Chislet
Durlock
Seasalter
Graveney
Yorkletts
Highstreet
Wildwood Wealden Forest Park
Hoath
Upstreet
West Stourmouth
Minster
Pegwell
Pegwell Bay
Viking Ship 'Hugin'
East Stourmouth
Westmarsh
Oostende
Oare
Faversham
Davington
Druidstone
Broad Oak
Hersden
Westbere
Stodmarsh
Goodnestone
Dargate
Hernhill
Denstroude
Tyler Hill
Sturry
Lewson Street
Ospringe
Preston
Staplestreet
Blean
Hales Place
Fordwich
Preston
Elmstone
Cop Street
Richborough Roman Fort
Prince's
Sandwich Bay
Painter's Forstal
North Street
Boughton St
Dunkirk
Upper Harbledown
Rough Common
Old Town Hall
Wickhambreaux
Hoaden
Littlebourne
Seaton
Ickham
Ash
Sandwich
Royal St George's
Sheldwich
South Street
Oversland
Harbledown
Canterbury
Durlock
Wingham
Marshborough
Eastling
Hogben's Hill
Selling
Thanington
Chartham Hatch
Howletts
Bramling
Stone Cross
Woodnesborough
Throwley Forstal
Badlesmere
Old Wives Lees
Chartham
Nackington
Bekesbourne
Patrixbourne
Goodnestone
Staple
Statenborough
Eastry
Worth
Shottenden
Shalmsford Street
Street End
Bridge
Adisham
Ratling
Chillenden
Ham
Hacklinge
Leaveland
Chilham
Lower Hardres
Bishopsbourne
Higham Park
Aylesham
Nonington
Finglesham
The Downs
Dane Street
Garlinge Green
North Downs Way
Betteshanger
Northbourne
Sholden
Deal
Castle
Challock
Molash
Godmersham
Petham
Kingston
Womenswold
Tilmanstone
Great Mongeham
Upper Deal
Elvington
Lower Eythorne
Eythorne
Ripple
Walmer
Castle
Sole Street
Elham Valley
Barham
Woolage Green
Barfrestone
Derringstone
Sutton
East Studdal
Ringwould
Crundale
Waltham
Bossingham
Shepherdswell
Sutton Downs
Kingsdown
13
Boughton Aluph
Wye
Wye Crown
Stelling Minnis
Westwell
Bodsham
Denton
Coldred
West Langdon
Martin
Lydden
Town Plan: Canterbury p

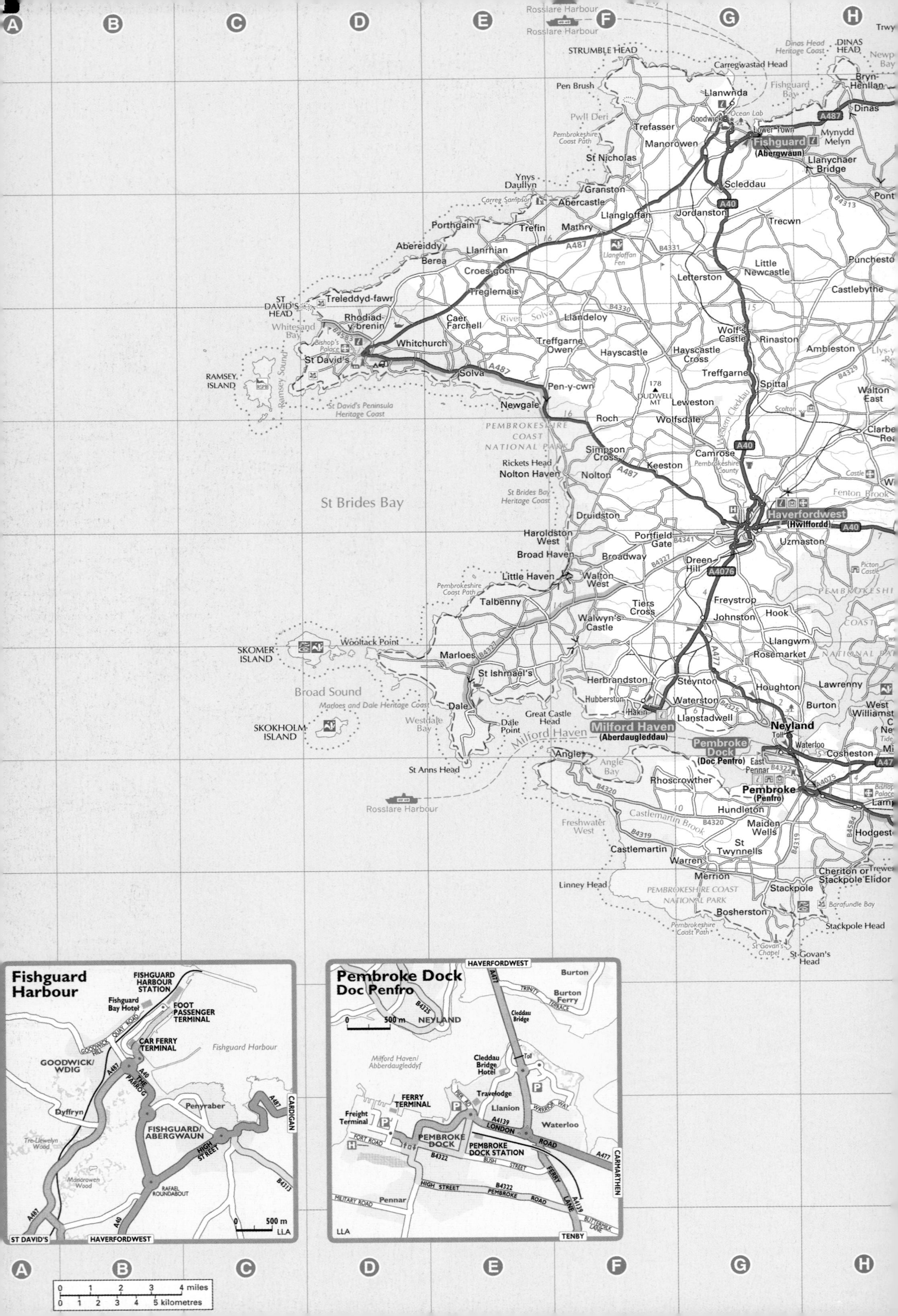

A
B
C
D
E
F
G
H
Rosslare Harbour
Rosslare Harbour
STRUMBLE HEAD
Dinas Head Heritage Coast
DINAS HEAD
Carregwastad Head
Pen Brush
Llanwnda
Fishguard Bay
Bryn-Henllan
Dinas
Pwll Deri
Goodwick
Ocean Lab
Trefasser
Lower Town
Pembrokeshire Coast Path
Manorowen
Fishguard
(Abergwaun)
Mynydd Melyn
St Nicholas
Llanychaer Bridge
Ynys Daullyn
Granston
Scleddau
Carreg Sampson
Abercastle
Jordanston
Llangloffan
Trecwn
Porthgain
Trefin
Mathry
Abereiddy
Llanrhian
Llangloffan Fen
Berea
Letterston
Little Newcastle
Punchesto
Croes-goch
Castlebythe
ST DAVID'S HEAD
Treleddyd-fawr
Treglemais
Whitesand Bay
Rhodiad-y-brenin
Caer Farchell
River Solva
Llandeloy
Wolf's Castle
Rinaston
Bishop's Palace
Whitchurch
Treffgarne Owen
Hayscastle
Hayscastle Cross
Ambleston
RAMSEY ISLAND
Ramsey Sound
St David's
Solva
Treffgarne
Pen-y-cwn
Spittal
Walton East
St David's Peninsula Heritage Coast
Newgale
178
DUDWELL MT
Leweston
Scolton
Roch
Wolfsdale
Western Cleddau
PEMBROKESHIRE COAST NATIONAL PARK
Simpson Cross
Camrose
Pembrokeshire County
Rickets Head
Keeston
Nolton Haven
Nolton
Castle
Fenton Brook
St Brides Bay
St Brides Bay Heritage Coast
Haverfordwest
(Hwlffordd)
Druidston
Haroldston West
Portfield Gate
Uzmaston
Broad Haven
Broadway
Dreen Hill
Picton Castle
Little Haven
Walton West
Pembrokeshire Coast Path
Talbenny
Freystrop
Tiers Cross
Johnston
Hook
Walwyn's Castle
SKOMER ISLAND
Wooltack Point
Llangwm
Marloes
Rosemarket
St Ishmael's
Herbrandston
Steynton
Houghton
Lawrenny
Broad Sound
Hubberston
Waterston
Burton
Marloes and Dale Heritage Coast
Dale
Hakin
Llanstadwell
West Williamston
SKOKHOLM ISLAND
Westdale Bay
Great Castle Head
Dale Point
Milford Haven
(Aberdaugleddau)
Neyland
Milford Haven
Pembroke Dock
(Doc Penfro)
Toll
Waterloo
Cosheston
Angle
Angle Bay
East Pennar
St Anns Head
Rhoscrowther
Pembroke
(Penfro)
Bishop's Palace
Rosslare Harbour
Hundleton
Castlemartin Brook
Freshwater West
Maiden Wells
Hodgeston
St Twynnells
Castlemartin
Warren
Cheriton or Stackpole Elidor
Merrion
Linney Head
PEMBROKESHIRE COAST NATIONAL PARK
Stackpole
Barafundle Bay
Bosherston
Pembrokeshire Coast Path
Stackpole Head
St Govan's Chapel
St Govan's Head
A487
A40
A4076
A477
A4075
B4313
B4331
B4330
B4583
B4329
B4341
B4327
B4325
B4322
B4320
B4319
B4584
Fishguard Harbour
FISHGUARD HARBOUR STATION
Fishguard Bay Hotel
FOOT PASSENGER TERMINAL
GOODWICK HILL
QUAY ROAD
CAR FERRY TERMINAL
Fishguard Harbour
GOODWICK/ WDIG
THE PARROG
Dyffryn
Penyraber
CARDIGAN
FISHGUARD/ ABERGWAUN
HIGH STREET
Tre-Llewelyn Wood
Manorowen Wood
RAFAEL ROUNDABOUT
0
500 m
LLA
ST DAVID'S
HAVERFORDWEST
Pembroke Dock
Doc Penfro
HAVERFORDWEST
Burton
TRINITY TERRACE
Burton Ferry
NEYLAND
Cleddau Bridge
Milford Haven/ Abberdaugleddyf
Toll
Cleddau Bridge Hotel
Travelodge
FERRY TERMINAL
Freight Terminal
Llanion
WARRIOR WAY
Waterloo
FORT ROAD
PEMBROKE DOCK
LONDON
ROAD
PEMBROKE DOCK STATION
BUSH STREET
CARMARTHEN
HIGH STREET
PEMBROKE ROAD
FERRY LANE
MILITARY ROAD
Pennar
BUTTERMILK LANE
LLA
TENBY
0 1 2 3 4 miles
0 1 2 3 4 5 kilometres

Pembroke peninsula
J
K
L
M
N
P
Q
R
Pen-y-bryn
Llechryd
Llandygwydd
Cilgerran
Afon Teifi
TIVY SIDE
Cwm-cou
Adpar
Llandyfriog
Penrhiw-llan
Capel Dewi
Rock Mill Woollen & Water Mill
Llandysul
Llanfihangel-ar-arth
Llanllwni
Abercych
Cenarth
Newcastle Emlyn
(Castell Newydd Emlyn)
36
Nevern
Felindre Farchog
Pengelli Forest
Newport
Castell Henllys
Eglwyswrw
Rhoshill
Pen-rhiw
Newchapel
Henllan
Teifi Valley Railway
Llangeler
Pontwelly
Drefach
National Wool
Felindre
Pentre-cwrt
Glynteg
Carreg Coetan
Boncath
Blaenffos
Pentre Ifan
Crosswell
Cwmhiraeth
Capel Iwan
Cwmpengraig
Pencader
New Inn
Mynydd Llanllwni
Brynberian
Bwlch-y-groes
Star
Rhos
Gwyddgrug
PEMBROKESHIRE COAST
Crymmych
MYNYDD PRESELI
NATIONAL PARK
Tegryn
Gwerno
Hermon
FOEL CWMCERWYN
Mynachlog ddu
Llanfyrnach
Hermon
Cwmduad
Alltwalis
Brechfa
Rosebush
FOEL DRYCH
Gors Fawr
Trelech
Glandwr
Llanpumsaint
Llandre Isaf
Maenclochog
Hebron
River Gwili
Pontarsais
Moat
Llangolman
Llanglydwen
Blaenwaun
Blaen-y-Coed
Cynwyl Elfed
New Moat
Cefn-y-pant
The Welsh Chocolate Farm
Cwmbach
Llanwinio
Talog
Gwili Railway
Rhydargaeau
26
Felingwm Uchaf
Llanycefn
Efailwen
Login
Llanboidy
Gellywen
Abernant
Bronwydd
Felingwm
Pont-ar-gothi
Llandissilio
Afon Gronw
Afon Cynin
Meidrim
Carmarthen
(Caerfyrddin)
Abergwili
Nantgaredig
Hetherston
Llanfallteg
Clunderwen
Llanfallteg West
Cwmfelin Boeth
Llangynin
Llangunnor
Capel Dewi
Llanarthne
Eastern Cleddau
Bethesda
Whitland Abbey
Bancyfelin
United Counties
Llanllwch
Johnstown
Tre-gynwr
Castle
Roberston Wathen
Llanddewi Velfrey
Whitland
Pwll Trap
St Clears
Cwmffrwd
Llanddarog
Croesyceiliog
Narberth
Crinow
Lampeter Velfrey
River Taf
Afon Cywyn
Llangynog
Idole
Bancycapel
Llangendeirne
Bluestone
Llanddowror
Tavernspite
Llanybri
Crwbin
Drefach
Templeton
Red Roses
Laugharne
Pontantwn
Bancffosfelen
Cwmmawr
Llansteffan
Ludchurch
Llanteg
Crunwear
Llansadurnen
Landyfaelog
Pontyberem
Meinciau
Ferryside
River Towy
Folly Farm
Colby Woodland Garden
Four Roads
Ponthenry
Reynalton
Stepaside
Amroth
Wharley Point
Pontyates
Mynydd Sylen
Begelly
Pendine
Llanmiloe
Museum of Speed
Ginst Point
Llansaint
Mynyddgarreg
Jeffreyston
Kilgetty
Summerhill
Broadmoor
Wiseman's Bridge
R Gwendraeth
Kidwelly
(Cydweli)
Carway
Ffos Las
Five Roads
Redberth
East Williamston
Saundersfoot
Trimsaran
Pen-y-Mynydd
Monkstone Point
Pembrey
New Hedges
Ffrwd Farm Mire
Gumfreston
St Florence
Manor House
Tenby
(Dinbych-y-Pysgod)
Pembrey
Archddu
Furnace
CARMARTHEN
BAY
Penally
Burry Port
Pwll
Llanelli
Millennium Coastal Park
Machynys
Gitar Point
Lydstep
Lydstep Point
Monastery
CALDEY ISLAND
Pembrokeshire Coast
Burry Inlet
Salthouse Point
Crofty
Broughton Bay
Llanmadoc
Landimore
Weobley Castle
Burry Holms
Llangennith
Cheriton
Oldwalls
Llanrhidian
Burry Green
Arthur's Stone
Wildfowl Trust
Rhossili Bay
Rhossili Downs
Reynoldston
Cefn-y-Bryn
GOWER
Llanddewi
Penmaen
Rhossili
Knelston
Visitor Centre
WORMS HEAD
Middleton
Penrice
Nicholaston
Paviland
Oxwich
Port Eynon
Horton
Oxwich Green
Oxwich Castle
Overton
Culver Hole
Port Einon Point
Port Einon Bay
Gower Heritage Coast
A487
A478
A484
A485
A486
A475
A40
A48
A477
A4066
A4075
A4115
A4118
A478
B4332
B4333
B4334
B4571
B4476
B4582
B4329
B4313
B4299
B4298
B4301
B4300
B4310
B4314
B4315
B4316
B4328
B4312
B4306
B4309
B4317
B4308
B4311
B4318
B4585
B4336
B4459
B4247
B4304

A
B
C
D
E
F
G
H
Croes-lan
Llanybydder
Rhandirmwyn
Penrhiw-llan
Rock Mill Woollen & Water Mill
Capel Dewi
Mynydd Pencarreg
Llandre
Cynghordy
Llandysul
Llanfihangel-ar-arth
Mynydd Llanybydder
37
Pumsaint
Dolaucothi Gold Mines
Cilycwm
Llangeler
Pontwelly
Llanllwni
Caeo
Pentre-cwrt
Mynydd Llanllwni
Rhydcymerau
River Cothi
Pencader
New Inn
Llansawel
Poor Man's Wood
Gwyddgrug
Llandovery
(Llanymddyfri)
Gwernogle
Abergorlech
Talley Abbey
Talley Lakes
Talley
MYNYDD CYNROS
Cwmduad
Alltwalis
Llansadwrn
Llanwrda
Brechfa
Mynydd Figyn
Myddfai
Mynydd Myddfai
Llanpumsaint
Llangadog
Pontarsais
Llanfynydd
River Gwili
Cynwyl Elfed
Gwili Railway
Rhydargaeau
RHIWIAU HILL
Twynllanan
25
Bethlehem
Felingwm Uchaf
Felingwm Isaf
Corn Goch
Bronwydd
Court Henry
Penybanc
Pont-ar-gothi
Llangathen
Cilsan
Llandeilo
Dinefwr Park
Aberglasney
Felindre
Ffairfach
CARMARTHEN VAN
Carmarthen
(Caerfyrddin)
Abergwili
Nantgaredig
Llanegwad
Castle
Gelli Aur
Llangunnor
Tre-gynwr
Johnstown
Llanllwch
Capel Dewi
Llanarthne
Paxton's Tower
Trapp
Carreg Cennen
BLACK MOUNTAIN
National Botanic Garden of Wales
CARREG LWYD
Carmel
CARREG GOCH
Dan-yr-ogof
Cwmffrwd
Llanddarog
Maesybont
Croesyceiliog
Porthyrhyd
Pentre-Gwenlais
Llandybie
Idole
Dyn Lech Owain
Bancycapel
Llangendeirne
Cefneithin
Gorslas
Glanaman
Brynamman
Cefn-bryn-brain
Abercraf
Pontantwn
Crwbin
Drefach
Penygroes
Saron
Penller-Fedwen
Cwmllynfell
Cwm-twrch Uchaf
Cwmgiedd
Bancffosfelen
Cwmmawr
Tumble
Cross Hands
Ammanford
(Rhydaman)
Gwaun-Cae-Gurwen
Pen Rhiwfawr
Onllwyn
Llandyfaelog
Pontyberem
Upper Tumble
Cwmgwili
Capel Hendre
Tycroes
Cwmgors
Cwm-twrch Isaf
Ystradgynlais
Meinciau
Gurnos
Glan-rhyd
Ferryside
Four Roads
Ponthenry
Llannon
Mynydd-y-Gwair
Ystalyfera
Seven Sisters
Pontyates
Mynydd Sylen
MYNYDD ALLT-Y-GRUG
FARTEG HILL
Mynyddgarreg
Pont Abraham
Craig-Fawr
Godre'r-graig
Hir Fynydd
Kidwelly
(Cydweli)
Carway
Ffos Las
Five Roads
Cilmaengwyn
Rhydyfro
Trimsaran
Fforest
CEFN DRUM
Craig Llangiwg
Cilybebyll
Crynant
Pen-y-Mynydd
Hendy
Pontardawe
Gellinudd
Mynydd March Hywel
Vale of Neath
Pembrey
Ffrwd Farm Mire
Llangennech
Pontarddulais
Alltwen
Rhos
Felindre
Pembrey
Archdiddu
Clydach
Faerdre
Ynystawe
Glais
Cilfrew
Clyne
Burry Port
Pwll
Furnace
Llanelli
Pemberton
Bryn
Grovesend
Pontlliw
Swansea (West)
Bryn-côch
Cadoxton Juxta-Neath
Aberdulais
Aberdulais Falls
Millennium Coastal Park
Machynys
Gorseinon
Mynydd-Bach
Morriston
Llansamlet
Birchgrove
Tonna
Burry Inlet
Loughor
National Wetlands Centre
Castle
Cadle
Neath
(Castell-nedd)
Cefn Morfydd
Skewen
Tonmawr
Salthouse Point
Penclawdd
Gowerton
Fforest Fach
Landore
Winshwen
Cimla
Efail-fach
Cynonville
Crofty
Waunarlwydd
Cockett
Cwmdu
Pentre-chwyth
Crymlyn Bog
Briton Ferry
Pont-rhyd-y-fen
Broughton Bay
Llanmadoc
Poundffald
Three Crosses
Dunvant
FOEL MYNYDDAU
Landimore
Weobley Castle
Killay
Sketty
Brynmill
National Waterfront
Pwll-y-glaw
Burry Holms
Llangennith
Cheriton
Oldwalls
Llanrhidian
Upper Killay
Baglan
Bryn
Burry Green
Arthur's Stone
Wildfowl Trust
Ilston
SWANSEA
(ABERTAWE)
Cwmafan
Rhossili Bay
Rhossili Downs
Reynoldston
Cefn-y-Bryn
Parc le Breos
Parkmill
Bishopston
Black Pill
Aberavon
Port Talbot
Mynydd Margam
Llanddewi
GOWER
Penmaen
Pennard
West Cross
Swansea Bay
Taibach
Rhossili
Knelston
Penrice
Nicholaston
Oystermouth
Visitor Centre
Middleton
Oxwich
Southgate
The Mumbles
Mumbles Head
Margam
Stones Museum
WORMS HEAD
Paviland
Horton
Oxwich Bay
Pwlldu Head
Margam Park
Port Eynon
Overton
Oxwich Green
Oxwich Castle
Oxwich Point
Culver Hole
Port Einon Point
Port Einon Bay
Gower Heritage Coast
Mawdlam
Pyle
Kenfig
Rest Bay
Nottage
Porthcawl
0 1 2 3 4 miles
0 1 2 3 4 5 kilometres
Town Plan: Swansea p.13

South Wales
37
38
28
16
J
K
L
M
N
P
Q
R
Mynydd Ekynt
475
463
BRYN DU
454
WRHYD
Llandulas
Ysgir Fawr
Ysgir Fechan
Gwenddwr
Erwood
Crickadarn
Upper Chapel
384
CEFN CLAWDD
B4520
Llaneglwys
456
YSGWYDD HWCH
LLANDEFALLE HILL
Llandefalle
Lower Chapel
Merthyr Cynog
Nant Bran
Llanfihangel Nant Bran
Pont-faen
Pwllgloyw
Pentre-bach
417
TWYRN DISGWYLFA
Battle
Cradoc
Llanddew
Llywel
Trallong
352
Sennybridge
Defynnog
Brecon
(Aberhonddu)
Roman Fort
R Usk
Llanspyddid
B4602
B4601
A40
A470
A438
A4215
Libanus
National Park
Crai
Afon Senni
BRECON BEACONS
604
634
886
PEN-Y-FAN
Cefn Cyff
561
BRYN
763
764
GWAUN RHUDD
Talybont Reservoir
Talybont-on-Usk
Cefn Crew
Gwaen Nant-Ddu
734
FAN FAWR
726
FAN GIHIRYCH
663
FAN NEDD
631
FAN LLIA
NATIONAL PARK
Ystradfellte
A4059
Garwnant Forest Centre
Llwyn-on Reservoir
Pen-twyn Reservoir
442
TWYN CROES
Pontsticill
Brecon Mountain Railway
Vaynor
Cwm Taf
River Hepste
Sgwd yr Eira (Waterfall)
Penderyn
Mynydd-y Glog
A4109
Pontneddfechan
A465
Hirwaun
Rhigos
Blaengwrach
Penywaun
Cwmdare
Llwydcoed
Aber-nant
Abercanaid
Pentrebach
Cefn Pennar
Trecynon
600
CRAIG-Y-LLYN
Aberdare
(Aberdâr)
Cwmbach
Mynydd Merthyr
Aberaman
A4061
Mynydd Ystradffernol
Blaenrhondda
Blaen-y-cwm
Cwmaman
Abercwmboi
B4275
Mountain Ash
A4233
Maerdy
Treherbert
478
Treorchy
Ferndale
Ystrad
Pentre
Cwmparc
Blaengwynfi
Abergwynfi
A4107
Croeserw
571
WERFA
550
MYNYDD CAERAU
Tylorstown
Rhondda Valley
Clydach Vale
Llwynypia
Trealaw
Ynyshir
Porth
Tonypandy
Penygraig
Nant-y-moel
Blaengarw
Mynydd Llangeinwyr
Pontycymer
Garw Fechan Woodland Park
Ogmore Vale
Gilfach Goch
Lewistown
A4093
A4064
A4061
Llangeinor
Betws
Brynmenyn
Blackmill
Mynydd Maendy
Heol-y-Cyw
Brynna Woods
Brynna
Tondu
Aberkenfig
Bridgend
(Pen-y-Bont-ar-Ogwr)
Coity
Pant-ffrwyth
Pencoed
Llanilid
Llanharry
Brynsadler
Dragon International Studios
Pontyclun
Llanharan
Llantrisant
Groes-faen
Miskin
Creigiau
Pentyrch
Radyr
M4
A473
A48
B4181
Coychurch
Treoes
Llangan
Corntown
Ewenny
Ogmore
Penllyn
Ystradowen
Clawdd-coch
Trerhyngyll
Pendoylan
Maendy
Welsh St Donats
Aberthin
Colwinston
Llysworney
Llandow
Cowbridge
Llanblethian
St Quentin's Castle
Peterston-super-Ely
St Brides super-Ely
St Fagans
St George's
St Nicholas
A4232
Bonvilston
Michaelston-le-Pit
Tinkinswood
Dowlais
A4060
Merthyr Tydfil
(Merthyr Tudful)
Troedyrhiw
Aberfan
Merthyr Vale
A4054
A470
Treharris
Trelewis
Penrhiwceiber
Ynysboeth
Abercynon
Ynysybwl
Cilfynydd
Rhondda Heritage Park
Trehafod
Cymmer
Pontypridd
Tonyrefail
Trefforest
Pen-y-coedcae
Llantwit Fardre
Beddau
Church Village
Tyn-y-nant
Efail Isaf
Taff's Well
Tongwynlais
Castell Coch
Tredegar
Bryn Bach
Llechrhyd
Rhymney
Pontlottyn
Fochriw
Rhymney Valley
Tirphil
New Tredegar
Deri
Bedlinog
Cwmfelin
Brithdir
Bargoed
Gilfach
Gelligaer
Nelson
Hengoed
Ystrad Mynach
Llancaiach Fawr
Mynydd Eglwysilan
Senghenydd
Abertridwr
Groes-Wen
Caerphilly
(Caerffili)
Rudry
Llanbradach
Bedwas
Ynysddu
Cwmfelinfach
Maesycwmmer
Pengam
Blackwood
Pontllanfraith
Oakdale
Penmaen
Ebbw Vale
(Glynebwy)
550
MYNYDD CARN-Y-CEFN
Sirhowy Valley
Ebbw Valley
Bedwellty
Argoed
Markham
Hollybush
Manmoel
Beaufort
Brynmawr
Nantyglo
Blaina
COITY MOUNTAIN
Cwmtillery
Abertillery
(Abertyleri)
Llanhilleth
Crumlin
Newbridge
Pentwynmawr
Mynydd Lan
Abercarn
Cwmcarn
Pontywaun
Cwmcarn Forest Drive
Crosskeys
Risca
Wattsville
Machen
Lower Machen
Rogerstone
Draethen
Michaelstone-y-Fedw
Park Cefn Onn
Lisvane
Rhiwbina
Llanishen
Whitchurch
Birchgrove
Llandaff
Fairwater
Canton
Roath
Pengam
Splottlands
Cardiff Gate
Llanedeyrn
St Mellons
Llanrumney
Rumney
CARDIFF
(CAERDYDD)
A48(M)
Castleton
Marshfield
St Brides Wentlooge
Peterstone Wentlooge
Hay-on-Wye
Llowes
Cwmbach
Boughrood
Glasbury
River Wye
Llyswen
Llanigon
Aberllynfi
Three Cocks
Tregoyd
Velindre
Bronllys
Talgarth
Llanelieu
Llanfilo
Llandefaelog-Tre'r-Graig
Trefecca
Llanywern
Castell Dinas
Llangors
Llangors Lake
Llanhamlach
Llanfrynach
Pennorth
Pencelli
Scethrog
Llansantffraed
Cathedine
Cwmdu
Bwlch
Tretower
Tretower Court & Castle
Cwm Crawnon
550
TOR-Y-FOEL
Canal
Llangynidr
Crickhowell
Llangattock
516
GARN CAWS
536
550
MYNYDD LLANGYNIDR
Mynydd Llangatwg
Clydach
Gilwern
Gofilon
Llanfoist
Abergavenny
Mardy
A4077
A479
A4078
A4079
B4558
B4560
B4350
Gader Ridge
811
WAUN FACH
800
PEN-Y-GADER FAWR
Grwyne Fechan
Penallt Mawr Range
BLACK MOUNTAINS
Crug Hywel
550
CRUG MAWR
Llanbedr
690
LORD HEREFORD'S KNOB
676
HAY BLUFF
Black Mountain
Ffawddog Ridge
Afon Honddu
Dorstone
VAGAR HILL
486
CEFN HILL
Craswall
Escley Brook
Michaelchurch Escley
River Monnow
Priory
Llanthony
Offa's Dyke Path
Oldcastle
Grwyne Fawr
596
SUGAR LOAF
Sugar Loaf
Llantilio Pertholey
SKIRRID-FAWR
A465
Ironworks
Blaenavon Industrial Landscape
Blaenavon
Big Pit
Llanellen
Llanover
A4042
Mynydd Garnclochdy
Abersychan
Goetre
Penperlleni
Mamhilad
Little Mill
Monkswood
Pontypool
(Pont-y-Pŵl)
A472
Griffithstown
New Inn
Mynydd Maen
Greenmeadow Community Farm
Pontnewydd
Croesyceiliog
Forge Hammer
Cwmbran
(Cwmbrân)
Llantarnam
Ponthir
Henllys
Malpas
Bettws
Maindee
Bassaleg
Rhiwderyn
A468
Tredegar

38
39
27
17
Bredwardine
Clyro
Hay-on-Wye
Arthur's Stone
Monnington on Wye
Byford
Bridge Sollers
Sugwas Pool
Cannon Bridge
Burghill
Stretton Sugwas
Pipe and Lyde
Shelwick
Withington
Shucknall
Yarkhill
Monkhide
Holmer
Weston Beggard
Ashperton
Lugwardine
Hagley
Tarrington
Preston on Wye
Dorstone
Blakemere
Lulham
Tyberton
Madley
Breinton
Ruckhall
Clehonger
Bartestree
Dormington
Perton
Stoke Edith
Hereford
Blackmarstone
Lower Bullingham
Rotherwas Chapel
Dinedor Hill
Dinedor
Hampton Bishop
Putley Green
Putley
Mordiford
Llanigon
Vagar Hill
Hinton
Golden Valley
Peterchurch
Cefn Hill
Craswall
Escley Brook
Hay Bluff
Tregoyd
Shenmore
Cublington
Turnastone
Vowchurch
Coldwell
Allensmore
Woolhope
Kingstone
Hungerstone
Holme Lacy
Thruxton
Fownhope
Lord Hereford's Knob
Black Mountain
Michaelchurch Escley
St Margarets
Callow
Aconbury
Sollers Hope
Kivernoll
Little Dewchurch
Newton
Bacton
Kingsthorne
Ballingham
Stocking
River Monnow
River Dore
Brockhampton
Little Birch
Much Dewchurch
Carey
Gader Ridge
Waun Fach
Ffawddog Ridge
Afon Honddu
Wormbridge
Kilpeck
Much Birch
Pen-allt
How Caple
Abbey Dore
The Parks
Wormelow Tump
Hoarwithy
Longtown
King's Caple
Foy
Pen-y-Gader Fawr
Priory
Offa's Dyke Path
Ewyas Harold
Harewood End
Strangford
Crow Hill
Brampton Abbotts
Black Mountains
Llanthony
Clodock
Pontrilas
Bagwy Llydiart
Orcop Hill
Sellack
Baysham
Upper Grove Common
Rowlstone
Kentchurch
Orcop
Michaelchurch
Penallt Mawr Range
Oldcastle
Grwyne Fawr
St Weonards
St Owens Cross
Bridstow
Tretire
Peterstow
Ross-on-Wye
Cwmdu
Grosmont
Wilton
Weston under Penyard
Crug Mawr
Pandy
Garway
Glewstone
Tretower
Crug Hywel
Llanbedr
Llanvihangel Crucorney
Llangattock Lingoed
Craig Serrfyn
Skenfrith Castle
Broad Oak
Llancloudy
Llangarron
Pencraig
Goodrich
East Dean
Walford
Hope Mansell
Skenfrith
Cross Ash
Llangrove
Marstow
Crickhowell
Sugar Loaf
Skirrid-Fawr
Welsh Newton
Whitchurch
Old Forge
Ruardean
Drybrook
Mitcheldean
Llangattock
Llantilio Pertholey
Llanvetherine
Newcastle
St Maughans Green
Lower Lydbrook
Ruardean Woodside
Ruardean Hill
White Castle
Llanthewy Skirrid
Tal-y-coed
Buckholt
Symonds Yat
English Bicknor
Brierley
Gilwern
Mardy
Hen Gwrt (Moat)
Llantilio-Crossenny
Rockfield
Dixton
Upper Lydbrook
Cinderford
Clydach
Gofilon
Abergavenny (Y Fenni)
Llanvapley
Monmouthshire
Monmouth (Trefynwy)
Staunton
The Kymin
Llanfoist
Llanddewi Rhydderch
Brynmawr
Penrhos
Penallt
Broadwell
Coleford
Upper Soudley
Nantyglo
Ironworks
Blaenavon Industrial Landscape
Llanellen
Llanarth
Great Oak
Tregare
Dingestow
Mitchel Troy
Redbrook
Whitecliffe
Milkwall
Llanover
Pen-twyn
Newland
Perrygrove Railway
Highbury Wood
Blaenavon
Clytha Hill
Bryngwyn
Raglan Castle
Parkend
Big Pit
Blaina
Coity Mountain
Raglan
Pen-y-clawdd
Cwmcarvan
Clearwell Caves
Clearwell
Ellwood
Newmills
Whitebrook
Bettws Newydd
Goetre
Mynydd Garnclochdy
Cwmtillery
Penperlleni
Kemeys Commander
Kingcoed
Trellech
Harold's Stones
St Briavels
Bream
Abertillery (Abertyleri)
Abersychan
Wye Valley
Llandenny
Llandogo
Mamhilad
Little Mill
Llanishen
Offa's Dyke Path
Hewelsfield
Aylburton
Monkswood
Llansoy
Forest Park
Brockweir
Woolaston Common
Alvington
Gwernesney
Tintern Parva
Tintern Abbey
Llanhilleth
Pontypool (Pont-y-Pŵl)
Llandegfedd Reservoir
Usk
Pentre
Gwent Rural Life
Netherend
Llangwm
Wolvesnewton
Chapel Hill
Woolaston
Griffithstown
New Inn
Llanbadoc
Springdale Farm
Kilgwrrwg Common
Devauden
Crumlin
Mynydd Maen
Llanllowell
Coed-y-paen
Newchurch
Stroat
Newbridge
Llangybi
Itton Common
St Arvans
Tidenham
Greenmeadow Community Farm
Pontnewydd
Croesyceiliog
Llantrisant
Gaerllwyd
Woodcroft
Pentwynmawr
Forge Hammer
Llandegveth
Mynydd-bach
Tutshill
Itton
Sedbury
Abercarn
Cwmbran (Cwmbrân)
Tredunnock
Mounton
Llanvair Discoed
Shirenewton
Pwllmeyric
Chepstow (Cas-Gwent)
River Severn
Oldbury-on-Severn
Mynydd Lan
Cwmcarn Forest Drive
Pontywaun
Llantarnam
Llanfrechfa
Llanhennock
Lower Morton
Crosskeys
Ponthir
Parc Seymour
Runston Chapel
Newton Green
Cowhill
Risca
Henllys
Caerleon
Llanvaches
Caerwent
Kington
Wattsville
Malpas
Celtic Manor
Llanbeder
Penhow
St Pierre
Mathern
Littleton-on-Severn
Thornbury
Machen
Bettws
Llandevaud
Caldicot (Cil-y-coed)
Severn Bridge
Severn View
Elberton
Lower Machen
Maindee
Christchurch
Llanmartin
Bishton
Roman Town
Magor
Llanfihangel Rogiet
Portskewett
Aust
Alveston
Rogerstone
Rhiwderin
Bassaleg
Llanwern
Liswerry
Rogiet
Ifton
Toll
Sudbrook
Ingst
Olveston
Draethen
Newport (Casnewydd-ar-Wysg)
Llandevenny
Magor Marsh
Undy
Second Severn Crossing
Redwick
Tockington
Rudry
Michaelstone-y-Fedw
Tredegar
Severn Beach
Pilning
Almondsbury
Nash
Solutia
Goldcliff
Whitson
Park Cefn Onn
Lisvane
Cardiff Gate
Castleton
Easter Compton
Compton Greenfield
Patchway
Bradley Stoke
Llanedeyrn
St Mellons
Marshfield
St Brides Wentlooge
Llanrumney
Rumney
Cardiff
Peterstone Wentlooge
Hallen
Filton
Stoke Gifford
Pengam
Severn Estuary
Battery Point
Avonmouth
Kings Weston
Shirehampton
Westbury-on-Trym
Horfield
Frenchay
Roath
Portishead
Splottlands
Cardiff (Caerdydd)
Weston-in-Gordano
Clapton-in-Gordano
Portbury
Easton-in-Gordano
Abbots Leigh
Noah's Ark
Bristol
Redland
Clifton
Eastville
Walton-in-Gordano
Lower Failand
0 1 2 3 4 miles
0 1 2 3 4 5 kilometres
A438
A4103
A465
A49
A466
A4137
A40
A4136
A4042
A449
A472
A48
A48(M)
A4232
A403
A4018
A4174
A4162
A369
A467
A4046
A4077
M4
M48
M49
M5
M32
B4348
B4349
B4352
B4224
B4399
B4347
B4521
B4233
B4234
B4228
B4231
B4293
B4235
B4245
B4246
B4598
B4239
B4055
B4057
B4461
B3124

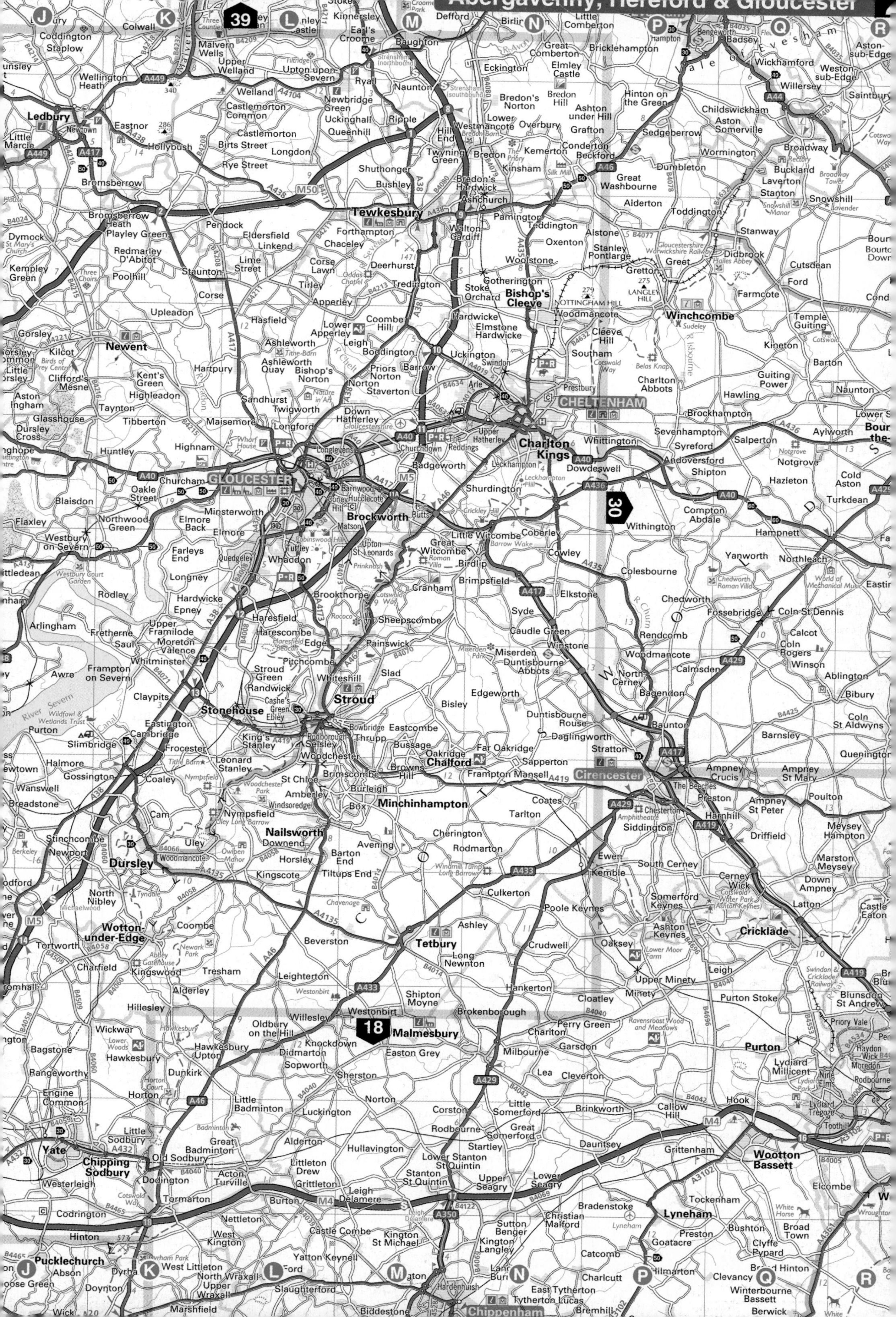

39
Colwall
Coddington
Staplow
Malvern Wells
Upper Welland
Kinnersley
Earl's Croome
Baughton
Defford
Birlin
Little Comberton
Great Comberton
Bricklehampton
Elmley Castle
Eckington
Hampton
Bengeworth
Badsey
Wickhamford
Aston-sub-Edge
Weston sub-Edge
Willersey
Saintbury
Wellington Heath
Upton upon Severn
Ryall
Naunton
Welland
Newbridge Green
Castlemorton Common
Ledbury
Eastnor
Uckinghall
Ripple
Little Marcle
Castlemorton
Queenhill
Hollybush
Birts Street
Longdon
Bredon's Norton
Bredon Hill
Hinton on the Green
Childswickham
Aston Somerville
Ashton under Hill
Grafton
Sedgeberrow
Lower Westmancote
Overbury
Hill End
Kemerton
Conderton
Beckford
Wormington
Broadway
Twyning Green
Bredon
Kinsham
Rye Street
Bromsberrow
Shuthonger
Bushley
Bredon's Hardwick
Great Washbourne
Dumbleton
Buckland
Laverton
Stanton
Snowshill
Ashchurch
Alderton
Toddington
Tewkesbury
Pamington
Bromsberrow Heath
Pendock
Dymock
Playley Green
Eldersfield
Forthampton
Walton Cardiff
Teddington
Alstone
Stanway
Linkend
Chaceley
Oxenton
Stanley Pontlarge
Didbrook
Redmarley D'Abitot
Lime Street
Corse Lawn
Deerhurst
Woolstone
Gretton
Greet
Cutsdean
Kempley Green
Poolhill
Staunton
Tirley
Tredington
Gotherington
Ford
Corse
Apperley
Stoke Orchard
Bishop's Cleeve
Farmcote
Upleadon
Hasfield
Coombe Hill
Hardwicke
Elmstone Hardwicke
Woodmancote
Winchcombe
Temple Guiting
Gorsley
Lower Apperley
Cleeve Hill
Sudeley
Newent
Ashleworth
Leigh
Boddington
Uckington
Southam
Kineton
Kilcot
Ashleworth Quay
Bishop's Norton
Swindon
Barton
Clifford's Mesne
Kent's Green
Hartpury
Priors Norton
Barrow
Charlton Abbots
Guiting Power
Highleadon
Norton
Staverton
Arle
Prestbury
Hawling
Naunton
Aston Ingham
Taynton
Sandhurst
Twigworth
Down Hatherley
CHELTENHAM
Brockhampton
Glasshouse
Tibberton
Maisemore
Longford
Sevenhampton
Aylworth
Dursley Cross
Highnam
Churchdown
The Reddings
Upper Hatherley
Charlton Kings
Whittington
Syreford
Salperton
Huntley
Badgeworth
Leckhampton
Dowdeswell
Andoversford
Shipton
Notgrove
Hazleton
Cold Aston
Churcham
GLOUCESTER
Barnwood
Hucclecote
Shurdington
Compton Abdale
Turkdean
Oakle Street
Blaisdon
Coney Hill
Brockworth
The Butts
30
Withington
Hampnett
Flaxley
Northwood Green
Minsterworth
Elmore Back
Elmore
Matson
Little Witcombe
Coberley
Westbury on Severn
Farleys End
Tuffley
Upton St Leonards
Great Witcombe
Birdlip
Cowley
Yanworth
Northleach
Quedgeley
Whaddon
Colesbourne
Longney
Cranham
Brimpsfield
Rodley
Hardwicke
Brookthorpe
Elkstone
Chedworth
Epney
Syde
Fossebridge
Coln St Dennis
Arlingham
Fretherne
Haresfield
Harescombe
Sheepscombe
Caudle Green
Rendcomb
Calcot
Upper Framilode
Saul
Moreton Valence
Edge
Painswick
Miserden
Winstone
Coln Rogers
Whitminster
Duntisbourne Abbots
Woodmancote
Winson
Frampton on Severn
Pitchcombe
North Cerney
Calmsden
Ablington
Awre
Stroud Green
Whiteshill
Slad
Edgeworth
Randwick
Stroud
Bisley
Bagendon
Bibury
Claypits
Cashe's Green
Ebley
Coln St Aldwyns
Stonehouse
Duntisbourne Rouse
Baunton
River Severn
Purton
Eastington
Cambridge
Bowbridge
Eastcombe
Barnsley
Daglingworth
Slimbridge
King's Stanley
Rodborough
Thrupp
Bussage
Stratton
Quenington
Frocester
Selsley
Oakridge
Far Oakridge
Halmore
Leonard Stanley
Woodchester
Browns Hill
Chalford
Sapperton
Ampney Crucis
Ampney St Mary
Gossington
Coaley
St Chloe
Brimscombe
Frampton Mansell
Cirencester
Wanswell
Amberley
Burleigh
The Beeches
Poulton
Breadstone
Nympsfield
Box
Minchinhampton
Coates
Preston
Ampney St Peter
Cam
Tarlton
Chesterton
Harnhill
Meysey Hampton
Nailsworth
Siddington
Stinchcombe
Uley
Downend
Cherington
Driffield
Newport
Avening
Rodmarton
Marston Meysey
Barton End
Dursley
Woodmancote
Horsley
Ewen
Kemble
South Cerney
Down Ampney
Kingscote
Tiltups End
Cerney Wick
Culkerton
North Nibley
Somerford Keynes
Latton
Castle Eaton
Poole Keynes
Coombe
Ashton Keynes
Cricklade
Wotton-under-Edge
Ashley
Tortworth
Beverston
Tetbury
Crudwell
Oaksey
Charfield
Long Newnton
Kingswood
Tresham
Leigh
Hankerton
Upper Minety
Alderley
Leighterton
Minety
Cloatley
Purton Stoke
Blunsdon St Andrew
Hillesley
Shipton Moyne
Westonbirt
Willesley
Brokenborough
Wickwar
Oldbury on the Hill
18
Malmesbury
Perry Green
Charlton
Priory Vale
Hawkesbury Upton
Knockdown
Garsdon
Bagstone
Hawkesbury
Didmarton
Easton Grey
Milbourne
Purton
Lydiard Millicent
Haydon Wick
Moredon
Rangeworthy
Dunkirk
Sopworth
Sherston
Lea
Cleverton
Nine Elms
Rodbourne
Engine Common
Horton
Little Badminton
Norton
Corston
Little Somerford
Brinkworth
Callow Hill
Hook
Lydiard Tregoze
Toothill
Luckington
Rodbourne
Great Somerford
Little Sodbury
Yate
Great Badminton
Alderton
Hullavington
Startley
Dauntsey
Grittenham
Wootton Bassett
Chipping Sodbury
Old Sodbury
Littleton Drew
Lower Stanton St Quintin
Westerleigh
Dodington
Acton Turville
Grittleton
Stanton St Quintin
Upper Seagry
Lower Seagry
Elcombe
Tormarton
Burton
Leigh Delamere
Bradenstoke
Tockenham
Codrington
Nettleton
Sutton Benger
Christian Malford
Lyneham
Broad Town
West Kington
Castle Combe
Kington St Michael
Kington Langley
Preston
Bushton
Hinton
Goatacre
Clyffe Pypard
Pucklechurch
Yatton Keynell
Catcomb
Abson
Dyrham
West Littleton
North Wraxall
Charlcutt
Hilmarton
Clevancy
Broad Hinton
Winterbourne Bassett
Upper Wraxall
Slaughterford
East Tytherton
Tytherton Lucas
Hardenhuish
Doynton
Marshfield
Biddestone
Chippenham
Berwick
Bremhill
Wick

Bromsgrove
Redditch
40
Beoley
Holt End
Tanworth in Arden
Lapworth
Wroxall
Beausale
Elmley Lovett
Bryan's Green
Finstall
Tardebigge
Forge Mill
Ullenhall
Lowsonford
Rowington
Leek Wootton
Norchard
Elmbridge
Stoke Prior
Avoncroft
Outhill
High Cross
Haseley
Hatton
Old Milverton
Cutnall Green
Upton Warren
Webheath
Headless Cross
Mappleborough Green
Henley-in-Arden
Preston Bagot
Shrewley
Warwick
Dunhampton
Broad Alley
Hampton Lovett
Wychbold
Woodgate
Upper Bentley
Lower Bentley
Grabbs Cross
Oldberrow
Pinley Green
Lye Green
Hampton Magna
Doverdale
Oldfield
Rashwood
Astwood
Walkwood
Studley
Wootton Wawen
Preston Green
Claverdon
Droitwich
Hadley
Hanbury
Hanbury Hall
Ham Green
Astwood Bank
Langley
Wolverton
Norton Lindsey
Sinton
Salwarpe
Hadzor
Woolmere Green
Edstone
Sherbourne
Feckenham
Sambourne
Coughton Court
Little Alne
Barford
Ladywood
Hawford Dovecote
Bradley Green
Broughton Green
Bradley
Coughton
Great Alne
Aston Cantlow
Bearley
Snitterfield
Fernhill Heath
Martin Hussingtree
Oddingley
Phepson
Stock Green
Holberrow Green
New End
Mary Arden's House
Wasperton
Hindlip
Himbleton
Earls Common
Cladswell
Cookhill
King's Coughton
Kinwarton Dovecote
Hampton Lucy
Newbold Pacey
Tibberton
Sale Green
Huddington
Stock Wood
Alcester
Arrow
Haselor
Wilmcote
Alveston
Charlecote
Crowle Green
Dormston
Inkberrow
Billesley
Charlecote Park
Grafton Flyford
Crowle
Abbots Morton
Weethley
Exhall
Temple Grafton
Shottery
Tiddington
Wellesbourne
39
Spetchley
Broughton Hackett
Kington
Flyford Flavell
Goom's Hill
Wood Bevington
Ragley Hall
Wixford
Ardens Grafton
Anne Hathaway's Cottage
Stratford-upon-Avon
Newtown
Churchill
Upton Snodsbury
North Piddle
Abberton
Rous Lench
Dunnington
Broom
Bidford-on-Avon
Binton
Luddington
Butterfly Farm
Whittington
White Ladies Aston
Naunton Beauchamp
Church Lench
Welford-on-Avon
Clifford Chambers
Loxley
Norton
Salford Priors
Atherstone on Stour
Combrook
Littleworth
Peopleton
Bishampton
Abbot's Salford
Preston on Stour
Stoulton
Marlcliff
Dorsington
Alderminster
Ettington
Drakes Broughton
Pinvin
Throckmorton
Harvington
Cleeve Prior
Long Marston
Wimpstone
Pillerton Priors
Wadborough
Norton
Lower Quinton
Crimscote
Wyre Piddle
Lower Moor
Lenchwick
North Littleton
Pebworth
Kerswell Green
Fladbury
Chadbury
Offenham
Middle Littleton
Tithe Barn
Broad Marston
Newbold on Stour
Pershore
Charlton
South Littleton
Fullready
Halford
Wick
Cropthorne
Armscote
Besford
Pensham
Evesham
Aldington
Bretforton
Honeybourne
Idlicote
Croome Park
Defford
Little Comberton
Mickleton
Kiftsgate Court
Hidcote Bartrim
Blackwell
Tredington
Kinnersley
Birlingham
Hampton
Bengeworth
Badsey
The Fleece Inn
Hidcote Manor Garden
Ilmington
Honington
Earl's Croome
Baughton
Bricklehampton
Vale of Evesham
Aston-sub-Edge
Darlingscott
Great Comberton
Wickhamford
Weston-sub-Edge
Hidcote Boyce
Ebrington
Shipston on Stour
Strensham (northbound)
Eckington
Elmley Castle
Willersey
Charingworth
Ryall
Naunton
Strensham (southbound)
Bredon's Norton
Bredon Hill
Hinton on the Green
Saintbury
Chipping Campden
Stretton on Fosse
Willington
Newbridge Green
Ashton under Hill
Childswickham
Aston Somerville
Tidmington
Burmington
Uckinghall
Ripple
Lower Westmancote
Overbury
Grafton
Sedgeberrow
Cotswold Way
Broad Campden
Paxford
Queenhill
Hill End
Bredon Barn
Broadway
Cherington
Twyning Green
Bredon
Kemerton
Conderton
Beckford
Wormington
Todenham
Shuthonger
Kinsham
The Priory
Silk Mill
Dumbleton
Buckland
Rectory
Broadway Tower
Blockley
Draycott
Aston Magna
Little Wolford
Bushley
Bredon's Hardwick
Great Washbourne
Laverton
Stanton
Snowshill
Snowshill Manor
Lavender
Batsford
Great Wolford
Ashchurch
Alderton
Toddington
Long Compton
Tewkesbury
Walton Cardiff
Pamington
Teddington
Alstone
Stanway
Bourton-on-the-Hill
Cotswold Falconry Centre
Moreton-in-Marsh
Barton-on-the-Heath
Forthampton
Oxenton
Stanley Pontlarge
Gloucestershire Warwickshire Railway
Didbrook
Hailes Abbey
Bourton Downs
Chaceley
Woolstone
Greet
Gretton
Cutsdean
Little Rollright
Rollright Stones
Deerhurst
Longborough
Chastleton
Little Compton
Odda's Chapel
Tredington
Gotherington
Langley Hill
Ford
Stoke Orchard
Bishop's Cleeve
Nottingham Hill
Farmcote
Condicote
Donnington
Evenlode
Salford
Winchcombe
Sudeley
Temple Guiting
Broadwell
Chastleton House
Adlestrop
Hardwicke
Woodmancote
Coombe Hill
Elmstone Hardwicke
Cleeve Hill
Cotswold
Stow-on-the-Wold
Cornwell
Lower Apperley
Leigh
Upper Swell
Lower Swell
Daylesford
Boddington
Uckington
Southam
Kineton
Barton
Oddington
Kingham
Churchill
Priors Norton
Barrow
Swindon
Belas Knap
Guiting Power
Maugersbury
Norton
Staverton
Arle
29
Charlton Abbots
Naunton
Upper Slaughter
Icomb
Bledington
Sarsden
Cheltenham
Hawling
Lower Slaughter
Wyck Rissington
Down Hatherley
Upper Hatherley
Brockhampton
Miniatures
Foscot
Bourton-on-the-Water
Gloucestershire
The Reddings
Sevenhampton
Salperton
Aylworth
Westcote
Nether Westcote
Churchdown
Charlton Kings
Whittington
Syreford
Notgrove
Model Village
Lyneham
Longlevens
Leckhampton
Dowdeswell
Andoversford
Shipton
Hazleton
Cold Aston
Little Rissington
Upper Rissington
Idbury
Fifield
Badgeworth
Leckhampton Hill
Motor & Toy
Clapton-on-the-Hill
Barnwood
Hucclecote
Shurdington
Turkdean
Milton-under-Wychwood
Shipton-under-Wychwood
Crickley Hill
Compton Abdale
Great Rissington
Brockworth
The Butts
Matson
Withington
Hampnett
Farmington
Habber Gallows Hill
Fullbrook Hill
Little Witcombe
Coberley
Barrow Wake
Great Witcombe
Upton St Leonards
Roman Villa
Cowley
Yanworth
Northleach
Sherborne
Great Barrington
Taynton
Prinknash
Birdlip
Colesbourne
Chedworth Roman Villa
World of Mechanical Music
Windrush
Eastington
Little Barrington
Fulbrook
Swinbrook
Brimpsfield
Cranham
Elkstone
Chedworth
Burford
Asthall
Brookthorpe
Cotswold Way
Fossebridge
Coln St Dennis
Syde
Calcot
Westwell
Sheepscombe
Caudle Green
Rendcomb
Coln Rogers
Aldsworth
Cotswold Wildlife Park
Painswick
Winstone
Woodmancote
Winson
Holwell
Shilton
Miserden
Miserden Park
Duntisbourne Abbots
Calmsden
North Cerney
Ablington
R Leach
Whiteshill
Slad
Carterton
Bibury
Edgeworth
Bagendon
Stroud
Bisley
Eastleach Turville
Eastleach Martin
Brize Norton
Duntisbourne Rouse
Coln St Aldwyns
Hatherop
Kencot
Alvescot
Bowbridge
Eastcombe
Thrupp
Baunton
Barnsley
Filkins
Bussage
Daglingworth
Stratton
Broadwell
Rodborough
Selsley
Far Oakridge
Oakridge
Chalford
Sapperton
Quenington
Broughton Poggs
Woodchester
Frampton Mansell
Cirencester
Ampney Crucis
Ampney St Mary
Southrop
Little Faringdon
Burleigh
Preston
Poulton
Coates
Ampney St Peter
Chesterton
Amphitheatre
Harnhill
Siddington
18
Fairford
0 1 2 3 4 miles
0 1 2 3 4 5 kilometres
A B C D E F G H
M5 M40 A38 A44 A46 A40 A417 A419 A429 A435 A436 A422 A441 A448 A435 A3400 A4189 A424 A361 B4077 B4035 B4425
Town Plans: Stratford-upon-Avon p.133, Warwick p.13

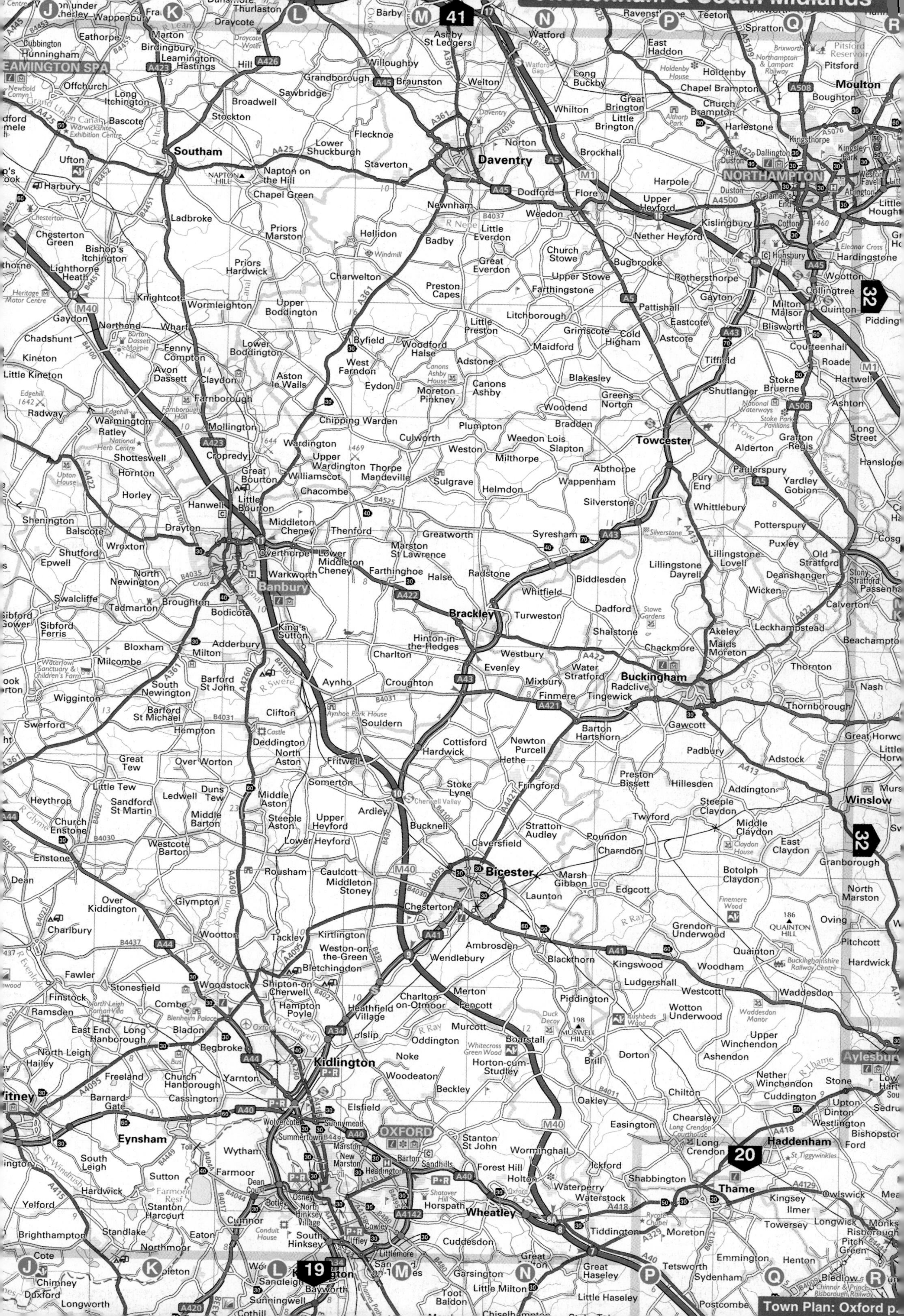
41
19
20
32
LEAMINGTON SPA
Cubbington
Hunningham
Eathorpe
Marton
Birdingbury
Leamington Hastings
Draycote
Thurlaston
Barby
Ashby St Ledgers
Watford
Ravensthorpe
Teeton
Spratton
East Haddon
Holdenby
Pitsford
Moulton
Offchurch
Long Itchington
Hill
Grandborough
Willoughby
Braunston
Welton
Long Buckby
Chapel Brampton
Boughton
Bascote
Broadwell
Sawbridge
Stockton
Flecknoe
Lower Shuckburgh
Great Brington
Little Brington
Whilton
Church Brampton
Harlestone
Kingsthorpe
Ufton
Southam
Napton on the Hill
Staverton
Daventry
Norton
Brockhall
Dallington
New Duston
Kingsley Park
Harbury
Chapel Green
Newnham
Dodford
Flore
Harpole
Upper Heyford
NORTHAMPTON
Duston
St James's End
Weston Favell
Little Houghton
Ladbroke
Priors Marston
Hellidon
Badby
Little Everdon
Weedon
Nether Heyford
Kislingbury
Far Cotton
Chesterton Green
Bishop's Itchington
Priors Hardwick
Great Everdon
Church Stowe
Bugbrooke
Hunsbury Hill
Hardingstone
Lighthorne Heath
Charwelton
Preston Capes
Upper Stowe
Farthingstone
Rothersthorpe
Wootton
Heritage Motor Centre
Knightcote
Wormleighton
Upper Boddington
Litchborough
Pattishall
Gayton
Milton Malsor
Collingtree
Quinton
Gaydon
Northend
Wharf
Little Preston
Grimscote
Cold Higham
Eastcote
Astcote
Blisworth
Chadshunt
Fenny Compton
Lower Boddington
Byfield
Woodford Halse
Adstone
Maidford
Tiffield
Courteenhall
Roade
Kineton
Avon Dassett
West Farndon
Canons Ashby
Little Kineton
Claydon
Aston le Walls
Eydon
Moreton Pinkney
Blakesley
Greens Norton
Stoke Bruerne
Hartwell
Edgehill 1642
Farnborough
Shutlanger
Ashton
Radway
Warmington
Chipping Warden
Plumpton
Woodend
Bradden
Ratley
Mollington
Wardington
Culworth
Weedon Lois
Towcester
Grafton Regis
Long Street
Upper Wardington
Weston
Slapton
Alderton
Shotteswell
Cropredy
Thorpe Mandeville
Milthorpe
Hanslope
Hornton
Great Bourton
Williamscot
Sulgrave
Abthorpe
Paulerspury
Upton House
Chacombe
Helmdon
Wappenham
Pury End
Yardley Gobion
Horley
Little Bourton
Silverstone
Whittlebury
Hanwell
Shenington
Middleton Cheney
Thenford
Greatworth
Syresham
Potterspury
Balscote
Drayton
Wroxton
Overthorpe
Marston St Lawrence
Puxley
Old Stratford
Shutford
Epwell
North Newington
Warkworth
Lower Middleton Cheney
Farthinghoe
Halse
Radstone
Biddlesden
Lillingstone Lovell
Lillingstone Dayrell
Deanshanger
Stony Stratford
Banbury
Swalcliffe
Tadmarton
Broughton
Bodicote
Whitfield
Dadford
Wicken
Calverton
Sibford Gower
Sibford Ferris
Brackley
Turweston
Stowe Gardens
Shalstone
Akeley
Leckhampstead
King's Sutton
Hinton-in-the-Hedges
Bloxham
Adderbury
Milton
Charlton
Westbury
Chackmore
Maids Moreton
Beachampton
Milcombe
Evenley
Water Stratford
Buckingham
Thornton
Barford St John
South Newington
Aynho
Croughton
Mixbury
Radclive
Finmere
Tingewick
Wigginton
Clifton
Barford St Michael
Aynhoe Park House
Souldern
Nash
Thornborough
Gawcott
Swerford
Hempton
Deddington
Barton Hartshorn
North Aston
Cottisford
Hardwick
Newton Purcell
Hethe
Great Horwood
Padbury
Adstock
Great Tew
Over Worton
Fritwell
Little Tew
Duns Tew
Somerton
Stoke Lyne
Fringford
Preston Bissett
Hillesden
Addington
Winslow
Heythrop
Sandford St Martin
Ledwell
Middle Aston
Ardley
Cherwell Valley
Steeple Claydon
Church Enstone
Middle Barton
Steeple Aston
Upper Heyford
Bucknell
Stratton Audley
Twyford
Middle Claydon
East Claydon
Enstone
Westcote Barton
Lower Heyford
Caversfield
Poundon
Charndon
Granborough
Dean
Rousham
Caulcott
Middleton Stoney
Bicester
Marsh Gibbon
Botolph Claydon
Over Kiddington
Glympton
Chesterton
Launton
Edgcott
North Marston
Charlbury
Wootton
Tackley
Kirtlington
Weston-on-the-Green
Ambrosden
Blackthorn
Kingswood
Grendon Underwood
Quainton
Oving
Pitchcott
Hardwick
Wendlebury
Bletchingdon
Woodham
Fawler
Stonesfield
Woodstock
Shipton-on-Cherwell
Merton
Ludgershall
Westcott
Waddesdon
Finstock
Combe
Hampton Poyle
Charlton-on-Otmoor
Fencott
Piddington
Wotton Underwood
Ramsden
Blenheim Palace
Heathfield Village
Murcott
Boarstall
Upper Winchendon
East End
Long Hanborough
Bladon
Islip
Oddington
Brill
Ashendon
North Leigh
Hailey
Begbroke
Kidlington
Noke
Horton-cum-Studley
Dorton
Aylesbury
Freeland
Church Hanborough
Yarnton
Woodeaton
Beckley
Nether Winchendon
Stone
Witney
Barnard Gate
Cassington
Elsfield
Oakley
Chilton
Cuddington
Upton
Dinton
Westlington
Eynsham
Wolvercote
Sunnymead
Summertown
OXFORD
Easington
Chearsley
Long Crendon
Haddenham
Bishopstone
Wytham
Marston
New Marston
Barton
Headington
Sandhills
Stanton St John
Worminghall
Ickford
Thame
South Leigh
Sutton
Farmoor
Forest Hill
Holton
Waterperry
Shabbington
Kingsey
Owlswick
Hardwick
Dean Court
Botley
Osney
North Hinksey Village
Cowley
Horspath
Wheatley
Waterstock
Ilmer
Yelford
Stanton Harcourt
Cumnor
South Hinksey
Iffley
Littlemore
Cuddesdon
Tiddington
Moreton
Towersey
Longwick
Monks Risborough
Brighthampton
Standlake
Eaton
Northmoor
Sandford-on-Thames
Garsington
Great Milton
Little Milton
Great Haseley
Little Haseley
Tetsworth
Sydenham
Emmington
Henton
Bledlow
Cote
Chimney
Duxford
Longworth
Appleton
Wootton
Kennington
Sunningwell
Bayworth
Toot Baldon
Chiselhampton
Postcombe
Cothill
Town Plan: Oxford p.

Braybrooke
Desborough
Geddington
Eleanor Cross
Woods
42
Aldwincle
Barnwell
All Saints
Luddington in the Brook
Sawtry
Great Gidding
Thurning
Triangular Lodge
Rushton
Boughton House
Sudborough
Rothwell
Weekley
Grafton Underwood
Lowick
Wigsthorpe
Thorpe Waterville
Winwick
Steeple Gidding
Hamerton Zoo Park
Coppingford
Monks Wood
Warkton
Slipton
Clopton
Orton
Kettering
Islip
Titchmarsh
Thrapston
Twywell
Hamerton
Upton
Loddington
Thorpe Malsor
Cranford St Andrew
Old Weston
Alconbury Weston
Great Cransley
Barton Seagrave
Buckworth
Wicksteed Park
Cranford St John
Denford
Woodford
Bythorn
Molesworth
Alconbury
Little Stukeley
Mawsley
Broughton
Keyston
Brington
Leighton Bromswold
Barham
Lamport
Lamport Hall
Burton Latimer
Great Addington
Ringstead
Woolley
Pytchley
Little Addington
Isham
Raunds
Catworth
Huntingdon
Old
Orlingbury
Finedon
Spaldwick
Ellington
Scaldwell
Walgrave
Little Harrowden
R. Nene
Hargrave
Easton
Brampton
Hannington
Great Harrowden
Irthlingborough
Stanwick
Covington
Stow Longa
Holcot
Hardwick
Chelveston
Lower Dean
Tilbrook
Grafham
Chichele College
Pitsford Reservoir
Higham Ferrers
Caldecott
Shelton
Upper Dean
Kimbolton
Grafham Water
Grafham Exhibition Centre
Buckden
Pitsford
Wellingborough
Yielden
West Perry
Stirtloe
Moulton
Sywell
Mears Ashby
Rushden
Swineshead
East Perry
Diddington
Irchester
Knuston
Boughton
Overstone
Wilby
Little Irchester
Newton Bromswold
Melchbourne
Staughton Green
Dillington
Sywell Reservoir
Little Wymington
Pertenhall
Great Doddington
Farndish
Wymington
Great Staughton
Southoe
Kingsley Park
Great Billing
Ecton
Earls Barton
Knotting
Little Staughton
Great Paxton
Weston Favell
Little Billing
Summer Leys
Strixton
Podington
Wollaston
Knotting Green
Riseley
Keysoe
Little Paxton
Hail Weston
Abington
Cogenhoe
Souldrop
Keysoe Row
Priory
Staploe
Duloe
St Neots
Hinwick
Santa Pod Raceway
Little Houghton
Whiston
Grendon
Bolnhurst
Sharnbrook
Thurleigh
Eaton Socon
Eynesbury
Brafield-on-the-Green
Castle Ashby
Great Houghton
Easton Maudit
Bozeat
Felmersham
Bletsoe
Colmworth
Eleanor Cross
Denton
Hardingstone
Odell
Radwell
Roothams Green
Wyboston
Yardley Hastings
Harrold
Chellington
Milton Ernest
Little Barford
Hackleton
Wilden
Carlton
Pavenham
Roxton
Tempsford
Quinton
Horton
Piddington
Warrington
Lavendon
Oakley
Ravensden
Wild Britain
Cold Brayfield
West End
Renhold
Great Barford
Gamlingay Great Heath
Stevington
Postmill
Olney
Turvey
Bromham
Clapham
Bedford
Blunham
Roade
Ravenstone
Newton Blossomville
Watermill
Everton
Hartwell
Clifton Reynes
Goldington
Willington
Weston Underwood
Emberton
Biddenham
Sandy
Potton
Ashton
Stoke Goldington
Cople
Moggerhanger
Stagsden
Kempston
Filgrave
Long Street
Beeston
RSPB
Tyringham
Astwood
Moot Hall
Cardington
Upper Caldecote
Sherington
R. Great Ouse
Shortstown
Elstow
Lower Caldecote
Hanslope
Gayhurst
Chicheley
Northill
Ickwell Green
Biggleswade
Grand Union Canal
Newport Pagnell
Little Linford
Lathbury
Bourne End
Wootton
Upper Shelton
Swiss Garden
Shuttleworth Collection
Old Warden
Castlethorpe
Haversham
North Crawley
Wharley End
Wilstead
Haynes (Silver End)
Old Warden
Broom
Lower Shelton
Haynes (Northwood End)
Cosgrove
New Bradwell
Great Linford
Cranfield
Stewartby
Houghton Conquest
Southill
Old Stratford
Bradwell
Willen
Moulsoe
Marston Moretaine
Haynes (Church End)
Langford
Wolverton
Stony Stratford
Broughton
Haynes (West End)
Stanford
Passenham
Gulliver's Land
Salford
Lidlington
Millbrook
Houghton House
Shefford
Clifton
Calverton
Milton Keynes
Woolstone
Woughton on the Green
Maulden
Beadlow
Astwick
Henlow
Lower End
Wavendon
Ampthill
Clophill
Campton
Church End
Stotfold
Beachampton
Shenley Church End
Loughton
Walton
Aspley Guise
Ridgmont
De Grey Mausoleum
Upper Gravenhurst
Meppershall
Arlesey
Simpson
Woburn Sands
Husborne Crawley
Steppingley
Flitton
Silsoe
Wrest Park
Upper & Lower Stondon
Shenley Brook End
Aspley Heath
Safari Park
Flitwick
Greenfield
Lower Gravenhurst
Shillington
Letchworth Garden City
Nash
Whaddon
Far Bletchley
Bow Brickhill
Woburn
Pulloxhill
Holwell
Bletchley
Eversholt
Westoning
Higham Gobion
Apsley End
Little Brickhill
Woburn Abbey
Newton Longville
Tingrith
Barton-le-Clay
Pirton
Ickleford
Great Horwood
Great Brickhill
Harlington
Hexton
Pegsdon
Little Horwood
Milton Bryan
Hitchin
Sharpenhoe
Barton Hills
Ravensburgh Castle
Walsworth
Drayton Parslow
Stockgrove
King's Wood
Mursley
Stoke Hammond
Toddington
Sundon Hills
Streatley
Winslow
Heath and Reach
Fancott
Upper Sundon
Little Wymondley
Warden Hill
Well Head
Hollingdon
Soulbury
Hockliffe
Tebworth
Great Offley
St Ippollitts
Swanbourne
Clipstone
Chalton
Lilley
Stewkley
Wingfield
Sundon Park
Marsh Farm
Hoggeston
Linslade
Eggington
Leygreen
Preston
Granborough
Dunton
Leighton Buzzard
Houghton Regis
Limbury
King's Walden
Burcott
Stanbridge
Tilsworth
Leagrave
Stopsley
Cockernhoe
St Paul's Walden
North Marston
Cublington
Wing
Ascott
Little Billington
Billington
Sewell
Totternhoe
Round Green
Darleyhall
Langley
Eaton Green
Luton
Oving
Whitchurch
Ledburn
Slapton
Eaton Bray
Dunstable
Stockwood
Breachwood Green
Whitwell
Aston Abbotts
Luton Airport
Someries
Pitchcott
Mentmore
Northall
Tree Cathedral
Church End
Caddington
Peter's Green
Kimpton
Codicote
Buckinghamshire Railway Centre
Hardwick
Edlesborough
Kensworth Common
Horton
Whipsnade
Slip End
Wingrave
Ivinghoe Aston
Woodside Animal Farm
Ayot St Lawrence
Weedon
Rowsham
ZSL Whipsnade
Holywell
Shaw's Corner
Addesdon
Cheddington
Studham
Markyate
Hulcott
Ivinghoe
Dagnall
Welwyn
Bierton
Long Marston
Ditstone
20
Flamstead
Harpenden
Batford
Wheathampstead
Wilstone
Marsworth
Ringshall
Little Gaddesden
Jockey End
Bridgewater
Gaddesden
Hertfordshire County
Thame
41
31
Town Plan: Milton Keynes p.13
0 1 2 3 4 miles
0 1 2 3 4 5 kilometres

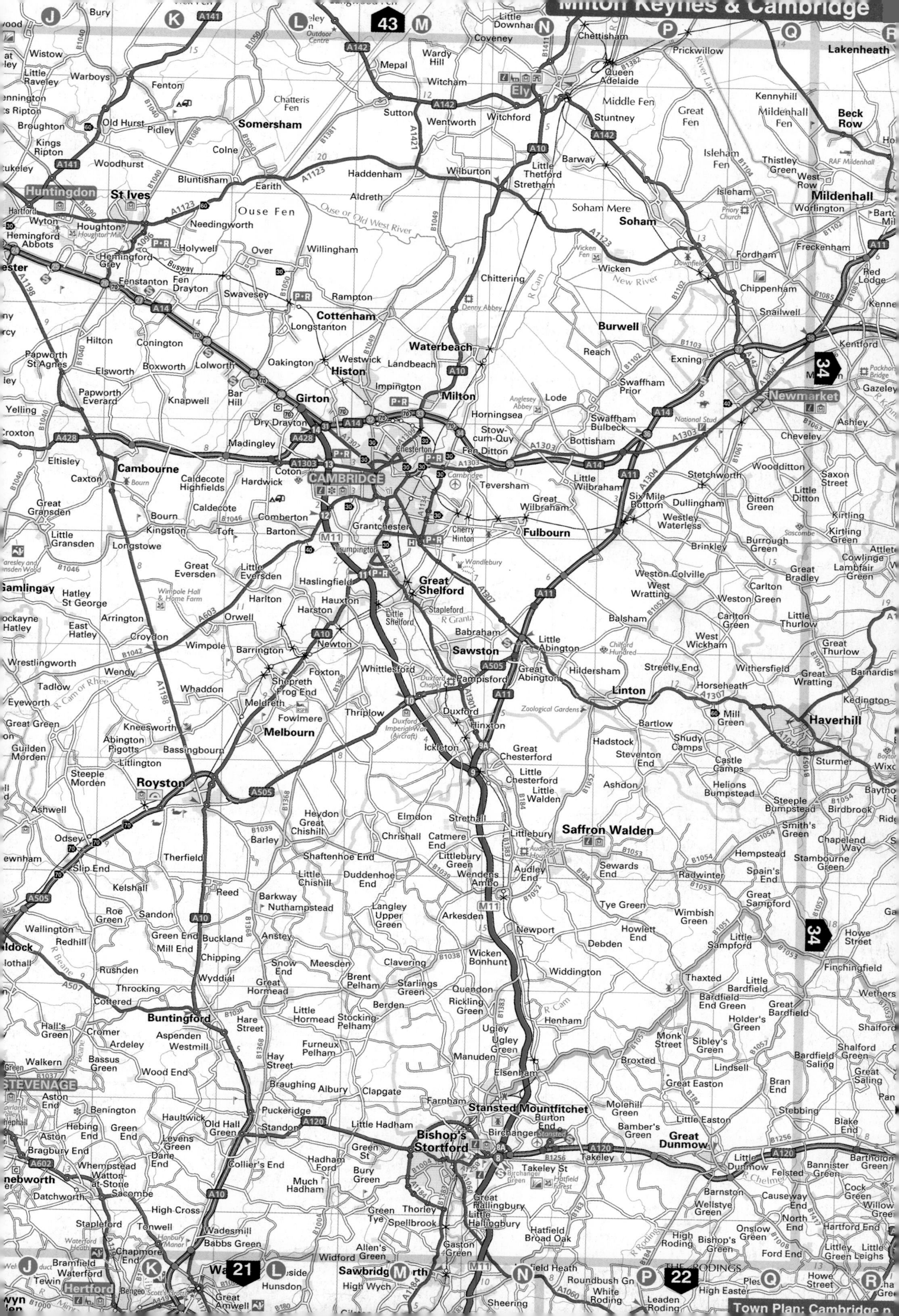

Milton Keynes & Cambridge
43
34
21
22
Town Plan: Cambridge
Bury
Wistow
Little Raveley
Warboys
Fenton
Chatteris Fen
Mepal
Wardy Hill
Witcham
Coveney
Little Downham
Chettisham
Prickwillow
Lakenheath
Queen Adelaide
Ely
Sutton
Wentworth
Witchford
Middle Fen
Stuntney
Great Fen
Kennyhill
Mildenhall Fen
Beck Row
Old Hurst
Pidley
Somersham
Broughton
Kings Ripton
Colne
Woodhurst
Bluntisham
Earith
Haddenham
Wilburton
Little Thetford
Stretham
Barway
Isleham Fen
Thistley Green
West Row
Huntingdon
St Ives
Aldreth
Ouse Fen
Needingworth
Ouse or Old West River
Soham Mere
Soham
Isleham
Mildenhall
Worlington
Hartford
Wyton
Houghton
Hemingford Abbots
Hemingford Grey
Holywell
Over
Willingham
Fordham
Freckenham
Wicken
Red Lodge
New River
Fenstanton
Fen Drayton
Swavesey
Rampton
Chittering
Chippenham
Cottenham
Longstanton
Denny Abbey
Burwell
Snailwell
Hilton
Conington
Papworth St Agnes
Elsworth
Boxworth
Lolworth
Oakington
Westwick
Histon
Landbeach
Waterbeach
Reach
Exning
Kentford
Papworth Everard
Knapwell
Bar Hill
Girton
Impington
Milton
Swaffham Prior
Newmarket
Gazeley
Yelling
Dry Drayton
Horningsea
Lode
Anglesey Abbey
Swaffham Bulbeck
Ashley
Croxton
Madingley
Chesterton
Stow-cum-Quy
Fen Ditton
Bottisham
Cheveley
Eltisley
Cambourne
Caldecote Highfields
Coton
Hardwick
CAMBRIDGE
Teversham
Little Wilbraham
Stetchworth
Woodditton
Saxon Street
Caxton
Great Gransden
Caldecote
Comberton
Great Wilbraham
Six Mile Bottom
Dullingham
Ditton Green
Little Ditton
Little Gransden
Bourn
Kingston
Toft
Barton
Grantchester
Cherry Hinton
Fulbourn
Westley Waterless
Kirtling
Kirtling Green
Longstowe
Trumpington
Wandlebury
Brinkley
Burrough Green
Cowlinge
Lambfair Green
Great Eversden
Little Eversden
Haslingfield
Great Shelford
Weston Colville
West Wratting
Great Bradley
Carlton
Gamlingay
Hatley St George
Harlton
Hauxton
Stapleford
Weston Green
Carlton Green
Little Thurlow
Cockayne Hatley
Arrington
East Hatley
Croydon
Orwell
Harston
Little Shelford
R Granta
Babraham
Balsham
Little Abington
West Wickham
Great Thurlow
Wrestlingworth
Wimpole
Barrington
Newton
Sawston
Chilford Hundred
Hildersham
Streetly End
Withersfield
Great Wratting
Barnardiston
Tadlow
Wendy
Shepreth
Foxton
Whittlesford
Pampisford
Great Abington
Horseheath
Linton
Eyeworth
Whaddon
Frog End
Meldreth
Fowlmere
Thriplow
Duxford
Hinxton
Zoological Gardens
Bartlow
Mill Green
Kedington
Haverhill
Great Green
Kneesworth
Abington Pigotts
Guilden Morden
Bassingbourn
Litlington
Melbourn
Ickleton
Great Chesterford
Hadstock
Steventon End
Shudy Camps
Castle Camps
Sturmer
Steeple Morden
Royston
Little Chesterford
Little Walden
Ashdon
Helions Bumpstead
Steeple Bumpstead
Birdbrook
Ashwell
Heydon
Great Chishill
Elmdon
Strethall
Littlebury
Saffron Walden
Smith's Green
Odsey
Barley
Chrishall
Catmere End
Chapelend Way
Therfield
Shaftenhoe End
Littlebury Green
Audley End
Hempstead
Stambourne Green
Slip End
Little Chishill
Duddenhoe End
Wendens Ambo
Sewards End
Radwinter
Spain's End
Kelshall
Reed
Barkway
Nuthampstead
Langley Upper Green
Arkesden
Tye Green
Great Sampford
Wimbish Green
Roe Green
Sandon
Newport
Howlett End
Debden
Little Sampford
Howe Street
Wallington
Redhill
Green End
Buckland
Mill End
Anstey
Snow End
Meesden
Clavering
Wicken Bonhunt
Widdington
Finchingfield
Chipping
Wyddial
Brent Pelham
Starlings Green
Thaxted
Little Bardfield
Rushden
Throcking
Great Hormead
Quendon
Bardfield End Green
Great Bardfield
Wethersfield
Cottered
Buntingford
Hare Street
Little Hormead
Stocking Pelham
Berden
Rickling Green
Henham
Holder's Green
Hall's Green
Cromer
Ardeley
Aspenden
Westmill
Ugley
Ugley Green
Monk Street
Sibley's Green
Shalford
Walkern
Bassus Green
Furneux Pelham
Hay Street
Manuden
Broxted
Bardfield Saling
Shalford Green
Wood End
STEVENAGE
Braughing
Albury
Clapgate
Elsenham
Lindsell
Great Saling
Great Easton
Bran End
Aston End
Benington
Farnham
Stansted Mountfitchet
Molehill Green
Stebbing
Puckeridge
Haultwick
Old Hall Green
Standon
Little Hadham
Burton End
Little Easton
Blake End
Hebing End
Green End
Levens Green
Bishop's Stortford
Birchanger
Bamber's Green
Great Dunmow
Aston
Bragbury End
Dane End
Green St
Takeley
Little Dunmow
Bannister Green
Bartholomew Green
Whempstead
Watton-at-Stone
Collier's End
Hadham Ford
Bury Green
Takeley St
Felsted
Knebworth
Much Hadham
Barnston
Cock Green
Datchworth
Sacombe
Causeway End
Great Hallingbury
Wellstye Green
High Cross
Thorley
Little Hallingbury
North End
Green Tye
Spellbrook
Hatfield Broad Oak
Onslow Green
Hartford End
Stapleford
Tonwell
Wadesmill
Babbs Green
High Roding
Bishop's Green
Littley Green
Little Leighs
Chapmore End
Gaston Green
Allen's Green
Ford End
Bramfield
Waterford
Widford
Sawbridgeworth
THE RODINGS
Tewin
Hertford
Bengeo
Hunsdon
High Wych
Roundbush Gn
White Roding
High Easter
Pleshey
Howe Street
Great Amwell
Sheering
Leaden Roding

A
B
C
D
E
F
G
H
44
33
22
Brandon
Lakenheath
Thetford
Brettenham
Rushford
Garboldisham
North Lopham
Fersfield
South Lopham
Bressingham
Shelfanger
Gasthorpe
A1066
River Little Ouse
Smallworth
Blo Norton
Redgrave and Lopham Fen
Steam Museum & Gardens
River Waveney
Roydon
Kennyhill
Mildenhall Fen
Beck Row
Eriswell
Elveden Forest
Elveden
Elveden War Memorial
Euston
Barnham
Coney Weston
Hopton
Market Weston
Thelnetham
Redgrave
Wortham
Holywell Row
RAF Mildenhall
Thistley Green
West Row
Mildenhall
A1065
A11
A134
A1088
Fakenham Magna
Barningham
Hinderclay
Botesdale
A143
Sapiston
Hepworth
Rickinghall
Mellis
Honington
Bardwell
Stanton
Wattisfield
Mill Street
Worlington
Barton Mills
A1101
Icklingham
Anglo-Saxon Village Reconstruction
Ixworth Thorpe
Walsham le Willows
Gislingham
Troston
Wyken
Freckenham
Tuddenham
Lackford Green
West Stow
Brockley
Ampton
Great Livermere
West Street
Crowland
Finningham
Fordham
Ixworth
Langham
Four Ashes
Westhorpe
Wickham Street
Red Lodge
Herringswell
Cavenham
Lackford
Culford
Ingham
Timworth
Badwell Ash
Long Thurlow
Wyverstone Street
Wickham Skeith
Chippenham
Flempton
Hengrave
Timworth Green
Conyer's Green
Upper Town
Grimstone End
Hunston
Stowlangtoft
Great Ashfield
Wyverstone
Cotton
Snailwell
Kennett
Fornham All Saints
Fornham St Martin
Great Barton
Pakenham
Stanton Street
Bacton
Kentford
Risby
A14
Thurston
Norton Little Green
Higham
Norton
Haughley Green
Mendlesham
Moulton
Packhorse Bridge
Burthorpe Green
Westley
Bury St Edmunds
Tostock
Elmswell
Gazeley
Barrow
Beyton Green
Beyton
Wetherden
Gipping
Newmarket
Little Saxham
Ickworth House
Blackthorpe
Kingshall Street
Woolpit
Haughley
Old Newton
Saxham Street
Ashley
Dalham
Horringer
Rushbrooke
Hessett
Rougham Green
Drinkstone
Stowupland
Cheveley
Denham
Sicklesmere
Bradfield St George
Drinkstone Green
Harleston
Woodditton
Saxon Street
Hargrave
Ousden
Chevington
Hawstead
Maypole Green
Rattlesden
Stowmarket
Little Ditton
Whepstead
Bradfield St Clare
Gedding
Buxhall
Mill Green
Great Finborough
Combs Ford
Ditton Green
Lidgate
Chedburgh
Bradfield Combust
Felsham
Combs
Kirtling
Depden
Hightown Green
Needham Market
Sascombe
Kirtling Green
Rede
Stanningfield
Cross Green
Great Green
Burrough Green
Attleton Green
Thorns
Brockley Green
Harrow Green
Windsor Green
Cockfield
Thorpe Green
Brettenham
Battisford Tye
Barking
Cowlinge
Lambfair Green
Wickhambrook
Pound Green
Stradishall
Great Bradley
Hawkedon
Somerton
Lawshall
Cross Green
Ringshall
Charles Tye
Carlton
Shimpling Street
Thorpe Morieux
Cooks Green
Barking Tye
Weston Green
Denston
Stansfield
Hartest
Gifford's Hall
Hitcham Causeway
Wattisham
Ringshall Stocks
Carlton Green
Little Thurlow
Assington Green
Upper Street
River Glem
Boxted
Shimpling
Alpheton
Preston
Hitcham Street
Hitcham
Nedging Tye
Great Bricett
Offton
Great Thurlow
Bridge Street
Lavenham
Kettlebaston
Bildeston
Guildhall
Stanstead
Brent Eleigh
Monks Eleigh
Naughton
Somersham
Withersfield
Great Wratting
Hundon
Barnardiston
Poslingford
Sue Ryder Foundation
Glemsford
Kentwell Hall
Chelsworth
Nedging
Ash Street
Mount Pleasant
Swingleton Green
Semer
Whatfield
Elmsett
Kedington
Brockley Green
Chilton Street
Nether Hall
Cavendish
Pentlow
Long Melford
Melford Hall
Little Waldingfield
Milden
Lindsey Tye
Haverhill
A1092
Clare
Clare Castle
Lindsey
Aldham
Mill Green
Boyton End
Stoke by Clare
Foxearth
Acton
Rose Green
St James' Chapel
Kersey
A1071
Castle Camps
Sturmer
Boyton
Wixoe
Borley
Newman's Green
Great Waldingfield
Wicker Street Green
Duke Street
Hadleigh
Helions Bumpstead
Ovington
Belchamp St Paul
Belchamp Otten
Mill Green
Groton
Chattisham
Baythorne End
Ashen
Belchamp Walter
Sudbury
Cornard Tye
Newton
Steeple Bumpstead
Birdbrook
Ridgewell
Little Yeldham
Great Cornard
Boxford
Layham
Bulmer
Little Cornard
Middleton
Great Wenham
Smith's Green
Chapelend Way
Stambourne
A1017
Bulmer Tye
Great Henny
Assington
Raydon
Capel St Mary
Hempstead
Stambourne Green
Great Yeldham
Gestingthorpe
Henny Street
Polstead
Shelley
Lower Raydon
Toppesfield
Rose Green
Leavenheath
Holton St Mary
Spain's End
Pool Street
Colne Valley
A131
Wickham St Paul
Twinstead
Stoke-by-Nayland
A12
Castle Hedingham
Alphamstone
Lamarsh
Honey Tye
Higham
Great Sampford
Gainsford End
Lucking Street
Nayland
Thorington Street
Stratford St Mary
East Bergholt
Howe Street
Sible Hedingham
Great Maplestead
Little Maplestead
Pebmarsh
Bures
Wissington
Boxted
Carters
Flatford
Little Sampford
Mount Bures
Wormingford
Boxted Cross
Dedham
Finchingfield
Little Horkesley
Langham
Little Bardfield
Boose's Green
Great Horkesley
Boxted
Manningtree
Lawford
Wethersfield
Blackmore End
Halstead
Colne Engaine
White Colne
Wakes Colne
Ardleigh Heath
Ardleigh
Great Bardfield
A1124
Horkesley Heath
Holder's Green
Shalford
Beazley End
Gosfield
Earls Colne
Chappel
Fordham
Rose Green
West Bergholt
Shalford Green
Church End
Greenstead Green
Fordstreet
Parson's Heath
Bardfield Saling
Jasper's Green
High Garrett
Burton's Green
Great Tey
Aldham
Eight Ash Green
Seven Star Green
Lexden
A120
Colchester
Lindsell
Great Saling
Bocking Churchstreet
Stisted
Marks Hall
Elmstead Market
Bran End
Panfield
Little Tey
Marks Tey
Stanway
Beacon End
Greenstead
Stebbing
Braintree
Bocking
Pattiswick
Coggeshall
A133
Blake End
B1256
Bradwell
Copford Green
Colchester Zoo
Wivenhoe
Rayne
Bartholomew Green
Great Notley
Surrex
Langley Green
Easthorpe
Heckfordbridge
Rowhedge
Alresford
Little Dunmow
Felsted
Bannister Green
Paycocke's
River Blackwater
Coggeshall Grange Barn
Skye Green
Hardy's Green
Layer-de-la-Haye
Fingringhoe
High Park Corner
Black Notley
Cressing
Feering
Birch
Barnston
Causeway End
Cock Green
Hawbush Green
Silver End
Smythe's Green
Abberton
Willows Green
The Green
Cressing Temple
Kelvedon
Messing
Birch Green
Langenhoe
Wellstye Green
North End
White Notley
Layer Breton
Onslow Green
Hartford End
Great Leighs
Faulkbourne
Inworth
Tiptree
Layer Marney
Abberton Reservoir
Peldon
Brightlingsea
Bishop's Green
Littley Green
Little Leighs
Fuller Street
Fairstead
Tiptree Heath
Ford End
Mersea Island
Pleshey
Chatham Green
Terling
Witham
Little Braxted
Oxley Green
Tolleshunt Knights
Great Wigborough
East Mersea
High Easter
Great Braxted
Salcott-cum-Virley
0 1 2 3 4 miles

Harwich International Port
PASSENGER & CRUISE TERMINAL
HARWICH INTERNATIONAL STATION
CAR FERRY TERMINAL
CONTAINER TERMINAL
EAST DOCK ROAD
WEST DOCK ROAD
REFINERY ROAD
STATION ROAD
Parkeston
Harwich Industrial Estate
Superstore
PARKESTON ROUNDABOUT
ST NICHOLAS ROUNDABOUT
Dovercourt
MAIN ROAD
HIGHFIELD AVENUE
FRONKS ROAD
Upper Dovercourt
IPSWICH, COLCHESTER
HARWICH
A120
B1352
0
400 m
LLA
Diss
Harleston
Halesworth
Southwold
Walberswick
Dunwich
Wrentham
Covehithe
South Cove
Wangford
Reydon
Blythburgh
Wenhaston
Blyford
Holton
Westhall
Brampton
Stoven
Uggeshall
Rumburgh
Spexhall
Wissett
Chediston
Cookley
Walpole
Bramfield
Thorington
Heveningham
Ubbeston Green
Peasenhall
Sibton
Yoxford
Darsham
Westleton
Middleton
Middleton Moor
Theberton
Eastbridge
Kelsale
Carlton
Saxmundham
Knodishall
Leiston
Aldringham
Thorpeness
Aldeburgh
Aldeburgh Bay
Friston
Sternfield
Benhall Green
Benhall Street
Farnham
Snape
Snape Street
Stratford St Andrew
Little Glemham
Great Glemham
Blaxhall
Tunstall
Campsea Ash
Wickham Market
Rendlesham
Ufford
Eyke
Bromeswell
Melton
Woodbridge
Sutton Hoo
Chillesford
Sudbourne
Butley
Orford
Orford Ness
Capel St Andrew
Boyton
Hollesley
Hollesley Bay
North Weir Point
Shottisham
Sutton
Waldringfield
Martlesham
Martlesham Heath
Kesgrave
IPSWICH
Chantry
Belstead
Wherstead
Freston
Nacton
Levington
Bucklesham
Brightwell
Newbourne
Hemley
Kirton
Falkenham
Alderton
Bawdsey
Trimley St Martin
Trimley St Mary
Walton
Old Felixstowe
Felixstowe
Landguard Fort
Landguard Point
Harwich
Harwich Harbour
Dovercourt
Upper Dovercourt
Ramsey
Little Oakley
Great Oakley
Pennyhole Bay
Horsey Island
The Naze
Walton on the Naze
Kirby le Soken
Kirby Cross
Frinton-on-Sea
Thorpe-le-Soken
Great Holland
Great Clacton
Holland-on-Sea
CLACTON-ON-SEA
Jaywick
Hoek van Holland
Esbjerg
Shotley
Shotley Street
Shotley Gate
Erwarton
Harkstead
Holbrook
Holbrook Bay
Stutton
Chelmondiston
Woolverstone
Tattingstone
River Stour
River Orwell
River Deben
River Ore
River Alde
Wrabness
Bradfield
Mistley
Wix
Framlingham
Saxtead
Dennington
Badingham
Bruisyard
Cransford
Rendham
Swefling
Parham
Hacheston
Easton
Marlesford
Kettleburgh
Brandeston
Cretingham
Earl Soham
Debenham
Stradbroke
Fressingfield
Laxfield
Eye
Hoxne
Scole
Dickleburgh
Mendham
Metfield
Weybread
Wingfield
Grundisburgh
Witnesham
Tuddenham
Westerfield
Playford
Great Bealings
Hasketon
Burgh
Clopton
Otley
Helmingham
Claydon
Henley
Suffolk Heritage Coast

A
B
C
D
E
F
G
H
Aberystwyth
200 m
Cardigan Bay
CARDIGAN
BAY
MACHYNLLETH, LLANGURIG
CARDIGAN
Royal Pier
Conference Centre
Coastguard Station
University (Old College)
Monument
North Tower
Castle
St Michael's
Clock Tower
Market Hall
Ceredigion Museum & Gallery
St Paul Methodist
St David's URC
Town Hall
Capel y Morfa
The Morlan Centre
Surgery
Bethel
CAB
Salvation Army
Eglwys y Santes Fair
ABERYSTWYTH STATION
Holy Trinity
Rheidol
Ystwyth Retail Park
Vale of Rheidol Steam Railway Station
Pont Aberystwyth
Slipway
Government Offices
Fire Station
Lifeboat Station
Marina
Ro-fawr
Aberystwyth Town FC
Police Station
TA Centre
Aqua Terra
Afon Rheidol
STRYD FAWR
ALEXANDRA ROAD
BRIDGE STREET
PENPARCAU ROAD
DAN DRE / MILL ST
LLA
Aberarth
Aberaeron
New Quay
Llanina
Ceredigion Heritage Coast
Maen-y-groes
Gilfachrheda
Llwyncelyn
Cross Inn
Llanarth
Oakford
Nanternis
Caerwedros
Dihewyd
Ynys-Lochtyn
Llwyndafydd
Mydroilyn
Llangranog
Pontgarreg
Plwmp
Penbryn
Pentregat
Cardigan Island
Aberporth
Tresaith
Sarnau
Brynhoffnant
Talgarreg
Gorsgoch
Cardigan Island Coastal Farm Park
Felinwynt Rainforest & Butterfly Centre
Y Ferwig
Tremain
Blaenannerch
Tan-y-groes
Glynarthen
Poppit Sands
Pembrokeshire Coast Path
Penparc
Blaenporth
Rhydlewis
Ffostrasol
Cwrt-newydd
St Dogmaels Moylgrove Heritage Coast
St Dogmaels
Cardigan (Aberteifi)
Bettws Evan
Hawen
Pontshaen
Beulah
Troedyraur
Penrhiw-pal
Tre-groes
Moylegrove
Maesllyn
Pren-gwyn
Rhydowen
Llanwenog
Ponthirwaun
Brongest
Llechryd
Croes-lan
Pen-y-bryn
Llandygwydd
Cilgerran
TIVY SIDE
Capel Dewi
Abercych
Cenarth
Cwm-cou
Adpar
Llandyfriog
Penrhiw-llan
Rhoshill
Pen-rhiw
Newcastle Emlyn (Castell Newydd Emlyn)
Henllan
Llandysul
Llanfihangel-ar-arth
Nevern
Felindre Farchog
Newchapel
Llangeler
Pontwelly
Llanllwni
Newport
Eglwyswrw
Drefach
Felindre
Pentre-cwrt
Boncath
Cwmhiraeth
Glynteg
Blaenffos
Capel Iwan
Pencader
New Inn
Crosswell
Bwlch-y-groes
Cwmpengraig
Rhos
Gwyddgrug
Brynberian
Tegryn
Hermon
PEMBROKESHIRE COAST
25
A487
A484
A486
A475
A478
0 1 2 3 4 miles
0 1 2 3 4 5 kilometres

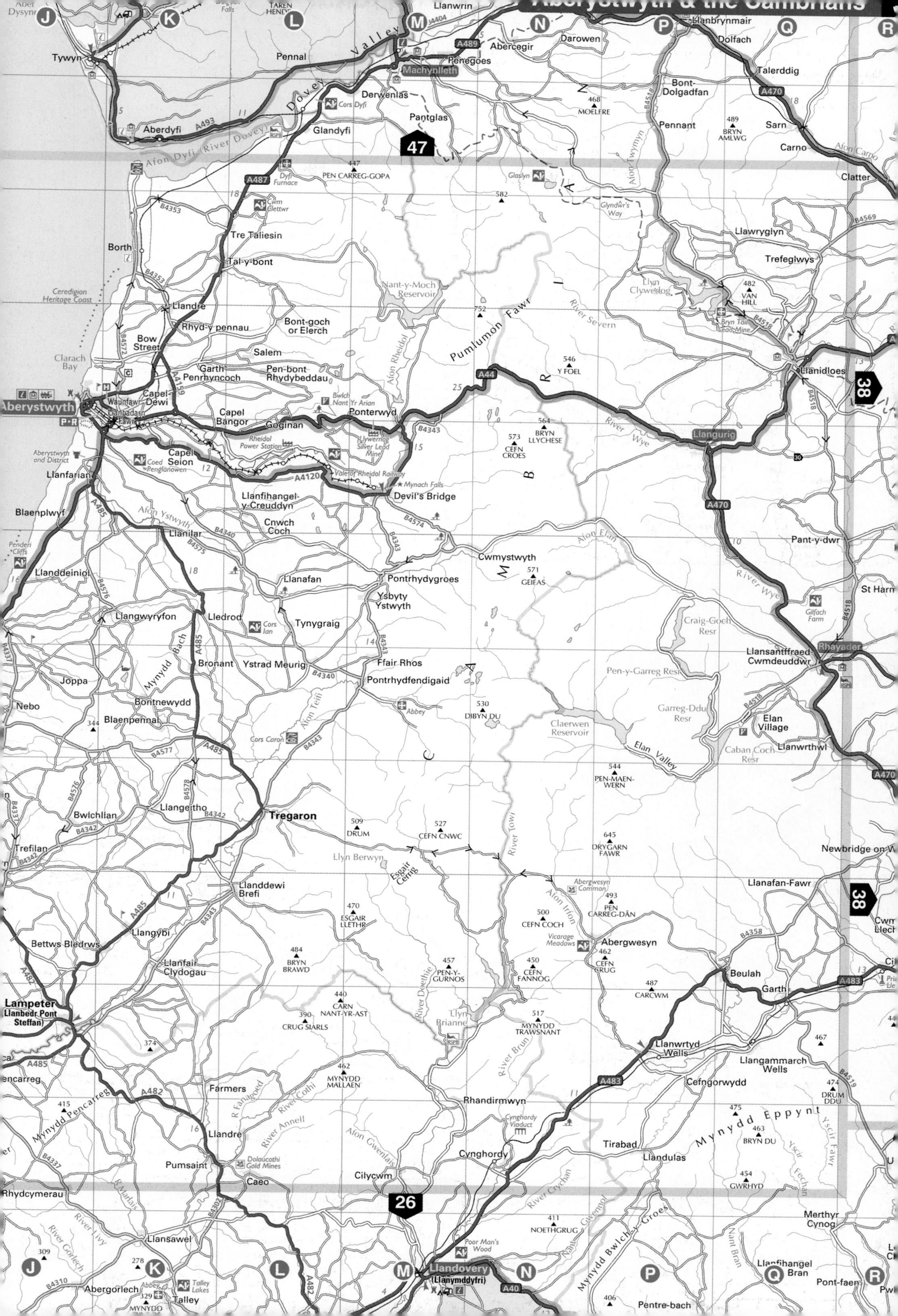

Aberystwyth & the Cambrians
J
K
L
M
N
P
Q
R
Tywyn
Pennal
Dovey Valley
Llanwrin
A489
Abercegir
Darowen
Llanbrynmair
Dolfach
Penegoes
Machynlleth
Talerddig
Bont-Dolgadfan
A470
Derwenlas
Cors Dyfi
468
MOELFERE
B4518
Pantglas
Pennant
489
BRYN AMLWG
Sarn
Aberdyfi
A493
Afon Dyfi (River Dovey)
Glandyfi
47
Carno
Afon Carno
A487
Dyfi Furnace
447
PEN CARREG-GOPA
Glaslyn
Afon Twymyn
Clatter
Cwm Clettwr
582
Glyndŵr's Way
B4353
Tre Taliesin
B4569
Llawryglyn
Borth
Tal-y-bont
Trefeglwys
Ceredigion Heritage Coast
Nant-y-Moch Reservoir
Llyn Clywedog
482
VAN HILL
Llandre
752
River Severn
Bryn Tail Lead Mine
B4518
Rhyd-y pennau
Bont-goch or Elerch
Bow Street
B4572
Salem
Pumlumon Fawr
Clarach Bay
Afon Rheidol
546
Y FOEL
Llanidloes
38
Garth
Penrhyncoch
Pen-bont Rhydybeddau
A4159
A44
Aberystwyth
Waunfawr
Capel-Dewi
Llanbadarn Fawr
Bwlch Nant Yr Arian
Ponterwyd
Capel Bangor
Goginan
B4343
564
BRYN LLYCHESE
573
CEFN CROES
River Wye
Llangurig
Rheidol Power Station
Llywernog Silver Lead Mine
Aberystwyth and District
Capel Seion
Coed Penglanowen
Vale of Rheidol Railway
Llanfarian
A4120
Mynach Falls
Devil's Bridge
A470
Llanfihangel-y-Creuddyn
Blaenplwyf
A485
Afon Ystwyth
B4574
Cnwch Coch
Llanilar
B4340
B4575
Pant-y-dwr
Penderi Cliffs
Afon Elan
Cwmystwyth
Llanddeiniol
B4576
571
GEIFAS
Llanafan
Pontrhydygroes
St Harmon
Ysbyty Ystwyth
Llangwyryfon
Lledrod
Cors Ian
Tynygraig
Gilfach Farm
Craig-Goch Resr
B4518
Mynydd Bach
B4343
Rhayader
Bronant
Ystrad Meurig
Ffair Rhos
Llansantffraed-Cwmdeuddwr
Joppa
B4340
Pontrhydfendigaid
Pen-y-Garreg Resr
Nebo
Bontnewydd
Abbey
530
DIBYN DU
Garreg-Ddu Resr
Blaenpennal
344
Afon Teifi
Claerwen Reservoir
Elan Village
Cors Caron
B4343
Caban Coch Resr
Llanwrthwl
B4577
A485
Elan Valley
544
PEN-MAEN-WERN
A470
B4576
B4578
B4337
Llangeitho
B4342
Tregaron
Bwlchllan
509
DRUM
527
CEFN CNWC
645
DRYGARN FAWR
B4342
Trefilan
River Towi
Newbridge on W
Llyn Berwyn
Esgair Cerrig
Llanddewi Brefi
Abergwesyn Common
Llanafan-Fawr
Afon Irfon
470
ESGAIR LLETHR
500
CEFN COCH
493
PEN CARREG-DÂN
A485
B4343
Llangybi
Vicarage Meadows
Abergwesyn
B4358
Bettws Bledrws
484
BRYN BRAWD
462
CEFN GRUG
457
PEN-Y-GURNOS
450
CEFN FANNOG
Beulah
A482
Llanfair Clydogau
487
CARCWM
Garth
A483
Lampeter (Llanbedr Pont Steffan)
440
CARN NANT-YR-AST
River Doethie
Llyn Brianne
517
MYNYDD TRAWSNANT
390
CRUG SIARLS
374
Llanwrtyd Wells
Llangammarch Wells
467
A485
Pencarreg
River Brun
462
MYNYDD MALLAEN
A482
Farmers
A483
Cefngorwydd
B4519
474
DRUM DDU
R Fanagoed
River Cothi
Rhandirmwyn
415
Mynydd Pencarreg
River Annell
Cynghordy Viaduct
Mynydd Eppynt
475
Ysgir Fawr
Llandre
Afon Gwenlais
463
BRYN DU
B4337
Pumsaint
Dolaucothi Gold Mines
Cynghordy
Tirabad
Llandulas
Ysgir Fechan
Caeo
Cilycwm
454
GWRHYD
Rhydcymerau
R Marlais
26
River Crychan
Nant Gwennol
B4302
River Livy
River Gorlech
411
NOETHGRUG
Merthyr Cynog
Llansawel
Mynydd Bwlch-y-Groes
309
Poor Man's Wood
Nant Bran
278
Llandovery (Llanymddyfri)
Llanfihangel Bran
Talley Lakes
B4310
Abergorlech
Abbey
329
MYNYDD
Talley
A482
A40
406
Pentre-bach
Pont-faen

A
B
C
D
E
F
G
H
48
47
37
27
28
Llangadfan
Llanerfyl
Glyndwr's Way
Sychtyn
A458
A495
B4389
B4392
Heniarth
Welshpool
(Y Trallwng)
Welshpool & Llanfair Light Railway
B4385
Powis Castle
Llyn Coed y Dinas
Buttington
B4381
B4388
Leighton
Llanfair Caereinion
Castle Caereinion
House
Yockleton
Hanw
Cruckmeole
Westbury
Hinton
Arscott
Asterley
Plealey
Pontesbury
Aston Rogers
Aston Pigott
Minsterley
Long
Brockton
Worthen
B4386
B4499
Wrentnall
Habberley
Snailbeach
The Hollies
Castle Pulverbatch
Llanllugan
B4390
Manafon
Marton
Adfa
Llanwyddelan
New Mills
Forden
Berriew
Glansevern Hall
Garthmyl
Rorrington
Mitchell's Fold Stone Circle
Stiperstones
Pennerley
Pickless
Shelve
536
Tregynon
Offa's Dyke Path
Chirbury
A490
Castle
B4385
B4386
Montgomery
Town Hill
Priest Weston
513
CORNDON HILL
Ratlinghope
A483
Bettws Cedewain
B4389
Afon Carno
Bwlch-y-ffridd
Dolforwyn Castle
Llandyssil
Churchstoke
Hyssington
516
Clatter
Llanwnog
B4568
228
Pwll Penarth
Abermule
353
CEFN Y COED
Norbury
Wentnor
Linley
The Long Mynd
Caersws
B4569
A489
Newtown
(Y Drenewydd)
Llanllwchaiarn
B4368
More
Whitcot
Asterton
Lydham
Minton
Kerry
A489
Sarn
Marshbrook
Mochdre
Bishop's Castle
Lea
Choulton
Whittingslow
Llandinam
Mainstone
Plowden
River Severn
Dolfor
Clun Forest
Colebatch
Lydbury North
Edgton
A470
A488
Brockton
Wistanstow
Cheney Longville
Llanidloes
A483
B4368
Lower Down
Whitcott Keysett
Newcastle
Kempton
Hopesay
Aston on Clun
Bicton
Clunton
B4518
B4355
Felindre
Clun
Castle
B4368
Broome
Clunbury
Beguildy
R. Teme
Rockhill
Offa's Dyke Path
B4385
B4367
Clungunford
River Ithon
478
MOEL WILYM
Llanbadarn Fynydd
493
RED LION HILL
Tylcau Hill
547
BEACON HILL
Hobarris
Obley
New Invention
Hopton Castle
Hoptonheath
Sheldern
Beckjay
Llanfair Waterdine
Pentre Hodrey
Bedstone
Chapel Lawn
Knucklas Viaduct
Glyndwr's Way
B4355
Knucklas
Bucknell
Stowe
Kinton
Leintwardine
Bwlch-y-sarnau
Offa's Dyke Heritage Centre
A4113
Walford
Llanbister
B4356
Knighton
(Tref-y-Clawdd)
Brampton Bryan
Adforton
St Harmon
471
Llangunllo
A488
Gilfach Farm
B4518
A483
B4355
Castle
386
HARLEYS MT
Birtley
Rhayader
Llanddewi Ystradenni
Bleddfa
B4356
B4357
B4355
Lingen
Whitton
Norton
Lower Lye
Nantmel
A488
RSPB
A4110
A44
Llanfihangel Rhydithon
Upper Lye
Radnor Forest
Stapleton
Kinsham
Aymestrey
R Lugg
Byton
B4356
The Judge's Lodging
Presteigne
Coombes-Moor
Uphampton
Easthampton
Penybont
660
GT RHOS
610
BACH HILL
Kinnerton
A483
B4362
B4362
Llandegley
Shobdon
Llanyre
Evenjobb
A470
A4081
Llandrindod Wells
(Llandrindod)
A44
New Radnor
B4372
Four Stones
B4357
Stansbatch
Knill
Titley
Staunton on Arrow
B4358
Howey
Walton
Old Radnor
BRADNOR HILL
Eardisland
GILWERN HILL
B4355
Pembridge
Newbridge on Wye
Hergest Ridge
Hergest Croft
Kington
Marston
A44
Bearwood
Llansantffraed-in-Elvel
A483
542
GWAUN-CESTE HILL
Gladestry
Lower Hergest
Upper Hergest
Lyonshall
A470
CARNEDDAU
Holme Marsh
A480
Lower Broxwood
Dilwyn
Cwmbach Llechrhyd
A481
Hundred House
482
LITTLE HILL
524
Hengoed
Huntington
Woonton
Weobley
Royal Welsh
Llanelwedd
Glascwm
B4594
Offa's Dyke Path
Cwmmau Farmhouse
Almeley
A4112
Ledgemoor
Cilmery
A483
Prince Llewelyn
Builth Wells
(Llanfair-ym-Muallt)
Newchurch
A4111
Lower Welson
508
RED HILL
Bryngwyn
Brilley
Kinnersley
Eardisley
B4230
Wormsley
441
467
B4567
467
LLANBEDR HILL
Millhalf
Norton Canon
467
B4520
Aberedw
LLANDEILO HILL
Rhosgoch
Toll
Whitney-on-Wye
Winforton
Willersley
Letton
Yazor
472
BANC-Y-CELYN
Llandeilo Graban
Painscastle
CLYRO HILL
River Wye
Clifford
B4350
B4352
Bredwardine
Staunton on Wye
A438
A480
Mansell Gamage
Bishopstone
474
DRUM DDU
B4519
The Begwns
Brobury House
Arthur's Stone
Monnington on Wye
Byford
Erwood
Clyro
B4348
B4348
Gwenddwr
Hay-on-Wye
A438
B4351
Bridge Sollers
Cricka
Llowes
B4350
Dorstone
Preston on Wye
Golden Valley
Blakemere
Lulham
Cwmbach
Llanigon
Vagar
Tyberton
A470
0 1 2 3 4 miles
0 1 2 3 4 5 kilometres

Telford & Worcester
49
40
30
28
29
Town Plan: Worcester p
J
K
L
M
N
P
Q
R
Bayston Hill
Atcham
Wroxeter
Uppington
Donnington
Aston
The Wrekin
407
Roman City
Berrington
Cross Houses
Eaton Constantine
Little Wenlock
Condover
Garmston
Exfordsgreen
Stapleton
Eaton Mascott
Eyton on Severn
Cound
Leighton
Buildwas
Great Ryton
Upper Cound
Harnage
Cressage
Pitchford
Sheinton
Ironbridge
Acton Burnell
Frodesley
Harley
Homer
Much Wenlock
Broseley
Coalport
Longnor
Ruckley
Kenley
Church Preen
Stretton Westwood
Leebotwood
Hughley
Willey
Plaish
Bourton
Cardington
Gretton
Easthope
Acton Round
Church Stretton
Longville in the Dale
Brockton
Monkhopton
Morville
Hope Bowdler
Weston
Upper Netchwood
Upton Cressett
Bridgnorth
Rushbury
Shipton
Ticklerton
Stanton Long
Netchwood
Chetton
Eaton
Broadstone
Holdgate
Acton Scott
Middlehope
Ditton Priors
Neenton
Middleton Scriven
Alcaston
Aston Munslow
Munslow
Tugford
Cleobury North
Westhope
Abdon
546
BROWN CLEE HILL
Burwarton
Diddlebury
Corfton
Bouldon
Clee St Margaret
Aston Botterell
Culmington
Stoke St Milborough
Wenlock Edge
Hope Dale
Corve Dale
Onibury
Stanton Lacy
Hopton Cangeford
Farlow
Silvington
Bitterley
533
TITTERSTONE CLEE HILL
Cleeton St Mary
Middleton
Doddington
Foxwood
Angelbank
Bromfield
Snitton
Knowbury
Cleehill
Hopton Wafers
Ludlow
Ludford
Hope
Caynham
Knowle
Bagot
Whitton
Coreley
Milson
Bransley
Neen Savage
Cleobury Mortimer
Bayton
Overton
Pipe Aston
Ashford Carbonell
Ashford Bowdler
Greete
Nash
Neen Sollars
Mamble
Clows Top
Richards Castle
Middleton
Little Hereford
Boraston
Knighton on Teme
Wooferton
Brimfield Cross
Burford
Newnham
Rochford
Lindridge
Comberton
Berrington
Tenbury Wells
Kyrewood
Upper Rochford
Hanley William
Stockton on Teme
Orleton
Brimfield
Berrington Green
Eardiston
Bircher
Middleton on the Hill
St Michaels
Hanley Child
Stanford on Teme
Moreton
Eye
Ashton
Leysters
Upper Sapey
Stoke Bliss
Luston
Eyton
Kimbolton
Stockton
Whyle
Collington
Harpley
Cholstrey
Leominster
Hatfield
Thornbury
Old Church
Tedstone Wafer
Tedstone Delamere
Steen's Bridge
Docklow
Edwyn Ralph
Bredenbury
Ivington
Stoke Prior
Risbury
Wharton
Bromyard
Brockhampton Estate
Upper Hill
Newton
Hope under Dinmore
Bowley
Pencombe
Munderfield Row
Stanford Bishop
Linley Green
Westhope
Bodenham
Little Cowarne
Stoke Cross
Munderfield Stocks
Acton Beauchamp
Suckley
Bodenham Moor
Ullingswick
Acton Green
Stoke Lacy
Bishop's Frome
Evesbatch
Wellington
Upper Town
Felton
Moreton Jeffries
Much Cowarne
Marden
Preston Wynne
Burley Gate
Ocle Pychard
Lower Eggleton
Castle Frome
Fromes Hill
Mathon
Sutton St Nicholas
Newtown
Upper Egleton
Stretton Grandison
Moreton on Lugg
Westhide
Monkhide
Burghill
Pipe and Lyde
Withington
Yarkhill
Stretton Sugwas
Shelwick
Shucknall
Canon Frome
Bosbury
Coddington
Colwall
Holmer
Lugwardine
Hagley
Ashperton
Staplow
Breinton
Bartestree
Perton
Stoke Edith
Tarrington
Trumpet
Munsley
Wellington Heath
Oakengates
Priorslee
Hollinswood
TELFORD
Dawley
Horsehay
Stirchley
Madeley
Shifnal
Tong Norton
Tong
White Ladies Priory
Boscobel House
Bishop's Wood
Brewood
Standeford
Coven
Chillington
Kemberton
Royal Air Force
Albrighton
Codsall
Codsall Wood
Kingswood Common
Ryton
Boningale
Oaken
Sutton Maddock
Beckbury
Burnhill Green
Badger
Norton
Stockton
Pattingham
Perton
Tettenhall
WOLVERHAMPTON
Stableford
Ackleton
Chesterton
Wightwick
Wightwick Manor
Merryhill
Lower Penn
Nordley
Astley Abbots
Cross Lane Head
Rindleford
Worfield
Wyken
Hilton
Orton
Seisdon
Bromley
Hopstone
Roughton
Aston
Trysull
Gospel End
Sedgley
Claverley
Ounsdale
Oldbury
Heathton
Smestow
Halfpenny Green
Wombourne
Himley
Quatford
Bobbington
Swindon
Wolverhampton Business
Eardington
Six Ashes
Highgate Common
Chelmarsh
Dudmaston
Quatt
Glazeley
Tuckhill
Sutton
Hampton
Enville
Wordsley
Sidbury
Birdsgreen
Brierley Hill
Billingsley
Alveley
Compton
Stourton
Amblecote
Chorley
Woodhill
Severn Valley
Dunsley
Wollaston
Stottesdon
Highley
Romsley
Kinver
Old Swinford
STOURBRIDGE
Fenn Green
Whittington
Pedmore
Bodenham Arboretum
Upper Arley
Kinlet
Shatterford
Hagley
Cookley
Churchill
Wolverley
Severn Valley Railway
Blakedown
Broome
Buttonoak
Wyre Forest
Habberley
Blakebrook
Franche
Broadwaters
Belbroughton
Bewdley
Wribbenhall
KIDDERMINSTER
Drayton
Long Bank
West Midland
Stone
Harvington
Bluntington
Ribbesford
Wilden
Shenstone
Chaddesley Corbett
Bliss Gate
Upper Milton
Rock
Heightington
Stourport-on-Severn
Areley Kings
Torton
Rushock
Hartlebury
Astley Cross
Titton
Elmley Lovett
Pensax
Dunley
Chadwick
Lincomb
Bryan's Green
Abberley
The Burf
Crossway Green
Norchard
Cutnall Green
Elmbridge
Astley
Abberley Common
Noutard's Green
Comhampton
Dunhampton
Broad Alley
Upton Warren
Redmarley
Great Witley
Sytchampton
Hampton Lovett
Frog Pool
Northampton
Doverdale
Sapey Common
Stanford Bridge
276
WOODBURY HILL
Witley Court
Shrawley
Oldfield
Rashwood
Uphampton
Ombersley
Droitwich
Sankyn's Green
Hadley
Shelsley Walsh
Little Witley
Holt
Sinton
Shelsley Beauchamp
Holt Heath
Salwarpe
Clifton upon Teme
Grimley
Sinton
Ladywood
Martley
Wichenford
Sinton Green
Hawford
Dovecote
Martin Hussingtree
Berrow Green
Moseley
Fernhill Heath
Shoulton
Hindlip
Horsham
Hallow
Northwick
Tibberton
Whitbourne
Lower Broadheath
Crowle Green
Knightwick
WORCESTER
Rainbow Hill
Broad Green
Upper Broadheath
Trotshill
Crowle
Lulsley
Broadwas
Henwick
Newtown
Spetchley
Bringsty Common
Leigh Court Barn
Leigh
Rushwick
St Johns
Cherry Orchard
Whittington
Alfrick
Brockamin
Bransford
Alfrick Pound
Leigh Sinton
Powick
Norton
Callow End
Littleworth
Deblin's Green
Kempsey
Stoulton
Newland
Madresfield
Malvern Link
Cradley
West Malvern
Great Malvern
Guarlford
Clifton
Kerswell Green
Wadborough
Severn Stoke
Croome Park
Besford
Defford
Kinnersley
Earl's Croome
Baughton
Three Counties
Hanley Swan
Hanley Castle
Malvern Wells
Upper Welland
Upton upon Severn
Strensham (northbound)
Malvern Hills
River Severn
Staffs & Worcs Canal
M54
M5
A49
A458
A4169
A442
A454
A449
A458
A4117
A456
A443
A4112
A44
A417
A465
A4103
A438
A4110
A4104
A451
A456
A448
A442
A4133
A38
A4538
A4440
A4103
A41
A464
A463
A459
A491
B4380
B4371
B4378
B4368
B4364
B4363
B4555
B4194
B4190
B4202
B4214
B4204
B4203
B4197
B4196
B4220
B4219
B4211
B4208
B4361
B4362
B4365
B4176
B4161
B4189
B4373
B4375
B4376
B5061

50
49
39
30
Town Plan: Birmingham p.12
Stone
Uttoxeter
Stafford
Rugeley
Cannock Chase
Lichfield
Burton upon Trent
Tutbury
Barton-under-Needwood
Penkridge
Hednesford
Cannock
Burntwood
Brownhills
Tamworth
Wolverhampton
Walsall
Sutton Coldfield
West Bromwich
Dudley
Birmingham
Halesowen
Stourbridge
Kidderminster
Bromsgrove
Redditch
Solihull
Coleshill
Knowle
Dorridge
Kenilworth
Balsall Common
Aldridge
Codsall
Wombourne
Hagley
Fazeley
Kingsbury
Polesworth
Dordon
Baddesley Ensor
Alvechurch
Great Wyrley
Cheslyn Hay
Norton Canes
Heath Hayes & Wimblebury
Pelsall
Romsley
Meriden
M6
M54
M5
M42
M40
M6 Toll
A38(M)
0 1 2 3 4 miles
0 1 2 3 4 5 kilometres

51
42
32
31
Stanton by Dale
Chaddesden
Spondon
Ockbrook
Risley
Borrowash
Beeston
Chilwell
Rylands
West Bridgford
Gamston
Edwalton
on Trent
Cropwell Butler
Tithby
Granby
Barnstone
Langar
Cropwell Bishop
Cotgrave
Tollerton
Clipston
Owthorpe
Normanton on the Wolds
Plumtree
Colston Bassett
Plungar
Barkestone le Vale
Crewton
Alvaston
Allenton
Breaston
Draycott
Elvaston
Thulston
Sinfin
Chellaston
Shardlow
Aston-upon-Trent
Weston-upon-Trent
Swarkestone
Barrow upon Trent
Stanton by Bridge
Castle Donington
Hemington
Melbourne
Long Eaton
Toton
Clifton
Barton in Fabis
Thrumpton
Ruddington
Bradmore
Gotham
Great Central (Nottingham) Railway
Keyworth
Stanton on the Wolds
Bunny
Kinoulton
Hickling
Hose
Harby
Stathern
Eastwell
Eaton
Long Clawson
Ratcliffe on Soar
Kingston on Soar
Kegworth
West Leake
East Leake
Costock
Wysall
Widmerpool
Willoughby-on-the-Wolds
Upper Broughton
Nether Broughton
Goadby Marwood
Wycomb
Chadwell
Holwell
Scalford
Ab Kettleby
East Midlands
Donington Park
Grand Prix Collection
Isley Walton
Diseworth
Wilson
Breedon on the Hill
Ticknall
Calke Abbey
Calke
Tonge
Long Whatton
Zouch
Sutton Bonington
Normanton on Soar
Rempstone
West Thorpe
Old Dalby
Wartnaby
Grimston
Saxelbye
Melton Mowbray
Thorpe Arnold
Staunton Harold Church
Lount
Worthington
Belton
Hathern
Stanford on Soar
Cotes
Hoton
Wymeswold
Burton on the Wolds
Shoby
Asfordby Hill
Asfordby
Kirby Bellars
Brentingby
Smisby
Shepshed
Osgathorpe
Loughborough
Walton on the Wolds
Barrow upon Soar
Seagrave
Ragdale
Hoby
Frisby on the Wreake
Ashby-de-la-Zouch
Thringstone
Nanpantan
Quorn
Sileby
Thrussington
Rotherby
Burton Lazars
Swannington
Whitwick
Charnwood Forest
Mount St Bernard
Beacon Hill
Woodhouse
Woodhouse Eaves
Mountsorrel
Ratcliffe on the Wreake
Cossington
Rearsby
Great Dalby
Little Dalby
Packington
Ravenstone
Coalville
Bardon
Copt Oak
Great Central Railway
Rothley
Swithland
East Goscote
Gaddesby
Queniborough
Ashby Folville
Thorpe Satchville
Burrough Hill
Leesthorpe
Pickwell
Normanton le Heath
Measham
Heather
Donington le Heath
Stanton under Bardon
Markfield
Bradgate Park
Newtown Linford
Cropston
Thurcaston
Wanlip
Syston
Barsby
Burrough on the Hill
Twyford
Somerby
Cold Overton
Snarestone
Swepstone
Newton Burgoland
Ellistown
Ibstock
Field Head
Anstey
Birstall
Thurmaston
Watermead
Barkby
South Croxton
Knossington
Odstone
Bagworth
Thornton
Barkby Thorpe
Beeby
Owston
Shackerstone
Barton in the Beans
Nailstone
Groby
Glenfield
Belgrave
Hungarton
Lowesby
Halstead
Bilstone
Congerstone
Barlestone
Ratby
Keyham
Carlton
Osbaston
Kirby Muxloe
LEICESTER
Humberstone
Scraptoft
Tilton on the Hill
Market Bosworth
The Battlefield Line
Tropical Birdland
Newbold Verdon
Desford
Kirby Fields
Leicester Forest East
Dane Hills
Braunstone
North Evington
Evington
Thurnby
Houghton on the Hill
Skeffington
Loddington
Sheepy Parva
Cadeby
Peckleton
Stoneygate
Stoughton
Billesdon
Tugby
Sibson
Sutton Cheney
Kirkby Mallory
Mallory Park
Aylestone
Knighton
Little Stretton
Gaulby
Rolleston
Upton
Shenton
Bosworth Battlefield
Stapleton
Earl Shilton
Thurlaston
Enderby
Glen Parva
Oadby
King's Norton
Illston on the Hill
East Norton
Dadlington
Huncote
Wigston
Great Glen
Burton Overy
Goadby
Fenny Drayton
Stoke Golding
Barwell
Potters Marston
Narborough
Whetstone
South Wigston
Blaby
Newton Harcourt
Carlton Curlieu
Hallaton
Higham on the Hill
Elmesthorpe
Croft
Littlethorpe
Cosby
Countesthorpe
Foston
Kilby
Shangton
Stonton Wyville
Glooston
Cranoe
Hinckley
Burbage Common & Woods
Stoney Stanton
Willoughby Waterleys
Kibworth Harcourt
Kibworth Beauchamp
Tur Langton
Church Langton
Slawston
Medbourne
Weddington
NUNEATON
Sketchley
Burbage
Sapcote
Peatling Magna
Fleckney
Saddington
Smeeton Westerby
East Langton
Thorpe Langton
Welham
Attleborough
Aston Flamville
Broughton Astley
Arnesby
Weston by Welland
Burton Hastings
Sharnford
Frolesworth
Ashby Magna
Shearsby
Bruntingthorpe
Gumley
Sutton Bassett
Wigston Parva
Leire
Dunton Bassett
Peatling Parva
Mowsley
Foxton
Great Bowden
Griff
Claybrooke Magna
Ashby Parva
Laughton
Stoke Albany
Bramcote
Wolvey
Wolvey Heath
Copston Magna
Wibtoft
Ullesthorpe
Gilmorton
Lubenham
Dingley
Bedworth
Bulkington
Bitteswell
Walton
Kimcote
Union Canal
Marston Trussell
Market Harborough
Exhall
Willey
Lutterworth
Magna Park
Theddingworth
East Farndon
Braybrooke
Withybrook
Shilton
Ansty
Monks Kirby
Newnham Paddox
Misterton
Walcote
Husbands Bosworth
North Kilworth
Great Oxendon
Arthingworth
Longford
Foleshill
Potters Green
Henley Green
Wyken
Walsgrave on Sowe
Coombe Abbey
Street Ashton
Stretton under Fosse
Pailton
Cotesbach
Shawell
South Kilworth
Welford
Sibbertoft
Clipston
Harrington
COVENTRY
Stoke
Binley
Easenhall
Brinklow
Churchover
Swinford
Stanford Hall
Stanford on Avon
Kelmarsh
Kelmarsh Hall
Harborough Magna
Newbold on Avon
Newton
Catthorpe
Naseby
Haselbech
Lodding
Binley Woods
Bretford
Long Lawford
Lilbourne
Clay Coton
Cold Ashby
Maidwell
Draughton
Willenhall
Brandon
Wolston
Church Lawford
Clifton upon Dunsmore
Yelvertoft
Thornby
Lamport
Lamport Hall
Ryton-on-Dunsmore
New Bilton
Bilton
RUGBY
Hillmorton
Winwick
Cottesbrooke
Cottesbrooke Hall
Hanging Houghton
Baginton
Ryton Wood
Stoneleigh
Bubbenhall
Stretton-on-Dunsmore
Bourton on Dunsmore
DIRFT Logistics Park
Crick
West Haddon
Guilsborough
Hollowell
Creaton
Old
Scaldwell
Princethorpe
Dunchurch
Kilsby
Coton Manor
Coton
Ravensthorpe
Teeton
Brixworth
Hanington
Weston under Wetherley
Wappenbury
Frankton
Thurlaston
Draycote
Draycote Water
Barby
Spratton
Watford
Eathorpe
Birdingbury
Leamington Hastings
Hunningham
Hill
Willoughby
Ashby
Pitsford Reservoir
Pitsford
Northampton & Lamport
LEAMINGTON SPA
Offchurch
Grandborough
Braunston
Welton
Watford Gap
Boughton
Town Plans: Coventry p.126, Derby p.127, Leicester p

A
B
C
D
E
F
G
H
52
51
41
32
Thorpe
Fernwood
Fenton
Claypole
Stubton
Fulbeck
Caythorpe
Cranwell
Leasingham
Anwick
South Kyme
Elston
Cotham
Dry Doddington
Brandon
Frieston
Hough-on-the-Hill
Normanton
North Rauceby
Holdingham
South Rauceby
Sleaford
Evedon
Kirkby la Thorpe
Ewerby
Howell
Asgarby
East Heckington
Sibthorpe
Shelton
Long Bennington
Gelston
Carlton Scroop
Sudbrook
Ancaster
Quarrington
Heckington
The Pearoom
Great Hale
Little Hale
Hawksworth
Flawborough
Kilvington
Westborough
Foston
Hougham
Marston
Honington
Wilsford
Silk Willoughby
Burton Pedwardine
Helpringham
Alverton
Normanton
Allington
Barkston
Syston
Kelby
Culverthorpe
Swarby
Aswarby
Scredington
Swineshead
Bottesford
Vale of Belvoir
Belton
Belton House
Great Gonerby
Heydour
Oasby
Aisby
Aunsby
Osbournby
Spanby
Swaton
Bicker
Elton
Sedgebrook
Londonthorpe
Welby
Dembleby
Muston
Barrowby
Gonerby Hill Foot
Grantham
New Somerby
Newton
Threekingham
Northorpe
Donington
Redmile
Haceby
Braceby
Walcot
Horbling
Billingborough
Barkestone-le-Vale
Belvoir
Belvoir Castle
Woolsthorpe
Ropsley
Sapperton
Pickworth
Folkingham
Quadring
Little Ponton
Old Somerby
Humby
South Forty Foot Drain
Denton
Harlaxton
Harston
Stroxton
Great Ponton
Boothby Pagnell
Laughton
Pointon
Westhorpe
Stathern
Knipton
Croxton Kerrial
Aslackby
Risegate
Branston
Lenton
Ingoldsby
Eastwell
Eaton
Bitchfield
Rippingale
Dowsby
Bassingthorpe
Hall
Stoke Rochford
Easton
Burton Coggles
Irnham
Kirkby Underwood
Dunsby
Goadby Marwood
Saltby
Skillington
Wycomb
Waltham on the Wolds
Woolsthorpe Manor
Proxton
Woolsthorpe-by-Colsterworth
Corby Glen
Hacconby
Chadwell
Stonesby
Colsterworth
Hanthorpe
Morton
Scalford
Buckminster
Stainby
Elsthorpe
Grimsthorpe
Dyke
Spalding
Coston
North Witham
Swayfield
Swinstead
Edenham
Garthorpe
Sewstern
Gunby
Bourne
Twenty
Melton Mowbray
Thorpe Arnold
Freeby
Saxby
Creeton
South Witham
Castle Bytham
Little Bytham
Brentingby
Stapleford
Wymondham
Cribbs Meadow
R Eye
Lound
Edmondthorpe
Thistleton
Witham on the Hill
Toft
Burton Lazars
Clipsham
Careby
Thurlby
R Glen
Deeping St Nicholas
Teigh
Market Overton
Manthorpe
Deeping Fen
Little Dalby
Whissendine
Barrow
Greetham
Stretton
Carlby
Ashwell
Rutland
Cottesmore
Pickworth
Braceborough
Wilsthorpe
Baston
Leesthorpe
Burrough Hill
Pickwell
Exton
Rutland Falconry & Owl Centre
Open Air Theatre
Essendine
Langtoft
Market Deeping
Cold Overton
Langham
Greatford
Barholm
Somerby
Barleythorpe
Vale of Catmose
Burley
Little Casterton
Ryhall
Frognall
Knossington
Whitwell
Tickencote
Empingham
West Deeping
Deeping Gate
Deeping St James
Great Casterton
Tallington
Northborough
Owston
Oakham
Egleton
Upper Hambleton
Rutland Water
Ingthorpe
Northfields
Stamford
Uffington
Maxey
Peakirk
Tinwell
Burghley
Bainton
Etton
Glinton
Newborough
Halstead
Braunston
Brooke
Prior's Coppice
River Chater
Manton
Lyndon
Edith Weston
Ketton
Barnack
Helpston
Werrington
Wing
North Luffenham
Aldgate
Geeston
Easton-on-the-Hill
Hills & Holes
Ufford
Southorpe
Loddington
Ridlington
Maze
Pilton
Collyweston
Wittering
Marholm
New England
Belton
Preston
South Luffenham
Ayston
Morcott
Duddington
Thornhaugh
Sacrewell Farm & Country Centre
Castor Hanglands
Upton
Tugby
Glaston
East Norton
Allexton
Wardley
Uppingham
Barrowden
Tixover
Bedford Purlieus
Ailsworth
Goadby
Bisbrooke
Wakerley
Wansford
Sutton
Stibbington
Castor
Nene Valley Railway
Ferry Meadows
Longthorpe
New Fletton
Woodston
Old Fletton
Stanground
Peterborough
Stockerston
Horninghold
Seaton
Lyddington
Lyddington Bede House
Harringworth
King's Cliffe
Yarwell
Sibson
Water Newton
Alwalton
Orton Waterville
Orton Longueville
Hallaton
Stoke Dry
Eyebrook Reservoir
Laxton
Thorpe by Water
Nassington
Prebendal Manor House
Chesterton
Cranoe
Blaston
Blatherwycke
Apethorpe
Woodnewton
East of England
Hampton
Farcet
Slawston
Nevill Holt
Great Easton
Caldecott
Gretton
Kirby Hall
Bulwick
Willow Brook
Elton
Elton Hall
Medbourne
Deene
Fotheringhay
Welham
Drayton
Bringhurst
Deene Park
Southwick
Haddon
Rockingham
Rockingham Castle
Deenethorpe
Morborne
Yaxley
Weston by Welland
Ashley
Middleton
Little Weldon
Short Wood
Glapthorn
Tansor
Warmington
Sutton Bassett
East Carlton
Cottingham
Rockingham Forest
Upper Benefield
Cotterstock
Folksworth
Stoke Albany
East Carlton
Wilbarston
Great Weldon
Oundle
Ashton
Stilton
Holme
Dingley
Lower Benefield
Caldecote
Brampton Ash
Corby
Little Oakley
Stanion
Polebrook
Lutton
Denton
Glatton
Market Harborough
West Lodge Rural Centre
Pipewell
Great Oakley
Brigstock
Stoke Doyle
Barnwell
Lyveden New Bield
Fermyn Woods
Hemington
Conington
Braybrooke
Barnwell St Andrew
Sawtry
Desborough
Pilton
Luddington in the Brook
Barnwell All Saints
Great Gidding
Triangular Lodge
Geddington
Eleanor Cross
Wadenhoe
Achurch
Wigsthorpe
Thurning
Rushton
Newton
Boughton House
Sudborough
Steeple Gidding
Hamerton
Rothwell
Weekley
Warkton
Grafton Underwood
Lowick
Thorpe Waterville
Winwick
Clopton
Slipton
Titchmarsh
Orton
Kettering
A1
A1(M)
A15
A17
A52
A151
A153
A427
A43
A47
A605
A606
A607
A6003
A6116
A6121
A1175
A6
0 1 2 3 4 miles
0 1 2 3 4 5 kilometres
Town Plan: Peterborough p.13

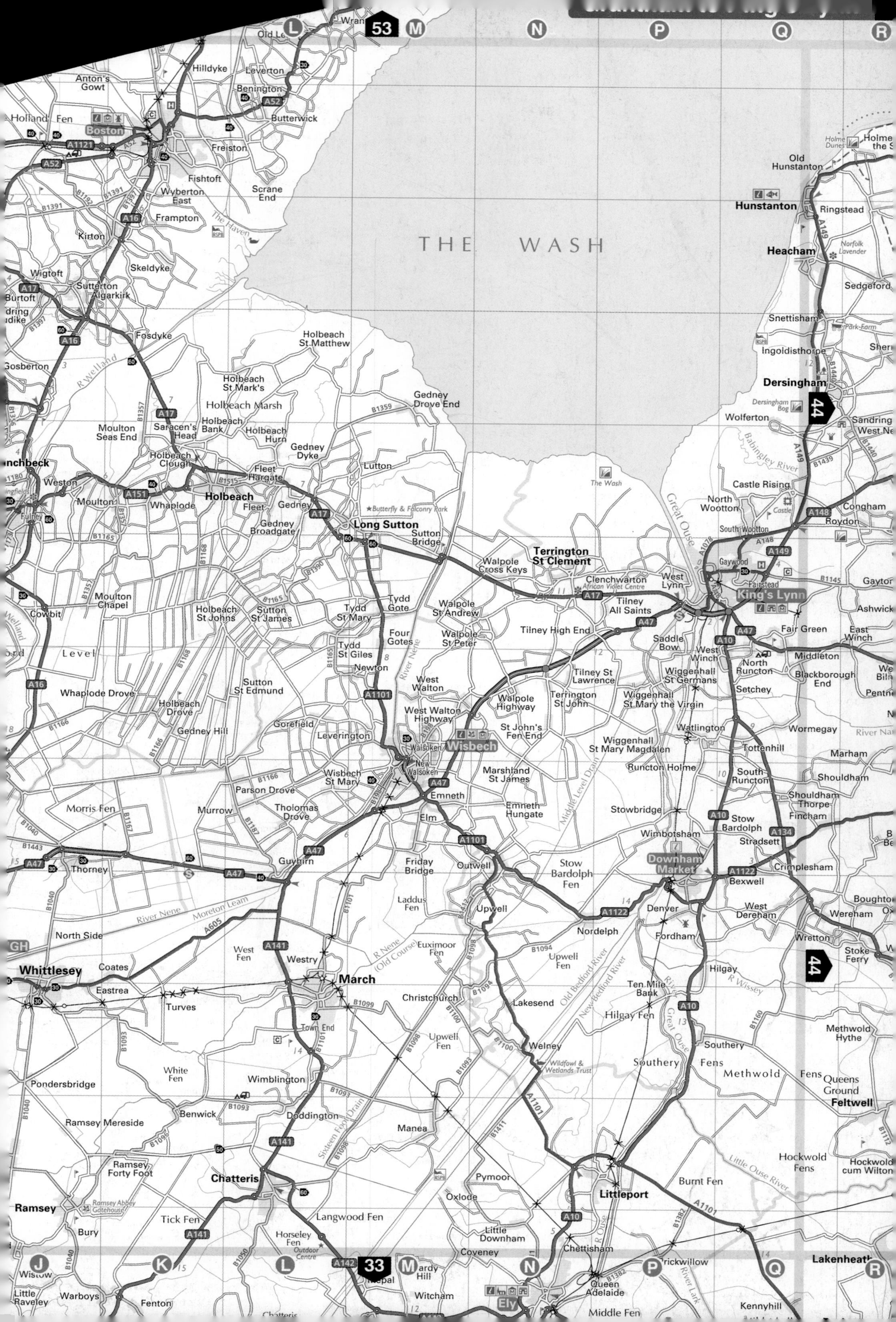

53
L
M
N
P
Q
R
Old Leake
Hilldyke
Leverton
Benington
Butterwick
Anton's Gowt
Holland Fen
Boston
A1121
A52
Freiston
Fishtoft
Wyberton East
Scrane End
Frampton
B1391
B1192
B1397
A16
The Haven
Kirton
Skeldyke
Wigtoft
Sutterton
Algarkirk
A17
Burtoft
Fosdyke
R Welland
Gosberton
Holbeach St Matthew
Holbeach St Mark's
Holbeach Marsh
Holbeach Bank
Holbeach Hurn
Gedney Drove End
B1359
Moulton Seas End
Saracen's Head
B1357
Holbeach Clough
Gedney Dyke
Lutton
Spalding
Pinchbeck
Weston
Moulton
A151
Whaplode
Holbeach
Fleet Hargate
B1515
Fleet
Gedney
Gedney Broadgate
B1165
Long Sutton
Butterfly & Falconry Park
Sutton Bridge
B1168
B1390
Moulton Chapel
Cowbit
Holbeach St Johns
Sutton St James
Tydd St Mary
Tydd Gote
Four Gotes
Tydd St Giles
Newton
River Nene
Level
Whaplode Drove
Holbeach Drove
Sutton St Edmund
Gedney Hill
Gorefield
Leverington
A1101
B1166
Parson Drove
Wisbech St Mary
Wisbech
Walsoken
New Walsoken
Morris Fen
Murrow
Tholomas Drove
B1187
B1167
B1040
B1443
A47
Thorney
Guyhirn
Emneth
Elm
Friday Bridge
River Nene
Moreton Leam
A605
North Side
Whittlesey
Coates
Eastrea
Turves
West Fen
Westry
A141
March
Laddus Fen
R Nene (Old Course)
Euximoor Fen
Christchurch
B1099
Town End
B1093
B1101
Pondersbridge
White Fen
Wimblington
Benwick
Doddington
Ramsey Mereside
Sixteen Foot Drain
Manea
Ramsey Forty Foot
B1096
Chatteris
Ramsey
Ramsey Abbey Gatehouse
Bury
Tick Fen
Langwood Fen
Horseley Fen
Outdoor Centre
A142
33
Mepal
Wistow
Little Raveley
Warboys
Fenton
THE WASH
The Wash
Terrington St Clement
Walpole Cross Keys
Clenchwarton
African Violet Centre
West Lynn
Tilney All Saints
Walpole St Andrew
Walpole St Peter
Tilney High End
Tilney St Lawrence
West Walton
West Walton Highway
Walpole Highway
Terrington St John
St John's Fen End
Marshland St James
Emneth Hungate
Middle Level Drain
A1101
Outwell
Upwell
Stow Bardolph Fen
A1122
Nordelph
Upwell Fen
B1094
Old Bedford River
New Bedford River
Lakesend
Welney
Wildfowl & Wetlands Trust
Upwell Fen
B1098
B1100
B1411
Pymoor
Oxlode
Little Downham
Coveney
Mardy Hill
Witcham
Ely
Great Ouse
Saddle Bow
Wiggenhall St Germans
Wiggenhall St Mary the Virgin
Wiggenhall St Mary Magdalen
Watlington
Runcton Holme
Stowbridge
Wimbotsham
Downham Market
Denver
Fordham
Ten Mile Bank
Hilgay Fen
River Great Ouse
Southery
Littleport
A10
Chettisham
R Ouse
Queen Adelaide
B1382
Prickwillow
River Lark
Middle Fen
Old Hunstanton
Holme Dunes
Holme next the Sea
Hunstanton
Ringstead
Heacham
Norfolk Lavender
A149
Sedgeford
Snettisham
Park Farm
Ingoldisthorpe
Dersingham
Dersingham Bog
44
Wolferton
Sandringham
West Newton
Babingley River
B1439
B1440
Castle Rising
North Wootton
South Wootton
Congham
Roydon
A148
A1078
Gaywood
King's Lynn
B1145
Gayton
Ashwick
Fair Green
East Winch
West Winch
North Runcton
Middleton
Blackborough End
Setchey
Wormegay
River Nar
Tottenhill
Marham
South Runcton
Shouldham
Shouldham Thorpe
Fincham
Stow Bardolph
A134
Stradsett
Crimplesham
Bexwell
West Dereham
Wereham
Boughton
Wretton
Stoke Ferry
Hilgay
R Wissey
Southery Fens
Methwold
B1160
Methwold Hythe
Fens
Queens Ground
Feltwell
B1112
Hockwold Fens
Hockwold cum Wilton
Little Ouse River
Burnt Fen
A1101
Lakenheath
Kennyhill

A
B
C
D
E
Leake Common Side
Sibsey
K
Sibsey Trader Windmill
Fishtoft Drove
Frithville
B1184
Holkham Bay
Scolt Head Island
Brancaster Bay
Peddars Way & Norfolk Coast Path
Blakeney Point
Holme Dunes
Holme next the Sea
Brancaster
Brancaster Staithe
Burnham Deepdale
Burnham Norton
Burnham Overy Staithe
Holkham
Wells-next-the-sea
Morston
Salthouse
Old Hunstanton
Titchwell
Thornham
Branodunum Roman Fort
Burnham Market
Burnham Overy
B1155
Holkham Hall
Warham St Mary
A149
Stiffkey
Cockthorpe
Wiveton
Langham
Glandford
Hunstanton
Ringstead
B1355
Burnham Thorpe
Warham All Saints
Wighton
B1156
Saxlingham
North Norfolk Railway
R Glaven
Binham
Binham Priory & Market Cross
Field Dalling
Letheringsett
Holt
A149
B1153
B1155
Summerfield
North Creake
Creake Abbey
Wells & Walsingham Light Railway
The Shrine of Our Lady
Heacham
Norfolk Lavender
Peddars Way & Norfolk Coast Path
Docking
Stanhoe
Little Walsingham
Great Walsingham
Hindringham
Sharrington
Bale
Holt
Hempstead
Sedgeford
B1454
South Creake
North Barsham
Houghton St Giles
Brinton
Thornage
Hunworth
Fring
Bircham Newton
B1110
Snettisham
Park Farm
West Barsham
East Barsham
Great Snoring
Thursford
Gunthorpe
Stody
Briningham
Edgefield
B1354
Ingoldisthorpe
Shernborne
Syderstone
R Stiffkey
Little Snoring
A148
Barney
Melton Constable
Briston
Great Bircham
Bircham Tofts
Wicken Green Village
Croxton
Swanton Novers
Dersingham
Sculthorpe
Kettlestone
Fulmodeston
43
B1440
Anmer
B1454
Dunton
Shereford
Fakenham
Pensthorpe Waterfowl Park
Hindolveston
Wolferton
Sandringham
Houghton Hall
West Rudham
Tattersett
Coxford
Hempton
Stibbard
Thurning
West Newton
New Houghton
East Rudham
Tatterford
Little Ryburgh
Babingley River
B1440
A148
Toftrees
Wood Norton
Flitcham
Helhoughton
East Raynham
Great Ryburgh
B1146
A1067
B1439
Harpley
Colkirk
R Wensum
Guestwick
Castle Rising
Hillington
Little Massingham
West Raynham
Guist
Foulsham
North Wootton
Congham
South Raynham
Gateley
Twyford
Themelthorpe
A148
Roydon
Great Massingham
Weasenham St Peter
Whissonsett
Horningtoft
Bintree
Reepham
South Wootton
Grimston
Foxley
Foxley Wood
B1145
A149
B1153
Weasenham All Saints
Wellingham
Brisley
North Elmham
North Elmham Chapel
Gaywood
Tittleshall
Stanfield
Billingford
Bawdeswell
Fairstead
B1145
Gayton
B1145
Rougham
East Bilney
Old Beetley
Worthing
B1145
Sparham
King's Lynn
Ashwicken
Gayton Thorpe
Mileham
B1147
Lyng
A1065
B1146
Beetley
Swanton Morley
Lenwade
A47
Fair Green
East Winch
Litcham
Gressenhall
Elsing
A10
Middleton
East Walton
West Acre
Castle Acre
West Lexham
East Lexham
Beeston
Gressenhall Green
Hoe
North Runcton
West Bilney
Priory
Newton
Longham
Gressenhall
B1147
North Tuddenham
Blackborough End
Pentney
South Acre
Little Dunham
Great Dunham
Dereham
Hockering
Setchey
B1153
Great Fransham
Wendling
A47
Mattishall Burgh
Narborough
Scarning
Dereham
Mattishall
Wormegay
River Nar
A47
Sporle
Little Fransham
Clint Green
East Tuddenham
Tottenhill
Ecotech Discovery Centre
A47
Westfield
Yaxham
South Green
Welborne
Marham
Necton
East Bradenham
Whinburgh
South Runcton
Shouldham
Swaffham
Holme Hale
A1075
Brandon Parva
A1122
West Bradenham
Shipdham
Runhall
Shouldham Thorpe
North Pickenham
Garvestone
Thuxton
Barnham Broom
Fincham
B1135
Coston
A10
Stow Bardolph
Barton Bendish
B1077
Reymerston
A134
South Pickenham
Cranworth
Southburgh
Stradsett
Beachamwell
Mid Norfolk Railway
Kimberley
Cockley Cley
Ashill
Saham Hills
Woodrising
Hardingham
Crownthorpe
A1122
Crimplesham
Bexwell
Iceni Village
A1065
Ovington
Hingham
Hackford
Great Cressingham
B1108
West Dereham
Boughton
Gooderstone
Carbrooke
Wicklewood
Wereham
Oxborough
Saham Toney
Deopham
Morley St Botolph
Wretton
Oxburgh Hall
Hilborough
Watton
Scoulton
R Wissey
B1108
Stoke Ferry
Whittington
Little Cressingham
Griston
B1077
Little Ellingham
Hilgay
Foulden
A1075
Merton
Rockland St Peter
Deopham Green
43
B1108
R Wissey
B1112
A134
Northwold
Caston
Great Ellingham
B1172
Thompson
Rockland All Saints
Besthorpe
Methwold Hythe
Stow Bedon
Lower Stow Bedon
Fen Street
B1160
Methwold
Cranwich
Ickburgh
Attleborough
Southery
Peddars Way & Norfolk Coast Path
Breckles
Carleton
Fens
Mundford
Shropham
Methwold
Fens
Queens Ground
Thetford
Great Hockham
B1077
Feltwell
East Wretham
Snetterton
Old Buckenham
Eccles Road
A1065
A134
B1111
Grime's Graves
Forest
B1112
Weeting
Castle
A1075
Snetterton
Wilby
A11
Larling
Hockwold Fens
Hockwold cum Wilton
Quidenham
Banham
Little Ouse River
Santon Downham
Banham
Fen
Brandon
Croxton
Bridgham
East Harling
Kenninghall
Town Street
High Lodge Forest Centre
Brandon
Park
Brettenham
Winfarthing
B1106
B1107
B1111
Warren Lodge
Shadwell
North Lopham
Shelfanger
Fersfield
Lakenheath
Thetford
A1066
34
River
Garboldisham
South Lopham
A
B
C
D
E
F
G
H
Rushford
Gasthorpe
A1066
Bressingham
Little Ouse
Redgrave and Lopham Fen
Smallworth
Blo Norton
Steam Museum & Gardens
0 1 2 3 4 miles
0 1 2 3 4 5 kilometres
Center Parcs Elveden Forest
Elveden
Euston
Coney
Hopton

J
K
L
M
N
P
Q
R
Sheringham
West Runton
East Runton
Cromer
Upper Sheringham
Beeston Regis
Norfolk Shire Horse Centre
Overstrand
Sidestrand
Aylmerton
Felbrigg
Felbrigg Hall
Northrepps
Trimingham
West Beckham
East Beckham
Gresham
Crossdale Street
Bessingham
Sustead
Metton
Southrepps
Gimingham
Baconsthorpe
Roughton
Hanworth
Mundesley
Plumstead
Thurgarton
Thorpe Market
Lower Street
Stow Mill
Paston
Matlask
Trunch
Knapton
Bacton
Aldborough
Bradfield
Walcott
Wickmere
Antingham
Edingthorpe
Erpingham
Suffield
Calthorpe
Mannington Gardens
Wolterton Park
Itteringham
Swafield
North Walsham
Edingthorpe Green
Witton
Ridlington
Happisburgh
Banningham
Ingworth
Blickling
Meeting House Hill
Whimpwell Green
Felmingham
Happisburgh Common
Honing
Oulton Street
Tuttington
Lessingham
Hempstead
Aylsham
Briggate
East Ruston
Ingham Corner
Sea Palling
Burgh next Aylsham
Ingham
Waxham
Worstead
Stalham
Calthorpe Street
Bure Valley Railway
Dilham
Swanton Abbott
Hickling
Marsham
Oxnead
Lamas
Smallburgh
Brampton
Barton Turf
Wood Street
Sutton
Hickling Green
Horsey
Eastgate
Buxton Heath
Buxton
Tunstead
Barton Broad
Hickling Broad
Horsey Windpump
Brandiston
Neatishead
Catfield
Hevingham
Stratton Strawless
Irstead
Potter Heigham
Swannington
Horstead
Coltishall
Winterton-on-Sea
Felthorpe
Hainford
Ludham
Martham
Upgate
Frettenham
Belaugh
Hoveton
Bastwick
Wroxham
Upper Street
Hemsby
Hemsby Hole
Attlebridge
Horsford
Newton St Faith
Hillside
Horning
Upper Street
Repps
Ormesby Broad
Crostwick
Ormesby St Margaret
Rollesby
Scratby
Thorpe Marriot
Horsham St Faith
Spixworth
Woodbastwick
Bure Marshes
Broadland Conservation Centre
Thurne
Burgh St Margaret
Ormesby St Michael
California
Taverham
Drayton
Rackheath
Salhouse
Ranworth
Pilson Green
Clippesby
Costessey
Norwich Aviation
New Rackheath
Little Plumstead
Panxworth
Fairhaven
Cargate Green
Billockby
Filby
Caister-on-Sea
Hellesdon
Old Catton
Sprowston
Thorpe End
South Walsham
Thrigby
Mautby
Easton
NORWICH
Upton
Acle
Stokesby
Thrigby Hall
Caister
West End
West Caister
New Costessey
Great Plumstead
Blofield Heath
North Burlingham
Runham
Royal Norfolk
Marlingford
Thorpe St Andrew
Witton
Stracey Arms Windpump
Bawburgh
Colney
Blofield
Lingwood
Damgate
Tunstall
Little Melton
Brundall
Beighton
THE BROADS
Postwick
Strumpshaw
Whitlingham
Lynch Green
Cringleford
Norfolk Ski Centre
South Burlingham
Halvergate
River Yare
Eaton
New Lakenham
Old Lakenham
Trowse Newton
Kirby Bedon
Buckenham
Moulton St Mary
Freethorpe
Burgh Castle
Southtown
GREAT YARMOUTH
Hethersett
Keswick
Arminghall
Surlingham
Hassingham
Wickhampton
Berney Arms Windmill
Burgh Castle
East Port
Bramerton
Rockland St Mary
Cantley
Freethorpe Common
Bradwell
Gorleston-on-Sea
Caistor St Edmund
Framingham Pigot
Claxton
Limpenhoe
Belton
Ketteringham
Caistor Roman Town
Swardeston
Framingham Earl
Upper Stoke
Yelverton
Ashby St Mary
Carleton St Peter
Langley Street
Pettitts Crafts & Animal Adventure Park
Reedham
East Carleton
Dunston
Poringland
Hardley Street
Wymondham
Mulbarton
Stoke Holy Cross
Thurton
Swainsthorpe
Howe
Bergh Apton
Fritton
Fritton Lake Countryworld
St Olave's Priory
Bracon Ash
Wreningham
Shotesham
Chedgrave
Hopton on Sea
Hawe's Green
Silfield
Newton Flotman
Brooke
R Chet
Loddon
Norton Subcourse
Lound
Toprow
Saxlingham Thorpe
Thurlton
St Olaves
Wellthorpe
Saxlingham Nethergate
Mundham
Herringfleet
Somerleyton Hall & Gardens
Fundenhall
Flordon
Seething
Hales
Corton
Hapton
Tasburgh
Kirstead Green
Haddiscoe
Somerleyton
Blundeston
Saxlingham Green
Raveningham
Pleasurewood Hills
Low Tharston
Thwaite St Mary
Maypole Green
Upper Tasburgh
Tharston
Stratton St Michael
Hempnall
Stockton
Toft Monks
Forncett End
Forncett St Mary
Woodton
Kirby Cane
Wheatacre
Oulton
Forncett St Peter
Fritton
Hedenham
Aldeby
Burgh St Peter
Lowestoft Ness
Hempnall Green
Topcroft
Ellingham
Oulton Broad
Morningthorpe
Topcroft Street
Gillingham
LOWESTOFT
Kirkley
Wacton
Long Stratton
Shelton
River Waveney
Aslacton
Great Moulton
Ditchingham
Broome
Geldeston
Pakefield
Bungay
Shipmeadow
Worlingham
High Green
Hardwick
Earsham
Barnby
Carlton Colville
Mettingham
Barsham
Colegate End
Ringsfield
Beccles
North Cove
Gisleham
Tivetshall St Margaret
Denton
Ilketshall St Andrew
Mutford
Rushmere
Alburgh
Aviation
Winter Flora
Kessingland
Flixton
Ringsfield Corner
Hulver Street
Tivetshall St Mary
Pulham Market
Pulham St Mary
Ilketshall St Margaret
Black Street
Wortwell
Homersfield
Henstead
Suffolk Wildlife Park
Starston
St Margaret South Elmham
Redisham
Sotterley
Garlic Street
Benacre
Benacre Ness
Shimpling
Rushall
Redenhall
St Cross South Elmham
Shadingfield
Harleston
Mendham
Wrentham
Dickleburgh
Stone Street
Stoven
35
Thelveton
Thorpe Abbotts
Weybread
St James South Elmham
Brampton
South Cove
Diss
Brockdish
Metfield
Spexhall
Westhall
Scole
Weybread Street
Wissett
Uggeshall
Town Plan: Norwich p.

A
B
C
D
E
F
G
H
BAY
54
Llandwrog
Groes
Carmel
Glynllifon
Slateworks
Penygroes
Talysarn
Pontlyfni
Llanllyfni
Nebo
Clynnog-fawr
Nasareth
Pant Glas
522
Y GYRN-DDU
A499
A487
Lleyn Heritage Coast
Trefor
Tre'r Ceiri
564
YR EIFL
Llanaelhaearn
PENINSULA
Bryncir
Garn-Dolben
Dol
Trwyn y Gorlech
Llithfaen
St Cybi's Well
Llangybi
B4411
Afon Dwyfawr
Carreg Ddu
Porth Nefyn
Morfa Nefyn
Pistyll
B4417
Nefyn
Y Ffor
B4354
Pentref
Edern
Llanystumdwy
Chwilog
Criccieth
Castle
Bodfuan
Porth Ysgaden
A497
Llannor
Abererch
Penarth Fawr Medieval House
Tudweiliog
Efailnewydd
Dinas
371
Carn Fadrun
LLEYN
B4415
Pen-ychain
Porth Colman
Rhyd-y-clafdy
Pwllheli
Bryn-mawr
Llaniestyn
Penrhos
Pen-y-graig
Llangwnnadl
Meyllteyrn
Llanbedrog
Sarn
Botwnnog
B4413
Trwyn Llanbedrog
Porthoer
Bryncroes
St Tudwal's Road
Rhoshirwaun
Plas yn Rhiw
Llangian
Abersoch
Y Rhiw
Llanengan
Aberdaron
Llanfaelrhys
Porth Neigwl or Hell's Mouth
Bwlchtocyn
Marchros
St Tudwal's Island East
St Tudwal's Island West
Porth Ysgo
Aberdaron Bay
Porth Ceiriad
Bardsey Sound
Lleyn Heritage Coast
St Mary's
BARDSEY ISLAND
CARDIGAN
BAY
0 1 2 3 4 miles
0 1 2 3 4 5 kilometres

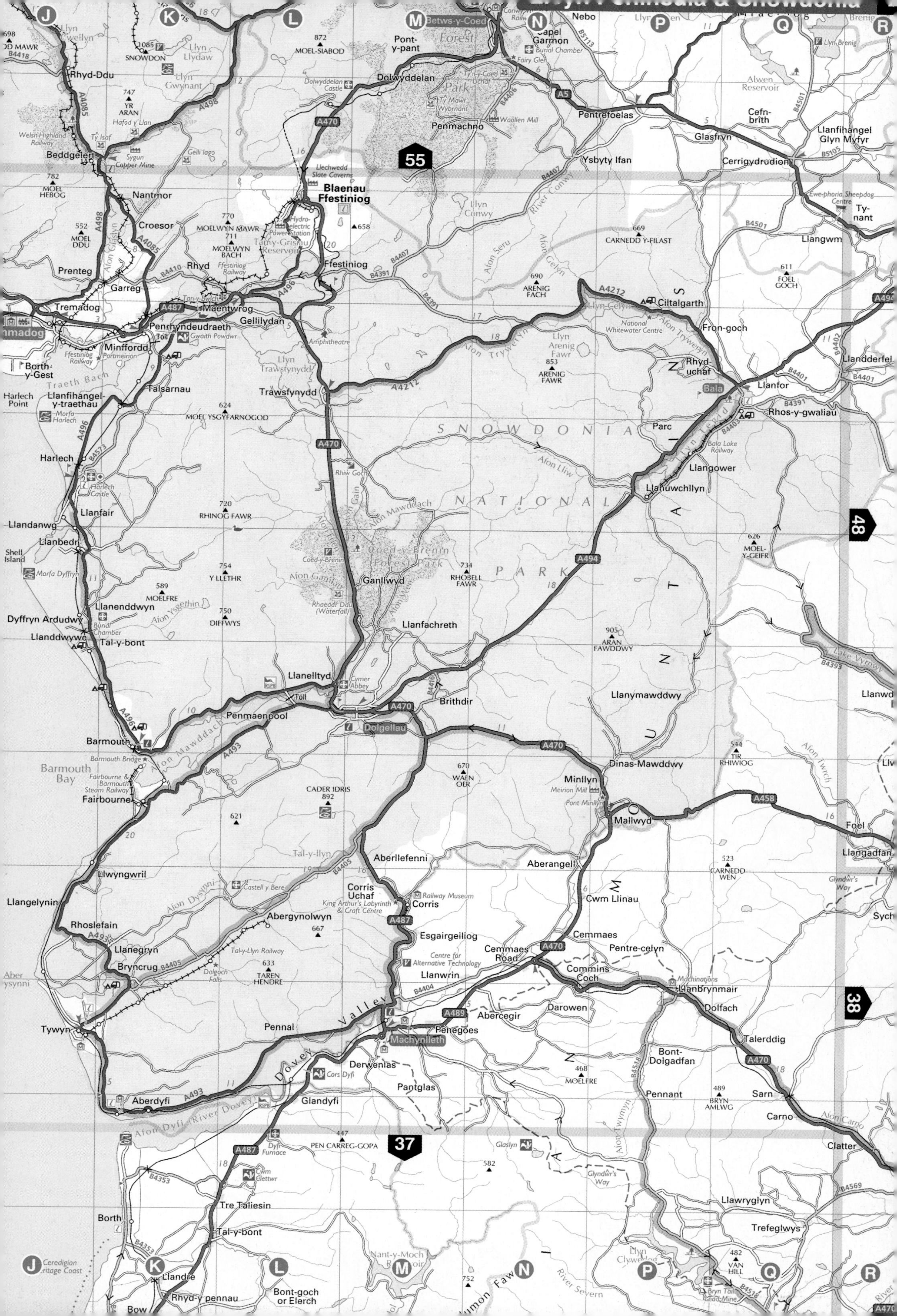

Llyn Cwellyn
SNOWDON
1085
Llyn Llydaw
Llyn Gwynant
Rhyd-Ddu
747
YR ARAN
Hafod y Llan
Welsh Highland Railway
Tŷ Isaf
Beddgelert
Sygun Copper Mine
Gelli Iago
782
MOEL HEBOG
Nantmor
Croesor
552
MOEL DDU
Afon Glaslyn
Prenteg
Garreg
Tremadog
Porthmadog
Borth-y-Gest
Penrhyndeudraeth
Minffordd
Ffestiniog Railway
Portmeirion
Toll
Traeth Bach
Harlech Point
Llanfihangel-y-traethau
Morfa Harlech
Talsarnau
Harlech
Harlech Castle
Llanfair
Llandanwg
Llanbedr
Shell Island
Morfa Dyffryn
Llanenddwyn
Dyffryn Ardudwy
Bondl Chamber
Llanddwywe
Tal-y-bont
Barmouth
Barmouth Bridge
Barmouth Bay
Fairbourne & Barmouth Steam Railway
Fairbourne
Llwyngwril
Llangelynin
Rhoslefain
Llanegryn
Bryncrug
Aber Dysynni
Tywyn
Aberdyfi
Afon Dyfi (River Dovey)
Dovey Valley
Pennal
872
MOEL-SIABOD
Pont-y-pant
Dolwyddelan
Dolwyddelan Castle
Betws-y-Coed
Gwydyr Forest
Tŷ Mawr Wybrnant
Tŷ-y-Coed Uchaf
Penmachno
Woollen Mill
Fairy Glen
Capel Garmon
Burial Chamber
Conwy Falls
Nebo
Llechwedd Slate Caverns
Blaenau Ffestiniog
658
770
MOELWYN MAWR
711
MOELWYN BACH
Hydro-electric Power Station
Tanygrisiau Reservoir
Ffestiniog
Rhyd
Ffestiniog Railway
Tan-y-Bwlch
Maentwrog
Gellilydan
Gwaith Powdwr
Amphitheatre
Llyn Trawsfynydd
Trawsfynydd
624
MOEL YSGYFARNOGOD
720
RHINOG FAWR
754
Y LLETHR
589
MOELFRE
750
DIFFWYS
Afon Ysgethin
Rhiw Goch
Afon Cain
Afon Mawddach
Afon Eden
Coed-y-Brenin
Coed-y-Brenin Forest Park
Afon Gamlan
Ganllwyd
Rhaeadr Du (Waterfall)
Afon Wen
Llanfachreth
Llanelltyd
Cymer Abbey
Toll
Penmaenpool
Afon Mawddach
Dolgellau
Brithdir
670
WAEN OER
CADER IDRIS
892
621
Tal-y-llyn
Aberllefenni
Corris Uchaf
Corris
Railway Museum
King Arthur's Labyrinth & Craft Centre
Castell y Bere
Afon Dysynni
Abergynolwyn
667
Tal-y-Llyn Railway
633
TAREN HENDRE
Dolgoch Falls
Esgairgeiliog
Centre for Alternative Technology
Llanwrin
Machynlleth
Penegoes
Derwenlas
Cors Dyfi
Pantglas
Glandyfi
Dyfi Furnace
Cwm Clettwr
447
PEN CARREG-GOPA
Tre Taliesin
Borth
Tal-y-bont
Ceredigion Heritage Coast
Llandre
Rhyd-y pennau
Bont-goch or Elerch
Bow Street
Nant-y-Moch Reservoir
Plynlimon Fawr
752
582
Glaslyn
Glyndŵr's Way
Afon Twymyn
Pentrefoelas
Ysbyty Ifan
Llyn Conwy
River Conwy
Afon Serw
Afon Gelyn
690
ARENIG FACH
Llyn Celyn
Ciltalgarth
National Whitewater Centre
Afon Tryweryn
Llyn Arenig Fawr
853
ARENIG FAWR
Fron-goch
Rhyd-uchaf
Bala
Llanfor
Rhos-y-gwaliau
Parc
Llyn Tegid
Bala Lake Railway
Llangower
Llanuwchllyn
Afon Lliw
SNOWDONIA NATIONAL PARK
734
RHOBELL FAWR
905
ARAN FAWDDWY
Llanymawddwy
Dinas-Mawddwy
Minllyn
Meirion Mill
Pont Minllyn
Mallwyd
Aberangell
Cwm Llinau
Cemmaes
Cemmaes Road
Pentre-celyn
Commins Coch
Darowen
Abercegir
Llanbrynmair
Machinations
Dolfach
Talerddig
Bont-Dolgadfan
468
MOELFRE
Pennant
489
BRYN AMLWG
Sarn
Carno
Afon Carno
Clatter
Llawryglyn
Trefeglwys
Llyn Clywedog
482
VAN HILL
Bryn Tail Lead Mine
River Severn
Alwen Reservoir
Llyn Brenig
Cefn-brith
Glasfryn
Llanfihangel Glyn Myfyr
Cerrigydrudion
Ewe-phoria Sheepdog Centre
Ty-nant
669
CARNEDD Y-FILAST
Llangwm
611
FOEL GOCH
Llandderfel
626
MOEL-Y-GEIFR
Lake Vyrnwy
Llanwddyn
544
TIR RHIWIOG
Afon Twrch
Foel
Llangadfan
523
CARNEDD WEN
Glyndŵr's Way
A5
A470
A487
A496
A493
A494
A4212
A458
A489
A498
A4085
B4405
B4404
B4353
B4391
B4407
B4501
B4402
B4401
B4403
B4393
B4518
B4569
55
48
38
37

56
55
47
38
A
B
C
D
E
F
G
H
Rhuddlan
Cwm
Whitford
Greenfield
Holywell
(Treffynnon)
Bagillt
Carmel
Pantasaph
Calcot
Bodelwyddan
St George
Rhuallt
St Asaph
Tremeirchion
Brynford
Dolphin
Flint
(Y Fflint)
Castle
Caerwys
Ysceifiog
Lixwm
Rhes-y-cae
Halkyn
Afon-wen
Trefnant
Bodfari
Llannefydd
Pen-y-felin
Nannerch
Northop
Northop Hall
Rhosesmor
Soughton
Henllan
Denbigh Friary
Vale of Clwyd
Clwydian Range
River Clwyd
Denbigh
(Dinbych)
Groes
Llandyrnog
Cilcain
Pant-y-mwyn
Gwernaffield
Mold
(Yr Wyddgrug)
Mynydd Isa
Buckley
(Bwcle)
Pentre Llanrhaeadr
Llanynys
Gellifor
Llangynhafal
Offa's Dyke Path
Loggerheads
555
MOEL FAMAU
Moel Famau
Bylchau
Nantglyn
Rhewl
Llanferres
Gwernymynydd
Nercwys
Leeswood
Pontybodkin
Pontblyddyn
Penymynydd
Penyffordd
Higher Kinnerton
Dodleston
Ruthin
(Rhuthun)
Llanbedr-Dyffryn-Clwyd
Eryrys
Treuddyn
Coed Talon
Hope
Caergwrle
Llanfwrog
Bontuchel
Y Gyffylliog
Llyn Brenig
Archaeological Trail
Gors Maen Llwyd
Llanarmon-yn-Ial
Llanfynydd
Ffrith
Llanfair Dyffryn Clwyd
Graig-fechan
Pentre-celyn
Efenechtyd
Pwll-glâs
Clocaenog
Clawdd-newydd
Llandegla
Bwlchgwyn
Minera
Lead Mines
Coedpoeth
Pen-y-stryt
Offa's Dyke Path
Cyrn-y-brain
Derwen
Llanelidan
Cross
Bryn Saith Marchog
Melin-y-wig
Llanfihangel Glyn Myfyr
417
Horseshoe Pass
Pentredwr
492
Rhosllanerchrugog
Penycae
Johnstown
Bersham
Rhostyllen
Erddig
Wrexham
(Wrecsam)
Marchwiel
Betws Gwerfil Goch
Gwyddelwern
Bryneglwys
578
MOEL Y GAMELIN
Llantysilio Mountain
Rhewl
Eliseg's Pillar
Valle Crucis Abbey
Ruabon Mountain
Dinas Bran
Ewe-phoria Sheepdog Centre
Ty-nant
Y Maerdy
Rug Chapel and Llangar Church
Druid
Corwen
Carrog
Llangollen Railway
Horseshoe Falls
Llangwm
Glyndyfrdwy
Llangollen
Ty'n-dwr
Garth
Trevor
Pontcysyllte Aqueduct
Ruabon
Rhosymedre
Cefn-mawr
Cefn Viaduct
Froncysyllte
Fron Isaf
Halton
Erbistock
Overton
Cynwyd
631
MOEL FFERNA
Plas Newydd
Glyn Ceiriog
Glyn Valley Tramway Museum
Chirk Castle
Chirk
Gledrid
Pontfadog
Bronygarth
Llwynmawr
Llandderfel
Llandrillo
Berwyn
784
CADER BRONWEN
827
CADER BERWYN
Y Berwyn
R. Dee
R. Ceiriog
Tregeiriog
444
PEN-Y-GWELY
Llanarmon Dyffryn Ceiriog
Weston Rhyn
Selattyn
Gobowen
St Martins
Dudleston Heath
Dudleston
Street Dinas
Knolton
Penley
Ellesmere
Perthy
Welsh Frankton
Tetchill
Whittington
Hordley
Old Oswestry Hill Fort
Oswestry
Pistyll Rhaeadr (Waterfall)
534
Moelfre
Llansilin
Llanrhaeadr-ym-Mochnant
Morda
Weston
Trefonen
Maesbury
Maesbury Marsh
Rednal
West Felton
Bagley
Grimpo
Haughton
Eardiston
Wykey
Pencraig
Llangynog
Pen-y-bont-fawr
Pen-y-Garnedd
Hirnant
Lake Vyrnwy
Llangedwyn
Pen-y-bont
Afon Tanat
Llanyblodwel
Morton
Llynclys
Woolston
Osbaston
Knockin
Pant
Maesbrook
Newtown
Ruyton-XI-Towns
Llansantffraid-ym-Mechain
Llanymynech
Kinnerley
Little Ness
Llanfechain
Four Crosses
Domgay
Nesscliffe
Kinton
Wilcott
Great Ness
Llanwddyn
Abertridwr
Tycrwyn
Llanfyllin
Deytheur
Llandrinio
Pentre
Felton Butler
Ensdon
Bwlch-y-cibau
Melverley
Fachwen
Llanfihangel-yng-Ngwynfa
Llwydiarth
Sarnau
Criggion
Crew Green
Shrawardine
Alberbury
Montford Bridge
Montford
364
BREIDDEN HILL
Rodney's Pillar
Pont Robert
Meifod
Geuffordd
River Vyrnwy
Dolanog
Afon Twrch
Guilsfield
Middletown
Wollaston
Foel
Llangadfan
River Banwy
Llanerfyl
Glyndŵr's Way
Halfway House
Yockleton
Westbury
Heniarth
Welshpool
(Y Trallwng)
Buttington
Welshpool & Llanfair Light Railway
Powis Castle
Hinton
Cruckmeole
Asterley
Rogers
Town Plan: Chester p.12
Willaston
Childer Thornton
Overpool
Ness Botanic Gardens
Burton
Capenhurst
Little Stanney
Blue Planet
Puddington
Shotwick
Backford
Wervin
Connah's Quay
Great Saughall
Mollington
Little Saughall
Shotton
Queensferry
Blacon
Upton
Newton
Wepre
Ewloe Castle
Aston
Mancot
Ewloe
Hawarden
CHESTER
Handbridge
Saltney
Huntington
Bretton
Broughton
Ecclest
Aldford
Pulford
Lavister
Rossett
Trevalyn
Marford
Llay
Gresford
Acton Park
Rhosnesni
Holt
Farnd
Crewe
Bangor-is-y-coed
Bangor-on-Dee
Worthe
Threapw
0 1 2 3 4 miles
0 1 2 3 4 5 kilometres

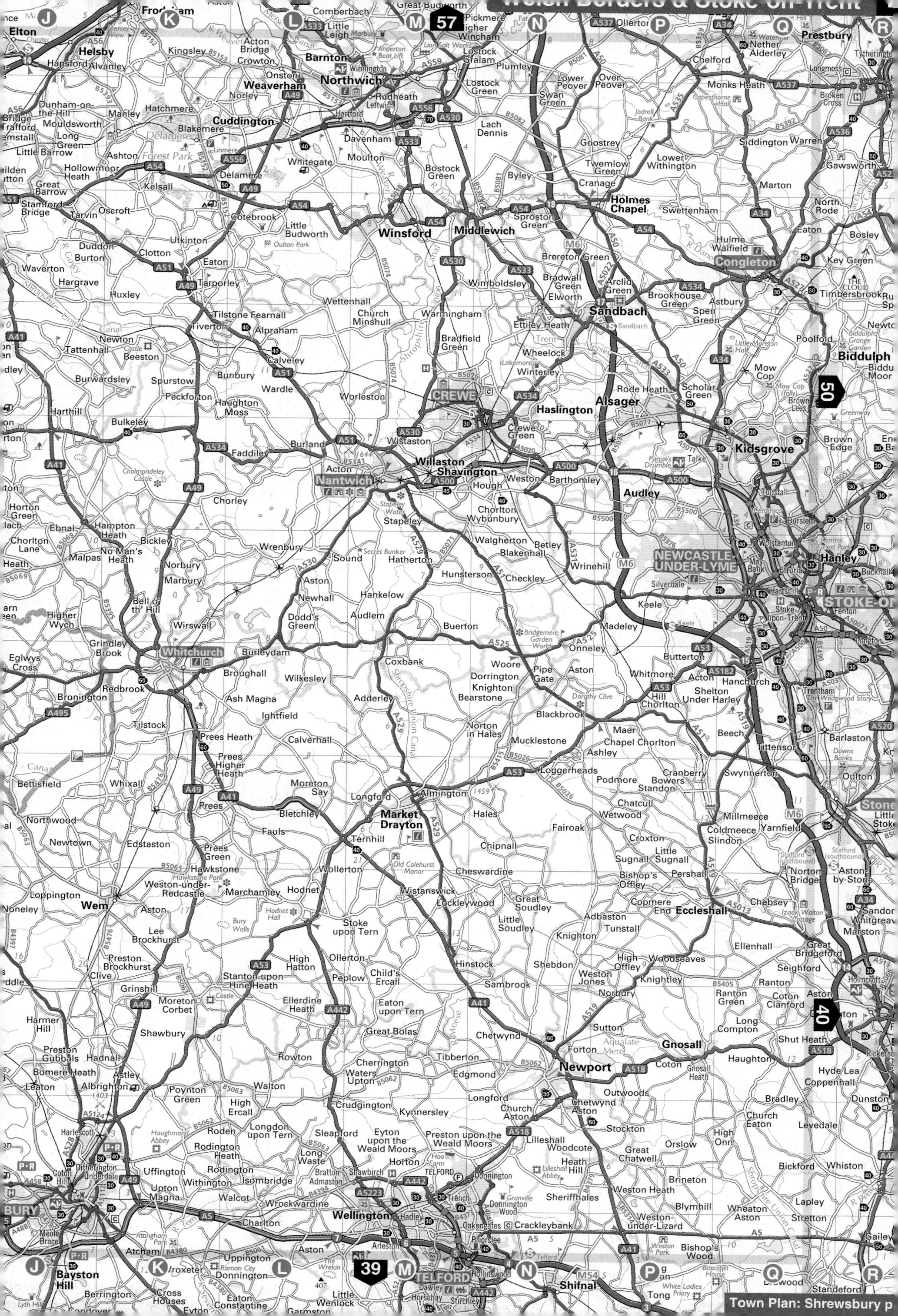

50
40
39
Town Plan: Shrewsbury p

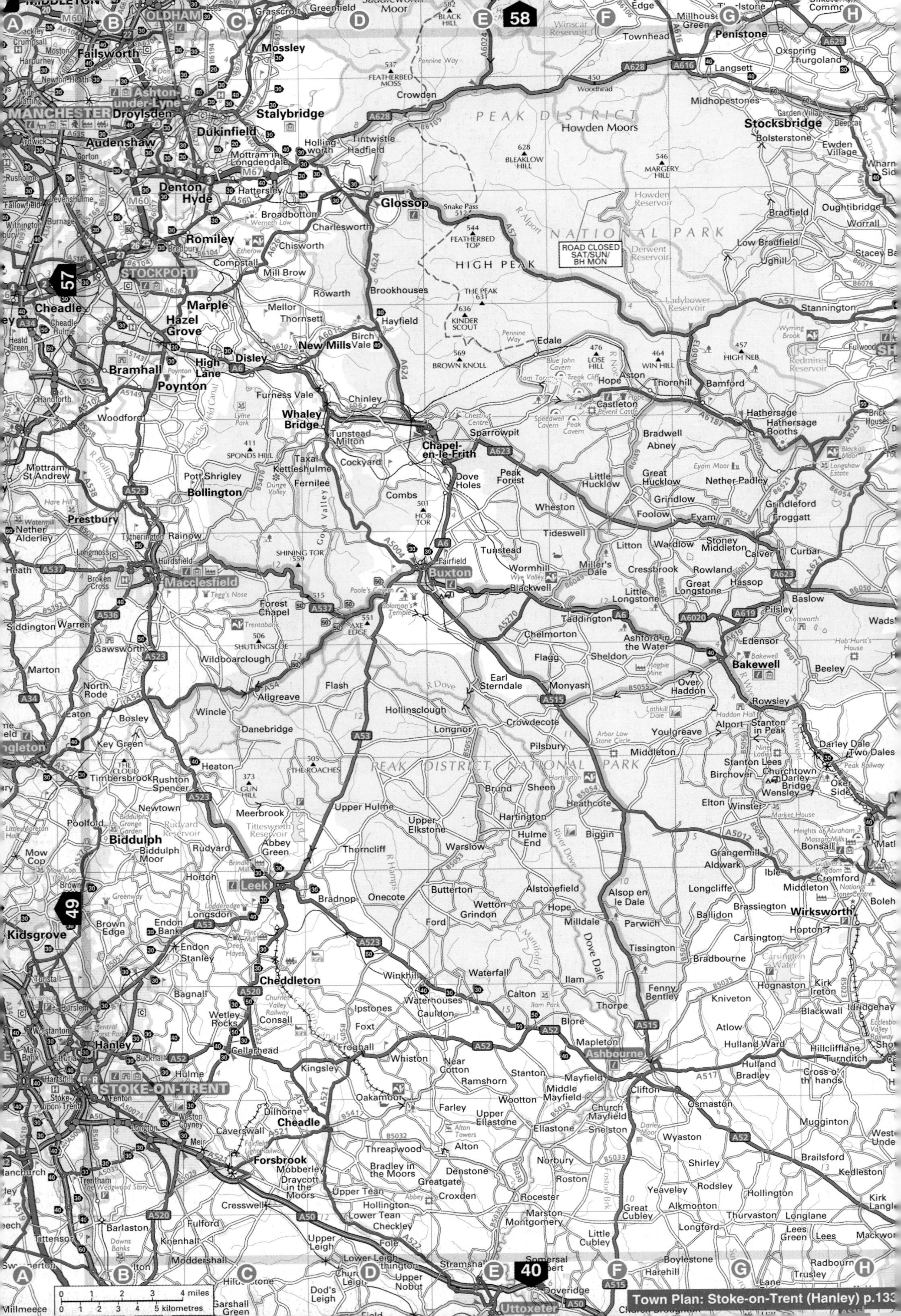

58
57
49
40
A
B
C
D
E
F
G
H
MIDDLETON
OLDHAM
Grasscroft
Greenfield
Saddleworth Moor
582 BLACK HILL
Winscar Reservoir
Edge
Millhouse Green
Thurlstone
Common
Penistone
Townhead
Oxspring
Thurgoland
Langsett
Midhopestones
Stocksbridge
Bolsterstone
Ewden Village
Deepcar
Wharncliffe Side
Oughtibridge
Worrall
Bradfield
Low Bradfield
Uighill
Stacey Bank
Failsworth
Moston
Crumpsall
Harpurhey
Newton Heath
MANCHESTER
Droylsden
Ashton-under-Lyne
Audenshaw
Ardwick
Gorton
Dukinfield
Stalybridge
Mossley
Hollingworth
Mottram in Longdendale
Tintwistle
Hadfield
Crowden
537 FEATHERBED MOSS
Pennine Way
Woodhead
PEAK DISTRICT
Howden Moors
628 BLEAKLOW HILL
546 MARGERY HILL
Howden Reservoir
Derwent Reservoir
NATIONAL PARK
ROAD CLOSED SAT/SUN/ BH MON
Rusholme
Levenshulme
Fallowfield
Withington
Burnage
Denton
Hyde
Hattersley
Broadbottom
Werneth Low
Glossop
Snake Pass 512
544 FEATHERBED TOP
HIGH PEAK
R Alport
Charlesworth
Chisworth
Romiley
Bredbury
Etherow
Compstall
STOCKPORT
Mill Brow
Rowarth
Brookhouses
THE PEAK 631
636 KINDER SCOUT
Ladybower Reservoir
Stannington
Cheadle
Cheadle Hulme
Heald Green
Marple
Hazel Grove
Mellor
Thornsett
Hayfield
Birch Vale
New Mills
Disley
High Lane
Bramhall
Poynton
Edale
569 BROWN KNOLL
476 LOSE HILL
464 WIN HILL
457 HIGH NEB
Wyming Brook
Redmires Reservoir
Fulwood
Handforth
Woodford
Furness Vale
Whaley Bridge
Chinley
Blue John Cavern
Mam Tor
Treak Cliff Cavern
Hope
Aston
Thornhill
Bamford
Castleton
Peveril Castle
Hathersage
Hathersage Booths
Brick Houses
Lyme Park
411 SPONDS HILL
Tunstead Milton
Taxal
Kettleshulme
Chapel-en-le-Frith
Chestnut Centre
Sparrowpit
Speedwell Cavern
Peak Cavern
Bradwell
Abney
Eyam Moor
Blacka Moor
Longshaw Estate
Mottram St Andrew
Pott Shrigley
Bollington
Cockyard
Fernilee
Dunge Valley
Goyt Valley
Dove Holes
Peak Forest
Little Hucklow
Great Hucklow
Nether Padley
Combs
501 HOB TOR
Grindlow
Grindleford
Froggatt
Prestbury
Hare Hill
Wheston
Foolow
Eyam
Nether Alderley
Tytherington
Rainow
Longmoss
SHINING TOR 559
Tideswell
Litton
Wardlow
Stoney Middleton
Calver
Curbar
Heath
Hurdsfield
Macclesfield
Broken Cross
Fairfield
Buxton
Tunstead
Wormhill
Wye Valley
Miller's Dale
Cressbrook
Rowland
Hassop
Baslow
Tegg's Nose
Forest Chapel
515
Poole's Cavern
Solomon's Temple
Blackwell
Little Longstone
Great Longstone
Pilsley
Chatsworth
Siddington
Warren
Trentabank
551 AXE EDGE
Taddington
Ashford in the Water
Edensor
Hob Hurst's House
Gawsworth
506 SHUTLINGSLOE
Chelmorton
Wildboarclough
Flagg
Sheldon
Magpie Mine
Bakewell
Beeley
Marton
North Rode
Flash
R Dove
Earl Sterndale
Monyash
Over Haddon
Allgreave
Wincle
Hollinsclough
Lathkill Dale
Haddon Hall
Rowsley
Eaton
Bosley
Danebridge
Longnor
Crowdecote
Youlgreave
Alport
Stanton in Peak
Congleton
Key Green
Pilsbury
Arbor Low Stone Circle
Middleton
Darley Dale
Two Dales
Nine Ladies
Stanton Lees
Churchtown
Darley Bridge
Wensley
Birchover
Peak Railway
Oker Side
505 THE ROACHES
THE CLOUD
Timbersbrook
Heaton
Rushton Spencer
373 GUN HILL
PEAK DISTRICT NATIONAL PARK
Hartington
Brund
Sheen
Heathcote
Elton
Winster
Market House
Newtown
Meerbrook
Upper Hulme
Poolfold
Biddulph Grange Garden
Rudyard Reservoir
Tittesworth Reservoir
Upper Elkstone
Hulme End
River Dove
Biggin
Heights of Abraham
Masson Mills
Bonsall
Matlock
Little Moreton Hall
Biddulph
Biddulph Moor
Rudyard
Abbey Green
Thorncliff
R Hamps
Warslow
Grangemill
Aldwark
Ible
Gulliver's Kingdom
Cromford
Mow Cop
Horton
Leek
Brindley Mill
Alstonefield
Alsop en le Dale
Longcliffe
Middleton
National Stone Centre
Brown Edge
Greenway
Bradnop
Onecote
Butterton
Wetton
Grindon
Hope
Milldale
Dove Dale
Parwich
Ballidon
Brassington
Wirksworth
Bolehill
Kidsgrove
Lodderedge
Longsdon
Endon Bank
Endon
Stanley
Flint Mill
Deep Hayes
Ford
R Manifold
Tissington
Carsington
Hopton
Carsington Water
Bradbourne
Tunstall
Bagnall
Cheddleton
Winkhill
Waterfall
Ilam
Fenny Bentley
Hognaston
Kirk Ireton
Churnet Valley Railway
Caldon Canal
Waterhouses
Cauldon
Calton
Ilam Park
Thorpe
Kniveton
Idridgehay
Burslem
Wetley Rocks
Consall
Ipstones
Foxt
Blore
Blackwall
Wolstanton
Central Forest Park
Hanley
Cellarhead
Froghall
Whiston
Mapleton
Ashbourne
Atlow
Hulland Ward
Hillcliffane
Turnditch
Ecclesbourne Valley Railway
Shottle
May Bank
Etruria
Bucknall
Hulme
Kingsley
Near Cotton
Ramshorn
Stanton
Mayfield
Hulland
Bradley
Cross o' th' hands
STOKE-ON-TRENT
Hartshill
Stoke-upon-Trent
Fenton
Werrington
Weston Coyney
Longton
Dilhorne
Cheadle
Oakamoor
Farley
Upper Ellastone
Wootton
Middle Mayfield
Church Mayfield
Clifton
Osmaston
Mugginton
Caverswall
Meir
Alton Towers
Alton
Ellastone
Snelston
Darley Moor
Wyaston
Weston Underwood
Hanchurch
Trentham
The Wedgwood Story
Forsbrook
Foxfield Light Railway
Mobberley
Draycott in the Moors
Threapwood
Bradley in the Moors
Denstone
Greatgate
Norbury
Roston
Shirley
Brailsford
Kedleston
Upper Tean
Hollington
Croxden
Abbey
Rocester
Yeaveley
Rodsley
Hollington
Kirk Langley
Cresswell
Lower Tean
Marston Montgomery
Great Cubley
Alkmonton
Thurvaston
Longlane
Tittensor
Barlaston
Fulford
Checkley
Little Cubley
Longford
Lees Green
Lees
Mackworth
Downs Banks
Knenhall
Upper Leigh
Fole
Foston Brk
Swynnerton
Barlaston
Moddershall
Hilderstone
Lower Leigh
Withington
Stramshall
Somersal Herbert
Boylestone
Harehill
Radbourne
Trusley
Church Leigh
Upper Nobut
Dod's Leigh
Doveridge
Lane
Millmeece
Garshall Green
Field
Uttoxeter
Church Broughton
0 1 2 3 4 miles
0 1 2 3 4 5 kilometres
Town Plan: Stoke-on-Trent (Hanley) p.133

Nottingham & Peak District
59
60
52
42
41
Wombwell
Worsbrough
Bolton Upon Dearne
Goldthorpe
Harlington
High Melton
Adwick upon Dearne
Sprotbrough
Mexborough
Hoyland Nether
Wath upon Dearne
Tankersley
Brampton
Swinton
Denaby
Cadeby
Conisbrough
Harley
Wentworth
Chapeltown
Nether Haugh
Rawmarsh
Thorpe Hesley
Scholes
Greasbrough
Thrybergh
Hooton Roberts
Ravenfield
Clifton
Micklebring
Ecclesfield
Kimberworth
ROTHERHAM
Bramley
Maltby
Tickhill
Stainton
Braithwell
Herringthorpe
Broom
Wickersley
Whiston
Brinsworth
Morthen
Thurcroft
Hooton Levitt
Slade Hooton
Stone
Roche Abbey
Laughton-en-le-Morthen
Brampton-en-le-Morthen
Brookhouse
Firbeck
Letwell
Catcliffe
Treeton
Ulley
Aughton
Aston
Fence
Dinnington
North Anston
Gildingwells
Langold
Todwick
Kiveton Park
South Anston
Woodsetts
Wales
Harthill
Shireoaks
Thorpe Salvin
Woodall
Killamarsh
Mosborough
Eckington
Ridgeway
Highlane
Hackenthorpe
Beighton
Handsworth
Richmond
Woodhouse
Intake
Troway
Ford
Marsh Lane
Apperknowle
Spinkhill
Renishaw
Dronfield
Unstone
West Handley
Middle Handley
Barlborough
Harlesthorpe
Whitwell
Hodthorpe
Mastin Moor
Staveley
Whittington
Barlow
Brimington
CHESTERFIELD
Newbold
Linacres Reservoirs
Clowne
Creswell
Stanfree
Elmton
Shuttlewood
Long Duckmanton
Holbeck
Whaley Thorns
Norton
Cuckney
Bolsover
Whaley
Upper Langwith
Nether Langwith
Langwith
Arkwright Town
Hills Town
Scarcliffe
Palterton
Temple Normanton
Heath
Walton
Wingerworth
Grassmoor
Glapwell
Shirebrook
Langwith Junction
Stony Houghton
New Houghton
Holmewood
North Wingfield
Ault Hucknall
Pleasley
Alton
Ashover
Clay Cross
Hardstoft
Teversal
Handley
Stretton
Pilsley
Tibshelf
Dunsill
Morton
Higham
Stonebroom
Newton
Shirland
Blackwell
Huthwaite
Sutton in Ashfield
Skegby
Brackenfield
Wessington
Westhouses
South Normanton
Alfreton
South Wingfield
Kirkby in Ashfield
Pinxton
Swanwick
Somercotes
Pye Bridge
Selston
Annesley
Annesley Woodhouse
Pentrich
Ironville
Ripley
Heage
Codnor
Loscoe
Underwood
Brinsley
Hucknall
Linby
Newstead
Newstead Abbey
Ravenshead
Papplewick
Blidworth Bottoms
Blidworth
Rainworth
Mansfield Woodhouse
MANSFIELD
Belper
Kilburn
Denby
Heanor
Horsley Woodhouse
Horsley
Smalley
Coxbench
Little Eaton
Eastwood
Newthorpe
Awsworth
Kimberley
Mapperley
Ilkeston
West Hallam
Cossall
Strelley
Morley
Stanley
Breadsall
Dale Abbey
Oakwood
DERBY
Chaddesden
Spondon
Stanton by Dale
Stapleford
Trowell
Beeston
Chilwell
Sandiacre
Risley
Ockbrook
Borrowash
Breaston
Toton
Attenborough
Wollaton
Lenton
Bilborough
Nuthall
Bulwell
Old Basford
Sherwood
Arnold
Daybrook
Mapperley Park
Carlton
Gedling
NOTTINGHAM
Bestwood Village
Calverton
Woodborough
Lowdham
Lambley
Burton Joyce
Shelford
Stoke Bardolph
Adbolton
Holme Pierrepont
West Bridgford
Radcliffe on Trent
Edwalton
Tollerton
Cotgrave
Clifton
Barton in Fabis
Gamston
Saxondale
Newton
Bingham
Cropwell Butler
Cropwell Bishop
Tithby
Langar
Granby
Car Colston
Scarrington
Aslockton
Whatton
Orston
Thoroton
Elton
Sutton
Bottesford
Flawborough
Hawksworth
Screveton
Shelton
Sibthorpe
Flintham
Kneeton
Syerston
Elston
Hoveringham
Caythorpe
Gunthorpe
East Bridgford
Thurgarton
Epperstone
Gonalston
Oxton
Bleasby
Fiskerton
Morton
Rolleston
Farndon
East Stoke
Thorpe
Hawton
Averham
Kelham
Upton
Normanton
Southwell
Halam
Edingley
Farnsfield
Halloughton
Hockerton
Kirklington
Winkburn
Bilsthorpe
Eakring
Maplebeck
Kersall
Kneesall
Ompton
Wellow
Ossington
Norwell Woodhouse
Norwell
Caunton
Bathley
North Muskham
Cromwell
Moorhouse
Laxton
Egmanton
Weston
Normanton on Trent
Skegby
Tuxford
Kirton
Boughton
Walesby
Ollerton
New Ollerton
Edwinstowe
Perlethorpe
Budby
Market Warsop
Church Warsop
Meden Vale
Old Clipstone
Clipstone
Rufford
Rufford Abbey
SHERWOOD FOREST
Bothamsall
Elkesley
West Drayton
Milton
Bevercotes
West Markham
Markham Moor
East Markham
Askham
Rockley
Gamston
Eaton
Ordsall
Retford
Babworth
Ranby
Worksop
Scofton
Carlton in Lindrick
Wigthorpe
North Carlton
South Carlton
Hodsock
Blyth
Oldcotes
Styrrup
Harworth
Bircotes
Spital Hill
Bawtry
Austerfield
Scaftworth
Scrooby
Harwell
Everton
Drakeholes
Mattersey
Mattersey Abbey
Ranskill
Torworth
Sutton cum Lound
Lound
Barnby Moor
Clarborough
Hayton
Welham
Grove
South Leverton
North Leverton with Habblesthorpe
Sturton le Steeple
North Wheatley
Saundby
Clayworth
Wiseton
Gringley on the Hill
Beckingham
Walkeringham
Misterton
Misson
West Stockwith
Graiseleound
Haxey
East Lound
Westwoodside
Blaxton
Auckley
Finningley
Branton
Old Cantley
Bessacarr
Rossington
New Rossington
Loversall
Wadworth
New Edlington
Old Edlington
Balby
Hexthorpe
DONCASTER
Warmsworth
Robin Hood Doncaster Sheffield
Treswell
Nether Headon
Headon
Stokeham
East Drayton
Upton
Darlton
Ragnall
Dunham
Fledborough
Laneham
Owston Ferry
Low Burnham
Wildsworth
Gunthorpe
Town Plans: Derby p.127, Nottingham p.130, Sheffield p

A
B
C
D
E
F
G
H
Eastoft
Burton upon Stather
Thealby
Normanby
Normanby Hall
Roxby
Winterton
Saxby All Saints
Bonby
Wootton
Curtis
Ulceby Skitter
South Killingholme
Immingham
Luddington
Flixborough
Amcotts
Flixborough Stather
Appleby
Low Santon
Worlaby
Elsham
Ulceby
Habrough
Immingham
Crowle
Ealand
Keadby
Gunness
Crosby
SCUNTHORPE
Melton Ross
Croxton
Kirmington
Stallingborough
Brocklesby
Keelby
Healing
Humberside
Great Limber
60
61
Burringham
Brumby
Ashby
Broughton
Wressle
Barnetby le Wold
Althorpe
Derrythorpe
Bottesford
Yaddlethorpe
Wrawby
Brigg
Bigby
Riby
Aylesby
Belton
Beltoft
East Butterwick
West Butterwick
Scawby
Somerby
Searby
Owmby
Grasby
Clixby
Irby upon Humber
Epworth
Old Rectory
Messingham
Sturton
Howsham
Cadney
Hibaldstow
North Kelsey Beck
Swallow
Low Burnham
Manton
North Kelsey
Caistor
Cabourne
Cuxwold
Owston Ferry
Scotterthorpe
Susworth
Scotter
Gainsthorpe Medieval Village
Redbourne
Nettleton
Rothwell
Haxey
East Lound
East Ferry
Scotton
Kirton in Lindsey
South Kelsey
Moortown
Brandy Wharf
Holton le Moor
Thornton le Moor
Thoresway
Thorganby
Wildsworth
Laughton
Northorpe
Gunthorpe
Grayingham
Waddingham
Snitterby
Normanby le Wold
Brookenby
West Stockwith
East Stockwith
Blyton
Blyborough
North Owersby
South Owersby
Claxby
Stainton le Vale
Walkerith
Pilham
Aisby
Willoughton
Atterby
Bishop Norton
Kingerby
Usselby
Kirkby
Osgodby
Walesby
Kirmond le Mire
Morton
Corringham
Gainsborough
Hemswell
Hemswell Cliff
Harpswell
Glentham
Bishopbridge
West Rasen
Middle Rasen
Tealby
Caenby
Toft next Newton
Market Rasen
North Willingham
Ludford
Springthorpe
Normanby
Saundby
Heapham
Glentworth
Newton by Toft
Sixhills
Bole
Lea
Upton
Owmby
Saxby
Linwood
Legsby
Fillingham
North Wheatley
Knaith
Kexby
Faldingworth
Hainton
South Willingham
Willingham by Stow
Ingham
Spridlington
Friesthorpe
Lissington
Fenton
Coates
Cold Hanworth
East Torrington
Gate Burton
Hackthorn
Snarford
Wickenby
Benniworth
Littleborough
Marton
Stow
Cammeringham
West Torrington
East Barkwith
Holton cum Beckering
Brattleby
Snelland
South Leverton
Ryland
West Barkwith
Cottam
Brampton
Sturton by Stow
Scampton
Aisthorpe
Fulnetby
Rand
Panton
Treswell
Sundown Adventureland
Rampton
Torksey
Bransby
Welton
Dunholme
Stainton by Langworth
Wragby
Sotby
Stokeham
Fenton
North Carlton
Lincolnshire
Scothern
Bullington
Hatton
Laneham
South Carlton
Langworth
Langton by Wragby
Great Sturton
East Drayton
Saxilby
Fossdyke Navigation
Sudbrooke
Nettleham
Apley
Kingthorpe
Laughterton
Kettlethorpe
Burton
North Greetwell
Barlings
Baumber
51
Dunham
Toll
Ragnall
Darlton
North Clifton
Newton on Trent
Thorney
Burton Waters
Skellingthorpe
Reepham
Bardney Limewoods
Minting
Cherry Willingham
Fiskerton
Gautby
Fledborough
High Marnham
South Clifton
Harby
Wigsley
LINCOLN
New Boultham
R. Witham
Washingborough
Edlington
Skegby
Low Marnham
Spalford
Doddington
Birchwood
Hartsholme
Swanpool Garden Suburb
Boultham
Canwick
Heighington
Branston Booths
Bardney
Bucknall
Normanton on Trent
Weston
Grassthorpe
Sutton on Trent
Whisby
Eagle
Road Transport
Swallow Beck
Bracebridge Heath
Bracebridge Low Fields
Branston
Potterhanworth Booths
Horsington
North Scarle
Southrey
Stixwould
Girton
Thorpe on the Hill
North Hykeham
Potterhanworth
Besthorpe
South Scarle
Carlton-on-Trent
South Hykeham
Waddington
Nocton
Woodhall Spa
Dunston
Metheringham Delph
Kirkstead
Cromwell
Swinderby
Haddington
Harmston
Aubourn
Collingham
Thurlby
Coleby
Metheringham
Martin
Norwell
Bassingham
Blankney
Dyke
Timberland Delph
Bathley
Holme
Boothby Graffoe
Tattershall Thorpe
North Muskham
Brough
Norton Disney
Kirkby Green
Scopwick
Timberland
Tattershall
Tattershall Castle
Carlton-le-Moorland
Navenby
Winthorpe
Langford
Nottinghamshire
Stapleford
R. Brant
Wellingore
Thorpe Tilney
Kelham
Aircraft
Ashby de la Launde
Rowston
Walcott
Dogdyke
Averham
Coddington
Newark-on-Trent
Brant Broughton
Beckingham
Welbourn
Digby
Billinghay
Chapel Hill
Bloxholm
Dorrington
Balderton
New Balderton
Stragglethorpe
Barnby in the Willows
North Kyme
Hawton
Leadenham
Ruskington
Fenton
Fernwood
Thorpe
Cranwell
Anwick
Fulbeck
Claypole
Stubton
Caythorpe
Leasingham
South Kyme
42
Brandon
Elston
Frieston
Evedon
Ewerby
North Rauceby
Holdingham
Kirkby
Syerston
Hough-on
0 1 2 3 4 miles
0 1 2 3 4 5 kilometres
A161
A18
M180
M181
A159
A15
A1077
B1216
B1392
B1450
B1398
B1400
B1206
B1207
B1208
B1204
B1218
B1211
B1210
A160
A180
A1173
B1205
B1434
B1225
B1203
A631
A1103
A46
B1241
A156
A1500
A158
A57
B1202
B1399
A157
B1190
B1188
B1178
B1131
A1434
A607
A1133
A17
B1202
B1191
B1189
B1192
B1188
A153
B1429
A1
A6065
B1164
B1395

J
K
L
M
N
P
Q
R
HUMBER
Kilnsea
Spurn Heritage Coast
SPURN HEAD
61
GRIMSBY
West Marsh
Cleethorpes
Old Clee
Nunsthorpe
Thrunscoe
The Jungle
Pleasure Island
Scartho
A16
A1098
A46
A180
B1203
B1219
Humberston
Rotterdam (Europoort)
Zeebrugge
New Waltham
Waltham Windmill
Holton le Clay
A1031
Brigsley
Ashby cum Fenby
Waithe
Tetney
North Cotes
Grainsby
North Thoresby
Marshchapel
Donna Nook
B1201
Grainthorpe
North Somercotes
Fulstow
Canal
Wold Newton
Lincolnshire Wolds Railway
Conisholme
Ludborough
Covenham St Bartholomew
North Ormsby
Covenham St Mary
Saltfleet
Yarburgh
Utterby
Fotherby
Alvingham
North Cockerington
Saltfleetby St Clement
Kelstern
A631
Saltfleetby All Saints
South Cockerington
Saltfleetby St Peter
Theddlethorpe St Helen
South Elkington
Grimoldby
B1200
Welton le Wold
Louth
Theddlethorpe All Saints
A157
Manby
Hallington
Little Carlton
Great Carlton
Mablethorpe
B1520
Raithby
Legbourne
Great Eau
North Reston
Gayton le Marsh
A1104
Trusthorpe
Withcall
A153
Little Cawthorpe
South Reston
Sutton on Sea
Tathwell
Withern
A52
Maltby le Marsh
Sandilands
Haugham
Muckton
Cadwell Park
Authorpe
B1373
A1111
Beesby
Burwell
Saleby
Asterby
Belleau
Markby
Scamblesby
Watermill & Wildfowl Gardens
Aby
White Pit
Swaby
Oxcombe
South Thoresby
Huttoft
Bilsby
Thurlby
Belchford
Anderby Creek
South Ormsby
Alford
Rigsby
B1449
Anderby
Tetford
B1196
Farlesthorpe
Mumby
Fulletby
Salmonby
Brinkhill
Well
Cumberworth
Chapel Point
Harrington
West Ashby
Somersby
Ulceby
Hogsthorpe
Chapel St Leonards
Bag Enderby
Sutterby
Willoughby
Horncastle
Ashby Puerorum
Langton
A1028
Sloothby
Greetham
Aswardby
Skendleby
A158
High Toynton
Habertoft
Addlethorpe
Fantasy Island
Hagworthingham
Sausthorpe
Ingoldmells
Snipe Dales
Partney
Welton le Marsh
Ingoldmells Point
Mareham on the Hill
Scremby
Lymn
Candlesby
Hameringham
Mavis Enderby
Raithby
Ashby by Partney
Gunby
Orby
B1195
Spilsby
Hundleby
Monksthorpe
B1183
Halton Holegate
Burgh le Marsh
Old Bolingbroke
Moorby
Toynton All Saints
Great Steeping
Bratoft
Wood Enderby
Miningsby
Bolingbroke Castle
Northcote
Skegness
A155
East Keal
Little Steeping
Irby in the Marsh
East Kirkby
Firsby
Keal Cotes
Revesby
Lincolnshire Aviation
Croft
Mareham le Fen
Stickford
Fendike Corner
Thorpe St Peter
Wainfleet Haven
Tumby Woodside
New Bolingbroke
Wainfleet All Saints
Stickney
New Leake
Wainfleet St Mary
Gibraltar Point
Eastville
Friskney
East Fen
West Fen
Northlands
B1192
Leake Common Side
Sibsey Trader Windmill
Sibsey
Gipsey Bridge
Frithville
B1184
Wrangle
Fishtoft Drove
Old Leake
43
Hilldyke
Leverton
Anton's Gowt
Benington

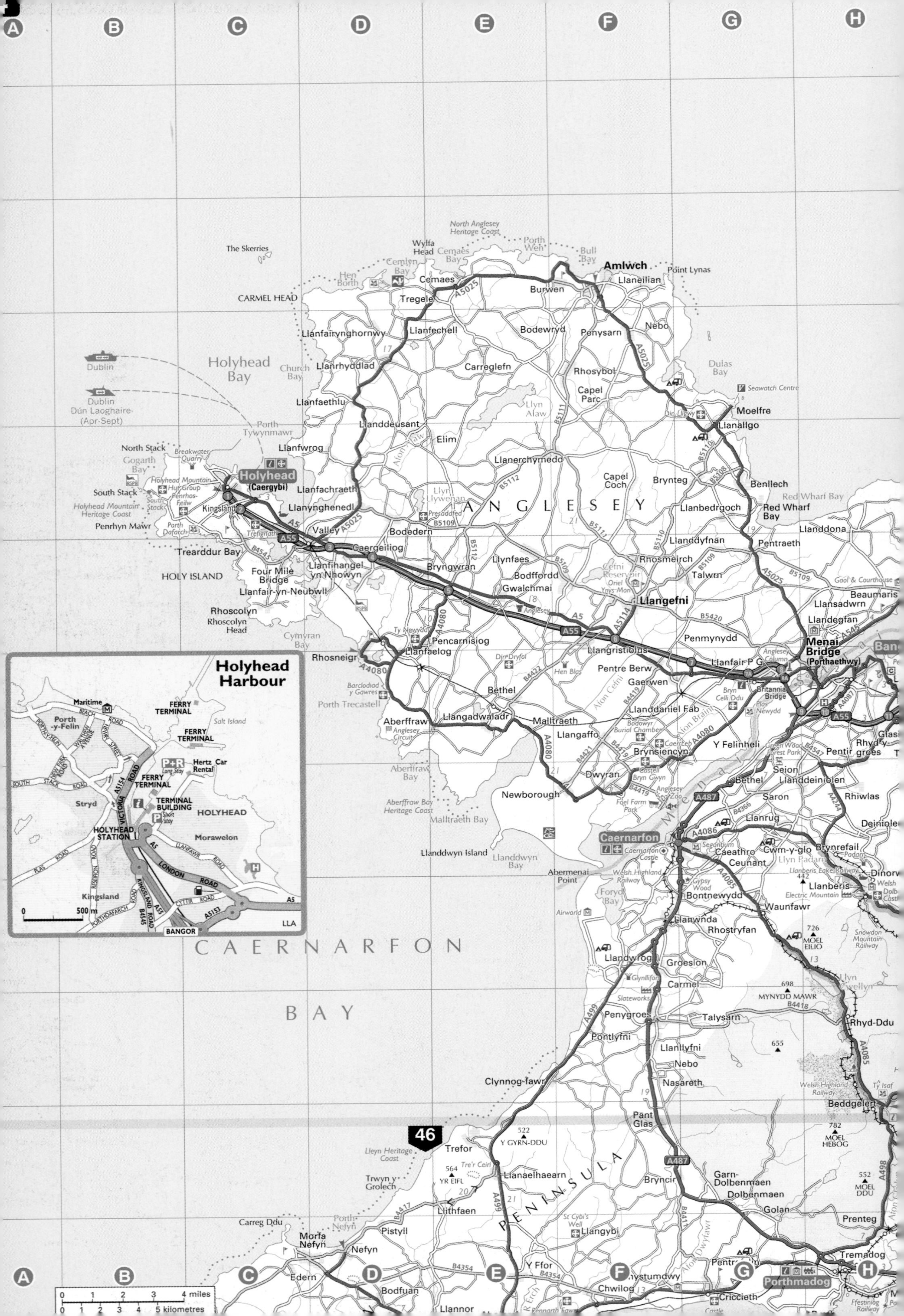

Holyhead Harbour
ANGLESEY
Holyhead Bay
HOLY ISLAND
CAERNARFON BAY
PENINSULA
Holyhead (Caergybi)
Amlwch
Llangefni
Menai Bridge (Porthaethwy)
Caernarfon
Porthmadog
Dublin
Dublin Dún Laoghaire (Apr-Sept)
46

J
K
L
M
N
P
Q
R
56
48
47
Great Orme Heritage Coast
GREAT ORMES HEAD
Puffin Island
Black Point
Little Ormes Head
Penrhyn Bay
Rhôs-on-Sea
Colwyn Bay
(Bae Colwyn)
Llandrillo-yn-Rhos
Conwy Bay
Llandudno
Deganwy
Llandudno Junction
Dwygyfylchi
Penmaenmawr
Conwy
Conwy Castle
Capelulo
Llanfairfechan
Henryd
Abergwyngregyn
Aber Waterfall
Afon Anafon
SNOWDONIA
NATIONAL
PARK
610
TAL-Y-FAN
Rowen
Ty'n-y-Groes
Llanbedr-y-Cennin
Tal-y-Bont
Dolgarrog
580
MOEL WINION
757
Y DROSGL
942
FOEL-FRAS
Bethesda
Afon Caseg
Afon Dulyn
Llyn Eigiau
Afon Ddu
1062
CARNEDD LLEWELYN
1044
CARNEDD DAFYDD
Llyn Cowlyd
Trefriw Woollen Mill
Trefriw
Llanrhychwyn
Llanrwst
Gwydir Castle
Llyn Crafnant
Llyn Geirionydd
Gwydir Uchaf Chapel
Llyn Ogwen
946
GARN
917
Y TRYFAN
1001
GLYDER FAWR
994
GLYDER-FACH
National Mountain Centre
Capel Curig
Gwydyr
Forest
Y Stablau
Betws-y-Coed
Conwy Valley Railway
872
MOEL-SIABOD
Pont-y-pant
Llyn Llydaw
Dolwyddelan
Dolwyddelan Castle
Park
Ty'n-y-Coed Uchaf
Ty Mawr Wybrnant
Penmachno
Woollen Mill
Llechwedd Slate Caverns
Blaenau Ffestiniog
658
770
MOELWYN MAWR
711
MOELWYN BACH
Hydro-electric Power Station
Tanysgrisiau Reservoir
Ffestiniog
Ffestiniog Railway
Rhyd
Maentwrog
Gellilydan
Gwaith Powdwr
Amphitheatre
Vale of Conwy
River Conwy
Bodnant
Graig
Tal-y-Cafn
Eglwysbach
Llansanffraid Glan Conwy
Bryn-y-Maen
Llanelian-yn-Rhos
Old Colwyn
Llysfaen
Llanddulas
Rhyd-y-foel
Abergele
Dolwen
Betws-yn-Rhos
Llanfair Talhaiarn
River Elwy
Llangernyw
Llansannan
Llanddoget
Pandy Tudur
Afon Derfyn
Pentre-tafarn-y-fedw
Gwytherin
Afon Aled
Llyn Aled
467
MOEL SEISIOG
448
MOEL LLYN
Llyn Alwen
Mynydd Hiraethog
Nebo
Capel Garmon
Burial Chamber
Fairy Glen
Pentrefoelas
Ysbyty Ifan
Llyn Conwy
Afon Serw
Afon Gelyn
690
ARENIG FACH
669
CARNEDD Y-FILAST
Llyn Celyn
Ciltalgarth
National Whitewater Centre
Afon Tryweryn
Llyn Arenig Fawr
853
Fron-goch
Rhyd-uchaf
Kinmel Bay
Abergele Roads
Rhyl
Towyn
Pensarn
St George
Bodelwyddan
Prestatyn
Gronant
Meliden
Gwaenysgor
Dyserth
Trelawnyd
Cwm
Rhuddlan
Offa's Dyke
Rhuallt
St Asaph
Tremeirchion
Trefnant
Vale of Clwyd
Bodfari
River Clwyd
Llannefydd
Henllan
Denbigh Friary
Denbigh
(Dinbych)
Castle
Groes
Pentre Llanrhaeadr
Bylchau
Nantglyn
Gors Maen Llwyd
Archaeological Trail
Llyn Brenig
Y Gyffylliog
Alwen Reservoir
Cefn-brith
Glasfryn
Llanfihangel Glyn Myfyr
Cerrigydrudion
Clocaenog
Clawdd-newydd
Derwen
Melin-y-wig
Bryn Saith Marchog
Betws Gwerfil Goch
Ewe-phoria Sheepdog Centre
Ty-nant
Llangwm
Y Maerdy
Druid
Rug Chapel and Llangar Church
Corwen
Cynwyd
611
FOEL GOCH
Llandderfel
A55
A470
A5
A4086
A498
A496
A547
A548
A543
A544
A525
A494
A4212
A5104
B5113
B5106
B5381
B5382
B5383
B5384
B5401
B5105
B4407
B4391
B4501

62
55
48
Isle of Man
0 1 2 3 4 5 miles
0 1 2 3 4 5 6 kilometres
POINT OF AYRE
Rue Point
Port Cranstal
The Lhen
Bride
Andreas
Shellag Point
Jurby Head
Jurby
Sandygate
St Jude's
Sulby
Ramsey Bay
Ramsey (Rhumsaa)
Churchtown
Glen Auldyn
Ballaugh
Orrisdale Head
ISLE OF MAN
ELLAN VANNIN
Maughold
Maughold Head
Ballajora
Kirk Michael
NORTH BARRULE
SNAEFELL
SLIEAU LHEAN
The Bungalow
Knocksharry
Laxey
Laxey Head
St Patrick's Isle
Peel (Purt ny-Hinshey)
Contrary Head
Patrick
St John's
SLIEAU RUY
Baldrine
Clay Head
Glen Maye
Crosby
Glen Vine
Strang
Union Mills
Onchan (Kiondroghad)
Onchan Head
Dalby
Foxdale
DOUGLAS (DOOLISH)
Belfast
Heysham
Liverpool
Birkenhead
Dublin
SOUTH BARRULE
St Marks
Douglas Head
Port Soderick
Grenaby
Santon Head
Bradda Head
Port Erin
Colby
Ballasalla
Castletown
Derbyhaven
Port St Mary
Cregneash
CALF OF MAN
Spanish Head
Scarlett Point
Castletown Bay
Dreswick Point
Caigher Point
Manx Heritage site
Liverpool Docks
FREEPORT FERRY TERMINAL
BOOTLE
New Brighton
WALLASEY
Kirkdale
Anfield
Everton
KINGSWAY
LIME STREET STATION
PIER HEAD FERRY TERMINAL
LIVERPOOL
12 QUAYS FERRY TERMINAL
QUEENSWAY
BIRKENHEAD
SPEKE
Cleveleys
Thornton
Stalnall
Hambleton
Out Rawcliffe
Little Singleton
Poulton-le-Fylde
Singleton
North Shore
BLACKPOOL
Staining
Thistleton
Great Marton
Weeton
Great Plumpton
South Shore
Westby
Wrea Green
St Anne's
Kellamergh
Warton
Fairhaven
Lytham
Lytham St Anne's
Banks
SOUTHPORT
Mere Brow
Holmeswood
Birkdale
Scarisbrick
Shirdley Hill
Bescar
Ainsdale
Halsall
Heaton's Bridge
Barton
Haskayne
Ormskirk
Formby
Formby Point
Great Altcar
Aughton
Hightown
Ince Blundell
Homer Green
Maghull
Lunt
Little Crosby
Sefton
Melling
Blundellsands
Brighton le Sands
CROSBY
Waterloo
Seaforth
Litherland
BOOTLE
Fazakerley
Croxteth
LIVERPOOL BAY
WALLASEY
New Brighton
LIVERPOOL
Hoylake
Moreton
Hilbre Island
Middle Eye
Little Eye
West Kirby
Greasby
BIRKENHEAD
Frankby
WIRRAL
Tranmere
Rock Ferry
Port Sunlight
Bebington
Thurstaston
Barnston
Brimstage
Heswall
Thornton Hough
Bromborough
Neston
Parkgate
Willaston
Childer Thornton
Overpool
Burton
Point of Ayr
Prestatyn
Gronant
Gwespyr
Rhyl
Llanasa
Ffynnongroyw
Gwaenysgor
Meliden
Trelogan
Mostyn
Glan-y-don
Kinmel Bay
Towyn
Trelawnyd
Dyserth
Cwm
Rhuddlan
Whitford
Gorsedd
Carmel
Greenfield
Lloc
Bodelwyddan
George
Rhuallt
Calcot
Brynford
Holywell (Treffynnon)
Flint
River Dee
River Mersey
0 1 2 3 4 miles
0 1 2 3 4 5 kilometres
Town Plans: Blackpool p.124, Liverpool p.12

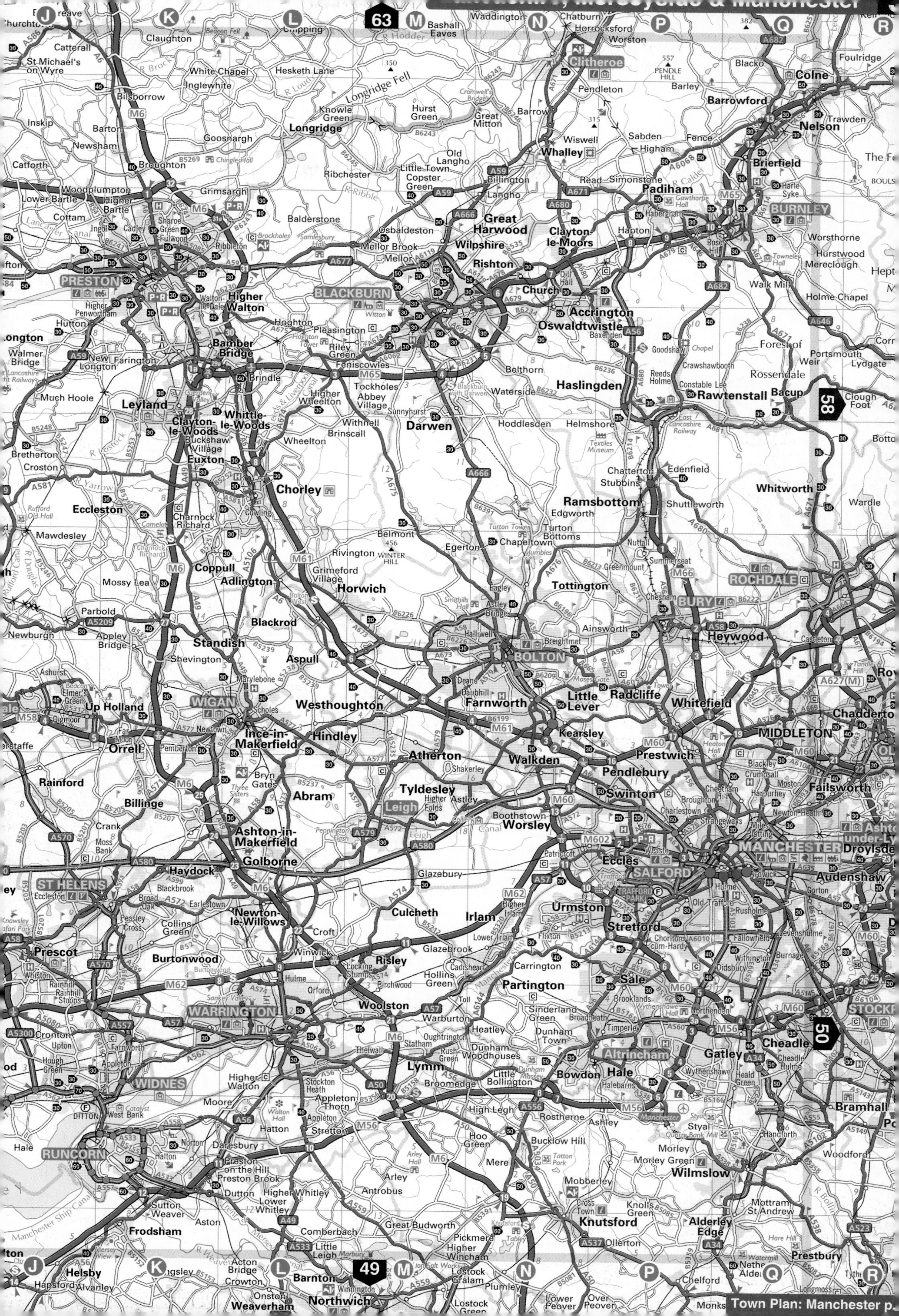63
58
50
49
Merseyside & Manchester
Town Plan: Manchester p.
Churchtown
Catterall
St Michael's on Wyre
Claughton
Chipping
Bashall Eaves
Waddington
Chatburn
Horrocksford
Worston
Clitheroe
Pendle Hill
Pendleton
Foulridge
Blacko
Colne
Barley
Barrowford
Trawden
Nelson
White Chapel
Inglewhite
Hesketh Lane
Longridge Fell
Bilsborrow
Knowle Green
Longridge
Hurst Green
Great Mitton
Barrow
Wiswell
Sabden
Fence
Higham
Whalley
Brierfield
Inskip
Barton
Newsham
Goosnargh
Old Langho
Catforth
Broughton
Little Town
Ribchester
Copster Green
Billington
Langho
Read
Simonstone
Padiham
Woodplumpton
Lower Bartle
Higher Bartle
Grimsargh
Cottam
Sharoe Green
Fulwood
Ribbleton
Balderstone
Great Harwood
Clayton-le-Moors
Hapton
Burnley
Worsthorne
Hurstwood
Mereclough
Osbaldeston
Mellor Brook
Mellor
Wilpshire
Rishton
Preston
Higher Walton
Blackburn
Church
Accrington
Walk Mill
Holme Chapel
Higher Penwortham
Hutton
Hoghton
Pleasington
Oswaldtwistle
Baxenden
Goodshaw
Crawshawbooth
Forest of Rossendale
Portsmouth
Weir
Lydgate
Longton
Walmer Bridge
New Longton
Farington
Bamber Bridge
Riley Green
Feniscowles
Belthorn
Haslingden
Reeds Holme
Constable Lee
Rawtenstall
Bacup
Clough Foot
Much Hoole
Leyland
Brindle
Tockholes
Abbey Village
Higher Wheelton
Waterside
Sunnyhurst
Darwen
Withnell
Brinscall
Hoddlesden
Helmshore
Clayton-le-Woods
Whittle-le-Woods
Buckshaw Village
Wheelton
Bretherton
Croston
Euxton
Chorley
Edenfield
Chatterton
Stubbins
Whitworth
Wardle
Eccleston
Cowling
Ramsbottom
Edgworth
Shuttleworth
Mawdesley
Charnock Richard
Belmont
Winter Hill
Turton Bottoms
Chapeltown
Egerton
Rivington
Nuttall
Summerseat
Coppull
Adlington
Grimeford Village
Horwich
Greenmount
Tottington
Rochdale
Mossy Lea
Eagley
Astley Bridge
Chesham
Bury
Parbold
Newburgh
Appley Bridge
Blackrod
Halliwell
Ainsworth
Heywood
Castleton
Standish
Shevington
Aspull
Bolton
Breightmet
Ashurst
Up Holland
Wigan
Scholes
Westhoughton
Deane
Daubhill
Farnworth
Little Lever
Radcliffe
Whitefield
Chadderton
Orrell
Pemberton
Ince-in-Makerfield
Hindley
Kearsley
Middleton
Prestwich
Atherton
Walkden
Pendlebury
Rainford
Bryn Gates
Shakerley
Swinton
Blackley
Crumpsall
Moston
Failsworth
Billinge
Abram
Tyldesley
Astley
Leigh
Boothstown
Worsley
Cheetham Hill
Harpurhey
Newton Heath
Crank
Moss Bank
Ashton-in-Makerfield
Golborne
Haydock
Patricroft
Eccles
Salford
Manchester
Droylsden
St Helens
Blackbrook
Earlestown
Glazebury
Ashton-under-Lyne
Audenshaw
Eccleston
Newton-le-Willows
Culcheth
Irlam
Urmston
Trafford Park
Old Trafford
Gorton
Stretford
Chorlton-cum-Hardy
Fallowfield
Levenshulme
Prescot
Collins Green
Peasley Cross
Croft
Lower Irlam
Flixton
Withington
Burnage
Burtonwood
Winwick
Risley
Glazebrook
Cadishead
Carrington
Didsbury
Whiston
Rainhill
Rainhill Stoops
Locking Stumps
Birchwood
Hollins Green
Partington
Sale
Brooklands
Hulme
Orford
Woolston
Warburton
Sinderland Green
Northenden
Stockport
Warrington
Cronton
Upton
Farnworth
Heatley
Oughtrington
Dunham Town
Timperley
Cheadle
Hough Green
Appleton
Statham
Thelwall
Rush Green
Dunham Woodhouses
Altrincham
Gatley
Cheadle Hulme
Heald Green
Widnes
Higher Walton
Stockton Heath
Lymm
Broomedge
Little Bollington
Bowdon
Hale
Wythenshawe
Halebarns
Bramhall
Ditton
West Bank
Moore
Appleton Thorn
High Legh
Rostherne
Ashley
Styal
Runcorn
Norton
Daresbury
Walton Hall
Hatton
Stretton
Hoo Green
Bucklow Hill
Handforth
Woodford
Halton
Preston on the Hill
Preston Brook
Arley Hall
Mere
Tatton Park
Morley
Morley Green
Wilmslow
Dutton
Higher Whitley
Lower Whitley
Arley
Antrobus
Mobberley
Sutton Weaver
Aston
Frodsham
Comberbach
Great Budworth
Pickmere
Cross Town
Knutsford
Knolls Green
Alderley Edge
Mottram St Andrew
Little Leigh
Higher Wincham
Ollerton
Prestbury
Helsby
Acton Bridge
Crowton
Barnton
Wincham
Lostock Gralam
Plumley
Chelford
Nether Alderley
Hapsford
Alvanley
Kingsley
Onston
Weaverham
Northwich
Lostock Green
Lower Peover
Over Peover
Monks
Manchester Ship Canal
Leeds & Liverpool Canal
Lancaster Canal

64
65
63
57
50
Hawkswick
Bouthwaite
Low Gill
High Grantley
Aldfield
Studley Royal
Studley Roger
Studley Royal Park
Fountains Abbey
Risplith
Sawley
Wath
Gouthwaite Reservoir
Pateley Bridge
Wilsill
Brimham Rocks (Rock formations)
Markington
Bishop Thornton
Bewerley
Glasshouses
Greenhow Hill
Stump Cross Caverns
Summerbridge
Hartwith
Shaw Mills
Dacre Banks
Dacre
Darley
Burnt Yates
Bedlam
Ripley
Birstwith
Hampsthwaite
Clint
Killinghall
Padside
Darley Head
Thornthwaite
Thruscross Reservoir
Kettlesing Bottom
Swincliffe
Kettlesing
Forest Moor
Blubberhouses
Fewston Reservoir
Fewston
Swinsty Res
Timble
HARROGATE
Harlow Carr
Beckwithshaw
Pannal Ash
Rossett Green
North Rigton
Huby
Dunkeswick
Leathley
Weeton
Castley
Arthington
Weardley
Bramhope
Pool
Otley
Chevin Forest Park
Newall
Farnley
Weston
Clifton
Askwith
Middleton
Denton
Nesfield
Langbar
Beamsley
Ilkley
Ben Rhydding
Burley in Wharfedale
Burley Wood Head
Menston
East Carlton
Guiseley
Old Bramhope
Eccup Reservoir
Yeadon
Leeds Bradford
Rawdon
Horsforth
Hawksworth
Park Gate
Baildon
Baildon Green
Charlestown
Thackley
Idle
Shipley
Saltaire
Greengates
Eccleshill
Frizinghall
Heaton
Manningham
Undercliffe
BRADFORD
Thornbury
Laisterdyke
Farsley
Pudsey
Bramley
Kirkstall
Armley
Wortley
Tong
Beeston
Churwell
Gildersome
Drighlington
Morley
Birkenshaw
Bowling
West Bowling
Wibsey
Odsal
Buttershaw
Queensbury
Shibden Head
Mountain
Clayton
Great Horton
Allerton
Thornton
Denholme
Keelham
Cullingworth
Harden
Wilsden
Cottingley
Bingley
Cross Flatts
East Morton
Riddlesden
East Riddlesden Hall
KEIGHLEY
Utley
Steeton
Eastburn
Sutton-in-Craven
Glusburn
Kildwick
Cowling
Ickornshaw
Silsden
Brunthwaite
Rombalds Moor
Addingham
Airedale
Skipton
Embsay
Embsay & Bolton Abbey Steam Railway
Draughton
Bolton Abbey
Bolton Priory
Halton East
Eastby
Stirton
Thorlby
Gargrave
Coniston Cold
Bell Busk
Hellifield
Flasby
Winterburn
Hetton
Rylstone
Cracoe
Airton
Otterburn
Kirkby Malham
Hanlith
Malham
National Park Centre
Malham Cove
Malham Tarn
Kilnsey
Kilnsey Park & Trout Farm
Conistone
CONISTONE MOOR
MEUGHER
Grass Wood
Threshfield
Grassington
Linton
Hebden
Thorpe
Burnsall
Grimwith Reservoir
New House Farm
Parcevall Hall
SIMON'S SEAT
Appletreewick
Barden Tower
West End Outdoor Centre
Broughton
East Marton
West Marton
Elslack
Carleton
Low Bradley
Bracewell
Thornton-in-Craven
Yorkshire Dales Lead Mining
Earby
Barnoldswick
Salterforth
Kelbrook
Lothersdale
Cononley
Foulridge
Colne
Nelson
Trawden
Brierfield
Harle Syke
BURNLEY
Worsthorne
Hurstwood
Mereclough
Towneley Hall
Walk Mill
Holme Chapel
The Forest of Trawden
BOULSWORTH HILL
Wycoller
Lund's Tower
Wainman's Pinnacle
Laycock
Keighley Moor
Oakworth
Keighley & Worth Valley Railway
Haworth
Stanbury
Penistone Hill
Oxenhope
Hare Croft
Wadsworth Moor
Heptonstall Moor
Pecket Well
Slack
Colden
Blackshaw Head
Heptonstall
Chisley
Wainstalls
Hebden Bridge
Mytholm
Charlestown
Cornholme
Booth
Midgley
Moor End
Mt Tabor
Luddenden
Bradshaw
Ambler Thorn
Northowram
Oakenshaw
Hunsworth
Wyke
HALIFAX
Warley Town
Hipperholme
Mytholmroyd
Luddenden Foot
Todmorden
Pennine Way
Stoodley Pike
Portsmouth
Lydgate
Forest of Rossendale
Weir
Bacup
Clough Foot
Walsden
Bottoms
Steep Lane
Sowerby
Sowerby Bridge
Southowram
Brighouse
Rastrick
Clifton
Hartshead
Cleckheaton
Heckmondwike
Liversedge
Norristhorpe
Roberttown
Birstall
Batley
Hanging Heaton
Dewsbury
Chidswell
Woodkirk
Kirkhamgate
Earlsheaton
Savile Town
Ravensthorpe
Northorpe
Mirfield
Ossett
Greetland
Lumb
Mill Bank
Soyland Town
Holywell Green
Elland
Ripponden
Barkisland
Stainland
Broad Carr
Clough Head
Netheroyd Hill
Fartown
Sheepridge
Upper Heaton
Upper Hopton
Kirkheaton
Thornhill
Whitley Lower
Middlestown
National Coal Mining Museum
Grange Moor
Overton
Flockton Green
Netherton
Hill Side
Houses Hill
HUDDERSFIELD
Lindley
Edgerton
Moldgreen
Greenside
Almondbury
Lower Houses
Newsome
Lepton
Flockton
Midgley
West Bretton
Yorkshire Sculpture Park
Emley
Highburton
Kirkburton
Kirklees Light Railway
Farnley Tyas
Shelley
Skelmanthorpe
Clayton West
High Hoyland
Scissett
Lower Cumberworth
Cannon Hall Open Farm
Cawthorne
Denby Dale
Upper Cumberworth
Upper Denby
Silkstone
Hoyland Swaine
Silkstone Common
Ingbirchworth
Thurlstone
Millhouse Green
Penistone
Oxspring
Thurgoland
Crow Edge
Winscar Reservoir
Townhead
Hepworth
Scholes
Birds Edge
Shepley
New Mill
Thurstonland
Brockholes
Honley
Netherthong
Upperthong
Holmfirth
Holmbridge
Holme
Holme Moss
BLACK HILL
Wilshaw
Meltham
Helme
Netherton
Blackmoorfoot
Linthwaite
Golcar
Scapegoat Hill
Slaithwaite
Marsden
Standedge Experience
Close Moor
Outlane
Sowood
Krumlin
Rishworth
Rishworth Moor
Deanhead
Saddleworth Moor
Hollingworth Lake
Littleborough
Wardle
Whitworth
Rawtenstall
Milnrow
ROCHDALE
Moss Moor
Denshaw
Delph
Diggle
Dobcross
Uppermill
Greenfield
Grasscroft
Saddleworth Moor
Mossley
Shaw
Royton
Castleton
Heywood
Chadderton
MIDDLETON
OLDHAM
Failsworth
Moston
Blackley
Harpurhey
Crumpsall
FEATHERBED MOSS
Pennine Way
0 1 2 3 4 miles
0 1 2 3 4 5 kilometres
Town Plans: Bradford p.124, Leeds p.128

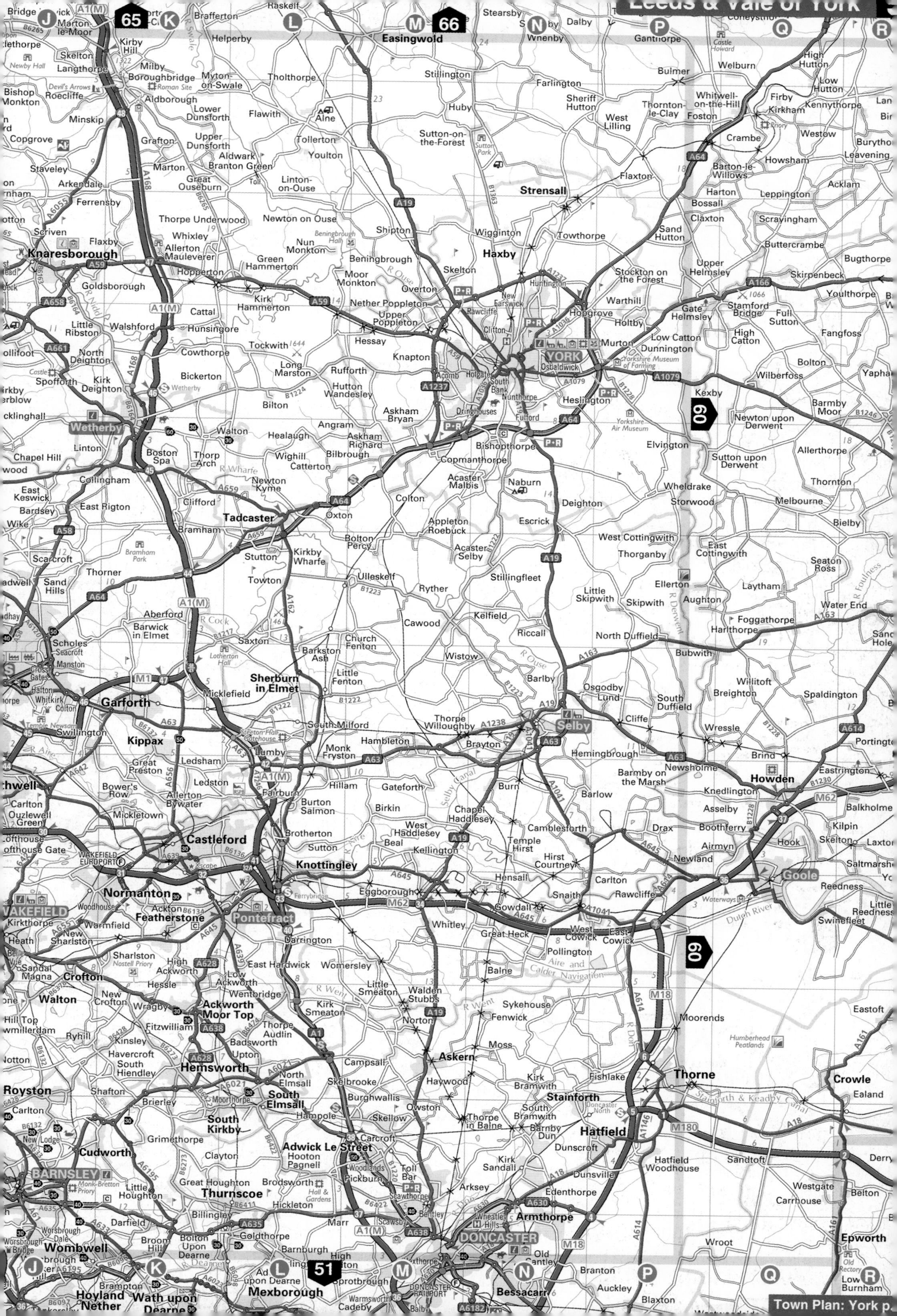
Leeds & Vale of York
65
66
51
Easingwold
Stillington
Huby
Strensall
Haxby
Wigginton
Skelton
YORK
Knaresborough
Wetherby
Tadcaster
Selby
Sherburn in Elmet
Garforth
Kippax
Castleford
Knottingley
Pontefract
Normanton
Featherstone
WAKEFIELD
Hemsworth
South Elmsall
South Kirkby
Adwick Le Street
Thurnscoe
BARNSLEY
Wombwell
Mexborough
DONCASTER
Armthorpe
Bessacarr
Hatfield
Thorne
Stainforth
Askern
Howden
Goole
Crowle
Epworth
Boroughbridge
Aldborough
Flawith
Alne
Tollerton
Youlton
Linton-on-Ouse
Newton on Ouse
Shipton
Beningbrough
Nun Monkton
Green Hammerton
Kirk Hammerton
Cattal
Hunsingore
Tockwith
Long Marston
Rufforth
Hutton Wandesley
Bilton
Askham Bryan
Askham Richard
Bilbrough
Copmanthorpe
Bishopthorpe
Naburn
Acaster Malbis
Colton
Appleton Roebuck
Acaster Selby
Stillingfleet
Escrick
Deighton
Wheldrake
Elvington
Heslington
Dunnington
Murton
Stamford Bridge
Full Sutton
Fangfoss
Wilberfoss
Kexby
Newton upon Derwent
Sutton upon Derwent
Melbourne
Thornton
Allerthorpe
Barmby Moor
Bielby
Seaton Ross
Laytham
Aughton
Ellerton
Thorganby
West Cottingwith
East Cottingwith
Skipwith
Little Skipwith
North Duffield
Bubwith
Foggathorpe
Harlthorpe
Willitoft
Breighton
Spaldington
Wressle
South Duffield
Cliffe
Osgodby
Lund
Hemingbrough
Barmby on the Marsh
Newsholme
Brind
Knedlington
Asselby
Boothferry
Airmyn
Hook
Kilpin
Skelton
Saltmarshe
Reedness
Swinefleet
Rawcliffe
Snaith
Carlton
Newland
Drax
Barlow
Camblesforth
Hirst Courtney
Temple Hirst
Hensall
Gowdall
West Cowick
East Cowick
Pollington
Balne
Sykehouse
Fenwick
Moss
Fishlake
Kirk Bramwith
South Bramwith
Barnby Dun
Dunscroft
Dunsville
Hatfield Woodhouse
Sandtoft
Westgate
Belton
Carrhouse
Wroot
Branton
Auckley
Blaxton
Edenthorpe
Kirk Sandall
Arksey
Bentley
Scawthorpe
Owston
Skellow
Burghwallis
Skelbrooke
Campsall
Norton
Kirk Smeaton
Little Smeaton
Walden Stubbs
Womersley
Whitley
Great Heck
Eggborough
Kellington
Beal
West Haddlesey
Chapel Haddlesey
Burn
Brayton
Thorpe Willoughby
Hambleton
Gateforth
Birkin
Burton Salmon
Hillam
Monk Fryston
South Milford
Lumby
Fairburn
Ledsham
Ledston
Brotherton
Sutton
Ferrybridge
Darrington
East Hardwick
Wentbridge
Ackworth Moor Top
Thorpe Audlin
Badsworth
Upton
North Elmsall
Hampole
Carcroft
Hooton Pagnell
Brodsworth
Pickburn
Clayton
Great Houghton
Little Houghton
Grimethorpe
Cudworth
Brierley
Shafton
Royston
Carlton
Havercroft
South Hiendley
Kinsley
Fitzwilliam
Wragby
Crofton
Walton
Sharlston
New Sharlston
Warmfield
Ackton
Whitwood
Mickletown
Allerton Bywater
Great Preston
Bower's Row
Swillington
Micklefield
Saxton
Barwick in Elmet
Aberford
Scholes
Thorner
Bramham
Clifford
Boston Spa
Thorp Arch
Walton
Collingham
Linton
East Keswick
Bardsey
Scarcroft
Wike
Spofforth
Kirk Deighton
North Deighton
Little Ribston
Walshford
Goldsborough
Flaxby
Allerton Mauleverer
Whixley
Hopperton
Thorpe Underwood
Great Ouseburn
Marton
Grafton
Arkendale
Ferrensby
Staveley
Copgrove
Minskip
Roecliffe
Langthorpe
Kirby Hill
Milby
Helperby
Brafferton
Myton-on-Swale
Tholthorpe
Lower Dunsforth
Upper Dunsforth
Aldwark
Branton Green
Sutton-on-the-Forest
Farlington
Sheriff Hutton
West Lilling
Thornton-le-Clay
Foston
Whitwell-on-the-Hill
Crambe
Barton-le-Willows
Flaxton
Harton
Bossall
Claxton
Sand Hutton
Upper Helmsley
Gate Helmsley
Warthill
Holtby
Stockton on the Forest
Hopgrove
Towthorpe
Huntington
New Earswick
Rawcliffe
Clifton
Nether Poppleton
Upper Poppleton
Hessay
Knapton
Acomb
Holgate
Dringhouses
Fulford
Osbaldwick
Low Catton
High Catton
Westow
Howsham
Leppington
Scrayingham
Buttercrambe
Bugthorpe
Skirpenbeck
Youlthorpe
Acklam
Kirkham
Firby
Bulmer
Welburn
Dalby
Gantnorpe
Stearsby
Whenby
Raskelf
Ulleskelf
Ryther
Cawood
Kelfield
Riccall
Wistow
Barlby
Church Fenton
Little Fenton
Barkston Ash
Towton
Stutton
Kirkby Wharfe
Bolton Percy
Oxton
Healaugh
Wighill
Catterton
Angram
Newton Kyme
Moorends
Eastoft
Ealand
Marr
Barnburgh
Goldthorpe
Bolton Upon Dearne
Billingley
Darfield
Hoyland Nether
Wath upon Dearne
Brampton
Hickleton
Old Cantley
Town Plan: York p

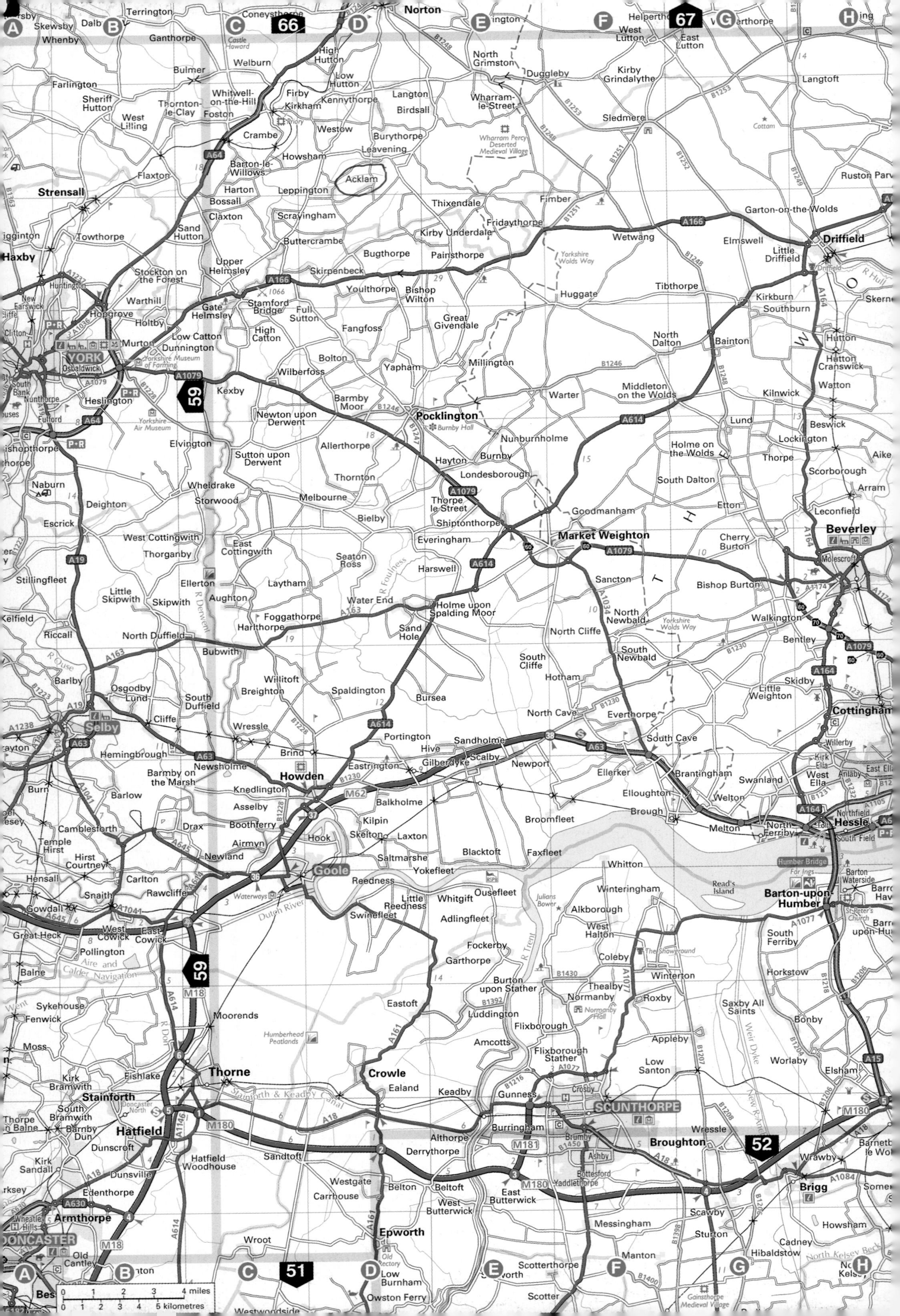

66
67
59
51
52
A
B
C
D
E
F
G
H
Norton
Skewsby
Dalby
Whenby
Terrington
Coneysthorpe
Ganthorpe
Castle Howard
Welburn
High Hutton
Low Hutton
North Grimston
Duggleby
Helperthorpe
West Lutton
East Lutton
Kirby Grindalythe
Langtoft
Bulmer
Farlington
Sheriff Hutton
Whitwell-on-the-Hill
Thornton-le-Clay
Foston
West Lilling
Firby
Kirkham
Priory
Kennythorpe
Langton
Birdsall
Wharram-le-Street
Wharram Percy Deserted Medieval Village
Sledmere
Cottam
Crambe
Westow
Burythorpe
Leavening
Howsham
Barton-le-Willows
Flaxton
Acklam
Strensall
Harton
Leppington
Bossall
Claxton
Scrayingham
Thixendale
Fimber
Fridaythorpe
Garton-on-the-Wolds
Ruston Parva
Driffield
Little Driffield
Elmswell
Wetwang
Kirby Underdale
Sand Hutton
Towthorpe
Haxby
Buttercrambe
Bugthorpe
Painsthorpe
Yorkshire Wolds Way
Upper Helmsley
Skirpenbeck
Stockton on the Forest
Huntington
New Earswick
Youlthorpe
Bishop Wilton
Huggate
Tibthorpe
Kirkburn
Southburn
Skerne
Warthill
Hopgrove
Holtby
Gate Helmsley
Stamford Bridge
1066
Full Sutton
High Catton
Low Catton
Fangfoss
Great Givendale
North Dalton
Bainton
Hutton
Hutton Cranswick
Clifton
York
Murton
Dunnington
Yorkshire Museum of Farming
Osbaldwick
Bolton
Millington
Yapham
Wilberfoss
South Bank
Nunthorpe
Heslington
Kexby
Barmby Moor
Pocklington
Burnby Hall
Warter
Middleton on the Wolds
Kilnwick
Watton
Fulford
Yorkshire Air Museum
Newton upon Derwent
Allerthorpe
Nunburnholme
Lund
Beswick
Bishopthorpe
Elvington
Sutton upon Derwent
Hayton
Burnby
Holme on the Wolds
Lockington
Thorpe
Aike
Scorborough
Naburn
Wheldrake
Thornton
Londesborough
South Dalton
Arram
Deighton
Storwood
Melbourne
Thorpe le Street
Goodmanham
Etton
Leconfield
Escrick
Bielby
Shiptonthorpe
Market Weighton
Beverley
West Cottingwith
East Cottingwith
Everingham
Cherry Burton
Thorganby
Seaton Ross
Molescroft
Stillingfleet
Harswell
Sancton
Bishop Burton
Ellerton
Laytham
R Foulness
Little Skipwith
Skipwith
Aughton
Water End
Holme upon Spalding Moor
North Newbald
Walkington
Kelfield
Foggathorpe
Harlthorpe
Riccall
North Duffield
Sand Hole
North Cliffe
Bentley
R Derwent
Bubwith
South Newbald
R Ouse
South Cliffe
Barlby
Hotham
Skidby
Willitoft
Little Weighton
Osgodby
Lund
Breighton
Spaldington
Bursea
Cottingham
South Duffield
North Cave
Everthorpe
Selby
Cliffe
Wressle
Portington
Sandholme
South Cave
Willerby
Hemingbrough
Brind
Hive
Gilberdyke
Scalby
Newport
Ellerker
Brantingham
Kirk Ella
Anlaby
East Ella
West Ella
Newsholme
Eastrington
Swanland
Barmby on the Marsh
Howden
Knedlington
Elloughton
Welton
Northfield
Burn
Barlow
Asselby
Balkholme
Brough
Hessle
Kilpin
Broomfleet
Melton
North Ferriby
Camblesforth
Drax
Boothferry
Temple Hirst
Airmyn
Hook
Skelton
Laxton
Blacktoft
Faxfleet
South Field
Hirst Courtney
Newland
Saltmarshe
Humber Bridge
Goole
Yokefleet
Whitton
Barton Waterside
Hensall
Carlton
Reedness
Ousefleet
Winteringham
Read's Island
Snaith
Rawcliffe
Waterways
Little Reedness
Whitgift
Julians Bower
Barton-upon-Humber
Gowdall
Dutch River
Swinefleet
Alkborough
St Peter's Church
Great Heck
West Cowick
East Cowick
Adlingfleet
West Halton
South Ferriby
Pollington
Fockerby
The Showground
Aire and Calder Navigation
Garthorpe
Coleby
R Trent
Balne
Winterton
Horkstow
Burton upon Stather
Thealby
Normanby
Normanby Hall
Roxby
Saxby All Saints
Sykehouse
Fenwick
Moorends
Eastoft
Luddington
Bonby
Humberhead Peatlands
Flixborough
Appleby
Weir Dyke
Moss
Amcotts
Worlaby
Flixborough Stather
Low Santon
Elsham
Kirk Bramwith
Fishlake
Thorne
Crowle
Crosby
Stainforth
Stainforth & Keadby Canal
Ealand
Keadby
Gunness
Scunthorpe
New R Ancholme
South Bramwith
Doncaster North
Thorpe in Balne
Barnby Dun
Hatfield
Burringham
Althorpe
Brumby
Wressle
Barnetby le Wold
Dunscroft
Sandtoft
Derrythorpe
Broughton
Ashby
Kirk Sandall
Hatfield Woodhouse
Dunsville
Westgate
Belton
Beltoft
East Butterwick
Bottesford
Yaddlethorpe
Wrawby
Brigg
Edenthorpe
Carrhouse
West Butterwick
Scawby
Armthorpe
Wheatley Hills
Epworth
Messingham
Howsham
Doncaster
Old Cantley
Wroot
Old Rectory
Sturton
Cadney
Manton
Hibaldstow
North Kelsey Beck
Scotterthorpe
Low Burnham
Owston Ferry
Scotter
Gainsthorpe Medieval Village
Westwoodside
York
P+R
A64
A166
A1079
A19
A163
A614
A63
A645
A1041
A1238
A1036
M62
M18
A614
M180
M181
A18
A1146
A630
A161
A1077
A1034
A164
A1174
A1105
A15
A1084
B1248
B1253
B1251
B1252
B1249
B1246
B1247
B1228
B1230
B1223
B1363
B1430
B1392
B1216
B1450
B1207
B1208
B1206
B1204
B1218
B1398
B1400
B1233
B1231
B1232
B1222
0 1 2 3 4 miles
0 1 2 3 4 5 kilometres

Town Plan: Kingston upon Hull p

St Bees
Egremont
70
71
LAKE DISTRICT
798
802
KIRK FELL
GREAT GABLE
780
GLARAMARA
LANK RIGG
Worm Gill
Wasdale Head
NATIONAL
762
HIGH WHITE STONES
Thornhill
Haile
691
SEATALLAN
River Bleng
910
GREAT END
Stickle Tarn
Grasmere
Wordsworth
Nethertown
Beckermet
978
964
SCAFELL
SCAFELL PIKE
902
BOW FELL
Great Langdale
Chapel Stile
Rydal
Rydal Water
White Moss Common
Rydal Mount
485
Kirkstone Pass
Calder Bridge
R Ehen
Wast Water
Nether Wasdale
Burnmoor Tarn
PARK
CUMBRIA
B5343
Elterwater
Armitt Museum
Ambleside
Bridge House
A592
Wellington
Cross
702
PIKE OF BLISCO
Little Langdale
Skelwith Bridge
Galava Fort
Stagshaw Garden
Troutbeck
Gosforth
R Irt
R Mite
393
Wrynose Pass
B5343
Santon Bridge
Boot
Hardknott Fort
393
Hardknott Pass
Low Wray
Townend
A591
Lake District
Troutbeck
Seascale
Eskdale Green
Hallsenna Moor
Drigg
Holmrook
Eskdale
652
HARTER FELL
Furness Fells
The Tarns
Outgate
High Wray
Windermere
Muncaster Mill
Ravenglass and Eskdale Railway
Levers Water
803
Coniston
THE OLD MAN OF CONISTON
Far End
Hawkshead Hill
Courthouse
Hawkshead
B5285
Windermere Steamboats & Museum
Hill Top
Bowness-on-Windermere
River Esk
Devoke Water
Seathwaite Tarn
Bowmanstead
Steam Yacht 'Gondola'
Far Sawrey
Ravenglass
Muncaster
Roman Bath House
A595
Hall Dunnerdale
Seathwaite
River Duddon
Esthwaite Water
Brantwood
Grizedale
Near Sawrey
Blackwell
Torver
Coniston Water
Grizedale Forest Park
Windermere
Waberthwaite
573
WHITFELL
Ulpha
A5084
Satterthwaite
Furness Fells
Graythwaite Hall
Thwaite Head
A593
Broughton Mills
High Nibthwaite
A592
321
GUMMERS HOW
Hycemoor
Selker Bay
Blawith
Stott Park Bobbin Mill
Rusland Cross
Finsthwaite
Bootle
Swinside Stone Circle
Broughton-in-Furness
Fell Foot Park
Oxen Park
Colton
Staveley
Newby Bridge
600
BLACK COMBE
A595
Lady Hall
Foxfield
Grizebeck
A5092
Lowick Green
Bouth
Lakeside and Haverthwaite Railway
Lakeland Motor Museum
Witherslack
Ayside
Gutterby Spa
Whitbeck
The Green
Gawthwaite
Spark Bridge
Haverthwaite
Penny Bridge
High Newton
Whicham
The Hill
A5093
Kirkby-in-Furness
Beck Side
B5281
Greenodd
B5278
Silecroft
Soutergate
Arrad Foot
Kirksanton
Millom
A595
Barrow Monument
222
HAMPSFELL
Priory Gatehouse
Lindale
Haverigg
Haverigg Point
Ulverston
Pennington
Cartmel
Ireleth
Askam in Furness
Swarthmoor
A590
Conishead Priory
Holker
Allithwaite
Grange-over-Sands
Lindal in Furness
Cark
B5278
Flookburgh
South Lakes Animal Park
Great Urswick
Bardsea
Sandscale Haws
Little Urswick
North Walney
Dalton-in-Furness
Humphrey Head
Scales
Baycliff
BARROW-IN-FURNESS
Newton
Furness Abbey
Bow Bridge
Stainton with Adgarley
Dendron
Watermill
Gleaston
Aldingham
MORECAMBE
Vickerstown
Barrow Island
Leece
A590
A5087
BAY
ISLE OF WALNEY
Rampside
Morecambe
Sheep Island
Piel Castle
Foulney Island
Piel Island
Sandylands
Piel Bar
Hilpsford Point
South Walney
Heysham
Higher Heysham
Douglas
Sunderland
Cockersand
Heysham Harbour
0
500 m
MORECAMBE
A589
Lower Heysham
HEYSHAM
Heysham Sands
BARROWS LANE
MIDDLETON WAY
Half Moon Bay
SMITHY LANE
Higher Heysham
PORT WAY
HEYSHAM PORT STATION
Freight Terminal
A683
A683
LANCASTER
ISLE OF MAN FERRY TERMINAL
Nuclear Power Stations
HONEY CLOSE LANE
MIDDLETON ROAD
LLA
Knott End-on-Sea
Pilling
Fleetwood
Preesall
Rossall Point
B5377
A588
A587
River Wyre
Stalmine
B5268
A585
Staynall
Cleveleys
Thornton
Hambleton
56
Little Singleton
A
B
C
D
E
F
G
H
0
1
2
3
4 miles
0
1
2
3
4
5 kilometres

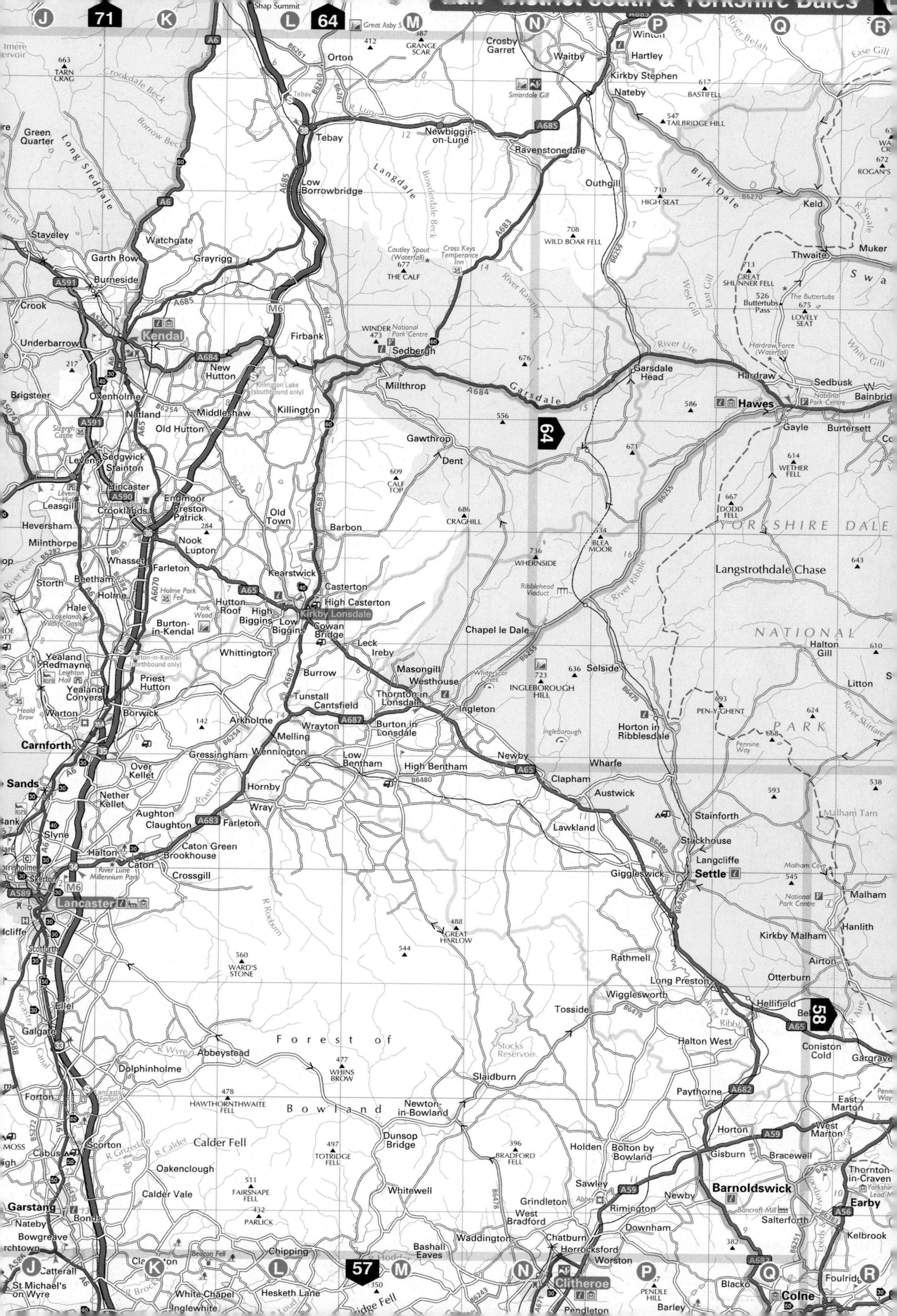

Lake District South & Yorkshire Dales
J
71
K
Shap Summit
L
64
Great Asby
M
N
P
Q
R
Orton
412
587
GRANGE SCAR
Crosby Garret
Winton
Hartley
Waitby
Kirkby Stephen
Nateby
617
BASTIFELL
547
TAILBRIDGE HILL
Smardale Gill
Tebay
R. Lune
Newbiggin-on-Lune
A685
Ravenstonedale
663
TARN CRAG
Crookdale Beck
Borrow Beck
Green Quarter
Long Sleddale
A6
Low Borrowbridge
Langdale
Bowderdale Beck
Outhgill
710
HIGH SEAT
Birk Dale
B6270
Keld
672
ROGAN'S
R. Swale
708
WILD BOAR FELL
Thwaite
Muker
Staveley
Watchgate
Grayrigg
Garth Row
Burneside
A591
Cautley Spout (Waterfall)
677
THE CALF
Cross Keys Temperance Inn
River Rawthey
713
GREAT SHUNNER FELL
526
Buttertubs Pass
The Buttertubs
675
LOVELY SEAT
West Gill
East Gill
Swa
Crook
A685
M6
Firbank
WINDER
473
National Park Centre
Sedbergh
River Ure
Hardraw Force (Waterfall)
Whity Gill
Underbarrow
Kendal
A684
New Hutton
676
Garsdale Head
Hardraw
Sedbusk
217
Killington Lake (southbound only)
Millthrop
A684
Garsdale
National Park Centre
Bainbridge
Brigsteer
Oxenholme
B6254
Killington
586
Hawes
Natland
Middleshaw
556
64
Gayle
Burtersett
Sizergh Castle
A591
A65
Old Hutton
Gawthrop
671
614
WETHER FELL
Levens
Sedgwick
Stainton
Dent
609
CALF TOP
Hincaster
Endmoor
A590
Crooklands
Preston Patrick
Old Town
686
CRAGHILL
B6255
667
DODD FELL
Leasgill
Heversham
Milnthorpe
Barbon
284
Nook
Lupton
534
BLEA MOOR
736
WHERNSIDE
YORKSHIRE DALES
Whasset
Farleton
Langstrothdale Chase
643
River Kent
Storth
Beetham
Holme
Kearstwick
Casterton
Holme Park Fell
A65
High Casterton
Ribblehead Viaduct
River Ribble
Hale
Lakeland Wildlife Oasis
Hutton Roof
Park Wood
High Biggins
Low Biggins
Kirkby Lonsdale
Cowan Bridge
Burton-in-Kendal
A6070
Chapel le Dale
NATIONAL
Halton Gill
610
Yealand Redmayne
Leighton Hall
Whittington
Leck
Ireby
B6255
Burton-in-Kendal (northbound only)
Priest Hutton
Yealand Conyers
Burrow
Masongill
Westhouse
White Scar Caves
723
INGLEBOROUGH HILL
636
Selside
Litton
Heald Brow
Warton
Old Rectory
Borwick
Tunstall
Cantsfield
Thornton in Lonsdale
Ingleton
B6479
693
PEN-Y-GHENT
624
River Skirfare
142
Arkholme
A683
A687
Wrayton
Burton in Lonsdale
Ingleborough
Horton in Ribblesdale
PARK
Carnforth
Melling
668
Pennine Way
Gressingham
Wennington
Low Bentham
High Bentham
Newby
Wharfe
Sands
Over Kellet
A65
Clapham
Hornby
B6480
Austwick
593
538
Nether Kellet
Wray
Malham Tarn
Aughton
Claughton
A683
Farleton
River Lune
Lawkland
Stainforth
Slyne
Caton Green
Brookhouse
Stackhouse
Halton
Caton
B6480
Langcliffe
River Lune Millennium Park
Crossgill
Giggleswick
Settle
Malham Cove
Skerton
M6
545
Malham
A589
Lancaster
National Park Centre
R Roeburn
488
GREAT HARLOW
B6480
Hanlith
Kirkby Malham
560
WARD'S STONE
544
Rathmell
Airton
Long Preston
Otterburn
Wigglesworth
Ellel
Tosside
B6478
Hellifield
58
Lancaster Canal
R Ribble
A65
Galgate
Forest of
Halton West
Coniston Cold
Stocks Reservoir
Gargrave
A588
R Wyre
Abbeystead
477
WHINS BROW
Dolphinholme
Slaidburn
Paythorne
A682
478
HAWTHORNTHWAITE FELL
Bowland
Newton-in-Bowland
East Marton
Forton
Lancaster (Forton)
Pennine Way
Horton
A59
West Marton
Calder Fell
497
TOTRIDGE FELL
Dunsop Bridge
396
BRADFORD FELL
Holden
Bolton by Bowland
Gisburn
Bracewell
Cabus
Scorton
R Grizedale
R Calder
B6478
Oakenclough
Sawley
Barnoldswick
B6252
Thornton-in-Craven
511
FAIRSNAPE FELL
Whitewell
A59
Newby
Calder Vale
Grindleton
Abbey
Rimington
Bancroft Mill
Earby
Garstang
432
PARLICK
Bonds
West Bradford
Salterforth
A56
Nateby
Downham
Bowgreave
Bashall Eaves
Waddington
Chatburn
382
Kelbrook
Leeds & Liverpool Canal
Horrocksford
Chipping
Beacon Fell
Worston
A682
Claughton
57
Hodder
Catterall
Clitheroe
Foulridge
St Michael's on Wyre
R Brock
White Chapel
Hesketh Lane
350
Pendle Hill
Blacko
Colne
Inglewhite
Pendleton
Barley
B6243
A671

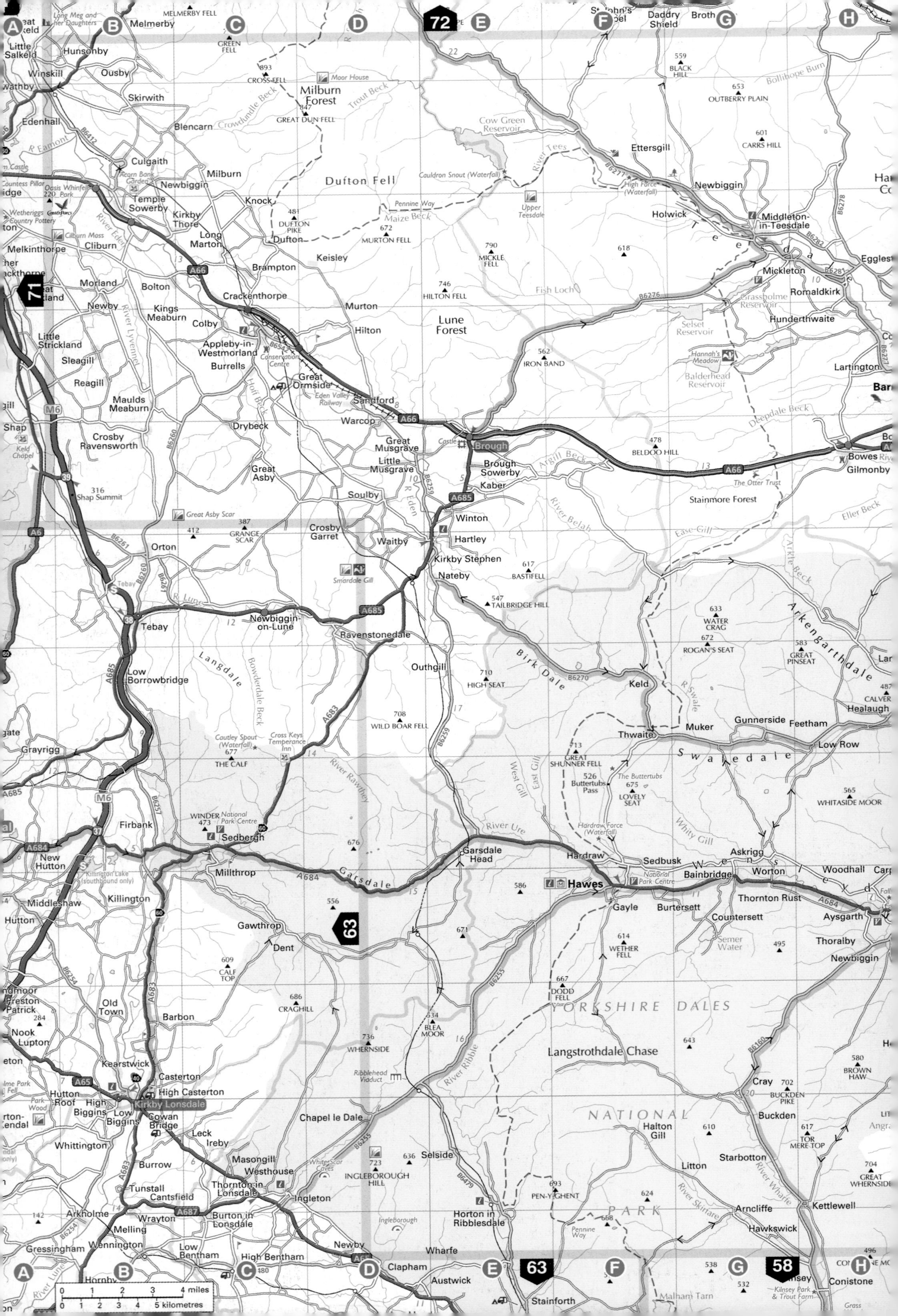

72
A
B
C
D
E
F
G
H
Long Meg and her Daughters
Melmerby
MELMERBY FELL
GREEN FELL
Daddry Shield
Little Salkeld
Hunsonby
Winskill
Ousby
893
CROSS FELL
Moor House
Milburn Forest
Skirwith
847
GREAT DUN FELL
Crowdundle Beck
Trout Beck
559
BLACK HILL
653
OUTBERRY PLAIN
Bollihope Burn
Edenhall
Blencarn
R Eamont
B6412
Cow Green Reservoir
601
CARRS HILL
Culgaith
Ettersgill
Acorn Bank Garden
Milburn
Newbiggin
Dufton Fell
Cauldron Snout (Waterfall)
River Tees
B6277
High Force (Waterfall)
Newbiggin
Countess Pillar
Oasis Whinfell
220
Park
Temple Sowerby
Kirkby Thore
Knock
Pennine Way
481
DUFTON PIKE
Maize Beck
Upper Teesdale
Holwick
Middleton-in-Teesdale
B6278
Wetheriggs Country Pottery
Cilburn Moss
River Eden
672
MURTON FELL
Long Marton
Dufton
Melkinthorpe
Cliburn
790
MICKLE FELL
618
Tees
Teesdale
B6282
Eggleston
Keisley
Brampton
A66
Mickleton
Romaldkirk
Morland
Bolton
746
HILTON FELL
Fish Loch
B6276
Grassholme Reservoir
71
Crackenthorpe
Newby
Kings Meaburn
River Lyvennet
Murton
Hunderthwaite
Colby
Lune Forest
Little Strickland
Appleby-in-Westmorland
Hilton
Selset Reservoir
Sleagill
B6542
Conservation Centre
562
IRON BAND
Hannah's Meadow
Lartington
Burrells
Reagill
Great Ormside
Balderhead Reservoir
Maulds Meaburn
Hoff Beck
Eden Valley Railway
Sandford
Deepdale Beck
M6
Warcop
A66
Shap
Drybeck
Castle
Brough
478
BELDOO HILL
Crosby Ravensworth
Great Musgrave
Keld Chapel
B6260
Little Musgrave
Brough Sowerby
Argill Beck
Bowes
Gilmonby
Great Asby
A66
39
316
Shap Summit
Kaber
R Eden
B6259
The Otter Trust
Soulby
A685
Stainmore Forest
Winton
Great Asby Scar
River Belah
Eller Beck
387
GRANGE SCAR
412
A6
Crosby Garret
Hartley
Ease Gill
B6261
Orton
Waitby
Kirkby Stephen
Arkle Beck
Tebay
Smardale Gill
617
BASTIFELL
B6260
B6261
R Lune
Nateby
547
TAILBRIDGE HILL
38
Tebay
Newbiggin-on-Lune
A685
633
WATER CRAG
Arkengarthdale
Ravenstonedale
672
ROGAN'S SEAT
583
GREAT PINSEAT
Langdale
Bowderdale Beck
Outhgill
A685
Low Borrowbridge
Birk Dale
B6270
710
HIGH SEAT
Keld
R Swale
487
CALVER
Healaugh
708
WILD BOAR FELL
Gunnerside
Feetham
Grayrigg
A683
B6259
Muker
Thwaite
Cautley Spout (Waterfall)
Cross Keys Temperance Inn
677
THE CALF
River Rawthey
713
GREAT SHUNNER FELL
Low Row
Swaledale
West Gill
East Gill
526
Buttertubs Pass
The Buttertubs
675
LOVELY SEAT
A685
565
WHITASIDE MOOR
M6
B6257
Firbank
WINDER
473
National Park Centre
River Ure
Hardraw Force (Waterfall)
Whity Gill
A684
37
Sedbergh
676
Garsdale Head
Hardraw
Askrigg
New Hutton
Killington Lake (southbound only)
Millthrop
A684
Garsdale
Sedbusk
National Park Centre
Bainbridge
Worton
Woodhall
Hawes
Wensleydale
Killington
586
Middleshaw
Gayle
Burtersett
Thornton Rust
A684
Aysgarth
556
Hutton
Countersett
63
671
Gawthrop
Dent
614
WETHER FELL
Semer Water
495
Thoralby
Newbiggin
609
CALF TOP
B6255
B6254
667
DODD FELL
686
CRAGHILL
Old Town
Barbon
Preston Patrick
YORKSHIRE DALES
284
534
BLEA MOOR
Nook
Lupton
643
736
WHERNSIDE
Langstrothdale Chase
B6160
Kearstwick
River Ribble
580
BROWN HAW
A65
Casterton
Cray
Ribblehead Viaduct
702
BUCKDEN PIKE
Hutton Roof
High Casterton
Kirkby Lonsdale
High Biggins
Low Biggins
Cowan Bridge
Chapel le Dale
Buckden
NATIONAL
Halton Gill
610
617
TOR MERE TOP
Leck
Whittington
Ireby
B6255
Masongill
Westhouse
White Scar Caves
636
Selside
723
INGLEBOROUGH HILL
Litton
Starbotton
River Wharfe
704
GREAT WHERNSIDE
Burrow
A683
Tunstall
Cantsfield
Thornton in Lonsdale
Ingleton
B6479
693
PEN-Y-GHENT
624
River Skirfare
142
Arkholme
A687
Wrayton
Burton in Lonsdale
Horton in Ribblesdale
Ingleborough
668
PARK
Arncliffe
Kettlewell
B6254
Melling
Pennine Way
Hawkswick
Gressingham
Wennington
Low Bentham
High Bentham
Newby
Wharfe
496
River Lune
Hornby
480
Clapham
63
538
58
Conistone
532
Austwick
Stainforth
Malham Tarn
Kilnsey Park & Trout Farm
Grass
0 1 2 3 4 miles
0 1 2 3 4 5 kilometres

Yorkshire Dales & Darlington
73
J
K
L
M
N
P
Q
R
Wolsingham
Thornley
Billy Row
Crook
Willington
Sunderland Bridge
Hett
Tudhoe
Quarrington Hill
Kelloe
Coxhoe
Trimdon Grange
Trimdon Colliery
Hutton Henry
Sheraton
Hart
River Wear
Fir Tree
Weardale Railway
Howden-le-Wear
Byers Green
Newfield
Spennymoor
Cornforth
Thrislington
Ferryhill
Trimdon
Elwick
Dalton Piercy
Hamsterley Forest
Toll
Witton le Wear
Hunwick
Middlestone
Kirk Merrington
Mainsforth
Bishop Middleham
Hardwick Hall
Fishburn
River Skerne
Summerhill
Hamsterley
Witton Park
Toronto
Auckland Castle
Escomb
Coundon
Leasingthorne
Sedgefield
Owton Manor
High Etherley
Toft Hill
Bishop Auckland
South Church
Eldon
Rushyford
Chilton
Bradbury
Woodland
Southside
St Helen Auckland
Tindale Crescent
Shildon
Greatham
High Lands
West Auckland
Mordon
Newton Bewley
Copley
Butterknowle
Gaunless
Evenwood
Bildershaw
Newton Aycliffe
Wynyard Woodland Park
Wolviston
Billingham
Cockfield
Stillington
Thorpe Thewles
Billingham Beck Valley
Langley Beck
Wackerfield
Bolam
Redworth
Heighington
Aycliffe
Whitton
Raby
Hilton
Great Stainton
Bishopton
Carlton
Roseworth
Norton
Staindrop
Brafferton
Little Stainton
Redmarshall
Ingleton
Killerby
Summerhouse
Stockton-on-Tees
Stainton
Cleatlam
Langton
Headlam
Denton
Walworth
Barmpton
Little Newsham
Gainford
Archdeacon Newton
Great Burdon
Sadberge
East Hartburn
Thornaby-on-Tees
Middlesbrough
Acklam
Nature's World
Startforth
Winston
Piercebridge
Carlbury
High Coniscliffe
Haughton le Skerne
Darlington
Elton
Longnewton
Egglestone Abbey
Whorlton
Rokeby Park
Ovington
Wycliffe
Caldwell
Eastbourne
Train Sculpture
Eaglescliffe
Ingleby Barwick
Stainton
Hemlington
Greta Bridge
Brignall
Hutton Magna
Eppleby
Manfield
Cleasby
Forcett
Middleton St George
Durham Tees Valley
Egglescliffe
Yarm
High Leven
Thornton
Maltby
Newby
Lane Head
West Layton
Aldbrough St John
Stapleton
Hurworth-on-Tees
Middleton One Row
Aislaby
Barningham
Newsham
East Layton
Croft-on-Tees
Low Dinsdale
Low Worsall
Hilton
Seamer
Neasham
Dalton
Ravensworth
Melsonby
Newton Morrell
Hurworth Place
Kirklevington
Stokesley
Barton
Eryholme
Girsby
Gayles
Dalton-on-Tees
Picton
Crathorne
Kirby Hill
Hartforth
Scotch Corner
Croft Circuit
Sockburn
Hutton Rudby
Rudby
River Leven
Whashton
Gilling West
Middleton Tyas
Hornby
Aske Hall
Moulton
North Cowton
Great Smeaton
Appleton Wiske
West Rounton
Potto
Richmond
Skeeby
East Cowton
Birkby
Welbury
East Rounton
Faceby
River Swale
Deighton
Swainby
Scorton
Ingleby Arncliffe
Marske
Hudswell
Easby
Brompton-on-Swale
Bolton-on-Swale
Whitwell
Fremington
Hipswell
Colburn
Catterick Bridge
Streetlam
Danby Wiske
East Harlsey
Cod Beck Reservoir
Marrick
Downholme
Ellerton
Mount Grace Priory
Catterick
Kiplin Hall
River Wiske
Ellerbeck
Osmotherley
Tunstall
Great Langton
Scotton
Kirkby Fleetham
Yafforth
Brompton
Foxton
Thimbleby
Black Hambleton
East Hauxwell
Hornby
Great Fencote
Thrintoft
Northallerton
Over Silton
Bellerby
Arrathorne
Hackforth
Little Fencote
Ainderby Steeple
Romanby
Nether Silton
Preston-under-Scar
Hunton
Langthorne
Scruton
Leyburn
Patrick Brompton
Little Crakehall
Morton-on-Swale
Warlaby
Thornton-le-Beans
Kepwick
Constable Burton
Newton-le-Willows
Swinithwaite
Harmby
Finghall
Crakehall
Leeming Bar
North Otterington
Wensley
Wensleydale Railway
Leeming
Cowesby
Spennithorne
Aiskew
Thornton-le-Moor
Borrowby
West Witton
Middleham
Cowling
Bedale
Gatenby
Thornton Steward
Rookwith
Londonderry
Knayton
Kirby Knowle
Agglethorpe
Coverham
Burrill
Exelby
South Otterington
Upsall
Jervaulx
River Ure
Thornton Watlass
Firby
Thornton-le-Street
Melmerby
Carlton
East Witton
Thirn
Thorp Perrow
Theakston
Maunby
Kirby Wiske
Boltby
Cover
Sowden Beck
Burneston
North Kilvington
West Scrafton
Snape
Carthorpe
Newsham
Felixkirk
Ellingstring
Pickhill
Birds of Prey Centre
South Kilvington
Thirlby
Sutton Bank
High Ellington
Well
Holme
Sandhutton
Thirsk
Sutton-under-Whitestonecliffe
Fearby
Theakston Brewery
Masham
Kirklington
Sinderby
Old Thirsk
Healey
Ainderby Quernhow
Nosterfield
Carlton Miniott
White Horse
Swinton
Thornborough
Sutton Howgrave
Howe
Sowerby
Bagby
Great Haw
Druid's Temple
Warthermaske
West Tanfield
Baldersby
Skipton-on-Swale
Thirkleby
Kilburn
Leighton Reservoir
Ilton
Marmion Tower
Middleton Quernhow
Catton
Roundhill Reservoir
Mickley
Wath
Norton Conyers
Baldersby St James
Little Hutton
Hutton Sessay
River Nidd
Grewelthorpe
North Stainley
Melmerby
Topcliffe
Dalton
Birdforth
Kirkby Malzeard
Lightwater Valley
Asenby
Rainton
Sessay
Middlesmoor
Nunwick
Stean
Lofthouse
Azerley
Thormanby
Laverton
Hutton Conyers
Galphay
Sharow
Dishforth
Cundall
Fawdington
Bouthwaite
Winksley
Studley Royal
Ripon
Copt Hewick
Bridge Hewick
Raskelf
Ramsgill
Low Grantley
Studley Roger
Marton-le-Moor
Norton-le-Clay
Brafferton
Gouthwaite Reservoir
High Grantley
Nidderdale
58
Risplith
Studley Royal Park
Littlethorpe
59
Kirby Hill
Helperby
Wath
Sawley
Fountains Abbey
Newby Hall
Langthorpe
Milby
Boroughbridge
Myton-on-Swale
Tholthorpe
A689
A688
A68
A6072
A167
A1(M)
A177
A179
A19
A689
A1185
A66
A67
A1150
A66(M)
A1(M)
A135
A1044
A6108
A6136
A684
A6055
A168
A61
A170
A172
A1032
A1130
B6282
B6279
B6274
B6275
B6444
B6280
B6278
B1280
B1278
B1274
B1275
B1263
B1264
B6271
B6270
B6287
B6268
B6285
B6267
B6265
B1448
B6443
319
399
544
1322

73
A
B
C
D
E
F
G
H
Wingate
Hesleden
Hutton Henry
Sheraton
Hart
Trimdon Grange
Trimdon Colliery
Trimdon
Elwick
Dalton Piercy
The Headland
Historic Quay
HARTLEPOOL
Hartlepool Bay
Fishburn
River Skerne
Summerhill
Owton Manor
Seaton Carew
Sedgefield
Greatham
Tees Bay
Newton Bewley
Billingham
Hartlepool Power Station Visitor Centre
Coatham Marsh
Redcar
Marske-by-the-Sea
Saltburn-by-the-Sea
Wynyard Woodland Park
Wolviston
Thorpe Thewles
Stillington
Billingham Beck Valley
River Tees
Whitton
Bishopton
Carlton
Roseworth
Norton
Kirkleatham
Old Hall
New Marske
Upleatham
Brotton
Skelton
Saltburn Smugglers
Hummersea Scar
Redmarshall
Grangetown
North Ormesby
Eston
Wilton
Dunsdale
Kilton
Loftus
Staithes
Heritage Centre
STOCKTON-ON-TEES
MIDDLESBROUGH
Normanby
Easington
Hinderwell
Sadberge
Elton
East Hartburn
Thornaby-on-Tees
Acklam
Nature's World
Ormesby
Ormesby Hall
Boosbeck
Margrove Park
Lingdale
Kilton Thorpe
Liverton
Runswick
Longnewton
Eaglescliffe
Marton
Guisborough
Stanghow
Woodhill
Ellerby
65
Ingleby Barwick
Stainton
Hemlington
Nunthorpe
Newton under Roseberry
Guisborough Forest
Hutton Lowcross
Cleveland Way
Moorsholm
Scaling
Gerrick
Mickleby
Durham Tees Valley
Yarm
Thornton
Maltby
Newby
Nunthorpe Village
Roseberry Topping
High Leven
West Barnby
Middleton One Row
Aislaby
Great Ayton
Captain Cook Monument
Commondale
Ugthorpe
Low Worsall
Hilton
Seamer
Little Ayton
Kirklevington
Stokesley
Kildale
Danby
The Moors Centre
Girsby
Picton
Crathorne
Easby
Battersby
Castleton
Ainthorpe
Lealholm
Egton
Hutton Rudby
Rudby
River Leven
Great Busby
Kirkby
Ingleby Greenhow
River Esk
The Green
Glaisdale
Hornby
Great Broughton
Westerdale
Egton Bridge
Appleton Wiske
West Rounton
Carlton-in-Cleveland
Potto
East Rounton
Welbury
Faceby
Urra
Urra Moor
NORTH YORK MOORS
Deighton
Swainby
Seave Green
Pike Hill
Goathland
Ingleby Arncliffe
East Harlsey
Chop Gate
Cod Beck Reservoir
Mount Grace Priory
Church Houses
NATIONAL PARK
Ellerbeck
Osmotherley
Bilsdale
Thorgill
Rosedale
Rosedale Abbey
NORTH YORK
CLEVELAND HILLS
Brompton
Foxton
Thimbleby
Low Mill
Black Hambleton
Fangdale Beck
Bransdale
Farndale
Stape
Newtondale Forest Drive
North Riding Forest Park
Northallerton
Over Silton
Nether Silton
River Rye
Warlaby
Thornton-le-Beans
Kepwick
Lastingham
Newton-on-Rawcliffe
Gillamoor
Hawnby
Hutton-le-Hole
Spaunton
Fadmoor
Appleton-le-Moors
Cropton
Thornton-le-Moor
Cowesby
The Hambleton Hills
Knayton
Kirby Knowle
Carlton
River Riccal
South Otterington
Upsall
Old Byland
Rievaulx Terrace & Temples
Kirkbymoorside
Pockley
Wrelton
Aislaby
Thornton-le-Street
Kirby Wiske
Boltby
Rievaulx
Nawton
Beadlam
Sinnington
Middleton
North Kilvington
Cold Kirby
Wombleton
Birds of Prey Centre
Newsham
Felixkirk
Thirlby
Sutton Bank
Rievaulx Abbey
Marton
South Kilvington
Sutton-under-Whitestonecliffe
Scawton
Helmsley
Pickering
Thirsk
Old Thirsk
Duncombe Park
Holme
Sandhutton
Spaunton
White Horse
Sproxton
Harome
Normanby
Ainderby Quernhow
Carlton Miniott
Sowerby
High Kilburn
Oldstead
Flamingo Land
Salton
Great Barugh
Bagby
Nunnington Hall
West Ness
Kirby Misperton
Skipton-on-Swale
Thirkleby
Kilburn
Wass
Oswaldkirk
Nunnington
East Ness
Brawby
Baldersby
Catton
Ampleforth
Shandy Hall
Butterwick
Baldersby St James
Little Hutton
Hutton Sessay
Carlton Husthwaite
Coxwold
Newburgh Priory
Gilling East
Stonegrave
Great Habton
Topcliffe
Dalton
Birdforth
Hovingham
Asenby
Rainton
Sessay
Husthwaite
Yearsley
Slingsby
Barton-le-Street
River Rye
Eden Camp
Thormanby
Oulston
Amotherby
Broughton
Dishforth
Cundall
Coulton
Scackleton
Appleton-le-Street
Swinton
Malton
Fawdington
Brandsby
Howardian Hills
Terrington
Coneysthorpe
Norton-le-Clay
Raskelf
Stearsby
Crayke
Skewsby
Dalby
Brafferton
Whenby
Ganthorpe
Castle Howard
Helperby
Easingwold
59
60
Welburn
Bulmer
Stillington
Farlington
Tholthorpe
Kirby Hill
Skelton
0 1 2 3 4 miles
0 1 2 3 4 5 kilometres
Town Plan: Middlesbrough p.12

Scarborough
North Bay
South Bay
Castle
Castle Hill
Coastguard Station
St Mary's
Friarage School
Lifeboat Station
Luna Park
Lighthouse
Town Hall
Olympia Scarborough
Grand Hotel
Rotunda Art Gallery
Brunswick
Stephen Joseph
SCARBOROUGH STATION
Yorkshire Coast College
Woodend Creative Workspace
Council Offices
Magistrates' Court
Police Sta
Balmoral Centre
YMCA
Fire Sta
Bowls Centre
WHITBY
FILEY
PICKERING, MALTON
Whitby
Sandsend
Ruswarp
Briggswath
Sleights
Sneaton
Ugglebarnby
High Hawsker
Stainsacre
Robin Hood's Bay
Fylingthorpe
Ravenscar
Staintondale
Cloughton
Burniston
Scalby
Hackness
Langdale End
Harwood Dale
Bickley
Broxa
Silpho
Suffield
Falsgrave
Osgodby
Eastfield
Crossgates
Cayton
Seamer
Irton
East Ayton
West Ayton
Hutton Buscel
Wykeham
Sawdon
Ebberston
Snainton
Ruston
Brompton-by-Sawdon
Allerston
Yedingham
Lebberston
Gristhorpe
Filey
Filey Brigg
Filey Bay
Folkton
Muston
Flixton
Staxton
Willerby
Sherburn
Ganton
Potter Brompton
Hunmanby
Fordon
Knapton
West Knapton
East Heslerton
West Heslerton
Wintringham
Thorpe Bassett
Foxholes
Wold Newton
Burton Fleming
Butterwick
Helperthorpe
Weaverthorpe
Thwing
Grindale
Reighton
Speeton
Buckton
Bempton
North Landing
Flamborough
FLAMBOROUGH HEAD
Selwicks Bay
Rudston
Boynton
Langtoft
Kirby Grindalythe
Duggleby
East Lutton
West Lutton
Bridlington
North Riding Forest Park
Dalby Forest
60
61

A
B
C
D
E
F
G
H
76
Woodland
Pinminnoch
Pinmore
Barr
Balligmorrie
Lendalfoot
A77
A714
Pinwherry
Muck Water
Bennane Head
Colmonell
B734
River Stinchar
B7044
Duisk River
Heronsford
Water of Tig
Ballantrae
Barrhill
Feoch Burn
Lochton
Belfast
Larne
(Mar-Oct)
Larne
Currarie Port
437 BENERAIRD
321 CARLOCK HILL
387 ALTIMEG HILL
Glen App
Milleur Point
Corsewall Point
305 BENBRAKE HILL
Loch Maberry
Southern Upland Way
Lady Bay
Barnhills
Portencalzie
Glenwhilly
Laggangairn Standing Stones
Main Water of Luce
Cross Water of Luce
Black Burn
Kirkcolm
B738
Cairnryan
Penwhirn Reservoir
271 ARTFIELD FELL
Loch Connell
Ervie
A718
B798
Low Barbeth
Braid Fell
Beoch Burn
New Luce
Low Salchrie
Knocknain
Leswalt
B7043
Loch Ryan
Innermessan
Castle of St John
A751
Black Loch
Castle Kennedy
White Loch
Chlenry
164 CRAIG FELL
Balgracie
Stranraer
Aird
Auchnotteroch
Castle Kennedy
A75
Glenluce Abbey
Glenluce
Dernaglar
Portslogan
Broadsea Bay
Glenwhan
Dunragit
Whitecrook
Lochans
181 CAIRN PAT
Kildrochet House
Piltanton Burn
B7084
Black Head
B7077
Ringdoo Point
A747
Milton
Castle Loch
Portpatrick
A716
Stairhaven
Stoneykirk
North Milmain
Auchenmalg
Mochrum Loch
B7042
Mull of Sinniness
Auchenmalg Bay
Sandhead
Cairngarroch
Kirkmadrine Stones
Money Head
THE RHINNS OF GALLOWAY
High Ardwell
Ardwell
Ardwell Bay
Ardwell House
Chapel Rossan
Drumbreddon
Balgowan
LUCE BAY
Logan
Port Logan Bay
Port Logan
B7065
Garrochtrie
Kilstay
Clanyard Bay
Laggantalluch Head
Kirkmaiden
Drummore
Barncorkrie
High Drummore
Killiness Point
Drumnaglaur
Maryport
B7041
Cardryne
Cardrain
West Cairngaan
MULL OF GALLOWAY
0 1 2 3 4 miles
0 1 2 3 4 5 kilometres

J
K
L
M
N
P
Q
R
76
77
78
70
Carsphairn
Knowehead
Glenhoul
Blawquhairn
Knocksheen
Garroch
St John's Town of Dalry
Bogue
Balmaclellan
New Galloway
Craigneston
Glencrosh
WETHER HILL
CORNHARROW HILL
Southern Upland Way
Loch Howie
Loch Urr
Corsock
LARGLEAR HILL
Ironmacannie
Knockvennie Smithy
Airds of Kells
Mossdale
Loch Ken
Crossmichael
Walbutt
Loch Roan
Clarebrand
Glenlochar
Townhead of Greenlaw
Threave Castle
Laurieston
Longwood
Bridge of Dee
Threave Garden
Rhonehouse
Ringford
Craigley
Airieland
Tongland
BENGAIRN
Little Sypland
Whinnie Liggate
Kirkcudbright
Culnaightrie
Mutehill
Dundrennan
Dundrennan Abbey
Orroland
Netherlaw
Abbey Head
Balmae
Little Ross
Ross
Kirkcudbright Bay
Balmangan
Borgue
Ringdoo Point
Borness
Kirkandrews
Gledpark
Kirkchrist
MacLellan's Castle
Twynholm
Compstonend
Margrie
Lennox Plunton
Girthon
Littleton
Gatehouse of Fleet
Anworth
Cardoness Castle
Fleet Valley
Skyre Burn
CAIRNHARROW
Kirkmabreck
Carsluith
Carsluith Castle
Cairnholy Chambered Cairns
Ravenshall Point
Mossyard
Fleet Bay
Islands of Fleet
Wigtown Bay
Creetown
Gem Rock
Upper Ruscoe
BENGRAY
Loch Whinyeon
WHITE TOP OF CULREACH
Big Water of Fleet
Little Water of Fleet
Woodhall Loch
Loch Skerrow
AUCHENCLOY HILL
CAIRN EDWARD
FELL OF FLEET
ROUND FELL
Loch Grannoch
Loch Fleet
Black Water of Dee
Clatteringshaws Loch
Clatteringshaws Forest & Wildlife Centre
Bruce's Stone
BENNAN
CAIRNSMORE OF FLEET
Galloway Deer Range
MILLFORE
LAMACHAN HILL
LARG HILL
GARLICK HILL
Loch Dee
Loch Trool
Bruce Memorial
Glen Trool Lodge
Glentrool Village
Glen Trool
Bargrennan
Creebank
Loch Ochiltree
Knowe
Carseriggan
Challoch
G A L L O W A Y
Penkill Burn
Minnigaff
Newton Stewart
Creebridge
Kirroughtree
Palnure
Shennanton
Kirkcowan
Baltersan
Causeway End
R. Bladnoch
Clugston
Torhouse Stone Circle
THE MACHARS
Wigtown
Bladnoch
Kirwaugh
Braehead
Kirkinner
Orchardton Bay
Malzie
Barrachan
Whauphill
Little Airies
Culscadden
Elrig
Druchtag Motte
Sorbie
Mochrum
Drumtrodden Cup & Ring
Drumtrodden Standing Stones
Drummoddie
Pouton
Garlieston
Cruggleton Bay
Broughton Mains
Big Balcraig
'Wren's Egg' Standing Stones
Monreith
Barsalloch Fort
Barsalloch Point
Point of Leg
Priory
Whithorn Story
Rispain Camp
Whithorn
Portyerrock
St Ninian's Cave
Kidsdale
Isle of Whithorn
St Ninian's Chapel (ruin)
Cutcloy
BURROW HEAD
Galloway Forest Park
Water of Minnoch
Loch Moan
GARWALL HILL
POLMADDIE HILL
SHALLOCH ON MINNOCH
Loch Recar
Loch Macaterick
MEAUL
Garryhorn Burn
Polmaddy Burn
CORSERINE
KIRRIEREOCH HILL
MERRICK
Loch Enoch
Loch Neldricken
Silver Flowe
MILFIRE
Loch Dungeon
Water of Deugh
Black Water
A713
A702
A712
A762
A75
A714
A746
A747
A711
A755
B7000
B7075
B729
B735
B733
B7052
B7005
B7085
B7004
B7021
B7063
B796
B727
B795
B794

A
B
C
D
E
F
G
H
78
Roucan
240
CARTHAT HILL
281
LARGLEAR HILL
Ironmacannie
Shawhead
Lincluden
Maxwell Town
Collin
Cargenbridge
Dumfries
Greenlea
Racks
Lochfoot
Eastlands
A75
Islesteps
Kingholm Quay
Crocketford
Auchenreoch Loch
Lochrutton Loch
Mouswald
Knockvennie Smithy
Milton Loch
Lochober Loch
Kirkconnell Flow
Kelton
Conheath
Mossdale
Airds of Kells
Milton
Kirkpatrick Durham
Springholm
Drumcoltran Tower
Beeswing
Glencaple
Bankend
Clarencefield
Loch Ken
Loch Roan
Walbutt
Old Bridge of Urr
Kirkconnell
Crossmichael
Kirkgunzeon
334
LOTUS HILL
Kinharvie
Nith Estuary
Woodhall Loch
Hardgate
Sweetheart Abbey
Corn Mill
New Abbey
Shearington
Caerlaverock Castle
Bowhouse
Ingleston
Blackshaw
Wildlife & Wetlands Trust Centre
Haugh of Urr
Redcastle
Clarebrand
Laurieston
Glenlochar
Townhead of Greenlaw
Hillowton
Urr Water
Glaisters Burn
Glensone Burn
Loch Kindar
430
CUIL HILL
Threave Castle
Castle Douglas
Edingham
569
CRIFFELL
Longwood
Carlingwark Loch
Little Knox
Dalbeattie
Carse Bay
Threave Garden
Bridge of Dee
Rhonehouse
Gelston
Kirkbean
Carsethorn
Craigley
Barlochan
Palnackie
Caulkerbush
Borron Point
Arbigland
Ringford
Airieland
Barnbarroch
Fairgirth
Mainsriddle
of Fleet
River Dee
343
SCREEL HILL
Orchardton Tower
Kippford or Scaur
Mote of Mark
Drumburn
Sandyhills
Loaningfoot
Gill Foot Bay
Southerness
390
BENGAIRN
Tongland
Colvend
East Stewartry Coast
Rockcliffe
Portling
Southerness Point
Twynholm
Compstonend
Little Sypland
Castlehill Point
69
Whinnie Liggate
Kirkchrist
MacLellan's Castle
Kirkcudbright
Auchencairn
Culnaightrie
Auchencairn Bay
Heston Island
Balcary
Balcary Point
SOLWAY FIRTH
Beckfoot
Gledpark
Borgue
Mutehill
Dundrennan
Rascarrel
Holme St Cuthbert
Orroland
Dundrennan Abbey
Kirkcudbright Bay
Dubmill Point
Balmangan
Ross
Balmae
Netherlaw
Abbey Head
Little Ross
Allonby
Allonby Bay
Allerby
Crosscanonby
Crosby
Fort
River Ellen
Maryport
Dearham
Flimby
Broughton Moor
Standingstone
Great Broughton
Camerton
Seaton
Great Clifton
Stainburn
Little Clifton
Eaglesfield
Greysouthen
Workington
Mossbay
Westfield
Moss Bay
Salterbeck
Deanscales
Dean
Harrington
Branthwaite
Ullock
Distington
Common End
Gilgarran
Lowca
Howgate
Parton
Low Moresby
Asby
Arlecdon
Rowrah
Kirkland
Whitehaven
Hensingham
Frizington
High Leys
Saltom Bay
Mirehouse
Cleator Moor
Ennerdale Bridge
Sandwith
River Ehen
St Bees Head
St Bees Head Heritage Coast
Rottington
Bigrigg
Cleator
River Calder
St Bees
Egremont
533
62
Haile
Nethertown
Beckermet
0 1 2 3 4 miles
0 1 2 3 4 5 kilometres

79
Ecclefechan
Annan
Gretna Green
Gretna
Longtown
Brampton
Carlisle
Wetheral
Wigton
Dalston
Caldbeck
Penrith
Cockermouth
Keswick
Bassenthwaite
Borrowdale
Buttermere
Glenridding
Patterdale
Shap
Ullswater
Haweswater
Lake District
Moricambe Bay
Bowness-on-Solway
Skiddaw
Helvellyn
Saddleback
Blencathra
72
64
62
63
Town Plan: Carlisle p.1

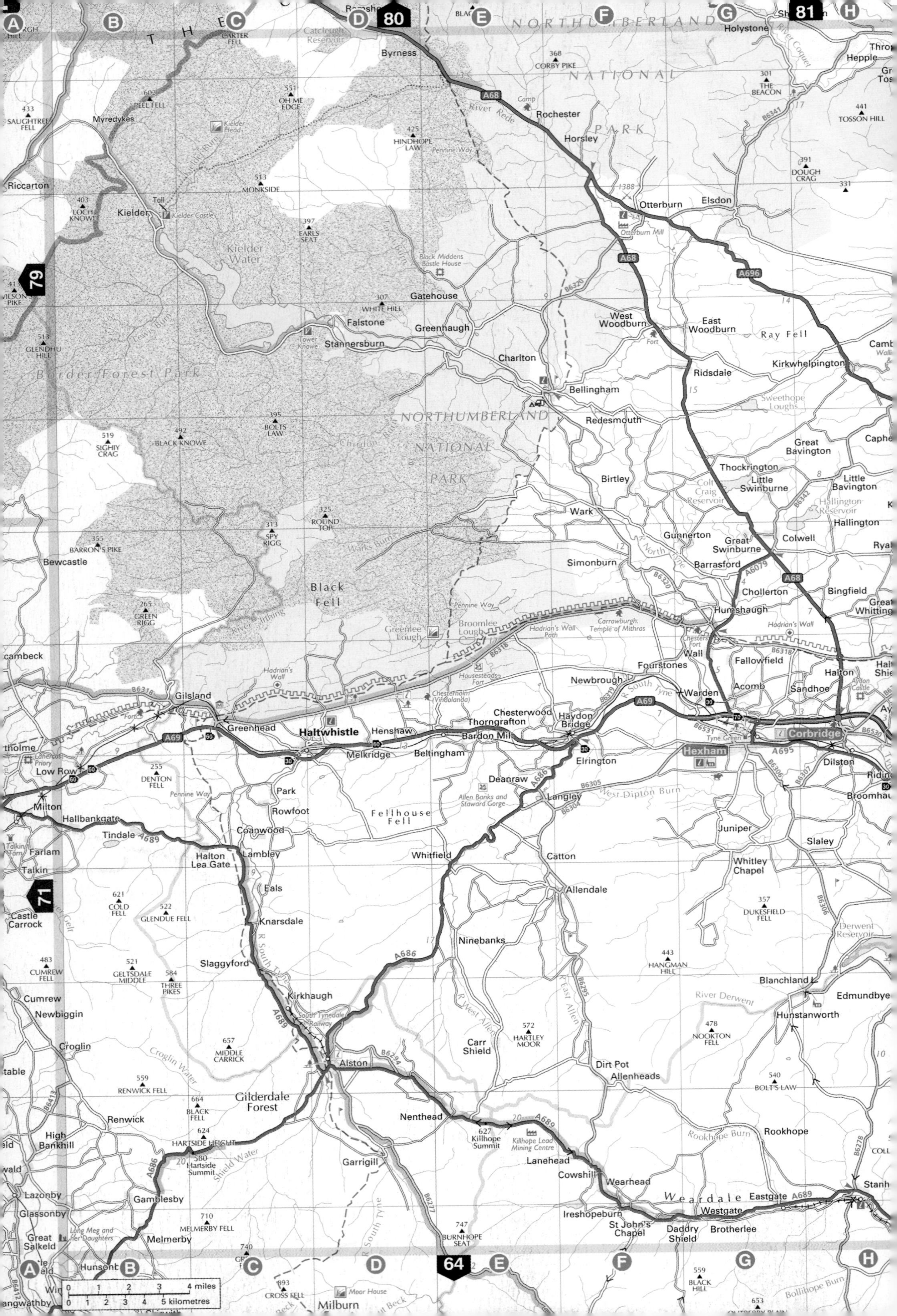

A
B
C
D
80
E
F
G
81
H
NORTHUMBERLAND
NATIONAL
PARK
Holystone
River Coquet
Hepple
Catcleugh Reservoir
CARTER FELL
Byrness
368 CORBY PIKE
301 THE BEACON
433 SAUGHTREE FELL
603 PEEL FELL
551 OH ME EDGE
Myredykes
Kielder Head
A68
River Rede
Camp
Rochester
441 TOSSON HILL
425 HINDHOPE LAW
Pennine Way
Horsley
B6341
391 DOUGH CRAG
Riccarton
513 MONKSIDE
331
403 LOCH KNOWE
Kielder
Toll
Kielder Castle
Otterburn
Elsdon
Otterburn Mill
397 EARLS SEAT
Kielder Water
Black Middens Bastle House
A696
79
WILSON PIKE
307 WHITE HILL
Gatehouse
B6320
513 GLENDHU HILL
Falstone
Greenhaugh
West Woodburn
East Woodburn
Ray Fell
Tower Knowe
Stannersburn
Fort
Charlton
Kirkwhelpington
Border Forest Park
Bellingham
Ridsdale
Sweethope Loughs
395 BOLTS LAW
519 SIGHTY CRAG
492 BLACK KNOWE
NORTHUMBERLAND
NATIONAL
PARK
Redesmouth
Great Bavington
Thockrington
Birtley
Colt Crag Reservoir
Little Swinburne
Little Bavington
Hallington Reservoir
B6342
325 ROUND TOP
Wark
Hallington
313 SPY RIGG
Warks Burn
Gunnerton
Great Swinburne
Colwell
355 BARRON'S PIKE
Bewcastle
R North Tyne
Simonburn
Barrasford
A6079
Black Fell
Chollerton
Bingfield
Pennine Way
Humshaugh
265 GREEN RIGG
River Irthing
Carrawburgh: Temple of Mithras
Hadrian's Wall
Greenlee Lough
Broomlee Lough
Hadrian's Wall Path
Chesters Fort
Wall
B6318
Fallowfield
Hadrian's Wall
Housesteads Fort
Fourstones
Halton
Newbrough
Acomb
Sandhoe
B6318
Gilsland
Chesterholm (Vindolanda)
R South Tyne
Warden
Fort
Chesterwood
Haydon Bridge
A69
Greenhead
Haltwhistle
Henshaw
Thorngrafton
B6531
Tyne Green
Corbridge
A69
Bardon Mill
Hexham
Lanercost Priory
Melkridge
Beltingham
Elrington
A695
Dilston
Low Row
255 DENTON FELL
Deanraw
B6306
B6307
Milton
Pennine Way
Park
A686
Langley
B6305
West Dipton Burn
Broomhaugh
Hallbankgate
Rowfoot
Allen Banks and Staward Gorge
B6304
Tindale
A689
Coanwood
Fellhouse Fell
Juniper
Farlam
Halton Lea Gate
Lambley
Whitfield
Catton
Slaley
Talkin
Whitley Chapel
71
Eals
Allendale
621 COLD FELL
522 GLENDUE FELL
357 DUKESFIELD FELL
Castle Carrock
Knarsdale
B6306
Derwent Reservoir
Ninebanks
A686
483 CUMREW FELL
521 GELTSDALE MIDDLE
584 THREE PIKES
Slaggyford
443 HANGMAN HILL
Blanchland
Cumrew
Kirkhaugh
R East Allen
B6295
River Derwent
Edmundbyers
Newbiggin
R West Allen
Hunstanworth
South Tynedale Railway
A689
478 NOOKTON FELL
657 MIDDLE CARRICK
572 HARTLEY MOOR
Croglin
Croglin Water
Carr Shield
Alston
B6294
Dirt Pot
Allenheads
559 RENWICK FELL
540 BOLT'S LAW
B6413
664 BLACK FELL
Gilderdale Forest
Renwick
Nenthead
627 Killhope Summit
A689
Killhope Lead Mining Centre
Rookhope Burn
Rookhope
High Bankhill
624 HARTSIDE HEIGHT
Garrigill
580 Hartside Summit
Shield Water
Lanehead
B6278
A686
Cowshill
Wearhead
Lazonby
Gamblesby
Weardale
Eastgate
A689
Stanhope
Glassonby
B6277
Ireshopeburn
Westgate
710 MELMERBY FELL
747 BURNHOPE SEAT
Long Meg and her Daughters
St John's Chapel
Daddry Shield
Brotherlee
Great Salkeld
Melmerby
R South Tyne
740
Hunsonby
64
559 BLACK HILL
893 CROSS FELL
Moor House
Milburn
Bollihope Burn
653
0 1 2 3 4 miles
0 1 2 3 4 5 kilometres

Northumberland & Tyneside
81
65
66
Town Plans: Newcastle upon Tyne p.130, Sunderland p.
Rothbury
Cragside House
Swarland
Felton
Gloster Hill
Acklington
Togston
Coquet Island
High Hauxley
Broomhill
Whitton
Longframlington
East Thirston
West Thirston
Pauperhaugh
South Broomhill
Red Row
Eshott
Brinkburn Priory
Druridge Bay
Stobswood
Widdrington
North Northumberland Heritage Coast
Causey Park Bridge
Longhorsley
Widdrington Station
Cresswell
Tritlington
Ulgham
Ellington
Lynemouth
Netherwitton
Stanton
Hebron
Longhirst
Woodhorn
Beacon Point
Longwitton
River Font
Hart Burn
Hartburn
Pegswood
Ashington
Bothal
Wansbeck Riverside
Newbiggin-by-the-Sea
Mitford
Morpeth
Hepscott
Guide Post
Stakeford
Middleton
Wansbeck
Meldon
Edington
Choppington
Bedlington
Bolam Lake
Whalton
Stannington Station
Cowpen
Blyth
Newsham
Plessey Woods
Belsay
Belsay Hall, Castle & Gardens
Ogle
Stannington
New Hartley
Seaton Sluice
River Blyth
Cramlington
Milbourne
Berwick Hill
Seaton
Seaton Delaval
St Mary's Lighthouse
Big Waters
Heugh
Ponteland
Dinnington
Brunswick Village
Dudley
Stamfordham
Dalton
Darras Hall
Wide Open
Earsdon
Monkseaton
Whitley Bay
Newcastle
Hazlerigg
Killingworth
Shiremoor
Cullercoats
River Pont
Black Callerton
Forest Hall
Tynemouth
Harlow Hill
Hadrian's Wall Path
Fawdon
Rising Sun
Tynemouth Priory & Castle
Rudchester
Gosforth
Longbenton
North Shields
IJmuiden
Throckley
Westerhope
South Gosforth
Willington Quay
South Shields
Horsley
Heddon-on-the-Wall
Kenton
Jesmond
Wallsend
Int. Ferry Terminal
George Stephenson's Birthplace
Newburn
Newcastle upon Tyne
Heaton
Jarrow
Tyne Tunnel
Westoe
Ovingham
Wylam
Claravale
Ryton
Walker
Harton
Marsden Bay
Crawcrook
Scotswood
Elswick
Byker
Hebburn
Marsden
Souter Lighthouse
Eltringham
Prudhoe
Blaydon
Metro Centre
Dunston
Felling
Monkton
Cleadon
Souter Point
Mickley Square
Greenside
Winlaton
Derwent Walk
West Boldon
Whitburn
Prestclose Wood
Gateshead
Wardley
High Mickley
Coalburns
Barlow
Whickham
East Boldon
Whitburn Bay
Painshawfield
Hedley on the Hill
High Spen
Team Valley
Low Fell
New Ridley
Highfield
Sunniside
Wrekenton
Seaburn
Fulwell
Southwick
Roker
Chopwell
Gibside
Bowes Railway & Museum
Hylton
Rowland's Gill
Blackhall Mill
Derwentcote Steel Furnace
Tanfield Railway
Lamesley
Springwell
Usworth
Wildfowl & Wetlands Trust
Castletown
Monkwearmouth
Hamsterley
Burnopfield
Angel of the North
Birtley
South Hylton
Sunderland
Newlands
Hobson
Causey Arch
Tanfield
Kibblesworth
Washington
Pennywell
Ebchester
Tantobie
Open Air
Hendon
Medomsley
Dipton
Tanfield Lea
Beamish
Ouston
Fatfield
Penshaw Monument
Penshaw
High Newport
Grangetown
Shotley Bridge
Stanley
West Pelton
Pelton
Herrington
New Silksworth
Tunstall
Ryhope
Durham Heritage Coast
Benfieldside
Bridgehill
Blackhill
Consett
Leadgate
Annfield Plain
South Moor
Grange Villa
River Wear
Shiney Row
Iveston
Templetown
Delves
Craghead
Chester-le-Street
Bournmoor
Houghton-le-Spring
Castleside
Holmside
Waldridge
Waldridge Fell
Chester Moor
Great Lumley
Rowley
Edmondsley
Nettlesworth
Hetton-le-Hole
Seaham
Burnhope
Plawsworth
West Rainton
East Rainton
Murton
Parkside
Dalton-le-Dale
Lanchester
Sacriston
Kimblesworth
Finchale Priory
Witton Gilbert
Dalton Park
South Hetton
River Browney
Diggerland
Pity Me
Low Moorsley
Hawthorn
Langley Park
Framwellgate Moor
Pittington
Easington Lane
Easington Colliery
Cornsay
Esh
Satley
Cornsay Colliery
Quebec
Bearpark
Crook Hall
Carrville
Hallgarth
Easington
Gilesgate Moor
Littletown
Haswell
Little Thorpe
Esh Winning
Ushaw Moor
Haswell Plough
Sherburn
Shotton Colliery
Durham
Hedleyhope Fell
New Brancepeth
Broompark
Sherburn Hill
Ludworth
Peterlee
Brandon
Shincliffe
Shadforth
Horden
Tow Law
East Hedleyhope
Thornley
Shotton
Blackhall Colliery
Meadowfield
Cassop Colliery
Wheatley Hill
Castle Eden
Blackhall Rocks
Waskerley Beck
Sunniside
Stanley Crook
Bowburn
Billy Row
Brancepeth
Sunderland Bridge
Quarrington Hill
Hesleden
Oakenshaw
Croxdale
Wingate
Wolsingham
Thornley
Hett
Kelloe
Crook
Willington
Tudhoe
Coxhoe
Trimdon Grange
Hutton Henry
Fir Tree
Byers Green
Weardale Railway
Howden-le-Wear
Port of Tyne
Tynemouth
Meadow Well
Percy Main
Howdon Road
Wet'n'Wild Water Park
Royal Quays Outlet Shopping Centre
Premier Inn
Royal Quays Marina
East Howdon
Check-in
International Passenger Terminal
Newcastle
The North
Tyne View
River Tyne
Priory Road
Jarrow
Sunderland
500 m

A
B
C
D
E
F
G
H
Machir Bay
Kilchiaran Bay
Loch Indaal
Bridgend
Bowmore
RHINNS OF ISLAY
Port Charlotte
231
BEINN TART A'MHILL
Lossit Bay
Nereabolls
A847
Rudha na Faing
Portnahaven
Port Wemyss
Orsay
RHINNS POINT
River Laggan
Duich R.
A846
B8016
82
Laggan Bay
Glenegedale
Islay
Rudha Mòr
Kintra
165
MAOL BUIDHE
THE OA
Lower Killeyan
Risabus
Kinnabus
American Monument
Loch Kinnabus
MULL OF OA
Rudha nan Leacan
Kilnaughton Bay
Port Ellen
Laphroaig
Texa
Lagavulin
Ardbeg
Rudha na Gainmhich
Eilean a' Chuirn
Kildalton Cross
Ardmore Point
Kintour
Claggain Bay
Ardtalla
Rudha Liath
454
BEINN URARAIDH
Loch Uraraidh
346
BEINN SHOLUM
490
BEINN BHEIGEIR
429
SGORR NAM FAOILEANN
471
Kilennan Burn
McArthur's Head
Rudha na Tràille
Port Askaig - Kennacraig
Port Ellen - Kennacraig
Earada
0 1 2 3 4 miles
0 1 2 3 4 5 kilometres

Kennacraig
Whitehouse
Kilchamaig
Loch Stornoway
Ardpatrick
West Loch Tarbert
Portachoillan
Clachan
Ronachan Point
Ronachan
Skipness
Skipness Point
Claonaig
83
Sound of Bute
84
Cock of Arran
Lochranza
Catacol
Kinerarach
Tarbert
GIGHA
Ardminish
Achamore
Rhunahaorine Point
Rhunahaorine
Tayinloan
Sound of Gigha
Cara
Loch Ciaran
Loch Garasdale
247 CRUACH MHIC GOUGAIN
264 CNOC-AN T-SAMHLAIDH
Crossaig
Cour Bay
Cour
Grogport
Barmollack
354 CRUACH NAN GABHAR
KILBRANNAN SOUND
Glen Catacol
Glen Chalmadale
A841
Sannox
North Arran
834 CAISTEAL ABHAIL
Loch Tanna
Corrie
Penrioch
Pirnmill
715 BEINN BHARRAIN
Glen Iorsa
874 GOATFELL
Whitefarland
Imachar
Balliekine
792 BEINN NUIS
Glen Rosa
Merkland Point
Brodick Castle, Garden & Country Club
Brodick Bay
76
Iorsa Water
ARRAN
Brodick
Strathwhillan
Corriegills
A83
Muasdale
Glenacardoch Point
Belloch
Barr Water
Glenbarr
MacAlister Clan
Carradale
Bridgend
Dippen
Carradale House
Carradale Point
Carradale Bay
Carradale Water
B842
B879
454 BEINN AN TUIRC
319
Cleongart
408 BORD MOR
Auchagallon Stone Circle
Machrie
Machrie Bay
Tormore
Machrie Moor Stone Circles
512 A'CHRUACH
B880
Moss Farm Road Stone Circle
Balmichael
503 BEINN BHREAC
Clauchland
Lamlash
Margnaheglish
Lamlash Bay
Holy Isla
Cordon
Bellochantuy Bay
Bellochantuy
Saddell
Saddell Bay
396 SGREADAN HILL
Ugadale
Tangy Loch
Torbeg
Shiskine
Blackwaterfoot
Drumadoon Bay
Kilpatrick
Kilpatrick Dun
Brown Head
Glen Scorrodale
Carn Ban
Auchencairn
Kingscross
Knockenkelly
Whiting Bay
Glen Ashdale
Glen Lussa
Peninver
Ardnacross Bay
Kilkenzie
Kilmichael
Corriecravie
Sliddery
Kilmory Water
Torr a' Chaisteal Fort
Largymore
Largybeg
Dippen Head
Dippen
Machrihanish Bay
Campbeltown
Machrihanish
Kilmory
Lagg
Torrylin Cairn
Bennan
Kildonan
Campbeltown Loch
Island Davarr
Drumlemble
B843
Bennan Head
Pladda
Kilkerran
Kildalloig
352 BEINN GHUILEAN
Achinhoan
385 THE STATE
Ru Stafnish
Dalsmeran
Conie Glen
Glen Kerran
Glen Breakerie
Strone Glen
Cattadale
Polliwilline Bay
Southend
Macharioch
Carskey
Dunaverty
Carskey Bay
Sanda Sound
Sheep Island
Borgadalemore Point
Sanda Island
76
340 Ailsa Craig
Inchmarnock
Midpark
Ballanlay
Meikle Kilmory
Ardscalpsie Bay
Stravanan Bay

84
75
68
69
FIRTH OF CLYDE
Irvine Bay
Ayr Bay
Bute
Kingarth
Kilchattan
Millport
Fairlie
Kilbirnie
Beith
Neilston
Uplawmoor
Lugton
Barrmill
Glengarnock
Drakemyre
Dalry
Burnhouse
Dunlop
Stewarton
Kingsford
West Kilbride
Seamill
Portencross
Farland Head
Little Cumbrae Island
Garroch Head
Kilwinning
Ardrossan
Saltcoats
Stevenston
Irvine
Dreghorn
Kilmaurs
Fenwick
KILMARNOCK
Hurlford
Crosshouse
Springside
Dundonald
Symington
Troon
Barassie
Monkton
Prestwick
New Prestwick
Tarbolton
Mauchline
Mossblown
St Quivox
Annbank
Ayr
Wallacetown
Whitletts
Alloway
Doonfoot
Heads of Ayr
Fisherton
Dunure
Culroy
Minishant
Dalrymple
Hollybush
Coylton
Drongan
Patna
Waterside
Rankinston
Maybole
Kirkmichael
Crosshill
Straiton
Kirkoswald
Maidens
Turnberry
Dipple
Kilgrammie
Dailly
Old Dailly
Girvan
Pinmore
Barr
Lendalfoot
Pinwherry
Ballantrae
Lamlash
Holy Island
Kildonan
Ailsa Craig
Whiting Bay
Cunninghame
Carrick
0 1 2 3 4 miles
0 1 2 3 4 5 kilometres

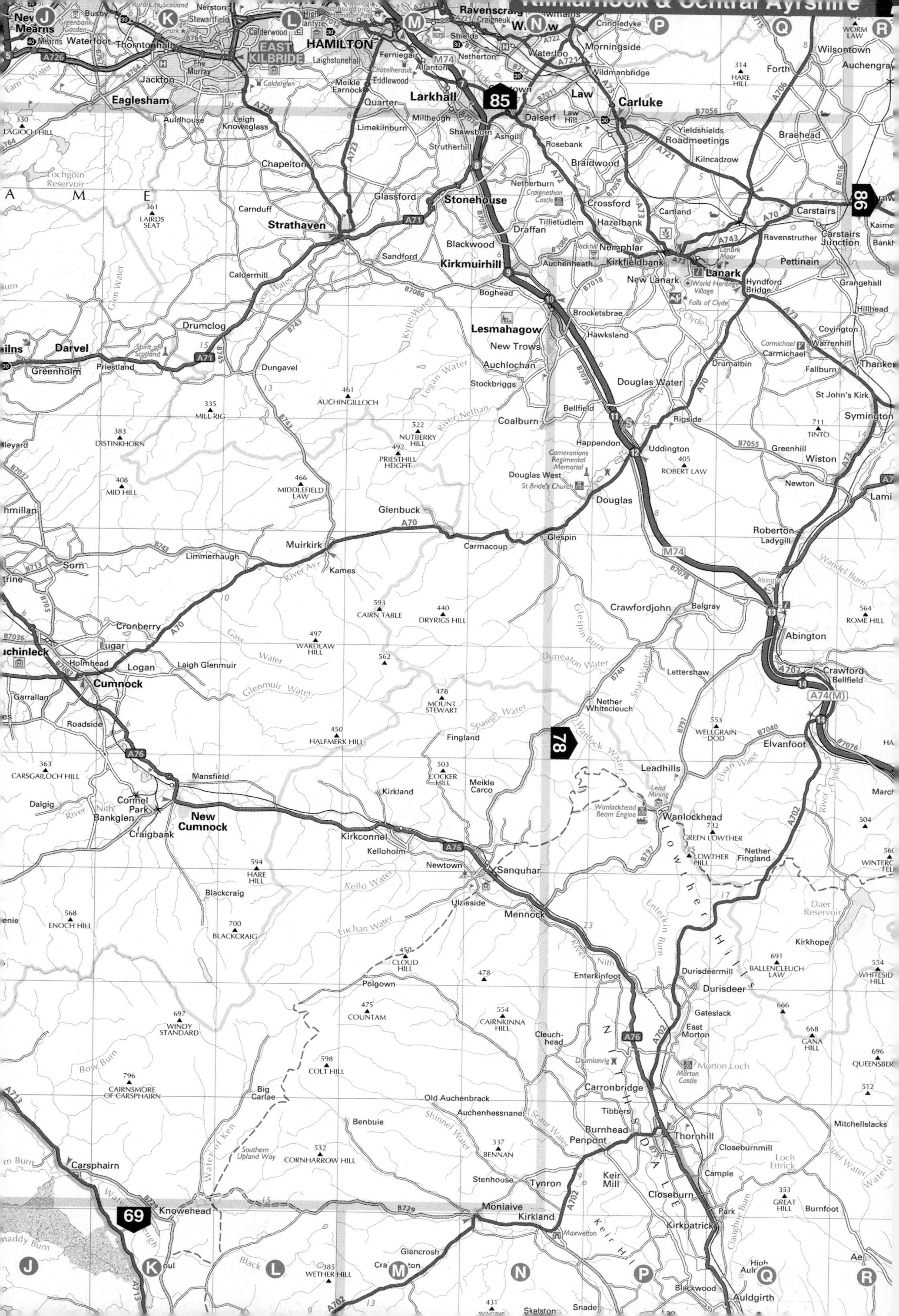

Kilmarnock & Central Ayrshire
J
K
L
M
N
P
Q
R
Newton Mearns
Busby
Nerston
Stewartfield
Ravenscraig
Newmains
Crindledyke
WORM LAW
Waterfoot
Thorntonhall
Calderwood
EAST KILBRIDE
HAMILTON
High Blantyre
Craigneuk
Wishaw
Morningside
Wilsontown
Auchengray
A726
The Murray
Laighstonehall
Shields
Netherton
Waterloo
Jackton
Calderglen
Ferniegair
M74
Wildmanbridge
314 HARE HILL
Forth
Meikle Earnock
Allanton
Earn Water
Eddlewood
Chatelherault
Larkhall
85
Law
Carluke
Eaglesham
Quarter
Dalserf
Law Hill
B7056
330 LAGIOCH HILL
Auldhouse
Leigh Knoweglass
Limekilnburn
Millheugh
Shawsburn
Ashgill
Yieldshields
Braehead
Roadmeetings
A726
Strutherhill
Rosebank
A721
Kilncadzow
Chapelton
Braidwood
Lochgoin Reservoir
A723
Netherburn
Craignethan Castle
A72
A M E
Glassford
Stonehouse
Crossford
Cartland
Carstairs
96
361 LAIRDS SEAT
Carnduff
Tillietudlem
A73
Hazelbank
Strathaven
A71
Draffan
Ravenstruther
Carstairs Junction
Kaimes
Bankhead
Blackwood
Nemphlar
A743
Blackhill
Lanark Moor
Sandford
Kirkmuirhill
Auchenheath
Kirkfieldbank
Pettinain
Caldermill
Lanark
Avon Water
New Lanark
World Heritage Village
Hyndford Bridge
Grangehall
Glen Water
Boghead
B7018
B7086
Falls of Clyde
Kype Water
Brocketsbrae
Hillhead
Lesmahagow
Covington
Drumclog
R Clyde
Darvel
Hawksland
A73
Carmichael
Warrenhill
B743
New Trows
Spirit of Scotland
A71
Logan Water
Auchlochan
Drumalbin
Fallburn
Thankerton
Greenholm
Priestland
Dungavel
B745
Stockbriggs
Douglas Water
A70
St John's Kirk
461 AUCHINGILLOCH
B7078
335 MILL RIG
B743
522 NUTBERRY HILL
River Nethan
Coalburn
Bellfield
Rigside
711 TINTO
Symington
383 DISTINKHORN
492 PRIESTHILL HEIGHT
Happendon
Uddington
B7055
Greenhill
Cameronians Regimental Memorial
405 ROBERT LAW
Wiston
B7037
408 MID HILL
466 MIDDLEFIELD LAW
Douglas West
St Bride's Church
Newton
Douglas
Glenbuck
A70
Robertonn
Ladygill
Muirkirk
Carmacoup
Glespin
M74
B743
Limmerhaugh
Kames
B7078
Sorn
B713
River Ayr
Abington
Wandel Burn
593 CAIRN TABLE
440 DRYRIGS HILL
Crawfordjohn
Balgray
564 ROME HILL
B705
Cronberry
A70
Glespin Burn
497 WARDLAW HILL
Abington
Gass Water
Lugar
Auchinleck
Holmhead
Logan
Laigh Glenmuir
562
Duneaton Water
Lettershaw
A702
Crawford
Bellfield
B7083
Cumnock
Glenmuir Water
Snar Water
B740
Garrallan
478 MOUNT STEWART
Nether Whitecleuch
A74(M)
Roadside
Spango Water
553 WELLGRAIN DOD
B7040
450 HALFMERK HILL
Fingland
78
Wanlock Water
Elvanfoot
A76
B797
B7076
Leadhills
363 CARSGAILOCH HILL
Mansfield
503 COCKER HILL
Meikle Carco
Elvan Water
Lead Mining
Dalgig
Connel Park
Kirkland
Wanlockhead Beam Engine
Wanlockhead
River Nith
Bankglen
New Cumnock
A702
504
Craigbank
732 GREEN LOWTHER
Kirkconnel
725 LOWTHER HILL
Nether Fingland
Kelloholm
A76
594 HARE HILL
Newtown
Sanquhar
B797
Kello Water
Blackcraig
Ulzieside
Dae Reservoir
568 ENOCH HILL
Mennock
Enterkin Burn
Lowther Hills
700 BLACKCRAIG
Euchan Water
23
17
Kirkhope
450 CLOUD HILL
River Nith
691 BALLENCLEUCH LAW
554 WHITESIDE HILL
478
Enterkinfoot
Durisdeermill
Polgown
Durisdeer
475 COUNTAM
554 CAIRNKINNA HILL
666
Gateslack
697 WINDY STANDARD
Cleuch-head
East Morton
668 GANA HILL
A76
A702
Nithsdale
Drumlanrig
Morton Loch
Morton Castle
696 QUEENSBERRY
Bow Burn
598 COLT HILL
796 CAIRNSMORE OF CARSPHAIRN
Big Carlae
Carronbridge
512
A713
Old Auchenbrack
Auchenhessnane
Tibbers
Benbuie
Shinnel Water
Scaur Water
Burnhead
Thornhill
Mitchellslacks
Penpont
Closeburnmill
Southern Upland Way
532 CORNHARROW HILL
337 BENNAN
Loch Ettrick
Carsphairn
Water of Ken
Cample
Stenhouse
Tynron
Keir Mill
Closeburn
353 GREAT HILL
Burnfoot
69
Knowehead
B729
Moniaive
Kirkland
A702
Park
Maxwelton
Kirkpatrick
Claughrie Burn
Keir Hills
Glencrosh
Craigdarroch
385 WETHER HILL
Black Water
Blackwood
Auldgirth
431
Skelston
Snade
A702
A713

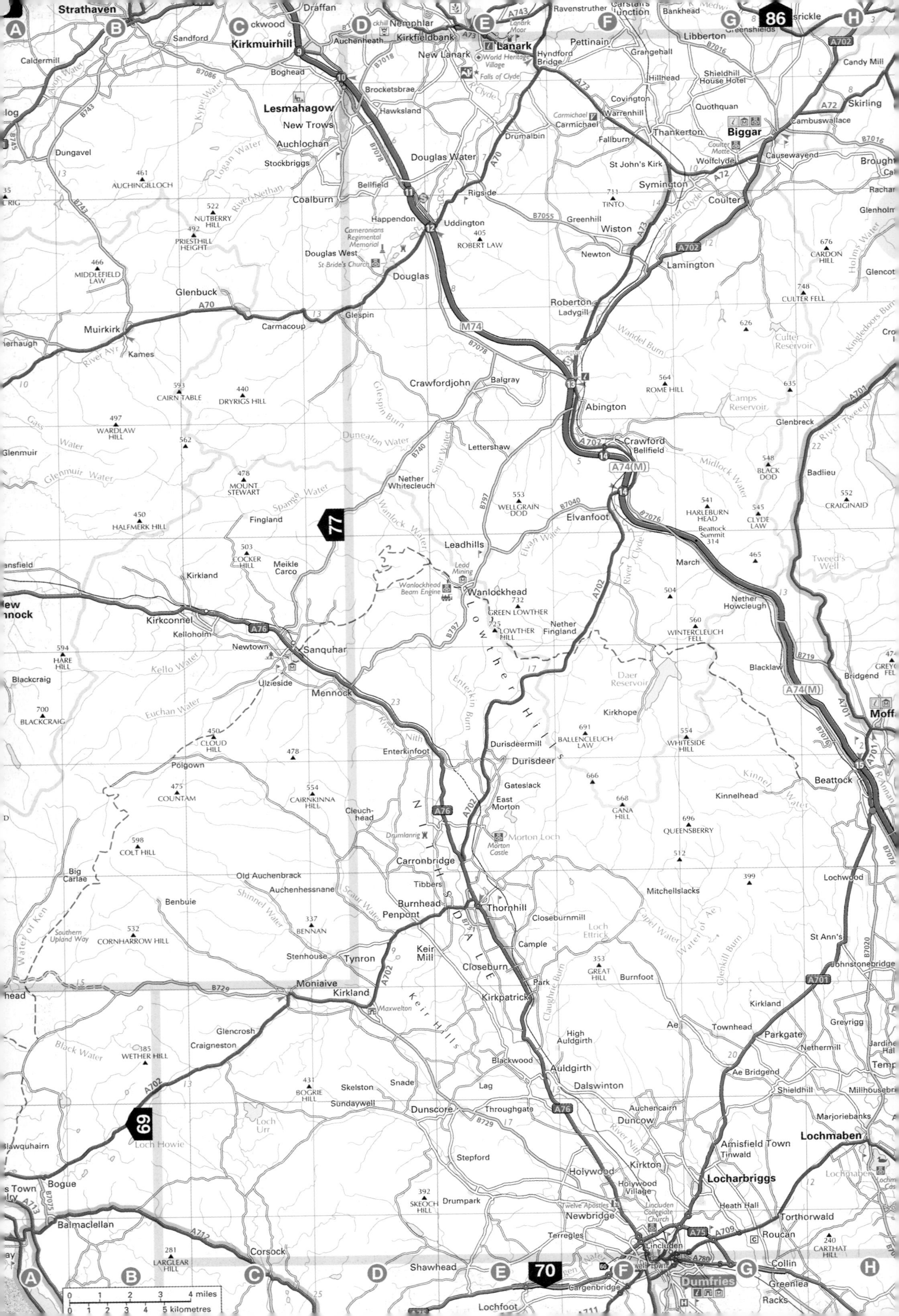
86
Strathaven
Draffan
Nemphlar
Lanark
Ravenstruther
Carstairs Junction
Bankhead
Kirkmuirhill
Sandford
Auchenheath
Kirkfieldbank
New Lanark
World Heritage Village
Falls of Clyde
Hyndford Bridge
Pettinain
Grangehall
Libberton
Greenshields
Candy Mill
Caldermill
Boghead
Brocketsbrae
Hillhead
Shieldhill House Hotel
Lesmahagow
New Trows
Hawksland
Carmichael
Covington
Warrenhill
Quothquan
Skirling
Cambuswallace
Thankerton
Biggar
Fallburn
Drumalbin
Auchlochan
Dungavel
Douglas Water
Stockbriggs
St John's Kirk
Wolfclyde
Coulter Motte
Causewayend
Broughton
461 AUCHINGILLOCH
Bellfield
Symington
Coulter
Coalburn
Rigside
711 TINTO
522 NUTBERRY HILL
492 PRIESTHILL HEIGHT
Happendon
Uddington
Greenhill
Wiston
Glenholm
Cameronians Regimental Memorial
405 ROBERT LAW
Douglas West
St Bride's Church
Newton
Lamington
676 CARDON HILL
466 MIDDLEFIELD LAW
Douglas
748 CULTER FELL
Glencot
Glenbuck
Roberton
Ladygill
Muirkirk
Carmacoup
Glespin
Kames
Culter Reservoir
Wandel Burn
Abington
593 CAIRN TABLE
440 DRYRIGS HILL
Crawfordjohn
Balgray
564 ROME HILL
635
Camps Reservoir
Abington
497 WARDLAW HILL
562
Glenbreck
Crawford
Bellfield
Lettershaw
Glenmuir
Glenmuir Water
478 MOUNT STEWART
Nether Whitecleuch
548 BLACK DOD
Badlieu
553 WELLGRAIN DOD
Elvanfoot
541 HARLEBURN HEAD
545 CLYDE LAW
552 CRAIGINAID
450 HALFMERK HILL
Fingland
Beattock Summit 314
503 COCKER HILL
Meikle Carco
Leadhills
Lead Mining
March
465
Tweed's Well
Kirkland
Wanlockhead Beam Engine
Wanlockhead
504
732 GREEN LOWTHER
Nether Howcleugh
Kirkconnel
Kelloholm
725 LOWTHER HILL
Nether Fingland
560 WINTERCLEUCH FELL
594 HARE HILL
Newtown
Sanquhar
Blacklaw
Bridgend
Blackcraig
Ulzieside
Mennock
Daer Reservoir
700 BLACKCRAIG
Euchan Water
Kirkhope
Moffat
691 BALLENCLEUCH LAW
554 WHITESIDE HILL
450 CLOUD HILL
478
Enterkinfoot
Durisdeermill
Durisdeer
Polgowan
666
Beattock
475 COUNTAM
554 CAIRNKINNA HILL
Gateslack
Kinnelhead
East Morton
668 GANA HILL
Cleuchhead
696 QUEENSBERRY
598 COLT HILL
Drumlanrig
Morton Loch
Morton Castle
512
Big Carlae
Old Auchenbrack
Carronbridge
399
Lochwood
Auchenhessnane
Tibbers
Mitchellslacks
Benbuie
Burnhead
Thornhill
Penpont
Closeburnmill
Southern Upland Way
532 CORNHARROW HILL
337 BENNAN
Loch Ettrick
Cample
St Ann's
Keir Mill
Stenhouse
Tynron
Closeburn
353 GREAT HILL
Burnfoot
Johnstonebridge
Moniaive
Kirkland
Park
Kirkpatrick
Maxwelton
Kirkland
Glencrosh
High Auldgirth
Ae
Townhead
Parkgate
Greyrigg
Craigneston
385 WETHER HILL
Nethermill
Black Water
Blackwood
Auldgirth
Ae Bridgend
431 BOGRIE HILL
Skelston
Snade
Lag
Dalswinton
Shieldhill
Millhousebridge
Sundaywell
Dunscore
Throughgate
Auchencairn
Duncow
Marjoriebanks
Loch Urr
Loch Howie
Amisfield Town
Tinwald
Lochmaben
Stepford
Holywood
Kirkton
Bogue
Locharbriggs
392 SKEOCH HILL
Drumpark
Holywood Village
Twelve Apostles
Lincluden Collegiate Church
Heath Hall
Newbridge
Torthorwald
Balmaclellan
Terregles
Roucan
281 LARGLEAR HILL
Corsock
Lincluden
240 CARTHAT HILL
Shawhead
Collin
Dumfries
Greenlea
Cargenbridge
Racks
Lochfoot
77
69
70
0 1 2 3 4 miles
0 1 2 3 4 5 kilometres

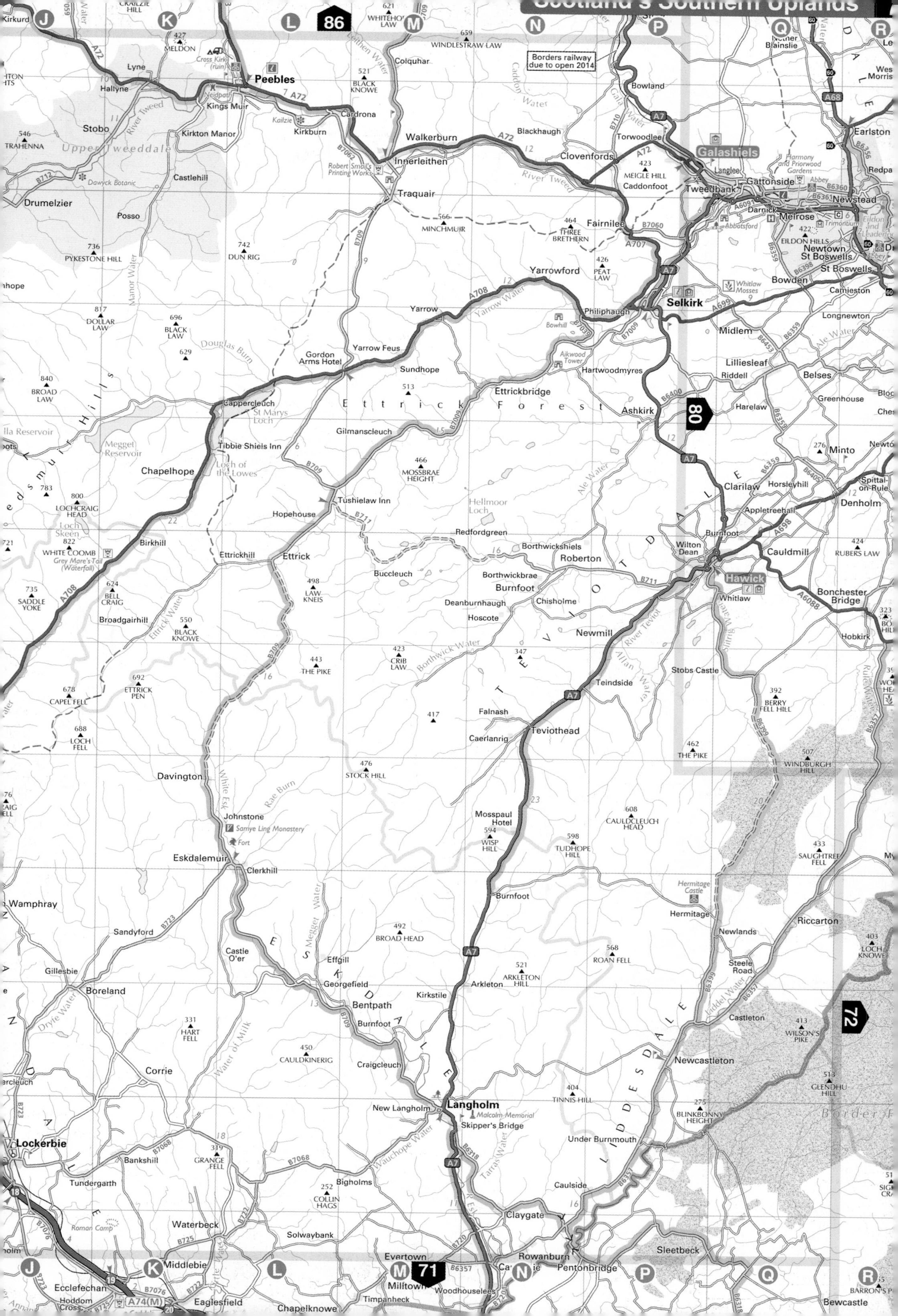

Borders railway due to open 2014
Peebles
Kirkurd
Lyne
Hallyne
Stobo
Kings Muir
Cross Kirk (ruin)
Cardrona
Kailzie
Kirkburn
Kirkton Manor
Upper Tweeddale
River Tweed
Dawyck Botanic
Drumelzier
Castlehill
Posso
Walkerburn
Innerleithen
Robert Smail's Printing Works
Traquair
Colquhar
Leithen Water
Blackhaugh
Clovenfords
Bowland
Torwoodlee
Galashiels
Langlee
Tweedbank
Gattonside
Darnick
Melrose
Abbotsford
Newstead
Trimontium
Eildon Hills
Newtown St Boswells
St Boswells
Bowden
Earlston
Redpath
Blainslie
Harmony and Priorwood Gardens
Meigle Hill
Caddonfoot
Fairnilee
Three Brethren
Minchmuir
Peat Law
Yarrowford
Selkirk
Philiphaugh
Bowhill
Whitlaw Mosses
Camieston
Longnewton
Midlem
Lilliesleaf
Riddell
Belses
Greenhouse
Harelaw
Minto
Yarrow
Yarrow Water
Yarrow Feus
Gordon Arms Hotel
Sundhope
Aikwood Tower
Hartwoodmyres
Ettrickbridge
Ashkirk
Ettrick Forest
Cappercleuch
St Marys Loch
Megget Reservoir
Tibbie Shiels Inn
Loch of the Lowes
Chapelhope
Gilmanscleuch
Mossbrae Height
Tushielaw Inn
Hopehouse
Hellmoor Loch
Redfordgreen
Borthwickshiels
Roberton
Borthwickbrae
Burnfoot
Chisholme
Deanburnhaugh
Hoscote
Newmill
Clarilaw
Horsleyhill
Appletreehall
Denholm
Spittal-on-Rule
Wilton Dean
Hawick
Cauldmill
Rubers Law
Whitlaw
Bonchester Bridge
Hobkirk
Dun Rig
Pykestone Hill
Manor Water
Dollar Law
Black Law
Douglas Burn
Broad Law
Lochcraig Head
Loch Skeen
White Coomb
Grey Mare's Tail (Waterfall)
Birkhill
Ettrickhill
Ettrick
Buccleuch
Law Kneis
Saddle Yoke
Bell Craig
Broadgairhill
Black Knowe
Ettrick Water
Ettrick Pen
Capel Fell
Loch Fell
The Pike
Crib Law
Borthwick Water
River Tevitor
Allan Water
Stobs Castle
Teindside
Berry Fell Hill
Falnash
Teviothead
Caerlanrig
Teviotdale
Windburgh Hill
Stock Hill
Davington
White Esk
Rae Burn
Johnstone
Samye Ling Monastery
Fort
Eskdalemuir
Clerkhill
Mosspaul Hotel
Wisp Hill
Tudhope Hill
Cauldcleuch Head
Saughtree Fell
Hermitage Castle
Hermitage
Burnfoot
Riccarton
Newlands
Steele Road
Wamphray
Sandyford
Broad Head
Megget Water
Castle O'er
Effgill
Georgefield
Arkleton Hill
Arkleton
Roan Fell
Loch Knowe
Gillesbie
Boreland
Bentpath
Kirkstile
Burnfoot
Eskdale
Liddesdale
Castleton
Wilson's Pike
Dryfe Water
Hart Fell
Water of Milk
Cauldkinerig
Craigcleuch
Newcastleton
Glendhu Hill
Corrie
Tinnis Hill
Blinkbonny Height
Langholm
New Langholm
Malcolm Memorial
Skipper's Bridge
Under Burnmouth
Tarras Water
Wauchope Water
Lockerbie
Bankshill
Grange Fell
Tundergarth
Collin Hags
Bigholms
Caulside
Roman Camp
Waterbeck
Solwaybank
Claygate
Sleetbeck
Middlebie
Evertown
Rowanburn
Pentonbridge
Canonbie
Milltown
Woodhouselees
Ecclefechan
Hoddom Cross
Eaglesfield
Timpanheck
Chapelknowe
Bewcastle
Barron's Pike

86
80
72
71

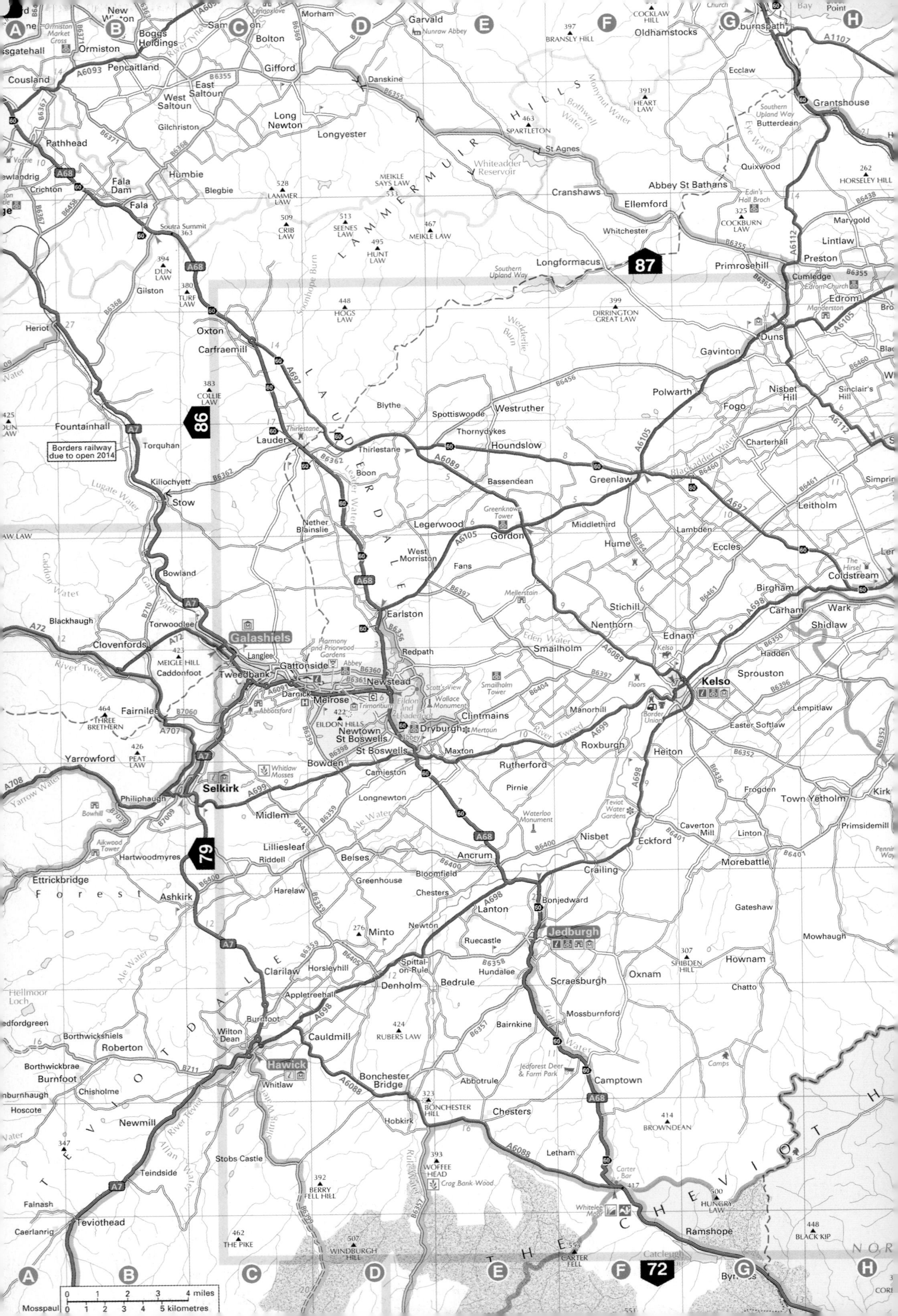

A
B
C
D
E
F
G
H
New Winton
Ormiston Market Cross
Ormiston
Boggs Holdings
Samuelston
Bolton
Morham
Garvald
Nunraw Abbey
397
BRANSLY HILL
COCKLAW HILL
Oldhamstocks
Cockburnspath
A1107
Cousland
A6093
Pencaitland
East Saltoun
West Saltoun
Gifford
Danskine
B6355
Ecclaw
391
HEART LAW
Grantshouse
Southern Upland Way
Butterdean
Eye Water
Gilchriston
Long Newton
Longyester
463
SPARTLETON
St Agnes
Bothwell Water
Monynut Water
Pathhead
A68
Crichton
Fala Dam
Fala
Humbie
Blegbie
528
LAMMER LAW
MEIKLE SAYS LAW
533
Whiteadder Reservoir
Cranshaws
Abbey St Bathans
Quixwood
262
HORSELEY HILL
Edin's Hall Broch
325
COCKBURN LAW
Ellemford
Whitchester
Marygold
Lintlaw
Soutra Summit
363
509
CRIB LAW
513
SEENES LAW
495
HUNT LAW
467
MEIKLE LAW
LAMMERMUIR HILLS
394
DUN LAW
380
TURF LAW
Gilston
Longformacus
87
Primrosehill
Preston
Cumledge
Edrom Church
Edrom
Manderston
Southern Upland Way
448
HOGS LAW
399
DIRRINGTON GREAT LAW
Heriot
Oxton
Carfraemill
Duns
Gavinton
A6105
A697
LAUDERDALE
383
COLLIE LAW
86
425
Fountainhall
Borders railway due to open 2014
Torquhan
Lauder
Thirlestane
Blythe
Spottiswoode
Westruther
Thornydykes
Houndslow
Polwarth
Fogo
Nisbet Hill
Sinclair's Hill
Charterhall
A6112
Killochyett
Stow
Lugate Water
B6362
Boon
A6089
Bassendean
Greenlaw
Blackadder Water
B6460
Leitholm
Nether Blainslie
Legerwood
Greenknowe Tower
Gordon
Middlethird
Lambden
Hume
Eccles
West Morriston
Fans
The Hirsel
Coldstream
Bowland
Caddon Water
Gala Water
B6397
Mellerstain
Birgham
Carham
Wark
Blackhaugh
A72
Torwoodlee
Galashiels
Earlston
Stichill
Nenthorn
Ednam
Shidlaw
Clovenfords
423
MEIGLE HILL
Caddonfoot
Langlee
Gattonside
Harmony and Priorwood Gardens
Abbey
Redpath
Eden Water
Smailholm
Kelso
Hadden
Sprouston
River Tweed
Tweedbank
Darnick
Melrose
Trimontium
Newstead
Scott's View
Eildon and Leaderfoot
Wallace Monument
Smailholm Tower
Floors
Border Union
Lempitlaw
464
THREE BRETHERN
Fairnilee
B7060
Abbotsford
422
EILDON HILLS
Newtown St Boswells
Dryburgh
Abbey
Clintmains
Mertoun
Manorhill
Roxburgh
Easter Softlaw
426
PEAT LAW
A707
St Boswells
Maxton
Heiton
Yarrowford
Bowden
Whitlaw Mosses
Camieston
Rutherford
Pirnie
A708
Yarrow Water
Selkirk
A699
Philiphaugh
Bowhill
Midlem
Longnewton
Ale Water
Waterloo Monument
Teviot Water Gardens
Frogden
Town Yetholm
Kirk
Primsidemill
Aikwood Tower
Hartwoodmyres
79
Lilliesleaf
Riddell
Belses
Ancrum
Nisbet
Eckford
Caverton Mill
Linton
Morebattle
Ettrickbridge
Forest
Ashkirk
B6400
Greenhouse
Bloomfield
Crailing
Chesters
Harelaw
A698
Lanton
Bonjedward
Gateshaw
276
Minto
Newton
Jedburgh
Ruecastle
Mowhaugh
Clarilaw
Horsleyhill
Spittal-on-Rule
Hundalee
B6358
307
SHIBDEN HILL
Hownam
Oxnam
Scraesburgh
Bedrule
Denholm
Chatto
Hellmoor Loch
Appletreehall
Mossburnford
Bedfordgreen
Burnfoot
Wilton Dean
Cauldmill
424
RUBERS LAW
Bairnkine
Jed Water
Borthwickshiels
Roberton
Hawick
B711
Borthwickbrae
Burnfoot
Whitlaw
Bonchester Bridge
Abbotrule
Jedforest Deer & Farm Park
Camptown
Camps
Chisholme
A6088
323
BONCHESTER HILL
Hobkirk
Chesters
414
BROWNDEAN
Hoscote
Newmill
River Teviot
Allan Water
347
TEVIOTDALE
Stobs Castle
393
WOFFEE HEAD
Crag Bank Wood
Letham
Carter Bar
417
500
HUNGRY LAW
CHEVIOT HILLS
Teindside
392
BERRY FELL HILL
Rule Water
Whitelee Moor
Falnash
A7
Teviothead
Caerlanrig
462
THE PIKE
507
WINDBURGH HILL
557
CARTER FELL
Ramshope
448
BLACK KIP
Catcleugh
72
Byrness
NOR
Mosspaul
0 1 2 3 4 miles
0 1 2 3 4 5 kilometres

ST ABB'S HEAD
St Abbs
Coldingham
Coldingham Bay
Eyemouth
Cairncross
Ayton
Burnmouth
Lamberton
Marshall Meadows Bay
Foulden
Edington
Hutton
Whiteadder Water
North Northumberland Heritage Coast
Berwick-upon-Tweed
Barracks
Castle
Town Ramparts
Tweedmouth
Spittal
Paxton
Hilton
Huds Head
Horndean
Horncliffe
Scremerston
Murton
Thornton
Norham
Upsettlington
Cheswick
CAUSEWAY FLOODED AT HIGH TIDE
Ancroft
Haggerston
HOLY ISLAND
Holy Island
Beal
Duddo
Bowsden
Lindisfarne Priory
Lindisfarne Castle
Castle Point
Guile Point
River Till
Etal
Heatherslaw Light Railway
Heatherslaw Corn Mill
Lady Waterford Hall
Lowick
Fenwick
Buckton
Crookham
Ford
Longstone Lighthouse
FARNE ISLANDS
Staple Sound
Inner Sound
St Cuthbert's Cave
Budle Bay
Bamburgh
Howtel
Milfield
Fenton
Belford
Nesbit
Doddington
Seahouses
North Sunderland
Lanton
Yeavering
Coupland
Kirknewton
Lucker
YEAVERING BELL
Akeld
Wooler
Chatton
Warenford
Beadnell
Swinhoe
NORTHUMBERLAND
Chathill
Newstead
Tughall
Beadnell Bay
Wild Cattle Park
Ros Castle
Ellingham
Preston
Newtown
Preston Pele Tower
Newton-by-the-Sea
Embleton & Newton Links
PRESTON HILL
CATERAN HILL
Christon Bank
Embleton
NATIONAL PARK
North Charlton
Fallodon
Embleton Bay
Ilderton
Old Bewick
Dunstanburgh Castle
South Charlton
THE CHEVIOT
Dunstan
Craster
New Bewick
Eglingham
Rock
DUNMOOR HILL
Rennington
Stamford
Beanley
Howick Hall
Howick
Cullernose Point
River Breamish
Branton
Powburn
Ingram
Longhoughton
Glanton
Denwick
CUSHAT LAW
COCHRANE PIKE
River Aln
Boulmer
Bolton
Alnwick
Seaton Point
Lesbury
Whittingham
River Alwin
Alnham
Castle
Alnmouth
Alnmouth Bay
Edlingham
Shilbottle
Netherton
Alwinton
LONG CRAG
Burradon
GLANTLEES HILL
Newton-on-the-Moor
Warkworth Castle & Hermitage
Warkworth
Harbottle
Amble
Coquet Island
Sharperton
Swarland
Gloster Hill
Holystone
Snitter
Cragside House
Guyzance
River Coquet
Rothbury
73
High Hauxley
Acklington
Thropton
Togston
Hepple
Whitton
Longframlington
Felton
Great Tosson
East Thirston
Broomhill

89
74
Torran Rocks
Eilean Dubh
Balnahard
Rudh' a' Geodha
Kiloran Bay
COLONSAY
Kiloran
Kilchattan
Scalasaig
B8086
B8087
Machrins
Colonsay
B8085
Garvard
Oronsay
Rudha Bàn
Dubh Eilean
ORONSAY
Eilean Ghurdmail
Colonsay-Port Askaig
Corpach Bay
Shian Bay
453 RAINBERG MÒR
JURA
Loch Righ Mòr
Rudh' ant-Sàilein
Loch Tarbert
Rudha a' Mhàil
Rudha Bholsa
363 SGARBH BREAC
ISLAY
506 SCRINADLE
398 BEINN TARSUINN
Nave Island
Ardnave Point
Gortantaoid Point
Jura Forest
784 BEINN AN OIR
734
Paps of Jura
Loch a' Chnuic Bhric
Bunnahabhain
316 GUIR-BHEINN
Sound of Islay
24
Knockrome
Ardfernal
Ton Mhòr
Kilnave
Loch Gruinart
Sanaigmore
Jura
Eilean Mòr
Loch Gòrr
Port Askaig
Feolin Ferry
560 GLASS BHEINN
A846
Finlaggan
Loch Finlaggan
Kiells
Keils
Small Isles
Rudha Lamanais
Lecht Gruinart
RSPB
529 DUBHA BHEINN
Craighouse
Saligo Bay
B8018
B8017
Gleann Mòr
Loch Ballygrant
Ballygrant
342 BRAT BHEINN
Rudha na Gaillich
Gruinart
Loch Gorm
8
Loch Lossit
Cabrach
Coul Point
Sunderland
266 BEINNE DUBH
Machir Bay
Kilchoman
Am Fraoch Eilean
Rudha na Tràille
Brosdale Island
Bridgend
Gartachossan
Bruichladdich
A847
Loch Indaal
429 SGÒRR NAM FAOILEANN
Kilchiaran Bay
Bowmore
3
Kilennan Burn
471
McArthur's Head
RHINNS OF ISLAY
15
Port Charlotte
V Port Askaig - Kennacraig
231 BEINN TART A'MHILL
River Laggan
490 BEINN BHEIGEIR
Lossit Bay
Duich
Nereabolls
Rudha Liath
Ardtalla
454 BEINN URARAIDH
Loch Uraraidh
B8016
Claggain Bay
Rudha na Faing
Portnahaven
Port Wemyss
11
Glenegedale
Laggan Bay
Kintour
Ardmore Point
Kildalton Cross
Port Ellen - Kennacraig
Orsay
RHINNS POINT
Islay
346 BEINN SHOLUM
Eilean a' Chuirn
Rudha Mòr
Kintra
Rudha na Gainmhich
MAOL BUIDHE
Port Ellen
Ardbeg
Lagavulin
Laphroaig
Texa
THE OA
0 1 2 3 4 miles
0 1 2 3 4 5 kilometres

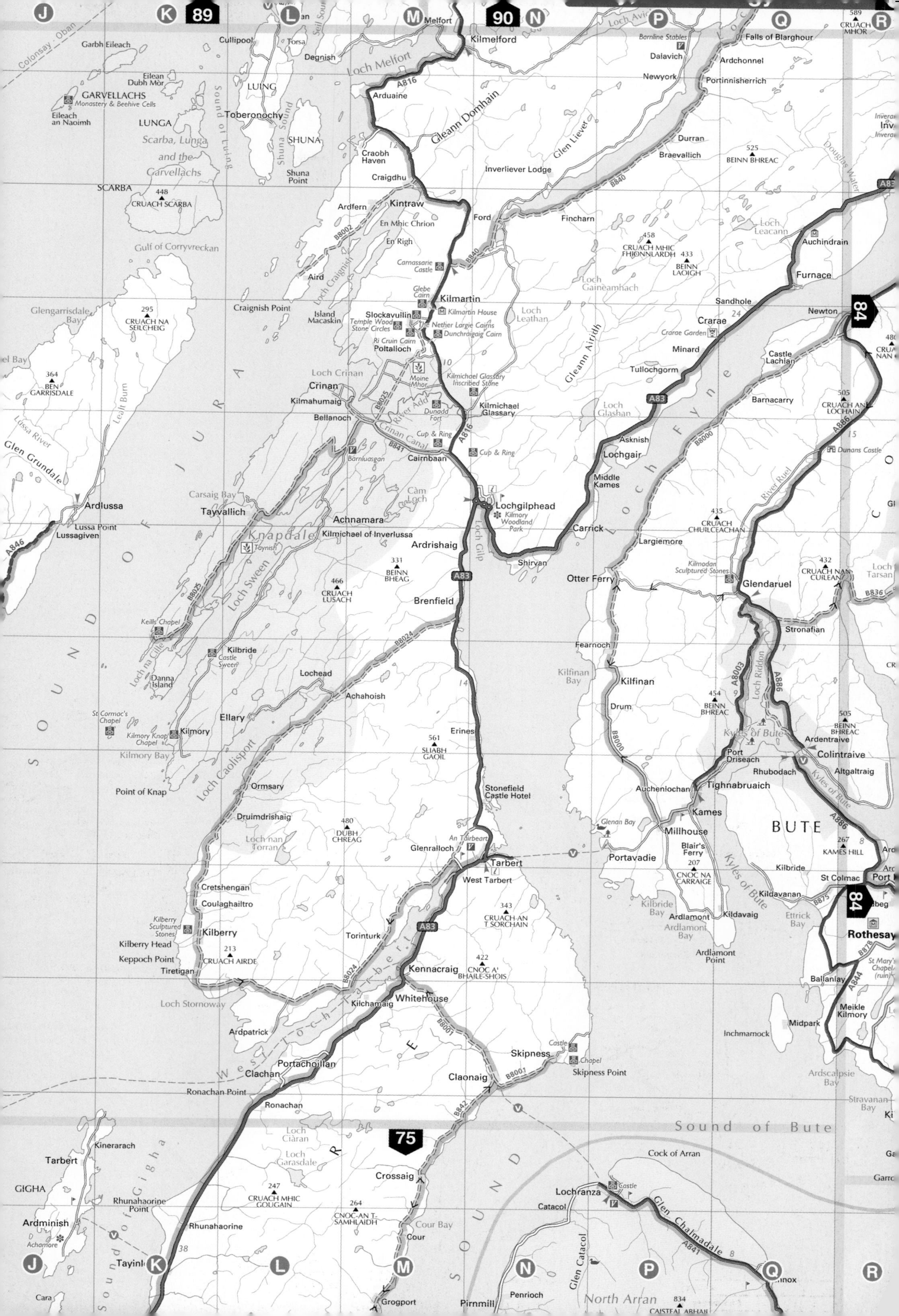

89
90
75
84
Kilmelford
Loch Melfort
Arduaine
Gleann Domhain
LUING
Toberonochy
LUNGA
SHUNA
GARVELLACHS
SCARBA
Gulf of Corryvreckan
Kilmartin
Crinan
Crinan Canal
Lochgilphead
Ardrishaig
Loch Fyne
Inveraray
Furnace
Crarae
Minard
Tullochgorm
Lochgair
Carrick
Otter Ferry
Glendaruel
Kilfinan
Tighnabruaich
Kames
Portavadie
Colintraive
BUTE
Rothesay
Port Bannatyne
Tayvallich
Knapdale
Loch Sween
Achnamara
Kilmory
Loch Caolisport
Ormsary
Tarbert
West Tarbert
Kilberry
Kennacraig
Whitehouse
Skipness
Claonaig
Clachan
Ronachan
Crossaig
Lochranza
Catacol
Glen Chalmadale
North Arran
Pirnmill
Grogport
GIGHA
Ardminish
Tayinloan
Sound of Gigha
SOUND OF JURA
Sound of Bute
Kyles of Bute
Ardlussa
Lussagiven
Glen Grundale

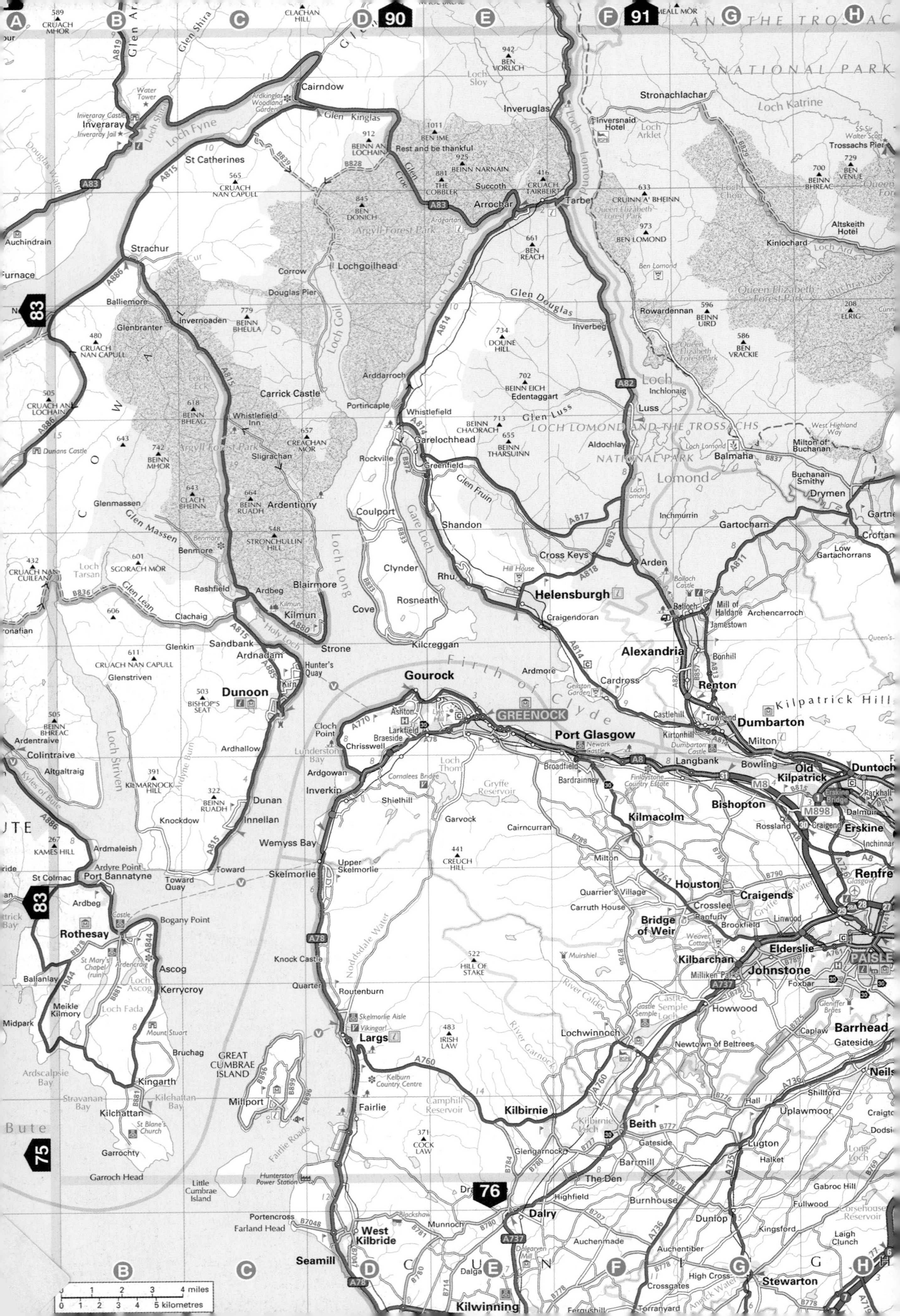

90
91
A
B
C
D
E
F
G
H
CLACHAN HILL
589 CRUACH MHOR
Glen Aray
Glen Shira
942 BEN VORLICH
MEALL MOR
THE TROSSACHS
NATIONAL PARK
Loch Sloy
Cairndow
Water Tower
Inveraray Castle
Inveraray
Inveraray Jail
Loch Shira
Ardkinglas Woodland Garden
Glen Kinglas
Inveruglas
Stronachlachar
Loch Katrine
Inversnaid Hotel
Loch Arklet
Sir Walter Scott
Trossachs Pier
Loch Fyne
St Catherines
Douglas Water
912 BEINN AN LOCHAIN
1011 BEN IME
Rest and be thankful
925 BEINN NARNAIN
881 THE COBBLER
Glen Croe
B828
B839
B829
A83
A815
565 CRUACH NAN CAPULL
845 BEN DONICH
Succoth
416 CRUACH TAIRBEIRT
Arrochar
Tarbet
Loch Lomond
633 CRUINN A' BHEINN
Queen Elizabeth Forest Park
700 BEINN BHREAC
729 BEN VENUE
Loch Chon
Ardgartan
Argyll Forest Park
973 BEN LOMOND
Altskeith Hotel
Kinlochard
Loch Ard
Auchindrain
Strachur
River Cur
661 BEN REACH
Ben Lomond
Furnace
A886
Corrow
Lochgoilhead
Loch Long
Glen Douglas
Queen Elizabeth Forest Park
Duchray Water
83
Balliemore
Douglas Pier
779 BEINN BHEULA
Invernoaden
Glenbranter
Loch Goil
A814
Inverbeg
Rowardennan
596 BEINN UIRD
208 ELRIG
480 CRUACH NAN CAPULL
734 DOUNE HILL
586 BEN VRACKIE
Loch Eck
Arddarroch
702 BEINN EICH
Edentaggart
A82
Loch
Inchlonaig
Luss
505 CRUACH AN LOCHAIN
618 BEINN BHEAG
Carrick Castle
Portincaple
Whistlefield
Whistlefield Inn
Glen Luss
LOCH LOMOND AND THE TROSSACHS
NATIONAL PARK
West Highland Way
Milton of Buchanan
643
742 BEINN MHOR
657 CREACHAN MOR
713 BEINN CHAORACH
655 BEINN THARSUINN
Garelochhead
Aldochlay
Loch Lomond
Balmaha
B837
Dunans Castle
Sligrachan
Rockville
Greenfield
B872
Lomond
Buchanan Smithy
Drymen
COWAL
643 CLACH BHEINN
Glen Fruin
Loch Lomond
Glenmassen
664 BEINN RUADH
Ardentinny
Coulport
Inchmurrin
Gartocharn
Gartness
Glen Massen
548 STRONCHULLIN HILL
Gare Loch
Shandon
A817
B832
Croftamie
Benmore
B833
Cross Keys
Low Gartachorrans
432 CRUACH NAN CUILEAN
Loch Tarsan
601 SGORACH MOR
Clynder
Arden
A811
Blairmore
Hill House
A818
Balloch Castle
B836
Glen Lean
Rashfield
Ardbeg
Kilmun
Rhu
Rosneath
Helensburgh
Balloch
Mill of Haldane
Archencarroch
Jamestown
606
Clachaig
Cove
Craigendoran
Holy Loch
A880
Kilcreggan
ronafian
Glenkin
Sandbank
A815
Strone
Ardnadam
Queen's
611 CRUACH NAN CAPULL
Hunter's Quay
Kirn
A885
Firth of Clyde
Alexandria
Bonhill
Glenstriven
Dunoon
Gourock
Ardmore
503 BISHOP'S SEAT
Cardross
Geilston Garden
A813
B857
Renton
Kilpatrick Hills
505 BEINN BHREAC
Loch Striven
Cloch Point
Ashton
Larkfield
Braeside
Chrisswell
A770
Lyle Hill
GREENOCK
Port Glasgow
Newark Castle
Castlehill
Townend
Dumbarton
Ardentraive
Colintraive
Ardyne Burn
Lunderston Bay
Loch Thom
Kirtonhill
Dumbarton Castle
Milton
A8
Langbank
Bowling
Old Kilpatrick
Duntocher
Altgaltraig
Ardhallow
Ardgowan
Cornalees Bridge
Gryffe Reservoir
Broadfield
Bardrainney
Finlaystone Country Estate
M8
B815
Erskine Bridge
Parkhall
391 KILMARNOCK HILL
Inverkip
Shielhill
Bishopton
M898
Dalmuir
Kyles of Bute
322 BEINN RUADH
Dunan
Innellan
Garvock
Kilmacolm
Rossland
Craigends
Erskine
BUTE
A886
Knockdow
Cairncurran
B788
Inchinnan
267 KAMES HILL
Ardmaleish
Wemyss Bay
441 CREUCH HILL
Milton
B789
Ardyne Point
Toward
Upper Skelmorlie
Renfrew
Port Bannatyne
St Colmac
Toward Quay
Skelmorlie
A761
Houston
B790
Glasgow
Quarrier's Village
Carruth House
Craigends
Gryffe Water
Ardbeg
Crosslee
Ranfurly
Bridge of Weir
Brookfield
Linwood
Castle
Bogany Point
Noddsdale Water
Rothesay
A844
A78
Weaver's Cottage
Elderslie
B878
St Mary's Chapel (ruin)
Ardencraig
Ascog
Knock Castle
522 HILL OF STAKE
Muirshiel
B786
Kilbarchan
PAISLEY
Ballanlay
Loch Ascog
Kerrycroy
Milliken Park
Johnstone
A737
Foxbar
Quarter
Routenburn
River Calder
Castle Semple
B787
Meikle Kilmory
Loch Fada
B881
Skelmorlie Aisle
Vikingar!
Howwood
Gleniffer Braes
Midpark
Mount Stuart
Largs
483 IRISH LAW
River Garnock
Lochwinnoch
B775
Caplaw
Barrhead
Bruchag
GREAT CUMBRAE ISLAND
Newtown of Beltrees
Gateside
A760
Ardscalpsie Bay
Kingarth
B896
B899
Kelburn Country Centre
A760
A736
Neilston
Kilchattan Bay
Stravanan Bay
Millport
Camphill Reservoir
Kilbirnie
Shillford
Hall
Uplawmoor
Kilchattan
St Blane's Church
Fairlie
Kilbirnie Loch
B776
Beith
B777
Craigton
Dodside
Bute
75
Fairlie Roads
371 COCK LAW
Gateside
Lugton
Long Loch
Garrochty
Glengarnock
B784
B780
B777
A735
Halket
Barrmill
B769
Garroch Head
Hunterston Power Station
Little Cumbrae Island
The Den
Gabroc Hill
76
Highfield
B706
Burnhouse
Fullwood
Corsehouse Reservoir
Dalry
Portencross
Farland Head
B7048
Blackshaw
Munnoch
B707
Dunlop
West Kilbride
B781
A737
Auchenmade
A736
Kingsford
Laigh Clunch
Dalgarven Mill
Auchentiber
Seamill
B7047
B780
B714
Dalgarven
CUNNINGHAME
B778
High Cross
Stewarton
A78
Kilwinning
Crossgates
Annick Water
Fergushill
Torranyard
0 1 2 3 4 miles
0 1 2 3 4 5 kilometres

91
92
98
77
Ardchullarie More
Loch Lubnaig
Queen Elizabeth Forest Park
BEN LEDI
Glen Finglas Reservoir
Callander (Calasraid)
Kilmahog
Coilantogle
Lendrick
Loch Venachar
Upper Drumbane
Auchterarder
Muirton
Gleneagles
Blackford
Braco
Greenloaning
Strathallan
Glen Eagles
STEELE'S KNOWE
Burnfoot
Kinbuck
Ashfield
Drumvaich
Burn of Cambus
Buchany
Doune
Deanston
Menteith Hills
BEINN DEARG
Aberfoyle
Port of Menteith
Ruskie
Thornhill
Lake of Menteith
Inchmahome Priory
Dykehead
Flanders Moss
River Forth
Blair Drummond
Dunblane
Sunnylaw
Bridge of Allan
Blairlogie
Menstrie
Tillicoultry
Alva
Dollar
BLAIRDENON HILL
BENCLEUCH
KING'S SEAT HILL
TARMANGIE HILL
Castlehill Reservoir
Yetts o'Muckhart
Pool of Muckhart
Castle Campbell
Dollarfield
Devonside
Coalsnaughton
Forest Mill
Tullibody
Glenochil
Fishcross
New Sauchie
Causewayhead
Raploch
Cambuskenneth
STIRLING
Cambus
Alloa
Clackmannan
Kennet
Buchlyvie
Arnprior
Kippen
Cauldhame
Gargunnock
Touch Hills
Cambusbarron
St Ninians
Fallin
Throsk
South Alloa
Bannockburn
Balfron
Fintry Hills
North Third
Chartershall
Cowie
North Third Reservoir
HART HILL
Dunmore
Kincardine
Airth
Killearn
Fintry
Auchenbowie
Loch Coulter
Plean
Letham
Carron Valley Reservoir
River Carron
EARL'S SEAT
CAMPSIE FELLS
MEIKLE BIN
TOMTAIN
Kilsyth Hills
Muirmill
Carron Bridge
Stoneywood
Dunipace
Torwood
Stenhousemuir
Larbert
Denny
Skinflats
Grangemouth
Carron
Netherton
Strathblane
Fin Glen
Clachan of Campsie
Haughhead
Lennoxtown
Milton of Campsie
Kilsyth
Banton
Braeface
Dennyloanhead
Banknock
Haggs
Bonnybridge
Camelon
Falkirk
Laurieston
Polmont
Redding
Westquarter
Brightons
Rumford
Maddiston
Shieldhill
California
Mugdock
Bardowie
Torrance
Kirkintilloch
Queenzieburn
Auchinstarry
Twechar
Dullatur
Croy
Cumbernauld Village
Abronhill
Castlecary
Balloch
Westfield
Cumbernauld
Condorrat
Waterside
Balmore
Cadder
Lenzie
Auchinloch
Bishopbriggs
Lumloch
Moodiesburn
Mollinsburn
Annathill
Luggiebank
Slamannan
Avonbridge
Standburn
Jawcraig
Binniehill
Limerigg
Southfield
Strathloanhead
Torphichen
Greengairs
Wattston
Longriggend
Muirhead
Glenboig
Riggend
Stand
Caldercruix
Garnkirk
Gartcosh
Stepps
Millerston
Springburn
Maryhill
GLASGOW
Scotstoun
Partick
Govan
Garthamlock
Provan Hall
Queenslie
Easterhouse
Barlanark
Shettleston
Baillieston
Glenmavis
Brackenhirst
Airdriehill
Plains
Hillend
Hillend Reservoir
Blackridge
Westrigg
Armadale
Woodend
Bathgate
Bathville
Boghall
Airdrie
Coatdyke
Craigneuk
Gartness
TORRANCE
Harthill
Whitburn
East Whitburn
Stoneyburn
Longridge
Loganlea
Addiewell
Pollokshields
Rutherglen
Bargeddie
COATBRIDGE
Calderbank
Chapelhall
Salsburgh
Kirk of Shotts
Eastfield
Tannochside
Carmyle
Newton
Viewpark
EUROCENTRAL
Bellshill
Holytown
Newhouse
Mossend
New Stevenston
Newarthill
Carfin
Cleekhimin
Parkside
Hartwood
Dykehead
Burnbrae
Shotts
Stane
Fauldhouse
Greenburn
Breich
Cambuslang
Uddingston
Bothwell
Flemington
Cathcart
Castlemilk
Carmunnock
Clarkston
Thornliebank
Giffnock
Sheddens
Busby
Nerston
Stewartfield
Blantyre
Motherwell
Ravenscraig
Cleland
Bellside
Bonkle
Allanbank
Allanton
Newmains
Wishaw
Crindledyke
Headlesscross
Gladsmuir Hills
WORM LAW
Newton Mearns
Waterfoot
Thorntonhall
EAST KILBRIDE
Calderwood
HAMILTON
Laighstonehall
Shields
Netherton
Waterloo
Morningside
Wilsontown
Auchengray
Forth
HARE HILL
Jackton
The Murray
Ferniegair
Allanton
Chatelherault
Eddlewood
Meikle Earnock
Larkhall
Overtown
Wildmanbridge
Law
Carluke
Eaglesham
Auldhouse
Leigh Knoweglass
Quarter
Limekilnburn
Millheugh
Shawsburn
Ashgill
Dalserf
Law Hill
Yieldshields
Roadmeetings
Braehead
Kilncadzow
Strutherhill
Rosebank
Braidwood
Chapelton
Lochgoin Reservoir
Netherburn
Stonehouse
Crossford
Carnwath
Carstairs
Kaimend
Carnduff
Strathaven
Tillietudlem
Hazelbank
Draffan
Blackwood
Nemphlar
LAIRDS SEAT
Town Plan: Glasgow p.

92
85
77
78
79
Condie
Glenfarg Reservoir
Deuglie
Glenfarg
Arngask
Newton of Balcanquhal
Dunshalt
Charlottetown
Ladybank
Craigrothie
Scotstarvit Tower
Struthers
Pitlessie
Gateside
Strathmiglo
River Eden
Kingskettle
Balmalcolm
Duncrievie
Drunzie
Burnside
Lomond Hills
Falkland Palace
Falkland
Freuchie
Kettlebridge
522 WEST LOMOND
448 EAST LOMOND
248 CLATTO HILL
Pratis
475 CORB LAW
486 STEELE'S KNOWE
497 INNERDOUNY HILL
O C H I L L S
Middleton
Tillyrie
Milnathort
Burleigh Castle
Glenlomond
Ballo Reservoir
Muirhead
Langdyke
River Devon
Glen Devon
Burnfoot
Glendevon
456 LENDRICK HILL
Carnbo
Dalqueich
Kinross
Lochleven Castle
Loch Leven
Kinross House
St Serf's Island
Kinnesswood
Holl Reservoir
Balfarg
Star
Baintown
Bonnybank
Kennoway
Castlehill Reservoir
Yetts o'Muckhart
Scotlandwell
Leslie
Cadham
Markinch
Windygates
Scoonie
Leven
Lundin Links
Pool of Muckhart
Drum
Crook of Devon
Auchmuirbridge
Glenrothes
Walkerton
Milton of Balgonie
Innerleven
Methilhill
Methil
Castle Campbell
Dollar Glen
Rumbling Bridge
Gairneybridge
River Leven
Pitteuchar
Coaltown of Balgonie
Kinglassie
Buckhaven
Dollar
Powmill
Cleish
Ballingry
Thornton
East Wemyss
Blairingone
264 CULT HILL
Cleish Hills
Hill End
379 DUMGLOW
Loch Glow
Lochore Meadows
Lochore
Crosshill
Dogton Stone
Auchterderran
River Ore
Coaltown of Wemyss
Cluny
Kelty
Glencraig
Cardenden
Lochgelly
West Wemyss
Black Devon
Gallatown
Chapel
Dysart
Balgonar
Saline
362 KNOCK HILL
Knockhill
Steelend
Forest Mill
Loch Fitty
Lumphinnans
Loch Gelly
Pathhead
Ravenscraig Castle
Kirkcaldy
Linktown
227 CRAIGLUSCAR HILL
Bowershall
Kingseat
Hill of Beath
Cowdenbeath
Auchtertool
Gowkhall
Townhill
Wellwood
Halbeath
Crossgates
Comrie
Oakley
Carnock
Milesmark
Blairhall
High Valleyfield
Donibristle
Fordell
Balmule
Kincardine
Cairneyhill
DUNFERMLINE
Kinghorn
Newmills
Culross Abbey
Culross Palace
Culross
Low Torry
Torryburn
Crossford
Aberdour
Castle
Pettycur Bay
Pettycur
Burntisland
Torry Bay
Crombie
Dalgety Bay
Charlestown
Rosyth
St Bridget's Kirk
Silversands Bay
Hillend
Limekilns
Inchcolm Abbey
Dalgety Bay
Inchkeith
Grangemouth
Bo'ness
Bo'ness & Kinneil Railway
Grangepans
Inverkeithing
Inverkeithing Bay
F I R T H O F F
Carriden
Blackness
House of the Binns
North Queensferry
Forth Road Bridge
Forth Railway Bridge
Kinneil House
Borrowstoun
Birkhill
Claymine
South Queensferry
Cramond Island
Hopetoun
Dalmeny
Polmont
Whitecross
Philpstoun
Newton
Eagle Rock
Cramond
Granton
Newhaven
Britannia
EDINBURGH
Cockenzie and Port Seton
Linlithgow
Loan
Union Canal
Muiravonside
Burnside
Lauriston Castle
Leith
Bridgend
Three Miletown
Kirkliston
Cramond Bridge
Barnton
Davidson's Mains
Warriston
St Triduana's Chapel
Preston Market Cross
Prestonpans
Heritage Museum
Cockleroy
Beecraigs
Winchburgh
Royal Highland (Ingliston)
Turnhouse
Blackhall
Portobello
Musselburgh
Westfield
Preceptory
Torphichen
Cairnpapple Hill
Ecclesmachan
Broxburn
Newbridge
Edinburgh
Dovecot
ARTHUR'S SEAT 251
Duddingston
Joppa
Newcraighall
Pinkie
Inveresk
Wallyford
Craigmillar
Craigmillar Castle
Elphinstone
Uphall
Ratho Viaduct
Ratho Station
Gogar
Corstorphine
South Gyle
Craiglockhart
Royal Observatory
Morningside
Dechmont
Dechmont Road
Almondell & Calderwood
Ratho
Hermiston
Juniper Green
Water of Leith
Blackford Hill
Liberton
Gilmerton
Newton
Danderhall
Whitecraig
Millerhill
Crossgatehall
Bathgate
Deans
Livingston
Pumpherston
Camps
Colinton
Bonaly
Dalkeith Park
Dalkeith
Cousland
Boghall
Almond Valley
Livingston Village
East Calder
Mid Calder
Wilkieston
Newmills
Currie
Kinleith
Malleny Garden
Balerno
Malleny Mills
Hillend
Straiton
Butterfly Farm
Eskbank
Lasswade
Newbattle
Mayfield
Oakbank
Kirknewton
493 ALLERMUIR HILL
Boghall
Loanhead
Bilston
Bonnyrigg
Polton
Chesterhill
Newtongrange
Dewarton
Whitburn
East Whitburn
Seafield
Blackburn
Bellsquarry
Woodhouselee
Castlelaw Hill Fort
Easter Howgate
Roslin
Mining Museum
Vogrie
Polbeth
Stoneyburn
Loganlea
Ainville
Threipmuir Reservoir
Pentland Hills
Milton Bridge
Newtonloan
Arniston
Newlandrig
Addiewell
West Calder
Linhouse Water
448 HARE HILL
579 SCALD LAW
576 CARNETHY HILL
Auchendinny
Rosewell
Crichton Castle
Crichton
Gorebridge
P E N T L A N D H I L L S
Harperrig Reservoir
Silverburn
Penicuik
Carrington
Breich
560 EAST CAIRN HILL
562 WEST CAIRN HILL
Pomathorn
Cobbinshaw Loch
Howgate
North Esk
North Middleton
Temple
Mount Lothian
Crosswood Reservoir
Baddinsgill Reservoir
Baddinsgill
Rosebery Reservoir
342 WORM LAW
Woolfords
Tarbrax
Carlops
Leadburn
Wilsontown
Auchengray
Craigburn
Heriot
Gladhouse Reservoir
South Tarbrax
415 HARROWS LAW
West Water
West Water Reservoir
Moorfoot Hills
Heriot Water
West Linton
Waterheads
Portmore Loch
369 LEFT LAW
451 MENDICK HILL
324 WHITE RIG
425 DUN LAW
651 BLACKHOPE SCAR
Dunsyre
South Medwin
Mountain Cross
Romanno Bridge
479 WETHER LAW
Eddleston
Carnwath
Dolphinton
Blyth Bridge
Lyne Water
Newbigging
Kaimend
Walston
476 CRAILZIE HILL
621 WHITEHOPE LAW
Carstairs Junction
Bankhead
Medwin
Netherurd
Elsrickle
Greenshields
Kirkurd
427 MELDON
659 WINDLESTRAW LAW
Libberton
Grangehall
Candy Mill
Cross Kirk (ruin)
Peebles
Colquhar
Lyne
571 BROUGHTON HEIGHTS
Hallyne
0 1 2 3 4 miles
0 1 2 3 4 5 kilometres
Town Plan: Edinburgh p.12

93
80
81
Anstruther
Crail
FIFE NESS
Isle of May
North Berwick
Dunbar
Haddington
Duns
Coldingham
Grantshouse
Cockburnspath
LAMMERMUIR HILLS
LAUDERDALE
Lauder
Greenlaw

A
B
C
D
E
F
96
G
H
Bagh a Chaisteil (Castlebay)
Loch Baghasdail (Lochboisdale)
Eilean Mòr
Rudha Mòr
Rudha Sgor-innis
Bousd
Sorisdale
Cliad Bay
B8072
Arnabost
Grishipoll
Clabhach
Loch Cliad
B8071
Coll - Oban
Hogh Bay
Ballyhaugh
Arinagour
COLL
Totronald
Coll
Acha
B8070
Feall Bay
Arileod
Uig
Eilean Ornsay
Caliach Point
RSPB
Calgary Point
Crossapol Bay
Loch Breachacha
Rudha Fàsachd
Gunna
Calgary Ba
Rudha Port Bhiosd
Clachan Mor
Balephetrish Bay
Caoles
B8069
Rudha Dubh
Treshnish Point
Loch Bhasapoll
Haugh Bay
B8068
Ruaig
Ballevullin
Cornoigmore
Kenovay
Gott Bay
Rudh' a' Chaoil
Kilkenneth
B8066
Tiree
B8065
Scarinish
Fladda
Moss
Heylipoll
Middleton
B8065
Crossapoll
TIREE
Hynish Bay
Lunga
Barrapoll
B8067
Balemartine
Loch a Phuill
TRESHNISH ISLES
Gometra
Mannel
Rinn Thorbhais
Balephuil Bay
Hynish
Bac Mòr or Dutchmans Cap
Bac Beag
Staffa
Little
Fingal's Cave
Rudha nan Cearc
Iona Abbey & Nunnery
IONA
Kintra
Baile Mòr
MacLean's Cross
Fionnphort
Aridhglas
Sound of Iona
St Columba Exhibition Centre
Soa Island
Erraid
Torran Rocks
A
B
C
D
E
F
82
G
H
0 1 2 3 4 miles
0 1 2 3 4 5 kilometres

MUCK
Port Mor
Sound of Arisaig
Rudha Choalais
Loch Ailort
Inverailort
Smearisary
Glenuig
ROIS-BHEINN
BEINN GAIRE
Eilean Shona
Rudha Aird Druimnich
Kinlochmoidart
Glen Forsian
Loch Moidart
Tioram
Ardmolich
Brunery
Glen Moidart
Ockle Point
Morar, Moidart and Ardnamurchan
Ockle
Kilmory
Sanna Point
Sanna Bay
Portuairk
Achnaha
Branault
BEINN BHREAC
Ardtoe
Shielfoot
Kentra
Arevegaig
Blain
Dalnabreck
MOIDART
Dalelia
Mingarrypark
Loch Shiel
Glen Hurich
Polloch
Loch Doilet
SGOR AN TARMAC
Scamoda
Ardnamurchan Point
Achosnich
MEALL NAN CON
ARDNAMURCHAN
Acharacle
Claish Moss
SUNART
BEINN RESIPOL
BEINN NA SEILG
Kilchoan
Ormsaigmore
Mingary
BEN HIANT
Loch Mudle
Glenbeg
Salen
Resipole
Glenborrodale
Ardslignish
Laga
BEN LAGA
Loch Sunart
Glencripesdale
GEARR CHREAG
Camasine
Anaheilt
Woodend
Strontian
Ardnastang
Camasachoirce
Liddesdale
Ardmore Point
Carna
Oronsay
Auliston Point
Sorne Point
Quinish Point
Glengorm Castle
Tobermory
Calve Island
Loch Teacuis
BEINN LADAIN
MEALL A' CHOISE
Lochuisge
GLAS BHEINN
'S AIRDE BEINN
Drimnin
Glen Dubh
Dervaig
Achnadrish House
BEINN BHUIDHE
SÌTHEAN NA RAPLAICH
Loch Arienas
BEINN MHEADHOIN
Acharn
SPEINNE MÒR
Loch Frisa
CÀRN MÒR
Claggan
Gleann Geal
Larachbeg
MEALL DAMH
SGURR A BHUIC
Sound of Mull
Rannoch River
Achranich
Loch Tearnait
Loch Aline
Fuinary
Glen Aros
Aros
Fanmore
CNOC AN DÀ CHINN
Glenaros House
Lochaline
Ballygown
Salen
Fishnish Point
Fishnish Pier
GLAIS BHEINN
AN SLEAGHOCH
Loch Tuath
Eas Fors (Waterfall)
BEINN NAN CARN
Killiechronan
Glen Forsa
LISMORE
ULVA
Oskamull
Gruline
BEINN NAN LUS
Macquarie Mausoleum
Scallastle Bay
Rudha an Ridire
Altcreich
Bernera Island
Kilcheran
Eorsa
Loch na Keal
Loch Bà
ISLE OF MULL
BEINN A' GHRÀIG
BEINN MHEADHON
DUN DA GHAOITHE
Craignure
Lynn of Lorne
Inch Kenneth
Inchkenneth Chapel (ruin)
Duart Bay
Duart Point
Torosay
Balnahard
Lochdonhead
Lochdon
BEN MORE
CRUACHAN DEARG
Gorten
Loch Don
Grass Point
BEIN NA SREINE
Strathcoil
CREACH BHEINN
Glen More
CARN BAN
KERRERA
Aird of Kinloch
Fossil Tree
Burg
Loch Scridain
Loch Fuaran
BEN BUIE
BEN CREACH
Loch Spelve
Croggan
Gallanachbeg
Gallanachmore
Pennycross
Pennyghael
BEINN NA CROISE
Lochbuie
Rudha Seanach
Sound of Kerrera
Ardentallen
Leidle Water
Loch Uisg
MAOL BAN
Loch Buie
Kilninver
Loch Assapol
CRUACHAN MIN
BEINN CHREAGACH
Carsaig
Rudha Dubh
DRUIM FADA
FIRTH OF LORNE
Uisken
Insh Island
Clachan
Clachan-Seil
SEIL
Ellenabeich
Easdale
Balvicar
Rudha nam Braithrean
Malcolm's Point
Colonsay · Oban
Cuan
Seil Sound
Melfort
Torsa
Degnish
Loch Melfort
Eilean Dubh Mòr
LUING
A861
A884
A848
A849
B8007
B8044
B8073
B8035
B849
B844
B8003
A816
96
97
90
82
83
J
K
L
M
N
P
Q
R

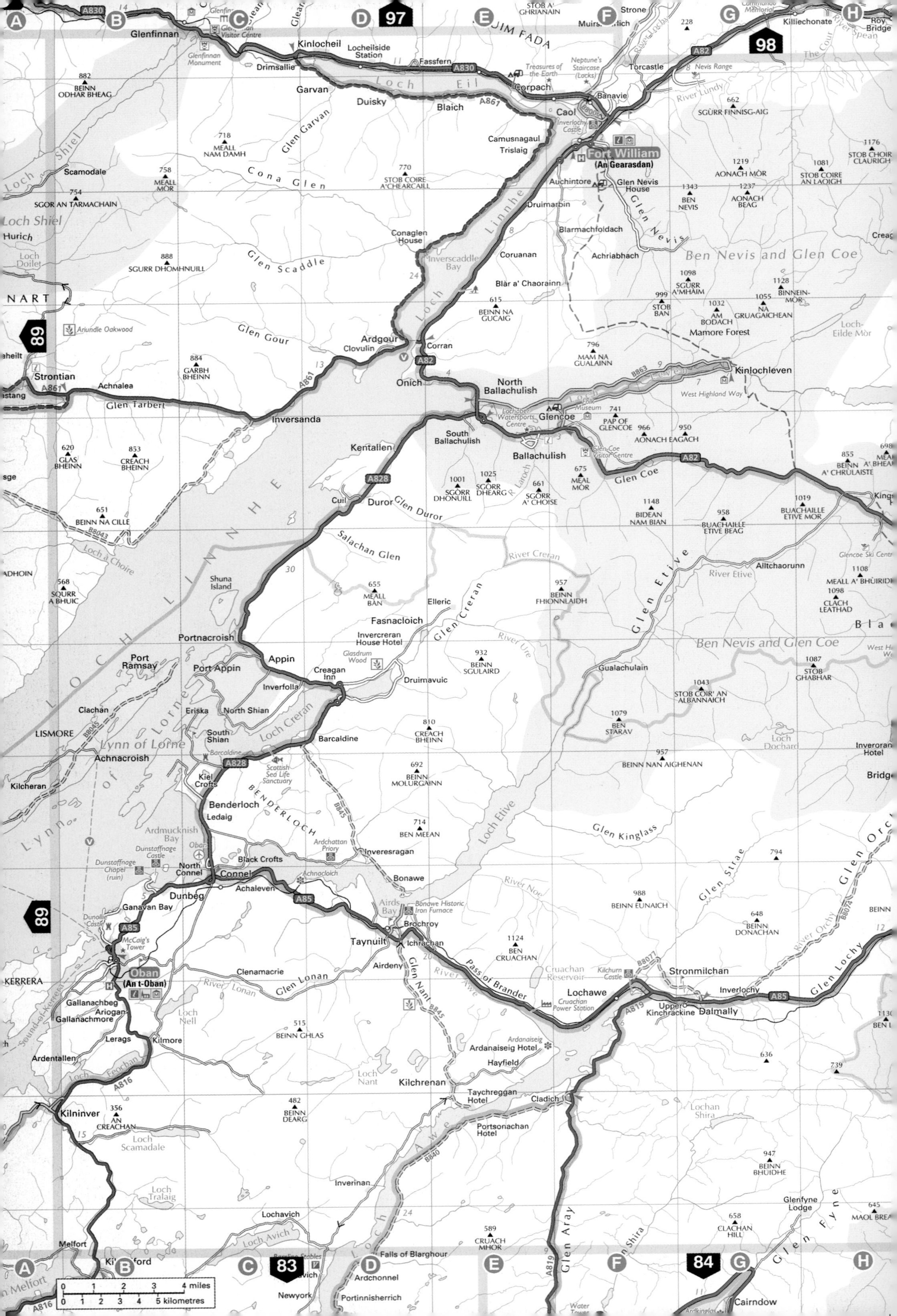

A
B
C
D
97
E
F
G
H
98
A830
Glenfinnan
Glenfinnan Visitor Centre
Glenfinnan Monument
Kinlocheil
Locheilside Station
Fassfern
Drimsallie
STOB A' GHRIANAIN
DRUIM FADA
Strone
Muirshearlich
River Lochy
228
Commando Memorial
Killiechonate
Roy Bridge
River Spean
The Cour
Treasures of the Earth
Neptune's Staircase (Locks)
Torcastle
A82
Nevis Range
Loch Eil
Corpach
Banavie
Caol
A861
882
BEINN ODHAR BHEAG
Garvan
Duisky
Blaich
Inverlochy Castle
River Lundy
662
SGÙRR FINNISG-AIG
718
MEALL NAM DAMH
Glen Garvan
Camusnagaul
Trislaig
Fort William
(An Gearasdan)
1176
STOB CHOIRE CLAURIGH
Loch Shiel
Scamodale
758
MEALL MÒR
Cona Glen
770
STOB COIRE A'CHEARCAILL
1219
AONACH MÒR
1081
STOB COIRE AN LAOIGH
754
SGOR AN TARMACHAIN
Auchintore
Glen Nevis House
1343
BEN NEVIS
1237
AONACH BEAG
Druimarbin
Loch Shiel
Hurich
Loch Linnhe
Glen Nevis
Blarmachfoldach
Conaglen House
Creag
Loch Doilet
888
SGURR DHOMHNUILL
Glen Scaddle
Coruanan
Achriabhach
Ben Nevis and Glen Coe
Inverscaddle Bay
24
Blàr a' Chaorainn
1098
SGURR A'MHAIM
1128
BINNEIN MÒR
NART
999
STOB BAN
1032
AM BODACH
1055
NA GRUAGAICHEAN
615
BEINN NA GUCAIG
Loch Linnhe
89
Ariundle Oakwood
Glen Gour
Mamore Forest
Loch Eilde Mòr
Ardgour
Clovulin
Corran
A82
796
MAM NA GUALAINN
heilt
884
GARBH BHEINN
13
Strontian
A861
Achnalea
Onich
North Ballachulish
B863
Loch Leven
Kinlochleven
West Highland Way
Glen Tarbert
Inversanda
Lochaber Watersports Centre
Folk Museum
Glencoe
741
PAP OF GLENCOE
966
AONACH EAGACH
950
620
GLAS BHEINN
853
CREACH BHEINN
Kentallen
South Ballachulish
Ballachulish
Glen Coe Visitor Centre
A82
698
855
BEINN A' CHRULAISTE
A828
1001
SGÒRR DHONUILL
1025
SGÒRR DHEARG
661
SGORR A' CHOISE
675
MEAL MÒR
Glen Coe
Cuil
Duror
Glen Duror
1148
BIDEAN NAM BIAN
958
BUACHAILLE ETIVE BEAG
1019
BUACHAILLE ETIVE MOR
Kings
651
BEINN NA CILLE
B8043
LOCH LINNHE
Loch a' Choire
Salachan Glen
River Creran
Glencoe Ski Centre
ADHOIN
30
Alltchaorunn
River Etive
568
SOURR A BHUIC
Shuna Island
655
MEALL BÀN
957
BEINN FHIONNLAIDH
1108
MEALL A' BHÙIRIDH
1098
CLACH LEATHAD
Elleric
Glen Creran
Glen Etive
Fasnacloich
Invercreran House Hotel
River Ure
Portnacroish
Port Ramsay
Appin
Glasdrum Wood
932
BEINN SGULAIRD
Ben Nevis and Glen Coe
Port Appin
Creagan Inn
Gualachulain
1087
STOB GHABHAR
Inverfolla
Druimavuic
1043
STOB COIR' AN ALBANNAICH
Clachan
Eriska
North Shian
Loch Creran
LISMORE
B8045
South Shian
Barcaldine
810
CREACH BHEINN
1079
BEN STARAV
Lynn of Lorne
Achnacroish
Barcaldine
Scottish Sea Life Sanctuary
A828
692
BEINN MOLURGAINN
957
BEINN NAN AIGHENAN
Loch Dochard
Inveroran Hotel
Kilcheran
Kiel Crofts
BENDERLOCH
Bridge
Benderloch
Ledaig
B845
714
BEN MEEAN
Loch Etive
Glen Kinglass
Lynn of Lorne
Ardmucknish Bay
Dunstaffnage Castle
Dunstaffnage Chapel (ruin)
Ardchattan Priory
Inveresragan
Glen Orchy
794
Black Crofts
North Connel
Connel
Achnacloich
Bonawe
Glen Strae
Achaleven
River Noe
Dunbeg
A85
988
BEINN EUNAICH
Ganavan Bay
Airds Bay
Bonawe Historic Iron Furnace
648
BEINN DONACHAN
B8074
BEINN
Dunollie Castle
A85
McCaig's Tower
Brochroy
Taynuilt
Ichrachan
1124
BEN CRUACHAN
River Orchy
12
KERRERA
Oban
(An t-Oban)
Clenamacrie
Airdeny
20
Glen Nant
River Awe
Cruachan Reservoir
Kilchurn Castle
B8077
Stronmilchan
Glen Lochy
Glen Lonan
River Lonan
Pass of Brander
Lochawe
Cruachan Power Station
Inverlochy
A85
Gallanachbeg
Ariogan
Gallanachmore
Loch Nell
B845
A819
Upper Kinchrackine
Dalmally
1130
BEN L
Sound of Kerrera
515
BEINN GHLAS
Lerags
Kilmore
Ardanaiseig
Ardanaiseig Hotel
636
739
Ardentallen
Loch Feochan
A816
Hayfield
Loch Nant
Kilchrenan
Taychreggan Hotel
Cladich
Kilninver
356
AN CREACHAN
482
BEINN DEARG
Lochan Shira
15
Loch Scamadale
Portsonachan Hotel
Loch Awe
B840
947
BEINN BHUIDHE
Loch Tralaig
Inverinan
Glen Aray
Glenfyne Lodge
645
MAOL BREA
Lochavich
Loch Avich
24
658
CLACHAN HILL
589
CRUACH MHOR
Glen Shira
Glen Fyne
Melfort
Loch Melfort
Kilmelford
Falls of Blarghour
Barbreck Stables
Dalavich
83
Ardchonnel
84
Newyork
Portinnisherrich
A819
Cairndow
Ardkinglas
A816
0 1 2 3 4 miles
0 1 2 3 4 5 kilometres

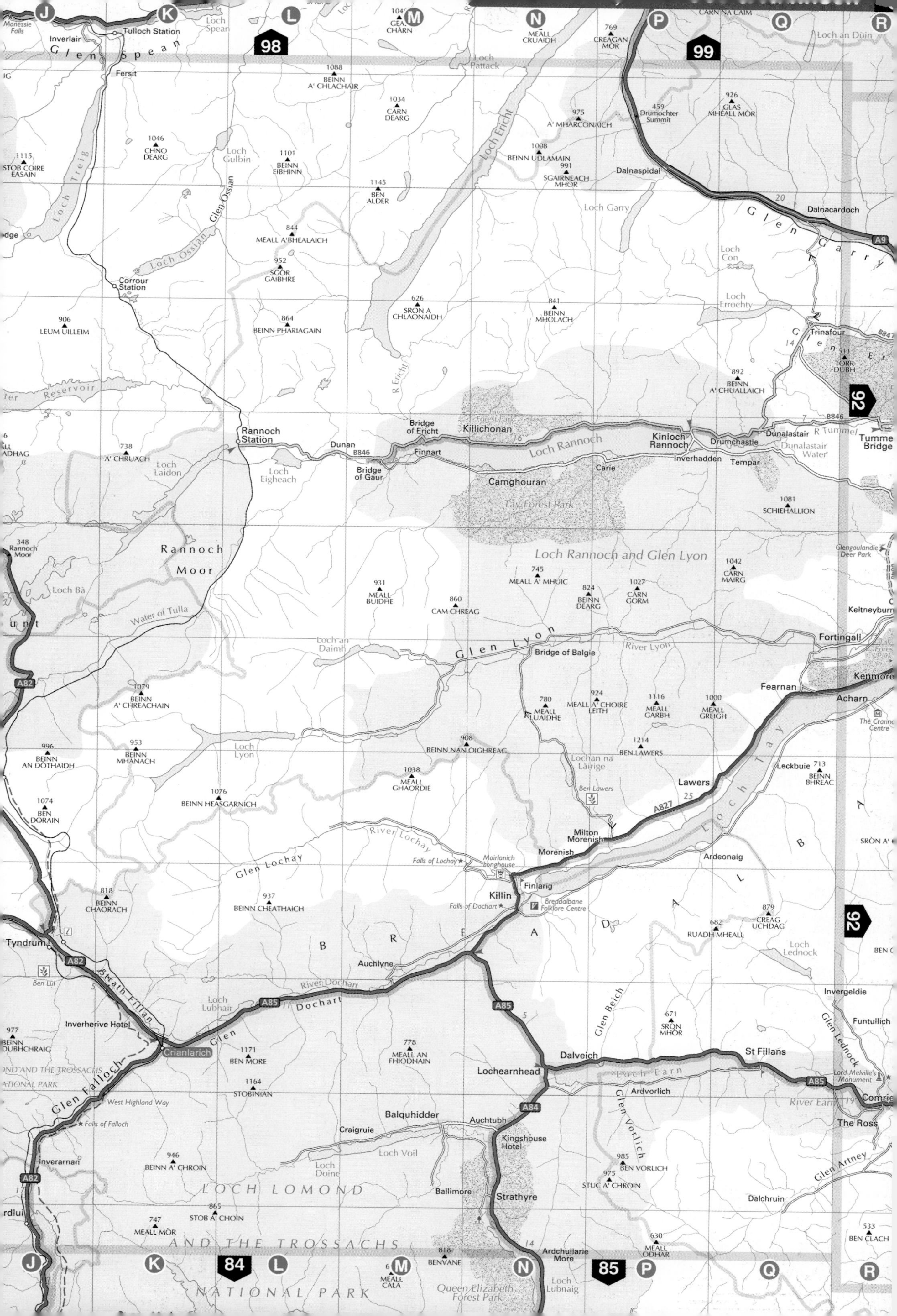

J
K
L
M
N
P
Q
R
98
99
92
84
85
Glen Spean
Tulloch Station
Inverlair
Fersit
Loch Spean
1046 GEAL CHÀRN
MEALL CRUAIDH
769 CREAGAN MOR
CARN NA CAIM
Loch an Dùin
Loch Pattack
1088 BEINN A' CHLACHAIR
1034 CARN DEARG
Loch Ericht
975 A' MHARCONAICH
459 Drumochter Summit
926 GLAS MHEALL MÒR
1046 CHNO DEARG
Loch Gulbin
1101 BEINN EIBHINN
1008 BEINN UDLAMAIN
991 SGAIRNEACH MHOR
Dalnaspidal
1115 STOB COIRE EASAIN
Loch Treig
Glen Ossian
1145 BEN ALDER
Loch Garry
Dalnacardoch
Glen Garry
A9
844 MEALL A' BHEALAICH
Loch Ossian
952 SGOR GAIBHRE
Loch Con
Corrour Station
626 SRON A CHLAONAIDH
841 BEINN MHOLACH
Loch Errochty
906 LEUM UILLEIM
864 BEINN PHARIAGAIN
Trinafour
B847
Glen Errochty
511 TORR DUBH
R Ericht
892 BEINN A' CHUALLAICH
Reservoir
Tay Forest Park
Bridge of Ericht
Killichonan
Rannoch Station
Kinloch Rannoch
Drumchastle
Dunalastair
B846
R Tummel
Tummel Bridge
738 A' CHRUACH
Dunan
B846
Finnart
Loch Rannoch
Dunalastair Water
Inverhadden
Tempar
Loch Laidon
Loch Eigheach
Bridge of Gaur
Carie
Camghouran
Tay Forest Park
1081 SCHIEHALLION
348 Rannoch Moor
Rannoch Moor
Loch Rannoch and Glen Lyon
Glengoulandie Deer Park
745 MEALL A' MHUIC
1042 CARN MAIRG
Loch Bà
931 MEALL BUIDHE
824 BEINN DEARG
1027 CARN GORM
860 CAM CHREAG
Keltneyburn
Water of Tulla
Loch an Daimh
Glen Lyon
Bridge of Balgie
River Lyon
Fortingall
A82
Fearnan
Kenmore
Acharn
1079 BEINN A' CHREACHAIN
780 MEALL LUAIDHE
924 MEALL A' CHOIRE LEITH
1116 MEALL GARBH
1000 MEALL GREIGH
The Crannog Centre
996 BEINN AN DOTHAIDH
953 BEINN MHANACH
Loch Lyon
908 BEINN NAN OIGHREAG
1214 BEN LAWERS
Lochan na Lairige
Leckbuie
713 BEINN BHREAC
Loch Tay
1038 MEALL GHAORDIE
Ben Lawers
Lawers
A827
1076 BEINN HEASGARNICH
1074 BEN DORAIN
River Lochay
Milton Morenish
Morenish
SRÒN A'
Ardeonaig
Glen Lochay
Falls of Lochay
Moirlanich Longhouse
BREADALBANE
Finlarig
Killin
Falls of Dochart
Breadalbane Folklore Centre
818 BEINN CHAORACH
937 BEINN CHEATHAICH
879 CREAG UCHDAG
682 RUADH MHEALL
Tyndrum
A82
Auchlyne
Loch Lednock
Ben Lui
Strath Fillan
River Dochart
Glen Beich
Invergeldie
Loch Lubhair
A85
Glen Dochart
A85
671 SRÒN MHOR
Funtullich
977 BEINN DUBHCHRAIG
Inverherive Hotel
Crianlarich
1171 BEN MORE
778 MEALL AN FHIODHAIN
Dalveich
St Fillans
Glen Lednock
Glen Falloch
Lochearnhead
Loch Earn
Lord Melville's Monument
1164 STOBINIAN
Ardvorlich
A85
West Highland Way
A84
River Earn
Comrie
Falls of Falloch
Balquhidder
Auchtubh
Glen Vorlich
The Ross
Craigruie
Kingshouse Hotel
Loch Voil
Inverarnan
946 BEINN A' CHROIN
985 BEN VORLICH
Glen Artney
Loch Doine
975 STUC A' CHROIN
A82
LOCH LOMOND AND THE TROSSACHS NATIONAL PARK
Ballimore
Strathyre
Dalchruin
865 STOB A' CHOIN
747 MEALL MÒR
630 MEALL ODHAR
533 BEN CLACH
818 BENVANE
Ardchullarie More
MEALL CALA
Loch Lubnaig
Queen Elizabeth Forest Park

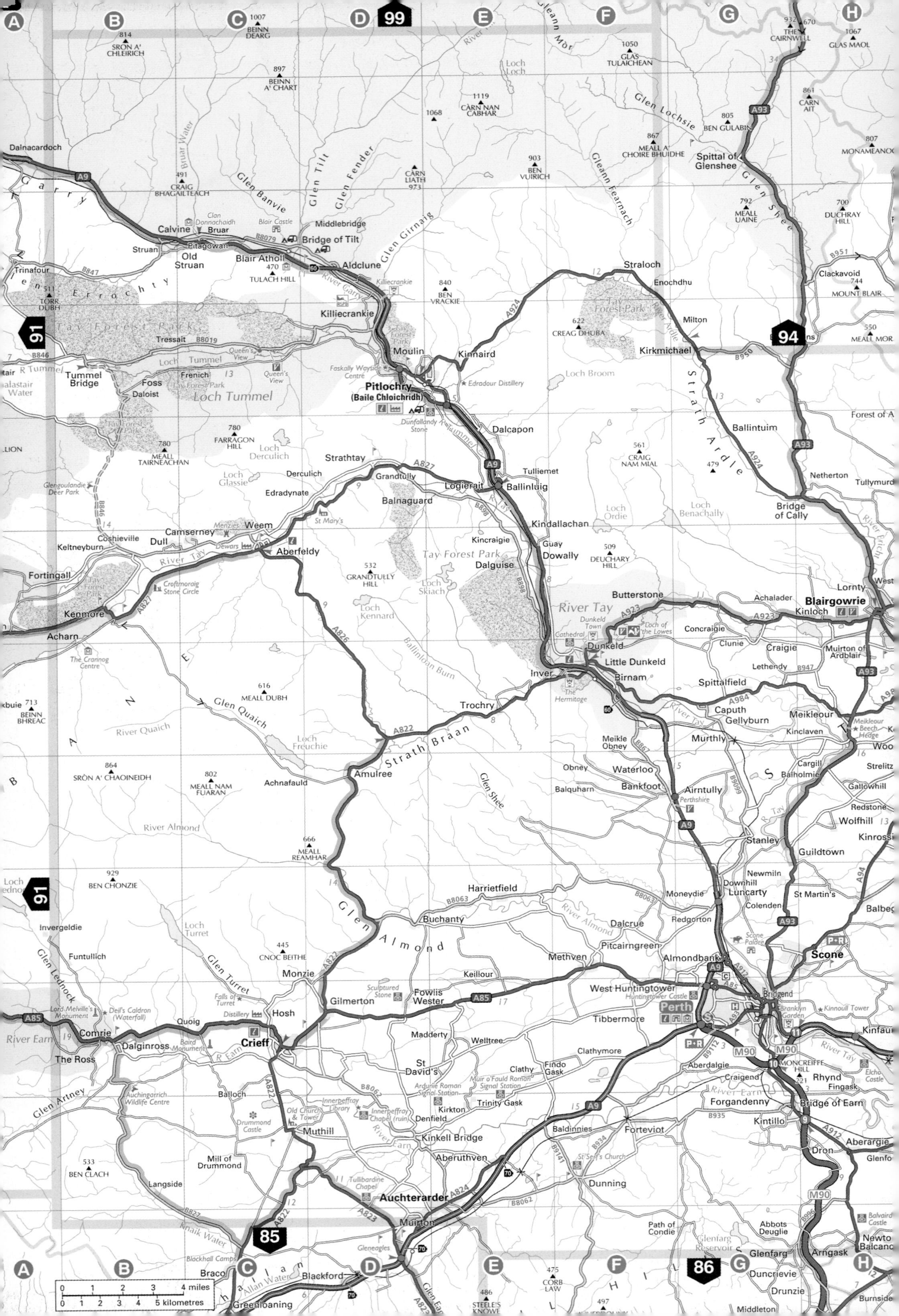

Perth & Tayside
J
K
L
M
N
P
Q
R
Glen Doll
831 LAIR OF ALDARARIE
Corrie Fee
928 MAYAR
946 DRIESH
896 BEN TIRRAN
739 CRUYS
693 WEST KNOCK
River North Esk
605 BULG
544 STURDY HILL
Glen Esk
Mains of Balnakettle
Fettercairn
B9120
Water of Saughs
677 HILL OF WIRREN
Clova
Glen Clova
649 CAIRN OF BAMS
755 FINBRACKS
Hunthill Lodge
West Water
Gannachy
Bogmuir
Edzell Castle & Garden
Sauchieburn
Rottal Lodge
579 HILL OF GARBET
Bridgend
Balfield
Edzell
Edzell Woods
Luthermuir
603 CAIRN DAUNIE
Glen Damff
Runtaleave
Glen Prosen
Cormuir
508
B955
Dunlappie
Brown Caterthun
White Caterthun
B966
River North Esk
A90
Glen Finlet
Pitcarity
River South Esk
490 NAKED TAM
Auchnacree
Kirkton of Menmuir
Tigerton
Inchbare
Newtonmill
Logie Pert
Keithock
Mains of Balhall
Little Brechin
Backwater Reservoir
Glencally
Glenquiech
Shandford
Lochty
Maison Dieu Chapel (ruin)
Trinity
Glenisla
94
Newmill of Inshewan
Fern
Careston
Brechin
95
House of Dun
Bellaty
Balintore
Dykehead
Cortachy
Burnside
Noran Water
Brechin Castle & Pictavia
R South Esk
A935
Caledonian Railway
B951
Dykends
Memus
Tannadice
B957
Inverquharity
Shielhill
Murthill
Doocot
Finavon
Netherton
Haughs of Kinnaird
Barnhead
Braes of Coul
Camera Obscura
B957
Crosston
Loch of Lintrathen
B951
Kingoldrum
Northmuir
Oathlaw
Sculptured Stones
Aberlemno
Maryton
River Isla
Reekie Linn Falls
Bridgend of Lintrathen
Kinnordy
Battledykes
A933
Farnell
A934
Dykehead
425 BALDUFF HILL
Bridge of Craigisla
Kirriemuir
A90
B9134
Mains of Melgunds
Westerton of Rossie
Westmuir
Southmuir
Ballinshoe
Kemp's Castle
B9113
Gauldswell
Kirkton of Airlie
Lunanhead
Restenneth Priory
Reswallie
Bolshan
132 WUDDY LAW
Padanaram
A926
Littleton
Forfar Loch
Guthrie
Glasterlaw
294 HILL OF ALYTH
B954
Airlie
Craigton of Airlie
Roundyhill
Drumgley
A932
Burnside
Kinnell
River Isla
St Orland's Stone
Forfar
A932
Pitmuies
Boysack
Ruthven
Leys of Cossans
A928
A94
Kingsmuir
Dunnichen
Friockheim
Lunan Water
Inverkeilor
Alyth
B952
Dean Water
Eassie Sculptured Stone
Angus Folk Museum
Douglastown
Bowriefauld
Letham
B965
New Alyth
Glamis
A94
B9127
Craichie
Leysmill
Chapelton
Cauldcots
A926
Balhary
Thornton
Letham Grange
Charleston
B9128
A933
Colliston
A92
Balkeerie Kirkinch
Eassie and Nevay
B961
Redford
Marywell
Longleys
Meigle
Sculptured Stone Museum
Inverarity
Whigstreet
B9127
Kirkbuddo
Greystone
Condor
St Vigeans
Gateside
A928
Hatton
Carmyllie
Newbigging
345 KINPURNEY HILL
Ardler
Newtyle
Nether Handwick
379 GALLOW HILL
Gallowfauld
Hayhillock
B9127
Elliot Water
Carlingheugh Bay
The Deil's Heid
Coupar Angus
B954
455 CRAIGOWL HILL
Petterden
259 CARROT HILL
Crombie
Bonnington
Arbirlot
Arbroath
Kettins
Tealing
Tealing Earth-House
Todhills
Monikie
Kirkton of Monikie
Bonnyton
Kirkton of Auchterhouse
Kirkton of Tealing
Tealing Dovecot
Newbigging
Craigton
Leys
Auchterhouse
B961
Muirdrum
A92
Campmuir
Sidlaw Hills
Lundie
Dronley
Kirkton of Strathmartine
Wellbank
Carlungie Earth-House
East Haven
Burnside of Duntrune
Newbigging
Upper Victoria
Panbride
Muirhead
A923
Claypotts Castle
Kellas
Ardestie Earth-House
Barry Mill
West Haven
Birkhill
Mains of Fintry
Murroes
Barry
Carnoustie
376 KINGS SEAT
Fowlis
Camperdown
Whitfield
B961
A930
Liff
Gourdie
Downfield
Douglas and Angus
Baldovie
B962
Carnoustie
B953
Abernyte
Denhead of Gray
Benvie
Lochee
Ancrum Outdoor Centre
B959
Claypotts Castle
Barnhill
Monifieth
Baledgarno
Mills Observatory
North Carr Lightship
DUNDEE
Broughty Ferry
Broughty Castle
Invergowrie
Longforgan
Ballindean
Inchture
Kingoodie
Dundee
Discovery Point & Verdant Works
HM Frigate 'Unicorn'
A92
Tay Bridge
Tayport
BUDDON NESS
Tentsmuir Point
Newport-on-Tay
Rait
A90
B946
Kilspindie
Inchmichael
FIRTH OF TAY
B945
Wormit
Balmerino Abbey
Kirkton
A914
Scottish National Golf Centre
Grange
Balmerino
Bottomcraig
Tentsmuir Point
Coultra
Gauldry
Errol
Kilmany
Creich
Hazelton Walls
Lucklawhill
A919
Leuchars
ST ANDREWS BAY
Brunton
Rathillet
Logie
RAF Leuchars
285 NORMANS LAW
A92
Balmullo
Lindores
Luthrie
Guardbridge
Glenduckie
Newburgh
Denbrae
River Eden
Kincaple
St Andrews
A91
Dunbog
Moonzie
Dairsie
A914
Castle
St Andrews
Den of Lindores
A913
Strathkinness
Grange of Lindores
B937
Fernie
Cupar
Botanic Garden
Brownhills
B983
Monimail
Letham
Kemback
Blebocraigs
Craigtoun
A917
Boarhills
Lochieheads
Collessie
Bow of Fife
A91
Cupar Muir
B940
Denhead
B9131
Auchtermuchty
Deer Centre
Bridgend
B939
Pitscottie
A915
Giffordtown
Springfield
Ceres
Cameron Reservoir
Baldinnie
Kingsbarns
Dunshalt
Charlottetown
Scotstarvit Tower
B940
Dunino
Ladybank
Craigrothie
Raderne
Balcomie Links
86
Peat Inn
87
FIFE NESS
River Eden
B936
Kingskettle
B9129
New Gilston
B941
Kingsmuir
B940
A912
A92
Balmalcolm
Lathones
Scotland's Secret Bunker
Falkland Palace
B936
Woodside
Largoward
B940
Lochty
Town Plan: Dundee p.

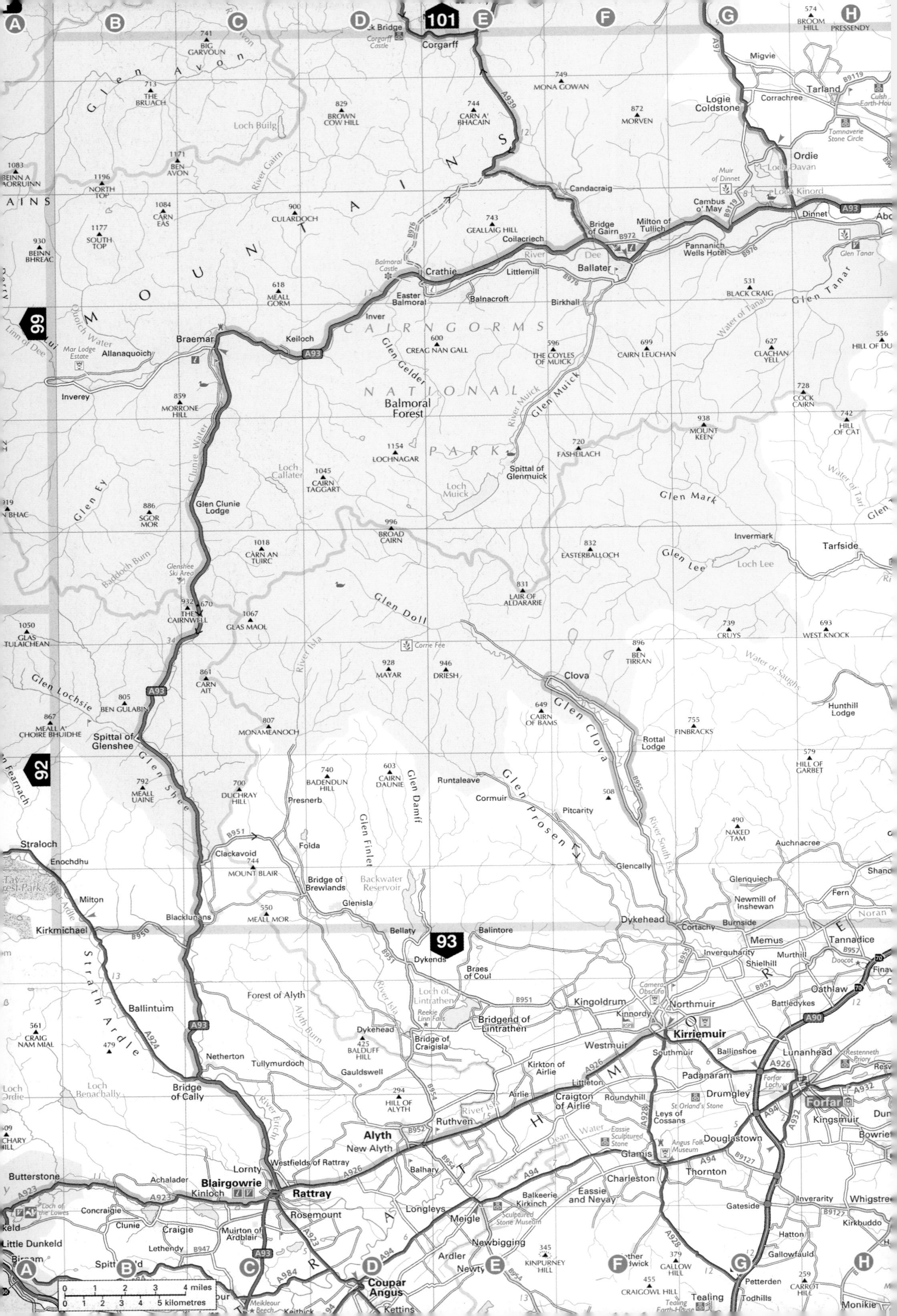

101
99
92
93
Corgarff
Corgarff Castle
741 BIG GARVOUN
Glen Avon
713 THE BRUACH
829 BROWN COW HILL
744 CARN A' BHACAIN
749 MONA GOWAN
872 MORVEN
Migvie
Tarland
Corrachree
Logie Coldstone
Culsh Earth-House
Tomnaverie Stone Circle
574 BROOM HILL
PRESSENDY
Loch Builg
1083 BEINN A' BHUIRD
1196 NORTH TOP
1171 BEN AVON
1084 CARN EAS
1177 SOUTH TOP
930 BEINN BHREAC
River Gairn
900 CULARDOCH
743 GEALLAIG HILL
Candacraig
Ordie
Muir of Dinnet
Loch Davan
Loch Kinord
Cambus o' May
Dinnet
Milton of Tullich
Bridge of Gairn
Coilacriech
Pannanich Wells Hotel
Glen Tanar
River Dee
Ballater
Balmoral Castle
Crathie
Littlemill
Easter Balmoral
Balnacroft
Birkhall
618 MEALL GORM
531 BLACK CRAIG
Water of Tanar
CAIRNGORMS NATIONAL PARK
MOUNTAINS
Quoich Water
Linn of Dee
Mar Lodge Estate
Allanaquoich
Braemar
Inver
Keiloch
600 CREAG NAN GALL
Glen Gelder
596 THE COYLES OF MUICK
699 CAIRN LEUCHAN
627 CLACHAN YELL
556 HILL OF DUB
Inverey
859 MORRONE HILL
Balmoral Forest
River Muick
Glen Muick
728 COCK CAIRN
742 HILL OF CAT
938 MOUNT KEEN
Clunie Water
1154 LOCHNAGAR
720 FASHEILACH
Spittal of Glenmuick
Loch Callater
1045 CAIRN TAGGART
Loch Muick
Water of Tarf
Glen Ey
886 SGOR MOR
Glen Clunie Lodge
Glen Mark
996 BROAD CAIRN
832 EASTERBALLOCH
Invermark
Tarfside
Glen Lee
Loch Lee
Baddoch Burn
1018 CARN AN TUIRC
Glenshee Ski Area
831 LAIR OF ALDARARIE
932 THE CAIRNWELL
670
1067 GLAS MAOL
Glen Doll
739 CRUYS
693 WEST KNOCK
1050 GLAS TULAICHEAN
Corrie Fee
896 BEN TIRRAN
River Isla
928 MAYAR
946 DRIESH
Water of Saughs
Clova
Glen Lochsie
861 CARN AIT
805 BEN GULABIN
649 CAIRN OF BAMS
Glen Clova
Hunthill Lodge
867 MEALL A' CHOIRE BHUIDHE
807 MONAMEANOCH
755 FINBRACKS
Spittal of Glenshee
Rottal Lodge
Glen Shee
579 HILL OF GARBET
740 BADENDUN HILL
603 CAIRN DAUNIE
Runtaleave
Glen Damff
Glen Prosen
508
Cormuir
792 MEALL UAINE
700 DUCHRAY HILL
Presnerb
Pitcarity
490 NAKED TAM
Glen Finlet
River South Esk
Straloch
Folda
Auchnacree
Enochdhu
Clackavoid
744 MOUNT BLAIR
Glencally
Bridge of Brewlands
Backwater Reservoir
Glenquiech
Milton
River Ardle
Glenisla
Newmill of Inshewan
Fern
Blacklunans
550 MEALL MOR
Dykehead
Noran
Kirkmichael
Bellaty
Balintore
Cortachy
Burnside
Memus
Tannadice
Dykends
Inverquharity
Murthill
Shielhill
Doocot
Strath Ardle
Braes of Coul
Forest of Alyth
Loch of Lintrathen
Camera Obscura
Kingoldrum
Northmuir
Oathlaw
Finavon
Ballintuim
Reekie Linn Falls
Bridgend of Lintrathen
Kinnordy
Battledykes
Alyth Burn
561 CRAIG NAM MIAL
479
Dykehead
425 BALDUFF HILL
Bridge of Craigisla
Kirriemuir
Westmuir
Southmuir
Ballinshoe
Lunanhead
Restenneth Priory
Netherton
Tullymurdoch
Gauldswell
Kirkton of Airlie
Padanaram
Forfar Loch
Forfar
Loch Benachally
Bridge of Cally
294 HILL OF ALYTH
Littleton
Airlie
Craigton of Airlie
Roundyhill
Drumgley
St Orland's Stone
River Ericht
Ruthven
Leys of Cossans
Kingsmuir
Alyth
New Alyth
Dean Water
Eassie Sculptured Stone
Angus Folk Museum
Douglastown
Glamis
Westfields of Rattray
Balhary
Lornty
Thornton
Butterstone
Achalader
Blairgowrie
Charleston
Kinloch
Rattray
Eassie and Nevay
Balkeerie
Kirkinch
Inverarity
Whigstreet
Loch of the Lowes
Concraigie
Rosemount
Longleys
Meigle
Sculptured Stone Museum
Gateside
Clunie
Craigie
Muirton of Ardblair
Kirkbuddo
Newbigging
Hatton
Little Dunkeld
Lethendy
345 KINPURNEY HILL
379 GALLOW HILL
Gallowfauld
Ardler
Newtyle
455 CRAIGOWL HILL
Petterden
259 CARROT HILL
Coupar Angus
Kettins
Tealing
Tealing Earth-House
Todhills
Monikie
Meikleour Beech
STRATHMORE
A93 A939 A97 A93 A923 A924 A926 A94 A984 A928 A90 A932
B976 B972 B9119 B951 B950 B954 B952 B947 B955 B957 B9127
0 1 2 3 4 miles
0 1 2 3 4 5 kilometres

Town Plan: Aberdeen p.

A
B
C
D
E
F
G
H
Dunvegan
Colbost Croft
Skinidin
Giant Angus
Kilmuir
A864
Lonmore
Caroy River
265
BEN AKETIL
271
CRUACHAN BEINN A' CHEARCAILL
104
Skeabost
Carbost
Borve
Uigshader
Drumuie
A855
312
Arnish
Brochel
SOUND
Roskhill
Glengrasco
Torvaig
469
HEALAVAL MORE
Orbost
Roag
amasaig
Vatten
Portree
Seafield
RAASAY
488
HEALAVAL BHEAG
Harlosh
Loch Caroy
A863
Glen Ose
Ose
B885
ISLE OF SKYE
417
BEINN NA GREINE
Penifiler
412
BEN TIANAVAIG
Glenmore
444
DÙN CAAN
368
BEINN NA BOINEID
Harlosh Island
Colbost Point
Tarner Island
Dun Beag
Bracadale
Loch Duagrich
Glenvarragill
Mugeary
A87
Camastianavaig
Tianavaig Bay
Oskaig
Rudha na' Leac
Loch Bracadale
Ullinish Lodge Hotel
Struan
Coillore
Ollach
Wiay
Clachan
310
BEINN NA LEAC
Idrigill Point
23
Glen Varragill
B883
Inverarish
Oronsay
Loch Harport
439
ROINEVAL
The Braes
Portnalong
Fiskavaig
B8009
444
BEN LEE
Peinchorran
Suisnish Point
Eyre Point
Rudha nan Clach
Fernilea
Sconser
SCA
Drynoch
369
ARNAVAL
Carbost
A863
Glen Drynoch
Merkadale
773
GLAMAIG
396
MULLACH NA CARN
Talisker Bay
Talisker
Glen Eynort
Sligachan
369
BEINN BHREAC
A87
Loch Ainort
Dunan
Luib
17
Caolas Scalpay
447
BEINN BHREAC
Grula
564
GLAS BHEIN MHÓRN
965
SGURR NAN GILLEAN
Cor
Loch Eynort
974
SGURR A' GHEADAIDH
The Cuillin Hills
732
BEINN NA CAILLICH
708
BEINN DEORG MHOR
Broadford
434
AN CRUACHIN
Glenbrittle House
Cuillin Hills
927
BLAVEN
B8083
Bualintur
1009
SGURR ALASDAIR
Loch Coruisk
Loch na Creitheach
Torrin
14
Loch Brittle
894
GARS BHEINN
225
CEANN NA BEINNE
Kirkibost
B8083
Loch Slapin
BEIN NAN C
Rudh' an Dùnain
Soay Sound
139
BEINN BHREAC
Loch Scavaig
344
BEN MEABOST
Suisnish
Rudha Suisnish
Loch Eishort
Mol-chlach
Elgol
Glasnakille
SOAY
Rudh' Aonghais
Tokavaig
Strathaird Point
Tarskavaig
Tarskavaig Bay
Achnacloich
CUILLIN SOUND
210
CANNA
CARN A' GHAILL
Garrisdale Point
A'Chill
Canna Harbour
Sanday
Rudha Shamhnan Insir
Clan Donald
Ardvasar
Calligarry
Sound of Canna
302
MULLACH MÒR
Aird of Sleat
Rudha na Roinne
A Bhrideanach
570
ORVAL
Kinloch
Loch Scresort
Ard Thurinish
Point of Sleat
Oigh-sgeir
RÙM
810
ASKIVAL
763
SGÙRR NAN GILLEAN
The Small Isles
Rudha nam Meirleach
Sound of Rum
Bay of Laig
Cleadale
Eilean Ighe
299
AN CRUACHAN
Rudha an Fhasaidh
Laig
EIGG
Luinga Mhòr
Kildonnan
393
AN SGÙRR
Sandavore
Rudh' Arisaig
103
Sound of Eigg
Eilean Chathastail
Eilean nan Each
MUCK
Port Mor
88
89
0 1 2 3 4 miles
0 1 2 3 4 5 kilometres

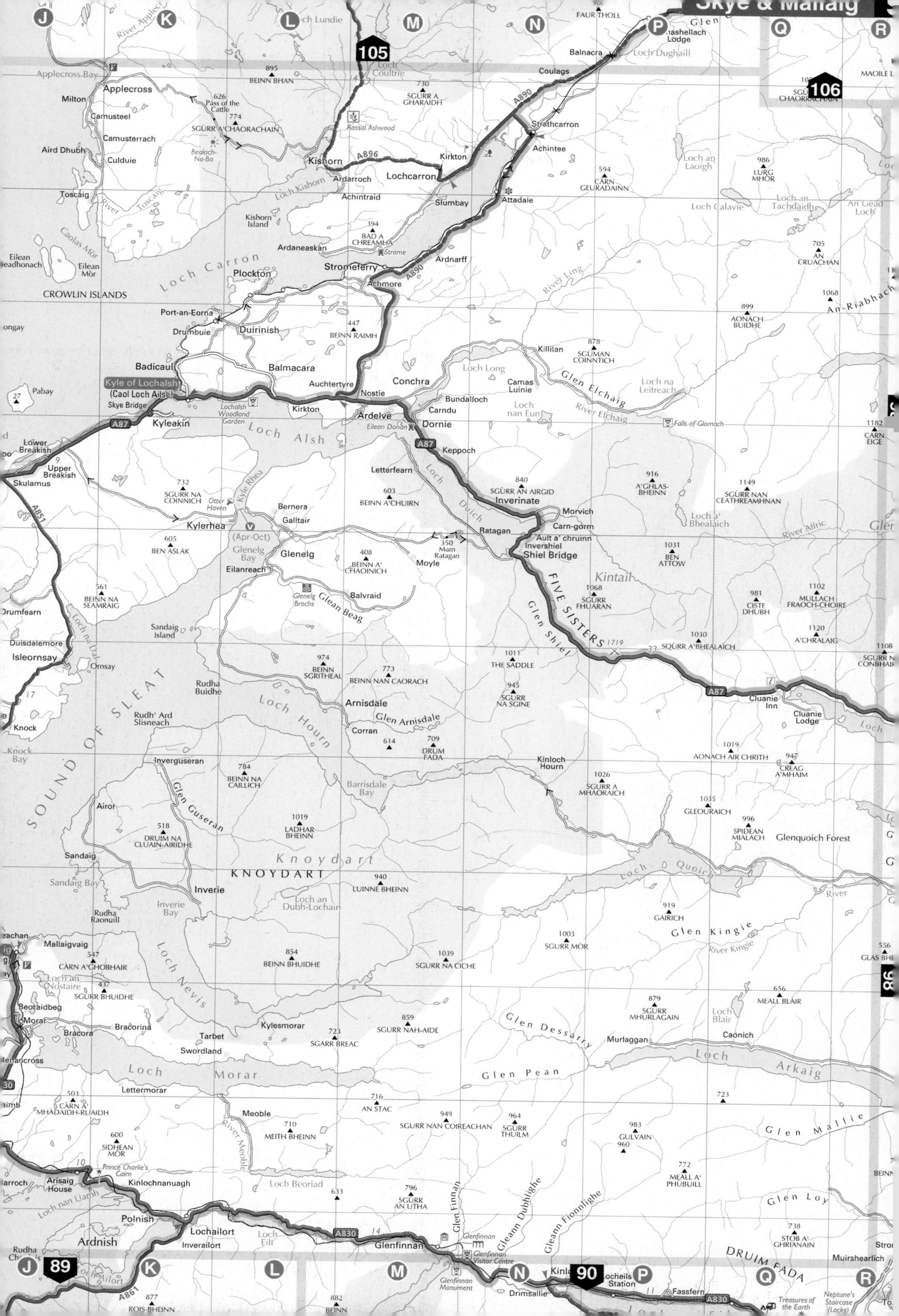

Skye & Mallaig
J
K
L
M
N
P
Q
R
105
106
89
90
98
Applecross Bay
Applecross
Milton
Camusteel
Camusterrach
Aird Dhubh
Culduie
Toscaig
River Toscaig
Caolas Mòr
Eilean Mòr
CROWLIN ISLANDS
Pabay
Pass of the Cattle
626
774
SGÙRR A' CHAORACHAIN
Bealach-Na-Ba
895
BEINN BHAN
Loch Coultrie
Rassal Ashwood
730
SGURR A GHARAIDH
A896
Kishorn
Loch Kishorn
Kishorn Island
Ardarroch
Achintraid
Lochcarron
Kirkton
Slumbay
Strathcarron
Achintee
Attadale
A890
Coulags
Balnacra
Loch Dughaill
Lodge
FAUR THOLL
Glen
Strome
394
BAD A CHREAMHA
Ardaneaskan
Stromeferry
Achmore
Ardnarff
Loch Carron
Plockton
Port-an-Eorna
Drumbuie
Duirinish
447
BEINN RAIMH
Badicaul
Balmacara
Kyle of Lochalsh
(Caol Loch Ailse)
Skye Bridge
Kyleakin
A87
Lochalsh Woodland Garden
Kirkton
Auchtertyre
Nostie
Ardelve
Eilean Donan
Dornie
Conchra
Bundalloch
Carndu
Loch Long
Camas Luinie
Loch nan Eun
Killilan
878
SGUMAN COINNTICH
Glen Elchaig
River Elchaig
Loch na Leitreach
Falls of Glomach
594
CARN GEURADAINN
Loch an Laoigh
Loch Calavie
986
LURG MHOR
Loch an Tachdaidh
An Gead Loch
705
AN CRUACHAN
River Ling
899
AONACH BUIDHE
1068
An Riabhach
1182
CARN EIGE
Loch Alsh
Lower Breakish
Upper Breakish
Skulamus
A851
732
SGURR NA COINNICH
Otter Haven
Kyle Rhea
Kylerhea
605
BEN ASLAK
Keppoch
Letterfearn
Loch Duich
603
BEINN A' CHUIRN
Bernera
Galltair
(Apr-Oct)
Glenelg Bay
Glenelg
Eilanreach
840
SGÙRR AN AIRGID
Inverinate
Morvich
Carn-gorm
Ratagan
Ault a' chruinn
Invershiel
Shiel Bridge
350
Mam Ratagan
Moyle
408
BEINN A' CHAOINICH
Glenelg Brochs
Glean Beag
Balvraid
916
A'GHLAS-BHEINN
1149
SGÙRR NAN CEATHREAMHNAN
Loch a' Bhealaich
River Affric
1031
BEN ATTOW
Kintail
FIVE SISTERS
1068
SGURR FHUARAN
Glen Shiel
561
BEINN NA SEAMRAIG
Drumfearn
Loch na Dal
Duisdalemore
Isleornsay
Ornsay
Sandaig Island
974
BEINN SGRITHEAL
773
BEINN NAN CAORACH
1011
THE SADDLE
945
SGURR NA SGINE
1030
SGÙRR A' BHEALAICH
1719
981
CISTE DHUBH
1102
MULLACH FRAOCH-CHOIRE
1120
A'CHRALAIG
1108
A87
Cluanie Inn
Cluanie Lodge
Rudha Buidhe
Rudh' Ard Slisneach
SOUND OF SLEAT
Loch Hourn
Arnisdale
Glen Arnisdale
Corran
614
709
DRUM FADA
Knock
Knock Bay
Inverguseran
784
BEINN NA CAILLICH
Glen Guseran
Barrisdale Bay
Kinloch Hourn
1026
SGURR A MHAORAICH
1019
AONACH AIR CHRITH
947
CREAG A'MHAIM
1035
GLEOURAICH
996
SPIDEAN MIALACH
Glenquoich Forest
Airor
518
DRUIM NA CLUAIN-AIRIDHE
1019
LADHAR BHEINN
Sandaig
Sandaig Bay
Knoydart
KNOYDART
Inverie
Inverie Bay
940
LUINNE BHEINN
Loch an Dubh-Lochain
Loch Quoich
River
919
GAIRICH
Rudha Raonuill
Mallaigvaig
547
CÀRN A'GHOBHAIR
Loch an Nostaire
437
SGURR BHUIDHE
Loch Nevis
854
BEINN BHUIDHE
1039
SGURR NA CICHE
1003
SGURR MOR
Glen Kingie
River Kingie
556
879
SGURR MHURLAGAIN
656
MEALL BLAIR
Loch Blair
Beoraidbeg
Morar
Bracora
Bracorina
Tarbet
Kylesmorar
859
SGURR NAH-AIDE
723
SGARR BREAC
Glen Dessarry
Murlaggan
Caonich
Swordland
Loch Morar
Glen Pean
Loch Arkaig
Lettermorar
503
CÀRN A' MHADAIDH-RUAIDH
716
AN STAC
723
Meoble
River Meoble
710
MEITH BHEINN
949
SGURR NAN COIREACHAN
964
SGURR THUILM
983
GULVAIN
960
Glen Mallie
600
SIDHEAN MÓR
Prince Charlie's Cairn
Arisaig House
Kinlochnanuagh
Loch nan Uamh
Loch Beoraid
633
796
SGURR AN UTHA
Glen Finnan
Gleann Dubhlighe
Gleann Fionnlighe
772
MEALL A' PHUBUILL
Glen Loy
Polnish
Ardnish
Lochailort
Inverailort
Loch Eilt
A830
Glenfinnan
Glenfinnan Visitor Centre
Glenfinnan Monument
738
STOB A' GHRIANAIN
DRUIM FADA
Muirshearlich
Loch Ailort
A861
877
ROIS-BHEINN
882
BEINN
Drimsallie
Locheils Station
Fassfern
Treasures of the Earth
Neptune's Staircase (Locks)

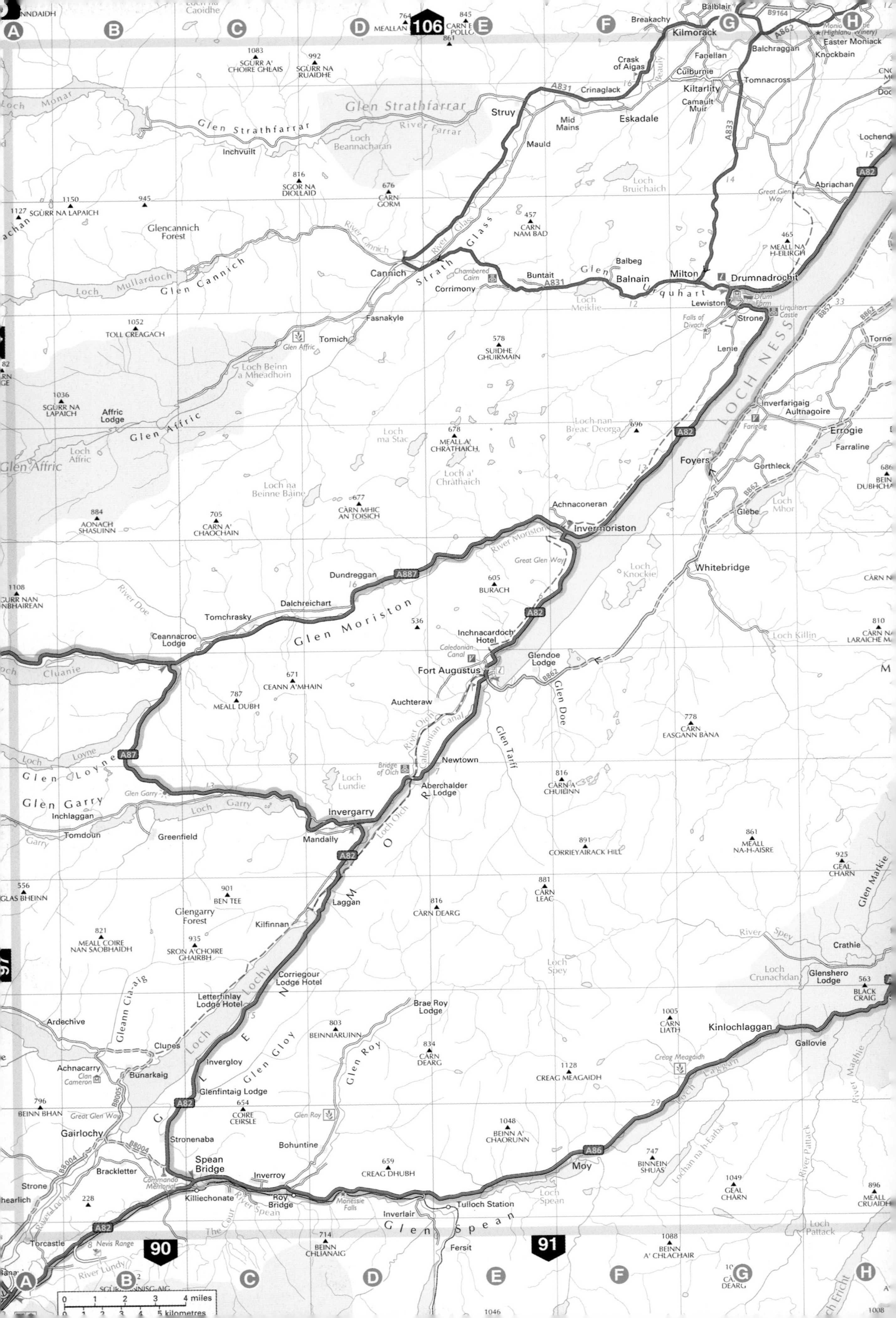
106
90
91
Kilmorack
Beauly
Kiltarlity
Struy
Glen Strathfarrar
Loch Monar
Inchvuilt
Loch Beannacharan
Eskadale
Mauld
Crinaglack
Drumnadrochit
Lewiston
Milton
Balnain
Buntait
Glen Urquhart
Cannich
Corrimony
Strath Glass
Glen Cannich
Loch Mullardoch
Glencannich Forest
Tomich
Fasnakyle
Glen Affric
Loch Affric
Affric Lodge
Loch Beinn a Mheadhoin
Strone
Lenie
Loch Ness
Inverfarigaig
Foyers
Errogie
Gorthleck
Achnaconeran
Invermoriston
Whitebridge
Glen Moriston
Dundreggan
Dalchreichart
Tomchrasky
Ceannacroc Lodge
Loch Cluanie
Inchnacardoch Hotel
Fort Augustus
Glendoe Lodge
Glen Doe
Auchteraw
Glen Tarff
Loch Loyne
Glen Loyne
Glen Garry
Inchlaggan
Tomdoun
Greenfield
Invergarry
Mandally
Newtown
Aberchalder Lodge
Loch Oich
Laggan
Kilfinnan
Glengarry Forest
Loch Lochy
Letterfinlay Lodge Hotel
Corriegour Lodge Hotel
Clunes
Achnacarry
Bunarkaig
Invergloy
Glenfintaig Lodge
Glen Gloy
Glen Roy
Brae Roy Lodge
Gairlochy
Stronenaba
Spean Bridge
Brackletter
Commando Memorial
Bohuntine
Inverroy
Roy Bridge
Killiechonate
Tulloch Station
Inverlair
Glen Spean
Fersit
Moy
Kinlochlaggan
Gallovie
Loch Laggan
Creag Meagaidh
Loch Spey
River Spey
Crathie
Glenshero Lodge
Loch Crunachdan
Glen Markie
Torcastle
A82
A87
A887
A831
A833
A862
A86
B862
B852
B8004
B8005
0 1 2 3 4 miles
0 1 2 3 4 5 kilometres

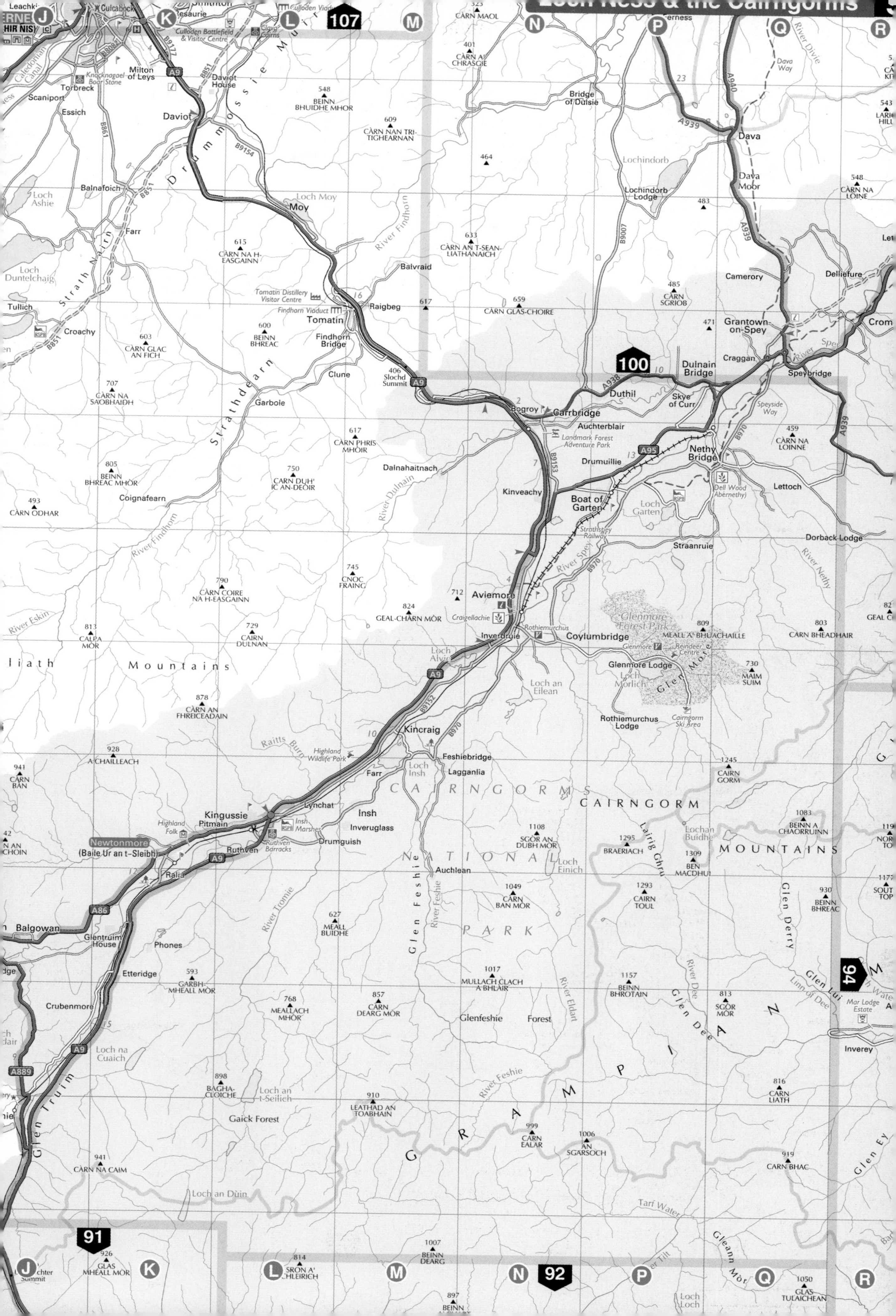

107
Culcabock
Culloden Battlefield & Visitor Centre
Clava Cairns
Milton of Leys
Knocknagael Boar Stone
Torbreck
Scaniport
Essich
Daviot
Daviot House
Drummossie Muir
CÀRN MAOL
401
CÀRN A' CHRASGIE
548
BEINN BHUIDHE MHOR
609
CÀRN NAN TRI-TIGHEARNAN
464
Bridge of Dulsie
Lochindorb
Lochindorb Lodge
Dava
Dava Moor
Dava Way
River Divie
543
548
CARN NA LOINE
483
Loch Ashie
Balnafoich
Loch Moy
Moy
Farr
Loch Duntelchaig
Strath Nairn
615
CÀRN NA H-EASGAINN
River Findhorn
633
CÀRN AN T-SEAN-LIATHANAICH
Balvraid
Camerory
Dellefure
485
CÀRN SGRIOB
Tullich
Tomatin Distillery Visitor Centre
Findhorn Viaduct
Raigbeg
617
659
CÀRN GLAS-CHOIRE
Tomatin
Croachy
603
CÀRN GLAC AN FICH
600
BEINN BHREAC
Findhorn Bridge
471
Grantown-on-Spey
Crom
Craggan
Speybridge
100
Dulnain Bridge
Clune
406
Slochd Summit
707
CÀRN NA SAOBHAIDH
Garbole
Strathdearn
Duthil
Skye of Curr
Bogroy
Carrbridge
Auchterblair
Landmark Forest Adventure Park
Speyside Way
617
CÀRN PHRIS MHÒIR
459
CÀRN NA LOINNE
Drumuillie
Nethy Bridge
805
BEINN BHREAC MHÒR
750
CÀRN DUH' IC AN-DEOIR
Dalnahaitnach
River Dulnain
Coignafearn
Kinveachy
Boat of Garten
Loch Garten
Dell Wood (Abernethy)
Lettoch
493
CÀRN ODHAR
Strathspey Railway
River Spey
Dorback Lodge
Straanruie
River Nethy
River Findhorn
745
CNOC FRAING
790
CÀRN COIRE NA H-EASGAINN
712
824
GEAL-CHARN MÒR
Aviemore
Craigellachie
Glenmore Forest Park
809
MEALL A' BHUACHAILLE
803
CARN BHEADHAIR
River Eskin
813
CALPA MÒR
729
CAIRN DULNAN
Inverdruie
Rothiemurchus
Coylumbridge
Glenmore
Reindeer Centre
Glenmore Lodge
Glen More
730
MAIM SUIM
Loch Alvie
Mountains
Loch an Eilean
Loch Morlich
878
CÀRN AN FHREICEADAIN
Kincraig
Rothiemurchus Lodge
Cairngorm Ski Area
Raitts Burn
Highland Wildlife Park
928
A' CHAILLEACH
Feshiebridge
Loch Insh
Lagganlia
1245
CAIRN GORM
941
CARN BAN
Farr
CAIRNGORMS
CAIRNGORM
Lynchat
Insh
Kingussie
Pitmain
Highland Folk
Insh Marshes
Inveruglass
1108
SGOR AN DUBH MOR
1083
BEINN A' CHAORRUINN
Lochan Buidhe
Lairig Ghru
1295
BRAERIACH
MOUNTAINS
Newtonmore
(Baile Ur an t-Sleibh)
Ruthven
Ruthven Barracks
Drumguish
1309
BEN MACDHUI
NATIONAL
Loch Einich
Ralia
Auchlean
1049
CARN BAN MÒR
1293
CAIRN TOUL
Glen Derry
930
BEINN BHREAC
River Tromie
Glen Feshie
River Feshie
627
MEALL BUIDHE
PARK
Balgowan
Glentruim House
Phones
Etteridge
593
GARBH-MHEALL MÒR
1017
MULLACH CLACH A' BHLAIR
River Eldart
1157
BEINN BHROTAIN
River Dee
94
Glen Lui
Linn of Dee
Mar Lodge Estate
768
MEALLACH MHÒR
857
CARN DEARG MÒR
Glenfeshie
Forest
Crubenmore
Glen Dee
813
SGOR MÒR
Inverey
Loch na Cuaich
GRAMPIAN
898
BAGHA-CLOICHE
Loch an t-Seilich
River Feshie
816
CARN LIATH
Gaick Forest
910
LEATHAD AN TOABHAIN
Glen Truim
999
CARN EALAR
1006
AN SGARSOCH
Glen Ey
941
CÀRN NA CAIM
919
CARN BHAC
Loch an Dùin
Tarf Water
91
926
GLAS MHEALL MÒR
1007
BEINN DEARG
814
92
Gleann Mòr
1050
GLAS TULAICHEAN
897
A9
A95
A938
A939
A940
A86
A889
B9153
B970
B9152
B851
B861
B9154
B9007
B9177

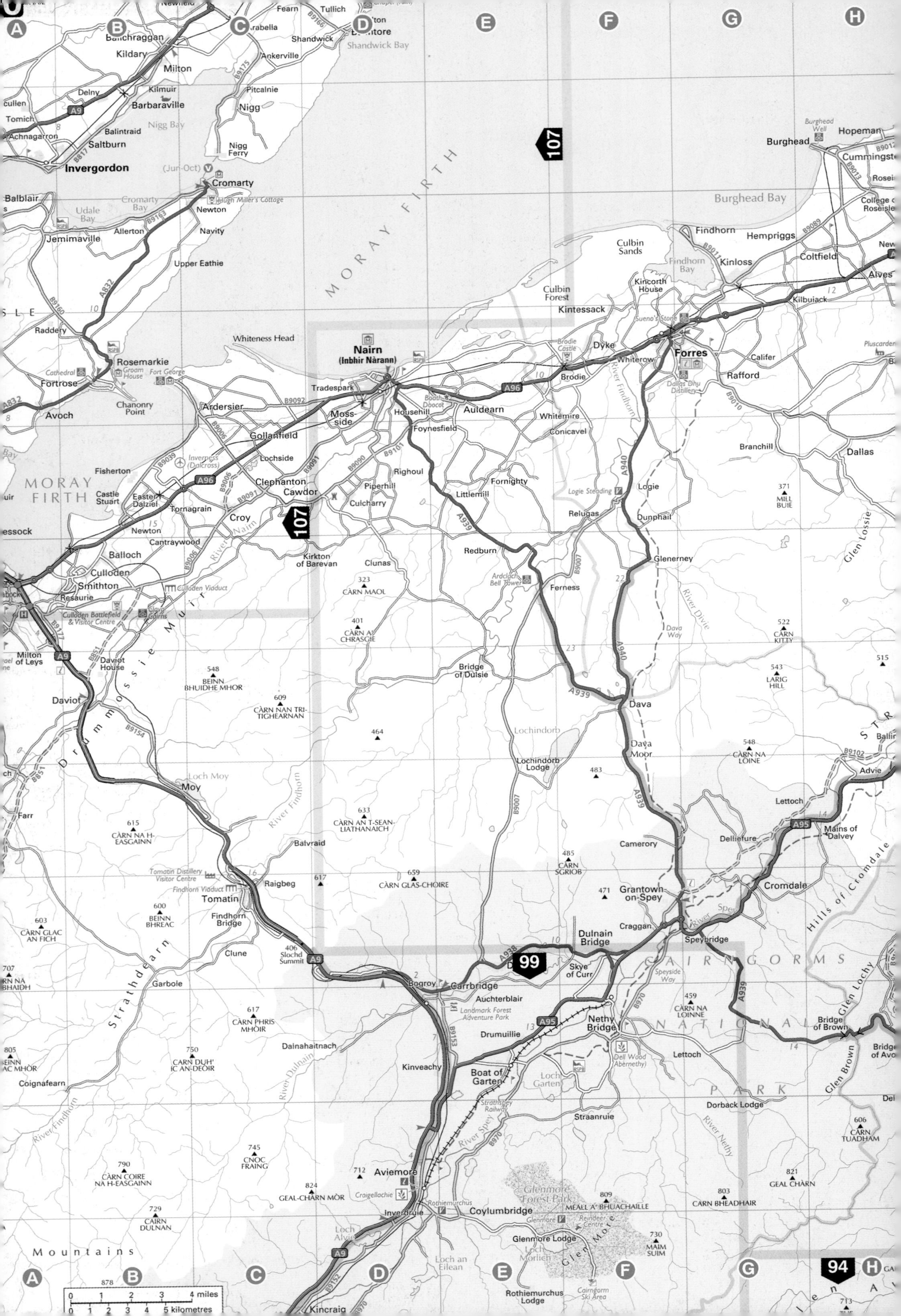

A
B
C
D
E
F
G
H
Fearn
Tullich
Balnabruich
Arabella
Shandwick
Balintore
Shandwick Bay
Balnchraggan
Kildary
Milton
Ankerville
107
Delny
Kilmuir
Pitcalnie
Barbaraville
Nigg
Tomich
A9
Balintraid
Nigg Bay
Achnagarron
Saltburn
Nigg Ferry
B817
Invergordon
(Jun-Oct)
Cromarty
Balblair
Cromarty Bay
Hugh Miller's Cottage
Udale Bay
Newton
B9163
Allerton
Navity
Jemimaville
Upper Eathie
MORAY FIRTH
Burghead Well
Hopeman
Burghead
Cummingston
Roseisle
Burghead Bay
College of Roseisle
Findhorn
Hempriggs
B9089
Culbin Sands
Findhorn Bay
B9011
Kinloss
Coltfield
Alves
Kincorth House
Culbin Forest
Kilbuiack
A832
B9160
Kintessack
Raddery
Sueno's Stone
Whiteness Head
Nairn
(Inbhir Nàrann)
Dyke
Brodie Castle
Forres
Pluscarden
Rosemarkie
Groam House
Cathedral
Fort George
Whiterow
River Findhorn
Califer
Fortrose
Brodie
Rafford
Dallas Dhu Distillery
Tradespark
Boath Doocot
A96
Chanonry Point
Ardersier
B9092
Auldearn
B9010
Avoch
Moss-side
Househill
Whitemire
Foynesfield
Conicavel
Gollanfield
B9006
Branchill
Dallas
Lochside
B9101
Inverness (Dalcross)
B9039
A940
Righoul
Fisherton
Clephanton
B9090
B9091
Logie Steading
Logie
Fornighty
Piperhill
Cawdor
Castle Stuart
Littlemill
371 MILL BUIE
Easter Dalziel
Tornagrain
Culcharry
Croy
Relugas
Dunphail
A939
River Nairn
Newton
Cantraywood
Redburn
Glen Lossie
Glenerney
Balloch
Kirkton of Barevan
Clunas
Ardclach Bell Tower
Culloden
Smithton
323 CÀRN MAOL
B9007
Ferness
Culloden Viaduct
Resaurie
Culloden Battlefield & Visitor Centre
Clava Cairns
River Divie
401 CÀRN A' CHRASGIE
Dava Way
522 CÀRN KITTY
B9177
Milton of Leys
A9
B851
Daviot House
548 BEINN BHUIDHE MHOR
Bridge of Dulsie
543 LARIG HILL
515
Drummossie Muir
Daviot
609 CÀRN NAN TRI-TIGHEARNAN
Dava
B9154
464
Lochindorb
Dava Moor
548 CÀRN NA LOINE
B9102
Advie
Lochindorb Lodge
483
Loch Moy
Moy
Lettoch
633 CÀRN AN T-SEAN-LIATHANAICH
Farr
615 CÀRN NA H-EASGAINN
Balvraid
A95
Mains of Dalvey
Cameroy
Dellefure
Tomatin Distillery Visitor Centre
485 CÀRN SGRIOB
Hills of Cromdale
Findhorn Viaduct
617
659 CÀRN GLAS-CHOIRE
Raigbeg
Tomatin
471
Grantown-on-Spey
Cromdale
600 BEINN BHREAC
River Spey
Findhorn Bridge
Craggan
603 CÀRN GLAC AN FICH
Dulnain Bridge
Speybridge
406 Slochd Summit
Clune
A938
99
Skye of Curr
CAIRNGORMS
707
Garbole
Strathdearn
Bogroy
Carrbridge
Speyside Way
Auchterblair
Landmark Forest Adventure Park
459 CÀRN NA LOINNE
Glen Lochy
617 CÀRN PHRIS MHÒIR
B970
Nethy Bridge
Bridge of Brown
NATIONAL
805
B9153
A95
Drumuillie
Lettoch
Bridge of Avon
750 CÀRN DUH' IC AN DEÒIR
Dalnahaitnach
Dell Wood (Abernethy)
Kinveachy
Boat of Garten
Loch Garten
Coignafearn
River Dulnain
PARK
Glen Brown
Dorback Lodge
Strathspey Railway
River Findhorn
River Spey
Straanruie
606 CÀRN TUADHAM
River Nethy
745 CNOC FRAING
790 CÀRN COIRE NA H-EASGAINN
712
Aviemore
Glenmore Forest Park
821 GEAL CHÀRN
824 GEAL-CHÀRN MÒR
Craigellachie
Rothiemurchus
809 MEALL A' BHUACHAILLE
803 CÀRN BHEADHAIR
Inverdruie
Coylumbridge
Glenmore
Reindeer Centre
729 CÀRN DULNAN
Loch Alvie
Glenmore Lodge
730 MAIM SUIM
Loch Morlich
Glen More
Mountains
Loch an Eilean
94
878
B9152
Rothiemurchus Lodge
Cairngorm Ski Area
Kincraig
713
0 1 2 3 4 miles
0 1 2 3 4 5 kilometres

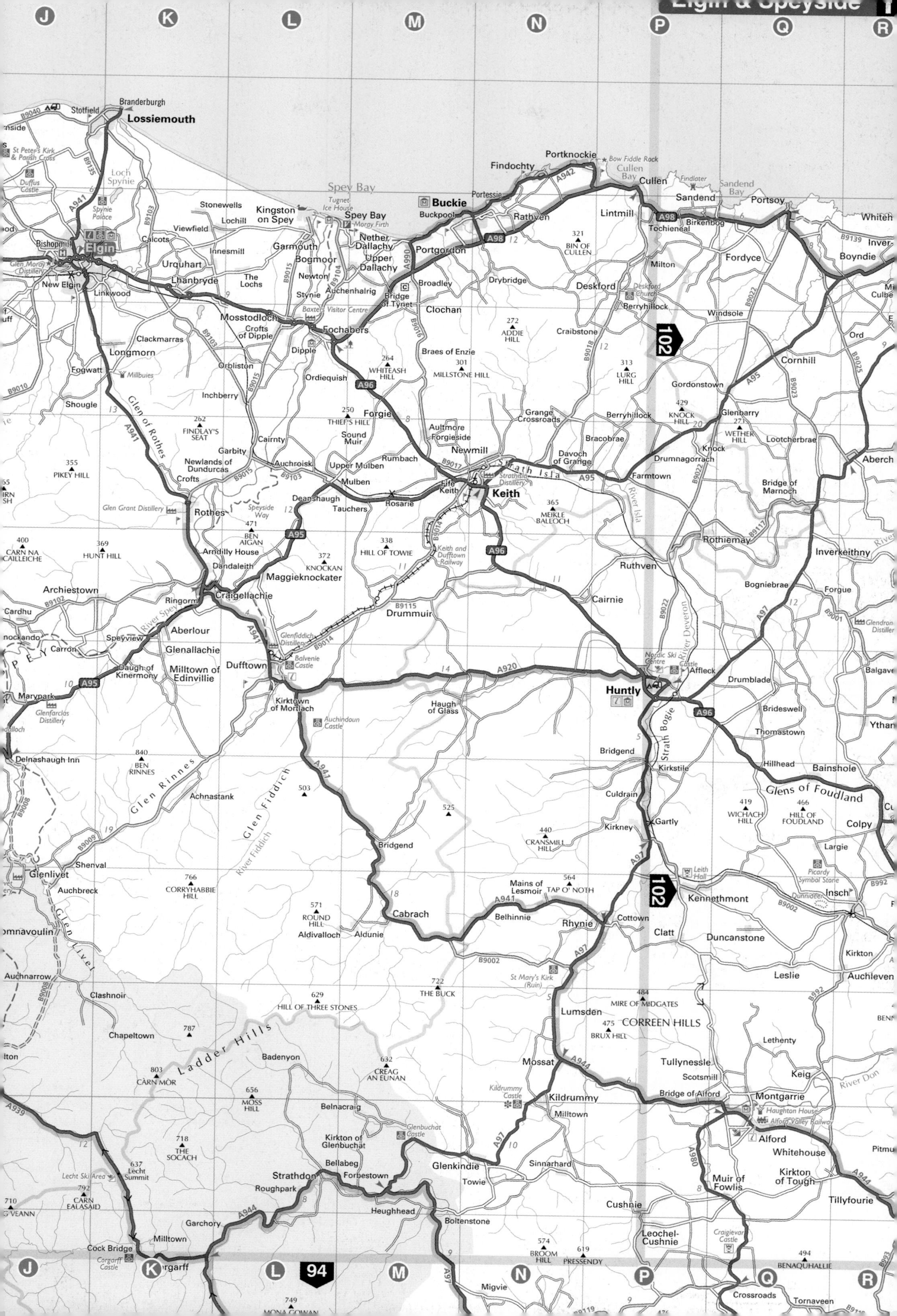
J
K
L
M
N
P
Q
R
Branderburgh
Stotfield
Lossiemouth
B9040
St Peter's Kirk & Parish Cross
Duffus Castle
Loch Spynie
B9135
A941
Spynie Palace
Stonewells
Lochill
Kingston on Spey
Spey Bay
Tugnet Ice House
Moray Firth
Buckie
Buckpool
Portessie
Findochty
Portknockie
Bow Fiddle Rock
Cullen Bay
Cullen
Findlater
Sandend Bay
Sandend
Portsoy
A942
Rathven
Lintmill
A98
Tochieneal
Birkenbog
B9139
Inver-
Bishopmill
Elgin
Glen Moray Distillery
New Elgin
Linkwood
Calcots
Viewfield
Innesmill
Urquhart
Lhanbryde
The Lochs
Garmouth
Bogmoor
Newton
Stynie
B9015
B9104
Nether Dallachy
Upper Dallachy
A990
Auchenhalrig
Bridge of Tynet
Portgordon
Broadley
Clochan
321 BIN OF CULLEN
Drybridge
Deskford
Deskford Church
Berryhillock
Milton
Fordyce
Boyndie
B9022
Windsole
Mosstodloch
Crofts of Dipple
Baxters Visitor Centre
Fochabers
Dipple
Clackmarras
Longmorn
B9103
Orbliston
Fogwatt
Millbuies
B9010
Shougle
Inchberry
Ordiequish
264 WHITEASH HILL
A96
B9016
Braes of Enzie
301 MILLSTONE HILL
272 ADDIE HILL
Craibstone
B9018
313 LURG HILL
102
Gordonstown
Cornhill
B9023
B9025
Ord
A95
Glen of Rothes
262 FINDLAY'S SEAT
250 THIEF'S HILL
Forgie
Sound Muir
Aultmore
Forgieside
Grange Crossroads
Berryhillock
429 KNOCK HILL
Glenbarry
271 WETHER HILL
Lootcherbrae
355 PIKEY HILL
Garbity
Cairnty
Newlands of Dundurcas
Auchroisk
Upper Mulben
Rumbach
Newmill
Bracobrae
Davoch of Grange
Knock
Drumnagorrach
Strath Isla
Strathisla Distillery
B9017
Farmtown
Aberch
Crofts
Mulben
Deanshaugh
Rosarie
Fife Keith
Keith
365 MEIKLE BALLOCH
River Isla
Bridge of Marnoch
Glen Grant Distillery
Rothes
Speyside Way
Tauchers
471 BEN AIGAN
A95
338 HILL OF TOWIE
B9014
Keith and Dufftown Railway
Rothiemay
B9117
400 CARN NA CAILLEICHE
369 HUNT HILL
Arndilly House
372 KNOCKAN
Inverkeithny
Dandaleith
Maggieknockater
Ruthven
Archiestown
B9102
Ringorm
Craigellachie
B9115
Drummuir
Cairnie
Bogniebrae
Forgue
Cardhu
River Spey
Aberlour
A941
Glenfiddich Distillery
B9022
River Deveron
A97
B9001
Glendron Distillery
Speyview
Carron
Glenallachie
Balvenie Castle
Nordic Ski Centre
Castle
Affleck
Daugh of Kinermony
Milltown of Edinvillie
Dufftown
A920
Huntly
Drumblade
Balgave
Marypark
Glenfarclas Distillery
Kirktown of Mortlach
Auchindoun Castle
Haugh of Glass
A96
Brideswell
Strath Bogie
Ythan
Thomastown
Delnashaugh Inn
840 BEN RINNES
Bridgend
Kirkstile
Hillhead
Bainshole
Glen Rinnes
Glen Fiddich
503
A941
Glens of Foudland
Achnastank
Culdrain
419 WICHACH HILL
466 HILL OF FOUDLAND
Colpy
525
River Fiddich
B9008
B9009
440 CRANSMILL HILL
Kirkney
Gartly
Bridgend
Largie
Shenval
Glenlivet
766 CORRYHABBIE HILL
Mains of Lesmoir
564 TAP O' NOTH
Leith Hall
Picardy Symbol Stone
Auchbreck
Kennethmont
B992
Insch
Dunnideer
571 ROUND HILL
Cabrach
A941
Belhinnie
Rhynie
Cottown
Clatt
B9002
Duncanstone
Glen Livet
Aldivalloch
Aldunie
Kirkton
B9002
Auchnarrow
St Mary's Kirk (Ruin)
Leslie
Auchleven
722 THE BUCK
Clashnoir
629 HILL OF THREE STONES
484 MIRE OF MIDGATES
B992
Lumsden
475 BRUX HILL
CORREEN HILLS
Chapeltown
787
Lethenty
Ladder Hills
Badenyon
632 CREAG AN EUNAN
Mossat
A944
Tullynessle
Scotsmill
Keig
803 CARN MÒR
656 MOSS HILL
Kildrummy Castle
Kildrummy
Bridge of Alford
Montgarrie
River Don
A939
Belnacraig
Milltown
Haughton House
Alford Valley Railway
Glenbuchat Castle
Kirkton of Glenbuchat
718 THE SOCACH
A97
Alford
A980
Whitehouse
637 Lecht Summit
Lecht Ski Area
Strathdon
Bellabeg
Forbestown
Glenkindie
Sinnarhard
Towie
Muir of Fowlis
Kirkton of Tough
A944
Tillyfourie
792 CARN EALASAID
Roughpark
710 VEANN
Heughhead
Cushnie
A944
Garchory
Boltenstone
Milltown
Leochel-Cushnie
Craigievar Castle
Cock Bridge
Corgarff Castle
Corgarff
574 BROOM HILL
619 PRESSENDY
494 BENAQUHALLIE
94
A97
Migvie
Crossroads
Tornaveen
749 MONA GOWAN

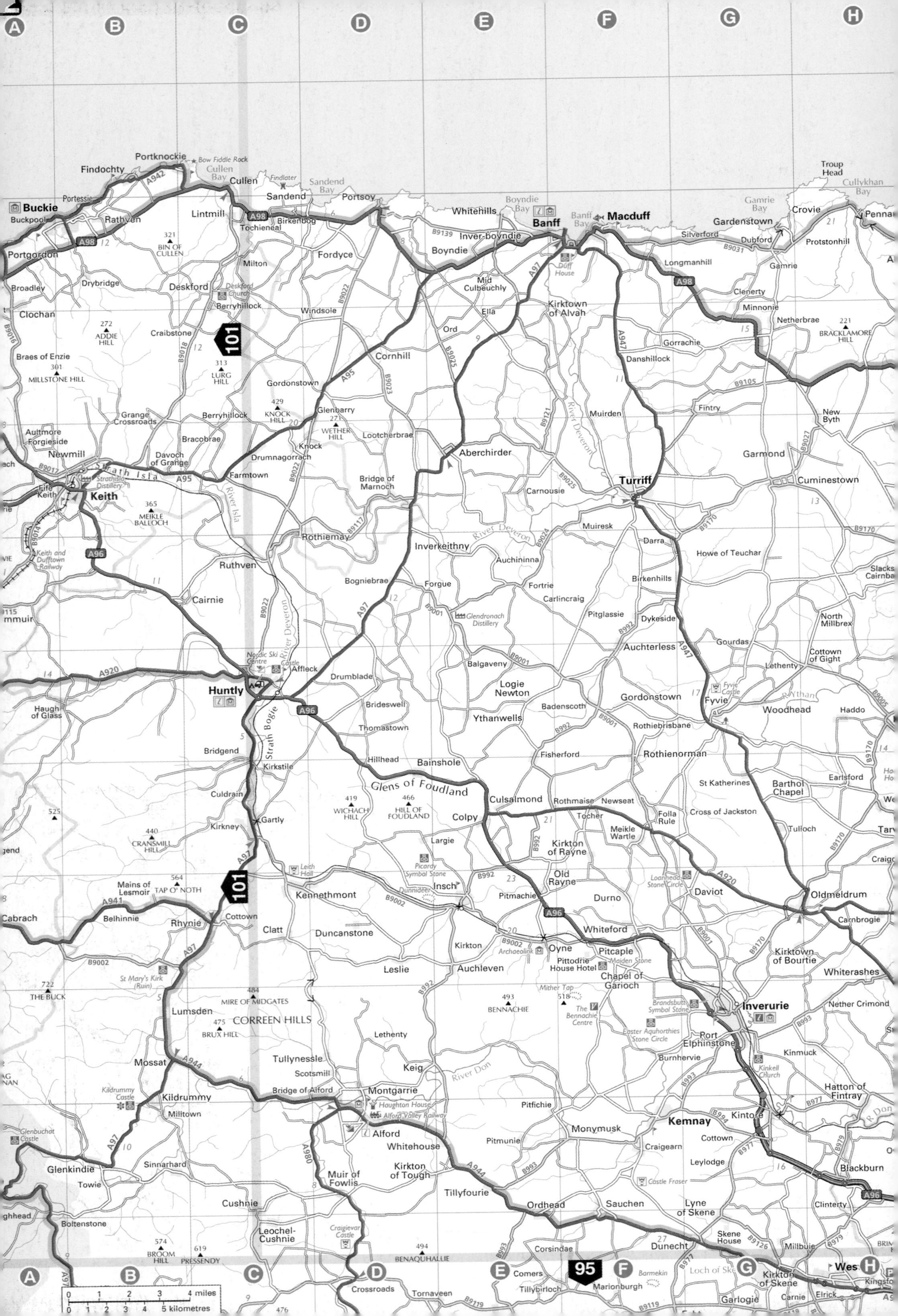
A
B
C
D
E
F
G
H
Buckie
Portgordon
Findochty
Portknockie
Cullen
Sandend
Portsoy
Whitehills
Banff
Macduff
Gardenstown
Crovie
Troup Head
Keith
Huntly
Turriff
Aberchirder
Fyvie
Oldmeldrum
Inverurie
Kemnay
Kintore
Alford
Rhynie
Lumsden
Insch
Glens of Foudland
CORREEN HILLS
River Deveron
River Don
River Isla
A96
A97
A98
A95
A920
A944
101
95
0 1 2 3 4 miles
0 1 2 3 4 5 kilometres

North Aberdeenshire
Rosehearty
Castle Lighthouse & Museum
Kinnaird Head
Pittulie
Sandhaven
Fraserburgh
Craigiefold
Peathill
Kirktown
Fraserburgh Bay
Cairnbulg
Inverallochy
Percyhorner
Coburby
Pitblae
Maggie's Hoosie
Whitelinks Bay
Mid Ardlaw
Boyndlie
Memsie
St Combs
Memsie Cairn
Rathen
Crofts of Savoch
Newburgh
Lonmay
Rattray Head
234
WAUGHTON HILL
Loch of Strathbeg
Crimond
Blackhill
Strichen
New Leeds
Leys
Denhead
Backfolds
Kirktown
St Fergus
Fetterangus
Rora
Deer Abbey
Dunshillock
Maud
River Ugie
Aden
Mintlaw
Inverugie
Old Deer
Longside
Buchanhaven
Peterhead
Blackhill of Clackriach
Drymuir
Bulwark
Stuartfield
Inverquhomery
Peterhead Bay
Millbreck
Nether Kinmundy
Hillhead of Cocklaw
Nethermuir
Burnhaven
Clola
Kinnadie
Buchan Ness
Blackhill
Stirling
Boddam
Auchnagatt
Lendrum Terrace
Kinknockie
Inkhorn
Longhaven
Coldwells
Bullers of Buchan
Hatton
Auchiries
North Haven
Arthrath
Muirtack
Slains
Cruden Bay
Bogbrae
Chapel Hill
Bay of Cruden
Ythanbank
Birness
Whinnyfold
The Skares
Auchedly
Artrochie
Kinharrachie
Ellon
Esslemont
Kirkton of Logie Buchan
Kirktown of Slains
Collieston
Pitmedden
Logierieve
Forvie
Housieside
Udny Station
Newburgh
Cultercullen
Foveran
Delfrigs
Causeyend
Whitecairns
Belhelvie
Balmedie
Potterton
Blackdog
Middleton Park
Denmore
Kirkwall Lerwick
Bridge of Don
95
Aberdeen
200 m
ELGIN
PETERHEAD
HUTCHEON STREET
Causeway End Primary School
Skene Square School
Aberdeen College Gallowgate Centre
Woolmanhill Hospital
RGU
Robert Gordon's College
Bon Accord Centre
City Council
City Council (Marischal College)
DVLA
Arts Centre
St Andrews Cathedral
Police HQ
Sheriff Court
Provost Skene's House
Health Centre
St Mark's
Kingdom Hall
His Majesty's
Art Gallery
RGU
St Nicholas
Gilcomston School
YMCA
HMRC
Surgery
Music Hall
ibis Hotel
Harbour Office
Maritime
Market
Terminal Building
St Mary's Cathedral
Government Offices
Jurys Inn Hotel
Northlink Ferries
ABERDEEN STATION
UnionSquare
Fish Market
Sports Centre
UNION STREET
WILLOWBANK ROAD
Ferryhill School
Pavilion
Victoria Bridge
River Dee
BANCHORY
FORFAR
Port Plan: Aberdeen

see page 111
for Western Isles
Fladda-chùain
Eilean Trodday
Rudha Hunish
North Duntulm
Duntulm
Kilmaluag
A855
Tairbeart (Tarbert)
Lùb Score
Skye Museum of Island Life
Flodigarry
Eilean Flodigarry
Borneskitaig
Kilmuir
Heribusta
Kilvaxter
542 MEAL NA SUIREAMACH
Digg
Staffin Bay
Staffin Island
Balgown
Brogaig
Loch nam Madadh (Lochmaddy)
Waternish Point
Linicro
Stenscholl
Staffin
Totscore
464 BIODA BUIDHE
Trotternish
Kilt Rock Waterfall
Ellishader
Maligar
Marishader
Valtos
Idrigill
River Rha
Ascrib Islands
Uig (Uige)
River Conon
611 BEINN EDRA
Garros
Rudha nam Brathairean
Culnaknock
Uig Bay
283 BEN GEARY
Geary
Loch Snizort
Lealt
Trumpan
Earlish
Tote
Gillen
Ardmore Point
Hallin
Peinlich
608 CREAG A' LAIN
A87
River Hinnisdal
DUNVEGAN HEAD
Isay
Mingay
Stein
Lusta
451 BEINN A' SGÀ
Loch Bay
214 BEN DIUBAIG
Greshornish House Hotel
Loch Greshornish
Kingsburgh
Loch Snizort Beag
Old Man of Storr
719 THE STORR
Loch Dunvegan
Claigan
Romesdal
River Romesdal
Boreraig
327 BEINN BHREAC
Bay
Treaslane
Eyre
Uig
Flashader
A850
Kensaleyre
River Haulton
Loch Pooltiel
B886
Upperglen
Loch Leathan
Feriniquarrie
Totaig
Edinbane
Bernisdale
Oisgill Bay
Milovaig
Glendale
Dunvegan
Tote
Loch Fada
Eilean Fladday
Manish Point
Lephin
B884
Colbost
Colbost Croft
B8036
Carbost
Borve
SOUND OF RAASAY
Waterstein
Toy
Dunvegan
Giant Angus MacAskill
Skeabost
Skinidin
Kilmuir
A864
Neist Point
Lonmore
265 BEN AKETIL
271 CRUACHAN BEINN A' CHEARCAILL
Uigshader
Drumuie
312
Moonen Bay
Roskhill
Caroy River
Glengrasco
96
469 HEALAVAL MORE
Roag
Torvaig
Ramasaig
B885
Portree
Seafield
Vatten
A863
Glen Ose
Harlosh
Ose
417 BEINN NA GREINE
Penifiler
412 BEN
0 1 2 3 4 miles
0 1 2 3 4 5 kilometres
A B C D E F G H

Skye & Wester Ross
108
106
97
Isle Ristol
Polbain
SUMMER ISLES
Achiltibuie
Polglass
Tanera Beg
Tanera Mòr
Badentarbat Bay
Steornabhagh (Stornoway)
Glas-leac Mòr
Glas-leac Beag
Horse Island
Horse Sound
Achduart
Culnacraig
Eilean Dubh
Priest Island
Greenstone Point
Cailleach Head
Leac Dhonn
Isle Martin
Rudha Beag
Scoraig
Annat Bay
Stattic Point
Rhireavach
635 BEINN GHOBHLACH
Mellon Udrigle
GRUINARD ISLAND
Badluachrach
Little Loch Broom
Badrallach
Foura
Rudha Reidh
Cove
Laide
Gruinard Bay
A832
Badcaul
Mellon Charles
Ormiscaig
Aultbea
Gruinard
Ardessie
Camusnagaul
Dundonnell
296 AN CUAIDH
ISLE OF EWE
764 SAIL MHÒR
Melvaig
Aultgrishin
Loch Ewe
B8057
Loch Fada
Little Gruinard River
Gruinard River
347 CREAG-MHEAL BEAG
Lochan Gaineamhaich
Strathnasheallag Forest
293 CNOC BREAC
Inverasdale
Naast
Inverewe Garden
1062 AN TEALLACH
North Erradale
B8021
Poolewe
Londubh
250 MEALL NA MEINE
681 BEINN A' CHAISGEIN BEAG
Loch na Sealga
Big Sand
906 BEINN DEARG MHOR
Fionn Loch
Wester Ross
Strath
Smithstown
Lonemore
A832
Auchtercairn
Heritage
Longa Island
Loch Gairloch
Gairloch
Dubh Loch
Charlestown
421 MEALL AN DOIREIN
791 BEINN AIRIDH CHARR
Eilean Horrisdale
Port Henderson
B8056
Badachro
Opinan
974 SGÙRRBAN
1019 MULLACH COIRE MHIC FHEARCHAIR
859 BEINN LAIR
South Erradale
Loch Bad an Sgalaig
Loch Maree Hotel
Letterewe
Loch Garbhaig
Lochan Fada
Redpoint
Talladale
Loch Maree
981 SLIOCH
Red Point
Loch Ghaineamhach
Loch a' Ghobhainn
875 BAOSBHEINN
Loch na h-Oidhche
680 BEINN A' MHÙINIDH
Kinlochewe Forest
619 BEINN BHREAC
855 BEINN AN EOIN
724
Loch a' Bhealaich
Loch Torridon
Craig River
Beinn Eighe
Incheril
Kinlochewe
Rudha na Fearn
Fearnmore
Lower Diabaig
985 BEINN ALLIGIN
914 BEINN DEARG
1009 RUADH-STAC MÒR
972
Glen Docherty
Òb Chuaig
Fearnbeg
Loch Diabaig
BEINN EIGHE
RONA
Arrina
Cuaig
Kenmore
Alligin Shuas
Inveralligin
1024 LIATHACH
1053
Torridon House
Glen Torridon
A896
Loch Clair
Loch Fhiarlaid
Callakille
Ardheslaig
Upper Loch Torridon
Torridon
782 SGURR DUBH
Loch Shieldaig
Shieldaig
Countryside Centre
Annat
Loch Coulin
Lonbain
492 AN GARBH-MHEALL
Wester Ross
677 CARN BREAC
493 CROIC-BHEINN
A896
Loch Damph
Glenshieldaig Forest
902 BEINN DAMPH
933 MAOL CHEAN-DEARG
958 SGORR RUADH
River Lair
Glencarron Lodge
River Applecross
907 FAUR THOLL
Craig
Glen Carron
Loch Lundie
Achnashellach Lodge
Balnacra
Loch Dughaill
Applecross Bay
Loch Coultrie
895 BEINN BHAN
Coulags
Applecross
730 SGURR A GHARAIDH
1052 SGURR A CHAORACHAIN
626
774 SGÙRR A' CHAORACHAIN
Camusteel
Rassal Ashwood
A890
Strathcarron
Camusterrach
Aird Dhubh
Achintee
A896
INNER S

108
105
97
98
COIGACH
Knockan
Elphin
Ledmore Junction
Knockan Cliff
Knockan Crag
Cromalt Hills
Rappach
STAC POLLAIDH
CUL BEAG
Loch Lurgainn
Ben mor Coigach
BEN MORE COIGACH
Achduart
Culnacraig
Drumrunie Lodge
Strathcanaird
Strath Canaird
Isle Martin
Ardmair
Morefield
Ullapool (Ulapul)
Loch Achall
Glen Achall
Loch Urigill
Loch a' Chroisg
NA DROMANNAN
CNOC NA GLAS CHOILLE
AN STICHD
BEINN AN EOIN
Loch Ailsh
River Oykel
Oykel Bridge Hotel
Loch na Claise Moire
River Cassley
Cassley
Rosehall
Doune
Strath Oykel
BEINN SGEIREACH
CNOC A' CH
Rappach Water
Glen Einig
BEINN ULBHAIDH
CREAG LOISGTE
BREAC BHEINN
MEALL DHEIRGIDH
Loch an Daimh
Strath Mulzie
Giasha Burn
CARN A' CHOIN DEIRG
Croick
River Carron
Glencalvie Forest
BEINN GHOBHLACH
Badrallach
BEINN EILIDEACH
Loch Broom
Leckmelm
MEALL DUBH
MEALL NAM BRADHAN
Loch a' Choire Mhoir
CARN BAN
Ardessie
Camusnagaul
Dundonnell
Ardindrean
Letters
Ardcharnich
Inverlael
CARN MOR
River Lael
Gleann Beag
Crom Loch
BEINN THARSUINN
CARN CHUINNEAG
AN TEALLACH
Strathnasheallag Forest
CARN BHIORAIN
Croftown
R Broom
BEINN DEARG
CARN BREAC BEAG
Braemore
Corrieshalloch Gorge
Falls of Measach
Loch Coire Lair
Loch a' Chaorunn
MEALL AN T-SITHE
MEALL LEACACHAIN
MEALL A' GHRIANAIN
Strathvaich Forest
Loch Vaich
BEINN NAN EUN
Loch a' Bhraoin
TOM BAN MOR
Loch Droma
BEINN LIATH BHEAG
Loch Glascarnoch
SGURR BAN
MULLACH COIRE MHIC FHEARCHAIR
SGURR MOR
A' CHAILLEACH
Aultguish Inn
Inchbae Lodge Hotel
BEINN DEARG
BEN WYVIS
Ben Wyvis
BEINN NAN RAMH
Loch Fannich
Fannich Lodge
Corriemoille Forest
CARN NA DUBH CHOILLE
Corriemoille
LITTLE WYVIS
Strath Garve
Kinlochewe Forest
AN CABAR
Lochluichart
Gorstan
Garve
CLOCH
Loch Luichart
FIONN BHEINN
Achanalt
Strath Bran
Loch Achanalt
Loch Garve
Glen Docherty
Achnasheen
Loch a' Chroisg
SGURR MARCASAIDH
Rogie Falls
Auchterneed
Strathpeffer
Highland Museum of Childhood
Loch Achilty
Little Scatwell
Loch Meig
R Conon
Contin
Jamestown
Loch Gowan
CARN MHARTUIN
SCUIR VUILLIN
Strathconon
Marybank
Muirton Mains
CARN BREAC
Loch Sgamhain
Strathconon Forest
MEALL NAN DAMH
CARN NACOINNICH
Glencarron Lodge
MORUISG
River Meig
Loch Beannacharain
Orrin Reservoir
Muir
Glen Carron
BAC AN EICH
River Orrin
Glen Orrin
SGURR COIRE NAN EUN
Loch na Caoidhe
MAOILE LUNNDAIDH
SGURR A' CHAORRACHAIN
MEALLAN BUIDHE
CARN BAN POLLON
Breakachy
Kilmorack
SGURR A' CHOIRE GHLAIS
SGURR NA RUAIDHE
Crask of Aigas
Culburnie
Kiltarlity
Crinaglack
A835
A837
A832
A890
A831
0 1 2 3 4 miles
0 1 2 3 4 5 kilometres

Ullapool, Easter Ross & Black Isle
109
110
100
99
Achnairn
Colaboll
Loch Beannach
317 SITHEAN ADH NAN EUN
Strath Brora
River Brora
Loch Brora
Lothmore
Lothbeg
COL-BHEINN
Ferrycroft Countryside Centre
Loch Craggie
323 BEN DOULA
Lairg
Tomich
Torrobull
A839
Dalreavoch Lodge
Loch Horn
520 BEN HORN
Dalchalm
Brora
378 CAGAR FEOSAIG
Golspie Burn
Rogart
Achany
B864
A836
313 CREAGAN GLAS
446 BEN LUNDIE
Doll
Carn Liath
Backies
A9
383 BEN BHRAGGIE
Rhives
Dunrobin Castle
Golspie
Linsidemore
333 MEALL EACHAINN
Falls of Shin
A837
Loch Buidhe
Torboll
Inveran
Invershin
Sleasdairidh
349 BEINN DONUILL
Cambusavie Platform
Loch Fleet
Culrain
River Evelix
Badninish
Skelbo
Skelbo Street
Achvaich
Fourpenny
Kyle of Sutherland
Embo
Rearquhar
Birichin
Lower Gledfield
Astle
B9168
Embo Street
Bonar Bridge
Pitgrudy
Dounie
Evelix
A949
Ardgay
Loch Migdale
Spinningdale
Clashmore
Camore
Dornoch
Kincardine
A949
Historylinks
Upper Ardchronie
Whiteface
Dornoch Firth
Cuthill
A836
Ferrytown
Tarbat Ness
Strule Hill
Ardmore
Innis Mhor
Bruceﬁeld
Wilkhaven
Cambuscurrie Bay
Ferry Point
Edderton
477 BEINN CLACH AN FHEADAIN
Glenmorangie Distillery
Portmahomack
Morangie
Inver
Rockfield
Aultnamain Inn
284
Tain (Baile Dhubhthaich)
Arboll
Toulvaddie
B9165
Lochslin
EASTER ROSS
692 BEINN THARSUINN
Loch Eye
Hill of Fearn
Rhynie
Balmuchy
379 CNOC AN T-SABHAIL
B9176
Newfield
B9165
Hilton of Cadboll Chapel (ruin)
Fearn
Tullich
Strath Rusdale
Arabella
Hilton
B9166
Balintore
Shandwick
Shandwick Bay
Ardross
Ballchraggan
Boath
Kildary
Milton
Ankerville
B9175
River Alness
Achandunie
Kilmuir
Delny
Pitcalnie
Rhicullen
Barbaraville
Moultavie
Millcraig
Tomich
Nigg
523 CNOC CEISLEIN
Achnagarron
Balintraid
Nigg Bay
Alness (Alanais)
Saltburn
B817
Nigg Ferry
Dalmore
Invergordon
(Jun-Oct)
Cromarty
MORAY FIRTH
Cromarty Firth
Balblair
Cromarty Bay
Hugh Miller's Cottage
Evanton
Resolis
Udale Bay
Newton
Swordale
B9163
Allerton
B9163
Navity
Teanord
Jemimaville
Cullicudden
Upper Eathie
Ardullie
Clanland & Seaport
Brae
Mountgerald House
Findon Mains
A832
Culbin Forest
Kintessack
BLACK ISLE
B9160
A862
B9169
Culbokie
255 MOUNT EAGLE
Raddery
Whiteness Head
Killen
Alcaig
Rosemarkie
Groam House
Nairn (Inbhir Nàrann)
Brodie Castle
Dyke
Maryburgh
Duncanston
Cathedral
Fortrose
Fort George
Belmaduthy
Corntown
Easter Kinkell
Knockbain
Tradespark
Brodie
A96
Riverford
A832
Chanonry Point
Ardersier
B9092
Moss-side
Boath Doocot
Auldearn
Munlochy
Avoch
Househill
Whitemire
Millbuie
A835
Tore
Littleburn
Munlochy Bay
B9006
Gollanfield
Foynesfield
Conicavel
Kilcoy
B9161
Fisherton
B9039
Inverness (Dalcross)
Lochside
B9101
Newton
A832
MORAY FIRTH
A96
B9090
Righoul
Bogallan
Black Isle Wildlife
Kilmuir
Castle Stuart
Easter Dalziel
Clephanton
Cawdor
Piperhill
Fornighty
A940
Redcastle
A9
Artafallie
Tornagrain
B9091
Culcharry
Littlemill
Logie Steading
Milton
Croy
Nairn
A939
Relugas
Charlestown
North Kessock
Newton
River Nairn
Beauly Firth
South Kessock
Cantraywood
Clachnaharry
Balloch
Kirkton of Barevan
Clunas
Redburn
Kirkhill
Bunchrew
Culloden
B9006
Leachkin
INVERNESS (INBHIR NIS)
Culcabock
Smithton
323 CARN MAOL
Ardclach Bell Tower
B9007
Moniack Castle (Highland Winery)
Resaurie
Culloden Viaduct
Ferness
Easter Moniack
Culloden Battlefield & Visitor Centre
Clava Cairns
Knockbain
B9177
B851
401 CARN A' CHRASGIE
316 CNOC NA MOINE
Caledonian Canal
Milton of Leys
Daviot House
Knocknagael Boar Stone
Dochgarroch
Torbreck
548
Bridge
A940

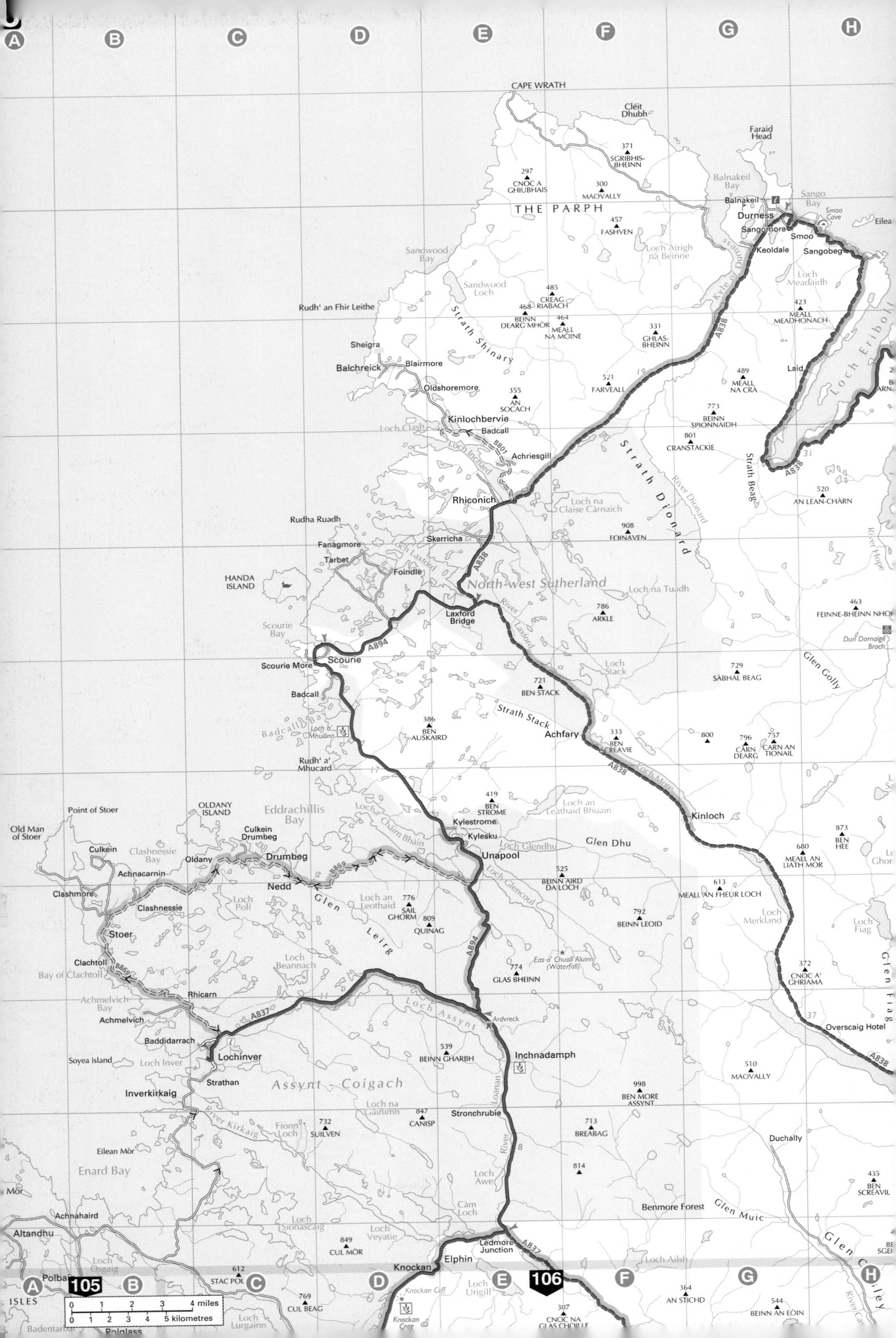

A
B
C
D
E
F
G
H
CAPE WRATH
Cléit Dhubh
371 SGRIBHIS-BHEINN
Faraid Head
297 CNOC A GHIUBHAIS
300 MAOVALLY
Balnakeil Bay
Sango Bay
THE PARPH
Balnakeil
Durness
Smoo Cave
Eilea
457 FASHVEN
Sangomore
Smoo
Loch Airigh na Beinne
Kyle of Durness
Keoldale
Sangobeg
Sandwood Bay
Loch Meadaidh
Sandwood Loch
485 CREAG RIABACH
423 MEALL MEADHONACH
Rudh' an Fhir Leithe
468 BEINN DEARG MHÒR
464 MEALL NA MOINE
331 GHLAS-BHEINN
A838
Strath Shinary
Sheigra
Loch Eriboll
Blairmore
Balchreick
489 MEALL NA CRA
Laid
521 FARVEALL
19
Oldshoremore
355 AN SOCACH
773 BEINN SPIONNAIDH
Kinlochbervie
Loch Clash
Badcall
801 CRANSTACKIE
B801
Loch Inchard
Achriesgill
Strath Dionard
Strath Beag
31
A838
River Dionard
520 AN LEAN-CHÀRN
Rhiconich
Loch na Claise Càrnaich
Rudha Ruadh
908 FOINAVEN
Skerricha
River Hope
Fanagmore
Loch Laxford
Tarbet
A838
Foindle
HANDA ISLAND
North-west Sutherland
Loch na Tuadh
463 FEINNE-BHEINN NHO
Laxford Bridge
River Laxford
786 ARKLE
Scourie Bay
7
A894
Dun Dornaigil Broch
Scourie More
Scourie
Loch Stack
Glen Golly
729 SÀBHAL BEAG
Badcall
721 BEN STACK
Strath Stack
Badcall Bay
386 BEN AUSKAIRD
Loch a' Mhuilinn
Achfary
333 BEN SCREAVIE
800
796 CARN DEARG
757 CARN AN TIONAIL
Rudh' a' Mhucard
A838
Loch More
17
419 BEN STROME
Loch an Leathaid Bhuain
Point of Stoer
OLDANY ISLAND
Eddrachillis Bay
Loch a' Chàirn Bhàin
Kinloch
Old Man of Stoer
Culkein Drumbeg
Kylestrome
873 BEN HEE
Kylesku
Loch Glendhu
Glen Dhu
Culkein
Clashnessie Bay
680 MEALL AN LIATH MOR
Drumbeg
Unapool
Oldany
Achnacarnin
B869
525 BEINN AIRD DA LOCH
Loch Glencoul
Clashmore
Nedd
613 MEALL AN FHEUR LOCH
Loch an Leothaid
776 SAIL GHORM
Clashnessie
Loch Poll
Glen Leirg
Loch Merkland
792 BEINN LEOID
809 QUINAG
Loch Fiag
Stoer
A894
Loch Beannach
Eas a' Chùal Aluinn (Waterfall)
Clachtoll
372 CNOC A' GHRIAMA
B869
774 GLAS BHEINN
Bay of Clachtoll
Glen Fiag
Rhicarn
Achmelvich Bay
11
Loch Assynt
A837
Ardvreck
37
Achmelvich
Overscaig Hotel
Baddidarrach
539 BEINN GHARBH
Inchnadamph
A838
Soyea Island
Loch Inver
Lochinver
510 MAOVALLY
Strathan
998 BEN MORE ASSYNT
Assynt - Coigach
Inverkirkaig
Loch na Gainimh
847 CANISP
Stronchrubie
732 SUILVEN
Fionn Loch
River Kirkaig
713 BREABAG
River Loanan
Duchally
Eilean Mòr
8
Enard Bay
814
Loch Awe
435 BEN SCREAVIL
Mòr
Càm Loch
Benmore Forest
Glen Muic
Achnahaird
Loch Sionascaig
Loch Veyatie
Altandhu
849 CUL MÒR
Ledmore Junction
A837
Glen Cassley
Loch Osgaig
Elphin
Loch Ailsh
612 STAC POL
Knockan
Polbain
105
106
ISLES
Knockan Cliff
Loch Urigill
364 AN STICHD
769 CUL BEAG
Knockan Crag
307 CNOC NA GLAS CHOILLE
544 BEINN AN EOIN
Loch Lurgainn
Badentarbat
Polglass
River Cassley
0 1 2 3 4 miles
0 1 2 3 4 5 kilometres

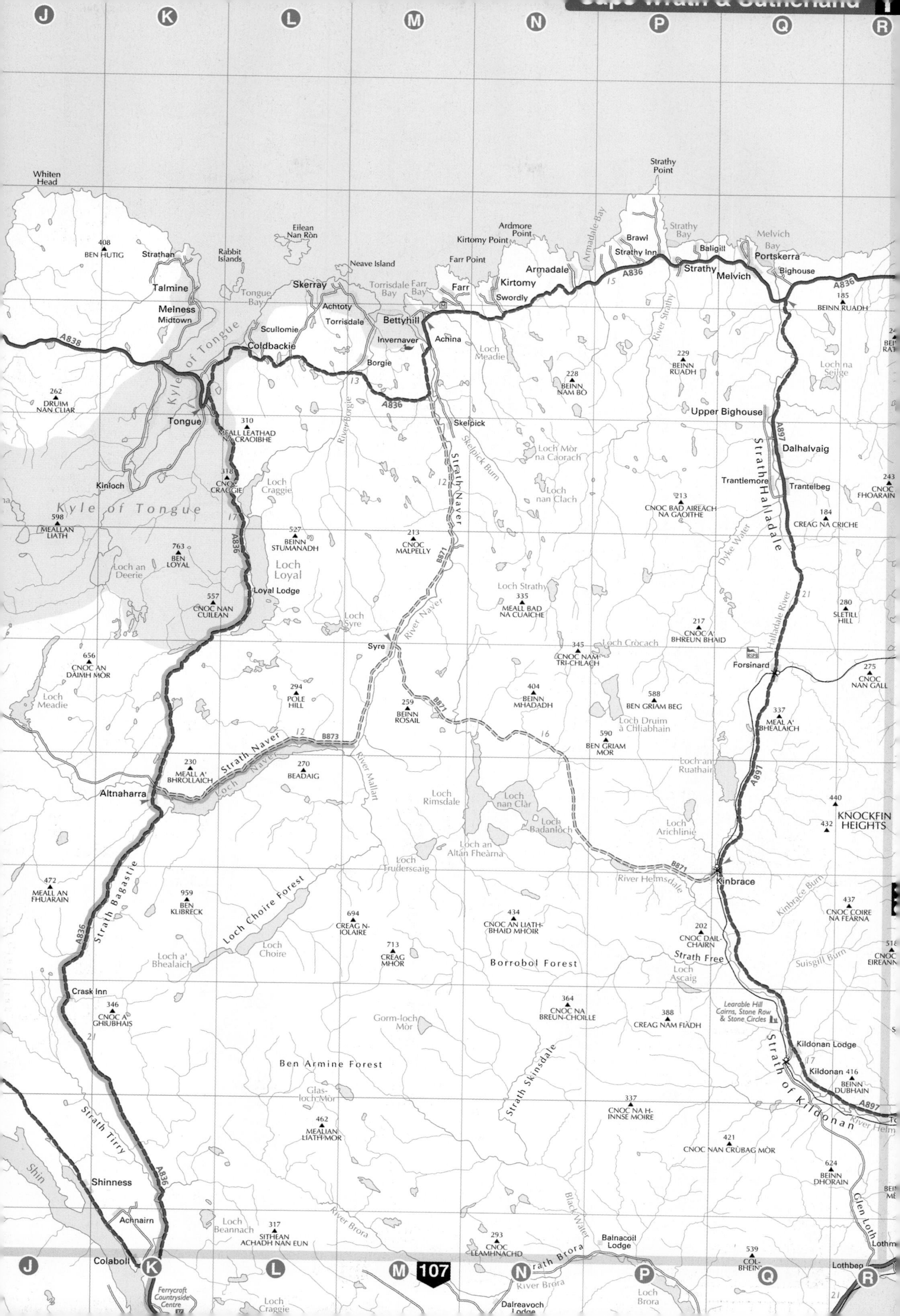

J
K
L
M
N
P
Q
R
Whiten Head
Strathy Point
Eilean Nan Ròn
Ardmore Point
Kirtomy Point
Armadale Bay
Brawl
Strathy Bay
Melvich Bay
408 BEN HUTIG
Strathan
Rabbit Islands
Neave Island
Farr Point
Strathy Inn
Baligill
Portskerra
Armadale
Strathy
Melvich
Bighouse
Talmine
Tongue Bay
Skerray
Torrisdale Bay
Farr Bay
Farr
Kirtomy
A836
Swordly
185 BEINN RUADH
Melness
Midtown
Achtoty
Torrisdale
Bettyhill
River Strathy
A838
Scullomie
Invernaver
Achina
Loch Meadie
Kyle of Tongue
Coldbackie
Borgie
229 BEINN RUADH
Loch na Seilge
228 BEINN NAM BO
262 DRUIM NAN CLIAR
13
Upper Bighouse
Tongue
310 MEALL LEATHAD NA CRAOIBHE
River Borgie
Skelpick
Loch Mòr na Caorach
A897
Dalhalvaig
318 CNOC CRAGGIE
Loch Craggie
Skelpick Burn
Strath Naver
Loch nan Clach
Trantlemore
Trantelbeg
243 CNOC FHOARAIN
Kinloch
Strath Halladale
213 CNOC BAD AIREACH NA GAOITHE
184 CREAG NA CRICHE
598 MEALLAN LIATH
17
527 BEINN STUMANADH
213 CNOC MALPELLY
Dyke Water
763 BEN LOYAL
Loch an Deerie
Loch Loyal
B871
Loch Strathy
335 MEALL BAD NA CUAICHE
21
280 SLETILL HILL
Loyal Lodge
557 CNOC NAN CUILEAN
Loch Syre
River Naver
217 CNOC A' BHREUN BHAID
Halladale River
656 CNOC AN DAIMH MÒR
Syre
345 CNOC NAM TRI-CHLACH
Loch Cròcach
Forsinard
275 CNOC NAN GALL
Loch Meadie
294 POLE HILL
259 BEINN ROSAIL
404 BEINN MHADADH
588 BEN GRIAM BEG
337 MEAL A' BHEALAICH
Loch Druim a Chliabhain
B873
590 BEN GRIAM MOR
16
230 MEALL A' BHROLLAICH
270 BEADAIG
River Mallart
Loch an Ruathair
Altnaharra
Loch Naver
Loch Rimsdale
Loch nan Clàr
440
432
KNOCKFIN HEIGHTS
Loch Badanloch
Loch Arichlinie
Loch an Altan Fheàrna
Loch Truderscaig
B871
River Helmsdale
Kinbrace
472 MEALL AN FHUARAIN
Strath Bagastie
959 BEN KLIBRECK
Loch Choire Forest
694 CREAG N-IOLAIRE
434 CNOC AN LIATH-BHAID MHÒIR
Kinbrace Burn
437 CNOC COIRE NA FEARNA
202 CNOC DAIL-CHAIRN
713 CREAG MHÒR
Loch Choire
Loch a' Bhealaich
Borrobol Forest
Strath Free
Suisgill Burn
Loch Ascaig
Crask Inn
346 CNOC A' GHIUBHAIS
364 CNOC NA BREUN-CHOILLE
388 CREAG NAM FIADH
Learable Hill Cairns, Stone Row & Stone Circles
Gorm-loch Mòr
Strath of Kildonan
Kildonan Lodge
Kildonan
416 BEINN DUBHAIN
Ben Armine Forest
Strath Skinsdale
A897
Glas-loch Mòr
337 CNOC NA H-INNSE MOIRE
River Helmsdale
Strath Tirry
462 MEALLAN LIATH MOR
421 CNOC NAN CRÙBAG MÒR
Shin
624 BEINN DHORAIN
Shinness
Glen Loth
Achnairn
Loch Beannach
317 SITHEAN ACHADH NAN EUN
River Brora
Black Water
293 CNOC LEAMHNACHD
Balnacoil Lodge
539 COL-BHEIN
Colaboll
Strath Brora
River Brora
Lothbeg
Ferrycroft Countryside Centre
Loch Craggie
Loch Brora
Dalreavoch Lodge

A
B
C
D
E
F
G
H
Nethertown
ISLAND OF STROMA
Uppertown
Mell Head
St John's Point
Inner Sound
St Margaret's Hope
DUNNET HEAD
127
Briga Head
Stromness
Scarfskerry
Castle of Mey
Gills Bay
A836
DUNCANSBY HEAD
Muckle
Huna
Kirkstyle
John o' Groats
Stacks of Duncansby
121
DUNNET HILL
Brough
St John's Loch
Rattar
Loch Mey
Mey
Gills
Canisbay
B855
West Dunnet
Dunnet Bay
Dunnet
Barrock
A99
Holborn Head
Brims Ness
Scrabster
St Mary's Chapel (ruin)
Crosskirk
A836
A9
Thurso Bay
Thurso
Castlehill
Inkstack
Brabstermire
Skirza
Loch Heilen
16
Bridge of Forss
Murkle
Castletown
Greenland
Gill Burn
Freswick
Freswick Bay
Sandside Bay
Upper Dounreay
Skiall
Achreamie
Lythmore
B874
Olrig House
Slickly
Ness Head
Isauld
Cnoc Freiceadain Long Cairns
Forss Water
Glengolly
A9
Weydale
Tain
B876
Auckengill
Kirk Burn
Broch
Nybster
Reay
Achvarasdal
Shebster
Hilliclay
Bowermadden
Sortat
17
Brough Head
Lyth
Bower
Howe
Sordale
Knockdee
Loch Calder
Roadside
B874
Loch Scarmclate
Halcro
Mireland
Keiss
Burn of Lyth
16
Broubster
Clayock
Gillock
Kirk
B870
Loch of Wester
Sinclair Bay
Halkirk
Georgemas Junction Station
Shurrery
B870
B874
21
Killimster
B876
Shurrery Lodge
Scotscalder Station
Loch Watten
Loch Scye
Harpsdale
176
SPITTAL HILL
B874
Reiss
Castle Girnigoe & Sinclair
Noss Head
290
BEIN NAM BAD MHOR
Loch Shurrery
Dorrery
Olgrinmore
River Thurso
Spittal
B870
Watten
Winless
Wick River
A882
Sibster
Ackergill
Staxigoe
160
BRAIGH FEITH HEMIGAL
132
DRUIM A CHRACAIRNIE
Mybster
Loch of Toftingall
Bilbster
A99
Wick
Janetstown
Papigoe
Loch Tuim Ghlais
Loch Caluim
Westerdale
23
Haster
Milton
Wick Bay
Old Wick
Newton
South Head
Castle of Old Wick
Whiterow
Strath Beg
Achairn Burn
Badlipster
203
CNOC PREAS A'MHADAIDH
200
CNOC BEUL NA FAIRE
136
BEINN CHAITEAG
Loch Hempriggs
Tannach
Altnabreac Station
A9
Thrumster
145
BALLHARN HILL
Grey Cairns of Camster
A99
17
Sarclet
Loch More
Loch Ruard
Loch Stemster
212
HILL OF YARROWS
Loch of Yarrows
Achavanich
Strathmore Water
Loch an Thulachan
Loch Sand
248
STEMSTER HILL
Loch Rangag
Cairn o'Get
Ulbster
Whaligoe
Rumsdale Water
226
COIRE NA BEINN
Whaligoe Steps
Dalnawillan Lodge
Roster
Bruan
Hill o'Many Stanes
348
BEN ALISKY
Glutt Water
287
BEN-A-CHIELT
Upper Lybster
Mid Clyth
Halberry Head
Glutt Lodge
264
CNOCAN CONACHREAG
Swiney
Clyth Ness
Occumster
Houstry
Invershore
Lybster
Lybster Bay
Land-hallow
Forse
Smerral
Latheron
317
CNOC LOCH MHADADH
Dunbeath Water
Latheronwheel
Janetstown
A9
Berriedale Water
Laidhay Croft
Braemore
Dunbeath
484
MAIDEN PAP
Knockally
705
MORVEN
518
NOC AN EANNAICH
626
SCARABEN
Ramscraigs
Borgue
Langwell Forest
20
Newport
554
CREAG SCALABSDALE
Langwell House
Berriedale
401
CNOC NA MAOILE
A9
404
CREAG THORARAIDH
Torrish
Helmsdale
Ord of Caithness
Timespan
Navidale House Hotel
West Helmsdale
East Helmsdale
Helmsdale
591
BEINN NA MEILICH
Gartymore
Portgower
Lothmore
107
0 1 2 3 4 miles
0 1 2 3 4 5 kilometres

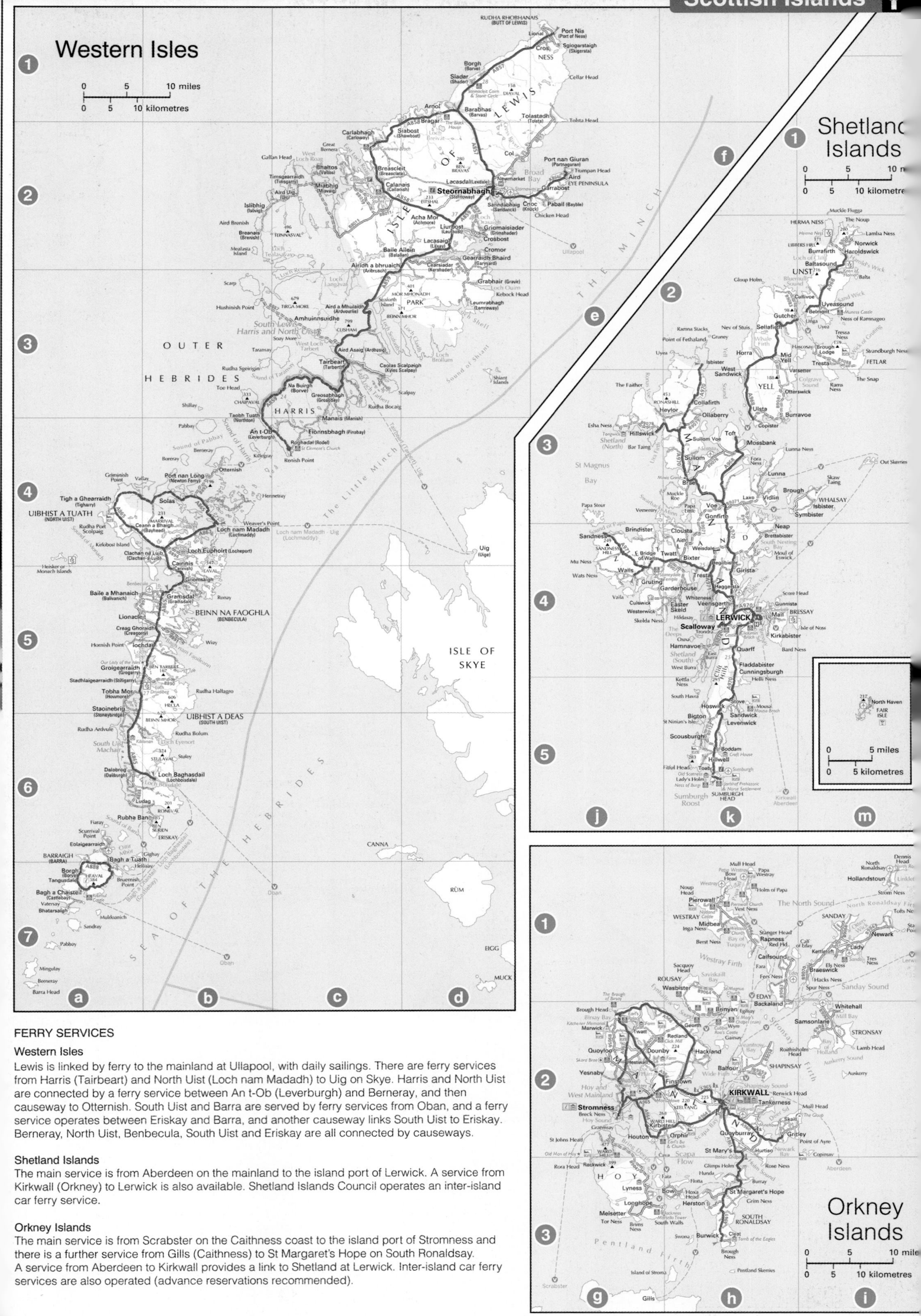

FERRY SERVICES

Western Isles

Lewis is linked by ferry to the mainland at Ullapool, with daily sailings. There are ferry services from Harris (Tairbeart) and North Uist (Loch nam Madadh) to Uig on Skye. Harris and North Uist are connected by a ferry service between An t-Ob (Leverburgh) and Berneray, and then causeway to Otternish. South Uist and Barra are served by ferry services from Oban, and a ferry service operates between Eriskay and Barra, and another causeway links South Uist to Eriskay. Berneray, North Uist, Benbecula, South Uist and Eriskay are all connected by causeways.

Shetland Islands

The main service is from Aberdeen on the mainland to the island port of Lerwick. A service from Kirkwall (Orkney) to Lerwick is also available. Shetland Islands Council operates an inter-island car ferry service.

Orkney Islands

The main service is from Scrabster on the Caithness coast to the island port of Stromness and there is a further service from Gills (Caithness) to St Margaret's Hope on South Ronaldsay. A service from Aberdeen to Kirkwall provides a link to Shetland at Lerwick. Inter-island car ferry services are also operated (advance reservations recommended).

114
A
B
C
D
E
Louisburgh
Inishturk
Caher Island
CROAGH PATRICK
PLAINS OF MAYO
Claremorris
Knock
Ballyhaunis
Castlerea
Ballinlough
Ballymoe
Ballintober
Partry
Lough Carra
Lough Mask
Ballindine
Inishbofin
Inishshark
Renvyle
Leenane
Ballinrobe
Kilmaine
Dunmore
Glennamaddy
Letterfrack
Connemara National Park
An Fhairche Clonbur
Cong
Neale
Shrule
Creegs
Athleague
Clifden
Sraith Salach Recess
Corr na Móna Cornamona
Tuam
Ballygar
Ballyconneely
Slyne Head
Lough Corrib
Headford
Mountbellew Bridge
Caltra
Cashel
Roundstone
Oughterard
Aughnanure
Glinsce Glinsk
Patrick Pearse's Cottage
Carna Carna
Monivea
Ahascragh
Kilconnell
Cruach na Caoile Croaghnakeela Island
Cill Chiaráin Kilkieran
Galway
GALWAY
Athenry
Garumna Gorumna Island
An Spidéal Spiddal
Salthill
Bearna Barna
Oranmore
Toll
Claribridge
Craughwell
Kilcolgan
Loughrea
An Sunda ó Thuaidh North Sound
Inis Mór Inishmore
Galway Bay
Killimor
Inis Meáin Inishmaan
Oileain Árann Aran Islands
Ballyvaughan
Kinvarra
Aillwee
THE BURREN
Thoor Ballylee
Gort
SLIEVE AUGHTY MTS
Portumna
Woodford
Inis Oírr Inisheer
South Sound
Lisdoonvarna
Burren National Park
Doolin
Kilfenora
Lough Cutra
Lough Graney
Cliffs of Moher
Ennistymon
Corrofin
Liscannor
Lahinch
Hags Head
Crusheen
Feakle
Scarriff
Mountshannon
Mal Bay
Tuamgraney
Ogonnelloe
Milltown Malbay
Tulla
Spanish Point
Ennis
Knappogue
Craggaunowen Bronze Age Project
Killaloe
Ballina
Doo Lough
Clarecastle
Broadford
Newmarket-on-Fergus
Sixmilebridge
Donegal Point
Doonbeg
Shannon
Cloniara
Newport
Cooraclare
Bunratty
Castleconnell
Kilkee
Killadysert
LIMERICK
River Shannon
Kilrush
Killimer
Tarbert
Loghill
Foynes
Askeaton
Patrickswell
Caherconlish
Pallas Grean New
Glin
Shanagolden
Adare
Loop Head
Mouth of the Shannon
Ballylongford
Croagh
Croom
Ballybunion
Ardagh
Rathkeale
Herbertstown
Ballyduff
Athea
Newcastle West
Ballingarry
Bruff
Hospital
Kerry Head
Causeway
Listowel
Duagh
Bruree
Ballyheige
Abbeydorney
Abbeyfeale
Kilmeedy
Charleville (An Ráth)
Kilmallock
Ballyheige Bay
Kilkinlea Lower
Broadford
Ballylanders
Rough Point
Ardfert
Dromcolliher
Brandon Bay
Tralee Bay
Tralee
Freemount
Liscarroll
Mitchelstown
Castlegregory
CNOC BREANAINN
BEENOSKEE
Camp
BAURTREGAUN
Castleisland
Buttevant
Ceann Sibéal Sybil Point
Anascaul
Inch
Castlemaine
Farranfore
Kerry
Scartaglin
Newmarket
Doneraile
Kildorrery
Glanworth
Ballydesmond
Kanturk
Castletownroche
An Daingean Dingle
Milltown
Boherbue
An Blascaod Mór Great Blasket Island
Ceann Sléibhe Slea Head
Killorglin
Banteer
Mallow
Annes Grove
Dingle Bay
Glenbeigh
Killarney
Rathmore
Beaufort
Lough Leane
Burnfort
Rathcormack
Millstreet
BOGGERAGH MTS
Killarney National Park
Muckross
Muckross House, Gardens & Farms
Poulgorm Bridge
CARRAUNTOOHIL
Carriganimmy
Watergrasshill
Doulus Head
Cahersiveen
MANGERTON MTN
Valencia Island
MULLAGHANATTIN
Kilgarvan
Baile Mhic Ire Ballymakeery
Macroom
Blarney
Glanmire
Kenmare
Dripsey
CORK
Passage West
Béal Átha an Ghaorthaidh Ballingeary
An Coireán Waterville
Sneem
Ovens
Douglas
Derrynane
Tahilla
Parknasilla
Cork
Ringaskiddy
Inchigeelagh
Kilmichael
Crookstown
Ballinhassig
Ceann Bhólais Bolus Head
Lauragh
KNOCKBOY
Cross Barry
Carrigaline
Skellig Michael
Cathair Dónall Caherdaniel
Kenmare River
Glengarriff
Bandon
An Scairbh Scariff Island
Ardgroom
Adrigole
Ballylickey
Dunmanway
Ballineen
Enniskean
Innishannon
Bantry
Dunderrow
Belgooly
Cod's Head
Allihies
Bantry Bay
Ballinascarty
Kilbrittain
Kinsale
Castletownbere
Ballinspittle
Dursey Island
Bear Island
Durrus
Drimoleague
Timoleague
Courtmacsherry
Old Head of Kinsale
Ballydehob
Leap
Ross Carbery
Clonakilty
Muntervary or Sheep's Head
Dunmanus Bay
Glandore
Clonakilty Bay
Skibbereen
Castletownshend
Galley Head
Schull
Toormore
Goleen
Mizen Head
Crookhaven
Baltimore
Toe Head
Oileán Cléire Clear Island
0 10 20 miles
0 10 20 30 kilometres

F
G
H
J
K
Longford
Kells
Drogheda
Edgeworthstown
Castlepollard
Navan
Balbriggan
Skerries
Mullingar
Trim
Athboy
Ballymahon
Kinnegad
Enfield
Dunboyne
Swords
Malahide
Portmarnock
Howth
Athlone
Moate
Kilbeggan
Tyrrellspass
Maynooth
Leixlip
Lucan
Celbridge
Edenderry
BOG OF ALLEN
DUBLIN
Dún Laoghaire
Killiney
Bray
Greystones
Tullamore
Clara
Daingean
Newbridge
NAAS
Kildare
Portarlington
Monasterevin
REPUBLIC OF IRELAND
Banagher
Birr
Mountmellick
Portlaoise
SLIEVE BLOOM MTS
Mountrath
Roscrea
Abbeyleix
Athy
Stradbally
Baltinglass
Blessington
Wicklow
Wicklow Head
Rathdrum
Arklow
Carlow
Tullow
Castlecomer
Bagenalstown
Gorey
Courtown
Kilkenny
Templemore
Thurles
Cashel
Callan
Thomastown
Graiguenamanagh
Enniscorthy
New Ross
Wexford
Rosslare
Rosslare Harbour
Cahir
Clonmel
Carrick-on-Suir
WATERFORD
Tramore
Dungarvan
Lismore
Youghal
KNOCKMEALDOWN MTS
Holyhead
Douglas (Apr-Sept)
Liverpool
Holyhead
Holyhead (Apr-Sept)
Fishguard (July-Sept)
Fishguard
Pembroke
Cherbourg
(Feb-Dec)
Roscoff
(May-Sept)
Roscoff
(Mar-Oct)
Toll-free motorway
Toll motorway and booth
Motorway junctions with and without number
Restricted motorway junctions
Motorway service area
National primary route (Republic of Ireland)
National secondary route (Republic of Ireland)
Regional road (Republic of Ireland)
Distance in kilometres between symbols (Republic of Ireland)
Primary route (Northern Ireland)
A road (Northern Ireland)
B road (Northern Ireland)
Distance in miles between symbols (Northern Ireland)
Minor road
Road under construction
Scenic route
International boundary
Vehicle ferry
Fast vehicle ferry or catamaran
National Park
Gaeltacht (Irish language area)
To reflect the distances shown on road signs, distances are shown in miles in Northern Ireland and kilometres in the Republic of Ireland.
16 kilometres = 10 miles
For key to touring information see page 1

Ireland index

F
G
H
J
K
G13 Mooncoin
J4 Moorfields
E9 Mountbellew Bridge
F5 Mountcharles
G10 Mountmellick
G10 Mountrath
E10 Mountshannon
G3 Moville
H6 Moy
H8 Moynalty
F9 Moyvore
C13 Muckross
G4 Muff
E6 Mullaghmore
G12 Mullinavat
G9 Mullingar
C7 Mulrany
H11 Myshall
H10 Naas
J8 Naul
H8 Navan
D8 Neale
E11 Nenagh
G7 Newbliss
H10 Newbridge
J6 Newcastle
D12 Newcastle West
F12 Newinn
D13 Newmarket
D11 Newmarket-on-Fergus
C7 Newport
E11 Newport
H12 New Ross
J6 Newry
G11 Newtown
J5 Newtownabbey
K5 Newtownards
G7 Newtownbutler
F8 Newtown Forbes
H6 Newtownhamilton
J10 Newtown Mount Kennedy
G5 Newtownstewart
H8 Nobber
E11 Ogonnelloe
H12 Oilgate
G8 Oldcastle
G5 Omagh
J7 Omeath
E12 Oola
D9 Oranmore
D9 Oughterard
E14 Ovens
E12 Pallas Green New
B14 Parknasilla
D8 Partry
H13 Passage East
E14 Passage West
E12 Patrickswell
H11 Paulstown
F5 Pettigo
G5 Plumbridge
H5 Pomeroy
H6 Portadown
K6 Portaferry
G10 Portarlington
K6 Portavogie
H3 Portballintrae
H4 Portglenone
G10 Portlaoise
J9 Portmarnock
E4 Portnoo
J9 Portraine
E11 Portroe
H3 Portrush
H3 Portstewart
E10 Portumna
C13 Poulgorm Bridge
J6 Poyntz Pass
G9 Raharney
J5 Randalstown
H4 Rasharkin
H10 Rathangan
J9 Rathcoole
E13 Rathcormack
G11 Rathdowney
J10 Rathdrum
J6 Rathfriland
D12 Rathkeale
F4 Rathmelton
D13 Rathmore
H9 Rathmoylon
G4 Rathmullan
J10 Rathnew
G8 Rathowen
H11 Rathvilly
J9 Ratoath
G4 Ray
C9 Recess
B8 Renvyle
E14 Ringaskiddy
G13 Ringville
H7 Rockcorry
F8 Roosky
H12 Rosbercon
F8 Roscommon
F10 Roscrea
F3 Rosepenna
D15 Ross Carbery
E6 Rosses Point
J13 Rosslare
J13 Rosslare Harbour
G6 Rosslea
F5 Rossnowlagh
J7 Rostrevor
B9 Roundstone
J10 Roundwood
J9 Rush
K6 Saintfield
G4 St Johnston
H9 Sallins
D9 Salthill
E11 Scarriff
C13 Scartaglin
J6 Scarva
C15 Schull
F8 Scramoge
G5 Seskinore
F14 Shanagarry
D12 Shanagolden
J9 Shankill
D11 Shannon
F9 Shannonbridge
H7 Shercock
H11 Shillelagh
F10 Shinrone
D9 Shrule
E11 Silvermines
G5 Sion Mills
D11 Sixmilebridge
J8 Skerries
D15 Skibbereen
H8 Slane
E6 Sligo
G6 Smithborough
B14 Sneem
C11 Spanish Point
D9 Spiddal
C9 Sraith Salach
H5 Stewartstown
J9 Stillorgan
G12 Stonyford
G4 Strabane
G10 Stradbally
G7 Stradone
H9 Straffan
E6 Strandhill
K6 Strangford
F5 Stranorlar
F8 Strokestown
H9 Summerhill
F6 Swanlinbar
H4 Swatragh
D7 Swinford
J9 Swords
H12 Taghmon
J13 Tagoat
C14 Tahilla
J9 Tallaght
F13 Tallow
F13 Tallowbridge
J6 Tandragee
F9 Tang
C12 Tarbert
F11 Templemore
F11 Templetouhy
J8 Termonfeckin
G12 Thomastown
F11 Thurles
G10 Timahoe
D15 Timoleague
J11 Tinahely
F12 Tipperary
E7 Tobercurry
H4 Tobermore
F11 Toomyvara
C15 Toormore
C13 Tralee
G13 Tramore
H8 Trim
D9 Tuam
E11 Tuamgraney
D11 Tulla
G9 Tullamore
H11 Tullow
E8 Tulsk
D7 Turlough
G9 Tyrrellspass
G11 Urlingford
G8 Virginia
J7 Warrenpoint
G13 Waterford
E13 Watergrasshill
B14 Waterville
C8 Westport
J12 Wexford
E14 Whitegate
K5 Whitehead
J10 Wicklow
J11 Woodenbridge
E10 Woodford
F14 Youghal
Malin Head
Inishtrahull Sound
Rathlin Island
Carndonagh
Buncrana
INISHOWEN
Portrush
Portstewart
Coleraine
Ballycastle
Ballymoney
Limavady
LONDONDERRY
DERRY
Letterkenny
Strabane
Lifford
Ballymena
Larne
Ballyclare
Antrim
Randalstown
Carrickfergus
NEWTOWNABBEY
BANGOR
Holywood
BELFAST
Newtownards
Donaghadee
Dundonald
Lisburn
Comber
Lough Neagh
NORTHERN IRELAND
SPERRIN MTS
Magherafelt
Cookstown
Omagh
Dungannon
Lurgan
Craigavon
Portadown
Banbridge
Armagh
Downpatrick
Newcastle
Newry
Warrenpoint
Kilkeel
MOURNE MTS
Enniskillen
Lower Lough Erne
Monaghan
Clones
Castleblayney
Dundalk
Dundalk Bay
Cavan
Carrickmacross
Bailieborough
Ardee
Drogheda
Kells
Navan
Balbriggan
Longford
Granard
Carrick-on-Shannon
IRON MTS
Manorhamilton
Donegal
Ballyshannon
Cairnryan
Troon
Douglas
Liverpool (Birkenhead)
113

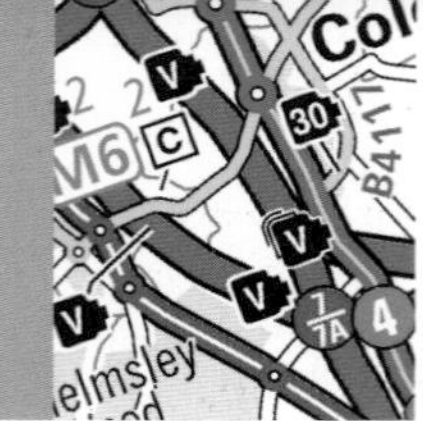

Restricted junctions

Motorway and Primary Route junctions which have access or exit restrictions are shown on the map pages thus: 3 56

M1 London - Leeds

Northbound
Access only from A1 (northbound)

Southbound
Exit only to A1 (southbound)

Northbound
Access only from A41 (northbound)

Southbound
Exit only to A41 (southbound)

Northbound
Access only from M25 (no link from A405)

Southbound
Exit only to M25 (no link from A405)

Northbound
Access only from A414

Southbound
Exit only to A414

Northbound
Exit only to M45

Southbound
Access only from M45

Northbound
Exit only to M6 (northbound)

Southbound
Access only from M6

Northbound
Exit only, no access

Southbound
Access only, no exit

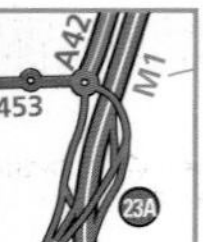

Northbound
Access only from A42

Southbound
No restriction

Northbound
No exit, access only

Southbound
Exit only, no access

Northbound
Exit only, no access

Southbound
Access only, no exit

Northbound
Exit only to M621

Southbound
Access only from M621

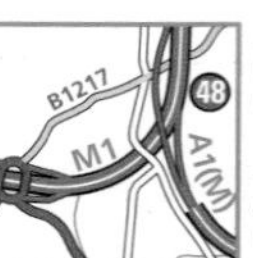

Northbound
Exit only to A1(M) (northbound)

Southbound
Access only from A1(M) (southbound)

M2 Rochester - Faversham

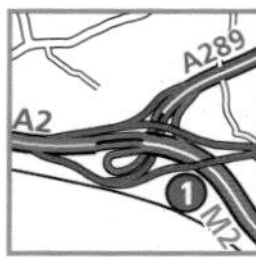

Westbound
No exit to A2 (eastbound)

Eastbound
No access from A2 (westbound)

M3 Sunbury - Southampton

Northeastbound
Access only from A303, no exit

Southwestbound
Exit only to A303, no access

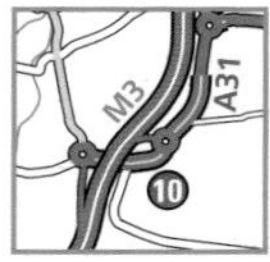

Northbound
Exit only, no access

Southbound
Access only, no exit

Northeastbound
Access from M27 only. No exit

Southwestbound
No access to M27 (westbound)

M4 London - South Wales

Westbound
Access only from A4 (westbound)

Eastbound
Exit only to A4 (eastbound)

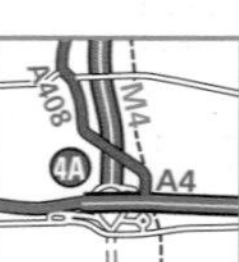

Westbound
No exit to A4 (westbound)

Eastbound
No restriction

Westbound
Exit only to M48

Eastbound
Access only from M48

Westbound
Access only from M48

Eastbound
Exit only to M48

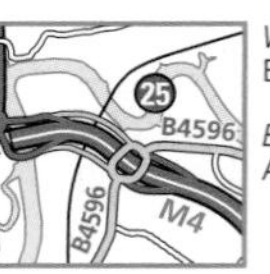

Westbound
Exit only, no access

Eastbound
Access only, no exit

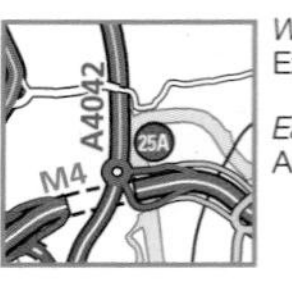

Westbound
Exit only, no access

Eastbound
Access only, no exit

Westbound
Exit only to A48(M)

Eastbound
Access only from A48(M)

Westbound
Exit only, no access

Eastbound
No restriction

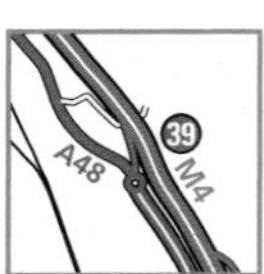

Westbound
Access only, no exit

Eastbound
No access or exit

M5 Birmingham - Exeter

Northeastbound
Access only, no exit

Southwestbound
Exit only, no access

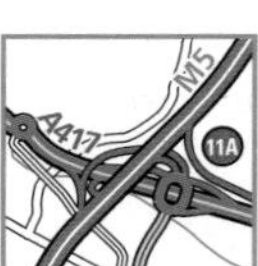

Northeastbound
Access only from A417 (westbound)

Southwestbound
Exit only to A417 (eastbound)

Northeastbound
No access, exit only

Southwestbound
No exit, access only

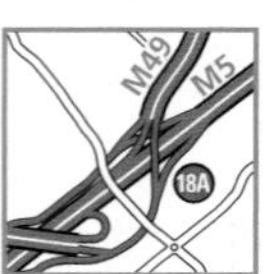

Northeastbound
Exit only to M49

Southwestbound
Access only from M49

Northeastbound
No restriction

Southwestbound
Access only from A30 (westbound)

M6 Toll Motorway

See M6 Toll Motorway map on page 121

M6 Rugby - Carlisle

Northbound
Exit only to M6 Toll

Southbound
Access only from M6 Toll

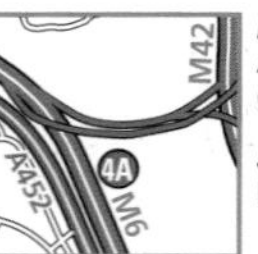

Northbound
Access only from M42 (southbound)

Southbound
Exit only to M42

Northbound
Exit only, no access

Southbound
Access only, no exit

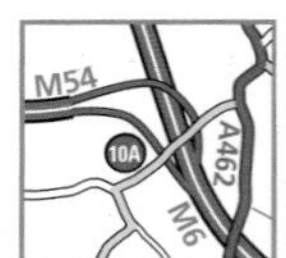

Northbound
Exit only to M54

Southbound
Access only from M54

Northbound
Access only from M6 Toll

Southbound
Exit only to M6 Toll

Northbound
No restriction

Southbound
Access only from M56 (eastbound)

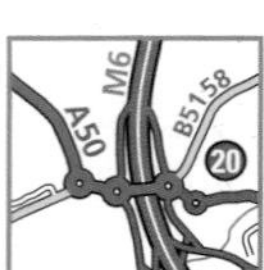

Northbound
Access only, no exit

Southbound
No restriction

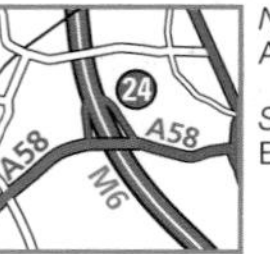

Northbound
Access only, no exit

Southbound
Exit only, no access

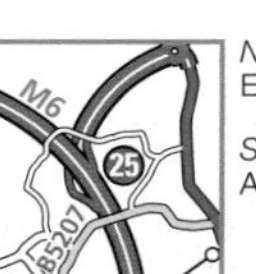

Northbound
Exit only, no access

Southbound
Access only, no exit

Northbound
No direct access, use adjacent slip road to jct 29A

Southbound
No direct exit, use adjacent slip road from jct 29A

Northbound
Acces only, no exit

Southbound
Exit only, no access

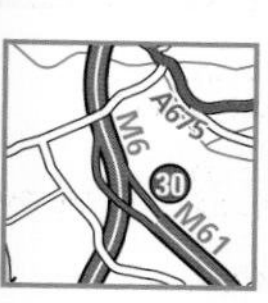

Northbound
Access only from M61

Southbound
Exit only to M61

Northbound
Exit only, no access

Southbound
Access only, no exit

Northbound
Exit only, no access

Southbound
Access only, no exit

M8 Edinburgh - Bishopton

See Glasgow District map on pages 138-139

M9 Edinburgh - Dunblane

Northwestbound
Exit only to M9 spur

Southeastbound
Access only from M9 spur

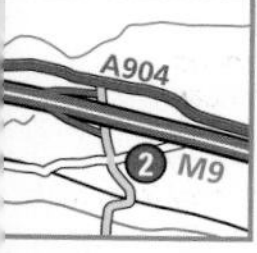

Northwestbound
Access only, no exit

Southeastbound
Exit only, no access

Northwestbound
Exit only, no access

Southeastbound
Access only, no exit

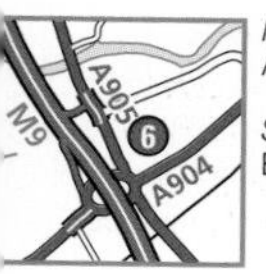

Northwestbound
Access only, no exit

Southeastbound
Exit only to A905

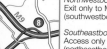

Northwestbound
Exit only to M876 (southwestbound)

Southeastbound
Access only from M876 (northeastbound)

M11 London - Cambridge

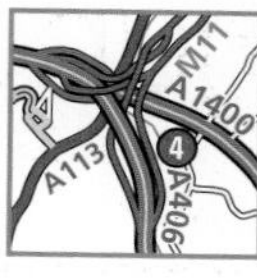

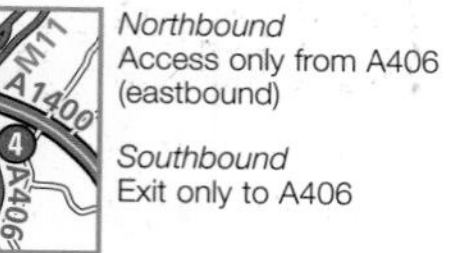

Northbound
Access only from A406 (eastbound)

Southbound
Exit only to A406

Northbound
Exit only, no access

Southbound
Access only, no exit

Northbound
Exit only to A11

Southbound
Access only from A11

Northbound
Exit only, no access

Southbound
Access only, no exit

Northbound
Exit only, no access

Southbound
Access only, no exit

M20 Swanley - Folkestone

Northwestbound
Staggered junction; follow signs - access only

Southeastbound
Staggered junction; follow signs - exit only

Northwestbound
Exit only to M26 (westbound)

Southeastbound
Access only from M26 (eastbound)

Northwestbound
Access only from A20

Southeastbound
For access follow signs - exit only to A20

Northwestbound
No restriction

Southeastbound
For exit follow signs

Northwestbound
Access only, no exit

Southeastbound
Exit only, no access

M23 Hooley - Crawley

Northbound
Exit only to A23 (northbound)

Southbound
Access only from A23 (southbound)

Northbound
Access only, no exit

Southbound
Exit only, no access

M25 London Orbital Motorway

See M25 London Orbital Motorway map on page 120

M26 Sevenoaks - Wrotham

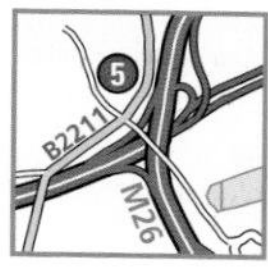

Westbound
Exit only to clockwise M25 (westbound)

Eastbound
Access only from anti-clockwise M25 (eastbound)

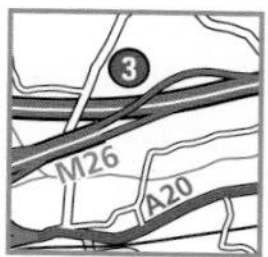

Westbound
Access only from M20 (northwestbound)

Eastbound
Exit only to M20 (southeastbound)

M27 Cadnam - Portsmouth

Westbound
Staggered junction; follow signs - access only from M3 (southbound). Exit only to M3 (northbound)

Eastbound
Staggered junction; follow signs - access only from M3 (southbound). Exit only to M3 (northbound)

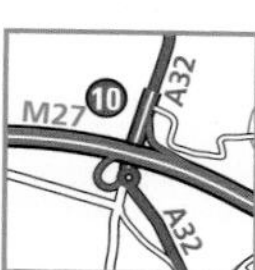

Westbound
Exit only, no access

Eastbound
Access only, no exit

Westbound
Staggered junction; follow signs - exit only to M275 (southbound)

Eastbound
Staggered junction; follow signs - access only from M275 (northbound)

M40 London - Birmingham

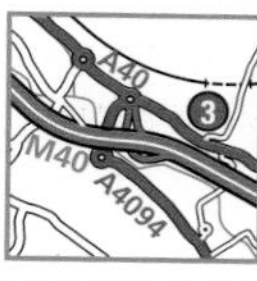

Northwestbound
Exit only, no access

Southeastbound
Access only, no exit

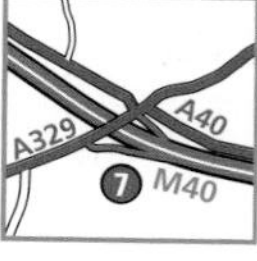

Northwestbound
Exit only, no access

Southeastbound
Access only, no exit

Northwestbound
Exit only to M40/A40

Southeastbound
Access only from M40/A40

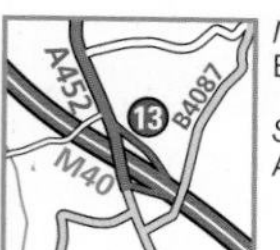

Northwestbound
Exit only, no access

Southeastbound
Access only, no exit

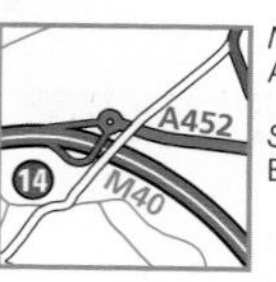

Northwestbound
Access only, no exit

Southeastbound
Exit only, no access

Northwestbound
Access only, no exit

Southeastbound
Exit only, no access

M42 Bromsgrove - Measham

See Birmingham District map on pages 136-137

M45 Coventry - M1

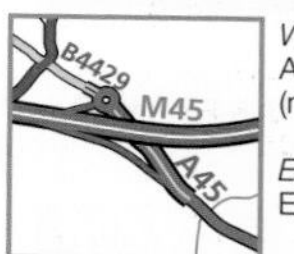

Westbound
Access only from A45 (northbound)

Eastbound
Exit only, no access

Westbound
Access only from M1 (northbound)

Eastbound
Exit only to M1 (southbound)

M53 Mersey Tunnel - Chester

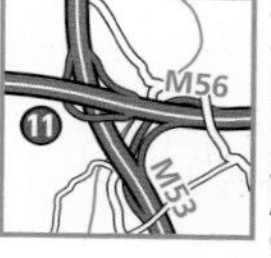

Northbound
Access only from M56 (westbound). Exit only to M56 (eastbound)

Southbound
Access only from M56 (westbound). Exit only to M56 (eastbound)

M54 Telford

Westbound
Access only from M6 (northbound)

Eastbound
Exit only to M6 (southbound)

M56 North Cheshire

For junctions 1,2,3,4 & 7 see Manchester District map on pages 140-141

Westbound
Access only, no exit

Eastbound
No access or exit

Westbound
Exit only to M53

Eastbound
Access only from M53

M57 Liverpool Outer Ring Road

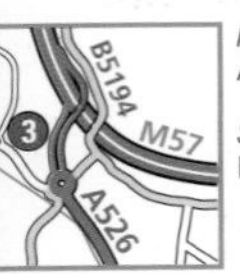

Northwestbound
Access only, no exit

Southeastbound
Exit only, no access

Northwestbound
Access only from A580 (westbound)

Southeastbound
Exit only, no access

M58 Liverpool - Wigan

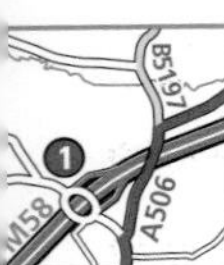

Westbound
Exit only, no access

Eastbound
Access only, no exit

M60 Manchester Orbital

ee Manchester District map on pages 40-141

M61 Manchester - Preston

Northwestbound
No access or exit

Southeastbound
Exit only, no access

Northwestbound
Exit only to M6 (northbound)

Southeastbound
Access only from M6 (southbound)

M62 Liverpool - Kingston upon Hull

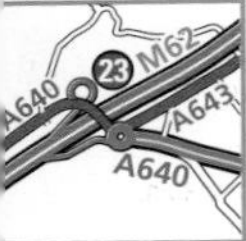

Westbound
Access only, no exit

Eastbound
Exit only, no access

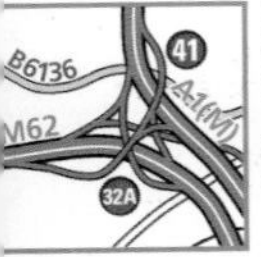

Westbound
No access to A1(M) (southbound)

Eastbound
No restriction

M65 Preston - Colne

Northeastbound
Exit only, no access

Southwestbound
Access only, no exit

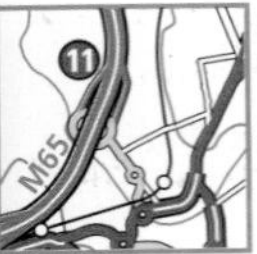

Northeastbound
Access only, no exit

Southwestbound
Exit only, no access

M66 Bury

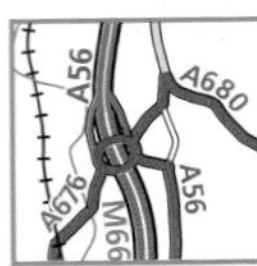

Northbound
Exit only to A56 (northbound)

Southbound
Access only from A56 (southbound)

Northbound
Exit only, no access

Southbound
Access only, no exit

M67 Hyde Bypass

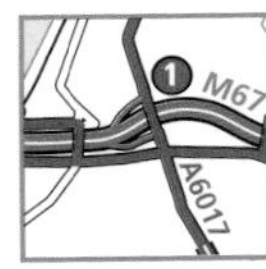

Westbound
Access only, no exit

Eastbound
Exit only, no access

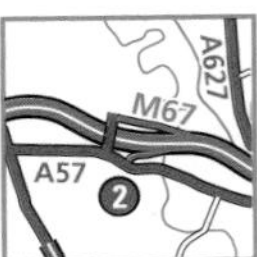

Westbound
Exit only, no access

Eastbound
Access only, no exit

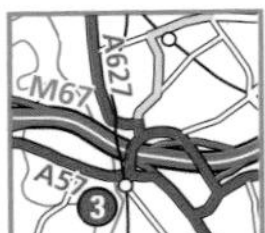

Westbound
Exit only, no access

Eastbound
No restriction

M69 Coventry - Leicester

Northbound
Access only, no exit

Southbound
Exit only, no access

M73 East of Glasgow

Northbound
No access from or exit to A89. No access from M8 (eastbound)

Southbound
No access from or exit to A89. No exit to M8 (westbound)

M74 and A74(M) Glasgow - Gretna

Northbound
Exit only, no access

Southbound
Access only, no exit

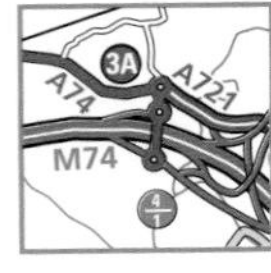

Northbound
Access only, no exit

Southbound
Exit only, no access

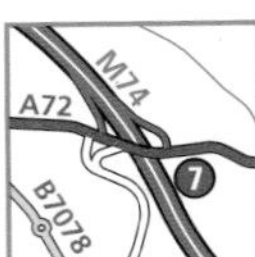

Northbound
Access only, no exit

Southbound
Exit only, no access

Northbound
No access or exit

Southbound
Exit only, no access

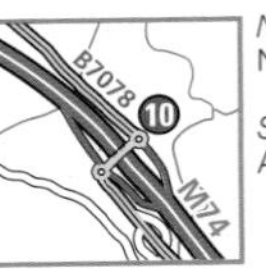

Northbound
No restriction

Southbound
Access only, no exit

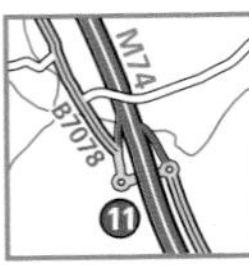

Northbound
Access only, no exit

Southbound
Exit only, no access

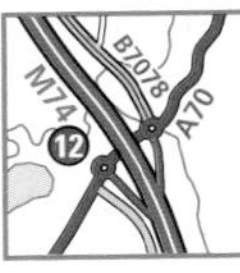

Northbound
Exit only, no access

Southbound
Access only, no exit

Northbound
Exit only, no access

Southbound
Access only, no exit

M77 South of Glasgow

Northbound
No exit to M8 (westbound)

Southbound
No access from M8 (eastbound)

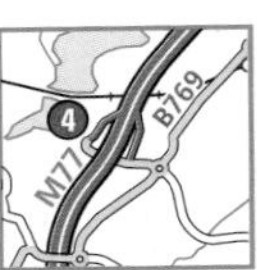

Northbound
Access only, no exit

Southbound
Exit only, no access

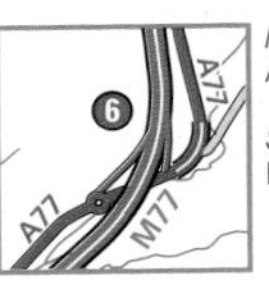

Northbound
Access only, no exit

Southbound
Exit only, no access

Northbound
Access only, no exit

Southbound
No restriction

M80 Glasgow - Stirling

Northbound
Exit only, no access

Southbound
Access only, no exit

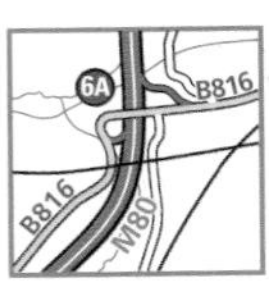

Northbound
Access only, no exit

Southbound
Exit only, no access

Northbound
Exit only to M876 (northeastbound)

Southbound
Access only from M876 (southwestbound)

M90 Forth Road Bridge - Perth

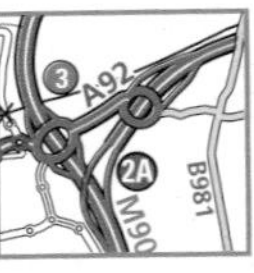

Northbound
Exit only to A92 (eastbound)

Southbound
Access only from A92 (westbound)

Northbound
Access only, no exit

Southbound
Exit only, no access

Northbound
Exit only, no access

Southbound
Access only, no exit

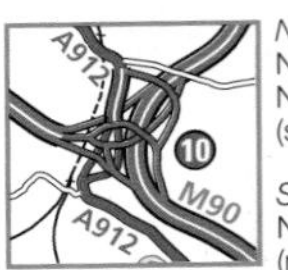

Northbound
No access from A912
No exit to A912 (southbound)

Southbound
No access from A912 (northbound).
No exit to A912

M180 Doncaster - Grimsby

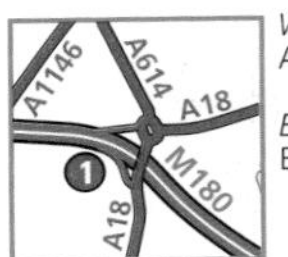

Westbound
Access only, no exit

Eastbound
Exit only, no access

M606 Bradford Spur

Northbound
Exit only, no access

Southbound
No restriction

M621 Leeds - M1

Clockwise
Access only, no exit

Anticlockwise
Exit only, no access

Clockwise
No exit or access

Anticlockwise
No restriction

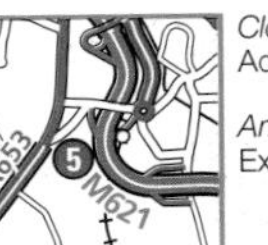

Clockwise
Access only, no exit

Anticlockwise
Exit only, no access

Clockwise
Exit only, no access

Anticlockwise
Access only, no exit

Clockwise
Exit only to M1 (southbound)

Anticlockwise
Access only from M1 (northbound)

M876 Bonnybridge - Kincardine Bridge

Northeastbound
Access only from M80 (northbound)

Southwestbound
Exit only to M80 (southbound)

Northeastbound
Exit only to M9 (eastbound)

Southwestbound
Access only from M9 (westbound)

A1(M) South Mimms - Baldock

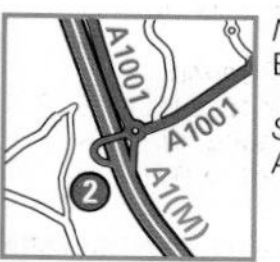

Northbound
Exit only, no access

Southbound
Access only, no exit

Northbound
No restriction

Southbound
Exit only, no access

Northbound
Access only, no exit

Southbound
No access or exit

A1(M) East of Leeds

Northbound
No access to M62 (eastbound)

Southbound
No restriction

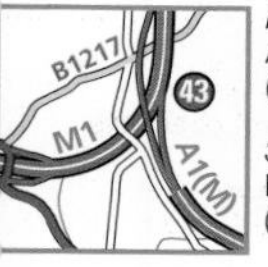

Northbound
Access only from M1 (northbound)

Southbound
Exit only to M1 (southbound)

A1(M) Scotch Corner - Newcastle upon Tyne

Northbound
Exit only to A66(M) (eastbound)

Southbound
Access only from A66(M) (westbound)

Northbound
No access. Exit only to A194(M) & A1 (northbound)

Southbound
No exit. Access only from A194(M) & A1 (southbound)

A3(M) Horndean - Havant

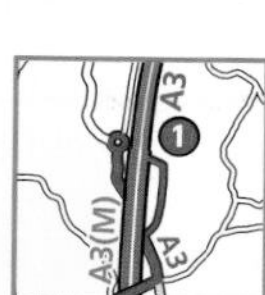

Northbound
Access only from A3

Southbound
Exit only to A3

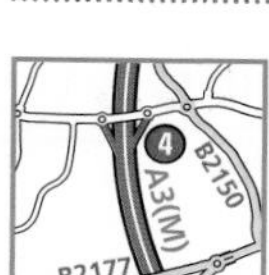

Northbound
Exit only, no access

Southbound
Access only, no exit

A48(M) Cardiff Spur

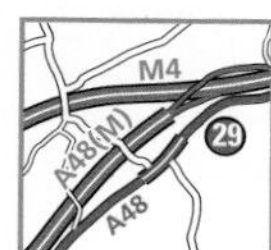

Westbound
Access only from M4 (westbound)

Eastbound
Exit only to M4 (eastbound)

Westbound
Exit only to A48 (westbound)

Eastbound
Access only from A48 (eastbound)

A66(M) Darlington Spur

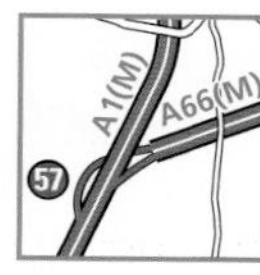

Westbound
Exit only to A1(M) (southbound)

Eastbound
Access only from A1(M) (northbound)

A194(M) Newcastle upon Tyne

Northbound
Access only from A1(M) (northbound)

Southbound
Exit only to A1(M) (southbound)

A12 M25 - Ipswich

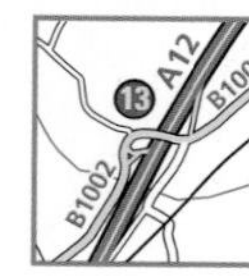

Northeastbound
Access only, no exit

Southwestbound
No restriction

Northeastbound
Exit only, no access

Southwestbound
Access only, no exit

Northeastbound
Exit only, no access

Southwestbound
Access only, no exit

Northeastbound
Access only, no exit

Southwestbound
Exit only, no access

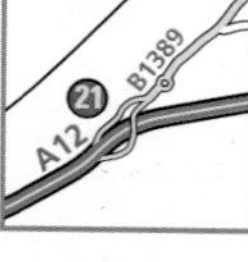

Northeastbound
No restriction

Southwestbound
Access only, no exit

Northeastbound
Exit only, no access

Southwestbound
Access only, no exit

Northeastbound
Access only, no exit

Southwestbound
Exit only, no access

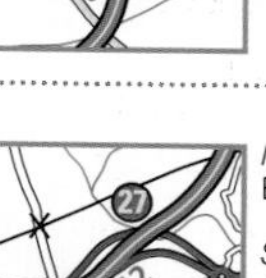

Northeastbound
Exit only, no access

Southwestbound
Access only, no exit

With A120
Northeastbound
Exit only, no access

Southwestbound
Access only, no exit

Northeastbound
Access only, no exit

Southwestbound
Exit only, no access

Northeastbound
Exit only (for Stratford St Mary and Dedham)

Southwestbound
Access only

A14 M1 Felixstowe

Westbound
Exit only to M6 & M1 (northbound)

Eastbound
Access only from M6 & M1 (southbound)

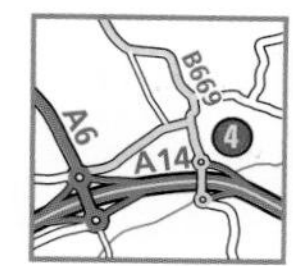

Westbound
Exit only, no access

Eastbound
Access only, no exit

Westbound
Access only from A1307

Eastbound
Exit only to A1307

Westbound
Access only, no exit

Eastbound
Exit only,no access

Westbound
Exit only to A11

Eastbound
Access only from A11

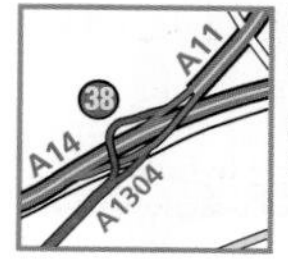

Westbound
Access only from A11

Eastbound
Exit only to A11

Westbound
Exit only, no access

Eastbound
Access only, no exit

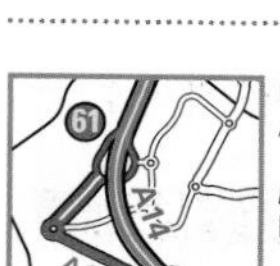

Westbound
Access only, no exit

Eastbound
Exit only, no access

A55 Holyhead - Chester

Westbound
Exit only, no access

Eastbound
Access only, no exit

Westbound
Access only, no exit

Eastbound
Exit only, no access

Westbound
Exit only, no access

Eastbound
No access or exit.

Westbound
Exit only, no access

Eastbound
No access or exit

Westbound
Exit only, no access

Eastbound
Access only, no exit

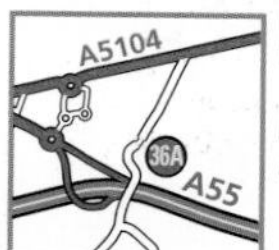

Westbound
Exit only to A5104

Eastbound
Access only from A5104

M25 London Orbital motorway

Refer also to atlas pages 20–21

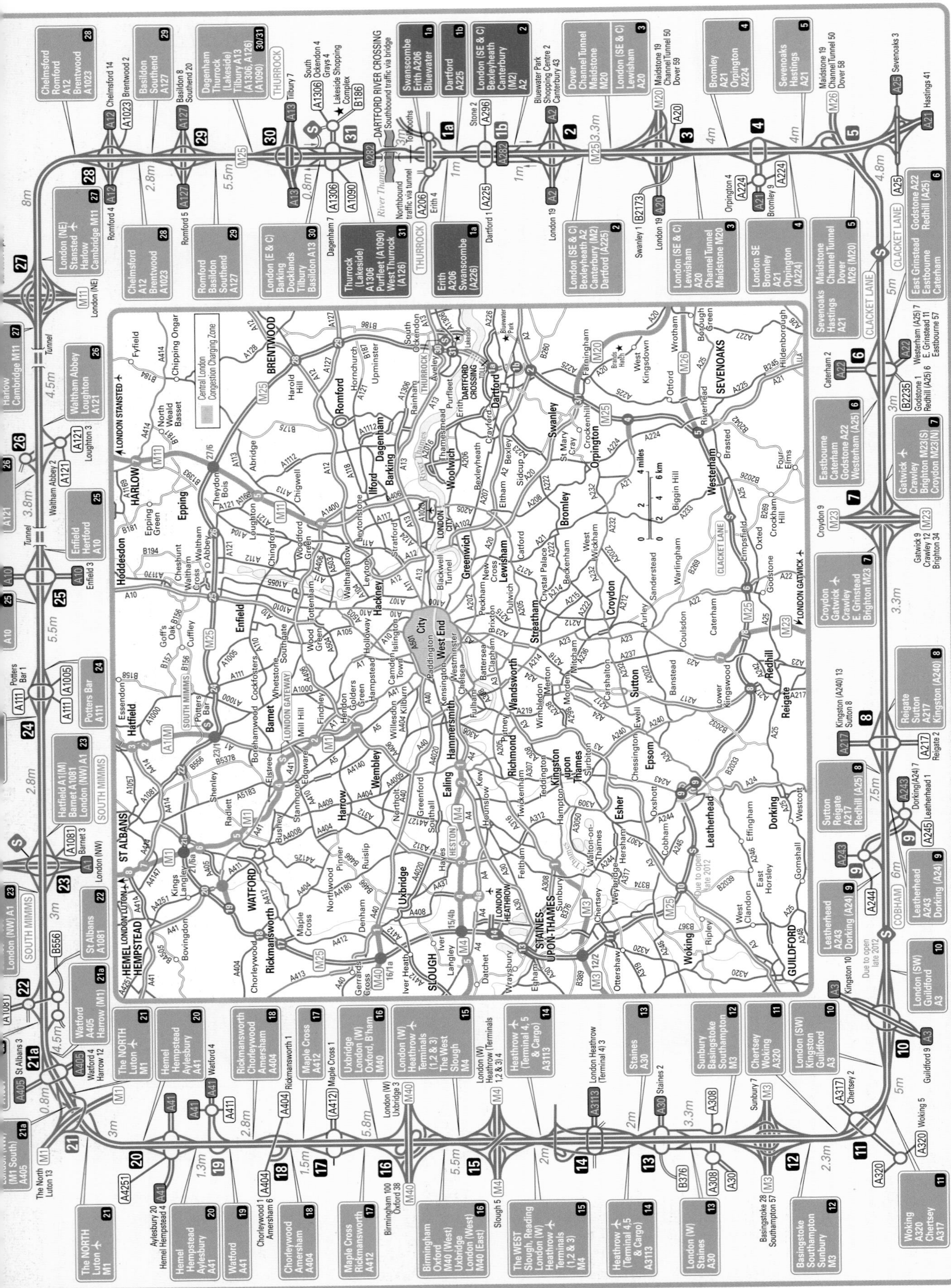

M6 Toll motorway

Refer also to atlas page 40

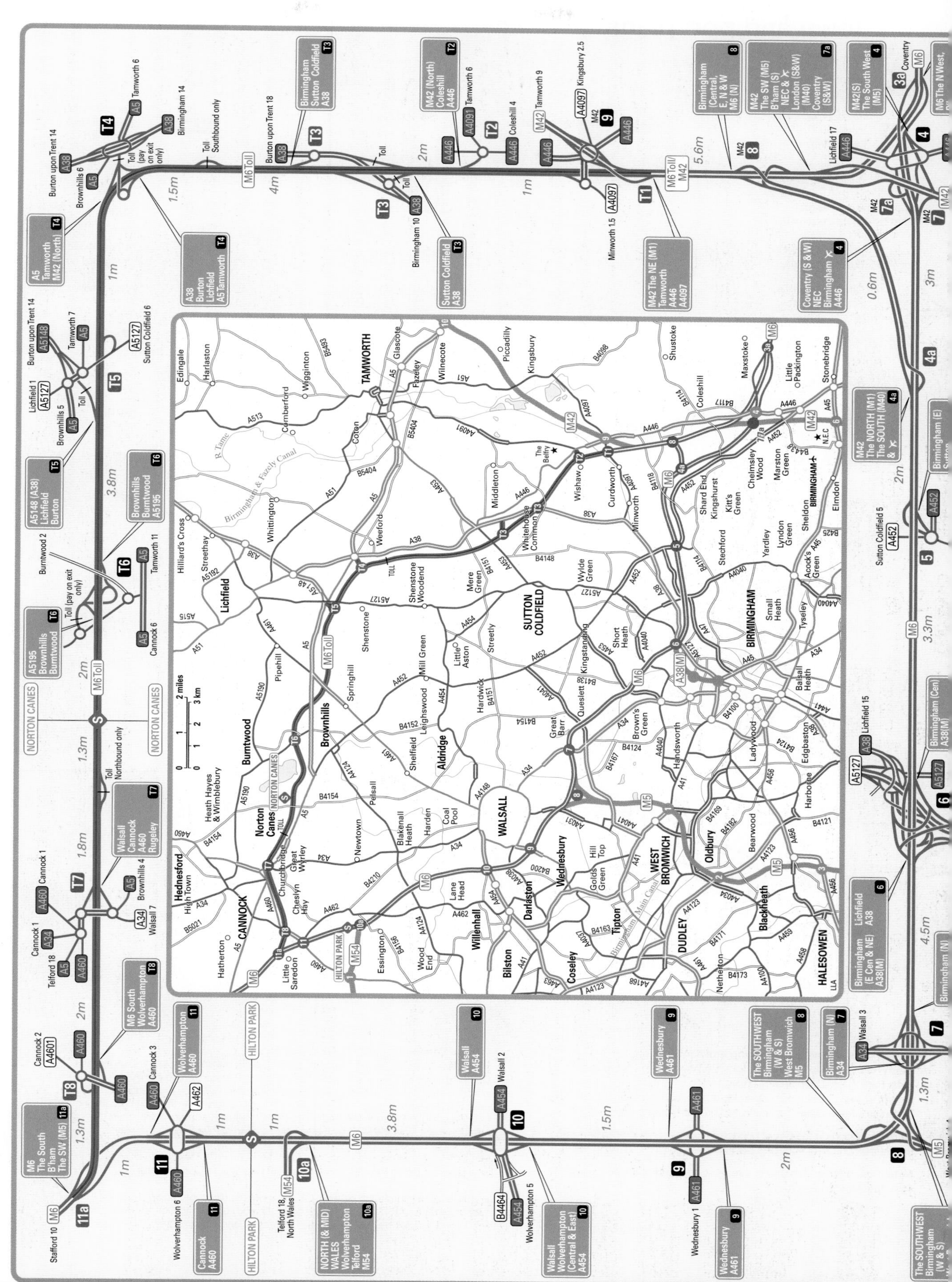

Street map symbols

Town and port plans

- Motorway and junction
- Primary road single/dual carriageway
- A road single/ dual carriageway
- B road single/ dual carriageway
- Local road single/ dual carriageway
- Other road single/ dual carriageway, minor road
- Building of interest
- Ruined building
- Tourist Information Centre
- Visitor or heritage centre
- World Heritage Site (UNESCO)
- English Heritage site
- Historic Scotland site
- Cadw (Welsh heritage) site
- National Trust site
- National Trust Scotland site

- One-way, gated/ closed road
- Restricted access road
- Pedestrian area
- Footpath
- Road under construction
- Road tunnel
- Museum
- Castle
- Castle mound
- Monument, statue
- Post Office
- Public library
- Shopping centre
- Shopmobility
- Viewpoint
- Toilet, with facilities for the less able

- Railway station
- Light rapid transit system station
- Level crossing
- Tramway
- Ferry route
- Airport, heliport
- Railair terminal
- Theatre or performing arts centre
- Cinema
- Abbey, chapel, church
- Synagogue
- Mosque
- Golf Course
- Racecourse
- Nature reserve
- Aquarium

- Car park
- Park and Ride (at least 6 days per week)
- Bus/coach station
- Hospital
- 24-hour Accident & Emergency hospital
- Petrol station, 24 hour
  Major suppliers only
- City wall
- Escarpment
- Cliff lift
- River/canal, lake
- Lock, weir
- Park/sports ground
- Cemetery
- Woodland
- Built-up area
- Beach

Central London street map (see pages 148 - 157)

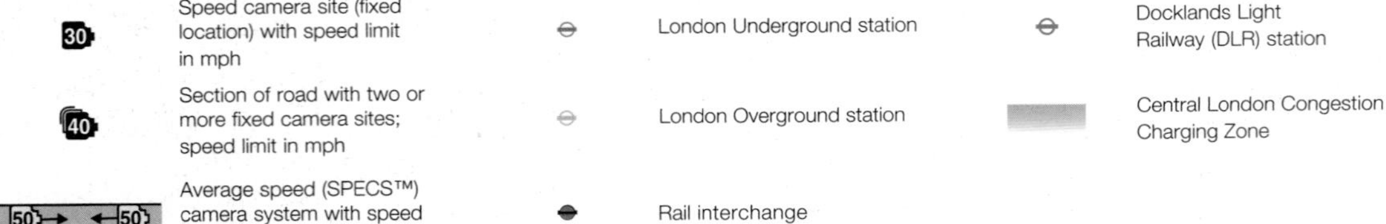

- Speed camera site (fixed location) with speed limit in mph
- Section of road with two or more fixed camera sites; speed limit in mph
- Average speed (SPECS™) camera system with speed limit in mph
- London Underground station
- London Overground station
- Rail interchange
- Docklands Light Railway (DLR) station
- Central London Congestion Charging Zone

Royal Parks (opening and closing times for traffic)

Green Park	Open 5am-midnight. Constitution Hill: closed Sundays
Hyde Park	Open 5am-midnight
Regent's Park	Open 5am-dusk. Most park roads closed midnight-7am
St James's Park	Open 5am-midnight. The Mall: closed Sundays

Traffic regulations in the City of London include security checkpoints and restrict the number of entry and exit points.

Note: Oxford Street is closed to through-traffic (except buses & taxis) 7am-7pm Monday-Saturday.

Central London Congestion Charging Zone

The daily charge for driving or parking a vehicle on public roads in the Congestion Charging Zone (CCZ), during operating hours, is £10 per vehicle per day in advance or on the day of travel. Alternatively you can pay £9 by registering with CC Auto Pay, an automated payment system. Drivers can also pay the next charging day after travelling in the zone but this will cost £12. Payment permits entry, travel within and exit from the CCZ by the vehicle as often as required on that day.

The CCZ operates between 7am and 6pm, Mon–Fri only. There is no charge at weekends, public holidays or betwen 25th Dec and 1st Jan inclusive.

For up to date information on the CCZ, exemptions, discounts or ways to pay, telephone 0845 900 1234, visit www.cclondon.com or write to Congestion Charging, P.O. Box 4782, Worthing BN11 9PS. Textphone users can call 020 7649 9123.

Transport for London
Congestion charging
Central ZONE
Mon - Fri
7am - 6pm

Town and port plans

Town plan contents

Central London

Ferry Po

Channel Tu

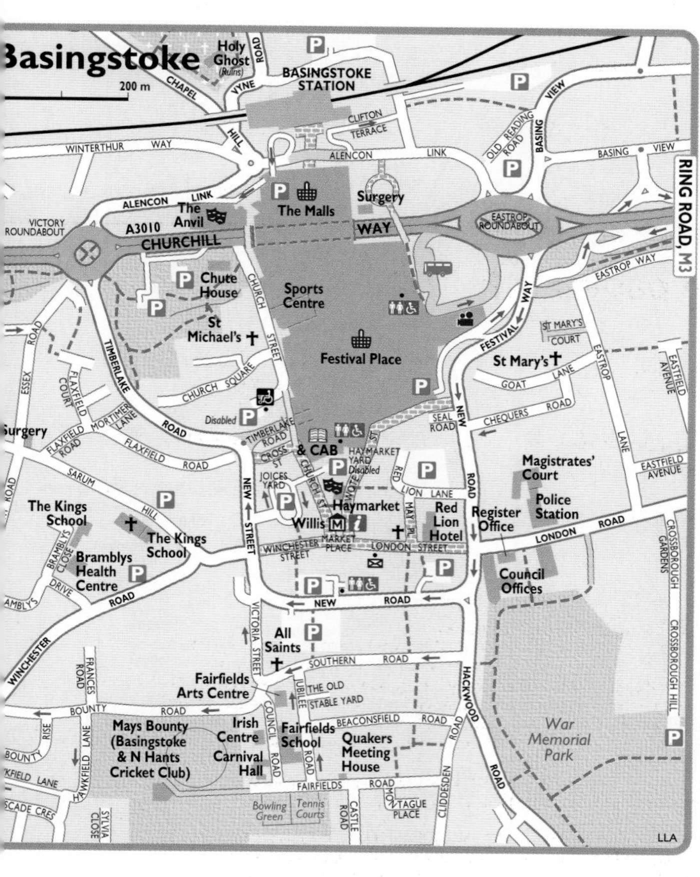

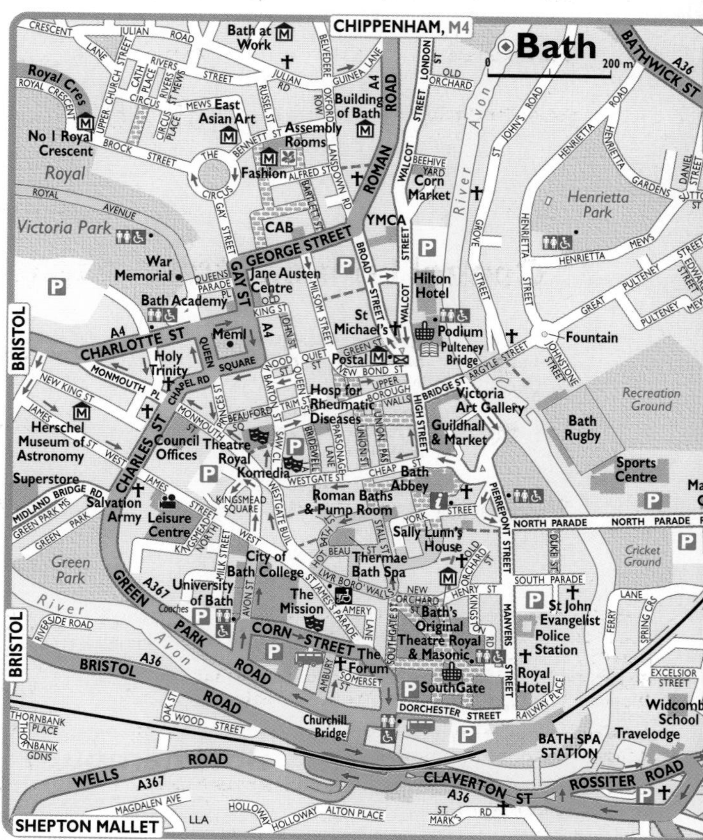

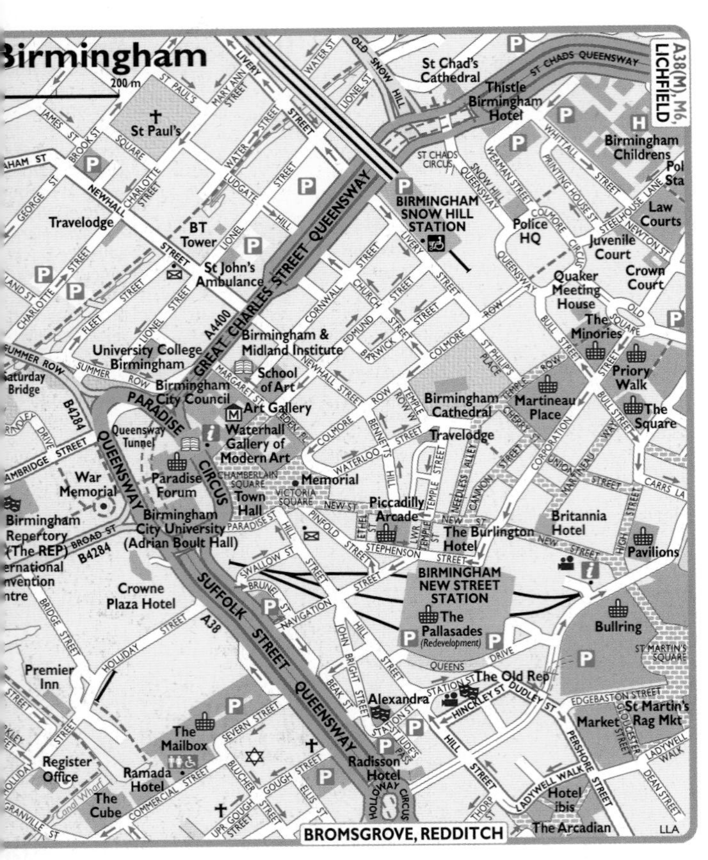
Birmingham
200 m
St Paul's
Travelodge
BT Tower
St John's Ambulance
St Chad's Cathedral
Thistle Birmingham Hotel
Birmingham Childrens
Police HQ
Law Courts
Juvenile Court
Crown Court
Quaker Meeting House
The Minories
BIRMINGHAM SNOW HILL STATION
GREAT CHARLES STREET QUEENSWAY
University College Birmingham
Birmingham & Midland Institute
School of Art
Birmingham City Council
Art Gallery
Waterhall Gallery of Modern Art
Birmingham Cathedral
Martineau Place
Priory Walk
The Square
Travelodge
War Memorial
Paradise Forum
Town Hall
Memorial
Piccadilly Arcade
Birmingham City University (Adrian Boult Hall)
Birmingham Repertory (The REP)
The Burlington Hotel
Britannia Hotel
Pavilions
BIRMINGHAM NEW STREET STATION
The Pallasades (Redevelopment)
Bullring
Crowne Plaza Hotel
Premier Inn
SUFFOLK STREET QUEENSWAY
Alexandra
The Old Rep
St Martin's Rag Mkt
Market
The Mailbox
Register Office
Ramada Hotel
Radisson Hotel
Hotel ibis
The Arcadian
The Cube
A38(M), M6, LICHFIELD
BROMSGROVE, REDDITCH
LLA

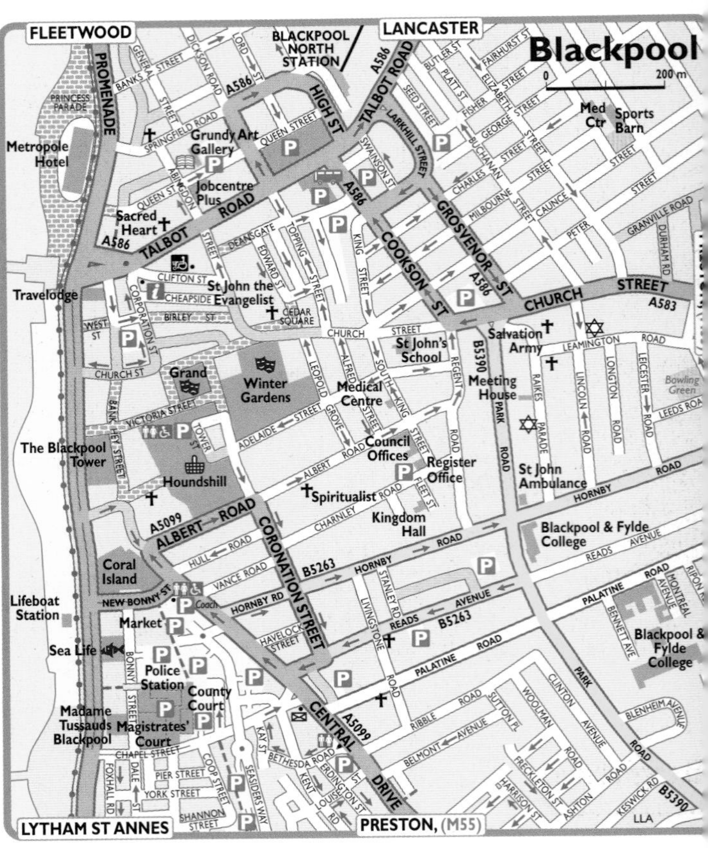
FLEETWOOD
BLACKPOOL NORTH STATION
LANCASTER
Blackpool
200 m
Metropole Hotel
Grundy Art Gallery
Jobcentre Plus
Sacred Heart
TALBOT ROAD
Med Ctr
Sports Barn
Travelodge
St John the Evangelist
CHURCH STREET
Salvation Army
St John's School
Meeting House
Grand
Winter Gardens
Medical Centre
The Blackpool Tower
Houndshill
Council Offices
Register Office
St John Ambulance
Spiritualist
Kingdom Hall
Blackpool & Fylde College
Coral Island
Lifeboat Station
Market
Sea Life
Police Station
County Court
Madame Tussauds Blackpool
Magistrates' Court
Blackpool & Fylde College
CENTRAL DRIVE
LYTHAM ST ANNES
PRESTON, (M55)
LLA

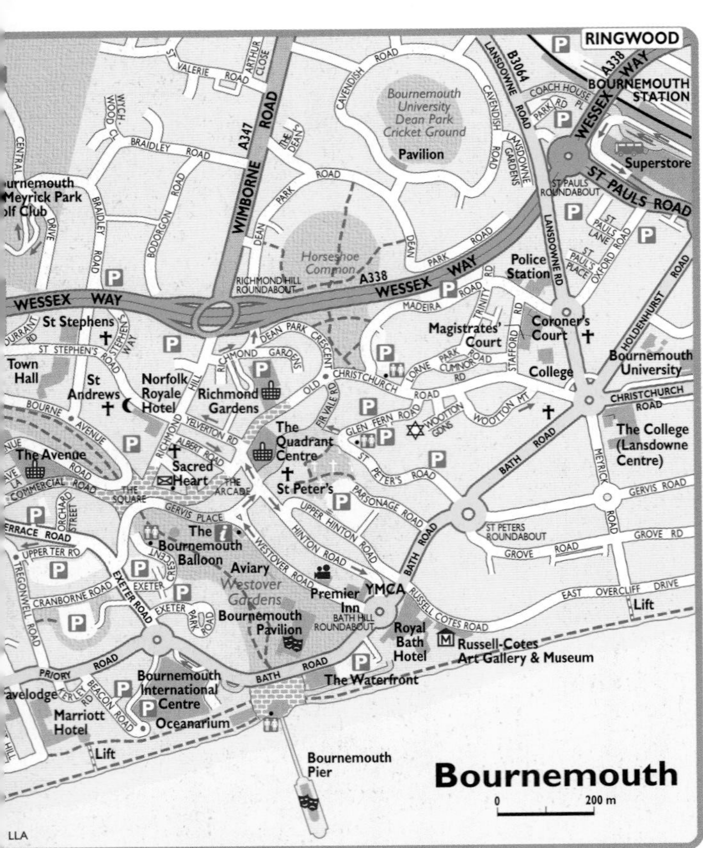
RINGWOOD
BOURNEMOUTH STATION
Superstore
Bournemouth University Dean Park Cricket Ground
Pavilion
Bournemouth Meyrick Park Golf Club
WIMBORNE ROAD
Horseshoe Common
WESSEX WAY
ST PAULS ROAD
Police Station
Coroner's Court
Magistrates' Court
St Stephens
Town Hall
St Andrews
Norfolk Royale Hotel
Richmond Gardens
College
Bournemouth University
The College (Lansdowne Centre)
The Avenue
Sacred Heart
The Quadrant Centre
St Peter's
The Bournemouth Balloon
Aviary
Westover Gardens
Bournemouth Pavilion
Premier Inn
YMCA
Royal Bath Hotel
Russell-Cotes Art Gallery & Museum
Lift
The Waterfront
Bournemouth International Centre
Oceanarium
Marriott Hotel
Lift
Bournemouth Pier
Bournemouth
200 m
LLA

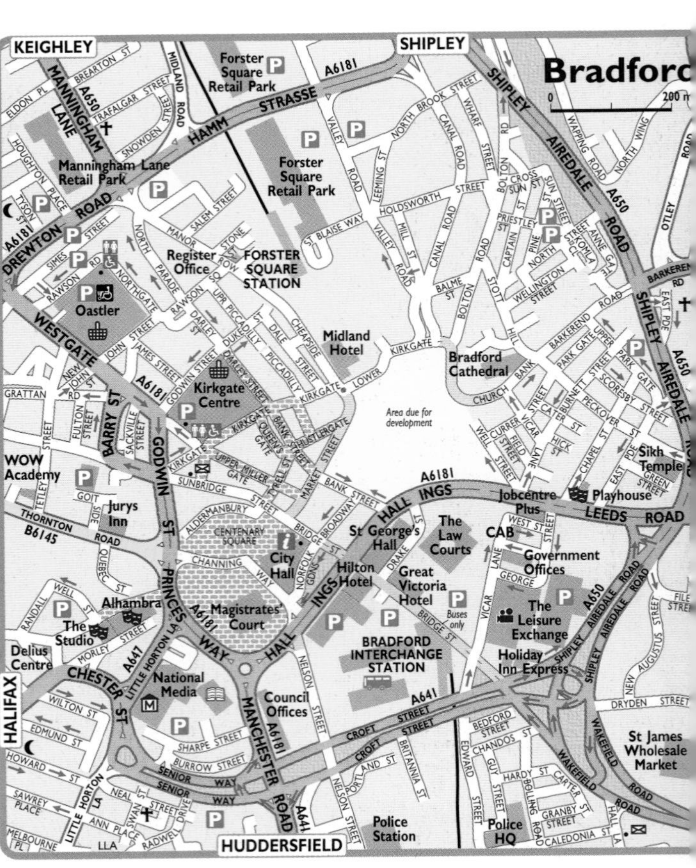
KEIGHLEY
SHIPLEY
Bradford
200 m
Forster Square Retail Park
Manningham Lane Retail Park
Forster Square Retail Park
Register Office
FORSTER SQUARE STATION
Oastler
Midland Hotel
Bradford Cathedral
Kirkgate Centre
Area due for development
WOW Academy
Jurys Inn
Sikh Temple
Playhouse
Jobcentre Plus
LEEDS ROAD
St George's Hall
The Law Courts
CAB
Government Offices
City Hall
Hilton Hotel
Great Victoria Hotel
Alhambra
The Studio
Magistrates' Court
The Leisure Exchange
BRADFORD INTERCHANGE STATION
Holiday Inn Express
Delius Centre
National Media
Council Offices
HALIFAX
St James Wholesale Market
Police Station
Police HQ
HUDDERSFIELD
LLA

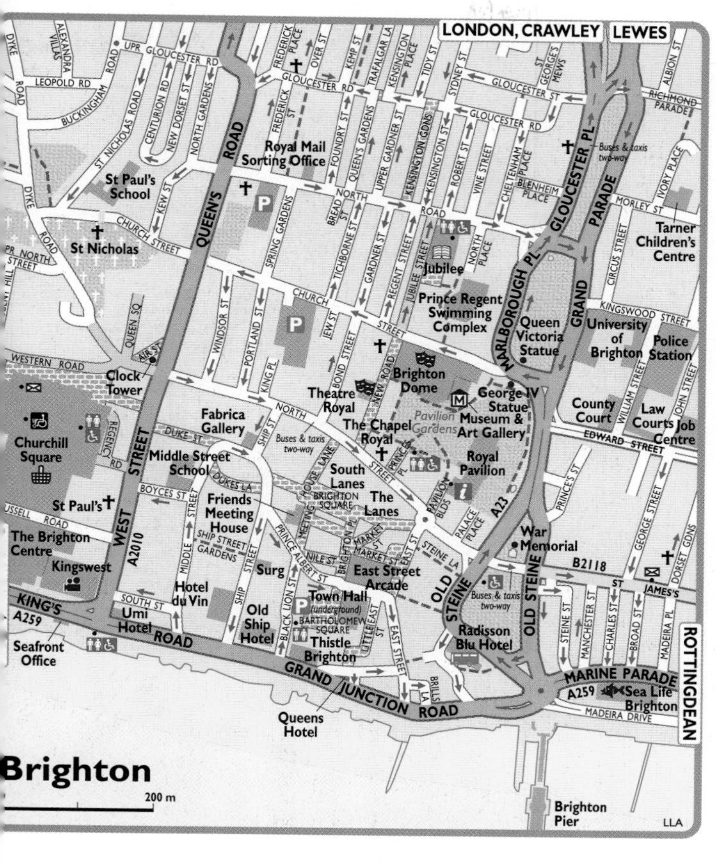
LONDON, CRAWLEY
LEWES
Brighton
200 m
St Paul's School
St Nicholas
Clock Tower
Churchill Square
St Paul's
The Brighton Centre
Kingswest
Seafront Office
Royal Mail Sorting Office
Jubilee
Prince Regent Swimming Complex
Queen Victoria Statue
University of Brighton
Police Station
Tarner Children's Centre
Brighton Dome
Theatre Royal
The Chapel Royal
George IV Statue
Museum & Art Gallery
Royal Pavilion
Pavilion Gardens
County Court
Law Courts
Job Centre
Fabrica Gallery
Middle Street School
Friends Meeting House
South Lanes
The Lanes
War Memorial
East Street Arcade
Hotel du Vin
Surg
Town Hall
Old Ship Hotel
Thistle Brighton
Radisson Blu Hotel
Umi Hotel
Queens Hotel
Sea Life Brighton
Brighton Pier
QUEEN'S ROAD
WEST STREET
KING'S ROAD
GRAND JUNCTION ROAD
MARINE PARADE
OLD STEINE
GRAND PARADE
MARLBOROUGH PL
GLOUCESTER PL
NORTH ST
CHURCH ST
ROTTINGDEAN
A259
A23
A2010
B2118
MADEIRA DRIVE
LLA

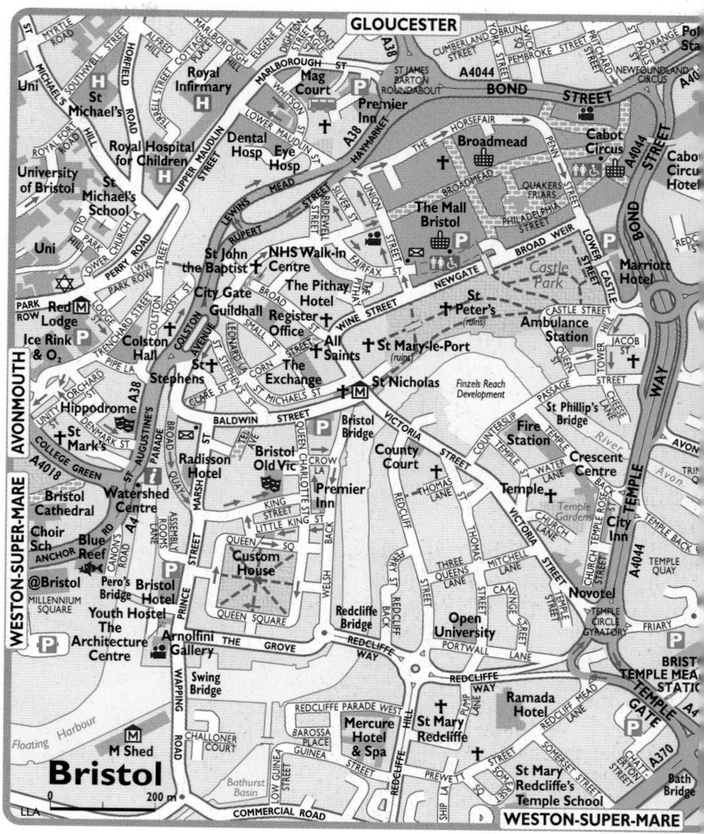
GLOUCESTER
Bristol
200 m
AVONMOUTH
WESTON-SUPER-MARE
Uni
St Michael's
Royal Infirmary
Mag Court
Premier Inn
Royal Hospital for Children
University of Bristol
St Michael's School
Dental Hosp
Eye Hosp
Broadmead
Cabot Circus
The Mall Bristol
Marriott Hotel
Castle Park
St John the Baptist
NHS Walk-In Centre
The Pithay
City Gate
Guildhall
Register Office
St Peter's (ruins)
Ambulance Station
Red Lodge
Ice Rink & O_2
Colston Hall
All Saints
St Mary-le-Port (ruins)
St Stephens
The Exchange
St Nicholas
Finzels Reach Development
Hippodrome
St Mark's
Bristol Bridge
St Phillip's Bridge
Fire Station
Radisson Hotel
Bristol Old Vic
County Court
Crescent Centre
Bristol Cathedral
Watershed Centre
Premier Inn
Temple
Choir Sch
Blue Reef
Custom House
City Inn
@Bristol
Pero's Bridge
Bristol Hotel
Novotel
Youth Hostel
The Architecture Centre
Arnolfini Gallery
Redcliffe Bridge
Open University
Swing Bridge
St Mary Redcliffe
Ramada Hotel
Mercure Hotel & Spa
M Shed
St Mary Redcliffe's Temple School
Floating Harbour
Bathurst Basin
BOND STREET
TEMPLE WAY
REDCLIFFE WAY
COMMERCIAL ROAD
A38
A4044
A4018
A4
A370
LLA

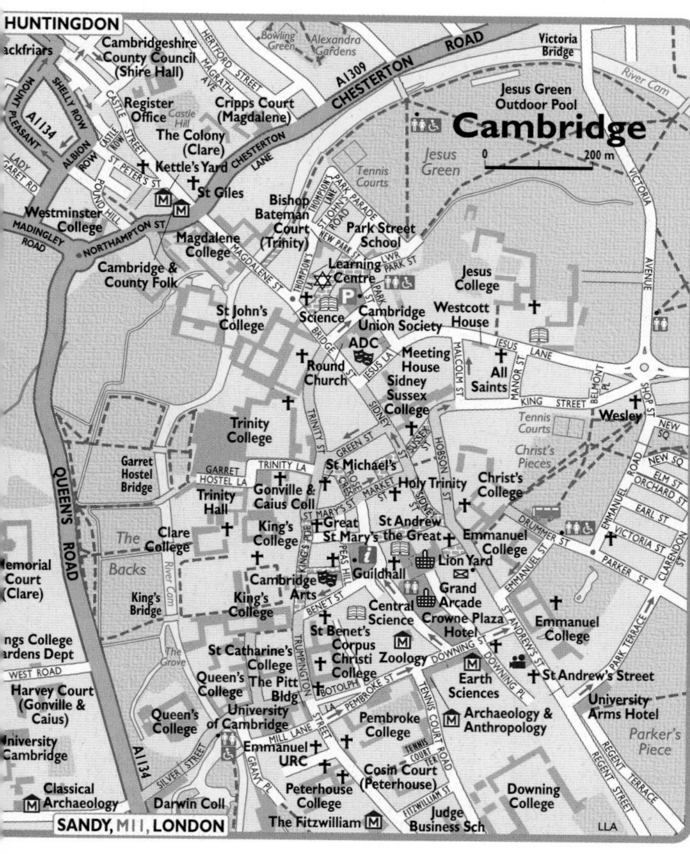
HUNTINGDON
Cambridge
200 m
Cambridgeshire County Council (Shire Hall)
Register Office
Cripps Court (Magdalene)
The Colony (Clare)
Kettle's Yard
St Giles
Westminster College
Magdalene College
Bishop Bateman Court (Trinity)
Park Street School
Cambridge & County Folk
Jesus Green Outdoor Pool
Jesus Green
Jesus College
Learning Centre
St John's College
Science
Cambridge Union Society
Westcott House
ADC
Round Church
Meeting House
Sidney Sussex College
All Saints
Wesley
Trinity College
Garret Hostel Bridge
Trinity Hall
St Michael's
Gonville & Caius Coll
Holy Trinity
Christ's College
Clare College
King's College
Great St Mary's
St Andrew the Great
Emmanuel College
Guildhall
Lion Yard
Grand Arcade
Cambridge Arts
King's Bridge
Central Science
Crowne Plaza Hotel
Emmanuel College
St Benet's
Corpus Christi College
Zoology
St Catharine's College
Queen's College
The Pitt Bldg
University of Cambridge
Earth Sciences
St Andrew's Street
University Arms Hotel
Parker's Piece
Archaeology & Anthropology
Pembroke College
Emmanuel URC
Cosin Court (Peterhouse)
Peterhouse College
Downing College
Darwin Coll
The Fitzwilliam
Judge Business Sch
Classical Archaeology
Harvey Court (Gonville & Caius)
QUEEN'S ROAD
CHESTERTON ROAD
SANDY, M11, LONDON
A1134
A1309
LLA

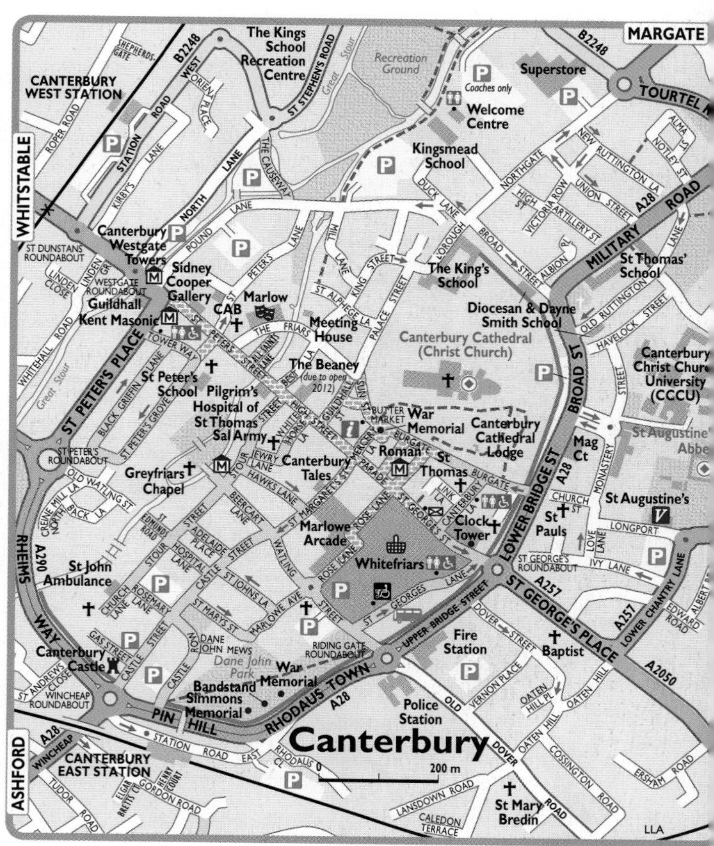
MARGATE
WHITSTABLE
ASHFORD
Canterbury
200 m
CANTERBURY WEST STATION
The Kings School Recreation Centre
Recreation Ground
Superstore
Welcome Centre
Kingsmead School
Canterbury Westgate Towers
Sidney Cooper Gallery
Marlow
CAB
Guildhall
Kent Masonic
The King's School
St Thomas' School
Diocesan & Payne Smith School
Meeting House
Canterbury Cathedral (Christ Church)
The Beaney (due to open 2012)
Canterbury Christ Church University (CCCU)
St Peter's School
Pilgrim's Hospital of St Thomas
Sal Army
War Memorial
Canterbury Cathedral Lodge
Greyfriars Chapel
Canterbury Tales
Roman
St Thomas
Mag Ct
St Augustine's Abbey
St Augustine's
Marlowe Arcade
Clock Tower
St Pauls
Whitefriars
St John Ambulance
Fire Station
Baptist
Canterbury Castle
Dane John Park
War Memorial
Bandstand Simmons Memorial
Police Station
CANTERBURY EAST STATION
St Mary Bredin
ST PETER'S PLACE
RHEIMS WAY
PIN HILL
RHODAUS TOWN
LOWER BRIDGE ST
ST GEORGE'S PLACE
BROAD ST
MILITARY ROAD
A28
A290
A257
A2050
B2248
LLA

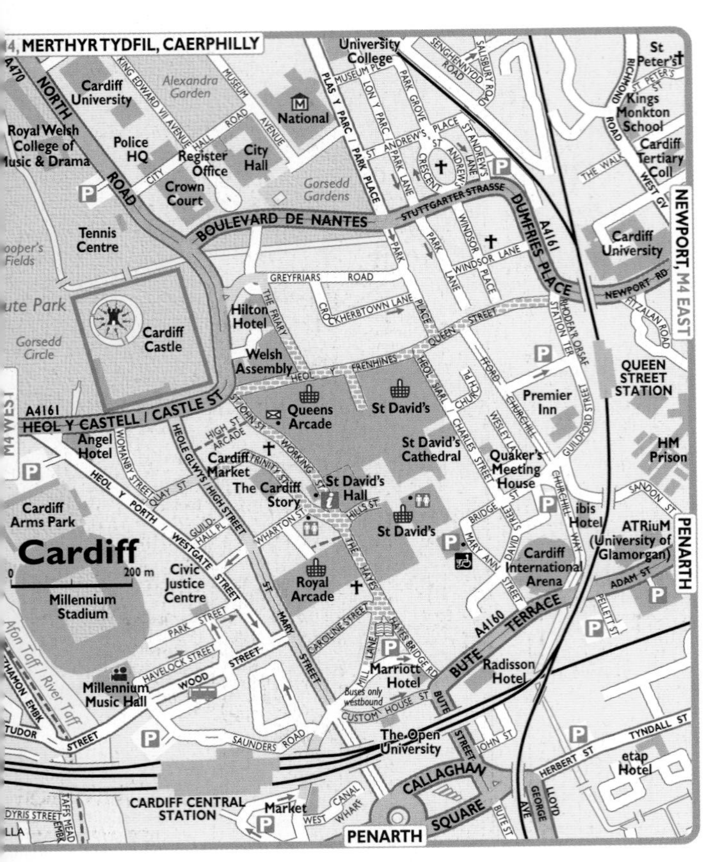
M4, MERTHYR TYDFIL, CAERPHILLY
Cardiff
0 200 m
Cardiff University
Alexandra Garden
National
Royal Welsh College of Music & Drama
Police HQ
Register Office
City Hall
Crown Court
Gorsedd Gardens
Tennis Centre
BOULEVARD DE NANTES
STUTTGARTER STRASSE
DUMFRIES PLACE
Cardiff Castle
Hilton Hotel
Welsh Assembly
Queens Arcade
St David's
St David's Cathedral
Premier Inn
QUEEN STREET STATION
HM Prison
Angel Hotel
Cardiff Market
The Cardiff Story
St David's Hall
Quaker's Meeting House
ibis Hotel
ATRiuM (University of Glamorgan)
Cardiff Arms Park
Cardiff International Arena
Civic Justice Centre
Royal Arcade
Millennium Stadium
Marriott Hotel
Radisson Hotel
Millennium Music Hall
The Open University
etap Hotel
CARDIFF CENTRAL STATION
Market
CALLAGHAN SQUARE
PENARTH
NEWPORT, M4 EAST
M4 WEST
University College
St Peter's
Kings Monkton School
Cardiff Tertiary Coll
Cardiff University
HEOL Y CASTELL / CASTLE ST
BUTE TERRACE
LLA

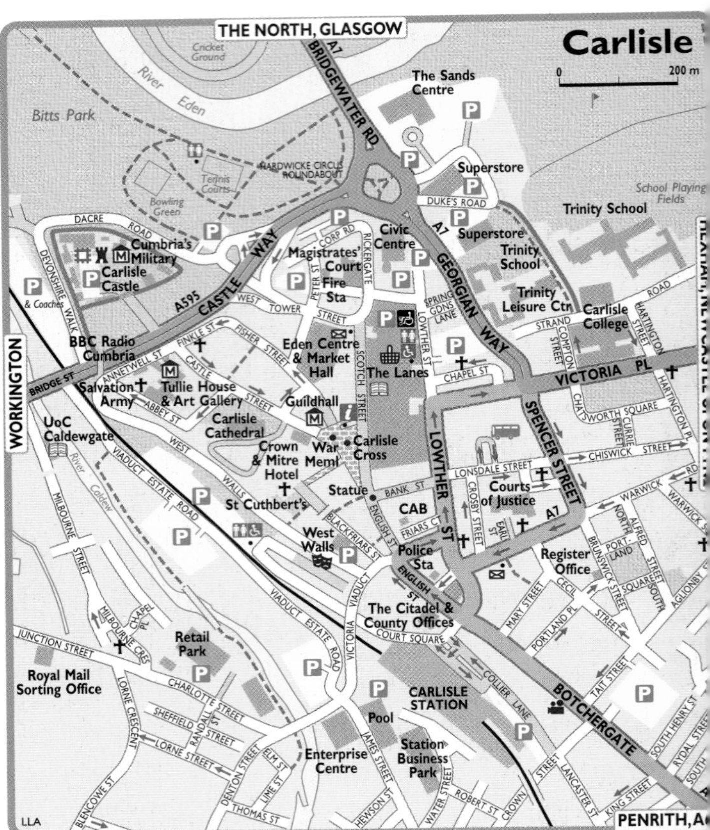
THE NORTH, GLASGOW
Carlisle
0 200 m
The Sands Centre
Bitts Park
River Eden
Superstore
Trinity School
School Playing Fields
Cumbria's Military
Carlisle Castle
Civic Centre
Magistrates' Court
Fire Sta
Superstore
Trinity School
Trinity Leisure Ctr
Carlisle College
BBC Radio Cumbria
Eden Centre & Market Hall
The Lanes
VICTORIA PL
Salvation Army
Tullie House & Art Gallery
Carlisle Cathedral
Guildhall
UoC Caldewgate
Crown & Mitre Hotel
War Meml
Carlisle Cross
St Cuthbert's
Statue
CAB
Courts of Justice
West Walls
Police Sta
Register Office
The Citadel & County Offices
Retail Park
Royal Mail Sorting Office
CARLISLE STATION
Pool
Station Business Park
Enterprise Centre
BOTCHERGATE
WORKINGTON
PENRITH, A6
LLA

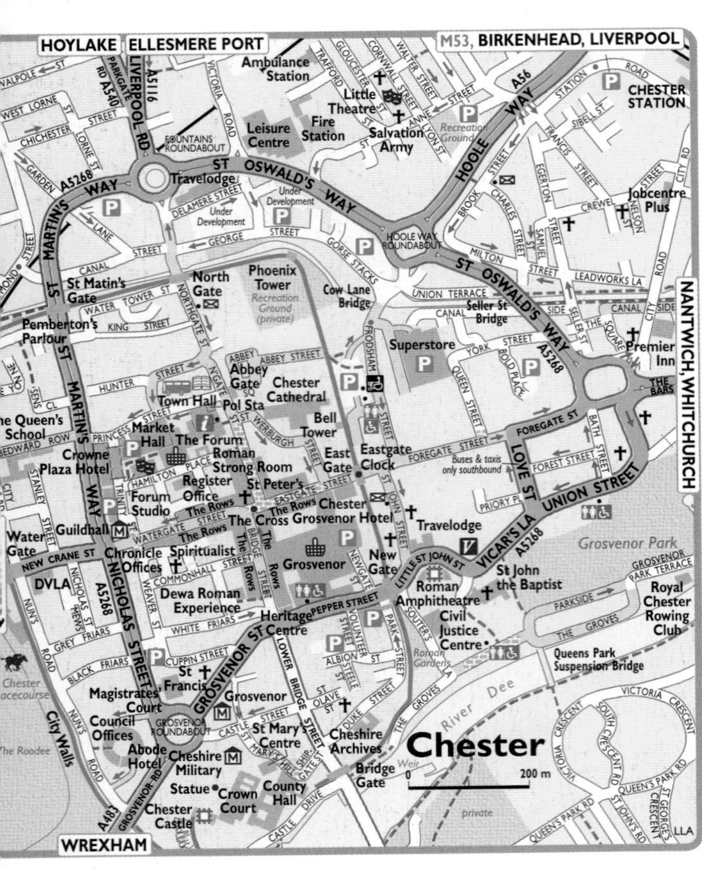
HOYLAKE
ELLESMERE PORT
M53, BIRKENHEAD, LIVERPOOL
Ambulance Station
CHESTER STATION
Little Theatre
Fire Station
Salvation Army
Leisure Centre
FOUNTAINS ROUNDABOUT
Travelodge
ST OSWALD'S WAY
HOOLE WAY
Jobcentre Plus
St Matin's Gate
North Gate
Phoenix Tower
Cow Lane Bridge
Seller St Bridge
Pemberton's Parlour
Superstore
Premier Inn
Abbey Gate
Chester Cathedral
Town Hall
Pol Sta
Bell Tower
The Queen's School
Market Hall
The Forum
Roman Strong Room
Eastgate Clock
Crowne Plaza Hotel
Register Office
St Peter's
Forum Studio
The Rows
Chester Grosvenor Hotel
Travelodge
Water Gate
Guildhall
The Cross
Chronicle Offices
Spiritualist
Grosvenor
New Gate
DVLA
Dewa Roman Experience
Heritage Centre
Roman Amphitheatre
St John the Baptist
Grosvenor Park
Royal Chester Rowing Club
Civil Justice Centre
St Francis
Queens Park Suspension Bridge
Magistrates' Court
Grosvenor
Council Offices
St Mary's Centre
Cheshire Archives
Abode Hotel
Cheshire Military
Chester
0 200 m
Statue
Crown Court
County Hall
Bridge Gate
Chester Castle
River Dee
City Walls
Chester Racecourse
The Roodee
NANTWICH, WHITCHURCH
WREXHAM
LLA

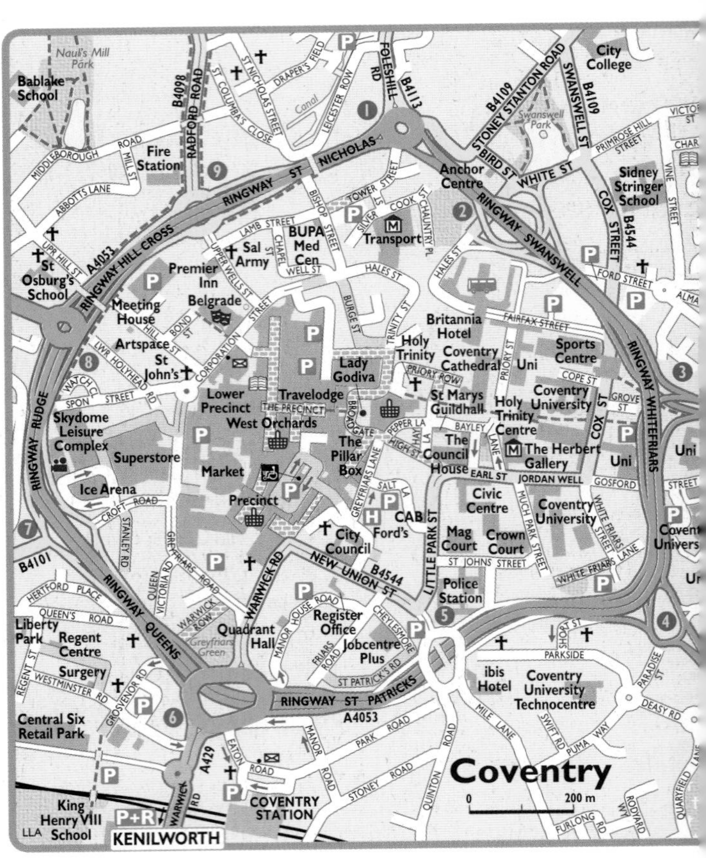
Naul's Mill Park
Bablake School
City College
Fire Station
Anchor Centre
Sidney Stringer School
RINGWAY ST NICHOLAS
Transport
St Osburg's School
Sal Army
BUPA Med Cen
Premier Inn
Belgrade
Meeting House
Artspace
St John's
Britannia Hotel
Sports Centre
Holy Trinity
Coventry Cathedral
Uni
Coventry University
Lady Godiva
Travelodge
Lower Precinct
West Orchards
St Marys Guildhall
Holy Trinity Centre
Skydome Leisure Complex
Superstore
The Pillar Box
The Council House
The Herbert Gallery
Uni
Ice Arena
Market
Precinct
Civic Centre
Coventry University
CAB
Ford's
City Council
Mag Court
Crown Court
Police Station
Register Office
Jobcentre Plus
Quadrant Hall
Liberty Park
Regent Centre
Surgery
Central Six Retail Park
ibis Hotel
Coventry University Technocentre
RINGWAY ST PATRICKS
RINGWAY QUEENS
RINGWAY WHITEFRIARS
RINGWAY SWANSWELL
RINGWAY HILL CROSS
King Henry VIII School
COVENTRY STATION
KENILWORTH
Coventry
0 200 m
LLA

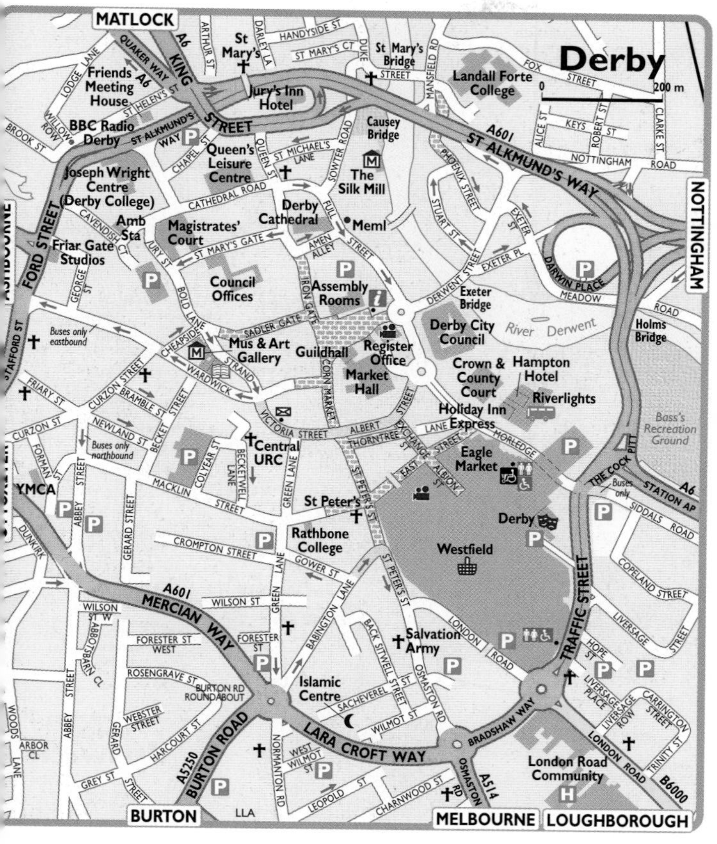
Derby
MATLOCK
NOTTINGHAM
BURTON
MELBOURNE
LOUGHBOROUGH
0
200 m
LLA
Friends Meeting House
BBC Radio Derby
Joseph Wright Centre (Derby College)
Amb Sta
Friar Gate Studios
St Mary's
Jury's Inn Hotel
Queen's Leisure Centre
Magistrates' Court
Council Offices
St Mary's Bridge
Landall Forte College
Causey Bridge
The Silk Mill
Derby Cathedral
Meml
Assembly Rooms
Mus & Art Gallery
Guildhall
Register Office
Market Hall
Exeter Bridge
Derby City Council
River Derwent
Holms Bridge
Crown & County Court
Hampton Hotel
Riverlights
Holiday Inn Express
Eagle Market
Boss's Recreation Ground
Central URC
St Peter's
Rathbone College
Westfield
Derby
YMCA
Salvation Army
Islamic Centre
London Road Community
KING STREET
ST ALKMUND'S WAY
FORD STREET
MERCIAN WAY
LARA CROFT WAY
BURTON ROAD
TRAFFIC STREET
CROMPTON STREET
WILSON ST
A601
A6
A5250
A514
B6000
Buses only eastbound
Buses only northbound

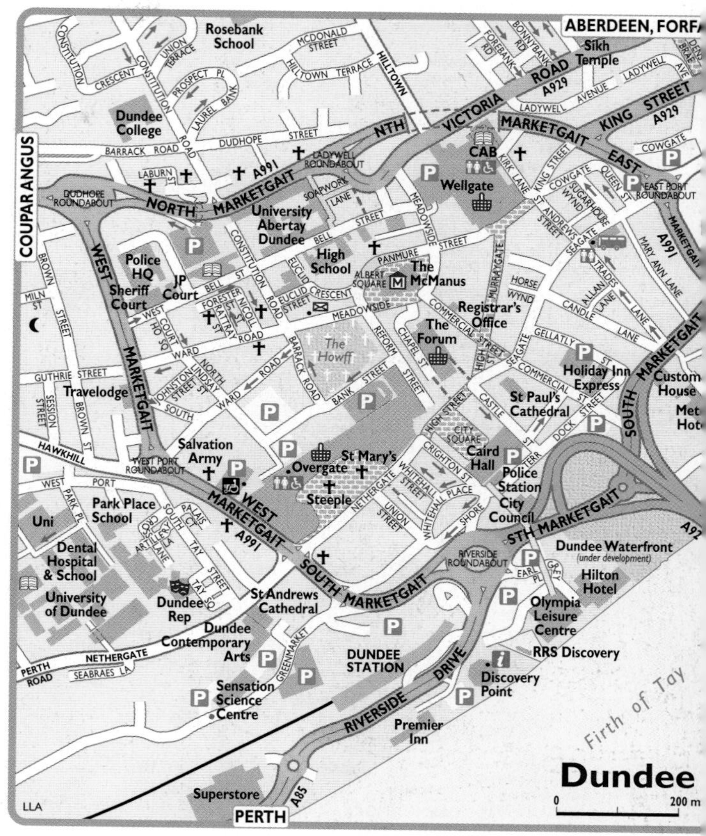
Dundee
ABERDEEN, FORFAR
COUPAR ANGUS
PERTH
0
200 m
LLA
Rosebank School
Sikh Temple
Dundee College
CAB
Wellgate
University Abertay Dundee
High School
The McManus
Police HQ
Sheriff Court
JP Court
Registrar's Office
The Forum
The Howff
Holiday Inn Express
St Paul's Cathedral
Custom House
Travelodge
Salvation Army
Overgate
St Mary's
Steeple
Caird Hall
Police Station
City Council
Uni
Park Place School
Dental Hospital & School
University of Dundee
Dundee Rep
St Andrews Cathedral
Dundee Contemporary Arts
Dundee Waterfront (under development)
Hilton Hotel
Olympia Leisure Centre
RRS Discovery
Discovery Point
DUNDEE STATION
Sensation Science Centre
Premier Inn
Superstore
Firth of Tay
NORTH MARKETGAIT
WEST MARKETGAIT
SOUTH MARKETGAIT
STH MARKETGAIT
VICTORIA ROAD
RIVERSIDE DRIVE
A991
A929
A85
A92

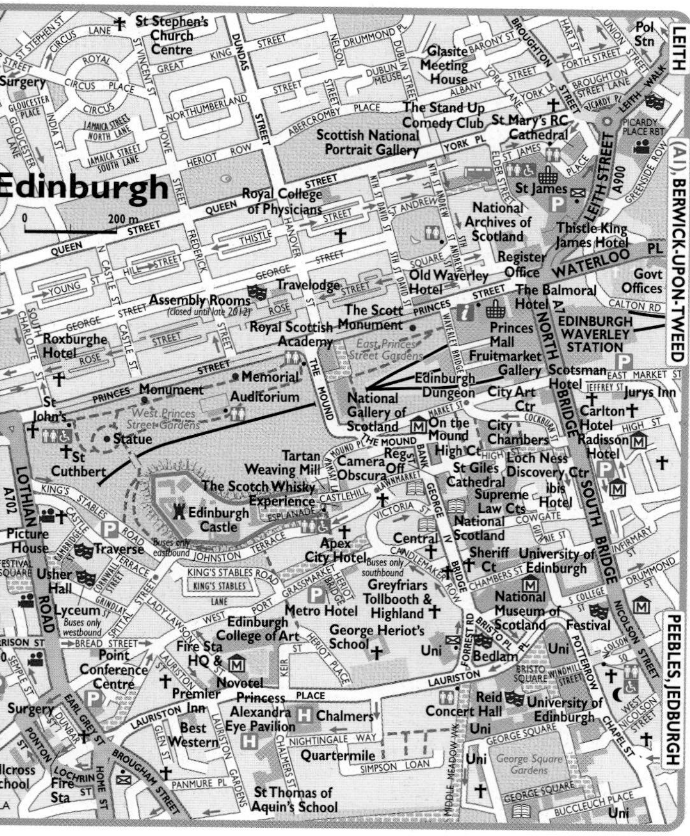
Edinburgh
0
200 m
LEITH
(A1), BERWICK-UPON-TWEED
PEEBLES, JEDBURGH
St Stephen's Church Centre
Surgery
Glasite Meeting House
Pol Stn
The Stand Up Comedy Club
St Mary's RC Cathedral
Scottish National Portrait Gallery
Royal College of Physicians
St James
National Archives of Scotland
Thistle King James Hotel
Register Office
Govt Offices
Travelodge
Old Waverley Hotel
The Balmoral Hotel
Assembly Rooms (closed until Nov 2012)
The Scott Monument
Royal Scottish Academy
Princes Mall
EDINBURGH WAVERLEY STATION
Roxburghe Hotel
Fruitmarket Gallery
Scotsman Hotel
Jurys Inn
East Princes Street Gardens
Monument
Memorial
Auditorium
National Gallery of Scotland
Edinburgh Dungeon
City Art Ctr
Carlton Hotel
Radisson Hotel
St John's
St Cuthbert
Statue
West Princes Street Gardens
Tartan Weaving Mill
Camera Obscura
On the Mound
Reg Off
High Ct
City Chambers
St Giles Cathedral
Loch Ness Discovery Ctr
The Scotch Whisky Experience
Edinburgh Castle
Supreme Law Cts
ibis Hotel
National Library of Scotland
Picture House
Traverse
Usher Hall
Apex City Hotel
Central Library
Sheriff Ct
University of Edinburgh
Lyceum
Greyfriars Tolbooth & Highland
National Museum of Scotland
Festival
Metro Hotel
Edinburgh College of Art
George Heriot's School
Fire Sta HQ
Uni
Bedlam
Point Conference Centre
Novotel
Premier Inn
Princess Alexandra Eye Pavilion
Chalmers
Reid Concert Hall
University of Edinburgh
Best Western
Quartermile
Surgery
Fire Sta
St Thomas of Aquin's School
George Square Gardens
PRINCES STREET
QUEEN STREET
GEORGE STREET
LEITH STREET
NORTH BRIDGE
SOUTH BRIDGE
WATERLOO PL
LOTHIAN ROAD
LAURISTON PLACE
A900
A702
Buses only eastbound
Buses only southbound
Buses only westbound

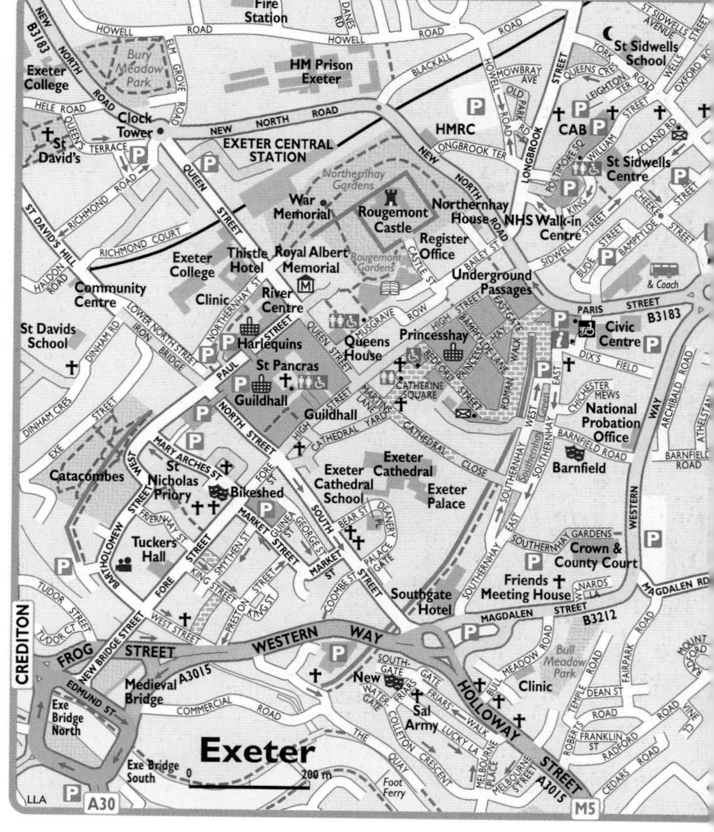
Exeter
0
200 m
CREDITON
A30
M5
LLA
Fire Station
Bury Meadow Park
HM Prison Exeter
St Sidwells School
Exeter College
Clock Tower
St David's
EXETER CENTRAL STATION
HMRC
CAB
St Sidwells Centre
Northernhay Gardens
War Memorial
Rougemont Castle
Northernhay House
NHS Walk-in Centre
Register Office
Rougemont Gardens
Exeter College
Thistle Hotel
Royal Albert Memorial Museum
Underground Passages
Community Centre
Clinic
River Centre
Civic Centre
St Davids School
Harlequins
Queens House
Princesshay
St Pancras
Guildhall
National Probation Office
Barnfield
Catacombes
St Nicholas Priory
Bikeshed
Exeter Cathedral
Exeter Cathedral School
Exeter Palace
Tuckers Hall
Crown & County Court
Friends Meeting House
Southgate Hotel
Bull Meadow Park
Medieval Bridge
New
Sal Army
Clinic
Exe Bridge North
Exe Bridge South
Foot Ferry
NEW NORTH ROAD
WESTERN WAY
FROG STREET
HOLLOWAY STREET
MAGDALEN ROAD
B3183
B3212
A3015

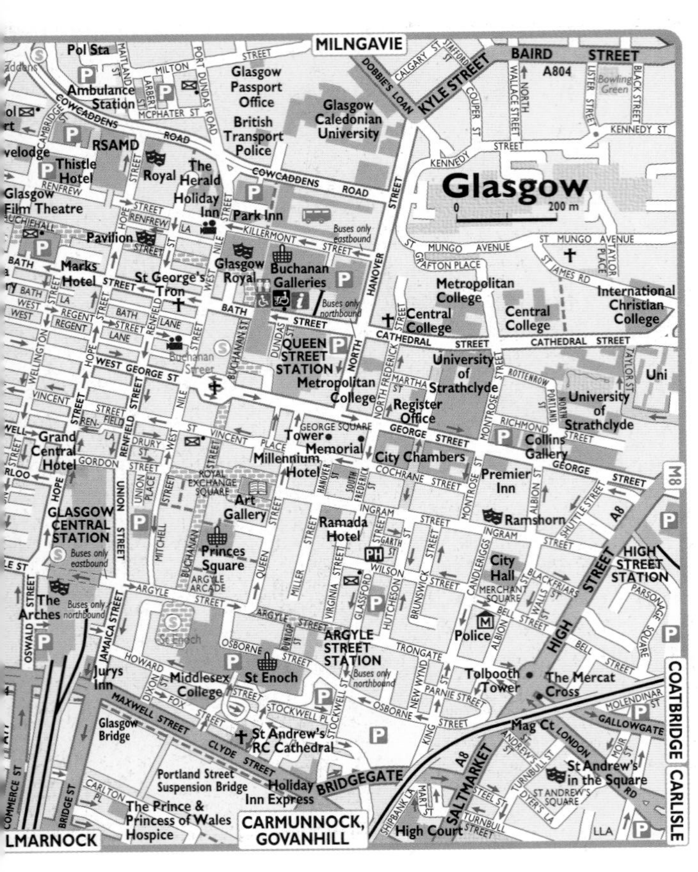

Glasgow
200 m
MILNGAVIE
BAIRD STREET
A804
KYLE STREET
Glasgow Passport Office
British Transport Police
Glasgow Caledonian University
COWCADDENS ROAD
Pol Sta
Ambulance Station
RSAMD
Thistle Hotel
Royal
The Herald
Holiday Inn
Park Inn
Glasgow Film Theatre
Pavilion
Marks Hotel
St George's Tron
Glasgow Royal
Buchanan Galleries
Metropolitan College
Central College
International Christian College
CATHEDRAL STREET
QUEEN STREET STATION
University of Strathclyde
Uni
Metropolitan College
Register Office
WEST GEORGE ST
Tower
Memorial
Millennium Hotel
City Chambers
GEORGE SQUARE
Collins Gallery
University of Strathclyde
Grand Central Hotel
Art Gallery
Premier Inn
GLASGOW CENTRAL STATION
Ramada Hotel
Ramshorn
HIGH STREET STATION
Princes Square
City Hall
M8
A8
The Arches
ARGYLE STREET STATION
Police
St Enoch
Middlesex College
Jurys Inn
Tolbooth Tower
The Mercat Cross
Glasgow Bridge
St Andrew's RC Cathedral
Mag Ct
St Andrew's in the Square
Portland Street Suspension Bridge
Holiday Inn Express
BRIDGEGATE
The Prince & Princess of Wales Hospice
CARMUNNOCK, GOVANHILL
SALTMARKET
High Court
COATBRIDGE
CARLISLE
LMARNOCK
LLA

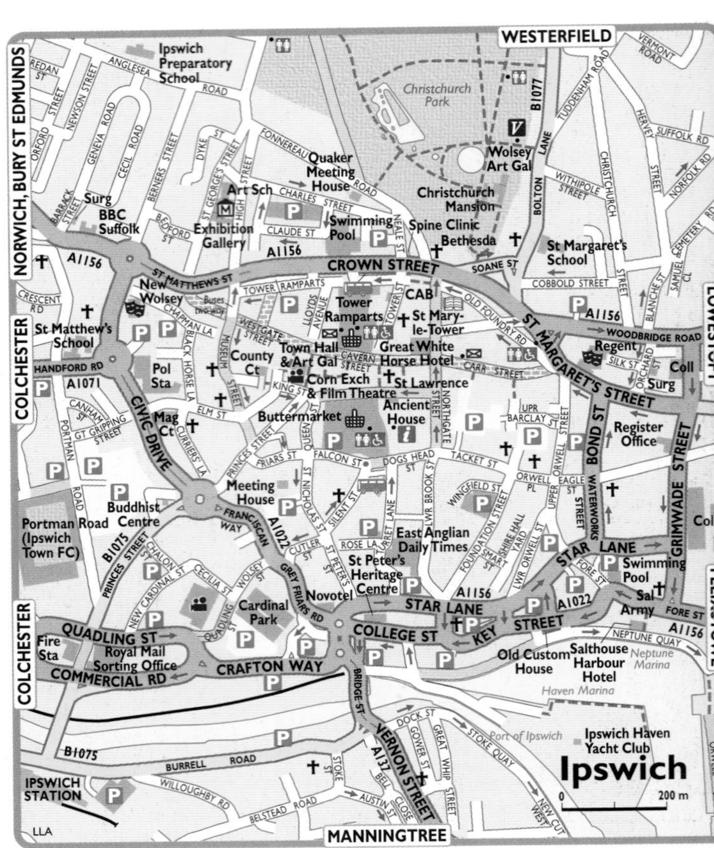

Ipswich
200 m
WESTERFIELD
NORWICH, BURY ST EDMUNDS
Ipswich Preparatory School
Christchurch Park
Wolsey Art Gal
Quaker Meeting House
Christchurch Mansion
Surg
BBC Suffolk
Art Sch
Exhibition Gallery
Swimming Pool
Spine Clinic
Bethesda
St Margaret's School
A1156
CROWN STREET
CAB
New Wolsey
Tower Ramparts
St Mary-le-Tower
St Matthew's School
Town Hall & Art Gal
Great White Horse Hotel
Regent
Coll
COLCHESTER
Pol Sta
County Ct
Corn Exch & Film Theatre
St Lawrence
Surg
ST MARGARET'S STREET
Mag Ct
Ancient House
Buttermarket
Register Office
CIVIC DRIVE
Meeting House
Buddhist Centre
Portman Road (Ipswich Town FC)
East Anglian Daily Times
St Peter's Heritage Centre
Novotel
Cardinal Park
STAR LANE
Swimming Pool
Sal Army
GRIMWADE STREET
QUADLING ST
Royal Mail Sorting Office
COLLEGE ST
KEY STREET
Fire Sta
COMMERCIAL RD
CRAFTON WAY
Old Custom House
Salthouse Harbour Hotel
Neptune Marina
Haven Marina
Port of Ipswich
Ipswich Haven Yacht Club
IPSWICH STATION
VERNON STREET
MANNINGTREE
LLA

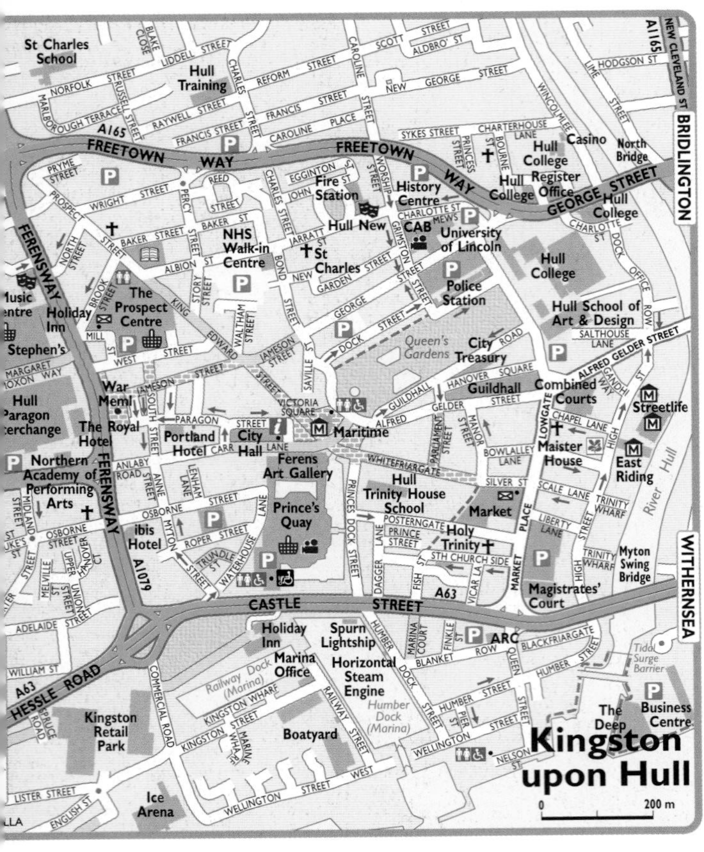

Kingston upon Hull
200 m
St Charles School
Hull Training
FREETOWN WAY
Casino
North Bridge
Hull College
Register Office
BRIDLINGTON
Fire Station
History Centre
Hull College
Hull New
CAB
University of Lincoln
Hull College
NHS Walk-in Centre
St Charles
FERENSWAY
The Prospect Centre
Police Station
Hull School of Art & Design
Holiday Inn
Queen's Gardens
City Treasury
Guildhall
Combined Courts
Streetlife
War Meml
The Royal Hotel
Portland Hotel
City Hall
Maritime
Maister House
East Riding
Hull Paragon Interchange
Northern Academy of Performing Arts
Ferens Art Gallery
Hull Trinity House School
Market
Prince's Quay
Holy Trinity
ibis Hotel
Mytton Swing Bridge
Magistrates' Court
CASTLE STREET
A63
WITHERNSEA
HESSLE ROAD
Holiday Inn
Spurn Lightship
Marina Office
Horizontal Steam Engine
ARC
Railway Dock (Marina)
Humber Dock (Marina)
Tidal Surge Barrier
The Deep
Business Centre
Kingston Retail Park
Boatyard
Ice Arena
LLA

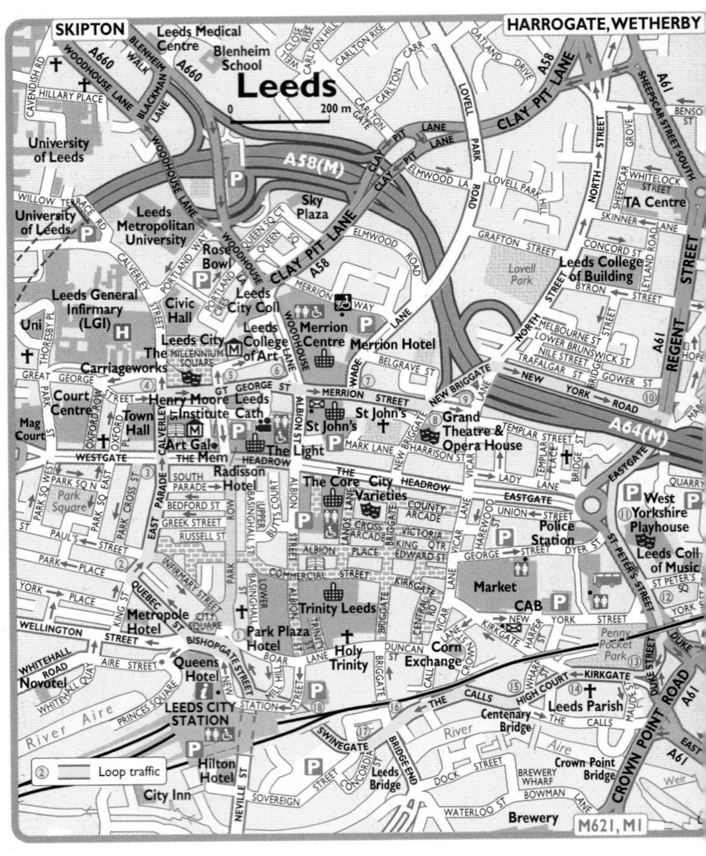

Leeds
200 m
SKIPTON
Leeds Medical Centre
Blenheim School
HARROGATE, WETHERBY
A660
A58
CLAY PIT LANE
A61
University of Leeds
A58(M)
Sky Plaza
TA Centre
University of Leeds
Leeds Metropolitan University
Rose Bowl
Leeds City Coll
Leeds College of Building
Leeds General Infirmary (LGI)
Civic Hall
Merrion Centre
Merrion Hotel
Uni
Leeds City College of Art
The Carriageworks
Court Centre
Henry Moore Institute
Leeds Cath
St John's
Grand Theatre & Opera House
Town Hall
Art Gal
The Light
A64(M)
Mag Court
Radisson Hotel
The Core
City Varieties
West Yorkshire Playhouse
Park Square
Police Station
Leeds Coll of Music
Market
CAB
Metropole Hotel
Trinity Leeds
Park Plaza Hotel
Holy Trinity
Corn Exchange
Novotel
Queens Hotel
LEEDS CITY STATION
Leeds Parish
Centenary Bridge
River Aire
Hilton Hotel
Leeds Bridge
Crown Point Bridge
CROWN POINT ROAD
City Inn
Brewery
Loop traffic
M621, M1

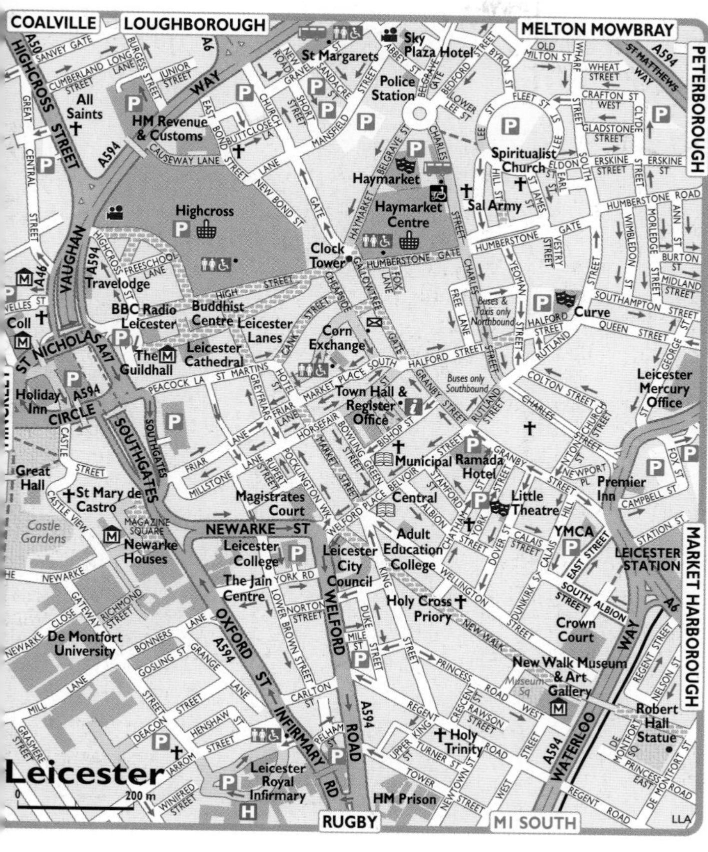
COALVILLE
LOUGHBOROUGH
MELTON MOWBRAY
PETERBOROUGH
MARKET HARBOROUGH
RUGBY
M1 SOUTH
Leicester
200 m
St Margarets
Sky Plaza Hotel
Police Station
All Saints
HM Revenue & Customs
Haymarket
Haymarket Centre
Spiritualist Church
Sal Army
Highcross
Clock Tower
Travelodge
BBC Radio Leicester
Buddhist Centre
Leicester Lanes
Curve
Corn Exchange
The Guildhall
Leicester Cathedral
Holiday Inn
Town Hall & Register Office
Leicester Mercury Office
Municipal
Ramada Hotel
Great Hall
St Mary de Castro
Magistrates Court
Central
Little Theatre
Premier Inn
Castle Gardens
Newarke Houses
Leicester College
Leicester City Council
Adult Education College
YMCA
LEICESTER STATION
The Jain Centre
Holy Cross Priory
Crown Court
De Montfort University
New Walk Museum & Art Gallery
Robert Hall Statue
Holy Trinity
Leicester Royal Infirmary
HM Prison
LLA

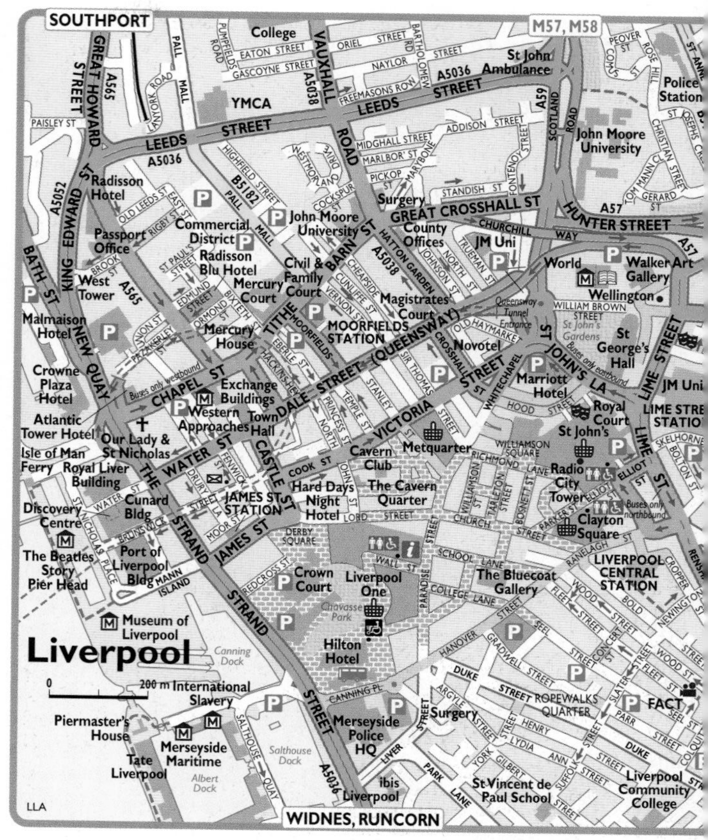
SOUTHPORT
M57, M58
WIDNES, RUNCORN
Liverpool
200 m
College
YMCA
St John Ambulance
Police Station
John Moore University
Radisson Hotel
Passport Office
Commercial District
Radisson Blu Hotel
John Moore University
Civil & Family Court
Mercury Court
Surgery
Great Crosshall St
County Offices
JM Uni
World Museum
Walker Art Gallery
Wellington
West Tower
Malmaison Hotel
Mercury House
Moorfields Station
Magistrates Court
Novotel
St George's Hall
Crowne Plaza Hotel
Exchange Buildings
Western Approaches
Marriott Hotel
Royal Court
JM Uni
Lime Street Station
Atlantic Tower Hotel
Our Lady & St Nicholas
Town Hall
St John's
Isle of Man Ferry
Royal Liver Building
Cavern Club
The Cavern Quarter
Metquarter
Radio City Tower
Discovery Centre
Cunard Bldg
James St Station
Hard Days Night Hotel
Clayton Square
The Beatles Story
Pier Head
Port of Liverpool Bldg
Crown Court
Liverpool One
The Bluecoat Gallery
Liverpool Central Station
Museum of Liverpool
Hilton Hotel
International Slavery
Piermaster's House
Merseyside Maritime
Tate Liverpool
Merseyside Police HQ
Surgery
Ropewalks Quarter
FACT
ibis Liverpool
St Vincent de Paul School
Liverpool Community College
LLA

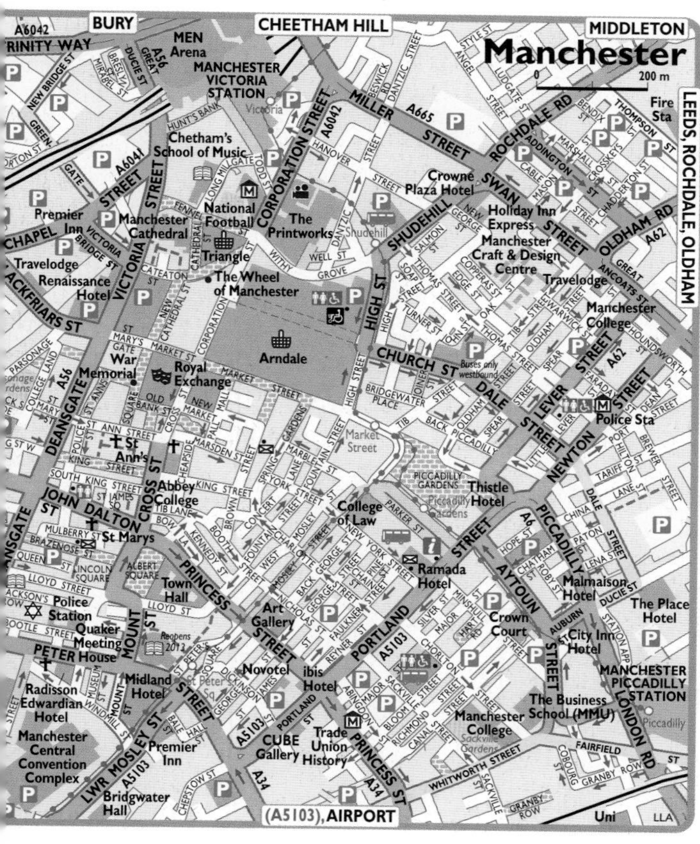
BURY
CHEETHAM HILL
MIDDLETON
LEEDS, ROCHDALE, OLDHAM
(A5103), AIRPORT
Manchester
200 m
MEN Arena
Manchester Victoria Station
Chetham's School of Music
Fire Sta
Crowne Plaza Hotel
Premier Inn
Manchester Cathedral
National Football
The Printworks
Holiday Inn Express
Manchester Craft & Design Centre
Travelodge
Renaissance Hotel
Triangle
The Wheel of Manchester
Travelodge
Manchester College
Arndale
War Memorial
Royal Exchange
Police Sta
St Ann's
Market Street
Thistle Hotel
Abbey College
College of Law
St Marys
Ramada Hotel
Town Hall
Police Station
Quaker Meeting House
Art Gallery
Malmaison Hotel
The Place Hotel
Crown Court
City Inn Hotel
Manchester Piccadilly Station
Radisson Edwardian Hotel
Midland Hotel
Novotel
ibis Hotel
The Business School (MMU)
Manchester College
Manchester Central Convention Complex
Premier Inn
CUBE Gallery
Trade Union History
Bridgwater Hall
Uni
LLA

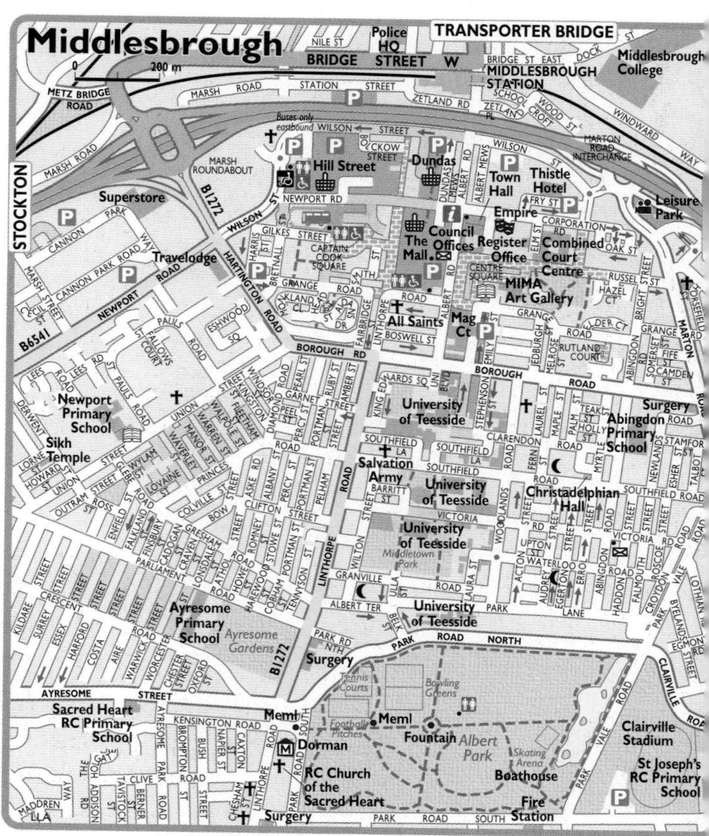
Middlesbrough
200 m
Police HQ
TRANSPORTER BRIDGE
Middlesbrough College
Middlesbrough Station
STOCKTON
Hill Street
Dundas
Town Hall
Thistle Hotel
Leisure Park
Superstore
Empire
Council Offices
Register Office
Combined Court Centre
The Mall
Travelodge
MIMA Art Gallery
All Saints
Mag Ct
Newport Primary School
University of Teesside
Surgery
Abingdon Primary School
Sikh Temple
Salvation Army
University of Teesside
Christadelphian Hall
University of Teesside
Ayresome Primary School
Ayresome Gardens
University of Teesside
Surgery
Sacred Heart RC Primary School
Meml
Dorman
Meml
Fountain
Albert Park
Boathouse
Clairville Stadium
St Joseph's RC Primary School
RC Church of the Sacred Heart
Surgery
Fire Station
LLA

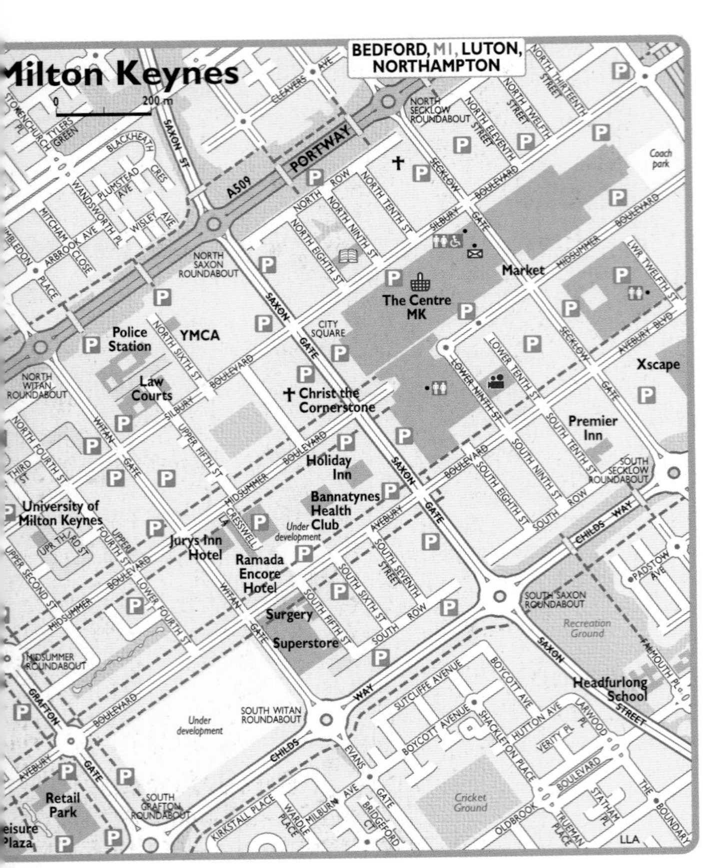
Milton Keynes
200 m
BEDFORD, M1, LUTON, NORTHAMPTON
PORTWAY
A509
NORTH SECKLOW ROUNDABOUT
NORTH SAXON ROUNDABOUT
NORTH WITAN ROUNDABOUT
CITY SQUARE
SILBURY BOULEVARD
MIDSUMMER BOULEVARD
AVEBURY BOULEVARD
SAXON GATE
SECKLOW GATE
WITAN GATE
Coach park
Market
The Centre MK
Police Station
YMCA
Law Courts
Christ the Cornerstone
Xscape
Premier Inn
Holiday Inn
Bannatynes Health Club
Under development
University of Milton Keynes
Jurys Inn Hotel
Ramada Encore Hotel
Surgery
Superstore
SOUTH SECKLOW ROUNDABOUT
SOUTH SAXON ROUNDABOUT
Recreation Ground
CHILDS WAY
Headfurlong School
MIDSUMMER ROUNDABOUT
SOUTH WITAN ROUNDABOUT
Under development
Cricket Ground
Retail Park
SOUTH GRAFTON ROUNDABOUT
Leisure Plaza
LLA

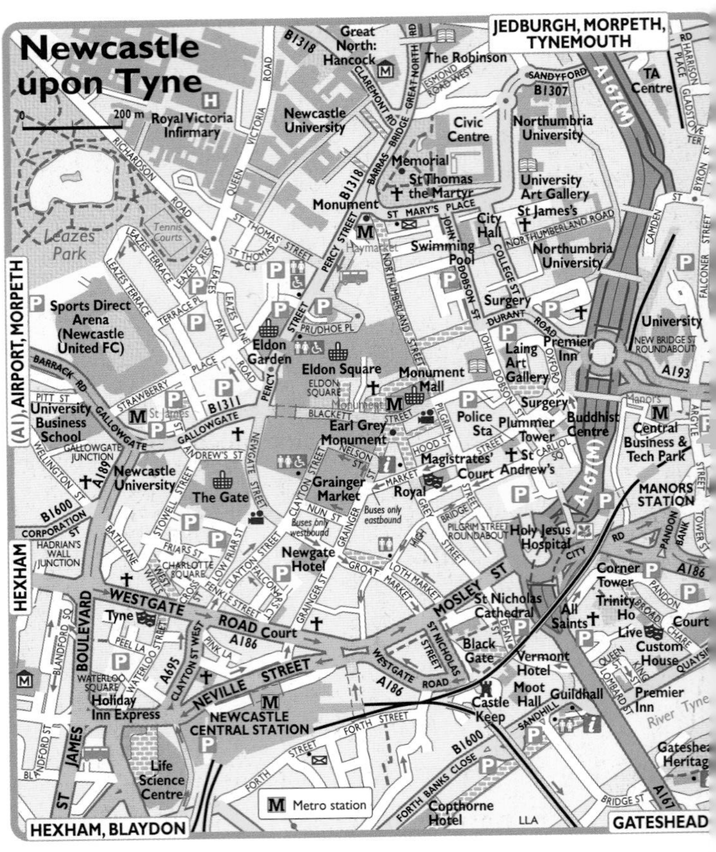
Newcastle upon Tyne
200 m
JEDBURGH, MORPETH, TYNEMOUTH
Great North: Hancock
The Robinson
TA Centre
Royal Victoria Infirmary
Newcastle University
Civic Centre
Northumbria University
Memorial
St Thomas the Martyr
University Art Gallery
St James's
Monument
City Hall
Swimming Pool
Northumbria University
Leazes Park
Tennis Courts
Sports Direct Arena (Newcastle United FC)
Surgery
University
NEW BRIDGE ST ROUNDABOUT
A193
Eldon Garden
Eldon Square
Laing Art Gallery
Premier Inn
(A1), AIRPORT, MORPETH
University Business School
St James
GALLOWGATE
Monument Mall
Earl Grey Monument
Police Sta
Plummer Tower
Buddhist Centre
Central Business & Tech Park
Newcastle University
The Gate
Grainger Market
Magistrates' Court
Royal
St Andrew's
MANORS STATION
Buses only eastbound
Buses only westbound
Newgate Hotel
Holy Jesus Hospital
HEXHAM
WESTGATE ROAD
Tyne
Court
A186
MOSLEY ST
St Nicholas Cathedral
All Saints
Corner Tower
Trinity Ho
Court
Live
Custom House
Black Gate
Vermont Hotel
Moot Hall
Guildhall
Castle Keep
Premier Inn
River Tyne
NEVILLE STREET
Holiday Inn Express
NEWCASTLE CENTRAL STATION
FORTH STREET
Gateshead Heritage
Life Science Centre
ST JAMES BOULEVARD
Metro station
Copthorne Hotel
HEXHAM, BLAYDON
GATESHEAD
LLA

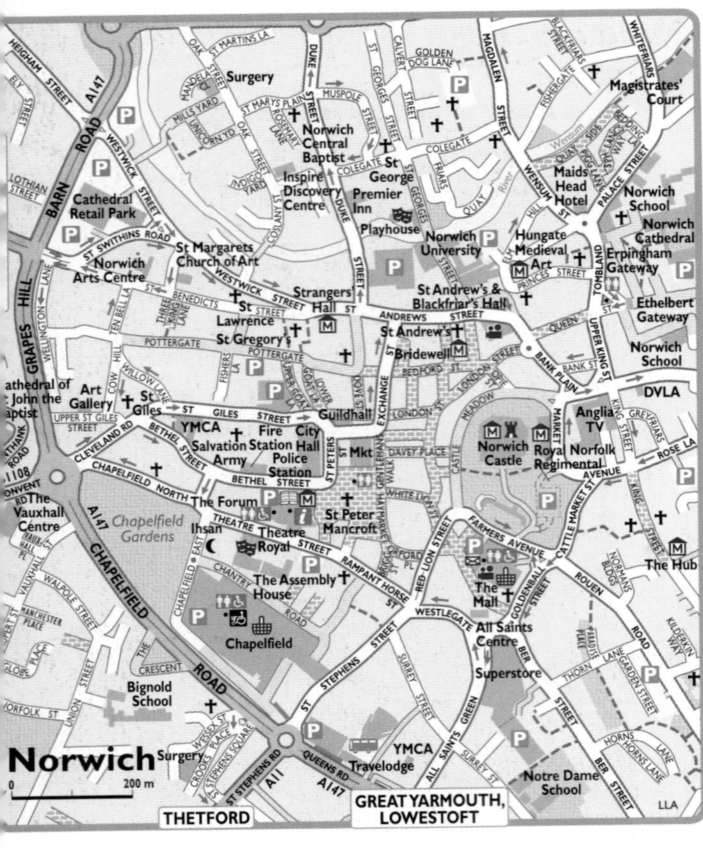
Surgery
Magistrates' Court
Norwich Central Baptist
St George
Inspire Discovery Centre
Premier Inn
Maids Head Hotel
Norwich School
Cathedral Retail Park
Norwich Cathedral
Playhouse
Norwich University
Hungate Medieval Art
Erpingham Gateway
St Margarets Church of Art
Norwich Arts Centre
Strangers Hall
St Andrew's & Blackfriar's Hall
Ethelbert Gateway
St Lawrence
St Andrew's
St Gregory's
Bridewell
Norwich School
Cathedral of St John the Baptist
Art Gallery
St Giles
Guildhall
DVLA
Anglia TV
YMCA
Salvation Army
Fire Station
City Hall
Police Station
Mkt
Norwich Castle
Royal Regimental
Norfolk
The Vauxhall Centre
Chapelfield Gardens
The Forum
St Peter Mancroft
Ihsan
Theatre Royal
The Assembly House
The Hub
CHAPELFIELD ROAD
Chapelfield
The Mall
All Saints Centre
Superstore
Bignold School
Norwich
Surgery
YMCA
Travelodge
Notre Dame School
200 m
THETFORD
GREAT YARMOUTH, LOWESTOFT
A147
A11
GRAPES HILL
BARN ROAD
LLA

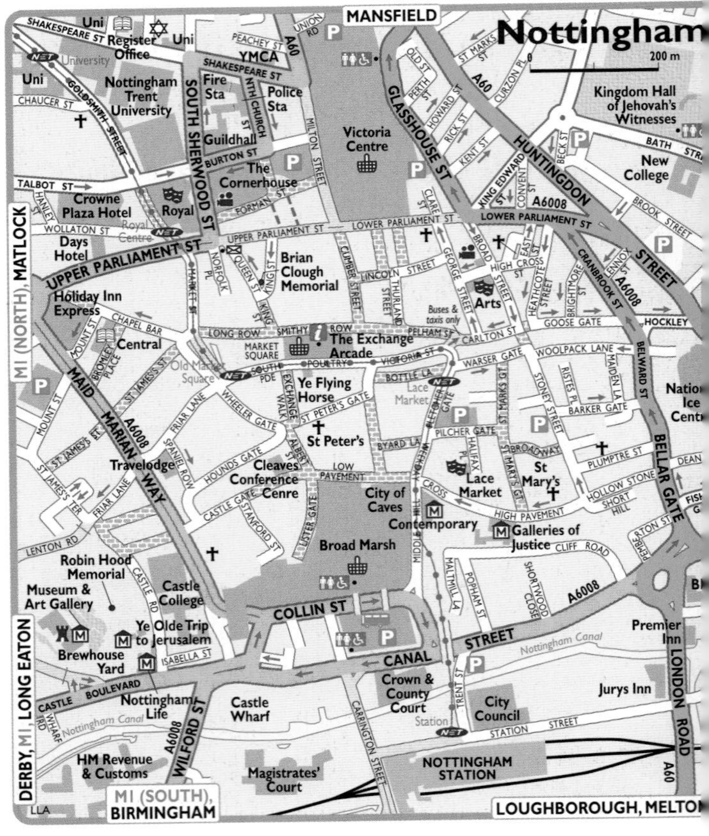
MANSFIELD
Nottingham
200 m
Uni
Register Office
Uni
YMCA
Uni
Nottingham Trent University
Fire Sta
Police Sta
Victoria Centre
Kingdom Hall of Jehovah's Witnesses
New College
Guildhall
The Cornerhouse
Crowne Plaza Hotel
Royal
Royal Centre
Days Hotel
UPPER PARLIAMENT ST
Brian Clough Memorial
Holiday Inn Express
Arts
Central
The Exchange Arcade
Old Market Square
Ye Flying Horse
Lace Market
St Peter's
National Ice Centre
Travelodge
Cleaves Conference Centre
City of Caves
Lace Market
St Mary's
Contemporary
Galleries of Justice
Broad Marsh
Robin Hood Memorial
Museum & Art Gallery
Castle College
COLLIN ST
Ye Olde Trip to Jerusalem
Brewhouse Yard
CANAL STREET
Crown & County Court
Premier Inn
Nottingham Life
Castle Wharf
City Council
Jurys Inn
HM Revenue & Customs
Magistrates' Court
NOTTINGHAM STATION
MAID MARIAN WAY
GLASSHOUSE ST
HUNTINGDON STREET
LONDON ROAD
M1 (NORTH), MATLOCK
DERBY, M1, LONG EATON
M1 (SOUTH), BIRMINGHAM
LOUGHBOROUGH, MELTO
LLA

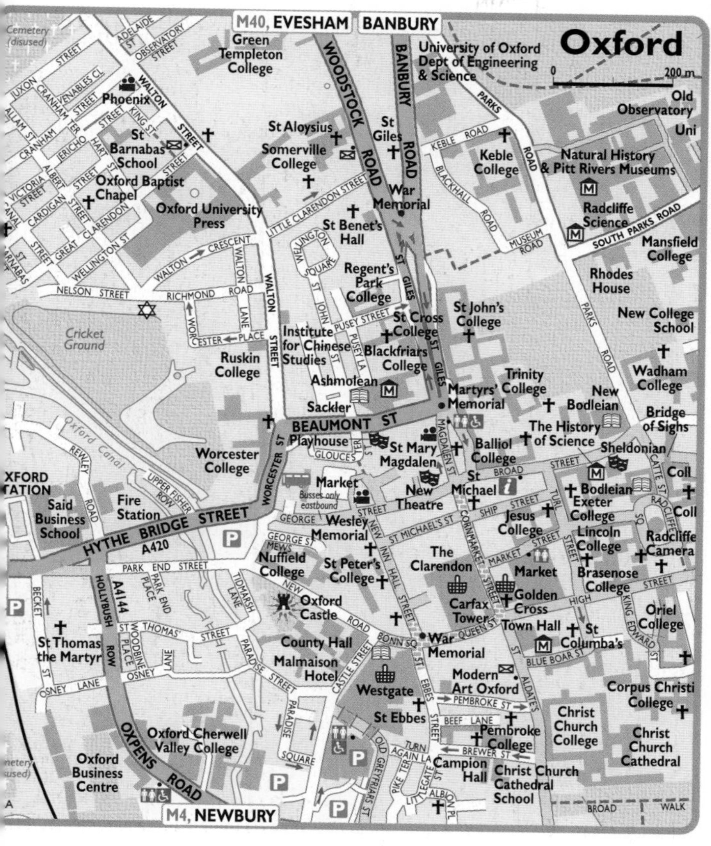
Oxford
M40, EVESHAM
BANBURY
M4, NEWBURY
Green Templeton College
University of Oxford Dept of Engineering & Science
Old Observatory
Phoenix
St Barnabas School
Oxford Baptist Chapel
Oxford University Press
St Aloysius
Somerville College
St Giles
Keble College
Natural History & Pitt Rivers Museums
Radcliffe Science
Mansfield College
War Memorial
St Benet's Hall
Regent's Park College
St John's College
Rhodes House
New College School
Cricket Ground
Ruskin College
Institute for Chinese Studies
St Cross College
Blackfriars College
Ashmolean
Sackler
Martyrs' Memorial
Trinity College
Wadham College
New Bodleian
Bridge of Sighs
BEAUMONT ST
Playhouse
Worcester College
St Mary Magdalen
Balliol College
The History of Science
Sheldonian
Said Business School
Fire Station
Market
Wesley Memorial
New Theatre
St Michael
Bodleian
Exeter College
Jesus College
Lincoln College
Radcliffe Camera
HYTHE BRIDGE STREET
A420
Nuffield College
St Peter's College
The Clarendon
Market
Brasenose College
Oxford Castle
Carfax Tower
Golden Cross
Town Hall
Oriel College
St Columba's
St Thomas the Martyr
County Hall
Malmaison Hotel
War Memorial
Modern Art Oxford
Corpus Christi College
Westgate
St Ebbes
Christ Church College
Pembroke College
Christ Church Cathedral
Oxford Cherwell Valley College
Oxford Business Centre
Campion Hall
Christ Church Cathedral School
OXPENS ROAD
Oxford Canal

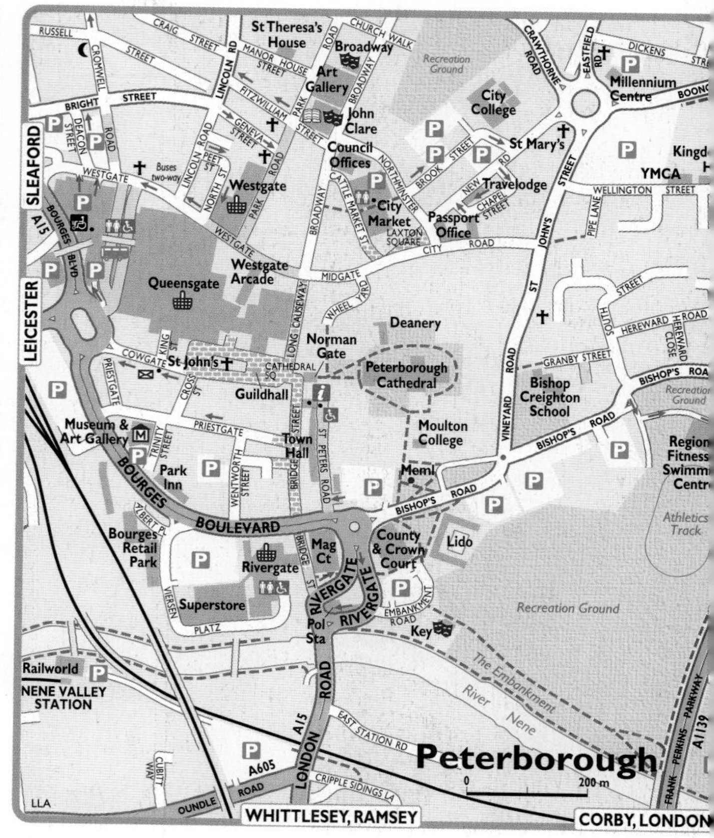
Peterborough
St Theresa's House
Broadway
Art Gallery
John Clare
City College
Millennium Centre
St Mary's
YMCA
Council Offices
Westgate
City Market
Passport Office
Travelodge
Westgate Arcade
Queensgate
SLEAFORD
A15
LEICESTER
Deanery
Norman Gate
Peterborough Cathedral
St John's
Guildhall
Bishop Creighton School
Museum & Art Gallery
Town Hall
Moulton College
Park Inn
BOURGES BOULEVARD
Bourges Retail Park
Rivergate
Mag Ct
County & Crown Court
Lido
Superstore
Pol Sta
Key
Recreation Ground
Railworld
NENE VALLEY STATION
River Nene
The Embankment
WHITTLESEY, RAMSEY
CORBY, LONDON
200 m

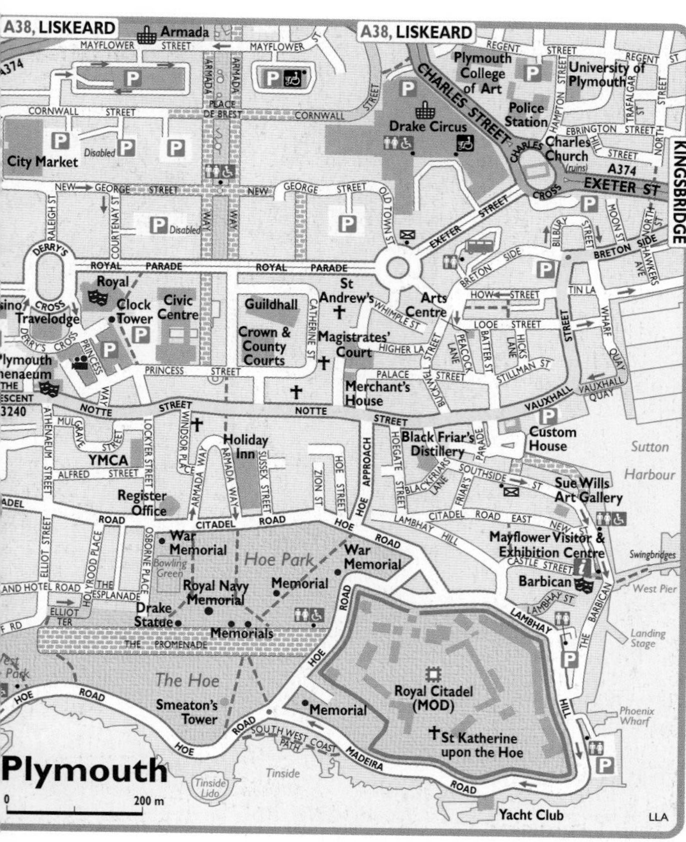
Plymouth
A38, LISKEARD
Armada
Plymouth College of Art
University of Plymouth
Police Station
Drake Circus
CHARLES STREET
Charles Church
KINGSBRIDGE
EXETER ST
City Market
Royal
Clock Tower
Civic Centre
Guildhall
St Andrew's
Arts Centre
Travelodge
Crown & County Courts
Magistrates' Court
Merchant's House
Holiday Inn
YMCA
Black Friar's Distillery
Custom House
Sutton Harbour
Sue Wills Art Gallery
Register Office
War Memorial
Hoe Park
War Memorial
Mayflower Visitor & Exhibition Centre
Barbican
Royal Navy Memorial
Drake Statue
Memorials
The Hoe
Smeaton's Tower
Memorial
Royal Citadel (MOD)
St Katherine upon the Hoe
Yacht Club
200 m

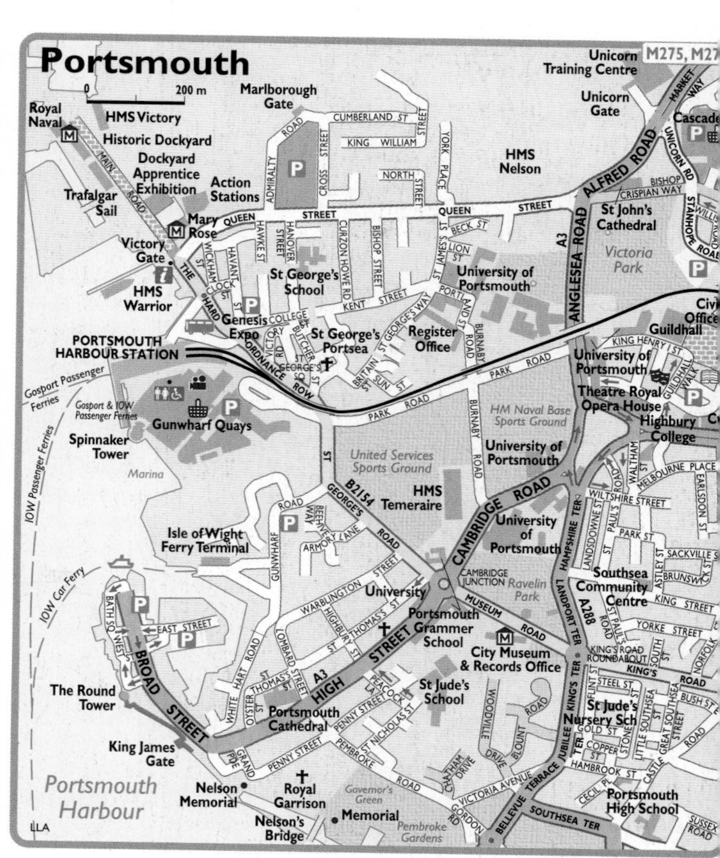
Portsmouth
Unicorn Training Centre
Unicorn Gate
M275, M27
Royal Naval
HMS Victory
Historic Dockyard
Dockyard Apprentice Exhibition
Marlborough Gate
Action Stations
HMS Nelson
Trafalgar Sail
Mary Rose
Victory Gate
HMS Warrior
St John's Cathedral
Victoria Park
St George's School
University of Portsmouth
Genesis Expo
St George's Portsea
Register Office
PORTSMOUTH HARBOUR STATION
Guildhall
University of Portsmouth
Theatre Royal Opera House
Gunwharf Quays
Spinnaker Tower
HM Naval Base Sports Ground
United Services Sports Ground
University of Portsmouth
Highbury College
HMS Temeraire
Isle of Wight Ferry Terminal
University of Portsmouth
Southsea Community Centre
University
Portsmouth Grammer School
City Museum & Records Office
The Round Tower
St Jude's School
Portsmouth Cathedral
St Jude's Nursery Sch
King James Gate
Portsmouth Harbour
Nelson Memorial
Royal Garrison
Memorial
Nelson's Bridge
Portsmouth High School
200 m

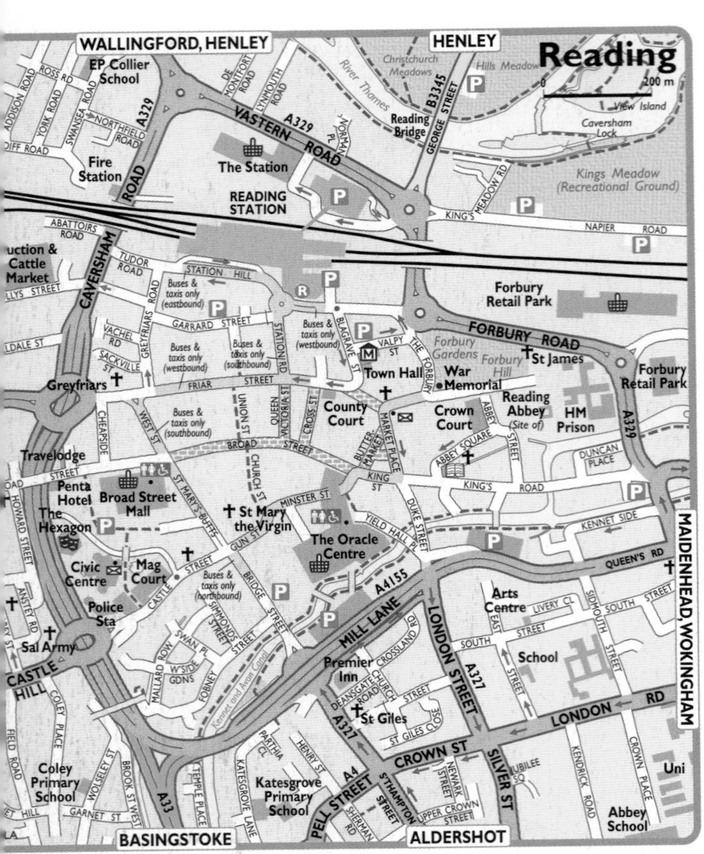
Reading
WALLINGFORD, HENLEY
HENLEY
EP Collier School
Fire Station
VASTERN ROAD
A329
The Station
READING STATION
Reading Bridge
Caversham Lock
View Island
Kings Meadow (Recreational Ground)
NAPIER ROAD
KING'S
CAVERSHAM ROAD
Forbury Retail Park
FORBURY ROAD
Forbury Gardens
St James
War Memorial
Forbury Retail Park
Town Hall
County Court
Crown Court
Reading Abbey (Site of)
HM Prison
A329
Greyfriars
FRIAR STREET
Travelodge
Penta Hotel
Broad Street Mall
St Mary the Virgin
The Hexagon
The Oracle Centre
KING'S ROAD
KENNET SIDE
QUEEN'S RD
Civic Centre
Mag Court
Police Sta
Sal Army
CASTLE HILL
A4155
MILL LANE
LONDON STREET
A327
Arts Centre
School
Premier Inn
St Giles
LONDON RD
CROWN ST
SILVER ST
Coley Primary School
Katesgrove Primary School
PELL STREET
Uni
Abbey School
A33
A4
MAIDENHEAD, WOKINGHAM
BASINGSTOKE
ALDERSHOT
200 m

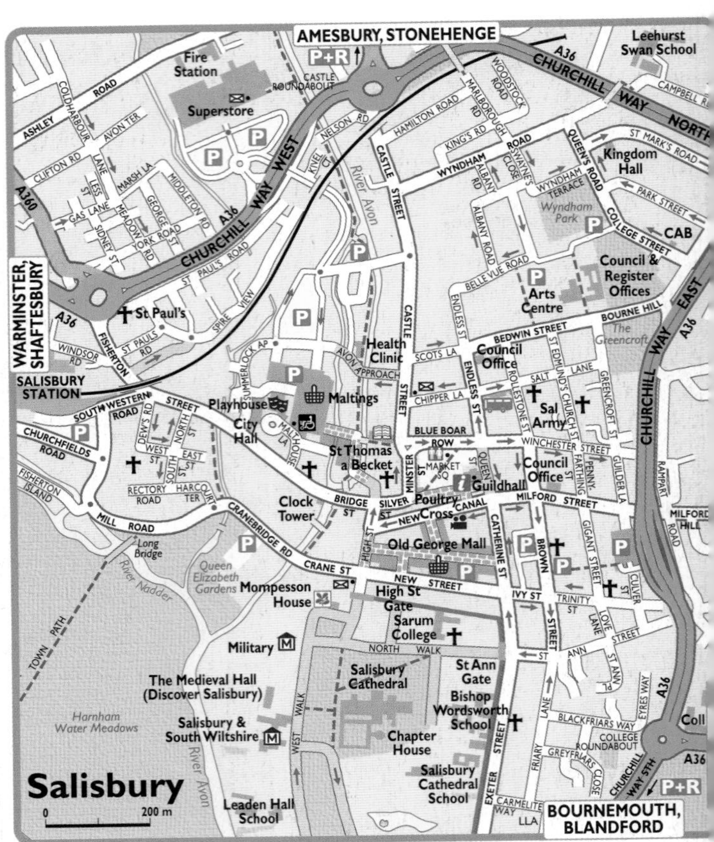
AMESBURY, STONEHENGE
Leehurst Swan School
Fire Station
Superstore
CASTLE ROUNDABOUT
A36
CHURCHILL WAY NORTH
CHURCHILL WAY WEST
WYNDHAM ROAD
Kingdom Hall
CAB
Wyndham Park
Council & Register Offices
WARMINSTER, SHAFTESBURY
A360
St Paul's
Health Clinic
Arts Centre
BEDWIN STREET
Council Office
The Greencroft
CHURCHILL WAY EAST
SALISBURY STATION
Playhouse
Maltings
City Hall
Sal Army
BLUE BOAR ROW
WINCHESTER STREET
St Thomas a Becket
Council Office
Guildhall
Clock Tower
Poultry Cross
MILFORD STREET
FISHERTON ISLAND
MILL ROAD
CRANEBRIDGE RD
Old George Mall
Long Bridge
River Nadder
Queen Elizabeth Gardens
Mompesson House
High St Gate
NEW STREET
Sarum College
Military
St Ann Gate
The Medieval Hall (Discover Salisbury)
Salisbury Cathedral
Bishop Wordsworth School
Harnham Water Meadows
Salisbury & South Wiltshire
Chapter House
Salisbury Cathedral School
Salisbury
Leaden Hall School
River Avon
COLLEGE ROUNDABOUT
BOURNEMOUTH, BLANDFORD
P+R
200 m

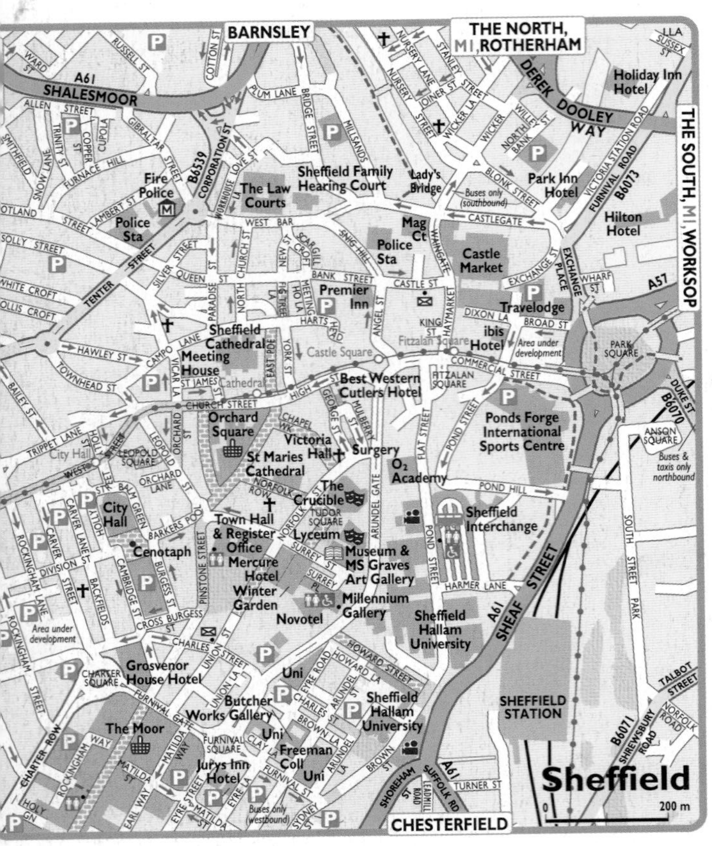
BARNSLEY
THE NORTH, M1, ROTHERHAM
A61
SHALESMOOR
DEREK DOOLEY WAY
Holiday Inn Hotel
THE SOUTH, M1, WORKSOP
Sheffield Family Hearing Court
Lady's Bridge
Park Inn Hotel
Fire Police
The Law Courts
Police Sta
Mag Ct
Castle Market
Hilton Hotel
Police Sta
Premier Inn
Travelodge
Sheffield Cathedral
ibis Hotel
Meeting House
Best Western Cutlers Hotel
Castle Square
Fitzalan Square
Ponds Forge International Sports Centre
Orchard Square
Victoria Hall
St Maries Cathedral
Surgery
O_2 Academy
The Crucible
City Hall
Town Hall & Register Office
Lyceum
Sheffield Interchange
Cenotaph
Mercure Hotel
Museum & MS Graves Art Gallery
Winter Garden
Millennium Gallery
Novotel
Sheffield Hallam University
SHEAF STREET
A61
Grosvenor House Hotel
Uni
Butcher Works Gallery
Sheffield Hallam University
SHEFFIELD STATION
The Moor
Uni
Freeman Coll
Uni
Jurys Inn Hotel
Sheffield
CHESTERFIELD
200 m

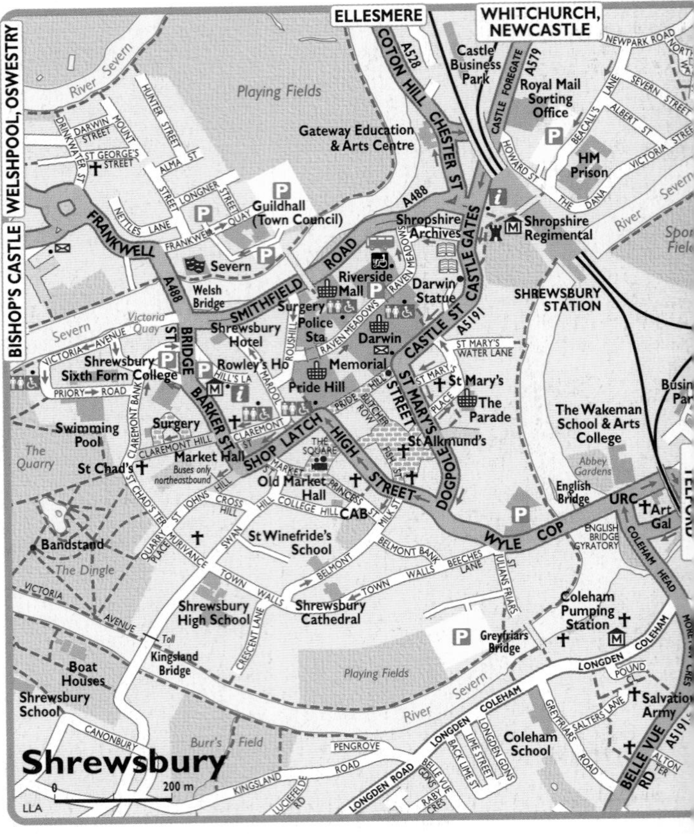
ELLESMERE
WHITCHURCH, NEWCASTLE
WELSHPOOL, OSWESTRY
River Severn
Playing Fields
Castle Business Park
Royal Mail Sorting Office
Gateway Education & Arts Centre
HM Prison
COTON HILL
CHESTER ST
Guildhall (Town Council)
Shropshire Archives
Shropshire Regimental
FRANKWELL
Severn
SMITHFIELD ROAD
Riverside Mall
Darwin Statue
CASTLE GATES
CASTLE ST
Welsh Bridge
Surgery
Police Sta
Darwin
SHREWSBURY STATION
BISHOP'S CASTLE
Shrewsbury Hotel
Shrewsbury Sixth Form College
Rowley's Ho
Memorial
St Mary's
Pride Hill
The Parade
The Wakeman School & Arts College
Swimming Pool
Surgery
The Quarry
Market Hall
SHOP LATCH
HIGH STREET
St Alkmund's
St Chad's
Old Market Hall
Abbey Gardens
English Bridge
CAB
WYLE COP
Art Gal
Bandstand
The Dingle
St Winefride's School
Shrewsbury High School
Shrewsbury Cathedral
Coleham Pumping Station
Greyfriars Bridge
Kingsland Bridge
Playing Fields
Boat Houses
Shrewsbury School
Burr's Field
Coleham School
Salvation Army
Shrewsbury
BELLE VUE RD
200 m

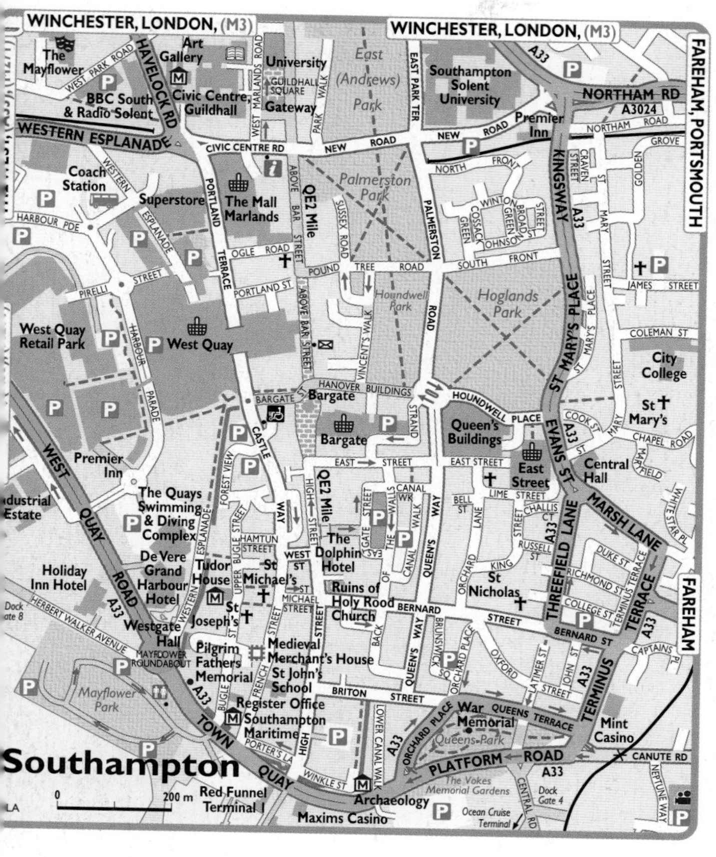
Southampton
WINCHESTER, LONDON, (M3)
FAREHAM, PORTSMOUTH
FAREHAM
The Mayflower
Art Gallery
BBC South & Radio Solent
Civic Centre, Guildhall
University Gateway
East (Andrews) Park
Southampton Solent University
Premier Inn
NORTHAM RD
WESTERN ESPLANADE
Coach Station
Superstore
The Mall Marlands
QE2 Mile
Palmerston Park
Houndwell Park
Hoglands Park
West Quay Retail Park
West Quay
Bargate
City College
St Mary's
Queen's Buildings
East Street
Central Hall
Premier Inn
The Quays Swimming & Diving Complex
Industrial Estate
De Vere Grand Harbour Hotel
Holiday Inn Hotel
Tudor House
St Michael's
The Dolphin Hotel
Ruins of Holy Rood Church
St Nicholas
Westgate Hall
St Joseph's
Pilgrim Fathers Memorial
Medieval Merchant's House
St John's School
Mayflower Park
Register Office
Southampton Maritime
War Memorial
Queens Park
Mint Casino
Red Funnel Terminal
Archaeology
Maxims Casino
The Vokes Memorial Gardens
Ocean Cruise Terminal
Dock Gate 4
Dock Gate 8
PLATFORM ROAD
TOWN QUAY
WEST QUAY ROAD
ST MARY'S PLACE
KINGSWAY
THREEFIELD LANE
MARSH LANE
TERMINUS TERRACE
200 m

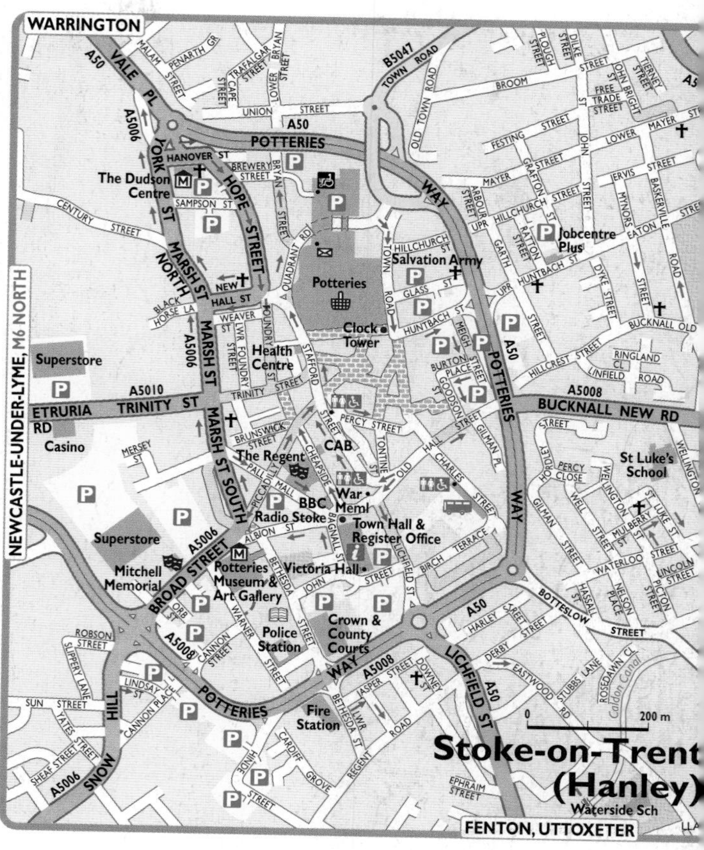
Stoke-on-Trent (Hanley)
WARRINGTON
NEWCASTLE-UNDER-LYME, M6 NORTH
FENTON, UTTOXETER
POTTERIES WAY
The Dudson Centre
Potteries
Clock Tower
Salvation Army
Jobcentre Plus
Superstore
Casino
Health Centre
ETRURIA TRINITY ST
BUCKNALL NEW RD
The Regent
CAB
War Meml
BBC Radio Stoke
Town Hall & Register Office
St Luke's School
Superstore
Mitchell Memorial
Potteries Museum & Art Gallery
Victoria Hall
Crown & County Courts
Police Station
Fire Station
BROAD STREET
MARSH ST
HOPE STREET
LICHFIELD ST
Waterside Sch
Caldon Canal
200 m

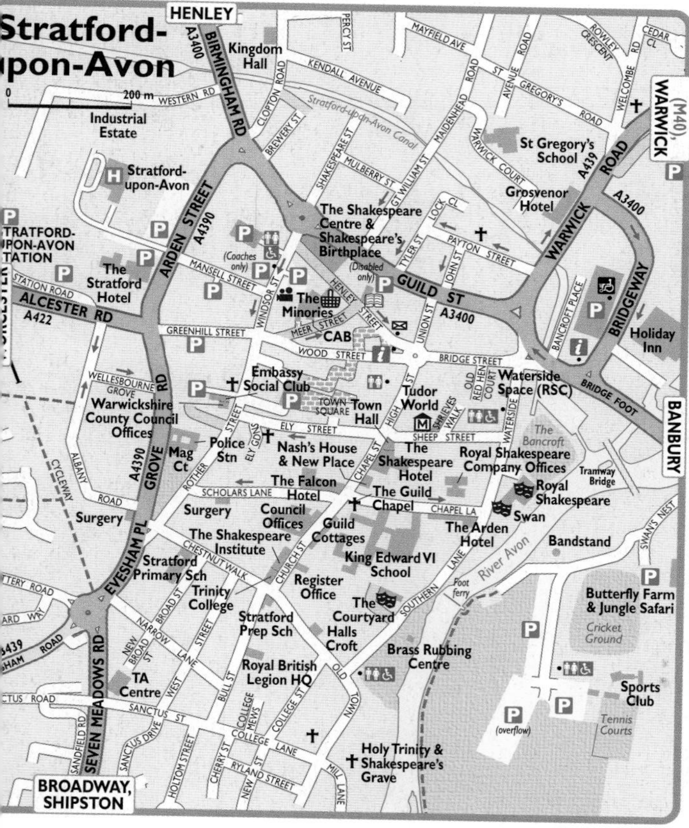
Stratford-upon-Avon
HENLEY
(M40) WARWICK
BANBURY
BROADWAY, SHIPSTON
Kingdom Hall
Industrial Estate
Stratford-upon-Avon
St Gregory's School
Grosvenor Hotel
The Shakespeare Centre & Shakespeare's Birthplace
Stratford-upon-Avon Station
The Stratford Hotel
ALCESTER RD
BIRMINGHAM RD
ARDEN STREET
GUILD ST
WARWICK ROAD
BRIDGEWAY
The Minories
CAB
Holiday Inn
Embassy Social Club
Tudor World
Waterside Space (RSC)
Town Hall
Warwickshire County Council Offices
Police Stn
Mag Ct
Nash's House & New Place
The Shakespeare Hotel
Royal Shakespeare Company Offices
Royal Shakespeare
Swan
The Falcon Hotel
The Guild Chapel
Surgery
Council Offices
Guild Cottages
The Arden Hotel
Bandstand
The Shakespeare Institute
King Edward VI School
River Avon
Stratford Primary Sch
Trinity College
Register Office
The Courtyard
Butterfly Farm & Jungle Safari
Stratford Prep Sch
Halls Croft
Brass Rubbing Centre
Cricket Ground
TA Centre
Royal British Legion HQ
Sports Club
Tennis Courts
Holy Trinity & Shakespeare's Grave
EVESHAM PL
SEVEN MEADOWS RD
GROVE RD
200 m

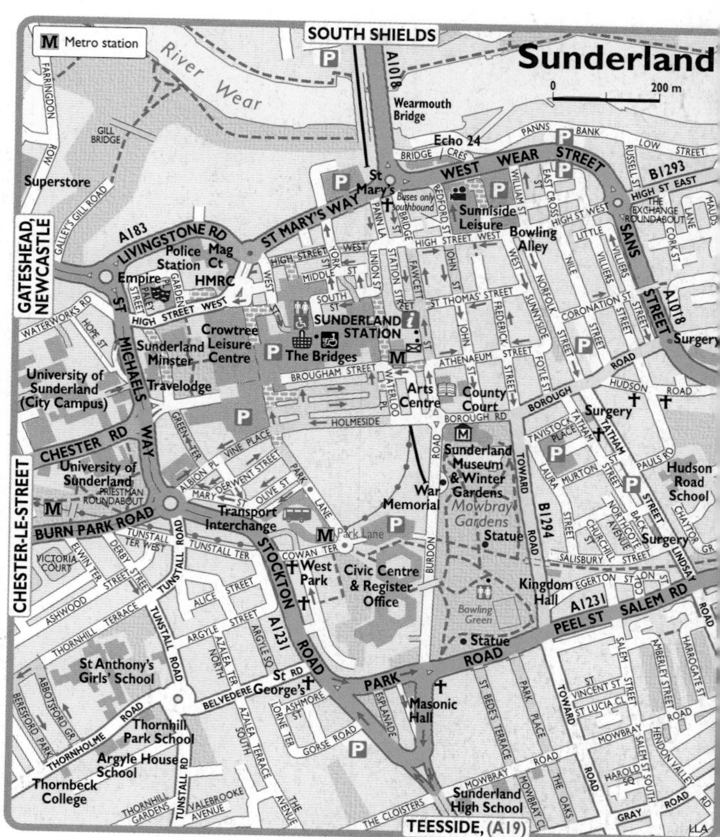
Sunderland
Metro station
SOUTH SHIELDS
GATESHEAD, NEWCASTLE
CHESTER-LE-STREET
TEESSIDE, (A19)
River Wear
Wearmouth Bridge
Echo 24
Superstore
St Mary's
WEST WEAR STREET
ST MARY'S WAY
Sunniside Leisure
Bowling Alley
LIVINGSTONE RD
Police Station
Mag Ct
HMRC
Empire
Crowtree Leisure Centre
Sunderland Minster
The Bridges
SUNDERLAND STATION
Travelodge
University of Sunderland (City Campus)
Arts Centre
County Court
Surgery
Hudson Road School
Sunderland Museum & Winter Gardens
Mowbray Gardens
University of Sunderland
War Memorial
CHESTER RD
BURN PARK ROAD
Transport Interchange
Park Lane
Statue
West Park
Civic Centre & Register Office
Kingdom Hall
Bowling Green
Statue
St Anthony's Girls' School
St George's
Masonic Hall
Thornhill Park School
Argyle House School
Thornbeck College
Sunderland High School
STOCKTON ROAD
PARK ROAD
PEEL ST
SALEM RD
SANS STREET
200 m

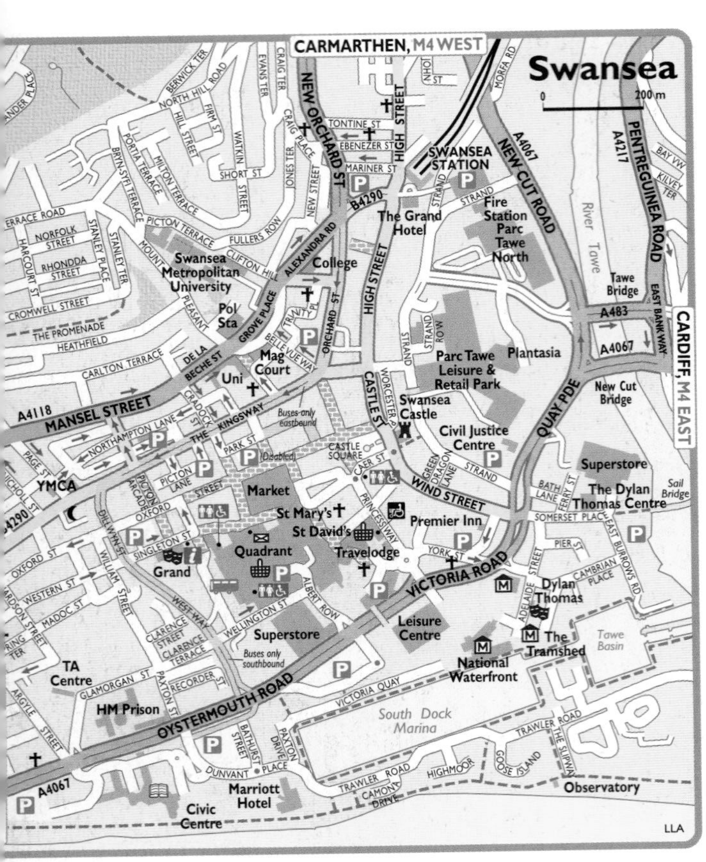
Swansea
0
200 m
CARMARTHEN, M4 WEST
CARDIFF, M4 EAST
SWANSEA STATION
The Grand Hotel
Fire Station
Parc Tawe North
River Tawe
Tawe Bridge
Swansea Metropolitan University
College
Pol Sta
Mag Court
Uni
Parc Tawe Leisure & Retail Park
Plantasia
New Cut Bridge
Swansea Castle
Civil Justice Centre
YMCA
Market
St Mary's
St David's
Quadrant
Grand
Premier Inn
Travelodge
Superstore
The Dylan Thomas Centre
Sail Bridge
Dylan Thomas
The Tramshed
Leisure Centre
National Waterfront
Tawe Basin
TA Centre
HM Prison
South Dock Marina
Marriott Hotel
Civic Centre
Observatory
MANSEL STREET
NEW ORCHARD ST
HIGH STREET
NEW CUT ROAD
PENTREGUINEA ROAD
QUAY PDE
WIND STREET
VICTORIA ROAD
OYSTERMOUTH ROAD
A4118
A4067
A4217
A483
B4290
Buses only eastbound
Buses only southbound
LLA

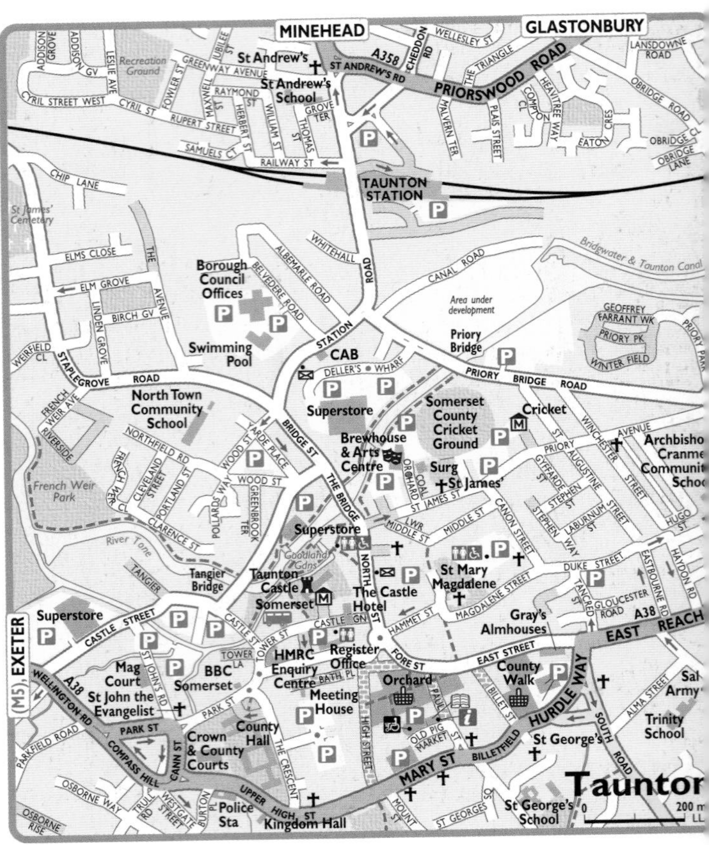
MINEHEAD
GLASTONBURY
(M5), EXETER
St Andrew's
St Andrew's School
PRIORSWOOD ROAD
TAUNTON STATION
Bridgwater & Taunton Canal
Borough Council Offices
Area under development
Priory Bridge
Swimming Pool
CAB
North Town Community School
Superstore
Somerset County Cricket Ground
Cricket
Brewhouse & Arts Centre
Surg
St James'
French Weir Park
River Tone
Archbishop Cranmer Community School
Tangier Bridge
Taunton Castle
Somerset
The Castle Hotel
St Mary Magdalene
Gray's Almshouses
Mag Court
BBC Somerset
St John the Evangelist
HMRC Enquiry Centre
Register Office
Meeting House
Orchard
County Walk
Sal Army
Trinity School
County Hall
Crown & County Courts
Police Sta
Kingdom Hall
St George's
St George's School
EAST REACH
HURDLE WAY
MARY ST
PRIORY BRIDGE ROAD
Taunton
200 m

TONBRIDGE
Kent & Sussex
YMCA
Royal Wells Hotel
Westfield Royal Victoria Place
Camden Centre
Clinic
Tunbridge Wells Gateway
Mus & Art Gallery
CAB
Trinity
Assembly Hall
Town Hall
Police Station
Medical Centre
Homeopathic
Hotel du Vin
St Augustine's
Calverley Park
Calverley Grounds
TUNBRIDGE WELLS STATION
The Great Hall
County Court
Mansion House (Register Office)
Fire Station
The Grove Bowling Club
The Grove
The Common
The Forum
Claremont School
King Charles the Martyr
The Pantiles
CHURCH ROAD
CRESCENT ROAD
CALVERLEY ROAD
LONDON ROAD
MOUNT EPHRAIM
A264
A26
B2023
A267
Tunbridge Wells
0
200 m
LEWES
HAILSHAM
LLA

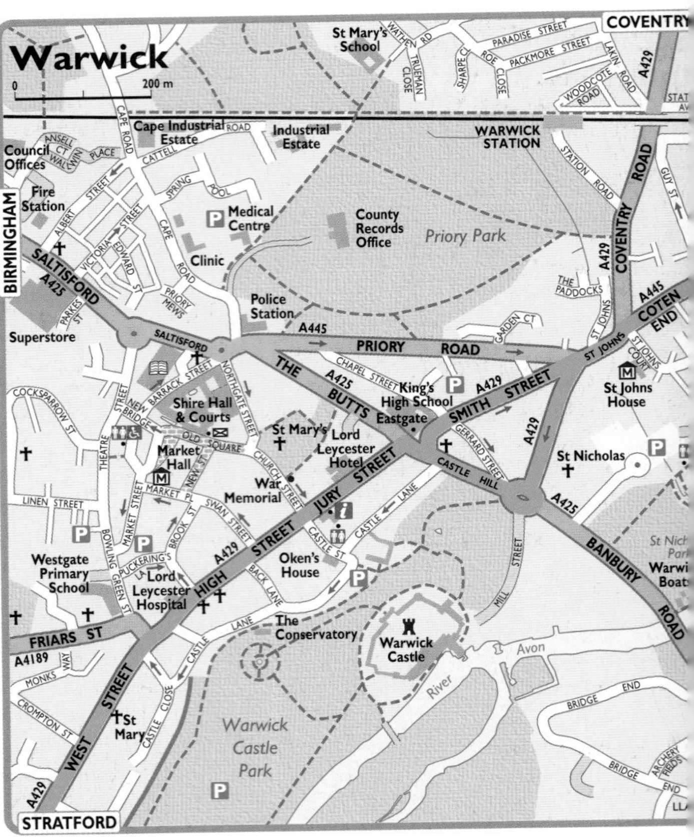
Warwick
0
200 m
COVENTRY
St Mary's School
Cape Industrial Estate
Industrial Estate
WARWICK STATION
Council Offices
Fire Station
Medical Centre
County Records Office
Priory Park
Clinic
Police Station
BIRMINGHAM
SALTISFORD
Superstore
PRIORY ROAD
THE BUTTS
King's High School
Eastgate
St Johns House
Shire Hall & Courts
St Mary's
Lord Leycester Hotel
Market Hall
War Memorial
St Nicholas
Westgate Primary School
Lord Leycester Hospital
Oken's House
The Conservatory
Warwick Castle
Avon
River
Warwick Castle Park
St Mary
SMITH STREET
JURY STREET
HIGH STREET
WEST STREET
BANBURY ROAD
COVENTRY ROAD
A429
A445
A425
A4189
STRATFORD

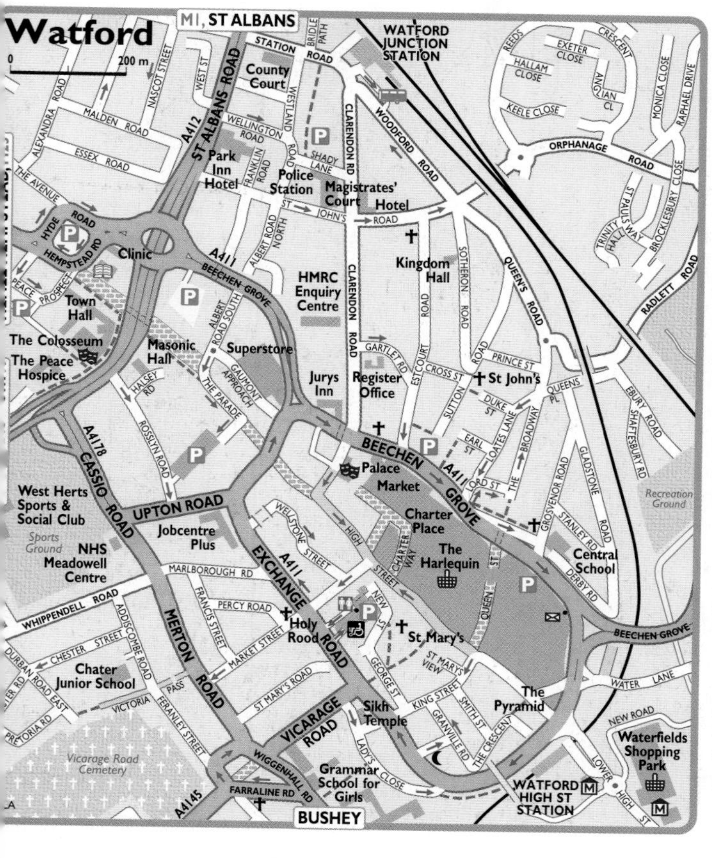
Watford
M1, ST ALBANS
200 m
WATFORD JUNCTION STATION
County Court
Park Inn Hotel
Police Station
Magistrates' Court
Hotel
Clinic
Town Hall
HMRC Enquiry Centre
Kingdom Hall
The Colosseum
The Peace Hospice
Masonic Hall
Superstore
Jurys Inn
Register Office
St John's
West Herts Sports & Social Club
Sports Ground
Jobcentre Plus
NHS Meadowell Centre
Palace
Market
Charter Place
The Harlequin
Central School
Recreation Ground
Holy Rood
St Mary's
Chater Junior School
Sikh Temple
The Pyramid
Waterfields Shopping Park
Vicarage Road Cemetery
Grammar School for Girls
WATFORD HIGH ST STATION
BUSHEY
ST ALBANS ROAD
BEECHEN GROVE
UPTON ROAD
CASSIO ROAD
MERTON ROAD
EXCHANGE ROAD
VICARAGE ROAD
CLARENDON ROAD
QUEEN'S ROAD
ORPHANAGE ROAD
WOODFORD ROAD
WHIPPENDELL ROAD

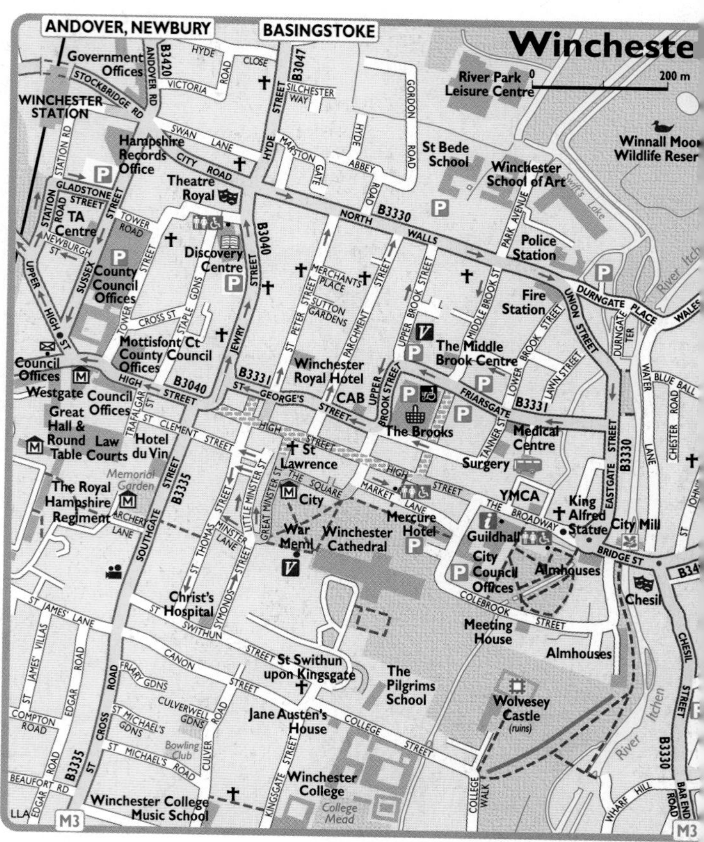
Winchester
ANDOVER, NEWBURY
BASINGSTOKE
200 m
Government Offices
WINCHESTER STATION
River Park Leisure Centre
Winnall Moors Wildlife Reserve
Hampshire Records Office
St Bede School
Winchester School of Art
Theatre Royal
TA Centre
Discovery Centre
Police Station
County Council Offices
Fire Station
Mottisfont Ct County Council Offices
The Middle Brook Centre
Council Offices
Westgate
Council Offices
Winchester Royal Hotel
CAB
The Brooks
Great Hall & Round Table
Law Courts
Hotel du Vin
Medical Centre
Surgery
St Lawrence
City
YMCA
King Alfred Statue
City Mill
The Royal Hampshire Regiment
Memorial Garden
War Meml
Winchester Cathedral
Mercure Hotel
Guildhall
City Council Offices
Almhouses
Chesil
Christ's Hospital
Meeting House
Almhouses
St Swithun upon Kingsgate
The Pilgrims School
Wolvesey Castle (ruins)
Jane Austen's House
Winchester College
College Mead
Winchester College Music School
Bowling Club
River Itchen
NORTH WALLS
HIGH STREET
SOUTHGATE STREET
COLLEGE STREET
M3

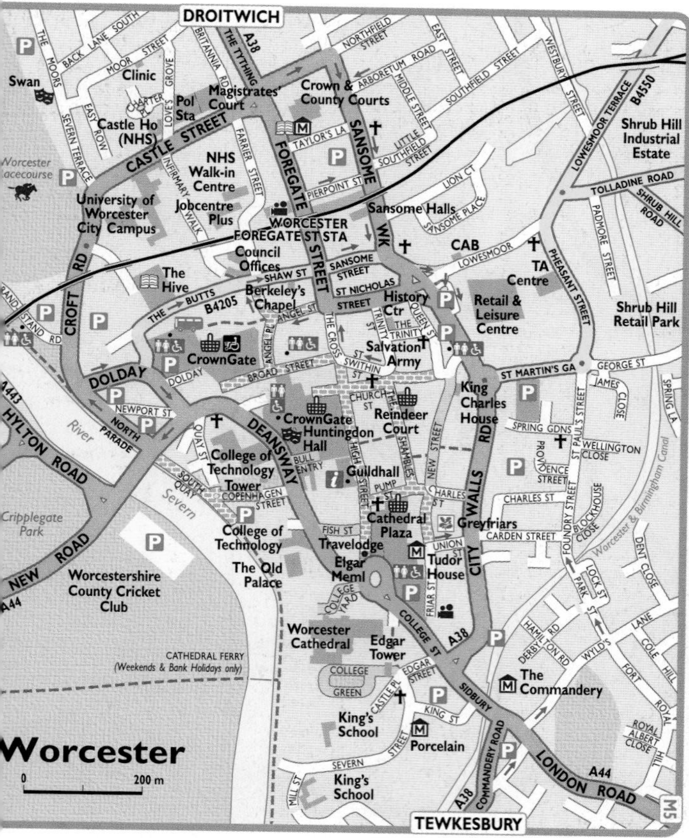
DROITWICH
Swan
Clinic
Pol Sta
Magistrates' Court
Crown & County Courts
Castle Ho (NHS)
NHS Walk-in Centre
Shrub Hill Industrial Estate
Worcester Racecourse
University of Worcester City Campus
Jobcentre Plus
Sansome Halls
WORCESTER FOREGATE ST STA
Council Offices
CAB
TA Centre
The Hive
Berkeley's Chapel
History Ctr
Retail & Leisure Centre
Shrub Hill Retail Park
CrownGate
Salvation Army
King Charles House
Reindeer Court
CrownGate
Huntingdon Hall
College of Technology Tower
Guildhall
Cripplegate Park
College of Technology
Cathedral Plaza
Greyfriars
The Old Palace
Travelodge
Elgar Meml
Tudor House
Worcestershire County Cricket Club
Worcester Cathedral
Edgar Tower
The Commandery
CATHEDRAL FERRY (Weekends & Bank Holidays only)
King's School
Porcelain
King's School
Worcester
200 m
TEWKESBURY
CASTLE STREET
FOREGATE STREET
SANSOME WK
CITY WALLS RD
DEANSWAY
LONDON ROAD
NEW ROAD
HYLTON ROAD
River Severn

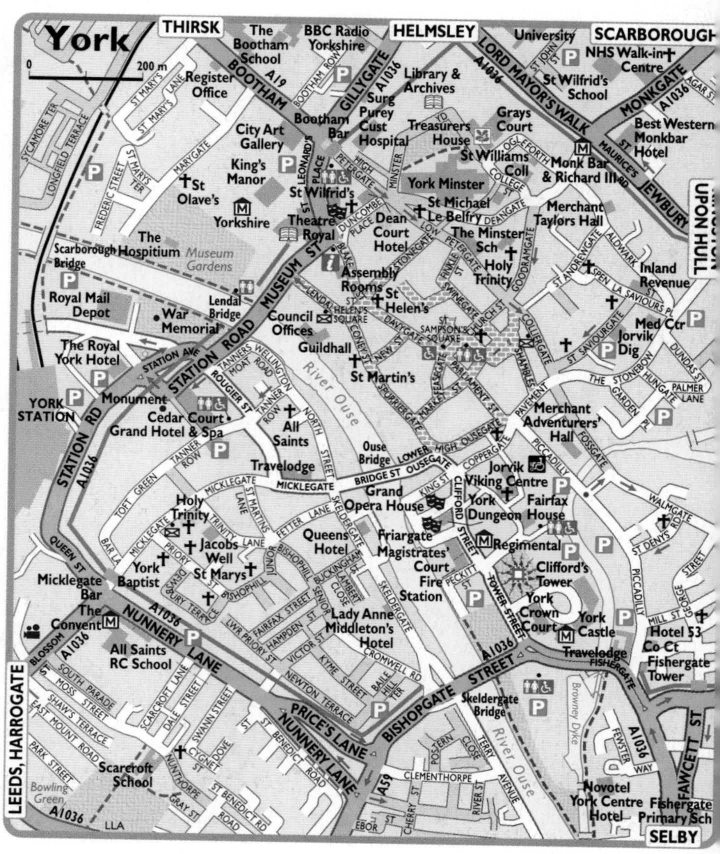
York
THIRSK
The Bootham School
BBC Radio Yorkshire
HELMSLEY
University
SCARBOROUGH
NHS Walk-in Centre
Register Office
Library & Archives
St Wilfrid's School
Surg
Purey Cust Hospital
Bootham Bar
Treasurers House
Grays Court
Best Western Monkbar Hotel
City Art Gallery
King's Manor
St Williams Coll
Monk Bar & Richard III
St Olave's
York Minster
St Wilfrid's
St Michael Le Belfry
Merchant Taylors Hall
Yorkshire
Theatre Royal
Dean Court Hotel
The Minster Sch
Holy Trinity
Inland Revenue
Scarborough Bridge
The Hospitium
Museum Gardens
Assembly Rooms
St Helen's
Royal Mail Depot
War Memorial
Lendal Bridge
Council Offices
Med Ctr
Jorvik Dig
The Royal York Hotel
Guildhall
St Martin's
YORK STATION
Monument
Cedar Court Grand Hotel & Spa
All Saints
Merchant Adventurers' Hall
Travelodge
Ouse Bridge
Jorvik Viking Centre
Grand Opera House
York Dungeon
Fairfax House
Holy Trinity
Jacobs Well
St Marys
Queens Hotel
Friargate
Magistrates' Court
Fire Station
Regimental
Clifford's Tower
York Baptist
Micklegate Bar
York Crown Court
York Castle
Hotel 53
The Convent
Travelodge
Co Ct
Fishergate Tower
All Saints RC School
Lady Anne Middleton's Hotel
Skeldergate Bridge
LEEDS, HARROGATE
Scarcroft School
Novotel York Centre Hotel
Fishergate Primary Sch
SELBY
UPON HULL
BOOTHAM
GILLYGATE
LORD MAYOR'S WALK
MONKGATE
STATION ROAD
MUSEUM ST
NUNNERY LANE
BISHOPGATE STREET
River Ouse
200 m

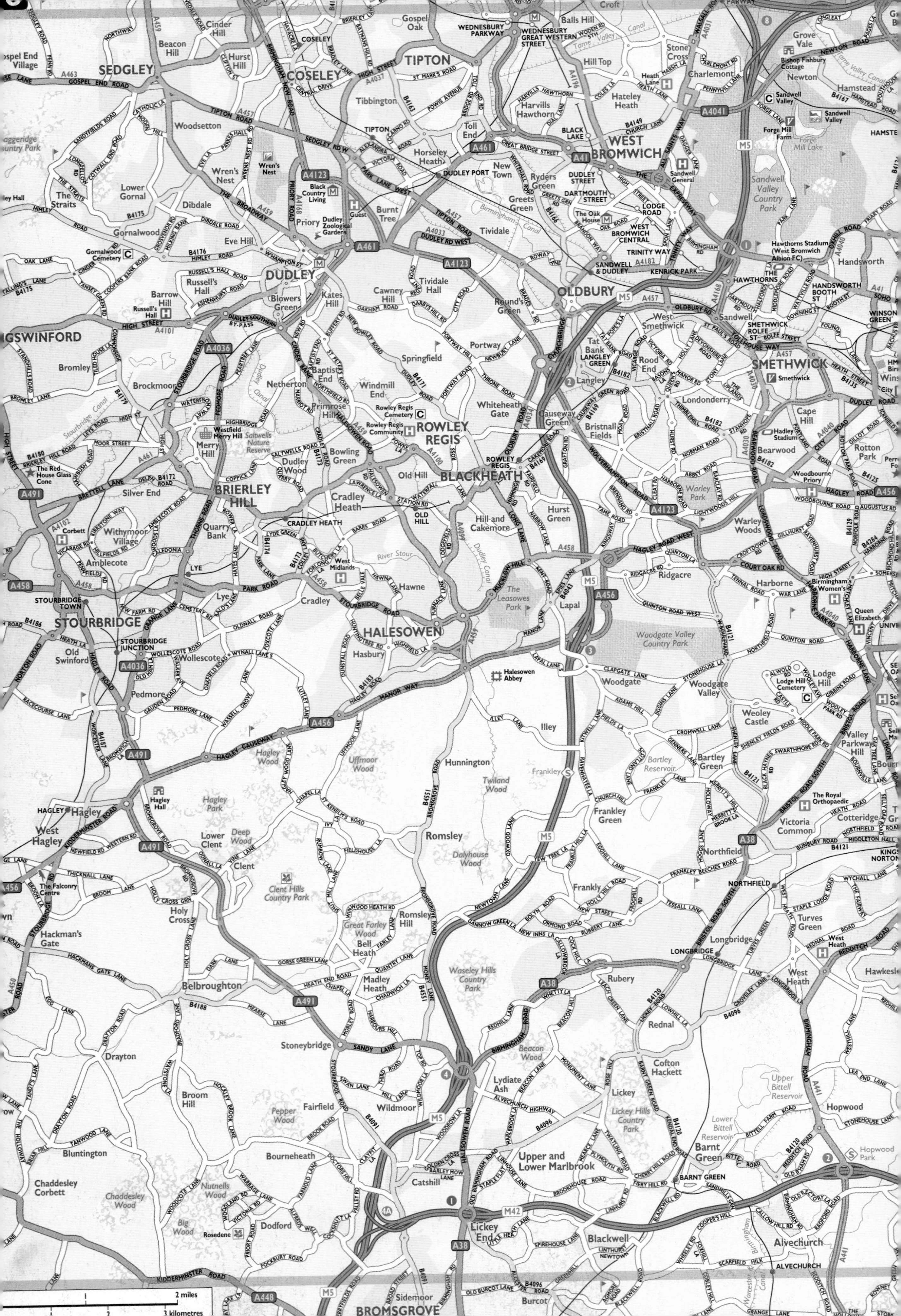

Sedgley
Coseley
Tipton
Gospel Oak
Wednesbury Parkway
Wednesbury Great Western Street
Balls Hill
Hill Top
Stone Cross
Charlemont
Grove Vale
Newton
Hamstead
Sandwell Valley
Gospel End Village
Beacon Hill
Cinder Hill
Hurst Hill
Tibbington
Harvills Hawthorn
Hateley Heath
Heath Lane
Woodsetton
Toll End
Black Lake
West Bromwich
Forge Mill Farm
Forge Mill Lake
Wren's Nest
Horseley Heath
Dudley Port
New Town
Ryders Green
Dudley Street
Dartmouth Street
Lodge Road
Sandwell General
Sandwell Valley Country Park
Lower Gornal
The Straits
Black Country Living
Burnt Tree
Greets Green
The Oak House
West Bromwich Central
Dibdale
Priory
Dudley Zoological Gardens
Tividale
Trinity Way
Hawthorns Stadium (West Bromwich Albion FC)
Handsworth
Gornalwood
Eve Hill
Gornalwood Cemetery
Dudley
Sandwell & Dudley
Kenrick Park
Hawthorns
Handsworth Booth St
Russell's Hall
Barrow Hill
Blowers Green
Kates Hill
Cawney Hill
Tividale Hall
Round's Green
Oldbury
Sandwell
Smethwick Rolfe St
Winson Green
Kingswinford
Bromley
Brockmoor
Netherton
Baptist End
Springfield
Portway
West Smethwick
Tat Bank
Langley Green
Rood End
Smethwick
Windmill End
Langley
Londonderry
Primrose Hill
Rowley Regis Cemetery
Rowley Regis Community
Rowley Regis
Whiteheath Gate
Causeway Green
Bristnall Fields
Cape Hill
Westfield Merry Hill
Saltwells Nature Reserve
Merry Hill
Dudley Wood
Bowling Green
Old Hill
Blackheath
Hadley Stadium
Bearwood
Rotton Park
The Red House Glass Cone
Brierley Hill
Silver End
Cradley Heath
Hurst Green
Warley Park
Woodbourne Priory
Withymoor Village
Quarry Bank
Hill and Cakemore
Warley Woods
Corbett
Amblecote
Lye
West Midlands
River Stour
Hawne
Dudley Canal
Ridgacre
Harborne
Birmingham's Women's
Stourbridge Town
Stourbridge
Cradley
The Leasowes Park
Lapal
Queen Elizabeth
Stourbridge Junction
Old Swinford
Wollescote
Halesowen
Hasbury
Woodgate Valley Country Park
Halesowen Abbey
Woodgate
Woodgate Valley
Lodge Hill
Lodge Hill Cemetery
Pedmore
Weoley Castle
Illey
Valley Parkway Hill
Hagley Wood
Uffmoor Wood
Hunnington
Frankley
Bartley Reservoir
Bartley Green
Twiland Wood
Hagley Hall
Hagley
West Hagley
Hagley Park
Romsley
Frankley Green
The Royal Orthopaedic
Cotteridge
Victoria Common
Lower Clent
Deep Wood
Clent
Dalyhouse Wood
Northfield
The Falconry Centre
Clent Hills Country Park
Frankly
Holy Cross
Hackman's Gate
Great Farley Wood
Romsley Hill
Bell Heath
Turves Green
Longbridge
West Heath
Belbroughton
Madley Heath
Waseley Hills Country Park
Rubery
Hawkesley
Rednal
Stoneybridge
Drayton
Beacon Wood
Lydiate Ash
Cofton Hackett
Upper Bittell Reservoir
Broom Hill
Fairfield
Wildmoor
Lickey
Lickey Hills Country Park
Hopwood
Pepper Wood
Lower Bittell Reservoir
Bluntington
Bourneheath
Upper and Lower Marlbrook
Barnt Green
Hopwood Park
Chaddesley Corbett
Chaddesley Wood
Nutnells Wood
Catshill
Big Wood
Rosedene
Dodford
Lickey End
Blackwell
Alvechurch
Sidemoor
Bromsgrove
Burcot
Worcester & Birmingham Canal
2 miles
3 kilometres

Birmingham district
Old Oscott
New Oscott
Wylde Green
Kingstanding
Boldmere
Oscott
Walmley
Over Green
Lea Marston
Perry Barr
Perry
Perry Common
Short Heath
Upper Witton
Chester Road
Pype Hayes
Pype Hayes Park
Curdworth
Ladywalk Nature Reserve
Alexander Stadium
Perry Park
Wilton Lakes
Erdington
John Taylor Hospice
Minworth
Perry Barr Greyhound Stadium
Tyburn
Castle Vale
Water Orton
River Tame
Witton
Gravelly Hill
Birches Green
Birmingham & Fazeley Canal
The Fort
Coleshill Parkway
Church Hill
Birchfield
Aston Villa FC
Aston Manor Transport
Aston Hall
Aston
Star City
Castle Bromwich
Lozells
Bromford
Buckland End
Kingshurst
Newtown
Aston New Town
Washwood Heath
Shard End
Coleshill
Woodlands
Jewellery Quarter
Hockley
New Town Row
Nechells Green
Duddeston
Saltley
Stechford
Glebe Farm
St Pauls
Birmingham Snow Hill
Children's
Birmingham
Moor Street
Adderley Park
Heartlands
Alum Rock
Kitts Green
Fordbridge
Chelmsley Wood
Lea Hall
Tile Cross
Birmingham New Street
Bullring
St Andrew's Stadium (Birmingham City FC)
Bordesley
Bordesley Green
Little Bromwich
Yardley
Blakesley Hall
Back to Backs
Lee Bank
Garretts Green
Brooklands
Marston Green
Highgate
Sparkbrook
Small Heath
Gilbertstone
Lyndon Green
Birmingham Business Park
Calthorpe Park
Warwickshire CCC
Hay Mills
Stockfield
Sheldon
National Exhibition Centre
LG Arena
Tyseley
Balsall Heath
Sparkhill
Acocks Green
Elmdon
Birmingham International Airport
Birmingham International
Birmingham Nature Centre
Cannon Hill
Showell Green
West Midlands Police
Spring Road
Moseley Hall
National Motorcycle
Moseley
Wake Green
Moseley Bog
GRA Hall Green Stadium
Olton
Elmdon Park
Highbury Park
King's Heath
Springfield
Sarehole Mill
Hall Green
Olton Reservoir
Grand Union Canal
Bickenhill
Ten Acres
Kineton Green
Elmdon Heath
Hampton-in-Arden
Stirchley
Billesley
Hall Green
Catherine-de-Barnes
Billesley Common
Yardley Wood
Robin Hood Cemetery
Solihull
Brandwood End
Shirley
Sharmans Cross
Warstock
Eastcote
Highter's Heath
Shirley Street
Blossomfield
Parkridge Centre
Shirley
Haslucks Green
Hillfield
Copt Heath
Shirley Heath
Barston
Major's Green
Widney Manor
Hollywood
Bateman's Green
Whitlock's End
Dickens Heath
Monkspath
Knowle
Headley Heath
Tilehouse Green
Stratford upon Avon Canal
Wythall
Tidbury Green
Cheswick Green
Bentley Heath
Temple Balsall
Wythal Green
Rumbush
Blythe Valley Park
Dorridge
Tanner's Green
Earlswood
New Fallings Coppice
Earlswood Lakes
Terry's Green
Weatheroak Hill
Hillcrest Park
The Lakes
Packwood
Chessetts Wood
Chadwick End
Hockley Heath
Arnold's Wood
Windmill Naps
Portway
Packwood House
Baddesley Clinton
Wood End
Lapworth

Milton
Auchentorlie Wood
McKellar's Wood
Lonendale Wood
Ledhill Wood
MILNGAVIE
Milngavie
Mains Plantation
CRAIGDHU RD
B8050
West of Scotland RFC
AUCHENHOWIE RD
A807
River Clyde
GREAT WESTERN ROAD
DUMBARTON ROAD
BOWLING
A82
Old Kilpatrick
KILPATRICK
Cyldebank
DUNTOCHER
Hardgate
Faifley
GLASGOW ROAD
A810
DUNTOCHER ROAD
BEARSDEN
Antonine Wall: Bearsden Bath House
HILLFOOT
Bearsden
Erskine Park
Erskine Bridge
A898
Mountblow
Parkhall
M8
A8
Erskine
B815
Bishopton
Dalmuir
B814
A814
Radnor Park
Drumry
Drumchapel
DALMUIR
CLYDEBANK
Golden Jubilee National
SINGER
Kilbowie
DRUMRY
A8014
Bargarran
North Barr
Rashielee
M898
Rossland
ERSKINE
West Craigend
BISHOPTON
OLD GREENOCK ROAD
Park Mains
Gamieland
Irchinnan
A726
Kilbowie
CLYDEBANK
Linnvale
Great Western
DRUMCHAPEL
Blairdardie
WESTERTON
High Knightswood
Acre
Forth and Clyde Canal
Whitecrook
YOKER
Netherton
KELVINDALE
MARYHILL
SUMMERSTON
Dawsholm
Knightswood
Temple
ANNIESLAND
GARSCADDEN
Anniesland
Yoker
Scotstounhill
SCOTSTOUNHILL
Jordanhill
Kelvindale
Gartnavel Royal
Glasgow Nuffield
JORDANHILL
Hyndland
HYNDLAND
Dowanhill
Blythswood
The King's Inch
A814
Scotstoun
Broomhill
River Gryfe
B790
HOUSTON ROAD
Robertson Park
RENFREW
Xscape
Braehead
Whiteinch
Western Infirmary
HILLHEAD
GLASGOW AIRPORT
Porterfield
Loanhead
PARTICK
KELVINHALL
Yorkhill
Clyde Tunnel
Shieldhall
Riverside
Southern General
Linthouse
The Tall Ship at Glasgow Harbour
GOVAN
Craigends
28A
29
28
27
26
25A
25
24
23
22
Gockston
Gallowhill
North Cardonald
Govan
Drumoyne
Summertown
Glasgow Science Centre
North Clippens
Linwood
East Fulton
Shotroods
Laigh Park
St Mirren Park Stadium (St Mirren FC)
PAISLEY ST JAMES
HILLINGTON WEST
HILLINGTON EAST
Hillington
West Drumoyne
Ibrox Stadium (Rangers FC)
IBROX
CESSNOCK
Ibrox
A737
Brookfield
Ferguslie Park
Coats Observatory, Paisley Museum & Art Galleries
PAISLEY GILMOUR ST
Whitehaugh
Greenlaw
Penilee
Oldhall
Cardonald
CARDONALD
Craighton
Craigton
House for an Art Lover
Bellahouston Park
DUMBRECK
PAISLEY
Barochan Cross
Woodside
Ralston
A761
Crookston
CROOKSTON
HAWKHEAD
PAISLEY ROAD WEST
South Cardonald
MOSSPARK
Mosspark
Dumbreck
Williamsburg
JOHNSTONE
Millarston
Castlehead
Royal Alexandra
PAISLEY CANAL
Blackhill
Ross Hall
Rosshall
MAXWELL PARK
Crossmyloof
Lounsdale
Meikleriggs
Charleston
A726
CORKERHILL
Corkerhill
M77
Elderslie
Quarrelton
Cartside
Howwood Road
Johnstone Castle
Carriagehill
Brodie Park
Lochfield
Lavendale
Crookston Castle
North Wood
Pollok Country Park
Brediland
Stanely
Thornly Park
Dykebar
Bull Wood
Cochrane Castle
Craigston Wood
Foxbar
Stanely Reservoir
Glenburn
Pollok
POLLOKSHAWS WEST
Pollok House
Pollokshaws
Spateston
Silverburn
Roughmussel
P+R
Bardrain Wood
Gleniffer Braes Country Park
Mansewood
Auldhouse
Nitshill
PRIESTHILL AND DARNLEY
KENNISHEAD
Kennishead
B769
Cross Stobbs
Boylestone
NITSHILL
A736
THORNLIEBANK
Camwadric
Darnley
Arden
Harelaw Reservoir
Crossmill
B773
South Nitshill
BARRHEAD
Hillside
Dunterlie
Cower Park
Thornliebank
Orchard Park
Leverside
BARRHEAD
Arthurlie
Lochlibo
Auchenback
M77
Rouken Glen Park
A727
WILLIAMWOOD
Waulkmill Glen Reservoir
PATTERTON
WHITECRAIGS
Williamwood
Nether Kirkton
Neilston
NEILSTON
Balgray Reservoir
Ryat Linn Reservoir
Crookfur
Whitecraigs
Greenbank Garden
Broom
Kirkhill
Loch Libo
Walton Dam
NEWTON MEARNS
Burnhouse
Mearns
Uplawmoor
Melons Wood
Crow Wood
Harelaw Dam
Lugton
Long Loch
White Loch
Brother Loch
Black Loch
A735
B775
Eagle
2 miles

KIRKINTILLOCH
West Balgrochan
Torrance
Balmore
Bardowie
Cleddans
Harestanes
Hillhead
Rosebank
Barleybank
Townhead
Westermains
Waterside
Oxgang
The Greens
High Gallowhill
Boghead
Lenzie
Millersneuk
Claddens
Cadder
Wilderness Plantation
Forth and Clyde Canal
River Kelvin
Auchinloch
Gadloch
Bishopbriggs
High Possil
Milton
Auchinairn
Lambhill
Stobhill General
Balornock
Robroyston
Parkhouse
Springburn
Barmulloch
Petershill
Possil Park
Port Dundas
Germiston
Blackhill
Millerston
Stepps
Muirhead
Chryston
Moodiesburn
Gartcosh
Marnoch
Glenboig
Johnston Loch
Orchardton Woods
Orchardton Plantation
Blackwood
Broadwood Stadium (Clyde FC)
Westfield
Dalshannon
Mollinsburn
Annathill
Craigend
Garthamlock
Gartloch
Bishop Loch
Woodend Loch
Hogganfield Loch
Hogganfield Park
Ruchazie
Riddrie
Carntyne
HMP Barlinnie
Cranhill
Queenslie
Provan Hall
Lochwood Plantation
Easterhouse
Townhead
Drumpellier Country Park
Drumpellier
Sunnyside
Blairhill
Royston
Alexandra Park
Glasgow Cathedral
Dennistoun
Haghill
GLASGOW
Glasgow Green
People's Palace
Laurieston
Gorbals
Hutchesontown
Bridgeton
Dalmarnock
Barrowfield
Celtic Park FC
Gallowgate
Parkhead
Shettleston
Tollcross
Tollcross Park
Dalbeth
Sandyhills
Mount Vernon
Baillieston
Garrowhill
Swinton
Balanark
Springboig
Greenfield
Lightburn
Bargeddie
Kirkwood
Dundyvan
Barrowfield
Old Monkland
Kirkshaws
Shawhead
Calderbraes
Birkenshaw
Tannochside
Viewpark
Uddingston
Bothwell
Bothwell Castle
Orbiston
Strathclyde Country Park
Strathclyde Loch
MOTHERWELL
Shawfield
Shawfield Greyhound Stadium
Farm Cross
Polmadie
Crosshill
Govanhill
Toryglen
Hampden Park Stadium & The Scottish Football Museum
Mount Florida
RUTHERGLEN
Kings Park
Cathcart
Croftfoot
Spittal
Burnside
Fernhill
Springhall
Cathkin
Carmyle
Fullerton
Daldowie
Cambuslang
Westburn
Newton
Vicarland
Whitlawburn
Greenlees
Cairns
Halfway
Hallside
Holmwood
Linn Park
Castlemilk
Big Wood
Quarry Wood
Carmunnock
Busby
Nerston
Blantyre
David Livingstone Centre
Silverwells
Bothwell
Kittochside
National Museum of Rural Life Scotland
James Hamilton Heritage Park
Castleglen
Stewartfield
Calderwood
College Milton
East Mains
West Mains
Hairmyres
Westwood
EAST KILBRIDE
Birniehill
Saint Leonards
Mossneuk
The Murray
Newlandsmuir
Greenhills
Whitehills
Kelvin
Calderglen Country Park
Lindsayfield
Hillhouse
Udston
Earnock
Chantinghall
Burnbank
Whitehill
Black Muir Plantation
Hamilton Park
New Douglas Park Stadium (Hamilton Academical FC)
HAMILTON
Hamilton West
Hamilton Central
Low Parks
Hamilton Low Parks
Laighstonehall
Little Earnock
Fairhill
Silvertonhill
Low Waters
Cadzow Castle
Meikle Earnock
Eddlewood
Old Oaks
Quarter
M&D's
South Lanarkshire

HEYWOOD
SHAW
ROYTON
OLDHAM
CHADDERTON
MIDDLETON
FAILSWORTH
DROYLSDEN
ASHTON-UNDER-LYNE
WHITEFIELD
PRESTWICH
RADCLIFFE
LITTLE LEVER
KEARSLEY
WALKDEN
PENDLEBURY
SWINTON
WORSLEY
ECCLES
Heaton Park
Heaton Park Reservoir
Castleton
Rochdale Canal
Manchester, Bolton & Bury Canal
River Irwell
Bridgewater Canal
2 miles

Manchester district
URMSTON
Davyhulme
Crofts Bank
Calder Bank
Trafford General
Trafford Centre
EventCity
Flixton
FLIXTON
Trafford Park
TRAFFORD PARK
EXCHANGE QUAY
POMONA
Old Trafford Stadium & Museum (Manchester United FC)
Lancashire CCC Old Trafford Cricket Ground
Gorse Hill
Old Trafford
OLD TRAFFORD
TRAFFORD BAR
St George's
Firswood
FIRSWOOD
STRETFORD
Longford Park
Spire
Whalley Range
CHORLTON
Moss Side
Bridgewater
University Dental
Whitworth Art Gallery
Whitworth Park
Alexandra Park
Manchester Royal Infirmary
Royal Manchester Childrens'
Manchester Royal Eye & St Marys
Victoria Park
Longsight
Gallery of Costume
Platt Fields Park
Rusholme
O2 Apollo Manchester
West Gorton
Belle Vue Greyhound Stadium
Gorton
BELLE VUE
RYDER BROW
Abbey Hey
Debdale
Debdale Park
Gorton Upper Reservoir
Audenshaw Reservoirs
DENTON
Hooley Hill
Haughton Green
Green Bank Fields
LEVENSHULME
Levenshulme
North Reddish
REDDISH NORTH
Denton Wood
REDDISH
Reddish Green
REDDISH SOUTH
Mid Reddish
South Reddish
BRINNINGTON
Brinnington
Bredbury
BREDBURY
Arden Park
Lower Bredbury
Barrack Hill
Hatherlow
Bredbury Green
Woodbank Memorial Park
Little Moor
Offerton
Offerton Green
Fallowfield
ST WERBURGH'S ROAD
Chorlton-cum-Hardy
Chorlton Park
Hough End Fields
(Due to open Summer 2013)
WHITHINGTON
Manchester
Mersey Valley
Sale Water Park
River Mersey
Barlow Moor
West Didsbury
WEST DIDSBURY
Withington
MAULDETH ROAD
Fog Lane Park
Burnage
BURNAGE
Heaton Chapel
HEATON CHAPEL
Heaton Moor
Heaton Norris
Lancashire Hill
Heaton Mersey
Didsbury
DIDSBURY VILLAGE
EAST DIDSBURY
East Didsbury
Hat Works
STOCKPORT
Edgeley
Cheadle Heath
Edgeley Park Stadium (Stockport County FC)
Shaw Heath
Stockport Cemetery
Heaviley
Cale Green
Mile End
Stockport Great Moor
Adswood
Davenport
Woods Moor
WOODSMOOR
Stepping Hill
HAZEL GROVE
Torkington
SALE
Ashton upon Mersey
BROOKLANDS
Brooklands
Northern Moor
Northenden
Wythenshawe Park
Wythenshawe Hall
TIMPERLEY
Timperley
Broadheath
Altrincham
NAVIGATION RD
Oldfield Brow
ALTRINCHAM
Dunham New Park
Dunham Massey
Dunham Park
Bowdon
Bowgreen
Rosehill
HALE
Ashley Heath
Hale Barns
Warburton Green
Thorns Green
Ashley
ASHLEY
Rostherne Mere
River Bollin
Birkin Brook
Baguley
Roundthorn
Wythenshawe
Newall Green
Benchill
WYTHENSHAWE
Sharston
GATLEY
Wythenshawe Centre
Woodhouse Park
Peel Hall
Well Green
Davenport Green
Painswick Park
MANCHESTER AIRPORT
Moss Nook
Styal
HEALD GREEN
Heald Green
Stanley Green
CHEADLE
Micker Brook
Bruntwood Park
Cheadle Royal
CHEADLE HULME
Bramhall Park
Bramall Hall
Bramhall Green
Bramhall Moor
Smithy Green
Gilbent
Carr Wood Park
Pownall Green
Kitt's Moss
BRAMHALL
Norbury Moor
Serpentine Wood
Poynton Pool
Poynton Brook
Lady Brook
River Goyt
River Tame

Smallburn
Carr Plantation
Ponteland
A696
PONTELAND ROAD
Dinnington
Big Waters
Seaton Burn
DUDLEY
Annitsford
Seghill
Fordley
A190
A19
A1
Wideopen
Brunswick Village
Weetslade Country Park
Burradon
Camperdown
Prestwick
NEWCASTLE INTERNATIONAL AIRPORT
AIRPORT
Darras Hall
Hazlerigg
SANDY LANE
K'WORTH WAY
Killingworth
High Callerton
CALLERTON PARKWAY
Woolsington Park
Newcastle
High Gosforth Park
Black Callerton
Brunton Park
Melton Park
West Moor
Forest Hall
Palmersville
Woolsington
Newcastle Great Park
Gosforth Lake
Kingston Park Stadium (Newcastle Falcons RFC)
Red House Farm
North Tyne Industrial Estate
Kingston Park
KINGSTON PARK
Fawdon
LONGBENTON
Benton
Kenton Bankfoot
BANK FOOT
FAWDON
WANSBECK ROAD
REGENT CENTRE
P+R
BENTON
FOUR LANE ENDS
LONGBENTON
Lowbiggin
Gosforth
St Nicholas
Newbiggin Hall Estate
Kenton
SOUTH GOSFORTH
Sanderson
Freeman
High Heaton
ILFORD ROAD
Throckley
Westerhope
Dukes Moor
West Denton
Cowgate
Nuns Moor
West Jesmond
WEST JESMOND
Jesmond
Bigges Main
A167
Blakelaw
Walkerville
Walbottle
East Denton
Northumberland CCC
A1058
Walkergate
Branding Village
WALKERGATE
Newburn Hall Motor Museum
Knop Law
A69
Denton Hall Turret
West Road
JESMOND
Heaton Park
CHILLINGHAM ROAD
Fenham
Spital Tongues
Royal Victoria Infirmary
A167(M)
Heaton
Newburn
Lemington
Denton Burn
HAYMARKET
Shieldfield
Holburn Dene
Benwell
Benwell Roman Temple
Newcastle General
ST JAMES
BYKER
Walker
RYTON
Hedgefield
Stella
Scotswood
Old Benwell
Arthur's Hill
MONUMENT
MANORS
Battle Field
Byker
Crookhill
NEWCASTLE UPON TYNE
Bessie Surtees House
Delaval
Blaydon Haugh
Stargate
BLAYDON
South Benwell
Elswick
NEWCASTLE CENTRAL
East Gateshead
St Peter's
St Anthony's
BLAYDON
Shibdon Pond Nature Reserve
River Tyne
GATESHEAD
GATESHEAD
Gateshead Stadium
Riverside Park
Felling Shore
Blaydon Burn
METROCENTRE (GATESHEAD)
Metro Centre
New Metroland
Gateshead International Stadium
Axwell Park
Dunston
A184
Winlaton
Bog Wood
Teams
Mount Pleasant
Felling
Swalwell
Shipcote
Beechgrove
DUNSTON
Derwent Walk Country Park & Derwenthaugh Park
Bensham
Deckham
Heworth
Winlaton Mill
Dunston Hill
Saltwell
Saltwell Park
Carr Hill
WHICKHAM
Windy Nook
Queen Elizabeth
Sheriff Hill
Fellside
Lobley Hill
Saltwell
Low Fell
Whitehills
Cockburn Wood
Team Valley
Beacon Lough
A692
Snipes Dene Wood
Hill Head Wood
Sunniside
Lyndhurst
Wrekenton
Bowes Railway
Chowdene
Springwell
Highfield
Rowlands Gill
SUNNISIDE
High Park Wood
Harlow Green
Allerdene
Angel of the North
Gibside
Blackman's Wood
Ladypark
Eighton Banks
West Wood
Scaife's Wood
Old Ravensworth
Bryan's Leap
ANDREWS HOUSE
High Friarside
Leazes
Burnopfield
Tanfield Railway
Birtley
North Side
WASHINGTON
Kibblesworth
Beckley Wood
Lintz
Crookgate Bank
Birtley
Hobson
A692
CAUSEY ARCH
Causey Arch
Tanfield
Portobello
Ayton
Washington
Mill Wood
Urpeth
Vigo
Ewehurst Wood
EAST TANFIELD
Mountsett
Beamish Wild
Tantoble
Tanfield Lea
Carrickshill Wood
Beamish Open Air
Ouston
Barley Mow
Flint Hill
Kip Hill
Hellhole Wood
The Haughs
Rickleton
Dipton
Broom Hill
Shield Row
Perkinsville
A1(M)
Cockshot Hill
High Handenhold
Pelton
A693
STANLEY
West
2 miles

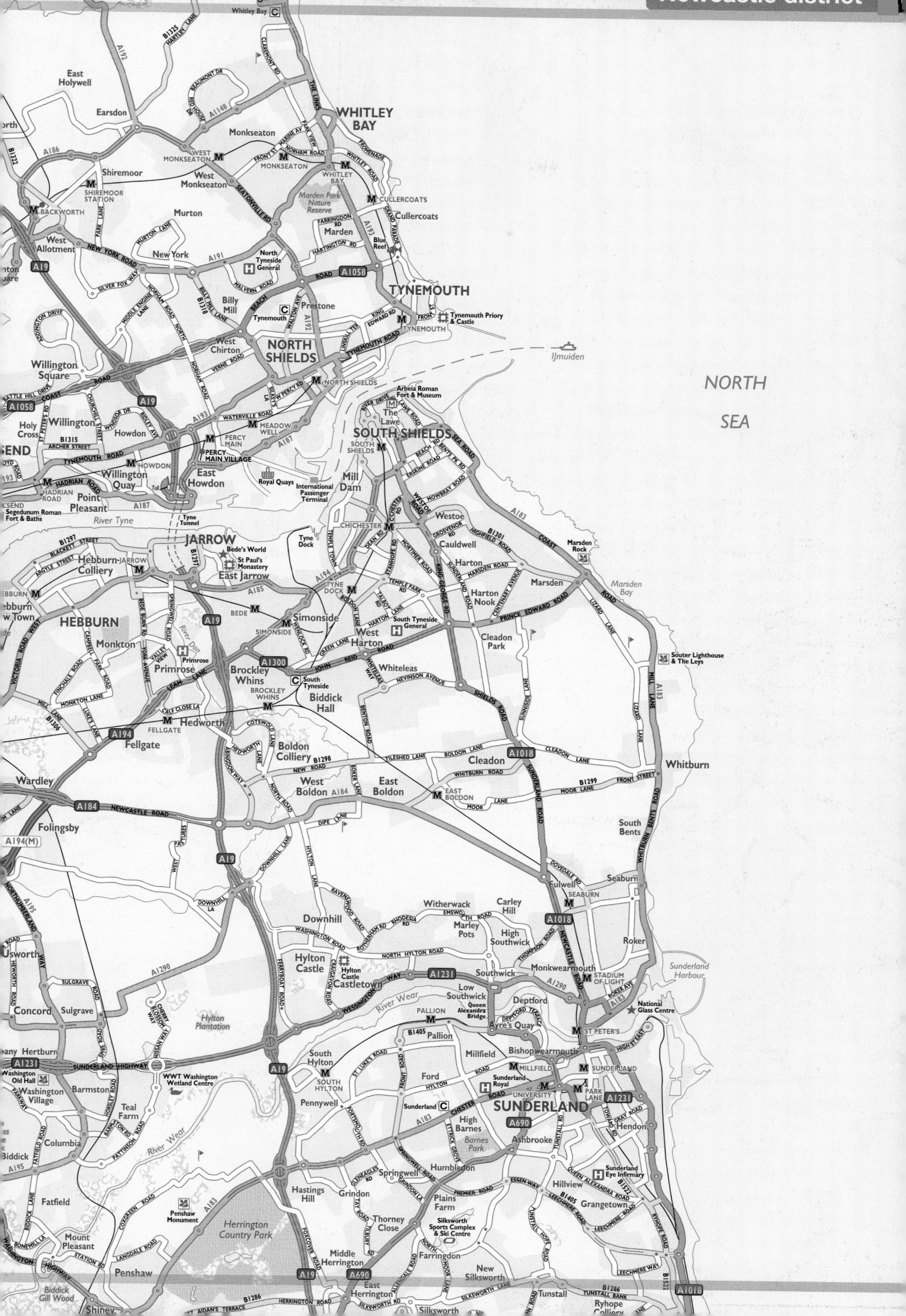

Whitley Bay C
B1325 HARTLEY LANE
A192
CLAREMONT RD
East Holywell
BEAUMONT DR
RED HOUSE DR
A1148
THE LINKS
Earsdon
WHITLEY BAY
Monkseaton
PARK VIEW
MARINE AV
A186
B1322
WEST MONKSEATON M
FRONT ST
NORHAM ROAD
PROMENADE
M MONKSEATON
M WHITLEY BAY
WHITLEY ROAD
Shiremoor
West Monkseaton
SEATONVILLE RD
M SHIREMOOR STATION
Marden Park Nature Reserve
M CULLERCOATS
M BACKWORTH
PARK LANE
Murton
FARRINGDON RD
GRAND PARADE
Cullercoats
MURTON LANE
Marden
A193
West Allotment
NEW YORK ROAD
HARTINGTON RD
Blue Reef
New York
A191
North Tyneside General H
A19
SILVER FOX WAY
MALVERN ROAD
ROAD A1058
TYNEMOUTH
NORHAM ROAD
B1318
BILLY MILL LANE
Billy Mill
BEACH
C Tynemouth
WALTON AVE
Prestone
A192
KING EDWARD RD
M
FRONT ST
Tynemouth Priory & Castle
TYNEMOUTH
MIDDLE ENGINE LANE
ADDINGTON DRIVE
NORTH ROAD
West Chirton
VERNE ROAD
NORTH SHIELDS
LINSKILL TER
TYNEMOUTH ROAD
IJmuiden
NORTH SEA
Willington Square
NORHAM ROAD
ROAD
M NORTH SHIELDS
Arbeia Roman Fort & Museum
BATTLE HILL DRIVE
COAST
A1058
A19
SILKEY'S LA
NEW PERCY RD
RIVER DRIVE
M
The Lawe
LAWE ROAD
Holy Cross
Willington
CHURCHILL STREET
WINDSOR DR
RIDLEY AVE
Howdon
A193
WATERVILLE ROAD
M MEADOW WELL
ST PETER'S RD
B1315
ARCHER STREET
M PERCY MAIN
A187
SOUTH SHIELDS
SEA ROAD
SOUTH SHIELDS M
BEACH RD
BENTS PK RD
WALLSEND
TYNEMOUTH ROAD
PERCY MAIN VILLAGE
M HOWDON
ERSKINE ROAD
Willington Quay
East Howdon
Royal Quays
International Passenger Terminal
Mill Dam
MOWBRAY ROAD
M HADRIAN ROAD
HADRIAN ROAD
Point Pleasant
Toll
A187
WESTOE ROAD
A183
WALLSEND Segedunum Roman Fort & Baths
River Tyne
Tyne Tunnel
CHICHESTER M
CHICHESTER RD
Westoe
COAST
Marsden Rock
GROSVENOR RD
B1301 HIGHFIELD ROAD
B1297
BLACKETT STREET
JARROW
Bede's World
Tyne Dock
DEAN RD
STANHOPE RD
MORTIMER ROAD
Cauldwell
ARGYLE STREET
Hebburn-Colliery
M JARROW
St Paul's Monastery
B1297
East Jarrow
TEMPLE TOWN
A194
TYNE DOCK M
KING GEORGE RD
SUNDERLAND ROAD
Harton
MARSDEN ROAD
CENTENARY AVENUE
Marsden
ROAD
Marsden Bay
M HEBBURN
Hebburn New Town
A185
TEMPLE PARK RD
Harton Nook
PRINCE EDWARD ROAD
LIZARD LANE
BEDE M
HEBBURN
VICTORIA ROAD WEST
BEDE BURN RD
SPRINGWELL ROAD
A19
M Simonside
SIMONSIDE
TALBOT RD
HARTON LANE
BOLDON LANE
South Tyneside General H
West Harton
ROAD
Cleadon Park
Monkton
River Don
WENLOCK RD
GREEN LANE
CAMPBELL PARK ROAD
YORK AVENUE
VALLEY VIEW
H Primrose
Primrose
A1300
JOHN REID ROAD
WHITELEAS WAY
Whiteleas
Souter Lighthouse & The Leys
FINCHALE ROAD
LEAM LANE
Brockley Whins
C South Tyneside
NEVINSON AVENUE
MILL LANE
A183
MONKTON LANE
BROCKLEY WHINS M
Biddick Hall
SHIELDS ROAD
SUNNISIDE LANE
MILL LANE
B1306
LUKES LANE
CALF CLOSE LA
M Hedworth
FELLGATE
A194
Fellgate
COTSWOLD LANE
HEDWORTH LANE
Boldon Colliery
BENTON ROAD
TILESHED LANE
BOLDON LANE
A1018
CLEADON LANE
LIZARD LANE
Cleadon
Whitburn
B1298
NEW ROAD
BOKER LANE
WHITBURN ROAD
B1299
FRONT STREET
ABINGDON WAY
West Boldon
A184
East Boldon
M EAST BOLDON
MOOR LANE
LANE
MOOR
SUNDERLAND ROAD
Wardley
NORTH ROAD
WHITBURN BENTS ROAD
A184
NEWCASTLE ROAD
DIPE LANE
South Bents
Folingsby
A194(M)
WEST PASTURES
A19
DOWNHILL LANE
HYLTON LANE
DOVEDALE RD
Seaburn
Fulwell
SEABURN M
NORTHUMBERLAND WAY
A195
DOWNHILL LA
RAVENSWOOD ROAD
Witherwack
EHSWORTH ROAD
Carley Hill
Downhill
ROTHERHAM RD
RHODESIA RD
A1018
Marley Pots
High Southwick
THOMPSON ROAD
NEWCASTLE ROAD
Roker
WASHINGTON ROAD
Usworth
NORTH HYLTON ROAD
HEWORTH ROAD
Hylton Castle
Monkwearmouth
Sunderland Harbour
A1290
FERRYBOAT ROAD
Hylton Castle
CRAIGAVON ROAD
WAY A1231
Southwick
M STADIUM OF LIGHT
SULGRAVE ROAD
Castletown
A1290
ROKER AVE
A183
Low Southwick
Deptford
Concord
Sulgrave
CHERRY BLOSSOM WAY
Hylton Plantation
WESSINGTON WAY
River Wear
Queen Alexandra Bridge
DEPTFORD TERRACE
National Glass Centre
SPRING LANE
PALLION M
Ayre's Quay
M ST PETER'S
NISSAN WAY
B1405 Pallion
Bishopwearmouth
HIGH ST EAST
Albany
Herrburn
South Hylton
ST LUKE'S ROAD
FRONT ROAD
Millfield
A1231
SUNDERLAND HIGHWAY
A19
M MILLFIELD
M SUNDERLAND
Washington Old Hall
WWT Washington Wetland Centre
M SOUTH HYLTON
Ford
ROAD
Sunderland Royal H
Washington Village
Barmston
HORSLEY ROAD
HYLTON
M UNIVERSITY
M PARK LANE
PARKWAY
Pennywell
Sunderland C
CHESTER ROAD
A1231
SUNDERLAND
Teal Farm
PORTSMOUTH RD
A183
High Barnes
A690
TUNSTALL RD
TOWARD RD
GRAY ROAD
Hendon
BARMSTON RD
Barnes Park
Ashbrooke
ETTRICK GROVE
FATFIELD ROAD
Columbia
PATTINSON ROAD
River Wear
Biddick
A195
SPRINGWELL ROAD
Humbledon
Sunderland Eye Infirmary H
GLENEAGLES RD
Springwell
GRINDON LA
QUEEN ALEXANDRA ROAD
B1522
Hastings Hill
Grindon
ESSEN WAY
Hillview
PREMIER ROAD
Fatfield
COXGREEN ROAD
B1405 Grangetown
Plains Farm
LEECHMERE ROAD
BIDDICK LANE
Penshaw Monument
A183
TAY ROAD
TUNSTALL HOPE ROAD
LEECHMERE ROAD
RYHOPE ROAD
Thorney Close
TILBURY RD
Silksworth Sports Complex & Ski Centre
Herrington Country Park
Mount Pleasant
BONEMILL LA
WASHINGTON HIGHWAY
STATION RD
LANGDALE ROAD
FOXCOVER ROAD
Middle Herrington
NORTH MOOR LANE
Farringdon
New Silksworth
LEECHMERE WAY
Penshaw
A19
A690
ALLENDALE ROAD
B1522
B1286
A1018
Biddick Gill Wood
East Herrington
SILKSWORTH LANE
ROAD
Tunstall
TUNSTALL BANK
B1286
HERRINGTON ROAD
Shiney Row
ST AIDAN'S TERRACE
SILKSWORTH RD
Silksworth
Ryhope Colliery

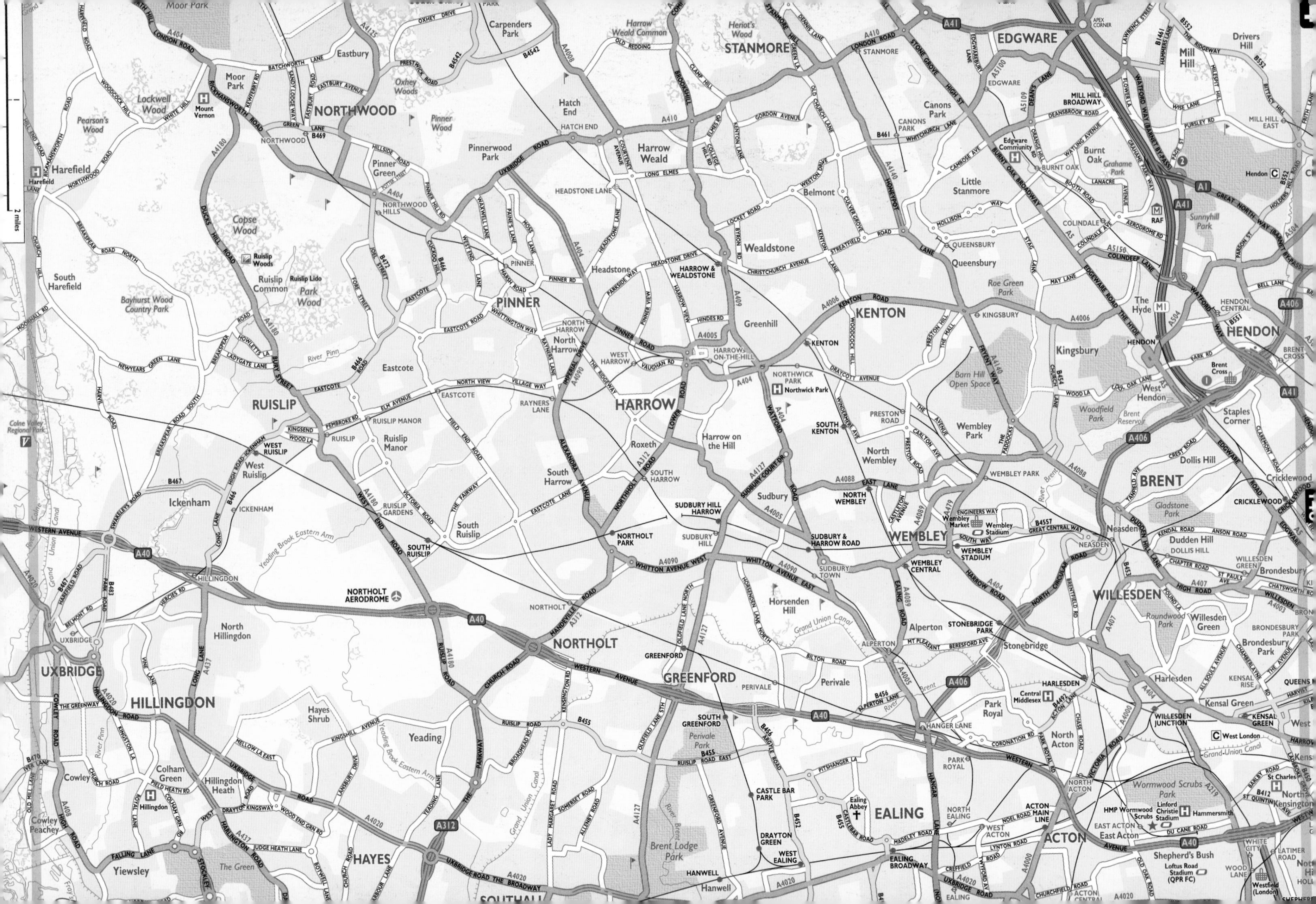

EDGWARE
Mill Hill
Drivers Hill
Burnt Oak
Colindale
Little Stanmore
Canons Park
STANMORE
Queensbury
Kingsbury
HENDON
Brent Cross
West Hendon
Staples Corner
Dollis Hill
BRENT
Cricklewood
Neasden
Dudden Hill
WILLESDEN
Willesden Green
Brondesbury
Harlesden
Kensal Green
KENTON
Wembley Park
North Wembley
WEMBLEY
Sudbury
Alperton
Stonebridge
Park Royal
North Acton
ACTON
East Acton
Shepherd's Bush
EALING
Perivale
Greenhill
Wealdstone
Belmont
Harrow Weald
Hatch End
HARROW
Harrow on the Hill
Roxeth
South Harrow
Headstone
North Harrow
PINNER
Pinnerwood Park
Carpenders Park
Eastbury
NORTHWOOD
Pinner Green
Moor Park
Eastcote
Ruislip Manor
RUISLIP
West Ruislip
South Ruislip
NORTHOLT
GREENFORD
Yeading
HAYES
Hanwell
Ickenham
North Hillingdon
HILLINGDON
Hillingdon Heath
UXBRIDGE
Colham Green
Yiewsley
Cowley
Cowley Peachey
Harefield
South Harefield
NORTHOLT AERODROME
2 miles

HAMMERSMITH
PUTNEY
WIMBLEDON
Barnes
Chiswick
Mortlake
East Sheen
Roehampton
Richmond Park
Wimbledon Common
Kingston Vale
Coombe
New Malden
RICHMOND UPON THAMES
KINGSTON UPON THAMES
SURBITON
Brentford
Syon Park
Old Deer Park
Isleworth
HOUNSLOW
TWICKENHAM
Teddington
Petersham
Ham
Bushy Park
Hampton Court Park
Hampton
Hanworth
FELTHAM
Hounslow Heath
Osterley Park
Heston
Cranford
Harlington
Hatton
HEATHROW AIRPORT
Sipson
Harmondsworth
Stanwell
East Bedfont
West Bedfont
Ashford
Sunbury-on-Thames
Lower Sunbury
Upper Halliford
Shepperton
Littleton
Laleham
Charlton
Queen Mary Reservoir
East Molesey
West Molesey
Thames Ditton
Chertsey

Central London Congestion Charging Zone
2 miles
3 kilometres
WOODFORD GREEN
REDBRIDGE
ILFORD
WALTHAM FOREST
WALTHAMSTOW
HARINGEY
TOTTENHAM
HACKNEY
NEWHAM
TOWER HAMLETS
ISLINGTON
CITY
CAMDEN
HAMPSTEAD
FINCHLEY
Stratford
Leyton
Leytonstone
Wanstead
Forest Gate
West Ham
Plaistow
Canning Town
Poplar
Stepney
Bethnal Green
Shoreditch
Hoxton
Dalston
Stoke Newington
Finsbury Park
Highbury
Kentish Town
Highgate
Hornsey
Crouch End
Muswell Hill
Wood Green
Upper Edmonton
East Finchley
Golders Green
West Hampstead
Kilburn
St John's Wood
Paddington
Bloomsbury
Holborn
Clerkenwell
Regent's Park
Hyde Park
LONDON CITY AIRPORT

144

LAMBETH
Imperial War
Bermondsey
Southwark Park
Surrey Quays
Greenwich Reach
Mudchute
Island Gardens
Cruise Terminal
New Charlton
Thames Barrier
WOOLWICH
Woolwich Dockyard
Kensington Olympia
West Kensington
Brompton
Belgravia
Victoria
Westminster Cathedral
South Kensington
CHELSEA
Pimlico
Vauxhall
Walworth
Newington
Kennington
For Central London see pages 148–157
South Bermondsey
Deptford
GREENWICH
Cutty Sark
Old Royal Naval College
Royal Observatory
Greenwich Park
Charlton
Queen Elizabeth
Woolwich Common
FULHAM
Parsons Green
Battersea Park
Nine Elms
South Lambeth
SOUTHWARK
Peckham
New Cross
St Johns
LEWISHAM
Blackheath
Blackheath Park
Kidbrooke
Sands End
River Thames
CLAPHAM
Stockwell
Camberwell
King's College
Ruskin Park
Nunhead
Brockley
Eltham
Putney
Wandsworth Town
WANDSWORTH
Battersea
Clapham Junction
Clapham Common
HMP Brixton
Brixton
Herne Hill
East Dulwich
Peckham Rye Park
Honor Oak
Ladywell
Hither Green
Lee
Eltham Palace
Southfields
Wandsworth Common
Clapham Park
Balham
Brockwell Park
Tulse Hill
Dulwich Village
Forest Hill
CATFORD
Mottingham
Wimbledon Park
Earlsfield
Upper Tooting
Streatham Hill
West Dulwich
Sydenham Hill Wood
Dulwich Wood
Bellingham
Grove Park
Summerstown
Tooting Bec Common
West Norwood
Upper Sydenham
Lower Sydenham
Bell Green
Downham
Tooting
Streatham Park
STREATHAM
Crystal Palace Park
Sydenham
Plaistow
Elmstead Wood
WIMBLEDON
South Wimbledon
Furzedown
Norwood New Town
New Beckenham
Beckenham Place Park
Elmstead
Colliers Wood
Streatham Vale
Norbury
Upper Norwood
Penge
BECKENHAM
Sundridge
Chislehurst
MERTON
Merton Park
MITCHAM
Thornton Heath
South Norwood
Elmers End
BROMLEY
Widmore
Shortlands
Bickley
Morden
Morden Hall Park
Mitcham Common
Croydon
Selhurst
South Norwood Country Park
Eden Park
Park Langley
Southborough
St Helier
Beddington Corner
Woodside
Monks Orchard
West Wickham
Hayes
Bromley Common
River Wandle

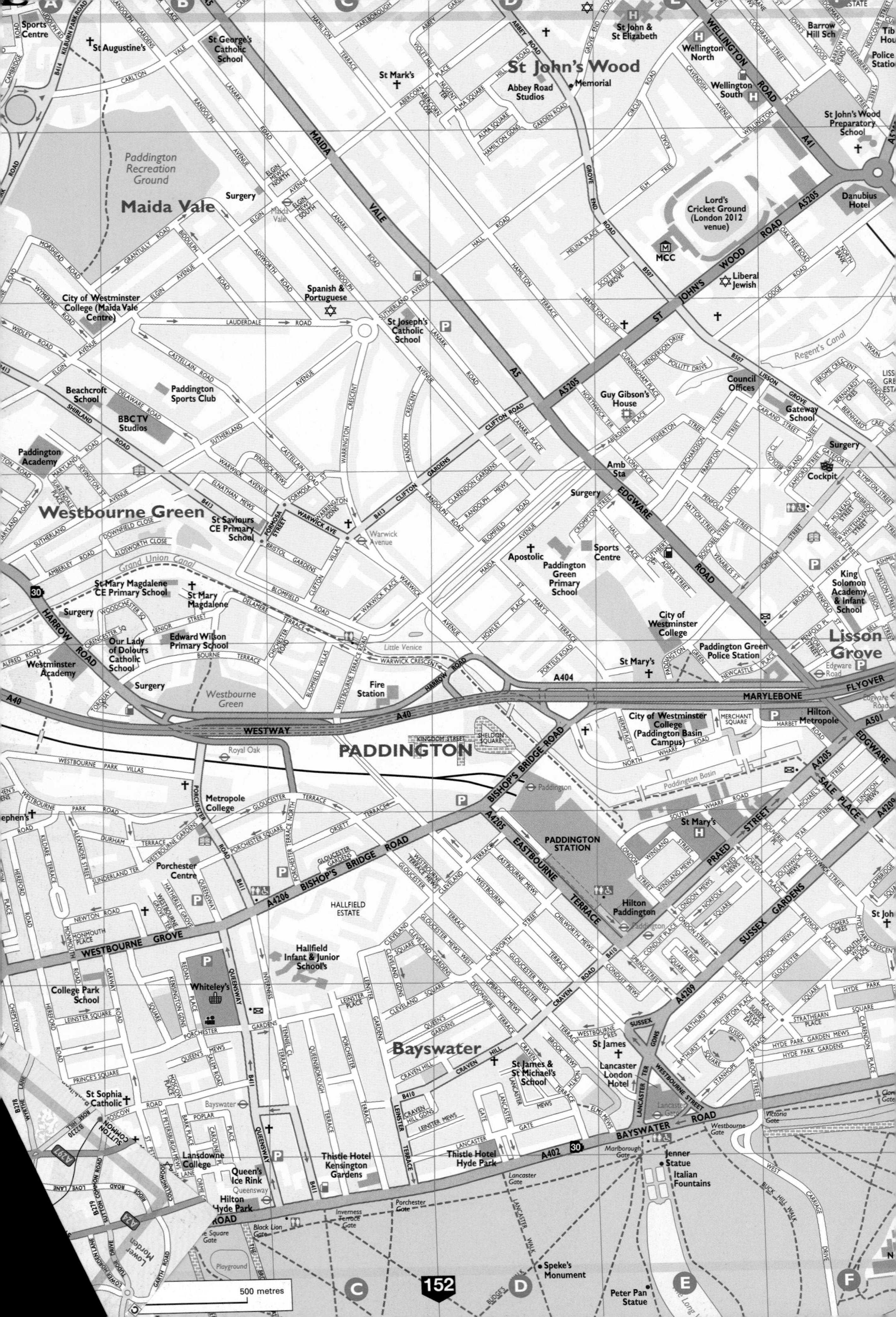
St John's Wood
Maida Vale
Westbourne Green
PADDINGTON
Bayswater
Lisson Grove
Sports Centre
St Augustine's
St George's Catholic School
St Mark's
Abbey Road Studios
Memorial
St John & St Elizabeth
Wellington North
Wellington South
Barrow Hill Sch
St John's Wood Preparatory School
Danubius Hotel
Lord's Cricket Ground (London 2012 venue)
MCC
Liberal Jewish
Paddington Recreation Ground
Surgery
Spanish & Portuguese
St Joseph's Catholic School
City of Westminster College (Maida Vale Centre)
Beachcroft School
Paddington Sports Club
BBC TV Studios
Paddington Academy
Council Offices
Guy Gibson's House
Gateway School
Cockpit
Amb Sta
St Saviours CE Primary School
Warwick Avenue
Apostolic
Paddington Green Primary School
Sports Centre
King Solomon Academy & Infant School
St Mary Magdalene CE Primary School
St Mary Magdalene
Edward Wilson Primary School
Our Lady of Dolours Catholic School
Westminster Academy
City of Westminster College
Paddington Green Police Station
St Mary's
Edgware Road
Little Venice
Fire Station
Westbourne Green
WESTWAY
MARYLEBONE
FLYOVER
City of Westminster College (Paddington Basin Campus)
Hilton Metropole
Royal Oak
Paddington Basin
Paddington
Metropole College
St Mary's
PADDINGTON STATION
Porchester Centre
HALLFIELD ESTATE
Hilton Paddington
Hallfield Infant & Junior School's
College Park School
Whiteley's
St James
St James & St Michael's School
Lancaster London Hotel
St Sophia Catholic
Bayswater
Lansdowne College
Queen's Ice Rink
Queensway
Hilton Hyde Park
Thistle Hotel Kensington Gardens
Thistle Hotel Hyde Park
Lancaster Gate
Marlborough Gate
Jenner Statue
Italian Fountains
Victoria Gate
Westbourne Gate
Porchester Gate
Inverness Terrace Gate
Black Lion Gate
Playground
Speke's Monument
Peter Pan Statue
500 metres
MAIDA VALE
EDGWARE ROAD
ST JOHN'S WOOD ROAD
WELLINGTON ROAD
BISHOP'S BRIDGE ROAD
HARROW ROAD
WESTBOURNE GROVE
QUEENSWAY
EASTBOURNE TERRACE
PRAED STREET
SUSSEX GARDENS
BAYSWATER ROAD
CLIFTON GARDENS
WARWICK AVE
A5
A40
A41
A404
A402
A4205
A4206
A4209
A5205
A501
B413
B507
B410
B411
30
152

Regent's Park
The Hub
Regent's Park Barracks
Winfield House
St John's Lodge
Open-air
Queen Mary's Gardens
Inner Circle
Capel Manor College
Chester Road
The Holme
Boating Lake
Royal College of Obstetricians & Gynaecologists
London Business School
Regent's College
Tennis Centre
Hanover Gate
London Central
Cumberland Gate
Christ Church School
St George's Cathedral
Allotments
Regent's Park Estate
Netley Primary School
Police Station
Schafer House
Royal College of Physicians
HMRC
Outer Circle
Park Square Gardens
Park Crescent
Great Portland Street
Royal National Orthopaedic
Fitzroy Square
Park Road
Francis Holland CE School
Sherlock Holmes'
Baker Street
Lost Property Office
Madame Tussauds
Royal Academy of Music
The Clinic
Marylebone Station
Travelodge
Landmark Hotel
Princess Grace
St Marylebone CE School
University of Westminster
Sherlock Holmes Hotel
Holiday Inn
Fitzrovia
Marylebone Road
Clinic
Western Eye
City of Westminster Courts
St Mary's CE Primary School
St Mary's
University College London
Heart
YHA
University of Westminster
Gloucester Place
York St
Paddington Street
Seymour Leisure Centre
Embassy of Switzerland
Sylvia Young Theatre School
Hampden Gurney CE Primary Sch
Fire Station
St Marylebone CE School
MARYLEBONE
Marylebone Hotel
Queen's College
Durrants Hotel
Wallace Collection
DLD College
Langham Hotel
College of Naturopathic Medicine
University of Westminster
Radisson Portman
School of Economic Science
University of Westminster
Royal College of Nursing
Animation Art Gal
London College of Fashion
Portman Sq
Churchill Hyatt Regency
Wigmore Street
Cavendish Sq
Edgware Road
Marylebone Police Station
Selfridges
Radisson Hotel
Oxford Street
London Palladium
Seymour St
Thistle Hotel
Cumberland Hotel
Marble Arch
Bond Street
Liberty
Tyburn Convent
Statue
Bayswater Road
Cumberland Gate
Speakers' Corner
West London College
Marriott Hotel
Claridges
Argentine Embassy
Italian Embassy
Canadian Embassy
Westbury Hotel
Police Station
Park Lane
Monument
US Embassy
Millennium Hotel
Connaught Hotel
Mayfair
Brook Gate
Grosvenor Gate
New Lodge
Grosvenor Chapel
St George's School
Berkeley Square
The Lookout
The Dorchester
May Fair Hotel
153

Somers Town
SOMERSTOWN ESTATE
Sports Centre
Edith Neville School
St Aloysius School
SS Mary & Pancras School
Maria Fidelis Convent School (Upper)
EVERSHOLT STREET
ST PANCRAS INTERNATIONAL STATION
KING'S CROSS STATION
Under development
Great Northern Hotel
King's Cross St Pancras
Premier Inn
CALEDONIA STREET
CALEDONIAN ROAD
Pentonville
PENTONVILLE ROAD
The British Library
St Pancras Renaissance Hotel
Camden Town Hall
St Pancras Camden Centre
Shaw
Novotel
EUSTON ROAD
EUSTON STATION
Thistle Hotel
Ibis
Travelodge
Fire Station
Premier Inn
Argyle School
St Pancras
Royal National Throat, Nose & Ear
Nuffield
Water Rats
SWINTON STREET
ACTON STREET
KING'S CROSS ROAD
GRAY'S INN ROAD
Peel Centre
University of London
Police Station
Travelodge
Clerkenwell
RNIB
Ambassadors Hotel
Friends House
Meeting House
Hilton London Euston
County Hotel
BMA House
Westminster Kingsway College
Health Centre
University of London
Foundling
Coram's Fields
Brunswick Square Gardens
Holiday Inn
Children's Society
Eastman Dental
London Welsh Centre
Goodenough College
Mount Pleasant (Royal Mail)
Wellcome Collection
University College
UCL
Bloomsbury (UCL)
Inst of Archaeology
Gandhi Memorial
Ambulance Station
Tavistock Hotel
Brunswick Centre
Chinese Art Gallery
University College London (UCL)
Royal Hotel National
Holiday Inn
Dickens
Christopher Hatton School
Petrie
Warburg Institute
Inst of Education (UCL)
School of Oriental & African Studies
Inst of Advanced Legal Studies
Hotel Russell
Hotel President
Royal London Hospital for Integrated Medicine
Great Ormond Street
St George the Martyr School
University of London
RADA
Birkbeck College
Brunei Gallery
Bloomsbury
Imperial Hotel
Language Centre
Italian
Police Station
Gray's Inn Gardens
School of Hygiene & Tropical Medicine
Senate House & Library (UCL)
Bedford Hotel
Park Inn Hotel
THEOBALD'S ROAD
Cavendish College
College of Law
Courtauld Institute Bio-chemistry
British Museum
Grange Holborn Hotel
October Gallery
City Law School
British Transport Police Station
University of London
Finnish Institute
Principal Registry
TOTTENHAM COURT ROAD
GOWER STREET
Radisson Edwardian Bloomsbury
Cartoon
HIGH HOLBORN
BLOOMSBURY WAY
Holborn
University of Westminster
YMCA
St Giles Hotel
Dominion
Bloomsbury Hotel
Berners Hotel
NEW OXFORD STREET
Dragon Hall
Sir John Soane's
Lincoln's Inn
Lincoln's Inn Fields
The Plaza
100 Club
OXFORD STREET
French Protestant
St Patrick's College
St Patrick's RC
Shaftesbury
St Giles
Travelodge
St Joseph's RC Primary School
Sports Centre
St Giles in the Fields
New London
City Lit
Civil Aviation Authority
LSE
Old Curiosity Shop
Royal College of Surgeons
Surgery
The Borderline
Phoenix
Youth Hostel
Central St Martin's College of Art & Design
Thomas Neal's
Peacock
London School of Economics (LSE)
The Royal Courts of Justice
Soho
Soho Hotel
Prince Edward
Ronnie Scott's
Cambridge
Ambassador
Fortune
Theatre Royal
St Clement Danes CE School
Aldwych
ALDWYCH
Australia House
St Clement Danes
Bush House
Royal Opera House
Waldorf Hotel
Novello
India House
HMRC
St Mary le Strand
Westminster Kingsway Coll
Best Western
Madame Jo Jo's
Palace
Fire Station
St Martin's
Covent Garden
London Transport
Jubilee Market Hall
St Anne's
Queen's
Soho Parish Sch
Gielgud
Apollo
Chinatown
Hippodrome
Leicester Square
Empire
Noel Coward
St Paul's
Strand
Duchess
Lyceum
Gibraltar House
Kings College
The Howard Hotel
Temple
Somerset House
Lyric
London Trocadero
Wyndhams
Odeon
Meeting House
Vaudeville
Prince of Wales
Radisson Edwardian
Capital Radio
Duke of York's
Garrick
Coliseum
Adelphi
Police Station
Savoy Hotel
Inst of Engineering & Technology
Royal Academy of Arts
Comedy
Royal Trafalgar Hotel
National Portrait Gallery
St Martin in the Fields
Theatre Royal Haymarket
Haymarket Hotel
The National Gallery
Trafalgar Square
Canada House
South African High Commission
Nelson's Column
Cleopatra's Needle
Victoria Embankment Gardens
Waterloo Bridge
Bandstand
Embankment
National
PICCADILLY
STRAND
CHARING CROSS ROAD
SHAFTESBURY AVENUE
KINGSWAY
VICTORIA EMBANKMENT
500 metres
154

Crafts Council
Old Red Lion
City & Islington 6th Form College
St Mark's
Sadler's Wells
FINSBURY
Hugh Myddelton Primary School
Tribunal Service
FINSBURY ESTATE
Youth Centre
Clerkenwell
Osteopathic Centre for Children
University of London
Holborn
St Ethelreda's Convent School
HOLBORN CIRCUS
CITY ROAD
GOSWELL ROAD
A501
A1
Industrial Estate
Boat Club
City Road Basin
Moreland Primary School
King's Square Gardens
City University
Community Centre
St Peter & St Paul RC Primary School
Dallington School
Sports Centre
County Court
Thistle Hotel
Dental Centre
Community Centre
Leisure Centre
LSO St Luke's
London School of Business Management
St Luke's
Willen House
City University
Moorfields Eye
Inst of Ophthalmology
St Luke's Prim Sch
Post Office HQ
Police Station
Regent's Vocational College
City College
Surgery
St John CE Primary Sch
Tennis Courts
Fire Station
SHOREDI
OLD STREET STATION
Central Foundation Boys School
Wesley House
Travelodge
Meeting House
Bunhill Fields Burial Ground
Armoury House
YMCA
Cass Business School
College of Law
Golden Lane Campus
Richard Cloudesley School
Barts & The London School of Medicine & Dentistry
Charterhouse
YMCA
Order of St John
Goldsmiths' Centre
FARRINGDON STATION
The Rookery Hotel
Barbican
Smithfield Market
Smithfield Market
The Barbican
Guildhall School of Music & Dance
City of London School for Girls
BARBICAN ESTATE
Museum of London
MOORGATE STATION
London Metropolitan University
LONDON WALL
St Bartholomew's
Police Station
CITY THAMESLINK STATION
Central Criminal Courts
London Stock Exchange
British Telecom Centre
Police Station
The Chartered Insurance Inst
Clockmakers
Guildhall Art Gallery & Roman Amphitheatre
Guildhall & City Business Libraries
The Mayor's & City of London Court
St Lawrence Jewry
ICAEW
Dutch
Tower 42
The Pinnacle (Bishopsgate Tower)
Bank of England
Royal Exchange Building
Wellington Statue
Dr Johnson's House
Shoe Lane
Congregational Memorial Hall
Saddlers Hall
St Paul's Cathedral
St Paul's Cathedral School
One New Change
Bridewell
CITY THAMESLINK STATION
Youth Hostel
The Grange St Paul's Hotel
Memorial
Church of Scientology
St Mary Aldermary
No.1 Poultry
City of London Magistrates' Court
St Mary Woolnoth
Leadenhall Market
Crowne Plaza Hotel
City of London School
BLACKFRIARS STATION
The Mermaid Conference Centre
Salvation Army
Mansion House
CANNON STREET STATION
London Capital Club
St James Garlickhythe
City of London School
CITY OF LONDON
HMS President
Blackfriars Millennium Pier
Blackfriars Bridge
River Thames
Millennium Bridge
New station complete mid 2012
Fire Station
The Monument
St Magnus the Martyr
Southwark Bridge
Bankside Pier
Bankside Gallery
The Oxo Tower
Tate Modern
Shakespeare's Globe
Financial Times
Clink Prison
Golden Hinde
London Bridge
London Bridge
G
H
J
K
L

148
Kensington Gardens
Round Pond
Sunken Gardens
Kensington Palace Green
Kensington Palace
'Time Flies' Clock Tower
Peter Pan Statue
The Long Water
Physical Energy Statue
Serpentine Bridge
Isis Statue
Serpentine Gallery
Diana Princess of Wales Memorial Fountain
The Lido
Bandstand
St Govor's Well
Mount Gate
Tennis Courts
Bowling Green
Prince of Wales Gate
Albert Memorial
Alexandra Gate
Queen's Gate
Palace Gate
THE FLOWER WALK
Embassy of Nepal
Embassy of Russia
Embassy of Lebanon
Romanian Embassy
Israel Embassy
Fire Station
Royal Garden Hotel
St Mary Abbots
St Mary Abbots CE Primary School
Kensington & Chelsea Town Hall
KENSINGTON
High Street Kensington
Milestone Hotel
Heythrop College
Thomas's Day School
KENSINGTON ROAD
KENSINGTON HIGH STREET
KENSINGTON CHURCH STREET
HYDE PARK GATE
KENSINGTON GORE
Royal College of Art
Royal Albert Hall
Royal Geographical Society
Knightsbridge
Royal College of Music
Imperial College London
Science
Natural History
Darwin Centre
Victoria & Albert
The Oratory
Royal College of Art
South Kensington
Health Centre
Baden Powell House
Superstore
Radisson Edwardian
Cromwell
Marriott Hotel
Holiday Inn
Emirates Hotel
Gloucester Road
Institute Francais
Lycée Francais
CROMWELL ROAD
South Kensington
Our Lady of Victories RC Primary School
OLD BROMPTON ROAD
EARL'S COURT ROAD
EARL'S COURT STATION
Earl's Court
St Cuthbert & St Matthais CE Primary School
Bousfield Primary School
THE BOLTONS
Royal Marsden
Royal Cancer
Royal Brompton & Harefield
CHELSEA
Gems Hampshire School
Fire Station
St Luke's
FULHAM ROAD
KING'S ROAD
WEST BROMPTON STATION
West Brompton
Brompton Cemetery
Servite RC Primary School
Chelsea & Westminster
Park Walk Primary School
REDCLIFFE GARDENS
FINBOROUGH ROAD
500 metres

Hyde Park
(London 2012 venue)
Police Station
The Lookout
Boat Hire
Serpentine
Bandstand
Holocaust Memorial Garden
The Dell
Rose Gdn
Memorial
Wellington Memorial
7th July Memorial
The Dorchester Hotel
Hilton Park Lane
Metropolitan Hotel
Intercontinental London Park Lane Hotel
Apsley House & Wellington
Hyde Park Corner
HYDE PARK CNR
Hard Rock Cafe
Athenaeum Hotel
Park Lane Hotel
Japanese Embassy
Limkokwing University
Shepherd Market
Washington Hotel
Holiday Inn
Portland Gallery
The Ritz Hotel
St James's Hotel
Stafford Hotel
Spencer House
Green Park
PICCADILLY
PARK LANE
Royal Artillery Meml
Wellington Arch
DUKE OF WELLINGTON PLACE
CONSTITUTION HILL
Canada Memorial
Queen Victoria Memorial
Buckingham Palace
Buckingham Palace Gardens (private)
Queen's Gallery
BUCKINGHAM GATE
Department for International Development
The Royal Mews
Rubens Hotel
St James
Thistle Hotel
The Goring Hotel
Victoria Palace
Cardinal Place
VICTORIA STREET
Apollo Victoria
St Vincent de Paul School
VICTORIA STATION
Victoria Place
The Grosvenor Hotel
St Peter's Eaton Sq CE Prim Sch
Hesperia London Victoria Hotel
Passport Office
Sports Centre
Premier Inn
BELGRAVE ROAD
The Colonnades
National Audit Office
Victoria Departures
Arrivals
Belgravia
Police Station
St Michael's
Francis Holland School
St Barnabas School
St Barnabas
PIMLICO ROAD
EBURY BRIDGE
Chelsea Barracks Site (area under development)
CHELSEA BRIDGE ROAD
Ranelagh Gardens
Lister
DEPOT
St Gabriels School
GROSVENOR ROAD
Grosvenor Bridge
Chelsea Bridge
River Thames
Battersea Power Station (disused)
Battersea
CHELSEA EMBANKMENT
Chelsea Physic Garden
Cadogan Pier
Christchurch CE Primary School
National Army
Royal Hospital Chelsea
Burton's Court
Chelsea
KING'S ROAD
Saatchi Gallery
DUKE OF YORK SQUARE
LOWER SLOANE STREET
SLOANE SQUARE
Royal Court
Sloane Square
Sloane Sq Hotel
Holy Trinity
Holy Trinity CE Prim Sch
Cadogan Hall
St Thomas More Language College
Holy Trinity CE Primary School
Sussex House School
St Simon Zelotes School
Police Station
Knightsbridge School
Cadogan Hotel
Hill House School
Icelandic Embassy
Danish Embassy
Jumeirah Carlton Tower Hotel
Pakistan High Commission
Jumeirah Lowndes Hotel
Harrods
Fire Station
Knightsbridge
KNIGHTSBRIDGE
Household Cavalry Barracks
Mandarin Oriental Hotel
Kuwait Embassy
French Embassy
Sheraton Park Tower Hotel
The Berkeley Hotel
The Lanesborough Hotel
St Paul's
Luxembourg Embassy
Belgian Embassy
The Halkin Hotel
Mexican Embassy
Turkish Emby
Trinidad & Tobago Emby
Emby of the Syrian Arab Republic
Portuguese Embassy
Malaysian High Comm
Belgrave Square
Ghana High Comm
Austrian Embassy
Royal College of Defence Studies
Irish Emby
Emby of the Côte d'Ivoire
Bahrain Embassy
Serbian Emby
Royal College of Psychiatrists
Brunei High Comm
Norwegian Embassy
German Embassy
Finnish Emby
Spanish Embassy
Hungarian Embassy
Italian Consulate
Bolivian Embassy
St Peter's
Abbey Coll
Diplomat Hotel
Chilean Embassy
SLOANE STREET
EATON SQUARE
ECCLESTON STREET
GROSVENOR PLACE
LOWER GROSVENOR PL
BUCKINGHAM PALACE ROAD
G
H
J
K
L

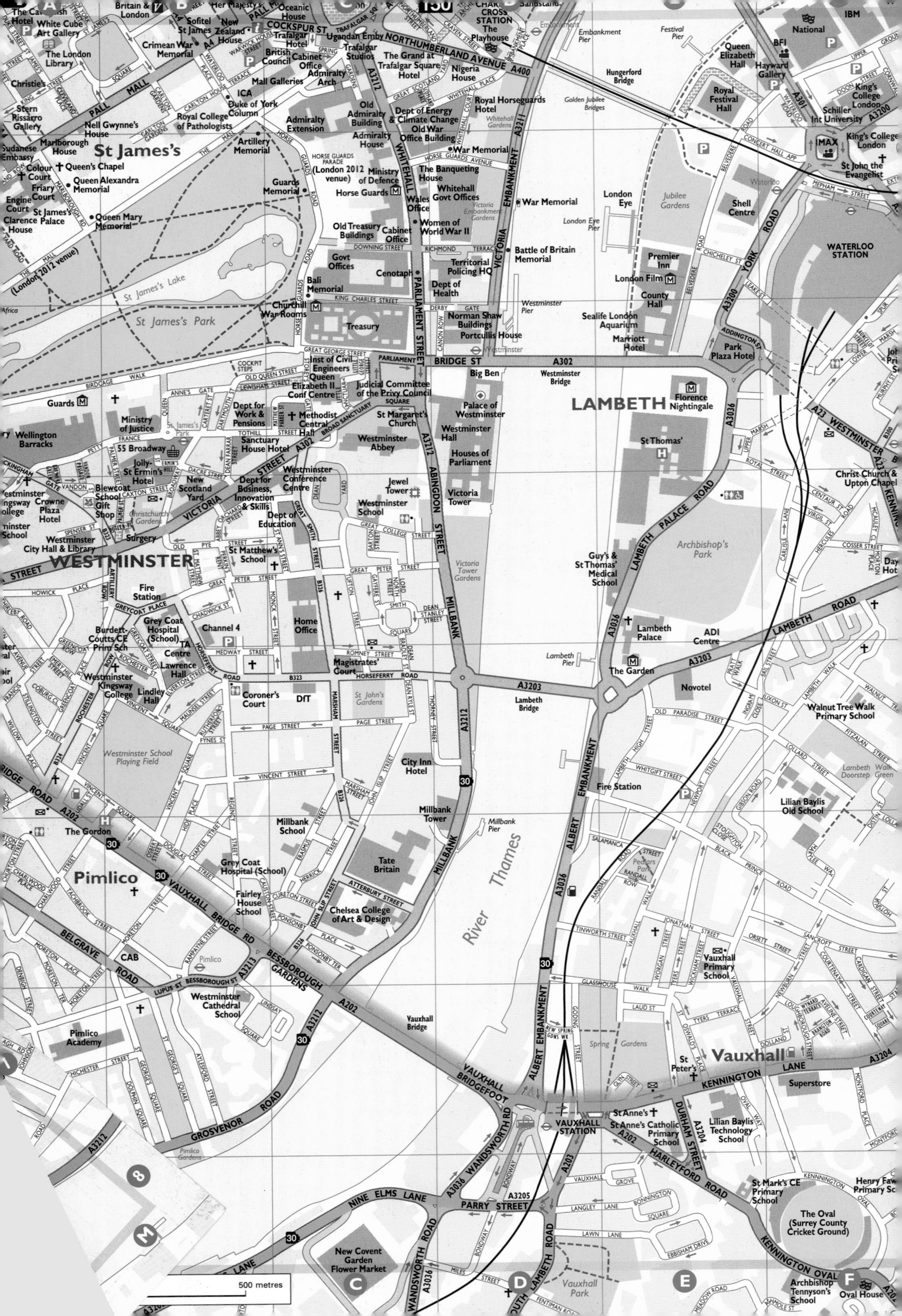

130
St James's
WESTMINSTER
LAMBETH
Pimlico
Vauxhall
River Thames
St James's Park
St James's Lake
Archbishop's Park
Jubilee Gardens
Victoria Tower Gardens
Westminster School Playing Field
Spring Gardens
Vauxhall Park
St John's Gardens
Christchurch Gardens
Pimlico Gardens
WATERLOO STATION
VAUXHALL STATION
CHARING CROSS STATION
The White Cube Art Gallery
The London Library
Christie's
Stern Rissarro Gallery
Sudanese Embassy
Marlborough House
Nell Gwynne's House
Queen's Chapel
Colour Court
Friary Court
Engine Court
Clarence House
St James's Palace
Queen Alexandra Memorial
Queen Mary Memorial
Crimean War Memorial
Sofitel St James
New Zealand House
Royal College of Pathologists
Duke of York Column
ICA
Mall Galleries
Artillery Memorial
British Council
Cabinet Office
Admiralty Arch
Trafalgar Hotel
Trafalgar Studios
Ugandan Emby
The Grand at Trafalgar Square Hotel
Nigeria House
The Playhouse
Oceanic House
Old Admiralty Building
Admiralty Extension
Admiralty House
Dept of Energy & Climate Change
Old War Office Building
Royal Horseguards Hotel
Whitehall Gardens
War Memorial
The Banqueting House
Whitehall Govt Offices
Ministry of Defence
Horse Guards
Horse Guards Parade (London 2012 venue)
Guards Memorial
Wales Office
Women of World War II
Old Treasury Buildings
Cabinet Office
Govt Offices
Cenotaph
Territorial Policing HQ
Dept of Health
Bali Memorial
Churchill War Rooms
Treasury
Norman Shaw Buildings
Portcullis House
Westminster
Victoria Embankment Gardens
War Memorial
Battle of Britain Memorial
Westminster Pier
London Eye Pier
London Eye
Embankment Pier
Festival Pier
Hungerford Bridge
Golden Jubilee Bridges
Queen Elizabeth Hall
National
BFI
IBM
Hayward Gallery
Royal Festival Hall
King's College London
Schiller Int University
King's College London
MAX
St John the Evangelist
Shell Centre
Premier Inn
London Film
County Hall
Sealife London Aquarium
Marriott Hotel
Park Plaza Hotel
Florence Nightingale
St Thomas'
Christ Church & Upton Chapel
Guy's & St Thomas' Medical School
Lambeth Palace
ADI Centre
Lambeth Pier
The Garden
Novotel
Walnut Tree Walk Primary School
Lambeth Walk Doorstep Green
Lilian Baylis Old School
Fire Station
Pedlars Park
Vauxhall Primary School
St Peter's
Superstore
St Anne's
St Anne's Catholic Primary School
Lilian Baylis Technology School
St Mark's CE Primary School
Henry Fawcett Primary School
The Oval (Surrey County Cricket Ground)
Archbishop Tennyson's School
Oval House
Big Ben
Palace of Westminster
Westminster Hall
Houses of Parliament
Victoria Tower
Westminster Bridge
Lambeth Bridge
Inst of Civil Engineers
Queen Elizabeth II Conf Centre
Judicial Committee of the Privy Council
St Margaret's Church
Westminster Abbey
Methodist Central Hall
Westminster Conference Centre
Jewel Tower
Westminster School
Dept for Work & Pensions
Dept for Business, Innovation & Skills
Dept of Education
Sanctuary House Hotel
Guards
Ministry of Justice
Wellington Barracks
55 Broadway
Jolly-St Ermin's Hotel
New Scotland Yard
Blewcoat School Gift Shop
Crowne Plaza Hotel
Westminster City Hall & Library
Surgery
St Matthew's School
Fire Station
Grey Coat Hospital (School)
Channel 4
TA Centre
Lawrence Hall
Burdett-Coutts CE Prim Sch
Westminster Kingsway College
Lindley Hall
Home Office
Magistrates' Court
Coroner's Court
DfT
City Inn Hotel
Millbank Tower
Millbank Pier
Millbank School
Tate Britain
Grey Coat Hospital (School)
Fairley House School
Chelsea College of Art & Design
The Gordon
CAB
Pimlico
Westminster Cathedral School
Pimlico Academy
Vauxhall Bridge
New Covent Garden Flower Market
PALL MALL
COCKSPUR ST
NORTHUMBERLAND AVENUE
WHITEHALL
PARLIAMENT STREET
BRIDGE ST
VICTORIA EMBANKMENT
ABINGDON STREET
MILLBANK
HORSEFERRY ROAD
VICTORIA STREET
BROAD SANCTUARY
BELVEDERE ROAD
YORK ROAD
WESTMINSTER BRIDGE ROAD
LAMBETH PALACE ROAD
LAMBETH ROAD
ALBERT EMBANKMENT
KENNINGTON LANE
HARLEYFORD ROAD
KENNINGTON OVAL
DURHAM STREET
VAUXHALL BRIDGE RD
BELGRAVE ROAD
BESSBOROUGH GARDENS
GROSVENOR ROAD
VAUXHALL BRIDGEFOOT
WANDSWORTH RD
NINE ELMS LANE
PARRY STREET
WANDSWORTH ROAD
SOUTH LAMBETH ROAD
A4
A400
A3212
A3211
A302
A3036
A3203
A3200
A301
A23
A202
A3213
A3204
A3205
A203
30
500 metres
A
B
C
D
E
F
8
M

151
Central London
Purdy Hicks Art Gallery
Modern
Times
Rose
The Anchor
Clink Prison
Golden Hinde
London Bridge City Pier
Site of original Globe Theatre
Vinopolis
Winchester Palace
London Bridge Experience
London Bridge
Cottons Centre
Hay's Galleria
The London Nautical School
Monument
LSE Bankside House
Peabody Estate
Southwark Cathedral
Duke St Hill
Tooley Street
Holiday Inn Express
Borough Market
Old Operating Theatre
London Dungeon
London Bridge Station
EF International Language School
Menier Theatre & Gallery
British Transport Police
London Bridge Hotel
The Shard
Britain at War
Southwark Playhouse
Waterloo East Station
Southwark
Travelodge
Union
Jerwood Space (Art Gallery)
London College of Advanced Studies
Guy's
Kings College London (Guy's Campus)
Thomas Street
Young Vic
Southwark College
Nolice's Gallery
London Fire Brigade HQ
St Saviour & St Mary Overy School
St Joseph's Catholic Primary School
Old Vic
Blackfriars Crown Court
Fire Station
London Fire Brigade
The Borough
Overseas Visitors Records Office
Royal British Legion
John Harvard
London Institute of Technology & Research
London School of Commerce
National Theatre Studios
Friars Primary School
Surgery
St George the Martyr
Borough
Coroner's Court
Snowsfields Primary School
Travelodge
Charles Dickens Primary School
Beormund Primary School
Kipling Estate
Ambulance HQ
London Christian School
London College of Accountancy
The Leather Market
Long Lane
Police Station
Crown Court
Tabard Gardens Estate
Henrywood Hall
Tabard Gardens
St George's Cathedral RC Primary School
St George's Cathedral
South Bank University
Institute of Optometry
Elim Estate
Inner London Crown Court
Decima Studios (Gallery)
Notre Dame RC Girls School
South Bank University
Buses only Northbound
Dickens Square Park
Chrysolyte Independent Christian School
Meakin Estate
Haddonhall Estate
St Jude's CE Primary School
The Perry
Elephant & Castle
Imperial War
Charlotte Sharman Primary School
Salvation Army
Globe Academy
Imperial War (All Saints Annexe)
London College of Communication
South Bank University
St Saviour's & St Olave's School
Bricklayer's Arms
New Kent Road
Elephant & Castle Station
Metropolitan Tabernacle
Newington
Heygate Estate
Victory Community Park
Victory Primary School
Townsend Primary School
The Olive School
Newington Butts
Walworth Road
Barlow/Congreve Estate
Cuming
St John's Walworth CE Primary School
English Martyrs Primary School
Kennington Lane
Crampton Primary School
Police Station
Walworth
Robert Browning Primary School
St Mary Newington
Surrey Square Infant School
Lambeth County Court
Kennington
Tibetan Buddhist Centre
Walworth Academy
City & Guilds of London Art School
TA Centre
Keyworth Primary School
Faraday Gardens
St Peter's CE Primary School
St Peter's
Pasley Park
St Paul's CE Primary School
Michael Faraday School
Kennington Park Road
Kennington
Kennington Park
Albany Road
Burgess Park
Brandon Estate
G
H
J
K
L
M

A
B
C
D
E
F
Old Spitalfields Market
Christ Church
Christ Church School
Bishopsgate Institute
Police Station
Brady Arts & Community Centre
WHITECHAPEL STATION
London Churchill College
Royal London
Barts & The London
East London Mosque
London Muslim Centre
Barts & The London School of Medicine & Dentistry
City University London
Whitechapel Bell Foundry
City of London College
Canon Barnett School
Petticoat Lane Market
East End Community School
Whitechapel Gallery
Icon College of Technology
Kobi Nazrul Primary School
London College
Queen Mary Innovation Centre
Madani Girls School
London School of Commerce & IT
Guildhall College
London Metropolitan University
Fire Station
Heron Tower
Travelodge
The Gherkin
Aldgate
Aldgate East
Beckett College
Harry Gosling Primary School
Mulberry Sports & Leisure Centre
Mulberry School for Girls
Bigland Green Primary School
Watney Market
Surgery
Sir John Cass's Prim Sch
English Martyrs Catholic School
City of London College
Islamic Sixth Form College
Lloyd's Register of Shipping
FENCHURCH STREET STATION
Premier Inn
Whitechapel
The Grange Hotel
Novotel
Ten Trinity Square
Trinity House
Tower Gateway
Tower Hill
Shapla Primary School
St Paul's Primary School
Swimming Pool
Latifiah Girls School
St George in the East
St George's Garden
Blue Coat School
All Hallows by the Tower
Tower of London
TOWER BRIDGE APPROACH
Tower Bridge House
Thomas More Square
St George in the East
News International
Tobacco Dock
West Dock
East Dock
St Katharine Docks
Tower Millennium Pier
Tower Hotel
St Katharine Pier
Tower Bridge
TOWER BRIDGE WHARF
HMS Belfast
MORE LONDON
The Scoop
City Hall
Hilton Hotel
Unicorn Theatre
Hermitage School
John Orwell Sports Centre
Wapping
St Peter's Primary School
The Captain Kidd
Police Station
River Thames
Alderman Stairs
BUTLER'S WHARF
Design
JAVA WHARF
ST SAVIOURS WHARF
JAMAICA WHARF
Cherry Garden Pier
King's Stairs
CHAMBERS WHARF
London City Mission
Magistrates' Court
Tower Bridge Primary School
Fire Station
St Michael's Catholic School
BERMONDSEY WALL ESTATE
Riverside Primary School
Most Holy Trinity
St Joseph's RC Primary School
Bosco College
Premier Inn
ARNOLD ESTATE
DICKENS ESTATE
Royal Marines Reserves (City of London)
St James CE Primary School
KIRBY ESTATE
Bermondsey
BERMONDSEY
St James's
Southwark College
BERMONDSEY SPA
Discovery Business Park
Buddhist Centre
Grange Primary School
Southwark Park
Tennis Courts
Bowling Green
Bermondsey Square Hotel
JAMAICA ROAD
TOWER BRIDGE ROAD
TOOLEY STREET
THE HIGHWAY
COMMERCIAL ROAD
WHITECHAPEL ROAD
COMMERCIAL STREET
LEMAN STREET
MANSELL STREET
0
250
500 metres

Smithy Street School
Stepney Green
STEPNEY
Stepney Green Maths & Computing College
Stepping Stones Farm
Sir John Cass Secondary School
St Dunstan's
Surgery
Ragged School
Halley Primary School
Stadium
Mile End Park
BURDETT ROAD
St Paul with St Luke Primary School
St Paul's
BURDETT ESTATE
Stebon Primary School
LOCKSLEY ESTATE
Cayley Primary School
Tower Hamlets College
Marion Richardson School
Ratcliff
Stephen Hawking School
Sir William Burrough Primary School
Stepney Greencoat CE Primary School
Our Lady's Catholic School
COMMERCIAL ROAD
A13
Bishop Challoner RC School
LIMEHOUSE STATION
The Mission
Tequila Wharf
Britannia Bridge
Limehouse Town Hall
St Anne's
EAST INDIA DOCK ROAD
WEST INDIA DOCK
Convent
CABLE STREET
St Mary's
BUTCHER ROW
Holiday Inn Express
Limehouse
Limehouse Basin
Limehouse Gallery
LIMEHOUSE LINK
Cyril Jackson School
THE HIGHWAY
Tennis Courts
NARROW STREET
River Thames
DUKE SHORE WHARF
DUNBAR WHARF
DUNDEE WHARF
Westferry Studios
WESTFERRY ROAD
Shadwell Basin Outdoor Activity Centre
LAVENDER WHARF
SOVEREIGN CRESCENT
KING & QUEEN WHARF
ROTHERHITHE STREET
Pumphouse Educational
CANARY RIVERSIDE
Four Seasons Hotel
ROTHERHITHE TUNNEL
SALTER ROAD
PACIFIC WHARF
Youth Hostel
Fisher Athletic FC
Lavender Nature Park
Hilton Hotel
CANADA WHARF
Nelson Dock
Canary Wharf Pier
WESTFERRY CIRCUS
Mellish Fields Sports Ground
Surrey Water
Bacon's College
CUMBERLAND WHARF
LAWRENCE WHARF
DURAND'S WHARF
ANCHORAGE POINT
Fire Station
Redriff Primary School
Surgery
MILLENNIUM HARBOUR
St John's Catholic Primary School
Alfred Salter Primary School
Albion Primary School
Russia Dock Woodland
Surrey Docks Farm
EXPRESS WHARF
HUTCHING'S WHARF
OCEAN WHARF
Works
CANADA ESTATE
Canada Water
Harmsworth Quays (Associated Newspapers)
Retail Park
Hollywood Bowl
Rotherhithe
Sir John McDougal Gardens
NEW ATLAS WHARF
Police Station
Surrey Quays
REDRIFF ROAD
Finland Quay
Rainbow Quay
Greenland Pier
Arnhem Wharf Primary School
Swedish Quay
Greenland Dock
KLEIN'S WHARF
G
H
J
K
L
M

Central London street index

this index, street and station names are listed in alphabetical order and written in full, but may be abbreviated on the map. Each ntry is followed by its Postcode District and each street name is preceded by the page number and the grid reference to the square in hich the name is found. Names are asterisked (*) in the index where there is insufficient space to show them on the map.

A

B

C

F

6 D3 Fairclough Street E1
6 B6 Fair Street SE1
5 K4 Falmouth Road SE1
1 J4 Fann Street EC1M
1 M1 Fanshaw Street N1
0 B6 Fareham Street W1D
2 A1 Farmer Street W8
2 A8 Farm Lane SW6
9 K8 Farm Street W1K
5 J1 Farnham Place SE1
7 M3 Farrance Street E14
1 G4 Farringdon ⇌ ⊖ EC1M
1 G4 Farringdon Lane EC1R
0 F3 Farringdon Road EC1R
1 H5 Farringdon Street EC1M
7 J5 Farrins Rents SE16
7 K7 Farrow Place SE16
6 F5 Farthing Fields * E1W
6 B1 Fashion Street E1
5 H7 Faunce Street SE17
2 C8 Fawcett Street SW10
1 L3 Featherstone Street EC1Y
6 A3 Fenchurch Avenue EC3M
6 A3 Fenchurch Buildings EC3M
6 A3 Fenchurch Place EC3M
6 A3 Fenchurch Street EC3M
6 A3 Fenchurch Street ⇌ EC3M
6 B8 Fendall Street SE1
5 M2 Fenning Street SE1
4 D8 Fentiman Road SW8
0 F2 Fernsbury Street WC1X
1 G6 Fetter Lane EC4A
6 D2 Fieldgate Street E1
5 J7 Fielding Street SE17
0 E1 Field Street WC1X
2 B8 Finborough Road SW10
1 L6 Finch Lane EC3V
7 K8 Finland Street SE16
1 L5 Finsbury Circus EC2M
1 G3 Finsbury Estate EC1R
1 M4 Finsbury Market EC2A
1 L4 Finsbury Square EC2A
1 L4 Finsbury Street EC2Y
3 G5 First Street SW3
7 J6 Fishermans Drive SE16
0 D5 Fisher Street WC1R
8 E3 Fisherton Street NW8
1 L7 Fish Street Hill EC3R
4 F5 Fitzalan Street SE11
9 J6 Fitzhardinge Street W1H
9 M4 Fitzroy Square W1T
9 M4 Fitzroy Street W1T
7 J3 Flamborough Street E14
6 C4 Flank Street E1
0 C3 Flaxman Terrace WC1H
1 G6 Fleet Street EC4A
5 H8 Fleming Road SE17
6 D3 Fletcher Street E1
5 L6 Flint Street SE17
0 C6 Flitcroft Street WC2H
6 D7 Flockton Street SE16
3 G7 Flood Street SW3
3 G7 Flood Walk SW3
0 D7 Floral Street WC2E
49 M5 Foley Street W1W
56 D3 Forbes Street E1
56 D2 Fordham Street E1
56 F2 Ford Square E1
51 K5 Fore Street EC2Y
48 C4 Formosa Street W9
49 G6 Forset Street W1H
55 H8 Forsyth Gardens SE17
56 B1 Fort Street E1
51 K4 Fortune Street EC1Y
51 J6 Foster Lane EC2V
52 E6 Foulis Terrace SW7
157 J5 Foundry Close SE16
156 B1 Fournier Street E1
156 E5 Fowey Close E1W
148 E4 Frampton Street NW8
154 A5 Francis Street SW1P
156 F8 Frankland Close SE16
153 H6 Franklin's Row SW3
155 G3 Frazier Street SE1
156 C8 Frean Street SE16
149 G7 Frederick Close W2
150 E2 Frederick Street WC1X
153 J3 Frederic Mews * SW1X
155 M6 Freemantle Street SE17
151 H2 Friend Street EC1V
150 B6 Frith Street W1D
156 E1 Fulbourne Street E1
156 F7 Fulford Street SE16
152 D8 Fulham Road SW10
152 F6 Fulham Road SW3
150 F5 Furnival Street EC4A
154 B5 Fynes Street SW1P

G

155 G1 Gabriel's Wharf SE1
156 B6 Gainsford Street SE1
157 G6 Galleon Close SE16
157 K2 Galsworthy Avenue E14
151 K2 Galway Street EC1V
155 H2 Gambia Street SE1
148 D1 Garden Road NW8
155 H4 Garden Row SE1
157 H1 Garden Street E1
151 M3 Garden Walk EC2A
151 J2 Gard Street EC1V
157 M4 Garford Street E14
151 G3 Garnault Place EC1R
156 F4 Garnet Street E1W
151 K3 Garrett Street EC1Y
150 C7 Garrick Street WC2E
157 H7 Garterway SE16
148 B6 Garway Road W2
156 E8 Gataker Street * SE16
152 F3 Gate Mews SW7
148 F3 Gateforth Street NW8
149 L3 Gate Mews NW1
151 M3 Gatesborough Street * EC2A
150 E5 Gate Street WC2A
153 K7 Gatliff Road SW1W
155 J4 Gaunt Street SE1
154 C4 Gayfere Street SW1P
155 H4 Gaywood Street SE1
155 H7 Gaza Street SE17
156 C7 Gedling Place SE1
151 J3 Gee Street EC1V
155 H5 George Mathers Road SE11
156 C7 George Row SE16
149 H6 George Street W1H
149 K7 George Yard W1K
155 H4 Geraldine Street SE1
153 K5 Gerald Road SW1W
150 B7 Gerrard Street W1D
155 G3 Gerridge Street SE1
152 D8 Gertrude Street SW10
154 E5 Gibson Road SE11
150 C5 Gilbert Place WC1A
155 G5 Gilbert Road SE11
149 K7 Gilbert Street W1K
149 L5 Gildea Street W1W
153 M5 Gillingham Street SW1V
157 L3 Gill Street E14
152 D7 Gilston Road SW10
151 H5 Giltspur Street EC1A
155 H4 Gladstone Street SE1
157 G4 Glamis Place E1W
157 G4 Glamis Road E1W
153 M7 Glasgow Terrace SW1V
155 J3 Glasshill Street SE1
150 A8 Glasshouse Street W1B
154 D7 Glasshouse Walk SE11
152 F7 Glebe Place SW3
152 C6 Gledhow Road SW5
149 H4 Glentworth Street NW1
157 J5 Globe Pond Road SE16
155 K3 Globe Street SE1
156 A4 Gloucester Court * EC3R
148 C6 Gloucester Gardens W2
148 D6 Gloucester Mews W2
148 C6 Gloucester Mews West W2
149 H3 Gloucester Place NW1
149 H5 Gloucester Place W1U
149 H5 Gloucester Place Mews W1U
152 C4 Gloucester Road SW7
152 D6 Gloucester Road SW7
152 C5 Gloucester Road ⊖ SW7
148 F6 Gloucester Square W2
153 M7 Gloucester Street SW1V
148 B5 Gloucester Terrace W2
148 D6 Gloucester Terrace W2
152 A2 Gloucester Walk W8
151 G2 Gloucester Way EC1R
154 E7 Glyn Street SE11
153 G6 Godfrey Street SW3
154 D7 Goding Street SE11
151 J7 Godliman Street EC4V
151 K1 Godwin Close N1
154 D1 Golden Jubilee Bridge WC2N
151 J4 Golden Lane EC1Y
150 A7 Golden Square W1F
156 E3 Golding Street E1
148 A4 Goldney Road W9
151 K6 Goldsmith Street EC2V
157 G8 Gomm Road SE16
150 A5 Goodge Place W1T
150 A5 Goodge Street W1T
150 B5 Goodge Street ⊖ W1T
156 C8 Goodwin Close SE16
152 A2 Gordon Place W8
150 B3 Gordon Square WC1H
150 B3 Gordon Street WC1H
152 D4 Gore Street SW7
156 A2 Goring Street * EC3A
149 L5 Gosfield Street W1W
150 B6 Goslett Yard WC2H
151 H1 Goswell Road EC1V
150 F3 Gough Street WC1X
156 B2 Goulston Street E1
150 B5 Gower Mews WC1E
150 A3 Gower Place NW1
150 B3 Gower Street WC1E
156 D2 Gower's Walk E1
151 M7 Gracechurch Street EC3V
150 B2 Grafton Place NW1
149 L8 Grafton Street W1S
150 A4 Grafton Way W1T
151 J1 Graham Street N1
153 J6 Graham Terrace SW1W
149 M1 Granby Terrace NW1
151 H5 Grand Avenue EC1A
156 B8 Grange Road SE1
156 A8 Grange Walk SE1
156 B8 Grange Yard SE1
148 B2 Grantully Road W9
149 J6 Granville Place W1H
148 A1 Granville Road NW6
150 F2 Granville Square WC1X
150 C6 Grape Street WC2H
156 B2 Gravel Lane E1
150 D2 Gray's Inn Road WC1X
150 F5 Gray's Inn Square WC1R
155 G3 Gray Street SE1
149 L6 Great Castle Street W1G
149 G4 Great Central Street NW1
150 B6 Great Chapel Street W1D
154 C4 Great College Street SW1P
149 H6 Great Cumberland Place W1H
155 K3 Great Dover Street SE1
151 M3 Great Eastern Street EC2A
154 C3 Great George Street SW1P
155 J1 Great Guildford Street SE1
150 E4 Great James Street WC1N
149 M7 Great Marlborough Street W1F
155 L2 Great Maze Pond SE1
150 C7 Great New Portland Street WC2H
156 D1 Greatorex Street E1
150 D4 Great Ormond Street WC1N
150 F2 Great Percy Street WC1X
154 B4 Great Peter Street SW1P
149 L4 Great Portland Street W1W
149 L4 Great Portland Street ⊖ W1W
150 A7 Great Pulteney Street W1F
150 D6 Great Queen Street WC2B
150 C5 Great Russell Street WC1B
154 C1 Great Scotland Yard SW1A
154 C4 Great Smith Street SW1P
155 H2 Great Sufffolk Street SE1
151 H4 Great Sutton Street EC1V
151 L6 Great Swan Alley EC2R
149 M4 Great Titchfield Street W1W
151 M7 Great Tower Street EC3M
156 A4 Great Tower Street EC3R
151 L6 Great Winchester Street EC2N
150 B7 Great Windmill Street W1D
150 B6 Greek Street W1D
157 J6 Greenacre Square SE16
156 E5 Green Bank E1W
148 F1 Greenberry Street NW8
154 A5 Greencoat Place SW1P
154 A4 Green Coat Row SW1P
156 D2 Greenfield Road E1
154 C5 Greenham Close SE1
153 M1 Green Park ⊖ W1J
149 J7 Green Street W1K
149 L4 Greenwell Street W1W
155 G2 Greet Street SE1
157 L4 Grenade Street E14
148 F3 Grendon Street NW8
152 C5 Grenville Place SW7
151 J6 Gresham Street EC2V
150 B5 Gresse Street W1T
151 G3 Greville Street EC1N
154 B4 Greycoat Place SW1P
154 B4 Greycoat Street SW1P
156 A8 Grigg's Place SE1
153 L8 Grosvenor Bridge SW8
153 J3 Grosvenor Crescent SW1X
153 J3 Grosvenor Crescent Mews SW1X
153 L4 Grosvenor Gardens SW1W
153 L4 Grosvenor Gardens Mews East SW1W
153 L4 Grosvenor Gardens Mews North SW1W
153 L4 Grosvenor Gardens Mews South * SW1W
149 H8 Grosvenor Gate W2
149 L7 Grosvenor Hill W1K
153 K3 Grosvenor Place SW1X
153 L8 Grosvenor Road SW1V
149 J7 Grosvenor Square W1K
149 K7 Grosvenor Street W1K
155 J8 Grosvenor Terrace SE5
148 D2 Grove End Road NW8
153 M5 Guildhouse Street SW1V
150 D4 Guilford Street WC1N
155 M5 Guinness Square SE1
157 K8 Gulliver Street SE16
151 G6 Gunpowder Square EC4A
156 B1 Gun Street E1
156 C2 Gunthorpe Street E1
151 J6 Gutter Lane EC2V
155 L3 Guy Street SE1

H

151 L2 Haberdasher Street N1
155 M4 Haddonhall Estate SE1
156 F3 Hainton Close E1
156 F2 Halcrow Street * E1
153 L1 Half Moon Street W1J
152 A8 Halford Road SW6
153 J4 Halkin Place SW1X
153 K3 Halkin Street SW1X
149 L5 Hallam Street W1W
157 K1 Halley Street E14
148 C6 Hallfield Estate W2
148 E4 Hall Place W2
148 D2 Hall Road NW8
151 H2 Hall Street EC1V
155 M6 Halpin Place SE17
153 G5 Halsey Street SW3
148 D2 Hamilton Close NW8
157 K7 Hamilton Close SE16
148 D2 Hamilton Gardens NW8
153 K2 Hamilton Place W1J
148 C1 Hamilton Terrace NW8
155 L3 Hamlet Way SE1
156 B4 Hammett Street EC3N
150 B1 Hampden Close NW1
149 H6 Hampden Gurney Street W2
149 M2 Hampstead Road NW1
155 J6 Hampton Street SE17
156 C1 Hanbury Street E1
150 E5 Hand Court WC1V
150 D3 Handel Street WC1N
155 L3 Hankey Place SE1
157 G1 Hannibal Road E1
149 L6 Hanover Square W1S
149 L7 Hanover Street W1S
153 H3 Hans Crescent SW3
149 M4 Hanson Street W1W
153 H4 Hans Place SW1X
153 G4 Hans Road SW3
153 H4 Hans Street SW1X
150 B6 Hanway Place W1T
150 B6 Hanway Street W1T
148 F5 Harbet Road W2
150 E4 Harbour Street WC1N
149 G5 Harcourt Street W1H
152 C7 Harcourt Terrace SW10
157 G3 Hardinge Street E1W
151 G2 Hardwick Street EC1R
155 M2 Hardwidge Street SE1
157 H6 Hardy Close SE16
149 L6 Harewood Place W1G
149 G4 Harewood Row NW1
149 G4 Harewood Avenue NW1
157 J1 Harford Street E1
154 E8 Harleyford Road SE11
152 D7 Harley Gardens SW10
149 K4 Harley Street W1G
155 G7 Harmsworth Street SE17
156 A8 Harold Estate SE1
155 K4 Harper Road SE1
153 H3 Harriet Street SW1X
153 H3 Harriet Walk SW1X
152 C6 Harrington Gardens SW7
152 E5 Harrington Road SW7
149 M1 Harrington Square NW1
149 M2 Harrington Street NW1
150 D2 Harrison Street WC1H
149 G6 Harrowby Street W1H
156 B2 Harrow Place E1
148 A4 Harrow Road W2
156 A3 Hart Street EC3R
153 G5 Hasker Street SW3
150 C2 Hastings Street WC1H
155 G1 Hatfields SE1
148 B6 Hatherley Grove W2
157 G6 Hatteraick Road SE16
151 G4 Hatton Garden EC1N
148 E4 Hatton Street W2
151 G4 Hatton Wall EC1N
157 H3 Havering Street E1
151 J1 Haverstock Street N1
157 H6 Hawke Place * SE16
156 B3 Haydon Street EC3N
149 G4 Hayes Place NW1
149 L8 Hay Hill W1J
155 H5 Hayles Street SE11
150 B8 Haymarket SW1Y
151 J4 Hayne Street EC1A
155 M1 Hay's Lane SE1
149 L8 Hay's Mews W1J
151 H3 Haywood Place EC1R
153 K3 Headfort Place SW1X
157 H2 Head Street E1
157 K2 Hearnshaw Street E14
151 M4 Hearn Street EC2A
150 E3 Heathcote Street WC1N
149 M7 Heddon Street W1B
150 A7 Heddon Street W1S
155 H5 Hedger Street SE11
155 J8 Heiron Street SE17
156 D5 Hellings Street E1W
151 K3 Helmet Row EC1V
157 L8 Helsinki Square SE16
148 E3 Henderson Drive NW8
156 A3 Heneage Lane EC3A
156 C1 Heneage Street E1
149 L6 Henrietta Place W1G
150 D7 Henrietta Street WC2E
156 D2 Henriques Street E1
155 L5 Henshaw Street SE17
151 G4 Herbal Hill EC1R
153 H4 Herbert Crescent SW1X
150 C3 Herbrand Street WC1H
154 F4 Hercules Road SE1
148 A6 Hereford Road W2
152 D6 Hereford Square SW7
148 E5 Hermitage Street W2
156 D5 Hermitage Wall E1W
151 H2 Hermit Street EC1V
157 K5 Heron Place SE16
157 M5 Heron Quay E14
154 C6 Herrick Street SW1P
153 K2 Hertford Street W1J
157 M4 Hertsmere Road E14
152 B6 Hesper Mews SW5
156 E3 Hessel Street E1
151 M3 Hewett Street EC2A
155 J5 Heygate Estate SE17
155 J5 Heygate Street SE17
154 B6 Hide Place SW1P
150 E5 High Holborn WC1V
152 A3 High Street Kensington ⊖ W8
152 A8 Hildyard Road SW6
156 F5 Hilliards Court E1W
155 J8 Hillingdon Street SE17
148 D1 Hill Road NW8
149 M6 Hills Place W1F
149 K8 Hill Street W1J
149 K6 Hinde Street W1U
157 M3 Hind Grove E14
157 M3 Hindgrove Area E14
157 G8 Hithe Grove SE16
153 K4 Hobart Place SW1W
152 D8 Hobury Street SW10
152 B6 Hogarth Road SW5
153 J6 Holbein Mews SW1W
153 J6 Holbein Place SW1W
151 G5 Holborn EC1N
150 E5 Holborn ⊖ WC2B
151 G5 Holborn Viaduct EC1A
150 F2 Holford Street WC1X
155 H1 Holland Street SE1
152 A3 Holland Street W8
150 A6 Hollen Street W1F
149 L6 Holles Street W1C
152 C8 Hollywood Road SW10
155 H5 Holyoak Road SE11
155 M2 Holyrood Street SE1
156 A6 Holyrood Street SE1
151 M4 Holywell Row EC2A
151 M1 Homefield Street * N1
149 G5 Homer Row W1H
149 G5 Homer Street W1H
156 D3 Hooper Street E1
156 C1 Hopetown Street E1
150 A7 Hopkins Street W1F
155 H1 Hopton Street SE1
155 L8 Hopwood Road SE17
152 A3 Hornton Place W8
152 A2 Hornton Street W8
150 B7 Horse & Dolphin Yard W1D
157 J3 Horseferry Road E14
154 B4 Horseferry Road SW1P
154 C2 Horse Guards Avenue SW1A
154 C2 Horse Guards Parade SW1A
154 C2 Horse Guards Road SW1A
156 B6 Horselydown Lane SE1
155 K8 Horsley Street SE17
151 H5 Hosier Lane EC1A
157 G8 Hothfield Place SE16
154 F6 Hotspur Street SE11
150 E6 Houghton Street WC2A
156 A2 Houndsditch EC3A
154 A4 Howick Place SW1E
150 A4 Howland Street W1T
157 K7 Howland Way SE16
148 D4 Howley Place W2
151 M2 Hoxton Square N1
151 M1 Hoxton Street N1
153 L6 Hugh Mews SW1V
153 L6 Hugh Street SW1V
153 L6 Hugh Street SW1V
157 J6 Hull Close SE16
151 J2 Hull Street EC1V
154 E1 Hungerford Bridge SE1
155 M4 Hunter Close SE1
150 D3 Hunter Street WC1N
150 A4 Huntley Street WC1E
155 M6 Huntsman Street SE17
149 H3 Huntsworth Mews NW1
157 H6 Hurley Crescent SE16
157 M7 Hutching's Street E14
151 G7 Hutton Street EC4Y
153 K2 Hyde Park Corner W1J
153 K2 Hyde Park Corner ⊖ W1J
152 D3 Hyde Park Court SW7
148 F6 Hyde Park Crescent W2
148 F7 Hyde Park Garden Mews W2
148 F7 Hyde Park Gardens W2
152 C3 Hyde Park Gate SW7
152 D3 Hyde Park Gate SW7
148 F7 Hyde Park Square W2
148 F7 Hyde Park Street W2

I

151 M7 Idol Lane EC3R
152 B8 Ifield Road SW10
155 J6 Iliffe Street SE17
155 J6 Iliffe Yard SE17
152 D4 Imperial College Road SW7
156 B3 India Street EC3N
150 A7 Ingestre Place W1F
150 F2 Inglebert Street EC1R
154 E5 Ingram Close SE11
149 J2 Inner Circle NW1
148 B6 Inverness Terrace W2
148 C8 Inverness Terrace Gate W2
155 H1 Invicta Plaza SE1
155 L7 Inville Road SE17
151 K6 Ironmonger Lane EC2V
151 K2 Ironmonger Row EC1V
150 C8 Irving Street WC2N
157 G6 Isambard Place SE16
157 K3 Island Row E14
152 A4 Iverna Court W8
152 A4 Iverna Gardens W8
153 G5 Ives Street SW3
149 G4 Ivor Place NW1
152 F6 Ixworth Place SW3

J

156 C6 Jacob Street SE1
156 F8 Jamaica Gate SE16
156 C7 Jamaica Road SE1
156 E7 Jamaica Road SE16
157 G2 Jamaica Street E1
156 C6 Jamaica Wharf SE1
149 K6 James Street W1U
150 D7 James Street WC2E
152 A1 Jameson Street W8
157 K1 Jamuna Close E14
156 D7 Janeway Street SE16
157 J4 Jardine Road E1W
156 C6 Java Wharf SE1
152 D3 Jay Mews SW7
150 A8 Jermyn Street SW1Y
148 F3 Jerome Crescent NW8
156 B3 Jewery Street EC3N
155 G2 Joan Street SE1
150 E4 Jockey's Fields WC1R
154 F3 Johanna Street SE1
150 D8 John Adam Street WC2N
151 G7 John Carpenter Street EC4Y
156 D7 John Felton Road SE16
156 C4 John Fisher Street E1
154 C5 John Islip Street SW1P
149 L6 John Prince's Street W1G
156 D7 John Roll Way SE16
155 J8 John Ruskin Street SE5
154 C6 John Slip Street SW1P
150 E4 John's Mews WC1N
154 A7 Johnson's Place SW1V
157 G3 Johnson Street E1
150 E4 John Street WC1N
155 L1 Joiner Street SE1
154 E6 Jonathan Street SE11
153 G6 Jubilee Place SW3
157 G2 Jubilee Street E1
152 B1 Jubilee Walk W8
150 C2 Judd Street WC1H
148 F5 Junction Mews W2
154 F5 Juxon Street SE11

K

157 H5 Katherine Close SE16
150 E6 Kean Street WC2B
157 J6 Keel Close SE16
150 E6 Keeley Street WC2B
156 E7 Keeton's Road SE16
155 H3 Kell Street SE1
152 B4 Kelso Place W8
150 E6 Kemble Street WC2B
152 A7 Kempsford Gardens SW5
155 G6 Kempsford Road SE11
149 J5 Kendall Place W1U
149 G6 Kendal Street W2
156 D5 Kennet Street E1W
157 G6 Kenning Street SE16
155 G7 Kennings Way SE11
155 H7 Kennington ⊖ SE11
154 E7 Kennington Lane SE11
154 E8 Kennington Oval SE11
155 G8 Kennington Park Gardens SE11
155 G7 Kennington Park Place SE11
155 G7 Kennington Park Road SE11
154 F4 Kennington Road SE1
155 G5 Kennington Road SE11
154 F8 Kennnington Oval SE11
149 J5 Kenrick Place W1U
152 A1 Kensington Church Street W8
152 B3 Kensington Court W8
148 B6 Kensington Gardens Square W2
152 C4 Kensington Gate W8
152 D3 Kensington Gore SW7
152 A4 Kensington High Street W8
152 B1 Kensington Palace Gardens W8
152 B2 Kensington Palace Gardens W8
152 A1 Kensington Place W8
153 G3 Kensington Road SW7
152 B3 Kensington Road W8
152 B3 Kensington Square W8
150 C3 Kenton Street WC1H
152 A6 Kenway Road SW5
150 D1 Keystone Close N1
155 H4 Keyworth Street SE1
148 A2 Kilburn Park Road NW6
148 A6 Kildare Terrace W2
150 E1 Killick Street N1
157 H6 Kinburn Street SE16
156 E2 Kinder Street E1
157 H5 King & Queen Wharf SE16
155 K6 King and Queen Street SE17
154 C2 King Charles Street SW1A
148 C5 Kingdom Street W2
151 J6 King Edward Street EC1A
155 G4 King Edward Walk SE1
155 H3 King James Street SE1
149 M7 Kingly Street W1F
151 L6 King's Arms Yard EC2R
155 H2 King's Bench Street SE1
151 H7 Kingscote Street EC4V
150 D1 King's Cross ⇌ N1C
150 E2 King's Cross Road WC1X
150 D1 King's Cross St Pancras ⊖ N1C
155 L1 King's Head Yard SE1
150 F4 King's Mews WC1N
148 E1 Kingsmill Terrace NW8
151 J2 King Square EC1V
152 E8 King's Road SW3
153 M5 King's Scholars Passage SW1P
156 F6 King's Stairs Close SE16
150 D7 King Street WC2E
154 A1 King Street SW1Y
151 K6 King Street EC2V
150 E6 Kingsway WC2B
151 L7 King William Street EC4N
153 J3 Kinnerton Place North * SW1X
153 J3 Kinnerton Place South * SW1X
153 J3 Kinnerton Street SW1X
153 J3 Kinnerton Yard * SW1X
155 L3 Kipling Estate SE1
155 L3 Kipling Street SE1
156 D7 Kirby Estate SE16
155 M3 Kirby Grove SE1
151 G4 Kirby Street EC1N

152 B5 Knaresborough Place SW5
151 J7 Knightrider Street EC4V
153 H3 Knightsbridge SW1X
153 H3 Knightsbridge ⊖ SW3
149 H4 Knox Street W1H
152 C4 Kynance Mews SW7
152 C4 Kynance Place SW7

L

151 L4 Lackington Street EC2A
156 B6 Lafone Street SE1
157 H5 Lagado Mews SE16
154 D5 Lambeth Bridge SW1P
154 E5 Lambeth High Street SE1
151 J7 Lambeth Hill EC4V
154 F3 Lambeth North ⊖ SE1
154 E4 Lambeth Palace Road SE1
154 F4 Lambeth Road SE1
154 F5 Lambeth Walk SE11
150 E4 Lamb's Conduit Street WC1N
151 K4 Lamb's Passage EC1Y
156 B1 Lamb Street E1
156 A7 Lamb Way SE1
155 H5 Lamlash Street SE11
148 D3 Lanark Place W9
148 B1 Lanark Road W9
148 D7 Lancaster Gate W2
148 D8 Lancaster Gate W2
148 E7 Lancaster Gate ⊖ W2
148 D7 Lancaster Mews W2
150 E7 Lancaster Place WC2E
155 H3 Lancaster Street SE1
148 E7 Lancaster Terrace W2
148 D8 Lancaster Walk W2
153 G3 Lancelot Place SW7
150 B2 Lancing Street NW1
153 J3 Lanesborough Place * SW1X
156 E3 Langdale Street E1
148 D1 Langford Place NW8
149 L5 Langham Place W1B
149 L5 Langham Street W1W
149 M5 Langham Street W1W
154 D8 Langley Lane SW8
150 C7 Langley Street WC2H
150 E3 Langton Close WC1X
148 A3 Lanhill Road W9
155 L4 Lansdowne Place SE1
155 J3 Lant Street SE1
155 K6 Larcom Street SE17
148 B3 Lauderdale Road W9
154 E7 Laud Street SE11
154 F3 Launcelot Street SE1
152 C4 Launceston Place W8
151 L7 Laurence Pountney Lane EC4V
157 K5 Lavender Road SE16
157 K4 Lavender Wharf SE16
155 J1 Lavington Street SE1
154 D8 Lawn Lane SW8
152 F8 Lawrence Street SW3
157 L6 Lawrence Wharf SE16
155 L4 Law Street SE1
149 L3 Laxton Place NW1
150 F4 Laystall Street EC1R
156 A3 Leadenhall Street EC3A
151 M6 Leadenhall Street EC3V
154 E2 Leake Street SE1
151 G4 Leather Lane EC1N
155 M3 Leathermarket Street SE1
150 E2 Leeke Street WC1X
149 J7 Lees Place W1K
150 B7 Leicester Square WC2H
150 C7 Leicester Square ⊖ WC2H
150 B7 Leicester Street WC2H
150 C3 Leigh Street WC1H
148 C6 Leinster Gardens W2
148 C7 Leinster Mews W2
148 C7 Leinster Place W2
148 A7 Leinster Square W2
148 C7 Leinster Terrace W2
156 C3 Leman Street E1
153 G4 Lennox Gardens SW1X
153 G5 Lennox Gardens Mews SW1X
151 L3 Leonard Street EC2A
157 M1 Leopold Estate E3
157 L1 Leopold Street E3
155 M5 Leroy Street SE1
151 J2 Lever Street EC1V
153 L4 Lewisham Street SW1H
152 A5 Lexham Gardens W8
152 A5 Lexham Mews W8
150 A7 Lexington Street W1F
156 B2 Leyden Street E1
157 H5 Leydon Close SE16
155 H3 Library Street SE1
150 A1 Lidlington Place NW1
148 F3 Lilestone Street NW8
156 D5 Lilley Close E1W
152 A7 Lillie Road SW6
152 A7 Lillie Yard SW6
151 H6 Limeburner Lane EC4M
156 D5 Lime Close E1W
157 L4 Limehouse Causeway E14
157 L3 Limehouse Link E14
157 J3 Limehouse ⇌⊖ E14
152 D8 Limerston Street SW10
151 M7 Lime Street EC3M
150 E6 Lincoln's Inn Fields WC2A
148 A8 Linden Gardens W2
156 F1 Lindley Street E1
154 B7 Lindsay Square SW1V
151 H4 Lindsey Street EC1A
149 G3 Linhope Street NW1
156 D8 Linsey Street SE16
150 D7 Lisle Street WC2H
148 F3 Lisson Green Estate NW8
149 G4 Lisson Grove NW1
148 F3 Lisson Grove NW8
148 F4 Lisson Street NW1
150 C7 Litchfield Street WC2H
149 M6 Little Argyll Street W1F
151 J5 Little Britain EC1A
153 K4 Little Chester Street SW1X
154 C3 Little George Street SW1P
150 A7 Little Marlborough Street W1F
151 G6 Little New Street EC4A
149 L6 Little Portland Street W1G
150 C5 Little Russell Street WC1A
153 M2 Little St James's Street SW1A
154 C3 Little Sanctuary SW1A
156 B3 Little Somerset Street E1
149 M5 Little Titchfield Street W1W
155 K7 Liverpool Grove SE17
151 M5 Liverpool Street EC2M
151 M5 Liverpool Street ⇌⊖ EC2M
151 K3 Lizard Street EC1V
156 D7 Llewellyn Street SE16
150 F2 Lloyd Baker Street WC1X
156 B3 Lloyd's Avenue EC3N
150 F2 Lloyd Square WC1X
151 G2 Lloyds Row EC1R
150 F2 Lloyd's Street WC1X
157 L2 Locksley Estate E14
157 L1 Locksley Street E14
155 L3 Lockyer Street SE1
148 F3 Lodge Road NW8
156 D7 Loftie Street SE16
152 A5 Logan Place W8
156 B1 Lolesworth Close E1
154 F5 Lollard Street SE11
154 F6 Lollard Street SE11
155 J2 Loman Street SE1
156 D1 Lomas Street E1
151 G6 Lombard Lane EC4Y
151 L7 Lombard Street EC3V
151 L8 London Bridge EC4R
155 L1 London Bridge ⇌⊖ SE1
155 L1 London Bridge Street SE1
148 E6 London Mews W2
155 H4 London Road SE1
156 A3 London Street EC3R
148 E6 London Street W2
151 K5 London Wall EC2M
150 D7 Long Acre WC2E
149 L3 Longford Street NW1
151 J5 Long Lane EC1A
155 L3 Long Lane SE1
153 M5 Longmoore Street SW1V
152 A5 Longridge Road SW5
155 H5 Longville Road SE11
156 A8 Long Walk SE1
150 E4 Long Yard WC1N
154 C4 Lord North Street SW1P
150 E1 Lorenzo Street WC1X
155 J8 Lorrimore Road SE17
155 H8 Lorrimore Square SE17
151 L6 Lothbury EC2R
154 F7 Loughborough Street SE11
151 M7 Lovat Lane EC3R
151 K6 Love Lane EC2V
157 K7 Lovell Place SE16
157 K2 Lowell Street E14
153 K4 Lower Belgrave Street SW1W
153 L4 Lower Grosvenor Place SW1W
150 A7 Lower James Street W1F
150 A7 Lower John Street W1F
154 F3 Lower Marsh SE1
157 G7 Lower Road SE16
153 J6 Lower Sloane Street SW1W
156 A4 Lower Thames Street EC3R
153 J4 Lowndes Close * SW1X
153 J4 Lowndes Place SW1X
153 H3 Lowndes Square SW1X
153 H4 Lowndes Street SW1X
152 F5 Lucan Place SW3
156 C8 Lucey Road SE16
151 H6 Ludgate Circus EC4M
151 H6 Ludgate Hill EC4M
151 M3 Luke Street EC2A
157 G3 Lukin Street E1
149 K7 Lumley Street W1K
153 L7 Lupus Street SW1V
154 B7 Lupus Street SW1V
148 E4 Luton Street NW8
149 J4 Luxborough Street W1U
153 J4 Lyall Mews SW1X
153 J4 Lyall Street SW1X
148 E3 Lyons Place NW8
155 K7 Lytham Street SE17

M

151 J2 Macclesfield Road EC1V
150 B7 Macclesfield Street * W1D
156 E5 Mace Close E1W
150 D6 Macklin Street WC2B
149 M2 Mackworth Street NW1
155 K7 Macleod Street SE17
149 M7 Maddox Street W1S
155 M2 Magdalen Street SE1
154 F8 Magee Street SE11
156 C6 Maguire Street SE1
148 D4 Maida Avenue W9
148 C2 Maida Vale W9
148 C2 Maida Vale ⊖ W9
155 K1 Maiden Lane SE1
150 D7 Maiden Lane WC2E
156 D7 Major Road SE16
153 G6 Makins Street SW3
150 B4 Malet Street WC1E
152 E8 Mallord Street SW3
148 F3 Mallory Street NW8
151 L3 Mallow Street EC1Y
151 H3 Malta Street EC1V
156 B7 Maltby Street SE1
149 J6 Manchester Square W1U
149 J5 Manchester Street W1U
155 L3 Manciple Street SE1
149 K3 Mandeville Place W1U
150 B6 Manette Street W1D
157 M6 Manilla Street E14
151 H2 Manningford Close EC1V
155 J7 Manor Place SE17
152 F7 Manresa Road SW3
156 C3 Mansell Street E1
149 K5 Mansfield Mews W1G
149 L5 Mansfield Street W1G
151 K7 Mansion House ⊖ EC4V
152 D5 Manson Mews SW7
152 D6 Manson Place SW7
157 J6 Mapleleaf Square SE16
156 F1 Maples Place E1
149 M4 Maple Street W1T
149 H7 Marble Arch ⊖ W1C
150 C3 Marchmont Street WC1H
149 L6 Margaret Street W1W
152 F7 Margaretta Terrace SW3
150 F3 Margery Street WC1X
156 E7 Marigold Street SE16
156 C7 Marine Street SE16
153 K1 Market Mews W1J
149 M6 Market Place W1W
153 G6 Markham Square SW3
153 G6 Markham Street SW3
156 A4 Mark Lane EC3R
148 E7 Marlborough Gate W2
148 C1 Marlborough Place NW8
154 A2 Marlborough Road SW1A
152 F6 Marlborough Street SW3
152 B4 Marloes Road W8
157 H6 Marlow Way SE16
157 K2 Maroon Street E14
150 A7 Marshall Street W1F
155 J2 Marshalsea Road SE1
154 C5 Marsham Street SW1P
157 M5 Marsh Wall E14
151 K3 Martha's Buildings EC1V
156 F3 Martha Street E1
151 L7 Martin Lane EC4V
148 A4 Maryland Road W9
148 A4 Marylands Road W9
149 G4 Marylebone ⇌⊖ NW1
149 K5 Marylebone High Street W1U
149 K6 Marylebone Lane W1U
149 G4 Marylebone Road NW1
149 K5 Marylebone Street W1G
154 F6 Marylee Way SE11
157 M2 Masjid Lane E14
155 M5 Mason Street SE17
155 M5 Massinger Street SE17
157 J1 Masters Street E1
157 J2 Matlock Street E14
154 C3 Matthew Parker Street SW1H
154 B5 Maunsel Street SW1P
153 L1 Mayfair Place W1J
156 F7 Mayflower Street SE16
150 A1 Mayford Estate NW1
156 F4 Maynards Quay E1W
150 C8 May's Street WC2N
154 F4 McAuley Close SE1
152 C5 McLeod's Mews SW7
155 G8 Meadcroft Road SE11
155 H8 Meadcroft Road SE11
154 E8 Meadow Road SW8
155 J5 Meadow Row SE1
154 F4 Mead Row SE1
155 M4 Meakin Estate SE1
150 E3 Mecklenburgh Square WC1N
154 B5 Medway Street SW1P
156 E5 Meeting House Alley E1W
149 G4 Melcombe Place NW1
149 H4 Melcombe Street W1U
148 D2 Melina Place NW8
155 M2 Melior Street SE1
150 A2 Melton Street NW1
153 K3 Memorial Gates SW1W
154 F2 Mepham Street SE1
150 C7 Mercer Street WC2H
148 E5 Merchant Square W2
150 F2 Merlin Street EC1R
155 K2 Mermaid Court SE1
155 K4 Merrick Square SE1
152 A8 Merrington Road SW6
155 L7 Merrow Street SE17
155 G7 Methley Street SE11
155 G2 Meymott Street SE1
151 K1 Micawber Street N1
152 A8 Micklethwaite Lane SW6
156 A1 Middlesex Street E1
156 B2 Middlesex Street E1
151 J5 Middle Street EC1A
150 F7 Middle Temple WC2R
150 F7 Middle Temple Lane EC4Y
157 H6 Middleton Drive SE16
150 C1 Midland Road NW1
157 J6 Midship Close SE16
152 D7 Milborne Grove SW10
155 H3 Milcote Street SE1
154 D8 Miles Street SW8
150 F7 Milford Lane WC2R
151 K6 Milk Street EC2V
157 G4 Milk Yard E1W
154 D4 Millbank SW1P
151 J8 Millennium Bridge SE1
157 M6 Millennium Harbour E14
157 L4 Milligan Street E14
150 E4 Millman Mews WC1N
150 E4 Millman Street WC1N
157 K3 Mill Place E14
156 B7 Millstream Road SE1
156 C6 Mill Street SE1
149 L7 Mill Street W1S
153 G5 Milner Street SW3
151 K4 Milton Street EC2Y
155 G7 Milverton Street SE11
156 A4 Mincing Lane EC3M
153 J5 Minera Mews SW1W
156 B3 Minories EC3N
151 J3 Mitchell Street EC1V
155 G2 Mitre Road SE1
156 A3 Mitre Street EC3A
149 G5 Molyneux Street W1H
154 C4 Monck Street SW1P
155 G5 Monkton Street SE11
151 K5 Monkwell Square EC2Y
148 A6 Monmouth Place W2
148 A6 Monmouth Road W2
150 C6 Monmouth Street WC2H
155 L1 Montague Close SE1
150 C5 Montague Place EC3R
150 C5 Montague Street WC1B
149 H5 Montagu Mansions W1U
149 H5 Montagu Mews North W1H
149 H6 Montagu Mews West W1H
149 H5 Montagu Place W1H
149 H5 Montagu Row W1U
149 H5 Montagu Square W1H
149 H6 Montagu Street W1H
154 F7 Montford Place SE11
156 C1 Monthorpe Road E1
153 G3 Montpelier Square SW7
153 G3 Montpelier Street SW7
152 G3 Montpelier Walk SW7
153 K3 Montrose Place SW1X
151 L7 Monument ⊖ EC4R
151 L7 Monument Street EC3R
151 M7 Monument Street EC3R
157 G4 Monza Street E1W
157 G7 Moodkee Street SE16
153 H5 Moore Street SW3
151 L5 Moorfields EC2Y
151 L6 Moorgate EC2R
151 L5 Moorgate ⇌⊖ EC2Y
151 K5 Moor Lane EC2Y
150 C7 Moor Street W1D
151 K2 Mora Street EC1V
155 K6 Morecambe Street SE17
151 H2 Moreland Street EC1V
156 A5 More London SE1
154 A6 Moreton Place SW1V
154 B6 Moreton Street SW1V
154 A6 Moreton Terrace SW1V
155 M2 Morgan's Lane SE1
156 A5 Morgan's Lane SE1
155 G3 Morley Street SE1
149 M1 Mornington Crescent NW1
149 L1 Mornington Place NW1
149 L1 Mornington Terrace NW1
156 A7 Morocco Street SE1
153 M5 Morpeth Terrace SW1P
156 F3 Morris Street E1
148 A2 Morshead Road W9
150 A4 Mortimer Market WC1E
150 A5 Mortimer Street W1T
149 M5 Mortimer Street W1W
154 F4 Morton Place SE1
150 B5 Morwell Street WC1B
148 B7 Moscow Place W2
148 B7 Moscow Road W2
153 G5 Mossop Street SW3
153 J4 Motcomb Street SW1X
152 E2 Mount Gate W2
151 J3 Mount Mills EC1V
150 F4 Mount Pleasant WC1X
149 K8 Mount Row W1K
149 K8 Mount Street W1K
149 K8 Mount Street Mews W1K
156 E1 Mount Terrace E1
149 J5 Moxon Street W1U
156 D2 Mulberry Street E1
152 E8 Mulberry Walk SW3
148 F4 Mulready Street NW8
151 M2 Mundy Street N1
149 L3 Munster Square NW1
155 K5 Munton Road SE17
154 F3 Murphy Street SE1
151 K1 Murray Grove N1
157 G2 Musbury Street E1
156 A4 Muscovy Street EC3N
150 C5 Museum Street WC1A
151 G2 Myddelton Passage EC1R
151 G1 Myddelton Square EC1R
151 G3 Myddelton Street EC1R
156 D2 Myrdle Street E1

N

150 F2 Naoroji Street WC1X
151 K1 Napier Grove N1
157 K4 Narrow Street E14
149 L2 Nash Street NW1
149 M5 Nassau Street W1W
156 C2 Nathaniel Close * E1
150 C6 Neal Street WC2H
156 C8 Neckinger SE1
157 H7 Needleman Street SE16
148 A1 Nelson Close NW6
151 H1 Nelson Place N1
155 H2 Nelson Square SE1
156 E2 Nelson Street E1
151 H1 Nelson Terrace N1
157 G7 Neptune Street SE16
156 D4 Nesham Street E1W
152 D8 Netherton Grove SW10
149 M2 Netley Street NW1
152 A6 Nevern Place SW5
152 A6 Nevern Square SW5
152 E6 Neville Street SW7
156 E2 Newark Street E1
157 M8 New Atlas Wharf E14
149 L7 New Bond Street W1S
149 L8 New Bond Street W1S
151 H6 New Bridge Street EC4V
151 M5 New Broad Street EC2M
149 M7 New Burlington Street W1S
154 F7 Newburn Street SE11
151 J5 Newbury Street EC1A
148 E5 Newcastle Place W2
149 K5 New Cavendish Street W1G
151 J6 New Change EC4M
155 L8 New Church Road SE5
155 K2 Newcomen Street SE1
148 F1 Newcourt Street NW8
157 L3 Newell Street E14
151 G6 New Fetter Lane EC4A
151 H6 Newgate Street WC1A
156 B2 New Goulston Street E1
156 A7 Newham's Row SE1
155 H6 Newington Butts SE1
155 J4 Newington Causeway SE1
155 K5 New Kent Road SE1
156 F4 Newlands Quay E1W
150 A5 Newman Street W1T
151 M3 New North Place EC2A
151 L1 New North Road N1
150 D4 New North Street WC1N
150 C6 New Oxford Street WC1A
154 E5 Newport Street SE11
149 H6 New Quebec Street W1H
152 E3 New Ride SW7
156 E2 New Road E1
150 C7 New Row WC2N
154 D7 New Spring Gardens Walk SE1
150 F6 New Square WC2A
156 A2 New Street EC2M
151 G6 New Street Square EC4A
148 A6 Newton Road W2
150 D5 Newton Street WC2B
151 K5 New Union Street EC2Y
151 L7 Nicholas Lane EC3V
155 H1 Nicholson Street SE1
152 D8 Nightingale Place SW10
151 K2 Nile Street N1
154 C8 Nine Elms Lane SW8
151 J6 Noble Street EC2V
151 J1 Noel Road N1
150 A6 Noel Street W1F
157 L2 Norbiton Road E14
149 G6 Norfolk Crescent W2
148 E6 Norfolk Place W2
148 E6 Norfolk Square W2
151 J3 Norman Street EC1V
150 B8 Norris Street SW1Y
151 G3 Northampton Road EC1R
151 H2 Northampton Square EC1V
149 J7 North Audley Street W1K
148 F2 North Bank NW8
151 H3 Northburgh Street EC1V
148 F7 North Carriage Drive W2
150 D1 Northdown Street N1
157 K4 Northey Street E14
150 A2 North Gower Street NW1
150 E4 Northington Street WC1N
150 E4 North Mews WC1N
149 G7 North Ride W2
149 J7 North Row W1K
156 C3 North Tenter Street E1
152 F5 North Terrace SW3
156 B3 Northumberland Alley EC3N
154 C1 Northumberland Avenue WC2N
148 A6 Northumberland Place W2
154 C1 Northumberland Street WC2N
148 E5 North Wharf Road W2
148 D3 Northwick Terrace NW8
157 L3 Norway Place E14
150 F5 Norwich Street EC4A
149 J4 Nottingham Place W1U
149 J4 Nottingham Street W1U
148 A8 Notting Hill Gate W11
152 A1 Notting Hill Gate ⊖ W11
148 D1 Nugent Terrace NW8
149 G6 Nutford Place W1H

O

155 G5 Oakden Street SE11
148 A3 Oakington Road W9
157 L3 Oak Lane E14
151 H1 Oakley Close EC1V
153 G8 Oakley Gardens SW3
150 A1 Oakley Square NW1
152 F8 Oakley Street SW3
148 F2 Oak Tree Road NW8
151 J5 Oat Lane EC2V
155 J6 Occupation Road SE17
157 J1 Ocean Square E1
157 L7 Odessa Street SE16
149 M5 Ogle Street W1W
151 H6 Old Bailey EC4M
153 J3 Old Barrack Yard SW1X
149 M8 Old Bond Street W1S
151 M6 Old Broad Street EC2N
152 B6 Old Brompton Road SW5
152 D6 Old Brompton Road SW7
149 M7 Old Burlington Street W1S
149 J4 Oldbury Place W1U
156 B2 Old Castle Street E1
149 L6 Old Cavendish Street W1G
157 H2 Old Church Road E1
152 E7 Old Church Street SW3
150 B7 Old Compton Street W1D
152 B3 Old Court Place W8
150 D4 Old Gloucester Street WC1N
156 C7 Old Jamaica Road SE16
151 K6 Old Jewry EC2R
155 M5 Old Kent Road SE1
149 G5 Old Marylebone Road NW1
156 C1 Old Montague Street E1
150 E5 Old North Street WC1X
154 E5 Old Paradise Street SE11
153 K2 Old Park Lane W1J
154 B4 Old Pye Street SW1P
154 B3 Old Queen Street SW1H
150 F6 Old Square WC2A
151 J3 Old Street EC1V
151 L3 Old Street ⇌⊖ EC1Y
151 L3 Oliver's Yard EC1Y
155 J8 Olney Road SE17
155 K2 O'Meara Street SE1
150 D1 Omega Place N1
157 J8 Onega Gate SE16
152 A8 Ongar Road SW6
152 D6 Onslow Gardens SW7
152 E5 Onslow Square SW7
152 E6 Onslow Square SW7
155 J4 Ontario Street SE1
157 M4 Ontario Way E14
155 H6 Opal Street SE1
157 G8 Orange Place SE16
153 K6 Orange Square SW1W
156 D5 Orange Street E1W
150 B8 Orange Street WC2H
155 L6 Orb Street SE17
148 E4 Orchardson Street NW8
149 J6 Orchard Street W1H
150 E4 Ordehall Street WC1N
155 H5 Orient Street SE11
148 B8 Orme Court W2
148 B8 Orme Lane W2
148 B8 Orme Square Gate W2
150 D4 Ormond Close WC1N
153 H7 Ormonde Gate SW3
150 A8 Ormond Yard SW1Y
154 E6 Orsett Street SE11
148 C6 Orsett Terrace W2
156 D5 Orton Street E1W
154 B6 Osbert Street SW1V
156 C2 Osborn Street E1
157 K7 Oslo Square SE16
149 L3 Osnaburgh Street NW1
149 L3 Osnaburgh Terrace NW1
149 J5 Ossington Buildings W1U
148 A7 Ossington Street W2
150 B1 Ossulston Street NW1
155 H5 Oswin Street SE11
155 H6 Othello Close SE1
155 H8 Otto Street SE17
149 H3 Outer Circle NW1
149 K1 Outer Circle NW1
154 F8 Oval ⊖ SE11
154 E7 Oval Way SE11
153 G4 Ovington Square SW3
153 G5 Ovington Street SW3
151 G1 Owen Street EC1V
150 B1 Oxendon Street SW1Y
149 M6 Oxford Circus ⊖ W1B
148 A1 Oxford Road NW6
148 F6 Oxford Square W2
149 L6 Oxford Street W1C
150 A6 Oxford Street WC1A

P

156 E3 Pace Place E1
157 H5 Pacific Wharf SE16
148 D6 Paddington ⇌⊖ W2
148 E5 Paddington Green W2
149 J5 Paddington Street W1U
157 K5 Pageant Crescent SE16
154 B5 Page Street SW1P
151 H2 Paget Street EC1V
150 E3 Pakenham Street WC1X
152 B2 Palace Avenue W8
148 A7 Palace Court W2
152 A1 Palace Gardens Terrace W8
152 C3 Palace Gate W8
152 B2 Palace Green W8
153 M4 Palace Place SW1E
153 M4 Palace Street SW1E
154 A1 Pall Mall SW1Y
154 B1 Pall Mall East SW1Y
154 B3 Palmer Street SW1H
151 K6 Pancras Lane EC4N
150 B8 Panton Street SW1Y
156 E7 Paradise Street SE16
153 H8 Paradise Walk SW3
155 L4 Pardoner Street SE1
151 H3 Pardon Street EC1V
156 D2 Parfett Street E1
155 G1 Paris Garden SE1

Q

R

S

T

U

V

W

Y

Z

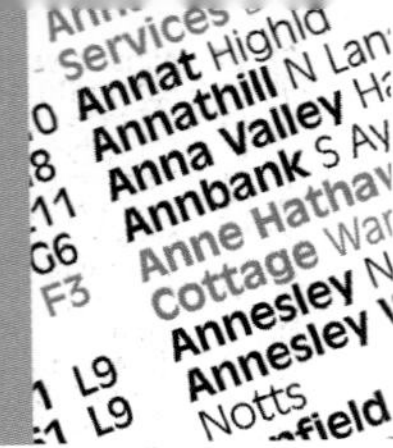

Index to place names

his index lists places appearing in the main-map section of the atlas in alphabetical order. The reference before each name gives the atlas page number and gri eference of the square in which the place appears. The map shows counties, unitary authorities and administrative areas, together with a list of the abbreviated ame forms used in the index.

he top 100 places of tourist interest are indexed in **red** (or **green** if a World Heritage site), motorway service areas in **blue** and airports in blue *italic*.

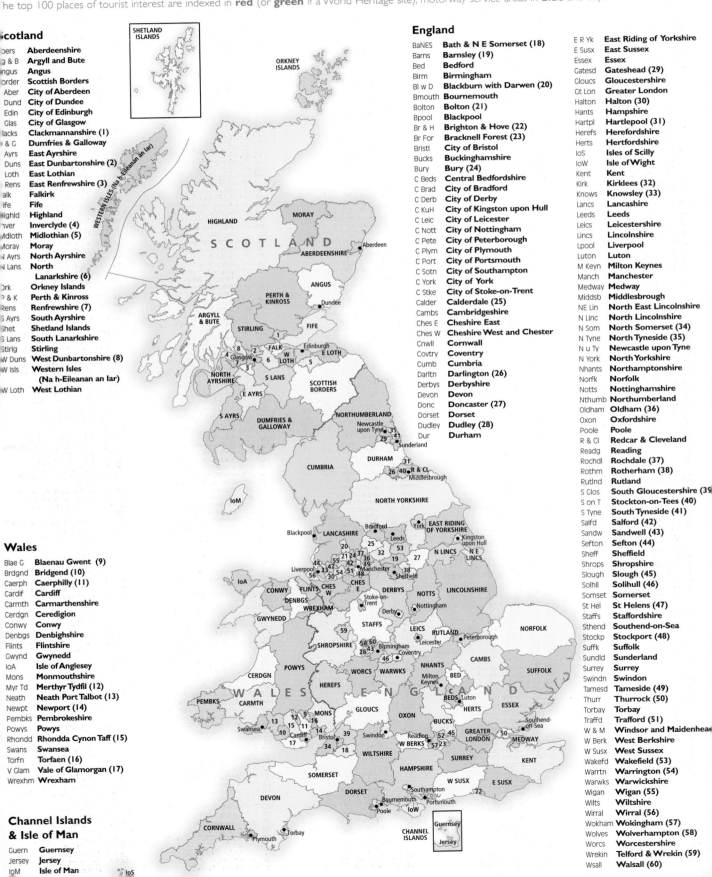

cotland

bers	**Aberdeenshire**
g & B	**Argyll and Bute**
ngus	**Angus**
order	**Scottish Borders**
Aber	**City of Aberdeen**
Dund	**City of Dundee**
Edin	**City of Edinburgh**
Glas	**City of Glasgow**
lacks	**Clackmannanshire (1)**
& G	**Dumfries & Galloway**
Ayrs	**East Ayrshire**
Duns	**East Dunbartonshire (2)**
Loth	**East Lothian**
Rens	**East Renfrewshire (3)**
alk	**Falkirk**
ife	**Fife**
lighld	**Highland**
nver	**Inverclyde (4)**
dloth	**Midlothian (5)**
Moray	**Moray**
N Ayrs	**North Ayrshire**
N Lans	**North Lanarkshire (6)**
Ork	**Orkney Islands**
P & K	**Perth & Kinross**
Rens	**Renfrewshire (7)**
S Ayrs	**South Ayrshire**
Shet	**Shetland Islands**
S Lans	**South Lanarkshire**
Stirlg	**Stirling**
W Duns	**West Dunbartonshire (8)**
W Isls	**Western Isles (Na h-Eileanan an Iar)**
W Loth	**West Lothian**

Wales

Blae G	**Blaenau Gwent (9)**
Brdgnd	**Bridgend (10)**
Caerph	**Caerphilly (11)**
Cardif	**Cardiff**
Carmth	**Carmarthenshire**
Cerdgn	**Ceredigion**
Conwy	**Conwy**
Denbgs	**Denbighshire**
Flints	**Flintshire**
Gwynd	**Gwynedd**
IoA	**Isle of Anglesey**
Mons	**Monmouthshire**
Myr Td	**Merthyr Tydfil (12)**
Neath	**Neath Port Talbot (13)**
Newpt	**Newport (14)**
Pembks	**Pembrokeshire**
Powys	**Powys**
Rhondd	**Rhondda Cynon Taff (15)**
Swans	**Swansea**
Torfn	**Torfaen (16)**
V Glam	**Vale of Glamorgan (17)**
Wrexhm	**Wrexham**

Channel Islands & Isle of Man

Guern	**Guernsey**
Jersey	**Jersey**
IoM	**Isle of Man**

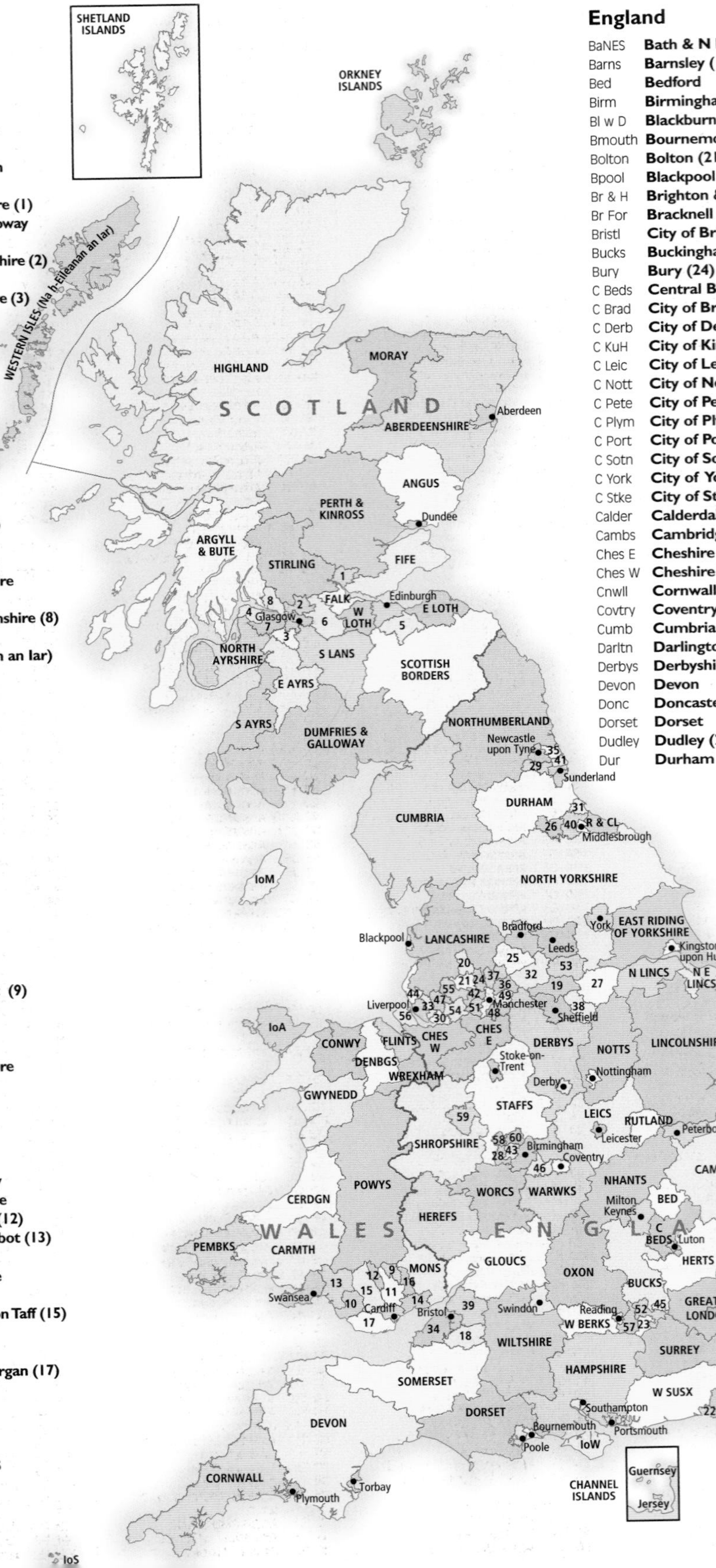

England

BaNES	**Bath & N E Somerset (18)**
Barns	**Barnsley (19)**
Bed	**Bedford**
Birm	**Birmingham**
Bl w D	**Blackburn with Darwen (20)**
Bmouth	**Bournemouth**
Bolton	**Bolton (21)**
Bpool	**Blackpool**
Br & H	**Brighton & Hove (22)**
Br For	**Bracknell Forest (23)**
Bristl	**City of Bristol**
Bucks	**Buckinghamshire**
Bury	**Bury (24)**
C Beds	**Central Bedfordshire**
C Brad	**City of Bradford**
C Derb	**City of Derby**
C KuH	**City of Kingston upon Hull**
C Leic	**City of Leicester**
C Nott	**City of Nottingham**
C Pete	**City of Peterborough**
C Plym	**City of Plymouth**
C Port	**City of Portsmouth**
C Sotn	**City of Southampton**
C York	**City of York**
C Stke	**City of Stoke-on-Trent**
Calder	**Calderdale (25)**
Cambs	**Cambridgeshire**
Ches E	**Cheshire East**
Ches W	**Cheshire West and Chester**
Cnwll	**Cornwall**
Covtry	**Coventry**
Cumb	**Cumbria**
Darltn	**Darlington (26)**
Derbys	**Derbyshire**
Devon	**Devon**
Donc	**Doncaster (27)**
Dorset	**Dorset**
Dudley	**Dudley (28)**
Dur	**Durham**
E R Yk	**East Riding of Yorkshire**
E Susx	**East Sussex**
Essex	**Essex**
Gatesd	**Gateshead (29)**
Gloucs	**Gloucestershire**
Gt Lon	**Greater London**
Halton	**Halton (30)**
Hants	**Hampshire**
Hartpl	**Hartlepool (31)**
Herefs	**Herefordshire**
Herts	**Hertfordshire**
IoS	**Isles of Scilly**
IoW	**Isle of Wight**
Kent	**Kent**
Kirk	**Kirklees (32)**
Knows	**Knowsley (33)**
Lancs	**Lancashire**
Leeds	**Leeds**
Leics	**Leicestershire**
Lincs	**Lincolnshire**
Lpool	**Liverpool**
Luton	**Luton**
M Keyn	**Milton Keynes**
Manch	**Manchester**
Medway	**Medway**
Middsb	**Middlesbrough**
NE Lin	**North East Lincolnshire**
N Linc	**North Lincolnshire**
N Som	**North Somerset (34)**
N Tyne	**North Tyneside (35)**
N u Ty	**Newcastle upon Tyne**
N York	**North Yorkshire**
Nhants	**Northamptonshire**
Norfk	**Norfolk**
Notts	**Nottinghamshire**
Nthumb	**Northumberland**
Oldham	**Oldham (36)**
Oxon	**Oxfordshire**
Poole	**Poole**
R & Cl	**Redcar & Cleveland**
Readg	**Reading**
Rochdl	**Rochdale (37)**
Rothm	**Rotherham (38)**
Rutlnd	**Rutland**
S Glos	**South Gloucestershire (39**
S on T	**Stockton-on-Tees (40)**
S Tyne	**South Tyneside (41)**
Salfd	**Salford (42)**
Sandw	**Sandwell (43)**
Sefton	**Sefton (44)**
Sheff	**Sheffield**
Shrops	**Shropshire**
Slough	**Slough (45)**
Solhll	**Solihull (46)**
Somset	**Somerset**
St Hel	**St Helens (47)**
Staffs	**Staffordshire**
Sthend	**Southend-on-Sea**
Stockp	**Stockport (48)**
Suffk	**Suffolk**
Sundld	**Sunderland**
Surrey	**Surrey**
Swindn	**Swindon**
Tamesd	**Tameside (49)**
Thurr	**Thurrock (50)**
Torbay	**Torbay**
Traffd	**Trafford (51)**
W & M	**Windsor and Maidenhea**
W Berk	**West Berkshire**
W Susx	**West Sussex**
Wakefd	**Wakefield (53)**
Warrtn	**Warrington (54)**
Warwks	**Warwickshire**
Wigan	**Wigan (55)**
Wilts	**Wiltshire**
Wirral	**Wirral (56)**
Wokham	**Wokingham (57)**
Wolves	**Wolverhampton (58)**
Worcs	**Worcestershire**
Wrekin	**Telford & Wrekin (59)**
Wsall	**Walsall (60)**

A

44 C7 Ardnadam Ag & B
96 H11 Ardnagrask Highld
97 M3 Ardnarff Highld
89 Q4 Ardnastang Highld
33 L10 Ardpatrick Ag & B
33 M6 Ardrishaig Ag & B
07 K7 Ardross Highld
76 D3 Ardrossan N Ayrs
58 H8 Ardsley East Leeds
89 L4 Ardslignish Highld
82 G11 Ardtalla Ag & B
89 M3 Ardtoe Highld
83 M2 Arduaine Ag & B
07 J9 Ardullie Highld
96 H8 Ardvasar Highld
91 P10 Ardvorlich P & K
11 c3 Ardvourlie W Isls
68 F9 Ardwell D & G
57 Q9 Ardwick Manch
39 P7 Areley Kings Worcs
89 N3 Arevegaig Highld
10 D3 Arford Hants
27 N8 Argoed Caerph
84 D3 Argyll Forest Park Ag & B
11 c3 Aribruach W Isls
88 H10 Aridhglas Ag & B
88 E5 Arileod Ag & B
88 F5 Arinagour Ag & B
90 B10 Ariogan Ag & B
97 J11 Arisaig Highld
97 J11 Arisaig House Highld
59 K2 Arkendale N York
33 M9 Arkesden Essex
63 L7 Arkholme Lancs
79 N10 Arkleton D & G
21 K4 Arkley Gt Lon
59 M11 Arksey Donc
51 K6 Arkwright Town Derbys
29 N4 Arle Gloucs
70 G10 Arlecdon Cumb
32 H9 Arlesey C Beds
49 M12 Arleston Wrekin
57 M11 Arley Ches E
40 H8 Arley Warwks
29 J6 Arlingham Gloucs
15 K4 Arlington Devon
12 B8 Arlington E Susx
96 H8 Armadale Highld
109 N3 Armadale Highld
85 Q8 Armadale W Loth
71 Q6 Armathwaite Cumb
45 L8 Arminghall Norfk
40 E4 Armitage Staffs
58 H7 Armley Leeds
30 G5 Armscote Warwks
59 N12 Armthorpe Donc
88 F4 Arnabost Ag & B
64 G12 Arncliffe N York
87 K2 Arncroach Fife
101 K6 Arndilly House Moray
8 E9 Arne Dorset
41 N8 Arnesby Leics
92 H12 Arngask P & K
97 L7 Arnisdale Highld
104 H11 Arnish Highld
86 G9 Arniston Mdloth
111 d1 Arnol W Isls
61 J6 Arnold E R Yk
51 N10 Arnold Notts
85 K4 Arnprior Stirlg
63 J6 Arnside Cumb
89 L7 Aros Ag & B
62 F6 Arrad Foot Cumb
60 H5 Arram E R Yk
75 P5 Arran N Ayrs
65 L8 Arrathorne N York
9 N9 Arreton IoW
105 L10 Arrina Highld
33 K6 Arrington Cambs
84 E3 Arrochar Ag & B
30 E3 Arrow Warwks
38 H1 Arscott Shrops
107 K6 Artafallie Highld
58 H5 Arthington Leeds
41 Q10 Arthingworth Nhants
103 K7 Arthrath Abers
103 L8 Artrochie Abers
10 G8 Arundel W Susx
70 H10 Asby Cumb
84 B9 Ascog Ag & B
20 E9 Ascot W & M
30 H9 Ascott-under-Wychwood Oxon
65 P11 Asenby N York
41 P4 Asfordby Leics
41 Q4 Asfordby Hill Leics
42 G2 Asgarby Lincs
22 C9 Ash Kent
23 P10 Ash Kent
17 L11 Ash Somset
20 E12 Ash Surrey
19 P5 Ashampstead W Berk
35 K6 Ashbocking Suffk
50 F10 Ashbourne Derbys
16 E11 Ashbrittle Somset
5 P6 Ashburton Devon
15 J11 Ashbury Devon
19 J4 Ashbury Oxon
52 C2 Ashby N Linc
53 L9 Ashby by Partney Lincs
53 J4 Ashby cum Fenby NE Lin
52 F11 Ashby de la Launde Lincs
41 J4 Ashby-de-la-Zouch Leics
41 P5 Ashby Folville Leics
41 M9 Ashby Magna Leics
41 M9 Ashby Parva Leics
53 K8 Ashby Puerorum Lincs
31 M1 Ashby St Ledgers Nhants
45 M9 Ashby St Mary Norfk
29 N3 Ashchurch Gloucs
6 C6 Ashcombe Devon
17 J4 Ashcombe N Som
17 L8 Ashcott Somset
33 P8 Ashdon Essex
19 N10 Ashe Hants
23 J3 Asheldham Essex
34 C8 Ashen Essex
31 P10 Ashendon Bucks
20 F3 Asheridge Bucks
85 N3 Ashfield Stirlg
35 K4 Ashfield cum Thorpe Suffk
35 L3 Ashfield Green Suffk
5 N9 Ashford Devon
15 J5 Ashford Devon
13 J2 Ashford Kent
20 H8 Ashford Surrey
39 K7 Ashford Bowdler Shrops
39 K7 Ashford Carbonell Shrops
19 P8 Ashford Hill Hants
50 G6 Ashford in the Water Derbys
77 N2 Ashgill S Lans
20 E12 Ash Green Surrey
41 J9 Ash Green Warwks
6 E1 Ashill Devon
44 E8 Ashill Norfk
17 J11 Ashill Somset
22 G5 Ashingdon Essex
73 M4 Ashington Nthumb
17 N11 Ashington Somset
11 J7 Ashington W Susx
79 P4 Ashkirk Border
29 L4 Ashleworth Gloucs
29 L4 Ashleworth Quay Gloucs
34 B5 Ashley Cambs
57 P11 Ashley Ches E
15 L9 Ashley Devon
29 N9 Ashley Gloucs
9 J8 Ashley Hants
9 L2 Ashley Hants
13 P1 Ashley Kent
42 B11 Ashley Nhants
49 N8 Ashley Staffs
18 B7 Ashley Wilts
20 F3 Ashley Green Bucks
49 K7 Ash Magna Shrops
19 M8 Ashmansworth Hants
14 F8 Ashmansworthy Devon
15 N7 Ash Mill Devon
8 D4 Ashmore Dorset
19 N6 Ashmore Green W Berk
30 H3 Ashorne Warwks
51 J8 Ashover Derbys
40 H12 Ashow Warwks
28 H1 Ashperton Herefs
5 Q8 Ashprington Devon
16 F9 Ash Priors Somset
15 L9 Ashreigney Devon
34 G7 Ash Street Suffk
21 J10 Ashtead Surrey
6 D1 Ash Thomas Devon
49 J2 Ashton Ches W
2 F9 Ashton Cnwll
6 B6 Ashton Devon
39 K8 Ashton Herefs
84 D7 Ashton Inver
31 Q4 Ashton Nhants
42 F11 Ashton Nhants
18 D8 Ashton Common Wilts
57 L8 Ashton-in-Makerfield Wigan
18 F2 Ashton Keynes Wilts
30 C6 Ashton under Hill Worcs
50 C2 Ashton-under-Lyne Tamesd
9 K5 Ashurst Hants
11 P3 Ashurst Kent
57 J7 Ashurst Lancs
11 J6 Ashurst W Susx
11 N3 Ashurstwood W Susx
20 E11 Ash Vale Surrey
5 J2 Ashwater Devon
33 J8 Ashwell Herts
42 C7 Ashwell Rutlnd
33 J8 Ashwell End Herts
45 J9 Ashwellthorpe Norfk
17 P6 Ashwick Somset
44 B6 Ashwicken Norfk
62 E6 Askam in Furness Cumb
59 M10 Askern Donc
7 M4 Askerswell Dorset
20 D3 Askett Bucks
71 Q10 Askham Cumb
51 Q6 Askham Notts
59 M5 Askham Bryan C York
59 M5 Askham Richard C York
83 P5 Asknish Ag & B
64 G8 Askrigg N York
58 F5 Askwith N York
42 F4 Aslackby Lincs
45 J11 Aslacton Norfk
51 Q11 Aslockton Notts
71 J7 Aspatria Cumb
33 K10 Aspenden Herts
32 D9 Aspley Guise C Beds
32 D9 Aspley Heath C Beds
57 L7 Aspull Wigan
60 C8 Asselby E R Yk
34 F8 Assington Suffk
34 C6 Assington Green Suffk
49 Q3 Astbury Ches E
31 P4 Astcote Nhants
53 J7 Asterby Lincs
38 G1 Asterley Shrops
38 H4 Asterton Shrops
30 H10 Asthall Oxon
30 H10 Asthall Leigh Oxon
107 M4 Astle Highld
49 K10 Astley Shrops
40 H9 Astley Warwks
57 M8 Astley Wigan
39 P8 Astley Worcs
39 N3 Astley Abbots Shrops
57 N6 Astley Bridge Bolton
39 P8 Astley Cross Worcs
49 L6 Aston Ches E
57 K12 Aston Ches W
50 F4 Aston Derbys
48 F3 Aston Flints
33 J11 Aston Herts
31 J12 Aston Oxon
51 L4 Aston Rothm
39 P4 Aston Shrops
49 K9 Aston Shrops
40 B3 Aston Staffs
49 N7 Aston Staffs
20 C6 Aston Wokham
49 L12 Aston Wrekin
32 C11 Aston Abbotts Bucks
39 L5 Aston Botterell Shrops
40 B2 Aston-by-Stone Staffs
30 F3 Aston Cantlow Warwks
20 E2 Aston Clinton Bucks
29 J4 Aston Crews Herefs
33 J11 Aston End Herts
40 C12 Aston Fields Worcs
41 L8 Aston Flamville Leics
29 J4 Aston Ingham Herefs
31 L4 Aston le Walls Nhants
30 G7 Aston Magna Gloucs
39 K5 Aston Munslow Shrops
38 H6 Aston on Clun Shrops
38 G2 Aston Pigott Shrops
38 G2 Aston Rogers Shrops
20 B4 Aston Rowant Oxon
30 D6 Aston Somerville Worcs
30 F6 Aston-sub-Edge Gloucs
19 P4 Aston Tirrold Oxon
41 K2 Aston-upon-Trent Derbys
19 P4 Aston Upthorpe Oxon
32 H8 Astwick C Beds
32 D7 Astwood M Keyn
30 C2 Astwood Worcs
30 D2 Astwood Bank Worcs
39 Q10 Astwood Crematorium Worcs
42 F3 Aswarby Lincs
53 L9 Aswardby Lincs
39 K1 Atcham Shrops
8 B8 Athelhampton Dorset
35 K3 Athelington Suffk
17 J9 Athelney Somset
87 K6 Athelstaneford E Loth
15 K7 Atherington Devon
40 H7 Atherstone Warwks
30 G4 Atherstone on Stour Warwks
57 M8 Atherton Wigan
50 G10 Atlow Derbys
97 N3 Attadale Highld
52 E5 Atterby Lincs
51 J3 Attercliffe Sheff
41 J7 Atterton Leics
44 H10 Attleborough Norfk
41 J8 Attleborough Warwks
45 J6 Attlebridge Norfk
34 C6 Attleton Green Suffk
61 K4 Atwick E R Yk
18 C7 Atworth Wilts
52 D10 Aubourn Lincs
101 J9 Auchbreck Moray
103 J8 Auchedly Abers
95 M6 Auchenblae Abers
85 N5 Auchenbowie Stirlg
70 D5 Auchencairn D & G
78 F11 Auchencairn D & G
75 Q6 Auchencairn N Ayrs
87 Q9 Auchencrow Border
86 F9 Auchendinny Mdloth
86 B10 Auchengray S Lans
101 M3 Auchenhalrig Moray
77 N3 Auchenheath S Lans
77 N11 Auchenhessnane D & G
83 P8 Auchenlochan Ag & B
76 F2 Auchenmade N Ayrs
68 G8 Auchenmalg D & G
76 F2 Auchentiber N Ayrs
83 Q3 Auchindrain Ag & B
106 C6 Auchindrean Highld
102 E6 Auchininna Abers
77 J7 Auchinleck E Ayrs
85 L8 Auchinloch N Lans
85 M7 Auchinstarry N Lans
90 F2 Auchintore Highld
103 M7 Auchiries Abers
99 M9 Auchlean Highld
95 P3 Auchlee Abers
102 E9 Auchleven Abers
77 N4 Auchlochan S Lans
95 J2 Auchlossan Abers
91 M9 Auchlyne Stirlg
77 J5 Auchmillan E Ayrs
93 R6 Auchmithie Angus
86 E3 Auchmuirbridge Fife
94 H8 Auchnacree Angus
103 J7 Auchnagatt Abers
101 J9 Auchnarrow Moray
68 D7 Auchnotteroch D & G
101 L5 Auchroisk Moray
92 E12 Auchterarder P & K
98 E7 Auchteraw Highld
99 N5 Auchterblair Highld
105 M7 Auchtercairn Highld
86 E3 Auchterderran Fife
93 L8 Auchterhouse Angus
102 F7 Auchterless Abers
93 J12 Auchtermuchty Fife
106 H9 Auchterneed Highld
86 E4 Auchtertool Fife
97 L4 Auchtertyre Highld
91 N11 Auchtubh Stirlg
110 G3 Auckengill Highld
51 P1 Auckley Donc
50 B2 Audenshaw Tamesd
49 M6 Audlem Ches E
49 P5 Audley Staffs
33 N8 Audley End Essex
33 N8 Audley End House Essex
60 C6 Aughton E R Yk
56 H7 Aughton Lancs
63 K8 Aughton Lancs
51 L4 Aughton Rothm
19 J9 Aughton Wilts
56 H7 Aughton Park Lancs
100 E4 Auldearn Highld
39 J10 Aulden Herefs
78 E10 Auldgirth D & G
77 K2 Auldhouse S Lans
97 N5 Ault a' chruinn Highld
105 N5 Aultbea Highld
105 L5 Aultgrishin Highld
106 F8 Aultguish Inn Highld
51 L7 Ault Hucknall Derbys
101 M5 Aultmore Moray
98 H4 Aultnagoire Highld
107 L6 Aultnamain Inn Highld
42 F3 Aunsby Lincs
28 G10 Aust S Glos
51 P2 Austerfield Donc
40 H6 Austrey Warwks
63 N8 Austwick N York
53 L7 Authorpe Lincs
18 G6 Avebury Wilts
22 C7 Aveley Thurr
29 M8 Avening Gloucs
51 Q9 Averham Notts
5 N10 Aveton Gifford Devon
99 N6 Aviemore Highld
19 L7 Avington W Berk
107 L10 Avoch Highld
8 G7 Avon Hants
85 Q8 Avonbridge Falk
31 K4 Avon Dassett Warwks
28 F12 Avonmouth Bristl
5 P8 Avonwick Devon
9 K3 Awbridge Hants
6 F3 Awliscombe Devon
29 J7 Awre Gloucs
51 L11 Awsworth Notts
17 L5 Axbridge Somset
19 Q11 Axford Hants
19 J6 Axford Wilts
6 H3 Axminster Devon
6 H5 Axmouth Devon
65 M3 Aycliffe Dur
72 H7 Aydon Nthumb
28 H8 Aylburton Gloucs
6 D4 Aylesbeare Devon
20 D1 Aylesbury Bucks
52 H3 Aylesby NE Lin
22 E10 Aylesford Kent
23 N11 Aylesham Kent
41 M7 Aylestone C Leic
45 K3 Aylmerton Norfk
45 K5 Aylsham Norfk
28 H2 Aylton Herefs
30 E9 Aylworth Gloucs
38 H8 Aymestrey Herefs
31 L7 Aynho Nhants
32 H12 Ayot St Lawrence Herts
76 F7 Ayr S Ayrs
64 H9 Aysgarth N York
16 E11 Ayshford Devon
62 H5 Ayside Cumb
42 C9 Ayston Rutlnd
81 J3 Ayton Border
65 M11 Azerley N York

B

6 C9 Babbacombe Torbay
33 L12 Babbs Green Herts
17 N9 Babcary Somset
33 N6 Babraham Cambs
51 P5 Babworth Notts
111 h1 Backaland Ork
103 L5 Backfolds Abers
48 H2 Backford Ches W
107 N3 Backies Highld
97 J11 Back of Keppoch Highld
17 L3 Backwell N Som
45 L3 Baconsthorpe Norfk
28 D3 Bacton Herefs
45 M4 Bacton Norfk
34 H4 Bacton Suffk
57 Q4 Bacup Lancs
105 L7 Badachro Highld
18 H5 Badbury Swindn
31 M3 Badby Nhants
108 D7 Badcall Highld
108 E5 Badcall Highld
105 Q4 Badcaul Highld
40 G11 Baddesley Clinton Warwks
40 H7 Baddesley Ensor Warwks
108 C10 Baddidarrach Highld
86 D10 Baddinsgill Border
102 F7 Badenscoth Abers
101 L10 Badenyon Abers
39 N3 Badger Shrops
29 M5 Badgeworth Gloucs
17 K5 Badgworth Somset
97 K4 Badicaul Highld
35 M3 Badingham Suffk
23 J11 Badlesmere Kent
78 H5 Badlieu Border
110 F6 Badlipster Highld
105 P4 Badluachrach Highld
107 M4 Badninish Highld
105 Q4 Badrallach Highld
30 E5 Badsey Worcs
10 D1 Badshot Lea Surrey
59 L10 Badsworth Wakefd
34 G3 Badwell Ash Suffk
17 Q12 Bagber Dorset
66 C10 Bagby N York
53 K8 Bag Enderby Lincs
30 D11 Bagendon Gloucs
111 a7 Bagh a Chaisteil W Isls
111 a7 Bagh a Tuath W Isls
48 E1 Bagillt Flints
41 J11 Baginton Warwks
26 G9 Baglan Neath
48 H9 Bagley Shrops
17 L7 Bagley Somset
50 B10 Bagnall Staffs
39 L7 Bagot Shrops
20 E10 Bagshot Surrey
29 J10 Bagstone S Glos
41 K6 Bagworth Leics
28 E4 Bagwy Llydiart Herefs
58 F6 Baildon C Brad
58 F6 Baildon Green C Brad
111 d2 Baile Ailein W Isls
111 b5 Baile a Mhanaich W Isls
88 G10 Baile Mor Ag & B
85 L9 Baillieston C Glas
64 G9 Bainbridge N York
102 D8 Bainshole Abers
42 F8 Bainton C Pete
60 G4 Bainton E R Yk
86 G2 Baintown Fife
80 E10 Bairnkine Border
50 G7 Bakewell Derbys
47 Q4 Bala Gwynd
111 d2 Balallan W Isls
98 F3 Balbeg Highld
92 H9 Balbeggie P & K
106 H12 Balblair Highld
107 L8 Balblair Highld
51 M1 Balby Donc
70 D5 Balcary D & G
98 G1 Balchraggan Highld
108 D4 Balchreick Highld
11 L4 Balcombe W Susx
87 M1 Balcomie Links Fife
65 N10 Baldersby N York
65 P11 Baldersby St James N York
57 L3 Balderstone Lancs
52 B12 Balderton Notts
93 M12 Baldinnie Fife
92 F11 Baldinnies P & K
33 J9 Baldock Herts
32 H9 Baldock Services Herts
93 M8 Baldovie C Dund
56 d5 Baldrine IoM
12 F7 Baldslow E Susx
44 G3 Bale Norfk
93 K9 Baledgarno P & K
88 C7 Balemartine Ag & B
86 D8 Balerno C Edin
86 F2 Balfarg Fife
95 J8 Balfield Angus
111 h2 Balfour Ork
85 J5 Balfron Stirlg
102 E7 Balgaveny Abers
86 B4 Balgonar Fife
68 F9 Balgowan D & G
99 J9 Balgowan Highld
104 E8 Balgown Highld
68 D7 Balgracie D & G
78 E4 Balgray S Lans
21 L8 Balham Gt Lon
93 J6 Balhary P & K
92 H8 Balholmie P & K
109 P3 Baligill Highld
93 K4 Balintore Angus
107 P7 Balintore Highld
107 M8 Balintraid Highld
111 b5 Balivanich W Isls
93 K6 Balkeerie Angus
60 D8 Balkholme E R Yk
90 E5 Ballachulish Highld
56 e4 Ballajora IoM
83 Q9 Ballanlay Ag & B
68 E3 Ballantrae S Ayrs
56 b6 Ballasalla IoM
94 F3 Ballater Abers
56 c3 Ballaugh IoM
107 M7 Ballchraggan Highld
87 J6 Ballencrieff E Loth
88 B7 Ballevullin Ag & B
50 G9 Ballidon Derbys
75 N5 Balliekine N Ayrs
84 B3 Balliemore Ag & B
68 G2 Balligmorrie S Ayrs
91 M11 Ballimore Stirlg
101 J7 Ballindalloch Moray
93 J9 Ballindean P & K
20 E3 Ballinger Common Bucks
28 G3 Ballingham Herefs
86 E3 Ballingry Fife
92 E5 Ballinluig P & K
93 M5 Ballinshoe Angus
92 G5 Ballintuim P & K
107 M11 Balloch Highld
85 M7 Balloch N Lans
92 C10 Balloch P & K
76 F11 Balloch S Ayrs
84 G6 Balloch W Duns
10 F5 Balls Cross W Susx
11 P3 Balls Green E Susx
89 J7 Ballygown Ag & B
82 E9 Ballygrant Ag & B
88 E5 Ballyhaugh Ag & B
69 P4 Balmaclellan D & G
69 P9 Balmae D & G
84 G5 Balmaha Stirlg
86 G1 Balmalcolm Fife
69 P9 Balmangan D & G
103 K10 Balmedie Abers
93 L10 Balmerino Fife
75 P6 Balmichael N Ayrs
94 D3 Balmoral Castle Grounds Abers
85 K8 Balmore E Duns
107 P6 Balmuchy Highld
86 E5 Balmule Fife
93 M10 Balmullo Fife
109 P12 Balnacoil Lodge Highld
105 P12 Balnacra Highld
94 E3 Balnacroft Abers
99 K2 Balnafoich Highld
92 E5 Balnaguard P & K
82 F3 Balnahard Ag & B
89 K9 Balnahard Ag & B
98 F3 Balnain Highld
108 G3 Balnakeil Highld
59 N9 Balne N York
92 F8 Balquharn P & K
91 M11 Balquhidder Stirlg
40 G11 Balsall Common Solhll
40 E9 Balsall Heath Birm
31 K6 Balscote Oxon
33 P6 Balsham Cambs
111 m2 Baltasound Shet
69 K6 Baltersan D & G
17 M8 Baltonsborough Somset
89 Q11 Balvicar Ag & B
97 M6 Balvraid Highld
99 M3 Balvraid Highld
57 K4 Bamber Bridge Lancs
33 P11 Bamber's Green Essex
81 N7 Bamburgh Nthumb
81 N7 Bamburgh Castle Nthumb
50 G4 Bamford Derbys
71 Q11 Bampton Cumb
16 C10 Bampton Devon
30 H12 Bampton Oxon
71 Q11 Bampton Grange Cumb
90 F2 Banavie Highld
31 L6 Banbury Oxon
31 L5 Banbury Crematorium Oxon
26 C6 Bancffosfelen Carmth
95 L3 Banchory Abers
95 P2 Banchory-Devenick Abers
25 P6 Bancycapel Carmth
25 N5 Bancyfelin Carmth
93 J9 Bandirran P & K
102 F3 Banff Abers
54 H7 Bangor Gwynd
54 H7 Bangor Crematorium Gwynd
48 H6 Bangor-is-y-coed Wrexhm
14 D11 Bangors Cnwll
44 H11 Banham Norfk
9 K6 Bank Hants
70 G2 Bankend D & G
92 F8 Bankfoot P & K
77 K8 Bankglen E Ayrs
103 J12 Bankhead C Aber
86 B12 Bankhead S Lans
85 N7 Banknock Falk
56 H5 Banks Lancs
79 K11 Bankshill D & G
45 K4 Banningham Norfk
34 B11 Bannister Green Essex
85 N5 Bannockburn Stirlg
21 K10 Banstead Surrey
5 N10 Bantham Devon
85 M7 Banton N Lans
17 K4 Banwell N Som
22 H10 Bapchild Kent
18 E12 Bapton Wilts
111 d1 Barabhas W Isls
76 F5 Barassie S Ayrs

65 Q11 Bracewell Lancs
51 J8 Brackenfield Derbys
85 M8 Brackenhirst N Lans
10 D10 Bracklesham W Susx
98 B11 Brackletter Highld
31 N6 Brackley Nhants
20 E9 Bracknell Br For
85 N2 Braco P & K
101 P5 Bracobrae Moray
45 K9 Bracon Ash Norfk
97 K10 Bracora Highld
97 K10 Bracorina Highld
50 G9 Bradbourne Derbys
65 N2 Bradbury Dur
31 N5 Bradden Nhants
20 D4 Bradenham Bucks
18 E5 Bradenstoke Wilts
6 E2 Bradfield Devon
35 J9 Bradfield Essex
45 L4 Bradfield Norfk
50 H3 Bradfield Sheff
19 P6 Bradfield W Berk
34 E5 Bradfield Combust Suffk
49 M4 Bradfield Green Ches E
35 J10 Bradfield Heath Essex
34 E5 Bradfield St Clare Suffk
34 E5 Bradfield St George Suffk
58 F7 Bradford C Brad
14 G10 Bradford Devon
17 N12 Bradford Abbas Dorset
18 C8 Bradford Leigh Wilts
18 C8 Bradford-on-Avon Wilts
16 G10 Bradford-on-Tone Somset
7 P4 Bradford Peverell Dorset
15 K5 Bradiford Devon
9 Q9 Brading IoW
50 G10 Bradley Derbys
19 Q11 Bradley Hants
53 J3 Bradley NE Lin
49 Q11 Bradley Staffs
40 C8 Bradley Wolves
30 C2 Bradley Worcs
30 C2 Bradley Green Worcs
50 D11 Bradley in the Moors Staffs
28 H11 Bradley Stoke S Glos
41 N2 Bradmore Notts
6 D3 Bradninch Devon
50 D9 Bradnop Staffs
7 L4 Bradpole Dorset
58 E8 Bradshaw Calder
4 H4 Bradstone Devon
49 N3 Bradwall Green Ches E
50 F5 Bradwell Derbys
34 D11 Bradwell Essex
32 B8 Bradwell M Keyn
45 Q8 Bradwell Norfk
49 Q5 Bradwell Crematorium Staffs
23 J3 Bradwell-on-Sea Essex
23 J2 Bradwell Waterside Essex
14 F8 Bradworthy Devon
107 L9 Brae Highld
111 k3 Brae Shet
85 N7 Braeface Falk
95 L10 Braehead Angus
69 K8 Braehead D & G
77 Q2 Braehead S Lans
94 C4 Braemar Abers
106 C6 Braemore Highld
110 C9 Braemore Highld
98 D10 Brae Roy Lodge Highld
84 D7 Braeside Inver
93 K4 Braes of Coul Angus
101 M4 Braes of Enzie Moray
111 i1 Braeswick Ork
83 P2 Braevallich Ag & B
65 N4 Brafferton Darltn
66 B12 Brafferton N York
32 B5 Brafield-on-the-Green Nhants
111 d1 Bragar W Isls
33 J11 Bragbury End Herts
77 P2 Braidwood S Lans
50 G11 Brailsford Derbys
34 C11 Braintree Essex
35 J3 Braiseworth Suffk
9 L3 Braishfield Hants
71 K10 Braithwaite Cumb
51 M2 Braithwell Donc
11 J7 Bramber W Susx
41 K9 Bramcote Warwks
51 L11 Bramcote Crematorium Notts
9 Q2 Bramdean Hants
45 L8 Bramerton Norfk
33 J12 Bramfield Herts
35 N3 Bramfield Suffk
35 J7 Bramford Suffk
50 B4 Bramhall Stockp
59 K5 Bramham Leeds
58 G5 Bramhope Leeds
19 Q8 Bramley Hants
58 G7 Bramley Leeds
51 L3 Bramley Rothm
10 G2 Bramley Surrey
19 Q8 Bramley Corner Hants
23 N11 Bramling Kent
6 C3 Brampford Speke Devon
32 H3 Brampton Cambs
64 C3 Brampton Cumb
71 Q4 Brampton Cumb
52 B7 Brampton Lincs
45 K5 Brampton Norfk
51 K1 Brampton Rothm
35 P1 Brampton Suffk
28 H4 Brampton Abbotts Herefs
42 B11 Brampton Ash Nhants
38 G7 Brampton Bryan Herefs
51 L4 Brampton-en-le-Morthen Rothm
40 D2 Bramshall Staffs
9 J4 Bramshaw Hants
10 D4 Bramshott Hants
17 L9 Bramwell Somset
89 L3 Branault Highld
44 C2 Brancaster Norfk
44 D2 Brancaster Staithe Norfk
73 L12 Brancepeth Dur
100 G5 Branchill Moray
101 K2 Branderburgh Moray
61 J5 Brandesburton E R Yk
35 L5 Brandeston Suffk
45 J6 Brandiston Norfk
73 M11 Brandon Dur
42 C1 Brandon Lincs
44 D11 Brandon Suffk
41 K11 Brandon Warwks
44 H8 Brandon Parva Norfk
66 E11 Brandsby N York
52 E4 Brandy Wharf Lincs
33 Q10 Bran End Essex
8 F8 Branksome Poole
8 F8 Branksome Park Poole
19 M11 Bransbury Hants
52 C7 Bransby Lincs
6 G5 Branscombe Devon
39 P10 Bransford Worcs
8 H7 Bransgore Hants
61 J7 Bransholme C KuH
39 M7 Bransley Shrops
42 B4 Branston Leics
52 E9 Branston Lincs
40 G4 Branston Staffs
52 F9 Branston Booths Lincs
9 P10 Branstone IoW
52 D11 Brant Broughton Lincs
35 J9 Brantham Suffk
70 H9 Branthwaite Cumb
71 L7 Branthwaite Cumb
60 G8 Brantingham E R Yk
51 N1 Branton Donc
81 L10 Branton Nthumb
59 K2 Branton Green N York
81 J6 Branxton Nthumb
50 G9 Brassington Derbys
21 P11 Brasted Kent
21 P11 Brasted Chart Kent
95 L3 Brathens Abers
53 M9 Bratoft Lincs
52 D7 Brattleby Lincs
18 D9 Bratton Wilts
49 L11 Bratton Wrekin
5 K2 Bratton Clovelly Devon
15 L5 Bratton Fleming Devon
17 P9 Bratton Seymour Somset
33 L10 Braughing Herts
31 M2 Braunston Nhants
42 B8 Braunston Rutlnd
41 M7 Braunstone Leics
14 H5 Braunton Devon
66 G11 Brawby N York
109 P3 Brawl Highld
20 E7 Bray W & M
41 Q9 Braybrooke Nhants
15 M5 Brayford Devon
4 H5 Bray Shop Cnwll
59 N7 Brayton N York
20 E7 Braywick W & M
32 G11 Breachwood Green Herts
51 J11 Breadsall Derbys
29 J8 Breadstone Gloucs
2 F9 Breage Cnwll
106 H12 Breakachy Highld
20 H5 Breakspear Crematorium Gt Lon
106 H4 Brealangwell Lodge Highld
28 H7 Bream Gloucs
8 H4 Breamore Hants
16 H5 Brean Somset
111 b2 Breanais W Isls
58 H3 Brearton N York
111 c2 Breascleit W Isls
111 c2 Breasclete W Isls
41 L2 Breaston Derbys
25 J3 Brechfa Carmth
95 K9 Brechin Angus
44 F10 Breckles Norfk
27 L3 Brecon Powys
27 L4 Brecon Beacons National Park
50 B3 Bredbury Stockp
12 G6 Brede E Susx
39 L10 Bredenbury Herefs
35 L6 Bredfield Suffk
22 G10 Bredgar Kent
22 F10 Bredhurst Kent
29 N2 Bredon Worcs
29 M2 Bredon's Hardwick Worcs
29 N2 Bredon's Norton Worcs
38 G12 Bredwardine Herefs
41 K3 Breedon on the Hill Leics
85 Q10 Breich W Loth
57 N7 Breightmet Bolton
60 C7 Breighton E R Yk
28 F2 Breinton Herefs
18 E6 Bremhill Wilts
12 D2 Brenchley Kent
15 N3 Brendon Devon
83 M6 Brenfield Ag & B
111 b2 Brenish W Isls
34 F7 Brent Eleigh Suffk
21 J7 Brentford Gt Lon
42 B6 Brentingby Leics
17 J6 Brent Knoll Somset
5 N8 Brent Mill Devon
33 M10 Brent Pelham Herts
22 C5 Brentwood Essex
13 J5 Brenzett Kent
13 J4 Brenzett Green Kent
40 D4 Brereton Staffs
49 P3 Brereton Green Ches E
111 k4 Bressay Shet
34 H1 Bressingham Norfk
40 H3 Bretby Derbys
40 H3 Bretby Crematorium Derbys
41 K11 Bretford Warwks
30 E5 Bretforton Worcs
57 J5 Bretherton Lancs
111 k4 Brettabister Shet
44 F12 Brettenham Norfk
34 F6 Brettenham Suffk
48 G3 Bretton Flints
40 B6 Brewood Staffs
8 B8 Briantspuddle Dorset
21 L2 Brickendon Herts
20 H3 Bricket Wood Herts
50 H5 Brick Houses Sheff
29 N1 Bricklehampton Worcs
56 e2 Bride IoM
71 J8 Bridekirk Cumb
5 L3 Bridestowe Devon
102 D7 Brideswell Abers
5 Q3 Bridford Devon
23 M11 Bridge Kent
17 N10 Bridgehampton Somset
65 N12 Bridge Hewick N York
73 K9 Bridgehill Dur
9 P6 Bridgemary Hants
101 P7 Bridgend Abers
75 M5 Bridgend Ag & B
82 E9 Bridgend Ag & B
95 J8 Bridgend Angus
27 J11 Bridgend Brdgnd
78 H7 Bridgend D & G
5 L9 Bridgend Devon
93 L12 Bridgend Fife
101 M8 Bridgend Moray
92 G10 Bridgend P & K
86 C7 Bridgend W Loth
93 K5 Bridgend of Lintrathen Angus
102 D10 Bridge of Alford Abers
85 N4 Bridge of Allan Stirlg
100 H10 Bridge of Avon Moray
101 J7 Bridge of Avon Moray
91 N7 Bridge of Balgie P & K
94 C9 Bridge of Brewlands Angus
100 H10 Bridge of Brown Highld
92 H5 Bridge of Cally P & K
95 K3 Bridge of Canny Abers
93 J5 Bridge of Craigisla Angus
70 C4 Bridge of Dee D & G
103 K12 Bridge of Don C Aber
100 E7 Bridge of Dulsie Highld
95 K5 Bridge of Dye Abers
92 G11 Bridge of Earn P & K
91 M5 Bridge of Ericht P & K
95 L3 Bridge of Feugh Abers
110 B3 Bridge of Forss Highld
94 F3 Bridge of Gairn Abers
91 M5 Bridge of Gaur P & K
102 D5 Bridge of Marnoch Abers
91 J8 Bridge of Orchy Ag & B
92 D3 Bridge of Tilt P & K
101 M3 Bridge of Tynet Moray
111 j4 Bridge of Walls Shet
84 G9 Bridge of Weir Rens
14 E10 Bridgerule Devon
28 E1 Bridge Sollers Herefs
34 E6 Bridge Street Suffk
16 C9 Bridgetown Somset
49 J2 Bridge Trafford Ches W
44 F11 Bridgham Norfk
39 N4 Bridgnorth Shrops
16 H8 Bridgwater Somset
17 J8 Bridgwater Services Somset
61 K2 Bridlington E R Yk
7 L4 Bridport Dorset
28 G4 Bridstow Herefs
57 Q2 Brierfield Lancs
59 K11 Brierley Barns
28 H6 Brierley Gloucs
40 B9 Brierley Hill Dudley
52 E3 Brigg N Linc
45 M5 Briggate Norfk
67 J6 Briggswath N York
70 H9 Brigham Cumb
61 J4 Brigham E R Yk
58 F9 Brighouse Calder
9 M10 Brighstone IoW
31 K12 Brighthampton Oxon
15 K11 Brightley Devon
12 D6 Brightling E Susx
34 H12 Brightlingsea Essex
11 L8 Brighton Br & H
56 F8 Brighton le Sands Sefton
85 Q7 Brightons Falk
19 M5 Brightwalton W Berk
35 L7 Brightwell Suffk
19 Q2 Brightwell Baldwin Oxon
19 P3 Brightwell-cum-Sotwell Oxon
19 Q2 Brightwell Upperton Oxon
65 J5 Brignall Dur
85 J2 Brig o'Turk Stirlg
53 J3 Brigsley NE Lin
63 J4 Brigsteer Cumb
42 D11 Brigstock Nhants
31 P10 Brill Bucks
2 G9 Brill Cnwll
38 F11 Brilley Herefs
39 K8 Brimfield Herefs
39 K8 Brimfield Cross Herefs
51 K6 Brimington Derbys
5 Q5 Brimley Devon
29 N6 Brimpsfield Gloucs
19 P7 Brimpton W Berk
29 M8 Brimscombe Gloucs
56 F11 Brimstage Wirral
51 J4 Brincliffe Sheff
60 C7 Brind E R Yk
111 j4 Brindister Shet
57 L4 Brindle Lancs
49 P11 Brineton Staffs
42 B10 Bringhurst Leics
39 M10 Bringsty Common Herefs
32 F2 Brington Cambs
44 G4 Briningham Norfk
53 L8 Brinkhill Lincs
33 Q6 Brinkley Cambs
41 K10 Brinklow Warwks
18 E4 Brinkworth Wilts
57 L5 Brinscall Lancs
51 L10 Brinsley Notts
51 K3 Brinsworth Rothm
44 G3 Brinton Norfk
111 h2 Brinyan Ork
44 F6 Brisley Norfk
17 N3 Brislington Bristl
12 H3 Brissenden Green Kent
17 N2 Bristol Bristl
17 M3 Bristol Airport N Som
17 N2 Bristol Zoo Bristl
44 H4 Briston Norfk
8 H2 Britford Wilts
27 N8 Brithdir Caerph
47 M7 Brithdir Gwynd
22 E11 British Legion Village Kent
26 G9 Briton Ferry Neath
19 R3 Britwell Salome Oxon
6 C10 Brixham Torbay
5 L9 Brixton Devon
21 L8 Brixton Gt Lon
18 C11 Brixton Deverill Wilts
41 Q12 Brixworth Nhants
30 H11 Brize Norton Oxon
30 H11 Brize Norton Airport Oxon
30 B1 Broad Alley Worcs
18 G3 Broad Blunsdon Swindn
50 C3 Broadbottom Tamesd
10 D8 Broadbridge W Susx
11 J4 Broadbridge Heath W Susx
30 F6 Broad Campden Gloucs
58 E9 Broad Carr Calder
8 F3 Broad Chalke Wilts
6 D4 Broadclyst Devon
84 F8 Broadfield Inver
96 H5 Broadford Highld
10 H6 Broadford Bridge W Susx
79 K6 Broadgairhill Border
39 P10 Broad Green Worcs
81 J4 Broadhaugh Border
24 F6 Broad Haven Pembks
57 N10 Broadheath Traffd
6 E2 Broadhembury Devon
5 Q7 Broadhempston Devon
18 G5 Broad Hinton Wilts
12 G6 Broadland Row E Susx
19 M8 Broad Layings Hants
101 M3 Broadley Moray
30 F5 Broad Marston Worcs
7 Q5 Broadmayne Dorset
25 J7 Broadmoor Pembks
7 L4 Broadoak Dorset
12 C5 Broad Oak E Susx
12 G6 Broad Oak E Susx
28 F5 Broad Oak Herefs
23 M10 Broad Oak Kent
57 K9 Broad Oak St Hel
22 E2 Broad's Green Essex
23 Q9 Broadstairs Kent
8 E8 Broadstone Poole
39 K4 Broadstone Shrops
12 G6 Broad Street E Susx
22 G11 Broad Street Kent
18 G5 Broad Town Wilts
39 N10 Broadwas Worcs
33 J11 Broadwater Herts
11 J8 Broadwater W Susx
39 Q6 Broadwaters Worcs
24 F6 Broadway Pembks
17 J11 Broadway Somset
30 E6 Broadway Worcs
28 G6 Broadwell Gloucs
30 G8 Broadwell Gloucs
30 G12 Broadwell Oxon
31 L2 Broadwell Warwks
7 L3 Broadwindsor Dorset
15 K10 Broadwood Kelly Devon
5 J3 Broadwoodwidger Devon
104 H12 Brochel Highld
90 D9 Brochroy Ag & B
39 P10 Brockamin Worcs
9 Q4 Brockbridge Hants
35 K2 Brockdish Norfk
9 K7 Brockenhurst Hants
78 D2 Brocketsbrae S Lans
35 J4 Brockford Street Suffk
31 N2 Brockhall Nhants
21 K12 Brockham Surrey
30 D9 Brockhampton Gloucs
10 B8 Brockhampton Hants
28 H3 Brockhampton Herefs
39 M10 Brockhampton Estate Herefs
58 F11 Brockholes Kirk
61 K11 Brocklesby Lincs
17 L3 Brockley N Som
34 D3 Brockley Suffk
34 C7 Brockley Green Suffk
34 D6 Brockley Green Suffk
38 G2 Brockton Shrops
38 G5 Brockton Shrops
39 L4 Brockton Shrops
28 G8 Brockweir Gloucs
29 M5 Brockworth Gloucs
40 C4 Brocton Staffs
75 Q5 Brodick N Ayrs
100 F4 Brodie Moray
59 L11 Brodsworth Donc
104 F8 Brogaig Highld
18 D3 Brokenborough Wilts
50 B6 Broken Cross Ches E
18 C9 Brokerswood Wilts
56 G11 Bromborough Wirral
35 J2 Brome Suffk
35 J2 Brome Street Suffk
35 M6 Bromeswell Suffk
71 J6 Bromfield Cumb
39 J6 Bromfield Shrops
32 E6 Bromham Bed
18 E7 Bromham Wilts
21 N9 Bromley Gt Lon
39 N3 Bromley Shrops
22 F9 Brompton Medway
65 P8 Brompton N York
67 K10 Brompton-by-Sawdon N York
65 L7 Brompton-on-Swale N York
16 E9 Brompton Ralph Somset
16 C9 Brompton Regis Somset
29 K3 Bromsberrow Gloucs
29 K3 Bromsberrow Heath Gloucs
40 C12 Bromsgrove Worcs
39 M10 Bromyard Herefs
37 K7 Bronant Cerdgn
36 E10 Brongest Cerdgn
49 J7 Bronington Wrexhm
27 N2 Bronllys Powys
25 P4 Bronwydd Carmth
48 F7 Bronygarth Shrops
55 M6 Bron-y-Nant Crematorium Conwy
9 J5 Brook Hants
9 L9 Brook IoW
13 K2 Brook Kent
10 E3 Brook Surrey
45 L9 Brooke Norfk
42 C8 Brooke Rutlnd
52 H4 Brookenby Lincs
84 G9 Brookfield Rens
17 P9 Brookhampton Somset
9 J5 Brook Hill Hants
63 K8 Brookhouse Lancs
51 L3 Brookhouse Rothm
49 P4 Brookhouse Green Ches E
50 D3 Brookhouses Derbys
13 J5 Brookland Kent
57 P10 Brooklands Traffd
21 K3 Brookmans Park Herts
22 C5 Brook Street Essex
12 H4 Brook Street Kent
29 L6 Brookthorpe Gloucs
20 F11 Brookwood Surrey
32 G8 Broom C Beds
51 K3 Broom Rothm
30 E4 Broom Warwks
45 M10 Broome Norfk
38 H6 Broome Shrops
40 B10 Broome Worcs
57 N10 Broomedge Warrtn
22 E2 Broomfield Essex
22 G11 Broomfield Kent
23 M9 Broomfield Kent
16 G9 Broomfield Somset
60 F8 Broomfleet E R Yk
72 H8 Broomhaugh Nthumb
59 K12 Broom Hill Barns
51 M10 Broom Hill Notts
73 M1 Broomhill Nthumb
73 M11 Broompark Dur
107 P2 Brora Highld
39 M2 Broseley Shrops
72 G12 Brotherlee Dur
59 L8 Brotherton N York
66 F4 Brotton R & Cl
110 B4 Broubster Highld
64 E5 Brough Cumb
60 F8 Brough E R Yk
110 E2 Brough Highld
52 B10 Brough Notts
111 m3 Brough Shet
49 K7 Broughall Shrops
111 m2 Brough Lodge Shet
64 E5 Brough Sowerby Cumb
78 H2 Broughton Border
33 J2 Broughton Cambs
48 G3 Broughton Flints
9 K2 Broughton Hants
57 K2 Broughton Lancs
32 C8 Broughton M Keyn
52 D2 Broughton N Linc
58 C4 Broughton N York
66 H11 Broughton N York
32 B2 Broughton Nhants
31 K6 Broughton Oxon
57 P8 Broughton Salfd
16 C3 Broughton V Glam
41 M8 Broughton Astley Leics
18 C7 Broughton Gifford Wilts
30 C2 Broughton Green Worcs
30 B3 Broughton Hackett Worcs
62 E5 Broughton-in-Furness Cumb
69 L9 Broughton Mains D & G
62 E4 Broughton Mills Cumb
70 H8 Broughton Moor Cumb
30 G12 Broughton Poggs Oxon
93 N9 Broughty Ferry C Dund
19 P11 Brown Candover Hants
50 B9 Brown Edge Staffs
102 H7 Brownhill Abers
93 P11 Brownhills Fife
40 D6 Brownhills Wsall
19 P8 Browninghill Green Hants
49 Q4 Brown Lees Staffs
8 F9 Brownsea Island Dorset
29 M8 Browns Hill Gloucs
5 N9 Brownston Devon
67 K8 Broxa N York
21 M3 Broxbourne Herts
87 N6 Broxburn E Loth
86 C7 Broxburn W Loth
33 P10 Broxted Essex
110 G7 Bruan Highld
92 C3 Bruar P & K
107 Q5 Brucefield Highld
84 B10 Bruchag Ag & B
82 C10 Bruichladdich Ag & B
35 M4 Bruisyard Suffk
35 M4 Bruisyard Street Suffk
52 C2 Brumby N Linc
50 E8 Brund Staffs
45 M8 Brundall Norfk
35 L3 Brundish Suffk
35 L3 Brundish Street Suffk
89 P2 Brunery Highld
73 M6 Brunswick Village N u Ty
58 D5 Brunthwaite C Brad
41 N9 Bruntingthorpe Leics
93 K10 Brunton Fife
19 J9 Brunton Wilts
15 L9 Brushford Devon
16 C10 Brushford Somset
17 P8 Bruton Somset
30 B1 Bryan's Green Worcs
8 C6 Bryanston Dorset
71 K2 Brydekirk D & G
2 b2 Bryher IoS
17 M11 Brympton Somset
26 D8 Bryn Carmth
26 H9 Bryn Neath
26 F6 Brynamman Carmth
25 J2 Brynberian Pembks
46 H3 Bryncir Gwynd
26 G8 Bryn-coch Neath
46 D5 Bryncroes Gwynd
47 K9 Bryncrug Gwynd
48 D6 Bryneglwys Denbgs
48 D1 Brynford Flints
57 L8 Bryn Gates Wigan
54 D6 Bryngwran IoA
28 D7 Bryngwyn Mons
38 E11 Bryngwyn Powys
24 H2 Bryn-Henllan Pembks
36 E9 Brynhoffnant Cerdgn
27 P6 Brynmawr Blae G
46 D5 Bryn-mawr Gwynd
27 J10 Brynmenyn Brdgnd
26 E9 Brynmill Swans
27 L11 Brynna Rhondd
54 H8 Brynrefail Gwynd
27 L11 Brynsadler Rhondd
48 C5 Bryn Saith Marchog Denbgs
54 F7 Brynsiencyn IoA
54 G5 Brynteg IoA
55 M6 Bryn-y-Maen Conwy
96 E5 Bualintur Highld
41 J11 Bubbenhall Warwks
60 C7 Bubwith E R Yk
79 M6 Buccleuch Border
84 H5 Buchanan Smithy Stirlg
103 M6 Buchanhaven Abers
92 D9 Buchanty P & K

C

D

E

43 M8 Elm Cambs
30 B1 Elmbridge Worcs
33 M8 Elmdon Essex
40 F10 Elmdon Solhll
21 M9 Elmers End Gt Lon
57 J7 Elmer's Green Lancs
41 L8 Elmesthorpe Leics
40 E5 Elmhurst Staffs
29 N1 Elmley Castle Worcs
39 Q8 Elmley Lovett Worcs
29 K6 Elmore Gloucs
29 K5 Elmore Back Gloucs
21 Q6 Elm Park Gt Lon
34 H7 Elmsett Suffk
34 H10 Elmstead Market Essex
13 L2 Elmsted Kent
23 N10 Elmstone Kent
29 M4 Elmstone Hardwicke Gloucs
60 G3 Elmswell E R Yk
34 G4 Elmswell Suffk
51 L6 Elmton Derbys
108 E12 Elphin Highld
86 H8 Elphinstone E Loth
95 N1 Elrick Abers
69 J9 Elrig D & G
72 F8 Elrington Nthumb
72 G3 Elsdon Nthumb
33 N10 Elsenham Essex
31 M11 Elsfield Oxon
60 H10 Elsham N Linc
44 H6 Elsing Norfk
58 B4 Elslack N York
9 P7 Elson Hants
86 C12 Elsrickle S Lans
10 E2 Elstead Surrey
10 D6 Elsted W Susx
42 F5 Elsthorpe Lincs
51 Q10 Elston Notts
32 F7 Elstow Bed
21 J4 Elstree Herts
61 L7 Elstronwick E R Yk
56 H2 Elswick Lancs
73 M7 Elswick N u Ty
33 K4 Elsworth Cambs
62 G2 Elterwater Cumb
21 N8 Eltham Gt Lon
21 N8 Eltham Crematorium Gt Lon
33 J5 Eltisley Cambs
42 F10 Elton Cambs
49 J1 Elton Ches W
50 G8 Elton Derbys
39 J7 Elton Herefs
51 Q11 Elton Notts
65 P4 Elton S on T
73 J8 Eltringham Nthumb
78 F5 Elvanfoot S Lans
41 K2 Elvaston Derbys
34 D2 Elveden Suffk
20 C11 Elvetham Heath Hants
87 J7 Elvingston E Loth
60 C5 Elvington C York
23 P12 Elvington Kent
66 C2 Elwick Hartpl
49 N3 Elworth Ches E
16 E8 Elworthy Somset
33 N1 Ely Cambs
16 F2 Ely Cardif
32 C6 Emberton M Keyn
71 J9 Embleton Cumb
81 P9 Embleton Nthumb
107 N4 Embo Highld
17 N6 Emborough Somset
107 N4 Embo Street Highld
58 D4 Embsay N York
9 K6 Emery Down Hants
58 G10 Emley Kirk
20 C3 Emmington Oxon
43 M8 Emneth Norfk
43 N8 Emneth Hungate Norfk
42 D8 Empingham Rutlnd
10 C4 Empshott Hants
49 K12 Emstrey Crematorium Shrops
10 C8 Emsworth Hants
19 M7 Enborne W Berk
19 M7 Enborne Row W Berk
41 M7 Enderby Leics
63 K5 Endmoor Cumb
50 B9 Endon Staffs
50 B9 Endon Bank Staffs
21 M4 Enfield Gt Lon
21 M4 Enfield Crematorium Gt Lon
21 M4 Enfield Lock Gt Lon
21 M4 Enfield Wash Gt Lon
18 G9 Enford Wilts
29 J11 Engine Common S Glos
19 Q6 Englefield W Berk
20 F8 Englefield Green Surrey
28 G5 English Bicknor Gloucs
17 Q4 Englishcombe BaNES
49 J9 English Frankton Shrops
19 L10 Enham-Alamein Hants
16 H8 Enmore Somset
8 C3 Enmore Green Dorset
70 H11 Ennerdale Bridge Cumb
92 F3 Enochdhu P & K
88 H6 Ensay Ag & B
8 F8 Ensbury Bmouth
48 H11 Ensdon Shrops
31 J8 Enstone Oxon
78 E7 Enterkinfoot D & G
39 P5 Enville Staffs
111 a6 Eolaigearraidh W Isls
29 K6 Epney Gloucs
51 P10 Epperstone Notts
21 P3 Epping Essex
21 N3 Epping Green Essex
21 N3 Epping Upland Essex
65 L5 Eppleby N York
21 K10 Epsom Surrey
31 J6 Epwell Oxon
52 A3 Epworth N Linc
48 G7 Erbistock Wrexhm
40 E8 Erdington Birm
12 B3 Eridge Green E Susx
83 N7 Erines Ag & B
90 C7 Eriska Ag & B
111 b6 Eriskay W Isls
34 C2 Eriswell Suffk
21 P7 Erith Gt Lon
18 E9 Erlestoke Wilts
5 M9 Ermington Devon
45 K4 Erpingham Norfk
98 H5 Errogie Highld
93 J10 Errol P & K
84 H8 Erskine Rens
68 D5 Ervie D & G
35 K9 Erwarton Suffk
38 C12 Erwood Powys
65 N6 Eryholme N York
48 E4 Eryrys Denbgs
65 L2 Escomb Dur
59 N5 Escrick N York
47 M9 Esgairgeiliog Powys
73 L11 Esh Dur
21 J9 Esher Surrey
73 L2 Eshott Nthumb
73 L11 Esh Winning Dur
98 F2 Eskadale Highld
86 G8 Eskbank Mdloth
62 D3 Eskdale Green Cumb
79 L8 Eskdalemuir D & G
56 H2 Esprick Lancs
42 F7 Essendine Rutlnd
21 L2 Essendon Herts
99 J2 Essich Highld
40 C6 Essington Staffs
103 J8 Esslemont Abers
66 D4 Eston R & Cl
81 K6 Etal Nthumb
18 F8 Etchilhampton Wilts
12 E5 Etchingham E Susx
13 M3 Etchinghill Kent
40 D4 Etchinghill Staffs
20 F7 Eton W & M
20 F7 Eton Wick W & M
49 Q6 Etruria C Stke
99 K9 Etteridge Highld
64 F2 Ettersgill Dur
49 N4 Ettiley Heath Ches E
40 B8 Ettingshall Wolves
30 H4 Ettington Warwks
42 G8 Etton C Pete
60 G5 Etton E R Yk
79 L6 Ettrick Border
79 N4 Ettrickbridge Border
79 L6 Ettrickhill Border
40 H2 Etwall Derbys
34 E2 Euston Suffk
57 K5 Euxton Lancs
107 K8 Evanton Highld
42 F1 Evedon Lincs
107 M4 Evelix Highld
38 F9 Evenjobb Powys
31 N7 Evenley Nhants
30 G8 Evenlode Gloucs
65 K3 Evenwood Dur
17 P8 Evercreech Somset
60 D6 Everingham E R Yk
18 H9 Everleigh Wilts
32 E9 Eversholt C Beds
7 N2 Evershot Dorset
20 C10 Eversley Hants
20 C10 Eversley Cross Hants
60 F7 Everthorpe E R Yk
32 H6 Everton C Beds
9 K8 Everton Hants
56 G9 Everton Lpool
51 P3 Everton Notts
71 M1 Evertown D & G
39 M11 Evesbatch Herefs
30 D5 Evesham Worcs
41 N6 Evington C Leic
50 H2 Ewden Village Sheff
21 K10 Ewell Surrey
13 N2 Ewell Minnis Kent
19 Q3 Ewelme Oxon
18 E2 Ewen Gloucs
27 J12 Ewenny V Glam
42 G1 Ewerby Lincs
10 H3 Ewhurst Surrey
12 F5 Ewhurst Green E Susx
10 H3 Ewhurst Green Surrey
48 F3 Ewloe Flints
5 J2 Eworthy Devon
20 D12 Ewshot Hants
28 D3 Ewyas Harold Herefs
15 K10 Exbourne Devon
16 C10 Exbridge Somset
9 M7 Exbury Hants
65 N9 Exelby N York
6 C4 Exeter Devon
6 D4 Exeter Airport Devon
6 C5 Exeter & Devon Crematorium Devon
6 C4 Exeter Services Devon
15 P5 Exford Somset
39 J2 Exfordsgreen Shrops
30 E3 Exhall Warwks
41 J9 Exhall Warwks
19 Q4 Exlade Street Oxon
6 C5 Exminster Devon
15 P4 Exmoor National Park
6 D6 Exmouth Devon
33 P4 Exning Suffk
6 D5 Exton Devon
9 Q4 Exton Hants
42 D7 Exton Rutlnd
16 C9 Exton Somset
6 B4 Exwick Devon
50 G5 Eyam Derbys
31 M4 Eydon Nhants
42 H9 Eye C Pete
39 J8 Eye Herefs
35 J3 Eye Suffk
81 K2 Eyemouth Border
33 J7 Eyeworth C Beds
22 G11 Eyhorne Street Kent
35 M6 Eyke Suffk
32 H5 Eynesbury Cambs
22 B9 Eynsford Kent
31 K11 Eynsham Oxon
7 L5 Eype Dorset
104 F10 Eyre Highld
23 P12 Eythorne Kent
39 J9 Eyton Herefs
48 H10 Eyton Shrops
39 L2 Eyton on Severn Shrops
49 M11 Eyton upon the Weald Moors Wrekin

F

19 L8 Faccombe Hants
66 C7 Faceby N York
48 B11 Fachwen Powys
49 L5 Faddiley Ches E
66 F9 Fadmoor N York
26 F8 Faerdre Swans
84 H8 Faifley W Duns
17 M2 Failand N Som
76 H6 Failford S Ayrs
50 B1 Failsworth Oldham
47 K8 Fairbourne Gwynd
59 L8 Fairburn N York
50 E6 Fairfield Derbys
40 C11 Fairfield Worcs
18 H1 Fairford Gloucs
70 E4 Fairgirth D & G
43 Q6 Fair Green Norfk
56 G4 Fairhaven Lancs
111 m5 Fair Isle Shet
20 F11 Fairlands Surrey
84 D11 Fairlie N Ayrs
12 G7 Fairlight E Susx
6 E4 Fairmile Devon
20 H10 Fairmile Surrey
79 P3 Fairnilee Border
9 N4 Fair Oak Hants
49 N8 Fairoak Staffs
19 Q8 Fair Oak Green Hants
22 D10 Fairseat Kent
34 C12 Fairstead Essex
43 Q6 Fairstead Norfk
11 P5 Fairwarp E Susx
27 N12 Fairwater Cardif
14 G7 Fairy Cross Devon
44 F4 Fakenham Norfk
34 E2 Fakenham Magna Suffk
87 J9 Fala Mdloth
87 J9 Fala Dam Mdloth
52 F6 Faldingworth Lincs
7 c2 Faldouet Jersey
29 J9 Falfield S Glos
35 L8 Falkenham Suffk
85 P7 Falkirk Falk
85 P6 Falkirk Crematorium Falk
86 F2 Falkland Fife
78 F2 Fallburn S Lans
85 N5 Fallin Stirlg
81 P9 Fallodon Nthumb
57 Q9 Fallowfield Manch
72 G7 Fallowfield Nthumb
83 Q1 Falls of Blarghour Ag & B
11 M8 Falmer E Susx
3 J8 Falmouth Cnwll
79 N7 Falnash Border
67 M9 Falsgrave N York
72 D4 Falstone Nthumb
108 D6 Fanagmore Highld
32 E10 Fancott C Beds
98 G1 Fanellan Highld
66 D8 Fangdale Beck N York
60 D4 Fangfoss E R Yk
89 J7 Fanmore Ag & B
106 D8 Fannich Lodge Highld
80 E6 Fans Border
32 C9 Far Bletchley M Keyn
42 H10 Farcet Cambs
31 Q3 Far Cotton Nhants
9 P6 Fareham Hants
62 F3 Far End Cumb
40 E5 Farewell Staffs
19 K2 Faringdon Oxon
57 K4 Farington Lancs
71 Q4 Farlam Cumb
17 M3 Farleigh N Som
21 M10 Farleigh Surrey
18 B8 Farleigh Hungerford Somset
19 Q10 Farleigh Wallop Hants
53 M8 Farlesthorpe Lincs
63 K6 Farleton Cumb
63 L8 Farleton Lancs
50 E11 Farley Staffs
9 J2 Farley Wilts
10 G2 Farley Green Surrey
20 C9 Farley Hill Wokham
29 K6 Farleys End Gloucs
10 B8 Farlington C Port
59 N1 Farlington N York
39 L6 Farlow Shrops
17 P4 Farmborough BaNES
30 D8 Farmcote Gloucs
37 K10 Farmers Carmth
30 F10 Farmington Gloucs
31 L11 Farmoor Oxon
57 K7 Far Moor Wigan
101 P5 Farmtown Moray
21 N9 Farnborough Gt Lon
20 E11 Farnborough Hants
19 M4 Farnborough W Berk
31 K4 Farnborough Warwks
20 E11 Farnborough Park Hants
20 E11 Farnborough Street Hants
10 F2 Farncombe Surrey
32 D4 Farndish Bed
48 H5 Farndon Ches W
51 Q9 Farndon Notts
81 Q6 Farne Islands Nthumb
93 Q5 Farnell Angus
8 E4 Farnham Dorset
33 M10 Farnham Essex
59 J3 Farnham N York
35 M5 Farnham Suffk
10 D1 Farnham Surrey
20 F6 Farnham Common Bucks
20 F6 Farnham Royal Bucks
22 B9 Farningham Kent
58 G7 Farnley Leeds
58 G5 Farnley N York
58 F10 Farnley Tyas Kirk
51 P9 Farnsfield Notts
57 N7 Farnworth Bolton
57 K10 Farnworth Halton
29 N7 Far Oakridge Gloucs
99 K3 Farr Highld
99 M8 Farr Highld
109 M3 Farr Highld
98 H5 Farraline Highld
6 D5 Farringdon Devon
17 P5 Farrington Gurney BaNES
62 H3 Far Sawrey Cumb
31 M6 Farthinghoe Nhants
31 N3 Farthingstone Nhants
58 F9 Fartown Kirk
58 G7 Fartown Leeds
90 D6 Fasnacloich Ag & B
98 D4 Fasnakyle Highld
90 D1 Fassfern Highld
73 N9 Fatfield Sundld
85 Q10 Fauldhouse W Loth
34 D12 Faulkbourne Essex
17 Q5 Faulkland Somset
49 L8 Fauls Shrops
23 K10 Faversham Kent
66 B11 Fawdington N York
73 M7 Fawdon N u Ty
22 C9 Fawkham Green Kent
31 J10 Fawler Oxon
20 C6 Fawley Bucks
9 M6 Fawley Hants
19 L5 Fawley W Berk
60 E8 Faxfleet E R Yk
11 K4 Faygate W Susx
56 G9 Fazakerley Lpool
40 G7 Fazeley Staffs
65 L10 Fearby N York
107 N7 Fearn Highld
91 Q7 Fearnan P & K
105 L9 Fearnbeg Highld
105 K9 Fearnmore Highld
83 P7 Fearnoch Ag & B
40 C6 Featherstone Staffs
59 K9 Featherstone Wakefd
30 D2 Feckenham Worcs
34 E11 Feering Essex
64 H7 Feetham N York
11 M3 Felbridge Surrey
45 K3 Felbrigg Norfk
11 M2 Felcourt Surrey
25 N2 Felindre Carmth
26 D5 Felindre Carmth
38 D6 Felindre Powys
26 E8 Felindre Swans
36 B11 Felindre Farchog Pembks
26 C4 Felingwm Isaf Carmth
26 C4 Felingwm Uchaf Carmth
66 C9 Felixkirk N York
35 L9 Felixstowe Suffk
73 M8 Felling Gatesd
32 E5 Felmersham Bed
45 L4 Felmingham Norfk
10 F9 Felpham W Susx
34 F5 Felsham Suffk
34 B11 Felsted Essex
20 H8 Feltham Gt Lon
20 H8 Felthamhill Surrey
45 J6 Felthorpe Norfk
39 L11 Felton Herefs
17 M3 Felton N Som
73 L2 Felton Nthumb
48 H11 Felton Butler Shrops
44 B11 Feltwell Norfk
57 P2 Fence Lancs
51 K4 Fence Rothm
31 M10 Fencott Oxon
53 M10 Fendike Corner Lincs
33 M5 Fen Ditton Cambs
33 K3 Fen Drayton Cambs
57 M4 Feniscowles Bl w D
6 F3 Feniton Devon
43 L10 Fenland Crematorium Cambs
39 P5 Fenn Green Shrops
22 F8 Fenn Street Medway
50 F10 Fenny Bentley Derbys
6 F3 Fenny Bridges Devon
31 K4 Fenny Compton Warwks
41 J7 Fenny Drayton Leics
33 K3 Fenstanton Cambs
44 G10 Fen Street Norfk
50 B11 Fenton C Stke
33 K2 Fenton Cambs
71 Q4 Fenton Cumb
52 B8 Fenton Lincs
52 C12 Fenton Lincs
52 B6 Fenton Notts
81 K7 Fenton Nthumb
87 K6 Fenton Barns E Loth
59 N10 Fenwick Donc
76 H3 Fenwick E Ayrs
73 J6 Fenwick Nthumb
81 M6 Fenwick Nthumb
3 J7 Feock Cnwll
82 F8 Feolin Ferry Ag & B
76 F3 Fergushill N Ayrs
104 B11 Feriniquarrie Highld
94 H9 Fern Angus
27 L9 Ferndale Rhondd
8 F7 Ferndown Dorset
100 E6 Ferness Highld
19 K3 Fernham Oxon
39 Q9 Fernhill Heath Worcs
10 E4 Fernhurst W Susx
93 K11 Fernie Fife
85 M11 Ferniegair S Lans
96 D3 Fernilea Highld
50 D5 Fernilee Derbys
52 B12 Fernwood Notts
59 J3 Ferrensby N York
97 J7 Ferrindonald Highld
10 H9 Ferring W Susx
59 L9 Ferrybridge Services Wakefd
95 M9 Ferryden Angus
65 M2 Ferryhill Dur
107 M5 Ferry Point Highld
25 N6 Ferryside Carmth
107 M5 Ferrytown Highld
44 H12 Fersfield Norfk
91 K2 Fersit Highld
99 M8 Feshiebridge Highld
21 J11 Fetcham Surrey
111 m2 Fetlar Shet
103 K5 Fetterangus Abers
95 K7 Fettercairn Abers
58 G4 Fewston N York
26 E5 Ffairfach Carmth
37 M7 Ffair Rhos Cerdgn
47 L3 Ffestiniog Gwynd
47 K3 Ffestiniog Railway Gwynd
26 D7 Fforest Carmth
26 E9 Fforest Fach Swans
36 F10 Ffostrasol Cerdgn
48 F4 Ffrith Flints
56 D11 Ffynnongroyw Flints
108 H9 Fiag Lodge Highld
21 M10 Fickleshole Surrey
16 G7 Fiddington Somset
8 B5 Fiddleford Dorset
3 J5 Fiddlers Green Cnwll
40 D2 Field Staffs
44 G3 Field Dalling Norfk
41 L5 Field Head Leics
8 B3 Fifehead Magdalen Dorset
8 B5 Fifehead Neville Dorset
8 B5 Fifehead St Quintin Dorset
101 M5 Fife Keith Moray
30 G9 Fifield Oxon
20 E7 Fifield W & M
18 H10 Figheldean Wilts
45 P7 Filby Norfk
67 N10 Filey N York
32 C7 Filgrave M Keyn
30 G12 Filkins Oxon
15 L6 Filleigh Devon
52 D6 Fillingham Lincs
40 H9 Fillongley Warwks
28 H11 Filton S Glos
60 F3 Fimber E R Yk
93 N4 Finavon Angus
44 B8 Fincham Norfk
20 C10 Finchampstead Wokham
83 N3 Fincharn Ag & B
10 B7 Finchdean Hants
34 B9 Finchingfield Essex
21 L5 Finchley Gt Lon
40 H2 Findern Derbys
100 G3 Findhorn Moray
99 M4 Findhorn Bridge Highld
101 N2 Findochty Moray
92 E10 Findo Gask P & K
95 Q3 Findon Abers
10 H8 Findon W Susx
107 K9 Findon Mains Highld
95 K2 Findrack House Abers
32 D3 Finedon Nhants
92 H10 Fingask P & K
20 C5 Fingest Bucks
65 L9 Finghall N York
77 M7 Fingland D & G
23 P11 Finglesham Kent
34 G11 Fingringhoe Essex
91 N9 Finlarig Stirlg
31 N7 Finmere Oxon
91 M5 Finnart P & K
34 H3 Finningham Suffk
51 P2 Finningley Donc
111 c4 Finsbay W Isls
40 C12 Finstall Worcs
62 G5 Finsthwaite Cumb
31 J10 Finstock Oxon
111 h2 Finstown Ork
102 G4 Fintry Abers
85 K5 Fintry Stirlg
95 K4 Finzean Abers
88 G10 Fionnphort Ag & B
111 c4 Fionnsbhagh W Isls
63 L4 Firbank Cumb
51 M3 Firbeck Rothm
60 C2 Firby N York
65 M9 Firby N York
11 P8 Firle E Susx
53 M10 Firsby Lincs
65 K1 Fir Tree Dur
9 P8 Fishbourne IoW
10 D8 Fishbourne W Susx
10 D8 Fishbourne Roman Palace W Susx
65 P2 Fishburn Dur
85 P4 Fishcross Clacks
102 E8 Fisherford Abers
86 G7 Fisherrow E Loth
9 N4 Fisher's Pond Hants
107 M11 Fisherton Highld
76 E7 Fisherton S Ayrs
18 E11 Fisherton de la Mere Wilts
24 G2 Fishguard Pembks
59 P10 Fishlake Donc
89 N7 Fishnish Pier Ag & B
17 P2 Fishponds Bristl
43 K2 Fishtoft Lincs
43 K1 Fishtoft Drove Lincs
96 D3 Fiskavaig Highld
52 F8 Fiskerton Lincs
51 Q9 Fiskerton Notts
18 G10 Fittleton Wilts
10 G6 Fittleworth W Susx
49 J11 Fitz Shrops
16 F9 Fitzhead Somset
59 K10 Fitzwilliam Wakefd
11 P5 Five Ash Down E Susx
12 B5 Five Ashes E Susx
17 J10 Fivehead Somset
4 F4 Fivelanes Cnwll
12 D2 Five Oak Green Kent
7 c2 Five Oaks Jersey
10 H4 Five Oaks W Susx
26 C7 Five Roads Carmth
20 E5 Flackwell Heath Bucks
30 C5 Fladbury Worcs
111 k4 Fladdabister Shet
50 F7 Flagg Derbys
67 Q12 Flamborough E R Yk
67 Q12 Flamborough Head E R Yk
66 H10 Flamingo Land Theme Park N York
20 H1 Flamstead Herts
10 F9 Flansham W Susx
58 H9 Flanshaw Wakefd
58 C3 Flasby N York
50 D7 Flash Staffs
104 D10 Flashader Highld
20 G4 Flaunden Herts
42 B2 Flawborough Notts
59 L2 Flawith N York
17 M3 Flax Bourton N Som
59 K3 Flaxby N York
29 J6 Flaxley Gloucs
16 F8 Flaxpool Somset
59 P2 Flaxton N York
41 P8 Fleckney Leics
31 L2 Flecknoe Warwks
52 B8 Fledborough Notts
7 P6 Fleet Dorset
20 D11 Fleet Hants
43 L5 Fleet Lincs
43 L5 Fleet Hargate Lincs
20 C11 Fleet Services Hants
62 G11 Fleetwood Lancs
16 D3 Flemingston V Glam
85 L10 Flemington S Lans
34 D3 Flempton Suffk
71 K7 Fletchertown Cumb
11 N5 Fletching E Susx
14 D10 Flexbury Cnwll
20 E12 Flexford Surrey
70 G8 Flimby Cumb
12 E4 Flimwell E Susx
48 E2 Flint Flints

G

H

I

J

K

L

M

31 Q3 Milton Malsor Nhants
91 P8 Milton Morenish P & K
95 J2 Milton of Auchinhove Abers
86 G3 Milton of Balgonie Fife
84 G5 Milton of Buchanan Stirlg
85 L7 Milton of Campsie E Duns
99 K1 Milton of Leys Highld
95 P2 Milton of Murtle C Aber
94 F3 Milton of Tullich Abers
8 B2 Milton on Stour Dorset
22 H9 Milton Regis Kent
30 H9 Milton-under-Wychwood Oxon
16 F10 Milverton Somset
30 H2 Milverton Warwks
40 C2 Milwich Staffs
83 P4 Minard Ag & B
29 M8 Minchinhampton Gloucs
16 C6 Minehead Somset
48 F5 Minera Wrexhm
18 F3 Minety Wilts
47 J4 Minffordd Gwynd
89 N3 Mingarrypark Highld
53 K10 Miningsby Lincs
4 G6 Minions Cnwll
76 F8 Minishant S Ayrs
47 P8 Minllyn Gwynd
69 K6 Minnigaff D & G
102 G4 Minnonie Abers
59 K2 Minskip N York
9 K5 Minstead Hants
10 D6 Minsted W Susx
23 J8 Minster Kent
23 P9 Minster Kent
38 G2 Minsterley Shrops
30 H10 Minster Lovell Oxon
29 K5 Minsterworth Gloucs
7 P2 Minterne Magna Dorset
52 H8 Minting Lincs
103 K6 Mintlaw Abers
43 Q6 Mintlyn Crematorium Norfk
80 D9 Minto Border
38 H4 Minton Shrops
70 F11 Mirehouse Cumb
110 G4 Mireland Highld
58 G9 Mirfield Kirk
29 N7 Miserden Gloucs
27 L11 Miskin Rhondd
51 P2 Misson Notts
41 M10 Misterton Leics
51 Q2 Misterton Notts
7 L2 Misterton Somset
35 J9 Mistley Essex
21 L9 Mitcham Gt Lon
29 J5 Mitcheldean Gloucs
3 J5 Mitchell Cnwll
78 F9 Mitchellslacks D & G
28 F6 Mitchel Troy Mons
73 L4 Mitford Nthumb
2 H5 Mithian Cnwll
31 N7 Mixbury Oxon
57 P11 Mobberley Ches E
50 D11 Mobberley Staffs
38 C4 Mochdre Powys
69 J9 Mochrum D & G
12 E1 Mockbeggar Kent
70 H10 Mockerkin Cumb
5 N9 Modbury Devon
50 B12 Moddershall Staffs
54 G4 Moelfre IoA
48 E9 Moelfre Powys
78 H7 Moffat D & G
32 G6 Moggerhanger C Beds
40 H4 Moira Leics
23 K11 Molash Kent
96 E7 Mol-chlach Highld
48 E3 Mold Flints
58 F10 Moldgreen Kirk
33 P10 Molehill Green Essex
60 H6 Molescroft E R Yk
32 F2 Molesworth Cambs
15 N6 Molland Devon
48 H2 Mollington Ches W
31 K5 Mollington Oxon
85 M8 Mollinsburn N Lans
95 M6 Mondynes Abers
35 L5 Monewden Suffk
92 F9 Moneydie P & K
78 C10 Moniaive D & G
93 N8 Monifieth Angus
93 N7 Monikie Angus
93 K11 Monimail Fife
21 K4 Monken Hadley Gt Lon
59 L8 Monk Fryston N York
39 L12 Monkhide Herefs
71 M4 Monkhill Cumb
39 L4 Monkhopton Shrops
39 J10 Monkland Herefs
14 H7 Monkleigh Devon
16 C3 Monknash V Glam
15 K10 Monkokehampton Devon
73 N6 Monkseaton N Tyne
34 F7 Monks Eleigh Suffk
11 K5 Monk's Gate W Susx
49 Q1 Monks Heath Ches E
19 Q9 Monk Sherborne Hants
16 E8 Monksilver Somset
41 L10 Monks Kirby Warwks
35 K4 Monk Soham Suffk
20 D3 Monks Risborough Bucks
53 M9 Monksthorpe Lincs
33 P10 Monk Street Essex
28 D8 Monkswood Mons
6 G3 Monkton Devon
23 P9 Monkton Kent
76 F6 Monkton S Ayrs
73 N8 Monkton S Tyne
18 B8 Monkton Combe BaNES
18 C12 Monkton Deverill Wilts
18 B7 Monkton Farleigh Wilts
16 H10 Monkton Heathfield Somset
7 J4 Monkton Wyld Dorset
73 P8 Monkwearmouth Sundld
9 Q2 Monkwood Hants
40 B7 Monmore Green Wolves
28 F6 Monmouth Mons
38 G12 Monnington on Wye Herefs
69 J10 Monreith D & G
17 M11 Montacute Somset
48 H11 Montford Shrops
48 H11 Montford Bridge Shrops
102 D10 Montgarrie Abers
38 E3 Montgomery Powys
95 L9 Montrose Angus
6 b2 Mont Saint Guern
19 K11 Monxton Hants
50 F7 Monyash Derbys
102 F11 Monymusk Abers
92 C9 Monzie P & K
85 L8 Moodiesburn N Lans
93 L11 Moonzie Fife
58 H6 Moor Allerton Leeds
53 J10 Moorby Lincs
8 E6 Moor Crichel Dorset
8 G8 Moordown Bmouth
57 L11 Moore Halton
58 D8 Moor End Calder
59 P10 Moorends Donc
58 F6 Moorhead C Brad
71 M4 Moorhouse Cumb
51 Q7 Moorhouse Notts
21 N11 Moorhouse Bank Surrey
17 K8 Moorlinch Somset
59 L3 Moor Monkton N York
66 F5 Moorsholm R & Cl
8 B4 Moorside Dorset
4 F7 Moorswater Cnwll
59 L11 Moorthorpe Wakefd
58 H6 Moortown Leeds
52 F4 Moortown Lincs
107 M5 Morangie Highld
97 J10 Morar Highld
101 M3 Moray Crematorium Moray
42 G10 Morborne Cambs
15 N10 Morchard Bishop Devon
7 K4 Morcombelake Dorset
42 D9 Morcott Rutlnd
48 F9 Morda Shrops
8 D8 Morden Dorset
21 K9 Morden Gt Lon
28 G2 Mordiford Herefs
65 N3 Mordon Dur
38 G4 More Shrops
16 C10 Morebath Devon
80 G8 Morebattle Border
62 H8 Morecambe Lancs
18 G4 Moredon Swindn
106 B4 Morefield Highld
13 N3 Morehall Kent
5 P9 Moreleigh Devon
91 N8 Morenish P & K
9 N3 Morestead Hants
8 B9 Moreton Dorset
21 Q3 Moreton Essex
39 J8 Moreton Herefs
20 B3 Moreton Oxon
56 F10 Moreton Wirral
49 K10 Moreton Corbet Shrops
5 P3 Moretonhampstead Devon
30 G7 Moreton-in-Marsh Gloucs
39 L11 Moreton Jeffries Herefs
30 H3 Moreton Morrell Warwks
39 J11 Moreton on Lugg Herefs
31 M4 Moreton Pinkney Nhants
49 L8 Moreton Say Shrops
29 K6 Moreton Valence Gloucs
46 E4 Morfa Nefyn Gwynd
87 K7 Morham E Loth
64 B3 Morland Cumb
57 P11 Morley Ches E
51 K11 Morley Derbys
58 H8 Morley Leeds
57 P11 Morley Green Ches E
44 H9 Morley St Botolph Norfk
86 F7 Morningside C Edin
85 N11 Morningside N Lans
45 K10 Morningthorpe Norfk
73 L4 Morpeth Nthumb
95 L8 Morphie Abers
40 E4 Morrey Staffs
26 F8 Morriston Swans
44 G2 Morston Norfk
14 H3 Mortehoe Devon
51 L3 Morthen Rothm
19 Q7 Mortimer W Berk
19 Q7 Mortimer West End Hants
21 K8 Mortlake Gt Lon
21 K8 Mortlake Crematorium Gt Lon
71 N5 Morton Cumb
51 K8 Morton Derbys
42 F5 Morton Lincs
52 B5 Morton Lincs
51 Q9 Morton Notts
48 F9 Morton Shrops
86 F8 Mortonhall Crematorium C Edin
65 N8 Morton-on-Swale N York
45 J6 Morton on the Hill Norfk
2 B8 Morvah Cnwll
97 N5 Morvich Highld
39 M4 Morville Shrops
5 J6 Morwellham Quay Devon
14 D8 Morwenstow Cnwll
51 K5 Mosborough Sheff
76 H4 Moscow E Ayrs
40 E10 Moseley Birm
40 C7 Moseley Wolves
39 P9 Moseley Worcs
88 B7 Moss Ag & B
59 N10 Moss Donc
101 N10 Mossat Abers
111 k3 Mossbank Shet
57 K8 Moss Bank St Hel
70 G9 Mossbay Cumb
76 G6 Mossblown S Ayrs
80 F10 Mossburnford Border
69 P5 Mossdale D & G
76 H9 Mossdale E Ayrs
62 H12 Moss Edge Lancs
85 M10 Mossend N Lans
50 C1 Mossley Tamesd
79 N8 Mosspaul Hotel Border
100 D4 Moss-side Highld
101 L4 Mosstodloch Moray
69 M8 Mossyard D & G
57 K6 Mossy Lea Lancs
7 L2 Mosterton Dorset
57 Q8 Moston Manch
56 D11 Mostyn Flints
8 C3 Motcombe Dorset
5 M10 Mothecombe Devon
71 N9 Motherby Cumb
85 M10 Motherwell N Lans
21 K9 Motspur Park Gt Lon
21 N8 Mottingham Gt Lon
9 K3 Mottisfont Hants
9 L10 Mottistone IoW
50 C2 Mottram in Longdendale Tamesd
57 Q12 Mottram St Andrew Ches E
49 J2 Mouldsworth Ches W
92 E4 Moulin P & K
11 M8 Moulsecoomb Br & H
19 P4 Moulsford Oxon
32 C8 Moulsoe M Keyn
107 K7 Moultavie Highld
49 M2 Moulton Ches W
43 K5 Moulton Lincs
65 M6 Moulton N York
32 B4 Moulton Nhants
34 B4 Moulton Suffk
16 E3 Moulton V Glam
43 J6 Moulton Chapel Lincs
45 N8 Moulton St Mary Norfk
43 K5 Moulton Seas End Lincs
4 E6 Mount Cnwll
58 E7 Mountain C Brad
27 L8 Mountain Ash Rhondd
86 D11 Mountain Cross Border
2 G7 Mount Ambrose Cnwll
34 E9 Mount Bures Essex
12 E6 Mountfield E Susx
107 J9 Mountgerald House Highld
2 G6 Mount Hawke Cnwll
3 K4 Mountjoy Cnwll
86 F10 Mount Lothian Mdloth
22 D4 Mountnessing Essex
28 F9 Mounton Mons
51 J10 Mount Pleasant Derbys
34 C7 Mount Pleasant Suffk
73 L9 Mountsett Crematorium Dur
41 M5 Mountsorrel Leics
58 D8 Mount Tabor Calder
10 F2 Mousehill Surrey
2 C9 Mousehole Cnwll
70 H2 Mouswald D & G
49 Q4 Mow Cop Ches E
80 H9 Mowhaugh Border
41 N9 Mowsley Leics
98 F11 Moy Highld
99 L3 Moy Highld
97 M6 Moyle Highld
36 B10 Moylegrove Pembks
75 K4 Muasdale Ag & B
95 P4 Muchalls Abers
28 F3 Much Birch Herefs
39 L11 Much Cowarne Herefs
28 F3 Much Dewchurch Herefs
17 K10 Muchelney Somset
17 L10 Muchelney Ham Somset
33 L11 Much Hadham Herts
57 J4 Much Hoole Lancs
4 F8 Muchlarnick Cnwll
28 H3 Much Marcle Herefs
39 L3 Much Wenlock Shrops
89 J1 Muck Highld
44 H2 Muckleburgh Collection Norfk
49 N7 Mucklestone Staffs
53 L7 Muckton Lincs
15 K5 Muddiford Devon
12 B7 Muddles Green E Susx
8 H8 Mudeford Dorset
17 N11 Mudford Somset
17 M11 Mudford Sock Somset
85 J7 Mugdock Stirlg
96 E2 Mugeary Highld
50 H11 Mugginton Derbys
102 F5 Muirden Abers
93 P8 Muirdrum Angus
102 F5 Muiresk Abers
93 L8 Muirhead Angus
86 F2 Muirhead Fife
85 L8 Muirhead N Lans
77 L6 Muirkirk E Ayrs
85 M6 Muirmill Stirlg
102 D11 Muir of Fowlis Abers
101 J4 Muir of Miltonduff Moray
107 J11 Muir of Ord Highld
98 A11 Muirshearlich Highld
103 K7 Muirtack Abers
85 Q1 Muirton P & K
106 H10 Muirton Mains Highld
92 H7 Muirton of Ardblair P & K
64 G7 Muker N York
45 K9 Mulbarton Norfk
101 L5 Mulben Moray
89 M8 Mull Ag & B
2 G11 Mullion Cnwll
2 F11 Mullion Cove Cnwll
53 N8 Mumby Lincs
39 M10 Munderfield Row Herefs
39 M11 Munderfield Stocks Herefs
45 M3 Mundesley Norfk
44 D10 Mundford Norfk
45 M9 Mundham Norfk
22 G3 Mundon Hill Essex
71 M9 Mungrisdale Cumb
107 K10 Munlochy Highld
76 E2 Munnoch N Ayrs
29 J1 Munsley Herefs
39 K5 Munslow Shrops
5 N3 Murchington Devon
31 N10 Murcott Oxon
110 D3 Murkle Highld
97 P10 Murlaggan Highld
93 N8 Murroes Angus
43 L8 Murrow Cambs
32 B10 Mursley Bucks
93 N4 Murthill Angus
92 G7 Murthly P & K
59 P4 Murton C York
64 D3 Murton Cumb
73 P10 Murton Dur
81 K5 Murton Nthumb
6 H4 Musbury Devon
86 G7 Musselburgh E Loth
42 B3 Muston Leics
67 N10 Muston N York
21 L5 Muswell Hill Gt Lon
69 P8 Mutehill D & G
45 P11 Mutford Suffk
92 C11 Muthill P & K
110 D5 Mybster Highld
26 G3 Myddfai Carmth
49 J10 Myddle Shrops
36 G9 Mydroilyn Cerdgn
3 J8 Mylor Cnwll
3 J8 Mylor Bridge Cnwll
25 K3 Mynachlog ddu Pembks
28 F9 Mynydd-bach Mons
26 E8 Mynydd-Bach Swans
25 P7 Mynyddgarreg Carmth
48 F3 Mynydd Isa Flints
95 M3 Myrebird Abers
72 B2 Myredykes Border
20 E11 Mytchett Surrey
58 C8 Mytholm Calder
58 D8 Mytholmroyd Calder
59 K2 Myton-on-Swale N York

N

105 M6 Naast Highld
111 c3 Na Buirgh W Isls
59 N5 Naburn C York
58 E6 Nab Wood Crematorium C Brad
23 M11 Nackington Kent
35 K8 Nacton Suffk
60 H3 Nafferton E R Yk
16 G9 Nailsbourne Somset
17 L3 Nailsea N Som
41 K6 Nailstone Leics
29 L8 Nailsworth Gloucs
100 D4 Nairn Highld
48 D2 Nannerch Flints
41 L4 Nanpantan Leics
3 L5 Nanpean Cnwll
3 M3 Nanstallon Cnwll
36 F8 Nanternis Cerdgn
26 C5 Nantgaredig Carmth
55 Q8 Nantglyn Denbgs
38 B8 Nantmel Powys
47 K3 Nantmor Gwynd
54 H9 Nant Peris Gwynd
49 M5 Nantwich Ches E
27 P6 Nantyglo Blae G
27 K9 Nant-y-moel Brdgnd
20 D4 Naphill Bucks
31 L2 Napton on the Hill Warwks
25 J6 Narberth Pembks
41 M7 Narborough Leics
44 C7 Narborough Norfk
54 F10 Nasareth Gwynd
41 P10 Naseby Nhants
32 B9 Nash Bucks
28 D11 Nash Newpt
39 L7 Nash Shrops
42 F10 Nassington Nhants
64 E6 Nateby Cumb
63 J12 Nateby Lancs
40 F5 National Memorial Arboretum Staffs
41 N6 National Space Science Centre C Leic
63 K4 Natland Cumb
34 G7 Naughton Suffk
30 E9 Naunton Gloucs
29 M2 Naunton Worcs
30 C4 Naunton Beauchamp Worcs
52 E10 Navenby Lincs
21 Q4 Navestock Essex
22 C4 Navestock Side Essex
110 B11 Navidale House Hotel Highld
107 N8 Navity Highld
66 F9 Nawton N York
34 F9 Nayland Suffk
21 N3 Nazeing Essex
111 k4 Neap Shet
50 E10 Near Cotton Staffs
62 G3 Near Sawrey Cumb
21 K6 Neasden Gt Lon
65 N5 Neasham Darltn
26 G8 Neath Neath
10 C3 Neatham Hants
45 M6 Neatishead Norfk
37 J7 Nebo Cerdgn
55 M9 Nebo Conwy
54 F10 Nebo Gwynd
54 F4 Nebo IoA
44 E8 Necton Norfk
108 C8 Nedd Highld
34 G7 Nedging Suffk
34 G6 Nedging Tye Suffk
35 K1 Needham Norfk
34 H6 Needham Market Suffk
33 K3 Needingworth Cambs
39 M6 Neen Savage Shrops
39 M7 Neen Sollars Shrops
39 M5 Neenton Shrops
46 E4 Nefyn Gwynd
84 H10 Neilston E Rens
27 M9 Nelson Caerph
57 Q2 Nelson Lancs
77 P3 Nemphlar S Lans
17 M4 Nempnett Thrubwell BaNES
72 E11 Nenthead Cumb
80 F6 Nenthorn Border
48 E4 Nercwys Flints
82 C11 Nereabolls Ag & B
85 L10 Nerston S Lans
81 K7 Nesbit Nthumb
58 E4 Nesfield N York
48 F1 Ness Botanic Gardens Ches W
48 H10 Nesscliffe Shrops
56 F12 Neston Ches W
18 C7 Neston Wilts
39 L4 Netchwood Shrops
49 Q1 Nether Alderley Ches E
18 G10 Netheravon Wilts
80 D5 Nether Blainslie Border
102 G4 Netherbrae Abers
41 P3 Nether Broughton Leics
77 N2 Netherburn S Lans
7 L3 Netherbury Dorset
59 J5 Netherby N York
7 P3 Nether Cerne Dorset
79 J10 Nethercleuch D & G
17 N11 Nether Compton Dorset
102 H10 Nether Crimond Abers
101 M3 Nether Dallachy Moray
28 G8 Netherend Gloucs
12 E6 Netherfield E Susx
78 F6 Nether Fingland S Lans
8 G2 Netherhampton Wilts
93 L7 Nether Handwick Angus
51 K2 Nether Haugh Rothm
7 K2 Netherhay Dorset
51 Q5 Nether Headon Notts
51 J10 Nether Heage Derbys
31 P3 Nether Heyford Nhants
78 G6 Nether Howcleugh S Lans
63 J8 Nether Kellet Lancs
103 L6 Nether Kinmundy Abers
51 M6 Nether Langwith Notts
70 C6 Netherlaw D & G
95 P4 Netherley Abers
78 G10 Nethermill D & G
103 J6 Nethermuir Abers
21 L11 Netherne-on-the-Hill Surrey
58 F9 Netheroyd Hill Kirk
50 G5 Nether Padley Derbys
85 J11 Netherplace E Rens
59 M4 Nether Poppleton C York
40 H5 Netherseal Derbys
66 C8 Nether Silton N York
16 G8 Nether Stowey Somset
58 F11 Netherthong Kirk
93 P4 Netherton Angus
6 B8 Netherton Devon
40 C9 Netherton Dudley
58 F10 Netherton Kirk
85 N11 Netherton N Lans
81 K11 Netherton Nthumb
92 H5 Netherton P & K
85 J7 Netherton Stirlg
58 H10 Netherton Wakefd
62 B1 Nethertown Cumb
110 G1 Nethertown Highld
40 E4 Nethertown Staffs
86 D12 Netherurd Border
19 K12 Nether Wallop Hants
62 D2 Nether Wasdale Cumb
30 G9 Nether Westcote Gloucs
40 G8 Nether Whitacre Warwks
78 D5 Nether Whitecleuch S Lans
31 Q10 Nether Winchendon Bucks
73 K3 Netherwitton Nthumb
99 Q5 Nethy Bridge Highld
9 M6 Netley Hants
9 K5 Netley Marsh Hants
20 B6 Nettlebed Oxon
17 P6 Nettlebridge Somset
7 M4 Nettlecombe Dorset
20 G2 Nettleden Herts
52 E8 Nettleham Lincs
22 D11 Nettlestead Kent
22 D12 Nettlestead Green Kent
9 Q8 Nettlestone IoW
73 M10 Nettlesworth Dur
52 G4 Nettleton Lincs
18 B5 Nettleton Wilts
18 G12 Netton Wilts
36 B11 Nevern Pembks
42 B10 Nevill Holt Leics
70 F3 New Abbey D & G
103 J3 New Aberdour Abers
21 M10 New Addington Gt Lon
58 G5 Newall Leeds
9 P2 New Alresford Hants
93 J6 New Alyth P & K
111 i1 Newark Ork
52 B11 Newark-on-Trent Notts
85 N10 Newarthill N Lans
22 C9 New Ash Green Kent
52 B11 New Balderton Notts
22 C9 New Barn Kent
21 L4 New Barnet Gt Lon
86 G8 Newbattle Mdloth
81 M9 New Bewick Nthumb
71 K3 Newbie D & G
64 B2 Newbiggin Cumb
71 P9 Newbiggin Cumb
71 Q6 Newbiggin Cumb
64 G3 Newbiggin Dur
64 H9 Newbiggin N York
73 N4 Newbiggin-by-the-Sea Nthumb
93 K7 Newbigging Angus
93 M8 Newbigging Angus
93 N8 Newbigging Angus
86 B11 Newbigging S Lans
63 N2 Newbiggin-on-Lune Cumb
41 L11 New Bilton Warwks
51 J6 Newbold Derbys
41 L11 Newbold on Avon Warwks
30 G5 Newbold on Stour Warwks
30 H3 Newbold Pacey Warwks
41 K6 Newbold Verdon Leics
53 K11 New Bolingbroke Lincs
42 H8 Newborough C Pete
54 F8 Newborough IoA
40 F3 Newborough Staffs
52 D8 New Boultham Lincs
35 L8 Newbourne Suffk
32 B8 New Bradwell M Keyn
51 J6 New Brampton Derbys
73 M11 New Brancepeth Dur
86 D7 Newbridge C Edin
27 P8 Newbridge Caerph
2 C9 Newbridge Cnwll
78 F11 Newbridge D & G
9 K4 Newbridge Hants
9 M9 Newbridge IoW
29 L2 Newbridge Green Worcs
38 B9 Newbridge on Wye Powys
56 F9 New Brighton Wirral
72 F7 Newbrough Nthumb
44 H11 New Buckenham Norfk
15 N10 Newbuildings Devon
103 K4 Newburgh Abers
103 K9 Newburgh Abers
93 J11 Newburgh Fife
57 J6 Newburgh Lancs
66 D11 Newburgh Priory N York
73 L7 Newburn N u Ty
17 Q6 Newbury Somset
19 M7 Newbury W Berk
21 N6 Newbury Park Gt Lon
64 B4 Newby Cumb
63 P11 Newby Lancs
63 N8 Newby N York
66 C5 Newby N York
62 G5 Newby Bridge Cumb

O

56 G8 Oakford Cerdgn
16 C11 Oakford Devon
42 C8 Oakham Rutlnd
10 C3 Oakhanger Hants
17 P6 Oakhill Somset
33 L4 Oakington Cambs
29 K5 Oakle Street Gloucs
32 E6 Oakley Bed
31 N10 Oakley Bucks
86 B4 Oakley Fife
19 P9 Oakley Hants
35 J2 Oakley Suffk
29 M7 Oakridge Gloucs
29 P9 Oaksey Wilts
40 H5 Oakthorpe Leics
51 J12 Oakwood C Derb
58 D6 Oakworth C Brad
23 J10 Oare Kent
15 N3 Oare Somset
18 H7 Oare Wilts
42 E3 Oasby Lincs
17 K10 Oath Somset
93 N4 Oathlaw Angus
20 H9 Oatlands Park Surrey
90 B9 Oban Ag & B
90 C8 *Oban Airport* Ag & B
38 G6 Obley Shrops
92 F8 Obney P & K
17 P11 Oborne Dorset
35 J3 Occold Suffk
110 F8 Occumster Highld
76 H7 Ochiltree E Ayrs
41 K1 Ockbrook Derbys
20 H11 Ockham Surrey
89 L3 Ockle Highld
11 J3 Ockley Surrey
39 L11 Ocle Pychard Herefs
17 M11 Odcombe Somset
17 Q4 Odd Down BaNES
30 B3 Oddingley Worcs
30 G8 Oddington Gloucs
31 M10 Oddington Oxon
32 D5 Odell Bed
20 C12 Odiham Hants
58 F8 Odsal C Brad
33 J8 Odsey Cambs
8 G3 Odstock Wilts
41 K6 Odstone Leics
31 J2 Offchurch Warwks
30 D5 Offenham Worcs
50 B3 Offerton Stockp
11 N7 Offham E Susx
22 D11 Offham Kent
10 G8 Offham W Susx
32 H4 Offord Cluny Cambs
32 H4 Offord D'Arcy Cambs
34 H6 Offton Suffk
6 G3 Offwell Devon
18 H6 Ogbourne Maizey Wilts
18 H6 Ogbourne St Andrew Wilts
18 H6 Ogbourne St George Wilts
73 K5 Ogle Nthumb
56 H11 Oglet Lpool
16 B2 Ogmore V Glam
16 B2 Ogmore-by-Sea V Glam
27 K10 Ogmore Vale Brdgnd
8 B5 Okeford Fitzpaine Dorset
5 M2 Okehampton Devon
50 H8 Oker Side Derbys
11 J3 Okewood Hill Surrey
32 B3 Old Nhants
95 Q1 Old Aberdeen C Aber
9 P1 Old Alresford Hants
108 C8 Oldany Highld
77 M11 Old Auchenbrack D & G
51 M11 Old Basford C Nott
19 Q9 Old Basing Hants
44 F6 Old Beetley Norfk
30 E2 Oldberrow Warwks
81 M9 Old Bewick Nthumb
53 K9 Old Bolingbroke Lincs
58 G5 Old Bramhope Leeds
51 J6 Old Brampton Derbys
70 C3 Old Bridge of Urr D & G
44 H10 Old Buckenham Norfk
19 M8 Old Burghclere Hants
40 C9 Oldbury Sandw
39 N4 Oldbury Shrops
40 H8 Oldbury Warwks
28 H9 Oldbury-on-Severn S Glos
18 B3 Oldbury on the Hill Gloucs
66 D9 Old Byland N York
51 N1 Old Cantley Donc
28 C4 Oldcastle Mons
45 K7 Old Catton Norfk
53 J2 Old Clee NE Lin
16 E7 Old Cleeve Somset
51 N7 Old Clipstone Notts
55 M6 Old Colwyn Conwy
51 N3 Oldcotes Notts
76 D10 Old Dailly S Ayrs
41 P3 Old Dalby Leics
103 K6 Old Deer Abers
51 M2 Old Edlington Donc
61 K6 Old Ellerby E R Yk
35 M9 Old Felixstowe Suffk
39 Q8 Oldfield Worcs
42 H10 Old Fletton C Pete
18 B10 Oldford Somset
28 G5 Old Forge Herefs
2 b1 Old Grimsby IoS
33 L11 Old Hall Green Herts
58 B12 Oldham Oldham
87 N7 Oldhamstocks E Loth
21 P2 Old Harlow Essex
44 B2 Old Hunstanton Norfk
33 J2 Old Hurst Cambs
63 K5 Old Hutton Cumb
84 H8 Old Kilpatrick W Duns
32 H11 Old Knebworth Herts
45 K8 Old Lakenham Norfk
17 P2 Oldland S Glos
57 M2 Old Langho Lancs
53 L12 Old Leake Lincs
66 H11 Old Malton N York
102 H9 Oldmeldrum Abers
4 H5 Oldmill Cnwll
30 H1 Old Milverton Warwks
17 J5 Oldmixon N Som
34 H4 Old Newton Suffk
38 F9 Old Radnor Powys
102 E9 Old Rayne Abers
13 K5 Old Romney Kent
11 K8 Old Shoreham W Susx
108 D4 Oldshoremore Highld
29 K11 Old Sodbury S Glos
42 D4 Old Somerby Lincs
66 D10 Oldstead N York
31 Q6 Old Stratford Nhants
92 C3 Old Struan P & K
40 B10 Old Swinford Dudley
66 B10 Old Thirsk N York
63 L5 Old Town Cumb
12 C9 Old Town E Susx
2 c2 Old Town IoS
57 P9 Old Trafford Traffd
71 P4 Oldwall Cumb
26 C9 Oldwalls Swans
32 G7 Old Warden C Beds
32 F2 Old Weston Cambs
110 G6 Old Wick Highld
20 F8 Old Windsor W & M
23 K11 Old Wives Lees Kent
20 G11 Old Woking Surrey
110 C5 Olgrinmore Highld
40 E4 Olive Green Staffs
9 M2 Oliver's Battery Hants
111 k3 Ollaberry Shet
96 F3 Ollach Highld
57 P12 Ollerton Ches E
51 P7 Ollerton Notts
49 M9 Ollerton Shrops
32 C6 Olney M Keyn
110 E3 Olrig House Highld
40 F10 Olton Solhll
28 H10 Olveston S Glos
39 Q8 Ombersley Worcs
51 P7 Ompton Notts
56 d5 Onchan IoM
50 D9 Onecote Staffs
39 J6 Onibury Shrops
90 E4 Onich Highld
26 H6 Onllwyn Neath
49 N6 Onneley Staffs
33 Q12 Onslow Green Essex
20 F12 Onslow Village Surrey
49 L1 Onston Ches W
105 L7 Opinan Highld
101 L4 Orbliston Moray
96 B2 Orbost Highld
53 M9 Orby Lincs
16 H10 Orchard Portman Somset
18 F10 Orcheston Wilts
28 F4 Orcop Herefs
28 F4 Orcop Hill Herefs
102 E4 Ord Abers
102 E12 Ordhead Abers
94 G2 Ordie Abers
101 L4 Ordiequish Moray
51 P5 Ordsall Notts
12 G7 Ore E Susx
35 N6 Orford Suffk
57 L10 Orford Warrtn
8 D8 Organford Dorset
13 J3 Orlestone Kent
39 J8 Orleton Herefs
39 M8 Orleton Worcs
32 C3 Orlingbury Nhants
66 D4 Ormesby R & Cl
45 P7 Ormesby St Margaret Norfk
45 P7 Ormesby St Michael Norfk
105 M4 Ormiscaig Highld
86 H8 Ormiston E Loth
89 K4 Ormsaigmore Highld
83 L8 Ormsary Ag & B
56 H7 Ormskirk Lancs
82 E5 Oronsay Ag & B
111 h2 Orphir Ork
21 P9 Orpington Gt Lon
56 G9 Orrell Sefton
57 K7 Orrell Wigan
70 C6 Orroland D & G
22 D7 Orsett Thurr
49 P11 Orslow Staffs
51 Q11 Orston Notts
63 L1 Orton Cumb
32 B2 Orton Nhants
39 Q3 Orton Staffs
42 G10 Orton Longueville C Pete
40 H6 Orton-on-the-Hill Leics
42 G10 Orton Waterville C Pete
33 K6 Orwell Cambs
57 M3 Osbaldeston Lancs
59 N4 Osbaldwick C York
41 K6 Osbaston Leics
48 G10 Osbaston Shrops
9 N8 Osborne House IoW
42 F3 Osbournby Lincs
49 J3 Oscroft Ches W
96 C2 Ose Highld
41 K4 Osgathorpe Leics
52 F5 Osgodby Lincs
59 N7 Osgodby N York
67 M9 Osgodby N York
96 G3 Oskaig Highld
89 K8 Oskamull Ag & B
50 G11 Osmaston Derbys
7 Q6 Osmington Dorset
7 Q6 Osmington Mills Dorset
59 J7 Osmondthorpe Leeds
66 C7 Osmotherley N York
31 L11 Osney Oxon
23 J10 Ospringe Kent
58 H9 Ossett Wakefd
51 Q7 Ossington Notts
21 J7 Osterley Gt Lon
66 E10 Oswaldkirk N York
57 N4 Oswaldtwistle Lancs
48 F9 Oswestry Shrops
21 Q10 Otford Kent
22 F11 Otham Kent
17 K9 Othery Somset
58 G5 Otley Leeds
35 K5 Otley Suffk
9 M3 Otterbourne Hants
72 Q9 Otterburn N York
72 F3 Otterburn Nthumb
83 P6 Otter Ferry Ag & B
4 E3 Otterham Cnwll
16 H7 Otterhampton Somset
111 b4 Otternish W Isls
20 G9 Ottershaw Surrey
111 k3 Otterswick Shet
6 E6 Otterton Devon
6 E4 Ottery St Mary Devon
13 M2 Ottinge Kent
61 M8 Ottringham E R Yk
71 J7 Oughterside Cumb
50 H3 Oughtibridge Sheff
57 M10 Oughtrington Warrtn
66 D11 Oulston N York
71 K5 Oulton Cumb
45 J4 Oulton Norfk
40 B1 Oulton Staffs
45 Q10 Oulton Suffk
45 Q10 Oulton Broad Suffk
45 J5 Oulton Street Norfk
42 E11 Oundle Nhants
39 Q4 Ounsdale Staffs
64 B1 Ousby Cumb
34 C5 Ousden Suffk
60 E9 Ousefleet E R Yk
73 M9 Ouston Dur
62 G3 Outgate Cumb
64 E7 Outhgill Cumb
30 E2 Outhill Warwks
58 E9 Outlane Kirk
56 H1 Out Rawcliffe Lancs
43 N8 Outwell Norfk
11 L2 Outwood Surrey
49 P11 Outwoods Staffs
59 J8 Ouzlewell Green Leeds
33 L3 Over Cambs
29 N2 Overbury Worcs
7 Q6 Overcombe Dorset
17 N11 Over Compton Dorset
57 M7 Overdale Crematorium Bolton
50 G7 Over Haddon Derbys
63 K8 Over Kellet Lancs
31 K9 Over Kiddington Oxon
17 L8 Overleigh Somset
30 H8 Over Norton Oxon
49 P1 Over Peover Ches E
56 H12 Overpool Ches W
108 H10 Overscaig Hotel Highld
40 H4 Overseal Derbys
66 C8 Over Silton N York
23 K11 Oversland Kent
32 B4 Overstone Nhants
16 G8 Over Stowey Somset
45 L3 Overstrand Norfk
17 L11 Over Stratton Somset
31 L6 Overthorpe Nhants
102 H11 Overton C Aber
19 N10 Overton Hants
62 H9 Overton Lancs
59 M3 Overton N York
39 J7 Overton Shrops
26 B10 Overton Swans
58 H10 Overton Wakefd
48 G7 Overton Wrexhm
85 N11 Overtown N Lans
19 K11 Over Wallop Hants
40 G8 Over Whitacre Warwks
31 K8 Over Worton Oxon
32 A11 Oving Bucks
10 E8 Oving W Susx
11 M8 Ovingdean Br & H
73 J7 Ovingham Nthumb
65 K5 Ovington Dur
34 C8 Ovington Essex
9 P2 Ovington Hants
44 F9 Ovington Norfk
73 J7 Ovington Nthumb
9 K4 Ower Hants
8 B9 Owermoigne Dorset
51 J3 Owlerton Sheff
20 D10 Owlsmoor Br For
20 C3 Owlswick Bucks
52 E6 Owmby Lincs
52 F3 Owmby Lincs
9 N3 Owslebury Hants
59 M11 Owston Donc
41 Q6 Owston Leics
52 B4 Owston Ferry N Linc
61 M7 Owstwick E R Yk
61 N8 Owthorne E R Yk
41 P2 Owthorpe Notts
66 C2 Owton Manor Hartpl
44 C9 Oxborough Norfk
53 K7 Oxcombe Lincs
63 K4 Oxenholme Cumb
58 D7 Oxenhope C Brad
62 G5 Oxen Park Cumb
17 L7 Oxenpill Somset
29 N3 Oxenton Gloucs
19 K8 Oxenwood Wilts
31 L11 Oxford Oxon
31 L10 *Oxford Airport* Oxon
31 M11 Oxford Crematorium Oxon
31 N12 Oxford Services Oxon
20 H4 Oxhey Herts
30 H5 Oxhill Warwks
40 B7 Oxley Wolves
22 H1 Oxley Green Essex
43 M11 Oxlode Cambs
80 F9 Oxnam Border
45 K5 Oxnead Norfk
21 J10 Oxshott Surrey
50 H1 Oxspring Barns
21 M11 Oxted Surrey
80 C4 Oxton Border
59 L5 Oxton N York
51 N9 Oxton Notts
26 C10 Oxwich Swans
26 C10 Oxwich Green Swans
106 F3 Oykel Bridge Hotel Highld
102 E9 Oyne Abers
26 E10 Oystermouth Swans

P

111 e2 Pabail W Isls
41 J5 Packington Leics
93 M5 Padanaram Angus
31 Q7 Padbury Bucks
21 L7 Paddington Gt Lon
13 M3 Paddlesworth Kent
22 D10 Paddlesworth Kent
12 D2 Paddock Wood Kent
57 P3 Padiham Lancs
58 F3 Padside N York
3 K1 Padstow Cnwll
19 Q7 Padworth W Berk
10 E9 Pagham W Susx
22 H5 Paglesham Essex
6 B10 Paignton Torbay
41 L10 Pailton Warwks
38 D11 Painscastle Powys
73 J8 Painshawfield Nthumb
60 E3 Painsthorpe E R Yk
29 M6 Painswick Gloucs
23 J10 Painter's Forstal Kent
84 H9 Paisley Rens
84 H9 Paisley Woodside Crematorium Rens
45 Q11 Pakefield Suffk
34 F4 Pakenham Suffk
20 E7 Paley Street W & M
40 D7 Palfrey Wsall
35 J2 Palgrave Suffk
8 B8 Pallington Dorset
76 H7 Palmerston E Ayrs
70 D4 Palnackie D & G
69 L6 Palnure D & G
51 L7 Palterton Derbys
19 Q8 Pamber End Hants
19 Q8 Pamber Green Hants
19 Q8 Pamber Heath Hants
29 N3 Pamington Gloucs
8 E7 Pamphill Dorset
33 N7 Pampisford Cambs
93 P8 Panbride Angus
14 F10 Pancrasweek Devon
28 D4 Pandy Mons
55 M8 Pandy Tudur Conwy
34 C10 Panfield Essex
19 Q5 Pangbourne W Berk
11 L7 Pangdean W Susx
58 H4 Pannal N York
58 H4 Pannal Ash N York
94 G3 Pannanich Wells Hotel Abers
48 F10 Pant Shrops
48 D1 Pantasaph Flints
27 K11 Pant-ffrwyth Brdgnd
46 H2 Pant Glas Gwynd
47 M10 Pantglas Powys
52 H7 Panton Lincs
37 R6 Pant-y-dwr Powys
48 E3 Pant-y-mwyn Flints
45 M7 Panxworth Norfk
111 h1 *Papa Westray Airport* Ork
70 H8 Papcastle Cumb
110 H5 Papigoe Highld
87 L7 Papple E Loth
51 M9 Papplewick Notts
33 J4 Papworth Everard Cambs
33 J4 Papworth St Agnes Cambs
3 N5 Par Cnwll
57 J6 Parbold Lancs
17 N8 Parbrook Somset
47 P5 Parc Gwynd
25 K6 Parc Gwyn Crematorium Pembks
28 E9 Parc Seymour Newpt
70 H9 Pardshaw Cumb
35 M5 Parham Suffk
78 E10 Park D & G
72 C8 Park Nthumb
20 B6 Park Corner Oxon
56 G3 Park Crematorium Lancs
28 H7 Parkend Gloucs
12 C1 Parkers Green Kent
13 J3 Park Farm Kent
56 F12 Parkgate Ches W
78 G10 Parkgate D & G
9 N6 Park Gate Hants
58 F6 Park Gate Leeds
11 K2 Parkgate Surrey
93 Q6 Parkgrove Crematorium Angus
84 H8 Parkhall W Duns
14 G7 Parkham Devon
26 D10 Parkmill Swans
21 K7 Park Royal Gt Lon
73 Q10 Parkside Dur
85 N10 Parkside N Lans
8 F8 Parkstone Poole
21 J3 Park Street Herts
58 E9 Park Wood Crematorium Calder
21 N2 Parndon Essex
21 N3 Parndon Wood Crematorium Essex
15 L3 Parracombe Devon
43 L8 Parson Drove Cambs
34 G10 Parson's Heath Essex
85 J9 Partick C Glas
57 N9 Partington Traffd
53 L9 Partney Lincs
70 F10 Parton Cumb
11 J6 Partridge Green W Susx
50 F9 Parwich Derbys
32 A8 Passenham Nhants
45 M4 Paston Norfk
11 L8 Patcham Br & H
10 H8 Patching W Susx
28 H11 Patchway S Glos
58 F2 Pateley Bridge N York
86 F4 Pathhead Fife
86 H9 Pathhead Mdloth
92 G12 Path of Condie P & K
76 G8 Patna E Ayrs
18 F8 Patney Wilts
56 b5 Patrick IoM
65 L8 Patrick Brompton N York
57 N8 Patricroft Salfd
61 M9 Patrington E R Yk
61 M9 Patrington Haven E R Yk
23 M11 Patrixbourne Kent
71 N11 Patterdale Cumb
39 P3 Pattingham Staffs
31 P4 Pattishall Nhants
34 D11 Pattiswick Green Essex
2 C9 Paul Cnwll
31 Q5 Paulerspury Nhants
61 K8 Paull E R Yk
8 G2 Paul's Dene Wilts
17 P5 Paulton BaNES
73 K2 Pauperhaugh Nthumb
32 E5 Pavenham Bed
16 H7 Pawlett Somset
30 F6 Paxford Gloucs
81 K4 Paxton Border
6 E3 Payhembury Devon
63 P10 Paythorne Lancs
11 N9 Peacehaven E Susx
50 F3 Peak District National Park
50 E5 Peak Forest Derbys
42 G8 Peakirk C Pete
17 Q5 Peasedown St John BaNES
44 H6 Peaseland Green Norfk
19 M5 Peasemore W Berk
35 M3 Peasenhall Suffk
11 L4 Pease Pottage W Susx
10 H2 Peaslake Surrey
57 K9 Peasley Cross St Hel
12 H5 Peasmarsh E Susx
103 J3 Peathill Abers
87 J1 Peat Inn Fife
41 N8 Peatling Magna Leics
41 N9 Peatling Parva Leics
34 E9 Pebmarsh Essex
30 F5 Pebworth Worcs
58 C8 Pecket Well Calder
49 K4 Peckforton Ches E
21 M8 Peckham Gt Lon
41 L7 Peckleton Leics
13 L3 Pedlinge Kent
40 B10 Pedmore Dudley
17 K8 Pedwell Somset
79 L2 Peebles Border
56 b4 Peel IoM
13 M3 Peene Kent
32 G9 Pegsdon C Beds
73 M4 Pegswood Nthumb
23 Q9 Pegwell Kent
96 G3 Peinchorran Highld
104 F10 Peinlich Highld
34 G12 Peldon Essex
40 D6 Pelsall Wsall
73 M9 Pelton Dur
4 F8 Pelynt Cnwll
26 D8 Pemberton Carmth
57 K7 Pemberton Wigan
25 P8 Pembrey Carmth
38 H9 Pembridge Herefs
24 H8 Pembroke Pembks
24 G7 Pembroke Dock Pembks
24 E5 Pembrokeshire Coast National Park Pembks
12 D2 Pembury Kent
28 G3 Pen-allt Herefs
28 F6 Penallt Mons
25 K8 Penally Pembks
16 G2 Penarth V Glam
37 L4 Pen-bont Rhydybeddau Cerdgn
36 E9 Penbryn Cerdgn
25 Q2 Pencader Carmth
87 J8 Pencaitland E Loth
54 D6 Pencarnisiog IoA
37 J10 Pencarreg Carmth
27 M4 Pencelli Powys
26 D9 Penclawdd Swans
27 K11 Pencoed Brdgnd
39 L10 Pencombe Herefs
28 G5 Pencraig Herefs
48 B9 Pencraig Powys
2 B8 Pendeen Cnwll
27 K7 Penderyn Rhondd
25 L7 Pendine Carmth
57 P8 Pendlebury Salfd
57 N2 Pendleton Lancs
29 K3 Pendock Worcs
4 C4 Pendoggett Cnwll
7 M1 Pendomer Somset
16 E2 Pendoylan V Glam
47 M10 Penegoes Powys
25 J4 Pen-ffordd Pembks
27 N8 Pengam Caerph
27 P12 Pengam Cardif
21 M8 Penge Gt Lon
4 D4 Pengelly Cnwll
2 H5 Penhallow Cnwll
2 G8 Penhalvean Cnwll
18 H3 Penhill Swindn
28 E10 Penhow Newpt
86 F9 Penicuik Mdloth
96 F2 Penifiler Highld
75 L7 Peninver Ag & B
50 G1 Penistone Barns
76 D10 Penkill S Ayrs
40 B5 Penkridge Staffs
48 H7 Penley Wrexhm
16 C2 Penllyn V Glam
55 L10 Penmachno Conwy
27 P8 Penmaen Caerph
26 D10 Penmaen Swans
55 K6 Penmaenmawr Conwy
47 L7 Penmaenpool Gwynd
16 E3 Penmark V Glam
3 J6 Penmount Crematorium Cnwll
54 G6 Penmynydd IoA
20 E5 Penn Bucks
47 L10 Pennal Gwynd
102 H3 Pennan Abers
47 P10 Pennant Powys
38 G3 Pennerley Shrops
58 C7 Pennines
62 F6 Pennington Cumb
27 M4 Pennorth Powys
20 E4 Penn Street Bucks
62 F5 Penny Bridge Cumb
89 L10 Pennycross Ag & B
89 L10 Pennyghael Ag & B
76 E8 Pennyglen S Ayrs
15 P9 Pennymoor Devon
73 P9 Pennywell Sundld
36 D10 Penparc Cerdgn
28 C7 Penperlleni Mons
4 E8 Penpoll Cnwll
2 F7 Penponds Cnwll
78 D9 Penpont D & G
36 D11 Pen-rhiw Pembks
27 M8 Penrhiwceiber Rhondd
26 G6 Pen Rhiwfawr Neath
36 F11 Penrhiw-llan Cerdgn
36 F10 Penrhiw-pal Cerdgn
46 F5 Penrhos Gwynd
28 E6 Penrhos Mons
55 M5 Penrhyn Bay Conwy
54 H7 Penrhyn Castle Gwynd
47 K4 Penrhyndeudraeth Gwynd
26 C10 Penrice Swans
75 N4 Penrioch N Ayrs
71 Q9 Penrith Cumb
3 K2 Penrose Cnwll
71 N9 Penruddock Cumb
2 H8 Penryn Cnwll
55 P6 Pensarn Conwy
39 N8 Pensax Worcs
17 R9 Penselwood Somset
17 N4 Pensford BaNES
30 C5 Pensham Worcs
73 N9 Penshaw Sundld

1 Q2 **Penshurst** Kent
4 G6 **Pensilva** Cnwll
3 M6 **Pentewan** Cnwll
4 H8 **Pentir** Gwynd
2 H4 **Pentire** Cnwll
4 D7 **Pentlow** Essex
4 C7 **Pentney** Norfk
9 P12 **Pentonbridge** Cumb
9 K10 **Penton Mewsey** Hants
4 G6 **Pentraeth** IoA
28 E8 **Pentre** Mons
27 K9 **Pentre** Rhondd
48 G11 **Pentre** Shrops
27 M7 **Pentrebach** Myr Td
27 J3 **Pentre-bach** Powys
54 F7 **Pentre Berw** IoA
48 F6 **Pentrebychan Crematorium** Wrexhm
48 D5 **Pentre-celyn** Denbgs
47 P9 **Pentre-celyn** Powys
26 F9 **Pentre-chwyth** Swans
25 P2 **Pentre-cwrt** Carmth
48 E6 **Pentredwr** Denbgs
47 J4 **Pentrefelin** Gwynd
55 M10 **Pentrefoelas** Conwy
36 F9 **Pentregat** Cerdgn
26 E5 **Pentre-Gwenlais** Carmth
38 G6 **Pentre Hodrey** Shrops
48 C3 **Pentre Llanrhaeadr** Denbgs
16 C2 **Pentre Meyrick** V Glam
55 M8 **Pentre-tafarn-y-fedw** Conwy
51 J9 **Pentrich** Derbys
8 F4 **Pentridge** Dorset
28 F7 **Pen-twyn** Mons
27 P9 **Pentwynmaur** Caerph
27 M11 **Pentyrch** Cardif
3 M5 **Penwithick** Cnwll
26 E4 **Penybanc** Carmth
38 C8 **Penybont** Powys
48 E10 **Pen-y-bont** Powys
48 C9 **Pen-y-bont-fawr** Powys
36 C11 **Pen-y-bryn** Pembks
48 F6 **Penycae** Wrexhm
28 E7 **Pen-y-clawdd** Mons
27 M10 **Pen-y-coedcae** Rhondd
24 E4 **Pen-y-cwn** Pembks
48 D2 **Pen-y-felin** Flints
48 F4 **Penyffordd** Flints
48 C10 **Pen-y-Garnedd** Powys
46 C5 **Pen-y-graig** Gwynd
27 L10 **Penygraig** Rhondd
26 D6 **Penygroes** Carmth
54 F10 **Penygroes** Gwynd
26 C7 **Pen-y-Mynydd** Carmth
48 F3 **Penymynydd** Flints
54 F4 **Penysarn** IoA
48 E5 **Pen-y-stryt** Denbgs
27 K7 **Penywaun** Rhondd
2 D9 **Penzance** Cnwll
2 D9 *Penzance Heliport* Cnwll
30 C4 **Peopleton** Worcs
49 L9 **Peplow** Shrops
76 F4 **Perceton** N Ayrs
103 K3 **Percyhorner** Abers
19 J10 **Perham Down** Wilts
16 C7 **Periton** Somset
21 J6 **Perivale** Gt Lon
6 D5 **Perkins Village** Devon
51 N6 **Perlethorpe** Notts
2 H7 **Perranarworthal** Cnwll
2 H5 **Perranporth** Cnwll
2 D9 **Perranuthnoe** Cnwll
2 H7 **Perranwell** Cnwll
2 H5 **Perranzabuloe** Cnwll
40 E8 **Perry Barr** Birm
40 E8 **Perry Barr Crematorium** Birm
18 E3 **Perry Green** Wilts
49 P9 **Pershall** Staffs
30 C5 **Pershore** Worcs
32 F4 **Pertenhall** Bed
92 G10 **Perth** P & K
92 G9 **Perth Crematorium** P & K
48 G8 **Perthy** Shrops
28 H2 **Perton** Herefs
39 Q3 **Perton** Staffs
42 H9 **Peterborough** C Pete
42 G9 **Peterborough Crematorium** C Pete
42 G10 **Peterborough Services** Cambs
28 D2 **Peterchurch** Herefs
95 N2 **Peterculter** C Aber
103 M6 **Peterhead** Abers
73 Q11 **Peterlee** Dur
10 C5 **Petersfield** Hants
32 G11 **Peter's Green** Herts
21 J8 **Petersham** Gt Lon
14 H9 **Peters Marland** Devon
28 B11 **Peterstone Wentlooge** Newpt
16 E2 **Peterston-super-Ely** V Glam
28 G4 **Peterstow** Herefs
5 K5 **Peter Tavy** Devon
23 L12 **Petham** Kent
4 G3 **Petherwin Gate** Cnwll
15 J9 **Petrockstow** Devon
12 G7 **Pett** E Susx
35 J5 **Pettaugh** Suffk
93 M7 **Petterden** Angus
78 F1 **Pettinain** S Lans
35 L6 **Pettistree** Suffk
16 D10 **Petton** Devon
21 N9 **Petts Wood** Gt Lon
86 F5 **Pettycur** Fife
103 J9 **Pettymuk** Abers
10 F6 **Petworth** W Susx
12 D8 **Pevensey** E Susx
12 D8 **Pevensey Bay** E Susx
18 H8 **Pewsey** Wilts
30 C3 **Phepson** Worcs
14 E7 **Philham** Devon
79 N4 **Philiphaugh** Border
2 E7 **Phillack** Cnwll
3 K7 **Philleigh** Cnwll
86 C6 **Philpstoun** W Loth
20 C11 **Phoenix Green** Hants
99 K9 **Phones** Highld
17 L10 **Pibsbury** Somset
59 L11 **Pickburn** Donc
66 H10 **Pickering** N York
40 H10 **Pickford** Covtry
65 N10 **Pickhill** N York
38 H3 **Picklescott** Shrops
57 M12 **Pickmere** Ches E
16 G9 **Pickney** Somset
42 B7 **Pickwell** Leics
42 F4 **Pickworth** Lincs
42 E7 **Pickworth** Rutlnd
48 H2 **Picton** Ches W
65 P6 **Picton** N York
11 N9 **Piddinghoe** E Susx
32 B6 **Piddington** Nhants
31 N10 **Piddington** Oxon
7 Q4 **Piddlehinton** Dorset
7 Q3 **Piddletrenthide** Dorset
33 K2 **Pidley** Cambs
65 L4 **Piercebridge** Darltn
111 h1 **Pierowall** Ork
22 C4 **Pilgrims Hatch** Essex
52 C5 **Pilham** Lincs
17 H7 **Pillaton** Cnwll
30 H4 **Pillerton Hersey** Warwks
30 H5 **Pillerton Priors** Warwks
51 J1 **Pilley** Barns
9 K7 **Pilley** Hants
62 H11 **Pilling** Lancs
28 G10 **Pilning** S Glos
50 E7 **Pilsbury** Derbys
7 K3 **Pilsdon** Dorset
50 G6 **Pilsley** Derbys
51 K8 **Pilsley** Derbys
45 N7 **Pilson Green** Norfk
11 N5 **Piltdown** E Susx
15 K5 **Pilton** Devon
42 E12 **Pilton** Nhants
42 D9 **Pilton** Rutlnd
17 N7 **Pilton** Somset
8 D5 **Pimperne** Dorset
43 J5 **Pinchbeck** Lincs
33 J10 **Pin Green** Herts
6 C4 **Pinhoe** Devon
30 G2 **Pinley Green** Warwks
76 D11 **Pinminnoch** S Ayrs
76 D11 **Pinmore** S Ayrs
6 E5 **Pinn** Devon
20 H5 **Pinner** Gt Lon
20 H5 **Pinner Green** Gt Lon
30 C4 **Pinvin** Worcs
68 G2 **Pinwherry** S Ayrs
51 L9 **Pinxton** Derbys
39 J12 **Pipe and Lyde** Herefs
39 J7 **Pipe Aston** Herefs
49 N7 **Pipe Gate** Shrops
100 D5 **Piperhill** Highld
42 B11 **Pipewell** Nhants
20 F11 **Pirbright** Surrey
80 E8 **Pirnie** Border
75 N4 **Pirnmill** N Ayrs
32 G9 **Pirton** Herts
20 B5 **Pishill** Oxon
46 E3 **Pistyll** Gwynd
92 C3 **Pitagowan** P & K
103 K3 **Pitblae** Abers
92 F9 **Pitcairngreen** P & K
107 N7 **Pitcalnie** Highld
102 F9 **Pitcaple** Abers
94 F8 **Pitcarity** Angus
29 L7 **Pitchcombe** Gloucs
31 Q9 **Pitchcott** Bucks
39 K2 **Pitchford** Shrops
20 C3 **Pitch Green** Bucks
101 J7 **Pitchroy** Moray
17 P9 **Pitcombe** Somset
87 M7 **Pitcox** E Loth
102 E11 **Pitfichie** Abers
102 F6 **Pitglassie** Abers
107 N4 **Pitgrudy** Highld
86 G1 **Pitlessie** Fife
92 D4 **Pitlochry** P & K
102 E9 **Pitmachie** Abers
99 L8 **Pitmain** Highld
103 J9 **Pitmedden** Abers
103 J9 **Pitmedden Garden** Abers
16 G11 **Pitminster** Somset
93 P6 **Pitmuies** Angus
102 E11 **Pitmunie** Abers
17 L9 **Pitney** Somset
93 J10 **Pitroddie** P & K
93 M11 **Pitscottie** Fife
22 E6 **Pitsea** Essex
31 Q1 **Pitsford** Nhants
20 F1 **Pitstone** Bucks
95 M7 **Pittarrow** Abers
87 K2 **Pittenweem** Fife
86 F3 **Pitteuchar** Fife
73 N11 **Pittington** Dur
102 F9 **Pittodrie House Hotel** Abers
8 H2 **Pitton** Wilts
103 K2 **Pittulie** Abers
73 M10 **Pity Me** Dur
21 J12 **Pixham** Surrey
85 N9 **Plains** N Lans
39 K3 **Plaish** Shrops
21 N6 **Plaistow** Gt Lon
10 G4 **Plaistow** W Susx
9 J4 **Plaitford** Hants
22 D11 **Platt** Kent
73 M10 **Plawsworth** Dur
22 C11 **Plaxtol** Kent
12 H6 **Playden** E Susx
35 K7 **Playford** Suffk
20 B7 **Play Hatch** Oxon
3 J7 **Playing Place** Cnwll
29 K3 **Playley Green** Gloucs
38 H2 **Plealey** Shrops
85 P5 **Plean** Stirlg
93 J12 **Pleasance** Fife
57 M4 **Pleasington** Bl w D
57 M4 **Pleasington Crematorium** Bl w D
51 L7 **Pleasley** Derbys
49 J2 **Plemstall** Ches W
22 D1 **Pleshey** Essex
97 L3 **Plockton** Highld
38 H5 **Plowden** Shrops
12 H2 **Pluckley** Kent
12 H2 **Pluckley Thorne** Kent
71 J7 **Plumbland** Cumb
49 N1 **Plumley** Ches E
71 P7 **Plumpton** Cumb
11 M7 **Plumpton** E Susx
31 N5 **Plumpton** Nhants
11 M6 **Plumpton Green** E Susx
21 N7 **Plumstead** Gt Lon
45 J3 **Plumstead** Norfk
41 N2 **Plumtree** Notts
41 Q1 **Plungar** Leics
12 H3 **Plurenden** Kent
7 Q3 **Plush** Dorset
36 F9 **Plwmp** Cerdgn
5 K8 **Plymouth** C Plym
5 K7 *Plymouth Airport* C Plym
5 L8 **Plympton** C Plym
5 L9 **Plymstock** C Plym
6 E3 **Plymtree** Devon
66 F9 **Pockley** N York
60 D4 **Pocklington** E R Yk
17 M10 **Podimore** Somset
32 D4 **Podington** Bed
49 P8 **Podmore** Staffs
42 G4 **Pointon** Lincs
8 G8 **Pokesdown** Bmouth
105 Q1 **Polbain** Highld
4 H8 **Polbathic** Cnwll
86 B9 **Polbeth** W Loth
2 G9 **Poldark Mine** Cnwll
42 F11 **Polebrook** Nhants
12 C8 **Polegate** E Susx
40 H7 **Polesworth** Warwks
105 Q2 **Polglass** Highld
3 M5 **Polgooth** Cnwll
77 M9 **Polgown** D & G
10 G8 **Poling** W Susx
10 G8 **Poling Corner** W Susx
4 D9 **Polkerris** Cnwll
59 N9 **Pollington** E R Yk
89 Q3 **Polloch** Highld
85 J10 **Pollokshaws** C Glas
85 J9 **Pollokshields** C Glas
3 L6 **Polmassick** Cnwll
85 Q7 **Polmont** Falk
97 K12 **Polnish** Highld
4 F9 **Polperro** Cnwll
4 E9 **Polruan** Cnwll
34 G8 **Polstead** Suffk
83 M4 **Poltalloch** Ag & B
6 C4 **Poltimore** Devon
86 F8 **Polton** Mdloth
80 G4 **Polwarth** Border
4 G4 **Polyphant** Cnwll
4 B4 **Polzeath** Cnwll
86 F9 **Pomathorn** Mdloth
43 J10 **Pondersbridge** Cambs
21 M4 **Ponders End** Gt Lon
2 H8 **Ponsanooth** Cnwll
5 N5 **Ponsworthy** Devon
26 D7 **Pont Abraham Services** Carmth
25 Q6 **Pontantwn** Carmth
26 F7 **Pontardawe** Neath
26 D7 **Pontarddulais** Swans
26 C5 **Pont-ar-gothi** Carmth
25 Q3 **Pontarsais** Carmth
48 F4 **Pontblyddyn** Flints
59 L9 **Pontefract** Wakefd
59 K9 **Pontefract Crematorium** Wakefd
73 L6 **Ponteland** Nthumb
37 M4 **Ponterwyd** Cerdgn
38 H2 **Pontesbury** Shrops
38 H2 **Pontesford** Shrops
48 E7 **Pontfadog** Wrexhm
24 H3 **Pontfaen** Pembks
27 L3 **Pont-faen** Powys
36 F9 **Pontgarreg** Cerdgn
26 C7 **Ponthenry** Carmth
28 C9 **Ponthir** Torfn
36 D10 **Ponthirwaun** Cerdgn
27 P9 **Pontllanfraith** Caerph
26 E8 **Pontlliw** Swans
27 N7 **Pontlottyn** Caerph
54 F10 **Pontlyfni** Gwynd
27 J7 **Pontneddfechan** Neath
28 C9 **Pontnewydd** Torfn
37 M7 **Pontrhydfendigaid** Cerdgn
26 H9 **Pont-rhyd-y-fen** Neath
37 M6 **Pontrhydygroes** Cerdgn
28 D4 **Pontrilas** Herefs
48 C11 **Pont Robert** Powys
36 G10 **Pontshaen** Cerdgn
27 M6 **Pontsticill** Myr Td
36 G11 **Pontwelly** Carmth
26 C7 **Pontyates** Carmth
26 C6 **Pontyberem** Carmth
48 F4 **Pontybodkin** Flints
27 L11 **Pontyclun** Rhondd
27 J9 **Pontycymer** Brdgnd
55 L10 **Pont-y-pant** Conwy
28 C8 **Pontypool** Torfn
27 M10 **Pontypridd** Rhondd
27 P9 **Pontywaun** Caerph
2 G7 **Pool** Cnwll
58 G5 **Pool** Leeds
8 E8 **Poole** Poole
8 E8 **Poole Crematorium** Poole
18 E2 **Poole Keynes** Gloucs
105 M6 **Poolewe** Highld
71 P10 **Pooley Bridge** Cumb
50 B8 **Poolfold** Staffs
29 K3 **Poolhill** Gloucs
86 B3 **Pool of Muckhart** Clacks
34 C8 **Pool Street** Essex
21 M7 **Poplar** Gt Lon
9 M8 **Porchfield** IoW
45 L9 **Poringland** Norfk
2 G8 **Porkellis** Cnwll
15 Q3 **Porlock** Somset
15 P3 **Porlock Weir** Somset
83 L10 **Portachoillan** Ag & B
97 K4 **Port-an-Eorna** Highld
90 C7 **Port Appin** Ag & B
82 F8 **Port Askaig** Ag & B
83 P8 **Portavadie** Ag & B
84 B9 **Port Bannatyne** Ag & B
17 M2 **Portbury** N Som
71 K3 **Port Carlisle** Cumb
82 C10 **Port Charlotte** Ag & B
9 Q6 **Portchester** Hants
9 Q6 **Portchester Crematorium** Hants
83 Q8 **Port Driseach** Ag & B
74 E4 **Port Ellen** Ag & B
102 G10 **Port Elphinstone** Abers
68 D5 **Portencalzie** D & G
76 C2 **Portencross** N Ayrs
56 a6 **Port Erin** IoM
7 N5 **Portesham** Dorset
101 N3 **Portessie** Moray
26 C10 **Port Eynon** Swans
24 G6 **Portfield Gate** Pembks
5 J3 **Portgate** Devon
4 C4 **Port Gaverne** Cnwll
84 F7 **Port Glasgow** Inver
101 M3 **Portgordon** Moray
110 B11 **Portgower** Highld
3 J4 **Porth** Cnwll
27 L9 **Porth** Rhondd
2 H10 **Porthallow** Cnwll
4 F9 **Porthallow** Cnwll
26 H12 **Porthcawl** Brdgnd
3 K2 **Porthcothan** Cnwll
2 B10 **Porthcurno** Cnwll
105 L7 **Port Henderson** Highld
24 E3 **Porthgain** Pembks
2 B10 **Porthgwarra** Cnwll
16 E3 **Porthkerry** V Glam
2 F9 **Porthleven** Cnwll
47 J4 **Porthmadog** Gwynd
2 H9 **Porth Navas** Cnwll
3 J10 **Porthoustock** Cnwll
3 M5 **Porthpean** Cnwll
2 G6 **Porthtowan** Cnwll
26 C5 **Porthyrhyd** Carmth
84 D4 **Portincaple** Ag & B
60 D7 **Portington** E R Yk
83 P2 **Portinnisherrich** Ag & B
71 L10 **Portinscale** Cumb
4 C4 **Port Isaac** Cnwll
17 L2 **Portishead** N Som
101 N2 **Portknockie** Moray
7 P8 **Portland** Dorset
95 Q3 **Portlethen** Abers
70 E5 **Portling** D & G
3 L7 **Portloe** Cnwll
68 E10 **Port Logan** D & G
107 Q5 **Portmahomack** Highld
47 J4 **Portmeirion** Gwynd
3 M7 **Portmellon** Cnwll
89 J1 **Port Mor** Highld
90 C6 **Portnacroish** Ag & B
111 e2 **Portnaguran** W Isls
74 B2 **Portnahaven** Ag & B
96 D3 **Portnalong** Highld
111 e2 **Port nan Giuran** W Isls
111 b4 **Port nan Long** W Isls
111 e1 **Port Nis** W Isls
86 G7 **Portobello** C Edin
40 C7 **Portobello** Wolves
85 K3 **Port of Menteith** Stirlg
111 e1 **Port of Ness** W Isls
18 H12 **Porton** Wilts
68 D8 **Portpatrick** D & G
4 B4 **Port Quin** Cnwll
90 B7 **Port Ramsay** Ag & B
2 F6 **Portreath** Cnwll
96 F2 **Portree** Highld
56 b7 **Port St Mary** IoM
3 K8 **Portscatho** Cnwll
9 Q7 **Portsea** C Port
109 Q3 **Portskerra** Highld
28 F10 **Portskewett** Mons
11 K8 **Portslade** Br & H
11 L8 **Portslade-by-Sea** Br & H
68 D7 **Portslogan** D & G
9 Q7 **Portsmouth** C Port
58 B8 **Portsmouth** Calder
56 c6 **Port Soderick** IoM
90 E11 **Portsonachan Hotel** Ag & B
102 D3 **Portsoy** Abers
56 G11 **Port Sunlight** Wirral
9 M5 **Portswood** C Sotn
26 G10 **Port Talbot** Neath
89 K3 **Portuairk** Highld
40 E11 **Portway** Worcs
74 B3 **Port Wemyss** Ag & B
69 J9 **Port William** D & G
4 H9 **Portwrinkle** Cnwll
69 L10 **Portyerrock** D & G
34 C7 **Poslingford** Suffk
79 K3 **Posso** Border
5 N4 **Postbridge** Devon
20 B4 **Postcombe** Oxon
13 M3 **Postling** Kent
45 L8 **Postwick** Norfk
95 K3 **Potarch** Abers
20 G2 **Potten End** Herts
67 L11 **Potter Brompton** N York
52 F9 **Potterhanworth** Lincs
52 F9 **Potterhanworth Booths** Lincs
45 N6 **Potter Heigham** Norfk
18 E8 **Potterne** Wilts
18 E8 **Potterne Wick** Wilts
21 K3 **Potters Bar** Herts
20 H3 **Potters Crouch** Herts
41 J10 **Potters Green** Covtry
41 L8 **Potters Marston** Leics
31 Q5 **Potterspury** Nhants
103 K11 **Potterton** Abers
66 C6 **Potto** N York
32 H6 **Potton** C Beds
50 C5 **Pott Shrigley** Ches E
14 D10 **Poughill** Cnwll
15 P9 **Poughill** Devon
8 H6 **Poulner** Hants
18 E8 **Poulshot** Wilts
18 G1 **Poulton** Gloucs
56 G2 **Poulton-le-Fylde** Lancs
26 D9 **Poundffald** Swans
11 P5 **Pound Green** E Susx
34 C6 **Pound Green** Suffk
11 L3 **Pound Hill** W Susx
31 N8 **Poundon** Bucks
5 N6 **Poundsgate** Devon
14 D11 **Poundstock** Cnwll
69 L9 **Pouton** D & G
11 L2 **Povey Cross** Surrey
81 M10 **Powburn** Nthumb
6 C6 **Powderham** Devon
7 M4 **Powerstock** Dorset
71 J3 **Powfoot** D & G
39 Q10 **Powick** Worcs
86 B3 **Powmill** P & K
7 Q6 **Poxwell** Dorset
20 G7 **Poyle** Slough
11 L7 **Poynings** W Susx
17 P11 **Poyntington** Dorset
50 B4 **Poynton** Ches E
49 K10 **Poynton Green** Wrekin
2 E9 **Praa Sands** Cnwll
21 P10 **Pratt's Bottom** Gt Lon
2 F8 **Praze-an-Beeble** Cnwll
49 K8 **Prees** Shrops
62 G11 **Preesall** Lancs
49 K8 **Prees Green** Shrops
49 K7 **Prees Heath** Shrops
49 K8 **Prees Higher Heath** Shrops
36 G10 **Pren-gwyn** Cerdgn
47 J3 **Prenteg** Gwynd
57 J9 **Prescot** Knows
16 E12 **Prescott** Devon
94 C8 **Presnerb** Angus
56 C11 **Prestatyn** Denbgs
50 B5 **Prestbury** Ches E
29 N4 **Prestbury** Gloucs
38 G8 **Presteigne** Powys
17 P7 **Prestleigh** Somset
87 P10 **Preston** Border
11 L8 **Preston** Br & H
6 B7 **Preston** Devon
7 Q6 **Preston** Dorset
61 K7 **Preston** E R Yk
18 F1 **Preston** Gloucs
32 H10 **Preston** Herts
23 K10 **Preston** Kent
23 N10 **Preston** Kent
57 K3 **Preston** Lancs
81 P8 **Preston** Nthumb
42 C9 **Preston** Rutlnd
16 E8 **Preston** Somset
34 F6 **Preston** Suffk
6 B9 **Preston** Torbay
18 F5 **Preston** Wilts
30 F2 **Preston Bagot** Warwks
31 P8 **Preston Bissett** Bucks
16 F10 **Preston Bowyer** Somset
49 K9 **Preston Brockhurst** Shrops
57 K11 **Preston Brook** Halton
19 Q11 **Preston Candover** Hants
31 M3 **Preston Capes** Nhants
57 L3 **Preston Crematorium** Lancs
30 F2 **Preston Green** Warwks
49 J10 **Preston Gubbals** Shrops
30 G4 **Preston on Stour** Warwks
57 K11 **Preston on the Hill** Halton
28 D1 **Preston on Wye** Herefs
86 H7 **Prestonpans** E Loth
63 K5 **Preston Patrick** Cumb
17 M11 **Preston Plucknett** Somset
65 J8 **Preston-under-Scar** N York
49 M11 **Preston upon the Weald Moors** Wrekin
39 K11 **Preston Wynne** Herefs
57 P7 **Prestwich** Bury
76 F6 **Prestwick** S Ayrs
76 F6 *Prestwick Airport* S Ayrs
20 E4 **Prestwood** Bucks
33 P1 **Prickwillow** Cambs
17 M6 **Priddy** Somset
63 K7 **Priest Hutton** Lancs
77 J4 **Priestland** E Ayrs
38 F3 **Priest Weston** Shrops
87 P10 **Primrosehill** Border
80 H8 **Primsidemill** Border
20 D3 **Princes Risborough** Bucks
41 K12 **Princethorpe** Warwks
5 M5 **Princetown** Devon
31 L3 **Priors Hardwick** Warwks
49 N12 **Priorslee** Wrekin
31 L3 **Priors Marston** Warwks
29 M4 **Priors Norton** Gloucs
18 G3 **Priory Vale** Swindn
17 Q4 **Priston** BaNES
22 G6 **Prittlewell** Sthend
10 B5 **Privett** Hants
15 J5 **Prixford** Devon
3 K6 **Probus** Cnwll
87 K6 **Prora** E Loth
71 J7 **Prospect** Cumb
2 F9 **Prospidnick** Cnwll
102 H3 **Protstonhill** Abers
73 K8 **Prudhoe** Nthumb
17 P4 **Publow** BaNES
33 L11 **Puckeridge** Herts
17 K11 **Puckington** Somset
17 Q2 **Pucklechurch** S Glos
48 G2 **Puddington** Ches W
15 P9 **Puddington** Devon
7 Q4 **Puddletown** Dorset
58 G7 **Pudsey** Leeds
10 G6 **Pulborough** W Susx
48 G4 **Pulford** Ches W
7 Q2 **Pulham** Dorset
45 K11 **Pulham Market** Norfk
45 K11 **Pulham St Mary** Norfk
32 F9 **Pulloxhill** C Beds
86 C8 **Pumpherston** W Loth
37 K11 **Pumsaint** Carmth
24 H3 **Puncheston** Pembks
7 M5 **Puncknowle** Dorset
12 C6 **Punnett's Town** E Susx
10 A8 **Purbrook** Hants
22 B7 **Purfleet** Thurr
17 J7 **Puriton** Somset
22 G3 **Purleigh** Essex
21 L10 **Purley** Gt Lon
19 Q5 **Purley** W Berk
17 Q11 **Purse Caundle** Dorset
7 K2 **Purtington** Somset
29 J7 **Purton** Gloucs
29 J7 **Purton** Gloucs
18 G4 **Purton** Wilts
18 G3 **Purton Stoke** Wilts
31 P5 **Pury End** Nhants
19 L2 **Pusey** Oxon
28 H2 **Putley** Herefs
28 H2 **Putley Green** Herefs
21 K8 **Putney** Gt Lon
21 K8 **Putney Vale Crematorium** Gt Lon
10 E1 **Puttenham** Surrey
31 Q6 **Puxley** Nhants
17 K4 **Puxton** N Som
26 C8 **Pwll** Carmth
48 C5 **Pwll-glas** Denbgs
27 L3 **Pwllgloyw** Powys
46 F4 **Pwllheli** Gwynd
28 F9 **Pwllmeyric** Mons
25 M5 **Pwll Trap** Carmth
26 H9 **Pwll-y-glaw** Neath
51 K9 **Pye Bridge** Derbys
11 L7 **Pyecombe** W Susx
26 H11 **Pyle** Brdgnd
16 F9 **Pyleigh** Somset
17 N8 **Pylle** Somset
43 M11 **Pymoor** Cambs
7 L4 **Pymore** Dorset
20 G10 **Pyrford** Surrey
20 B4 **Pyrton** Oxon
32 C2 **Pytchley** Nhants
14 F10 **Pyworthy** Devon

Q

42 H4 Quadring Lincs
43 J4 Quadring Eaudike Lincs
31 Q9 Quainton Bucks
16 G8 Quantock Hills Somset
111 k4 Quarff Shet
19 J11 Quarley Hants
51 J11 Quarndon Derbys
84 F9 Quarrier's Village Inver
42 F2 Quarrington Lincs
73 N12 Quarrington Hill Dur
40 B9 Quarry Bank Dudley
101 J3 Quarrywood Moray
84 D10 Quarter N Ayrs
85 M11 Quarter S Lans
39 N4 Quatford Shrops
39 N5 Quatt Shrops
73 L11 Quebec Dur
29 L6 Quedgeley Gloucs
33 P1 Queen Adelaide Cambs
22 H8 Queenborough Kent
17 N10 Queen Camel Somset
17 P3 Queen Charlton BaNES
84 H3 Queen Elizabeth Forest Park Stirlg
29 M2 Queenhill Worcs
8 B2 Queen Oak Dorset
9 P9 Queen's Bower IoW
58 E7 Queensbury C Brad
48 G2 Queensferry Flints
85 J10 Queenslie C Glas
85 L7 Queenzieburn N Lans
33 N10 Quendon Essex
41 N5 Queniborough Leics
30 F12 Quenington Gloucs
40 E8 Queslett Birm
4 G7 Quethiock Cnwll
44 G11 Quidenham Norfk
8 G2 Quidhampton Wilts
31 R4 Quinton Nhants
3 J4 Quintrell Downs Cnwll
87 P9 Quixwood Border
92 C10 Quoig P & K
41 M4 Quorn Leics
78 G2 Quothquan S Lans
111 h2 Quoyburray Ork
111 g2 Quoyloo Ork

R

96 G2 Raasay Highld
79 J3 Rachan Mill Border
55 J7 Rachub Gwynd
15 P8 Rackenford Devon
10 G7 Rackham W Susx
45 L7 Rackheath Norfk
70 G1 Racks D & G
111 g3 Rackwick Ork
40 H1 Radbourne Derbys
57 P7 Radcliffe Bury
51 N11 Radcliffe on Trent Notts
31 P7 Radclive Bucks
107 L9 Raddery Highld
87 J1 Radernie Fife
41 J10 Radford Covtry
31 J2 Radford Semele Warwks
21 J4 Radlett Herts
19 N2 Radley Oxon
22 D3 Radley Green Essex
20 C4 Radnage Bucks
17 P5 Radstock BaNES
31 N6 Radstone Nhants
31 J5 Radway Warwks
32 E5 Radwell Bed
32 H9 Radwell Herts
33 P8 Radwinter Essex
27 N11 Radyr Cardif
100 G4 Rafford Moray
41 P4 Ragdale Leics
28 E7 Raglan Mons
52 B8 Ragnall Notts
99 M4 Raigbeg Highld
39 Q10 Rainbow Hill Worcs
57 J8 Rainford St Hel
21 Q7 Rainham Gt Lon
22 F9 Rainham Medway
57 J9 Rainhill St Hel
57 J10 Rainhill Stoops St Hel
50 C6 Rainow Ches E
65 P11 Rainton N York
51 N8 Rainworth Notts
93 J9 Rait P & K
53 K6 Raithby Lincs
53 L9 Raithby Lincs
10 C5 Rake Hants
99 K9 Ralia Highld
96 A2 Ramasaig Highld
2 G8 Rame Cnwll
5 J9 Rame Cnwll
7 N3 Rampisham Dorset
62 E8 Rampside Cumb
33 L3 Rampton Cambs
52 B7 Rampton Notts
57 P5 Ramsbottom Bury
19 J6 Ramsbury Wilts
110 D9 Ramscraigs Highld
10 B5 Ramsdean Hants
19 P8 Ramsdell Hants
31 J10 Ramsden Oxon
22 E5 Ramsden Bellhouse Essex
43 J11 Ramsey Cambs
35 K10 Ramsey Essex
56 e3 Ramsey IoM
43 K11 Ramsey Forty Foot Cambs
43 J12 Ramsey Heights Cambs
23 J3 Ramsey Island Essex
24 C4 Ramsey Island Pembks
43 J11 Ramsey Mereside Cambs
43 J11 Ramsey St Mary's Cambs
23 Q9 Ramsgate Kent
65 K12 Ramsgill N York
80 G12 Ramshope Nthumb
50 E10 Ramshorn Staffs
10 F4 Ramsnest Common Surrey
52 H7 Ranby Lincs
51 P5 Ranby Notts
52 G7 Rand Lincs
21 J11 Randalls Park Crematorium Surrey
29 L7 Randwick Gloucs
84 G9 Ranfurly Rens
40 F3 Rangemore Staffs
29 J10 Rangeworthy S Glos
76 H8 Rankinston E Ayrs
91 L5 Rannoch Station P & K
16 C7 Ranscombe Somset
51 P4 Ranskill Notts
49 Q10 Ranton Staffs
49 Q10 Ranton Green Staffs
45 M7 Ranworth Norfk
85 N4 Raploch Stirlg
111 h1 Rapness Ork
70 D6 Rascarrel D & G
84 C6 Rashfield Ag & B
30 B2 Rashwood Worcs
66 C12 Raskelf N York
58 F9 Rastrick Calder
97 N6 Ratagan Highld
41 L6 Ratby Leics
41 J7 Ratcliffe Culey Leics
41 L2 Ratcliffe on Soar Notts
41 N5 Ratcliffe on the Wreake Leics
103 K3 Rathen Abers
93 L10 Rathillet Fife
63 P9 Rathmell N York
86 D7 Ratho C Edin
86 D7 Ratho Station C Edin
101 N3 Rathven Moray
31 J5 Ratley Warwks
23 N11 Ratling Kent
38 H3 Ratlinghope Shrops
110 F2 Rattar Highld
5 P7 Rattery Devon
34 F5 Rattlesden Suffk
12 C9 Ratton Village E Susx
92 H6 Rattray P & K
32 E3 Raunds Nhants
51 L2 Ravenfield Rothm
62 C3 Ravenglass Cumb
45 N10 Raveningham Norfk
67 L7 Ravenscar N York
85 N10 Ravenscraig N Lans
32 F6 Ravensden Bed
51 M9 Ravenshead Notts
58 G9 Ravensthorpe Kirk
41 P12 Ravensthorpe Nhants
41 K5 Ravenstone Leics
32 C6 Ravenstone M Keyn
63 N2 Ravenstonedale Cumb
77 Q3 Ravenstruther S Lans
65 K6 Ravensworth N York
59 M4 Rawcliffe C York
59 P9 Rawcliffe E R Yk
58 G6 Rawdon Leeds
58 G6 Rawdon Crematorium Leeds
22 H10 Rawling Street Kent
51 K2 Rawmarsh Rothm
22 F5 Rawreth Essex
6 G2 Rawridge Devon
57 P4 Rawtenstall Lancs
34 H8 Raydon Suffk
22 F5 Rayleigh Essex
34 C11 Rayne Essex
21 K9 Raynes Park Gt Lon
33 P4 Reach Cambs
57 P2 Read Lancs
20 B8 Reading Readg
20 B8 Reading Crematorium Readg
20 A9 Reading Services W Berk
12 H4 Reading Street Kent
23 Q9 Reading Street Kent
64 B4 Reagill Cumb
2 F8 Realwa Cnwll
107 M4 Rearquhar Highld
41 P5 Rearsby Leics
110 A3 Reay Highld
23 N9 Reculver Kent
16 E11 Red Ball Devon
25 J7 Redberth Pembks
20 H2 Redbourn Herts
52 D4 Redbourne N Linc
28 G6 Redbrook Gloucs
49 K7 Redbrook Wrexhm
12 H3 Redbrook Street Kent
100 E6 Redburn Highld
66 E3 Redcar R & Cl
70 D3 Redcastle D & G
107 J11 Redcastle Highld
85 Q7 Redding Falk
85 Q7 Reddingmuirhead Falk
30 D1 Redditch Worcs
30 D1 Redditch Crematorium Worcs
34 D5 Rede Suffk
45 L12 Redenhall Norfk
72 F5 Redesmouth Nthumb
95 M7 Redford Abers
93 P6 Redford Angus
10 D5 Redford W Susx
79 M6 Redfordgreen Border
92 G9 Redgorton P & K
34 H2 Redgrave Suffk
95 M2 Redhill Abers
8 G8 Red Hill Bmouth
33 J9 Redhill Herts
17 M4 Redhill N Som
21 L12 Redhill Surrey
45 N12 Redisham Suffk
17 N2 Redland Bristl
111 h2 Redland Ork
35 K3 Redlingfield Suffk
35 K3 Redlingfield Green Suffk
34 B3 Red Lodge Suffk
17 Q9 Redlynch Somset
8 H3 Redlynch Wilts
39 N8 Redmarley Worcs
29 K3 Redmarley D'Abitot Gloucs
65 P4 Redmarshall S on T
42 B3 Redmile Leics
65 J8 Redmire N York
95 M6 Redmyre Abers
48 G9 Rednal Shrops
80 D7 Redpath Border
105 K8 Redpoint Highld
25 L6 Red Roses Carmth
73 M2 Red Row Nthumb
2 G7 Redruth Cnwll
92 H8 Redstone P & K
54 G5 Red Wharf Bay IoA
28 E11 Redwick Newpt
28 G10 Redwick S Glos
65 M3 Redworth Darltn
33 K9 Reed Herts
45 N9 Reedham Norfk
60 D9 Reedness E R Yk
57 P4 Reeds Holme Lancs
52 E8 Reepham Lincs
44 H5 Reepham Norfk
65 J7 Reeth N York
40 H11 Reeves Green Solhll
17 M4 Regil N Som
108 A11 Reiff Highld
21 K12 Reigate Surrey
67 N11 Reighton N York
103 J10 Reisque Abers
110 G5 Reiss Highld
2 E8 Relubbus Cnwll
100 F5 Relugas Moray
20 C6 Remenham Wokham
20 C6 Remenham Hill Wokham
41 M3 Rempstone Notts
30 D11 Rendcomb Gloucs
35 M4 Rendham Suffk
35 M6 Rendlesham Suffk
84 H9 Renfrew Rens
32 F6 Renhold Bed
51 K5 Renishaw Derbys
81 P9 Rennington Nthumb
84 G7 Renton W Duns
72 B11 Renwick Cumb
45 N6 Repps Norfk
40 H3 Repton Derbys
107 L12 Resaurie Highld
89 P4 Resipole Highld
2 F7 Reskadinnick Cnwll
107 L8 Resolis Highld
26 H8 Resolven Neath
84 D2 Rest and be thankful Ag & B
87 R9 Reston Border
93 N5 Reswallie Angus
51 P5 Retford Notts
22 F4 Rettendon Essex
53 J10 Revesby Lincs
6 C3 Rewe Devon
9 M8 Rew Street IoW
35 P2 Reydon Suffk
44 G8 Reymerston Norfk
25 J7 Reynalton Pembks
26 C10 Reynoldston Swans
4 H5 Rezare Cnwll
37 M11 Rhandirmwyn Carmth
37 Q7 Rhayader Powys
106 H11 Rheindown Highld
48 E2 Rhes-y-cae Flints
48 C4 Rhewl Denbgs
48 D6 Rhewl Denbgs
108 C10 Rhicarn Highld
108 E5 Rhiconich Highld
107 L7 Rhicullen Highld
27 K7 Rhigos Rhondd
105 Q4 Rhireavach Highld
107 N3 Rhives Highld
27 N11 Rhiwbina Cardif
28 B10 Rhiwderyn Newpt
54 H8 Rhiwlas Gwynd
12 D2 Rhoden Green Kent
13 M2 Rhodes Minnis Kent
24 D4 Rhodiad-y-brenin Pembks
70 C4 Rhonehouse D & G
16 E3 Rhoose V Glam
25 P2 Rhos Carmth
26 G8 Rhos Neath
54 C6 Rhoscolyn IoA
24 F8 Rhoscrowther Pembks
48 E2 Rhosesmor Flints
38 E11 Rhosgoch Powys
36 C11 Rhoshill Pembks
46 C5 Rhoshirwaun Gwynd
47 J9 Rhoslefain Gwynd
48 F6 Rhosllanerchrugog Wrexhm
54 F6 Rhosmeirch IoA
54 D7 Rhosneigr IoA
48 G5 Rhosnesni Wrexhm
55 M5 Rhôs-on-Sea Conwy
25 P10 Rhossili Swans
54 G9 Rhostryfan Gwynd
48 F6 Rhostyllen Wrexhm
54 F4 Rhosybol IoA
47 Q4 Rhos-y-gwaliau Gwynd
48 F7 Rhosymedre Wrexhm
84 E6 Rhu Ag & B
48 C1 Rhuallt Denbgs
83 Q8 Rhubodach Ag & B
55 Q6 Rhuddlan Denbgs
75 K3 Rhunahaorine Ag & B
47 K3 Rhyd Gwynd
25 Q4 Rhydargaeau Carmth
26 D2 Rhydcymerau Carmth
54 H10 Rhyd-Ddu Gwynd
36 F10 Rhydlewis Cerdgn
36 G10 Rhydowen Cerdgn
47 P4 Rhyd-uchaf Gwynd
46 E4 Rhyd-y-clafdy Gwynd
55 N6 Rhyd-y-foel Conwy
26 F7 Rhydyfro Neath
54 H8 Rhyd-y-groes Gwynd
37 K4 Rhyd-y pennau Cerdgn
55 Q5 Rhyl Denbgs
27 N7 Rhymney Caerph
92 H10 Rhynd P & K
101 P9 Rhynie Abers
107 P6 Rhynie Highld
39 P7 Ribbesford Worcs
57 K3 Ribbleton Lancs
57 M2 Ribchester Lancs
52 H3 Riby Lincs
59 N6 Riccall N York
79 Q9 Riccarton Border
76 G4 Riccarton E Ayrs
39 J8 Richards Castle Herefs
21 J8 Richmond Gt Lon
65 L7 Richmond N York
51 K4 Richmond Sheff
40 B4 Rickerscote Staffs
17 L4 Rickford N Som
5 P11 Rickham Devon
34 H2 Rickinghall Suffk
33 N10 Rickling Green Essex
20 G5 Rickmansworth Herts
80 C8 Riddell Border
15 K8 Riddlecombe Devon
58 E5 Riddlesden C Brad
8 D9 Ridge Dorset
21 K4 Ridge Herts
8 D2 Ridge Wilts
40 H8 Ridge Lane Warwks
51 K5 Ridgeway Derbys
34 C8 Ridgewell Essex
11 P6 Ridgewood E Susx
32 D9 Ridgmont C Beds
72 H8 Riding Mill Nthumb
45 M4 Ridlington Norfk
42 C9 Ridlington Rutlnd
72 G4 Ridsdale Nthumb
66 E9 Rievaulx N York
66 E9 Rievaulx Abbey N York
71 L3 Rigg D & G
85 M8 Riggend N Lans
100 D5 Righoul Highld
53 L8 Rigsby Lincs
78 E2 Rigside S Lans
57 L4 Riley Green Lancs
4 G5 Rilla Mill Cnwll
67 J11 Rillington N York
63 P11 Rimington Lancs
17 N10 Rimpton Somset
61 M8 Rimswell E R Yk
24 H4 Rinaston Pembks
39 N3 Rindleford Shrops
69 Q7 Ringford D & G
45 J7 Ringland Norfk
11 N7 Ringmer E Susx
5 N10 Ringmore Devon
6 C8 Ringmore Devon
101 K6 Ringorm Moray
45 N11 Ringsfield Suffk
45 N11 Ringsfield Corner Suffk
20 F1 Ringshall Herts
34 G6 Ringshall Suffk
34 H6 Ringshall Stocks Suffk
32 E2 Ringstead Nhants
44 B3 Ringstead Norfk
8 H6 Ringwood Hants
13 Q1 Ringwould Kent
11 P7 Ripe E Susx
51 K10 Ripley Derbys
8 H7 Ripley Hants
58 H3 Ripley N York
20 G11 Ripley Surrey
9 Q3 Riplington Hants
65 N12 Ripon N York
42 F5 Rippingale Lincs
23 Q12 Ripple Kent
29 M2 Ripple Worcs
58 D9 Ripponden Calder
74 D4 Risabus Ag & B
39 K10 Risbury Herefs
34 D4 Risby Suffk
27 P9 Risca Caerph
61 K6 Rise E R Yk
42 H4 Risegate Lincs
32 F4 Riseley Bed
20 B10 Riseley Wokham
35 J3 Rishangles Suffk
57 N3 Rishton Lancs
58 D9 Rishworth Calder
41 L1 Risley Derbys
57 M9 Risley Warrtn
58 G1 Risplith N York
13 P2 River Kent
10 F5 River W Susx
107 J10 Riverford Highld
21 P11 Riverhead Kent
57 L6 Rivington Lancs
31 Q4 Roade Nhants
77 P2 Roadmeetings S Lans
77 K7 Roadside E Ayrs
110 D4 Roadside Highld
16 D8 Roadwater Somset
96 C2 Roag Highld
76 E9 Roan of Craigoch S Ayrs
27 P12 Roath Cardif
79 N6 Roberton Border
78 F3 Roberton S Lans
12 E5 Robertsbridge E Susx
58 G9 Roberttown Kirk
25 J5 Robeston Wathen Pembks
71 L2 Robgill Tower D & G
40 E10 Robin Hood Crematorium Solhll
51 P2 Robin Hood Doncaster Sheffield Airport Donc
67 K6 Robin Hood's Bay N York
5 K7 Roborough Devon
15 K8 Roborough Devon
56 H10 Roby Knows
50 E11 Rocester Staffs
24 F5 Roch Pembks
58 B10 Rochdale Rochdl
57 Q6 Rochdale Crematorium Rochdl
3 L4 Roche Cnwll
22 E9 Rochester Medway
72 E2 Rochester Nthumb
22 G5 Rochford Essex
39 L8 Rochford Worcs
3 L1 Rock Cnwll
81 P9 Rock Nthumb
39 N7 Rock Worcs
6 D4 Rockbeare Devon
8 G4 Rockbourne Hants
71 M4 Rockcliffe Cumb
70 D5 Rockcliffe D & G
6 C9 Rockend Torbay
56 G10 Rock Ferry Wirral
107 Q6 Rockfield Highld
28 F6 Rockfield Mons
15 N3 Rockford Devon
28 H9 Rockhampton S Glos
38 F6 Rockhill Shrops
42 C10 Rockingham Nhants
44 G10 Rockland All Saints Norfk
45 M8 Rockland St Mary Norfk
44 G9 Rockland St Peter Norfk
51 Q6 Rockley Notts
84 D5 Rockville Ag & B
20 C6 Rockwell End Bucks
29 L7 Rodborough Gloucs
18 G4 Rodbourne Swindn
18 D4 Rodbourne Wilts
7 N6 Rodden Dorset
18 B9 Rode Somset
49 P4 Rode Heath Ches E
111 c4 Rodel W Isls
49 L11 Roden Wrekin
16 D8 Rodhuish Somset
49 L11 Rodington Wrekin
49 L11 Rodington Heath Wrekin
29 K6 Rodley Gloucs
29 N8 Rodmarton Gloucs
11 N8 Rodmell E Susx
22 H10 Rodmersham Kent
22 H10 Rodmersham Green Kent
17 L6 Rodney Stoke Somset
50 G11 Rodsley Derbys
59 J2 Roecliffe N York
21 K2 Roe Green Herts
33 K9 Roe Green Herts
21 K8 Roehampton Gt Lon
11 K4 Roffey W Susx
107 M2 Rogart Highld
10 D5 Rogate W Susx
28 C10 Rogerstone Newpt
111 c4 Roghadal W Isls
28 E10 Rogiet Mons
19 Q3 Roke Oxon
73 P8 Roker Sundld
45 P7 Rollesby Norfk
41 Q7 Rolleston Leics
51 Q9 Rolleston Notts
40 G3 Rolleston on Dove Staffs
61 L5 Rolston E R Yk
12 G4 Rolvenden Kent
12 G4 Rolvenden Layne Kent
64 H3 Romaldkirk Dur
17 Q3 Roman Baths & Pump Room BaNES
65 P8 Romanby N York
86 D11 Romanno Bridge Border
15 M7 Romansleigh Devon
104 E10 Romesdal Highld
8 F5 Romford Dorset
21 P5 Romford Gt Lon
50 C3 Romiley Stockp
9 L3 Romsey Hants
39 P5 Romsley Shrops
40 C10 Romsley Worcs
105 J10 Rona Highld
83 L11 Ronachan Ag & B
72 G11 Rookhope Dur
9 N9 Rookley IoW
17 K5 Rooks Bridge Somset
16 E9 Rooks Nest Somset
65 L9 Rookwith N York
61 M7 Roos E R Yk
32 F5 Roothams Green Bed
9 Q2 Ropley Hants
9 Q2 Ropley Dean Hants
42 E4 Ropsley Lincs
103 L5 Rora Abers
38 F3 Rorrington Shrops
101 M5 Rosarie Moray
2 H5 Rose Cnwll
15 N7 Rose Ash Devon
77 N2 Rosebank S Lans
25 J3 Rosebush Pembks
66 G8 Rosedale Abbey N York
34 E10 Rose Green Essex
34 F7 Rose Green Suffk
34 F8 Rose Green Suffk
10 E9 Rose Green W Susx
106 H2 Rosehall Highld
103 J2 Rosehearty Abers
57 P3 Rose Hill Lancs
100 H2 Roseisle Moray
12 C9 Roselands E Susx
24 G7 Rosemarket Pembks
107 M10 Rosemarkie Highld
16 F12 Rosemary Lane Devon
92 H7 Rosemount P & K
3 L3 Rosenannon Cnwll
86 F9 Rosewell Mdloth
65 Q3 Roseworth S on T
71 Q11 Rosgill Cumb
96 C1 Roskhill Highld
71 M6 Rosley Cumb
86 F9 Roslin Mdloth
40 G4 Rosliston Derbys
84 E6 Rosneath Ag & B
69 P9 Ross D & G
48 G4 Rossett Wrexhm
58 H4 Rossett Green N York
51 N2 Rossington Donc
84 G8 Rossland Rens
28 H4 Ross-on-Wye Herefs
110 F7 Roster Highld
57 N11 Rostherne Ches E
71 L11 Rosthwaite Cumb
50 F11 Roston Derbys
86 D5 Rosyth Fife
73 J1 Rothbury Nthumb
41 P4 Rotherby Leics
12 B4 Rotherfield E Susx
20 B7 Rotherfield Greys Oxon
20 B7 Rotherfield Peppard Oxon
51 K3 Rotherham Rothm
51 L3 Rotherham Crematorium Rothm
31 Q3 Rothersthorpe Nhants
31 Q3 Rothersthorpe Services Nhants
20 B11 Rotherwick Hants
101 K5 Rothes Moray
84 B9 Rothesay Ag & B
102 G7 Rothiebrisbane Abers
102 D5 Rothiemay Moray
99 P7 Rothiemurchus Lodge Highld
102 F7 Rothienorman Abers
41 N5 Rothley Leics
102 F8 Rothmaise Abers
59 J8 Rothwell Leeds
52 G4 Rothwell Lincs
32 B1 Rothwell Nhants
94 F7 Rottal Lodge Angus
11 M9 Rottingdean Br & H
70 F11 Rottington Cumb
78 G12 Roucan D & G
78 G12 Roucan Loch Crematorium D & G
44 D6 Rougham Norfk
34 E4 Rougham Green Suffk
23 L10 Rough Common Kent
101 L11 Roughpark Abers
53 J9 Roughton Lincs
45 K3 Roughton Norfk
39 N4 Roughton Shrops
22 C1 Roundbush Green Essex
32 F11 Round Green Luton
7 K2 Roundham Somset
59 J6 Roundhay Leeds
18 E7 Roundway Wilts
93 L5 Roundyhill Angus
111 h1 Rousay Ork
6 H5 Rousdon Devon
31 L8 Rousham Oxon
30 D4 Rous Lench Worcs
84 D10 Routenburn N Ayrs
61 J6 Routh E R Yk

S

16 H7 **Stockland Bristol** Somset
15 P10 **Stockleigh English** Devon
15 P10 **Stockleigh Pomeroy** Devon
18 E7 **Stockley** Wilts
17 K11 **Stocklinch** Somset
50 B3 **Stockport** Stockp
50 B3 **Stockport Crematorium** Stockp
50 H2 **Stocksbridge** Sheff
73 J8 **Stocksfield** Nthumb
39 K9 **Stockton** Herefs
45 N10 **Stockton** Norfk
39 N3 **Stockton** Shrops
31 K2 **Stockton** Warwks
18 E12 **Stockton** Wilts
49 P11 **Stockton** Wrekin
57 L10 **Stockton Heath** Warrtn
66 C4 **Stockton-on-Tees** S on T
39 N8 **Stockton on Teme** Worcs
59 P3 **Stockton on the Forest** C York
17 P3 **Stockwood** Bristl
7 N2 **Stockwood** Dorset
30 D3 **Stock Wood** Worcs
23 N10 **Stodmarsh** Kent
44 H3 **Stody** Norfk
108 B9 **Stoer** Highld
17 N12 **Stoford** Somset
8 F1 **Stoford** Wilts
16 E8 **Stogumber** Somset
16 G7 **Stogursey** Somset
41 J10 **Stoke** Covtry
14 E7 **Stoke** Devon
10 B9 **Stoke** Hants
19 L9 **Stoke** Hants
22 G8 **Stoke** Medway
7 L3 **Stoke Abbott** Dorset
42 B11 **Stoke Albany** Nhants
35 J3 **Stoke Ash** Suffk
51 N11 **Stoke Bardolph** Notts
39 M9 **Stoke Bliss** Worcs
31 Q4 **Stoke Bruerne** Nhants
34 C7 **Stoke by Clare** Suffk
34 G9 **Stoke-by-Nayland** Suffk
6 C3 **Stoke Canon** Devon
19 N11 **Stoke Charity** Hants
4 H5 **Stoke Climsland** Cnwll
39 L11 **Stoke Cross** Herefs
20 H10 **Stoke D'Abernon** Surrey
42 E11 **Stoke Doyle** Nhants
42 C10 **Stoke Dry** Rutlnd
28 H1 **Stoke Edith** Herefs
8 F3 **Stoke Farthing** Wilts
44 B9 **Stoke Ferry** Norfk
6 B11 **Stoke Fleming** Devon
8 C9 **Stokeford** Dorset
6 B10 **Stoke Gabriel** Devon
28 H11 **Stoke Gifford** S Glos
41 K7 **Stoke Golding** Leics
32 B7 **Stoke Goldington** M Keyn
52 A7 **Stokeham** Notts
32 C10 **Stoke Hammond** Bucks
45 K9 **Stoke Holy Cross** Norfk
6 C8 **Stokeinteignhead** Devon
39 L11 **Stoke Lacy** Herefs
31 M8 **Stoke Lyne** Oxon
20 D2 **Stoke Mandeville** Bucks
20 C4 **Stokenchurch** Bucks
21 M6 **Stoke Newington** Gt Lon
5 Q10 **Stokenham** Devon
50 B10 **Stoke-on-Trent** C Stke
29 M3 **Stoke Orchard** Gloucs
20 F6 **Stoke Poges** Bucks
39 K10 **Stoke Prior** Herefs
30 C1 **Stoke Prior** Worcs
15 L5 **Stoke Rivers** Devon
42 D5 **Stoke Rochford** Lincs
20 B6 **Stoke Row** Oxon
17 J10 **Stoke St Gregory** Somset
16 H10 **Stoke St Mary** Somset
17 P6 **Stoke St Michael** Somset
39 K5 **Stoke St Milborough** Shrops
38 H6 **Stokesay Castle** Shrops
45 N7 **Stokesby** Norfk
66 D6 **Stokesley** N York
17 L11 **Stoke sub Hamdon** Somset
20 B4 **Stoke Talmage** Oxon
17 Q9 **Stoke Trister** Somset
49 M9 **Stoke upon Tern** Shrops
49 Q6 **Stoke-upon-Trent** C Stke
16 G7 **Stolford** Somset
22 C4 **Stondon Massey** Essex
20 C2 **Stone** Bucks
29 J9 **Stone** Gloucs
51 M3 **Stone** Rothm
40 B1 **Stone** Staffs
39 Q7 **Stone** Worcs
17 K6 **Stone Allerton** Somset
17 N5 **Ston Easton** Somset
17 K4 **Stonebridge** N Som
40 G10 **Stonebridge** Warwks
51 K8 **Stonebroom** Derbys
23 P11 **Stone Cross** Kent
12 E4 **Stonecrouch** Kent
61 J7 **Stoneferry** C KuH
83 N8 **Stonefield Castle Hotel** Ag & B
12 D4 **Stonegate** E Susx
66 F11 **Stonegrave** N York
95 P5 **Stonehaven** Abers
18 G11 **Stonehenge** Wilts
5 K9 **Stonehouse** C Plym
29 L7 **Stonehouse** Gloucs
77 M3 **Stonehouse** S Lans
12 H5 **Stone in Oxney** Kent
41 J11 **Stoneleigh** Warwks
42 B5 **Stonesby** Leics
31 K10 **Stonesfield** Oxon
35 J10 **Stones Green** Essex
22 C11 **Stone Street** Kent
35 N1 **Stone Street** Suffk
101 K3 **Stonewells** Moray
111 a5 **Stoneybridge** W Isls
86 B9 **Stoneyburn** W Loth
41 N7 **Stoneygate** C Leic
68 E8 **Stoneykirk** D & G
50 G6 **Stoney Middleton** Derbys
41 L8 **Stoney Stanton** Leics
17 Q9 **Stoney Stoke** Somset
17 P8 **Stoney Stratton** Somset
103 J11 **Stoneywood** C Aber
85 N6 **Stoneywood** Falk
35 J5 **Stonham Aspal** Suffk
40 E6 **Stonnall** Staffs
20 B6 **Stonor** Oxon
41 Q8 **Stonton Wyville** Leics
51 L7 **Stony Houghton** Derbys
32 B8 **Stony Stratford** M Keyn
15 L6 **Stoodleigh** Devon
16 C11 **Stoodleigh** Devon
13 L3 **Stop 24 Services** Kent
10 G6 **Stopham** W Susx
32 F11 **Stopsley** Luton
111 d2 **Stornoway** W Isls
111 d2 *Stornoway Airport* W Isls
10 H7 **Storrington** W Susx
63 J6 **Storth** Cumb
60 C5 **Storwood** E R Yk
101 J2 **Stotfield** Moray
32 H9 **Stotfold** C Beds
39 M5 **Stottesdon** Shrops
41 N7 **Stoughton** Leics
20 F12 **Stoughton** Surrey
10 C7 **Stoughton** W Susx
30 B4 **Stoulton** Worcs
40 B10 **Stourbridge** Dudley
40 B10 **Stourbridge Crematorium** Dudley
8 C5 **Stourpaine** Dorset
39 P7 **Stourport-on-Severn** Worcs
8 B3 **Stour Provost** Dorset
8 B3 **Stour Row** Dorset
39 Q5 **Stourton** Staffs
30 H6 **Stourton** Warwks
8 B1 **Stourton** Wilts
17 Q12 **Stourton Caundle** Dorset
111 k5 **Stove** Shet
35 P1 **Stoven** Suffk
87 J12 **Stow** Border
52 C7 **Stow** Lincs
43 P8 **Stow Bardolph** Norfk
44 F10 **Stow Bedon** Norfk
43 P8 **Stowbridge** Norfk
33 N5 **Stow-cum-Quy** Cambs
38 F7 **Stowe** Shrops
40 D3 **Stowe by Chartley** Staffs
17 P10 **Stowell** Somset
17 N4 **Stowey** BaNES
5 J3 **Stowford** Devon
34 F3 **Stowlangtoft** Suffk
32 G3 **Stow Longa** Cambs
22 G4 **Stow Maries** Essex
34 H5 **Stowmarket** Suffk
30 F8 **Stow-on-the-Wold** Gloucs
13 L2 **Stowting** Kent
13 L2 **Stowting Common** Kent
34 H5 **Stowupland** Suffk
99 P6 **Straanruie** Highld
95 L4 **Strachan** Abers
84 B3 **Strachur** Ag & B
35 K3 **Stradbroke** Suffk
34 C6 **Stradishall** Suffk
43 Q8 **Stradsett** Norfk
52 C11 **Stragglethorpe** Lincs
86 F8 **Straiton** Mdloth
76 G9 **Straiton** S Ayrs
102 H10 **Straloch** Abers
92 F3 **Straloch** P & K
40 E1 **Stramshall** Staffs
56 c5 **Strang** IoM
57 P8 **Strangeways** Salfd
28 G4 **Strangford** Herefs
68 E7 **Stranraer** D & G
19 Q7 **Stratfield Mortimer** W Berk
20 B10 **Stratfield Saye** Hants
20 B10 **Stratfield Turgis** Hants
21 M6 **Stratford** Gt Lon
35 M5 **Stratford St Andrew** Suffk
34 H9 **Stratford St Mary** Suffk
8 G3 **Stratford Tony** Wilts
30 G3 **Stratford-upon-Avon** Warwks
105 L6 **Strath** Highld
108 C10 **Strathan** Highld
109 K3 **Strathan** Highld
77 L3 **Strathaven** S Lans
85 J7 **Strathblane** Stirlg
106 C3 **Strathcanaird** Highld
97 N2 **Strathcarron** Highld
89 N9 **Strathcoil** Ag & B
101 L11 **Strathdon** Abers
93 M11 **Strathkinness** Fife
85 Q8 **Strathloanhead** W Loth
98 H10 **Strathmashie House** Highld
86 E1 **Strathmiglo** Fife
106 H10 **Strathpeffer** Highld
92 D5 **Strathtay** P & K
75 Q5 **Strathwhillan** N Ayrs
109 P3 **Strathy** Highld
109 P3 **Strathy Inn** Highld
91 N11 **Strathyre** Stirlg
14 E10 **Stratton** Cnwll
7 P4 **Stratton** Dorset
30 D12 **Stratton** Gloucs
31 N8 **Stratton Audley** Oxon
17 P6 **Stratton-on-the-Fosse** Somset
18 H4 **Stratton St Margaret** Swindn
45 K10 **Stratton St Michael** Norfk
45 K6 **Stratton Strawless** Norfk
11 M7 **Streat** E Susx
21 L8 **Streatham** Gt Lon
32 F10 **Streatley** C Beds
19 P5 **Streatley** W Berk
6 G5 **Street** Devon
17 L8 **Street** Somset
41 L10 **Street Ashton** Warwks
48 G7 **Street Dinas** Shrops
23 M11 **Street End** Kent
10 D9 **Street End** W Susx
40 F5 **Streethay** Staffs
65 N7 **Streetlam** N York
40 E7 **Streetly Crematorium** Wsall
33 P7 **Streetly End** Cambs
17 N8 **Street on the Fosse** Somset
92 H8 **Strelitz** P & K
51 L11 **Strelley** Notts
59 N3 **Strensall** C York
29 M1 **Strensham Services (northbound)** Worcs
29 M2 **Strensham Services (southbound)** Worcs
16 H7 **Stretcholt** Somset
5 R10 **Strete** Devon
57 P9 **Stretford** Traffd
33 M8 **Strethall** Essex
33 N2 **Stretham** Cambs
10 E8 **Strettington** W Susx
51 K8 **Stretton** Derbys
42 D7 **Stretton** Rutlnd
40 B5 **Stretton** Staffs
40 G3 **Stretton** Staffs
57 L11 **Stretton** Warrtn
39 L12 **Stretton Grandison** Herefs
41 K11 **Stretton-on-Dunsmore** Warwks
30 G6 **Stretton on Fosse** Warwks
28 E1 **Stretton Sugwas** Herefs
41 L10 **Stretton under Fosse** Warwks
39 L3 **Stretton Westwood** Shrops
103 K4 **Strichen** Abers
16 G7 **Stringston** Somset
32 C4 **Strixton** Nhants
28 G8 **Stroat** Gloucs
110 G1 **Stroma** Highld
97 M3 **Stromeferry** Highld
111 g2 **Stromness** Ork
84 G2 **Stronachlachar** Stirlg
83 Q6 **Stronafian** Ag & B
108 E11 **Stronchrubie** Highld
84 D6 **Strone** Ag & B
98 A11 **Strone** Highld
98 G4 **Strone** Highld
98 B11 **Stronenaba** Highld
90 F10 **Stronmilchan** Ag & B
111 i2 **Stronsay** Ork
111 i2 *Stronsay Airport* Ork
89 Q4 **Strontian** Highld
22 E9 **Strood** Medway
29 L7 **Stroud** Gloucs
10 B5 **Stroud** Hants
29 L7 **Stroud Green** Gloucs
42 C4 **Stroxton** Lincs
96 D3 **Struan** Highld
92 B3 **Struan** P & K
45 M8 **Strumpshaw** Norfk
77 M2 **Strutherhill** S Lans
86 H1 **Struthers** Fife
98 E2 **Struy** Highld
103 K6 **Stuartfield** Abers
9 P6 **Stubbington** Hants
57 P5 **Stubbins** Lancs
42 C1 **Stubton** Lincs
8 H5 **Stuckton** Hants
32 E12 **Studham** C Beds
8 F10 **Studland** Dorset
30 E2 **Studley** Warwks
18 E6 **Studley** Wilts
65 N12 **Studley Roger** N York
65 M12 **Studley Royal** N York
33 N2 **Stuntney** Cambs
34 B7 **Sturmer** Essex
8 B5 **Sturminster Common** Dorset
8 D7 **Sturminster Marshall** Dorset
8 B5 **Sturminster Newton** Dorset
23 M10 **Sturry** Kent
52 D3 **Sturton** N Linc
52 C7 **Sturton by Stow** Lincs
52 B6 **Sturton le Steeple** Notts
35 J2 **Stuston** Suffk
59 L6 **Stutton** N York
35 J9 **Stutton** Suffk
57 Q11 **Styal** Ches E
101 L3 **Stynie** Moray
51 N3 **Styrrup** Notts
84 E2 **Succoth** Ag & B
39 N10 **Suckley** Worcs
32 D1 **Sudborough** Nhants
35 N6 **Sudbourne** Suffk
42 D2 **Sudbrook** Lincs
28 F10 **Sudbrook** Mons
52 E8 **Sudbrooke** Lincs
40 F2 **Sudbury** Derbys
21 J6 **Sudbury** Gt Lon
34 E8 **Sudbury** Suffk
67 L8 **Suffield** N York
45 K4 **Suffield** Norfk
49 P8 **Sugnall** Staffs
28 E1 **Sugwas Pool** Herefs
96 H6 **Suisnish** Highld
56 d3 **Sulby** IoM
31 M5 **Sulgrave** Nhants
31 M5 **Sulgrave Manor** Nhants
19 Q6 **Sulham** W Berk
19 Q7 **Sulhamstead** W Berk
111 k3 **Sullom** Shet
111 k3 **Sullom Voe** Shet
16 F3 **Sully** V Glam
111 k5 *Sumburgh Airport* Shet
58 G2 **Summerbridge** N York
3 K5 **Summercourt** Cnwll
44 C3 **Summerfield** Norfk
25 K7 **Summerhill** Pembks
65 L4 **Summerhouse** Darltn
10 D8 **Summersdale** W Susx
57 P6 **Summerseat** Bury
31 L11 **Summertown** Oxon
20 H9 **Sunbury** Surrey
78 D11 **Sundaywell** D & G
82 C9 **Sunderland** Ag & B
71 J8 **Sunderland** Cumb
62 H10 **Sunderland** Lancs
73 P9 **Sunderland** Sundld
73 M12 **Sunderland Bridge** Dur
73 P9 **Sunderland Crematorium** Sundld
79 M4 **Sundhope** Border
32 F10 **Sundon Park** Luton
21 P11 **Sundridge** Kent
20 F9 **Sunningdale** W & M
20 F9 **Sunninghill** W & M
19 N1 **Sunningwell** Oxon
73 K12 **Sunniside** Dur
73 L8 **Sunniside** Gatesd
41 J2 **Sunnyhill** C Derb
57 M4 **Sunnyhurst** Bl w D
85 N4 **Sunnylaw** Stirlg
31 L11 **Sunnymead** Oxon
21 J9 **Surbiton** Gt Lon
43 J5 **Surfleet** Lincs
45 M8 **Surlingham** Norfk
34 E11 **Surrex** Essex
11 L3 **Surrey & Sussex Crematorium** W Susx
45 K3 **Sustead** Norfk
52 B3 **Susworth** Lincs
14 F9 **Sutcombe** Devon
14 F9 **Sutcombemill** Devon
53 L8 **Sutterby** Lincs
43 J3 **Sutterton** Lincs
32 H7 **Sutton** C Beds
42 F9 **Sutton** C Pete
33 M2 **Sutton** Cambs
5 N10 **Sutton** Devon
11 P9 **Sutton** E Susx
21 K9 **Sutton** Gt Lon
23 P12 **Sutton** Kent
59 L8 **Sutton** N York
45 N5 **Sutton** Norfk
51 Q12 **Sutton** Notts
31 K11 **Sutton** Oxon
39 N5 **Sutton** Shrops
49 N10 **Sutton** Staffs
35 M7 **Sutton** Suffk
10 F7 **Sutton** W Susx
22 B9 **Sutton at Hone** Kent
41 Q9 **Sutton Bassett** Nhants
18 D5 **Sutton Benger** Wilts
41 L3 **Sutton Bonington** Notts
43 M6 **Sutton Bridge** Lincs
41 K7 **Sutton Cheney** Leics
40 E8 **Sutton Coldfield** Birm
40 F7 **Sutton Coldfield Crematorium** Birm
19 N2 **Sutton Courtenay** Oxon
51 P4 **Sutton cum Lound** Notts
20 G11 **Sutton Green** Surrey
65 N10 **Sutton Howgrave** N York
51 L8 **Sutton in Ashfield** Notts
58 D5 **Sutton-in-Craven** N York
39 N2 **Sutton Maddock** Shrops
17 K8 **Sutton Mallet** Somset
8 E2 **Sutton Mandeville** Wilts
17 P10 **Sutton Montis** Somset
61 J7 **Sutton-on-Hull** C KuH
53 N7 **Sutton on Sea** Lincs
59 M2 **Sutton-on-the-Forest** N York
40 G2 **Sutton on the Hill** Derbys
52 B9 **Sutton on Trent** Notts
43 L7 **Sutton St Edmund** Lincs
43 L6 **Sutton St James** Lincs
39 K11 **Sutton St Nicholas** Herefs
19 M11 **Sutton Scotney** Hants
30 H6 **Sutton-under-Brailes** Warwks
66 C10 **Sutton-under-Whitestonecliffe** N York
60 C5 **Sutton upon Derwent** E R Yk
12 F1 **Sutton Valence** Kent
18 D11 **Sutton Veny** Wilts
8 C4 **Sutton Waldron** Dorset
57 K11 **Sutton Weaver** Ches W
17 N4 **Sutton Wick** BaNES
19 N2 **Sutton Wick** Oxon
53 L7 **Swaby** Lincs
40 H4 **Swadlincote** Derbys
44 D8 **Swaffham** Norfk
33 N4 **Swaffham Bulbeck** Cambs
33 P4 **Swaffham Prior** Cambs
45 L4 **Swafield** Norfk
66 C7 **Swainby** N York
45 K9 **Swainsthorpe** Norfk
18 B7 **Swainswick** BaNES
31 J6 **Swalcliffe** Oxon
23 L9 **Swalecliffe** Kent
52 H3 **Swallow** Lincs
52 D9 **Swallow Beck** Lincs
8 E3 **Swallowcliffe** Wilts
20 B9 **Swallowfield** Wokham
8 F10 **Swanage** Dorset
32 B10 **Swanbourne** Bucks
49 N2 **Swan Green** Ches W
60 G8 **Swanland** E R Yk
21 P9 **Swanley** Kent
21 Q9 **Swanley Village** Kent
9 P4 **Swanmore** Hants
41 K4 **Swannington** Leics
45 J6 **Swannington** Norfk
52 D9 **Swanpool Garden Suburb** Lincs
22 C8 **Swanscombe** Kent
26 E9 **Swansea** Swans
26 D9 *Swansea Airport* Swans
26 E8 **Swansea Crematorium** Swans
26 E8 **Swansea West Services** Swans
45 L5 **Swanton Abbot** Norfk
44 G6 **Swanton Morley** Norfk
44 G4 **Swanton Novers** Norfk
51 K9 **Swanwick** Derbys
9 N5 **Swanwick** Hants
42 F3 **Swarby** Lincs
45 K9 **Swardeston** Norfk
41 J2 **Swarkestone** Derbys
81 N12 **Swarland** Nthumb
19 P12 **Swarraton** Hants
62 F6 **Swarthmoor** Cumb
42 G3 **Swaton** Lincs
33 K3 **Swavesey** Cambs
9 J7 **Sway** Hants
42 E5 **Swayfield** Lincs
9 M4 **Swaythling** C Sotn
15 Q11 **Sweetham** Devon
11 P4 **Sweethaws** E Susx
4 E2 **Sweets** Cnwll
3 N4 **Sweetshouse** Cnwll
35 M4 **Swefling** Suffk
41 J5 **Swepstone** Leics
31 J7 **Swerford** Oxon
49 P3 **Swettenham** Ches E
35 K6 **Swilland** Suffk
59 J7 **Swillington** Leeds
15 L6 **Swimbridge** Devon
15 K6 **Swimbridge Newland** Devon
30 H10 **Swinbrook** Oxon
58 G3 **Swincliffe** N York
52 C10 **Swinderby** Lincs
29 N4 **Swindon** Gloucs
39 Q4 **Swindon** Staffs
18 G4 **Swindon** Swindn
61 K7 **Swine** E R Yk
60 D9 **Swinefleet** E R Yk
32 F4 **Swineshead** Bed
43 J3 **Swineshead** Lincs
110 E8 **Swiney** Highld
41 M10 **Swinford** Leics
13 N2 **Swingfield Minnis** Kent
13 N2 **Swingfield Street** Kent
34 F7 **Swingleton Green** Suffk
81 P8 **Swinhoe** Nthumb
65 J9 **Swinithwaite** N York
71 K10 **Swinside** Cumb
42 E5 **Swinstead** Lincs
80 H5 **Swinton** Border
65 L10 **Swinton** N York
66 G11 **Swinton** N York
51 K2 **Swinton** Rothm
57 P8 **Swinton** Salfd
41 M5 **Swithland** Leics
107 J8 **Swordale** Highld
97 L10 **Swordland** Highld
109 N3 **Swordly** Highld
49 Q8 **Swynnerton** Staffs
7 M5 **Swyre** Dorset
38 B1 **Sychtyn** Powys
29 N6 **Syde** Gloucs
21 M8 **Sydenham** Gt Lon
20 B3 **Sydenham** Oxon
5 J5 **Sydenham Damerel** Devon
44 D4 **Syderstone** Norfk
7 P3 **Sydling St Nicholas** Dorset
19 N8 **Sydmonton** Hants
51 Q10 **Syerston** Notts
54 H10 **Sygun Copper Mine** Gwynd
59 N10 **Sykehouse** Donc
111 k3 **Symbister** Shet
76 G5 **Symington** S Ayrs
78 G2 **Symington** S Lans
7 L4 **Symondsbury** Dorset
28 G5 **Symonds Yat** Herefs
109 M7 **Syre** Highld
30 D9 **Syreford** Gloucs
31 N6 **Syresham** Nhants
41 N5 **Syston** Leics
42 D2 **Syston** Lincs
39 Q8 **Sytchampton** Worcs
32 B4 **Sywell** Nhants

T

31 L9 **Tackley** Oxon
45 J10 **Tacolneston** Norfk
59 L5 **Tadcaster** N York
50 F6 **Taddington** Derbys
19 P8 **Tadley** Hants
33 J7 **Tadlow** Cambs
31 K6 **Tadmarton** Oxon
21 K11 **Tadworth** Surrey
27 N11 **Taff's Well** Rhondd
26 G10 **Taibach** Neath
107 M6 **Tain** Highld
110 E3 **Tain** Highld
111 c3 **Tairbeart** W Isls
33 P11 **Takeley** Essex
33 N11 **Takeley Street** Essex
6 E3 **Talaton** Devon
24 E6 **Talbenny** Pembks
6 E4 **Taleford** Devon
47 Q10 **Talerddig** Powys
36 G9 **Talgarreg** Cerdgn
27 N3 **Talgarth** Powys
96 D4 **Talisker** Highld
49 P5 **Talke** Staffs
71 Q4 **Talkin** Cumb
105 N8 **Talladale** Highld
79 J5 **Talla Linnfoots** Border
76 G10 **Tallaminnock** S Ayrs
49 J6 **Tallarn Green** Wrexhm
70 H8 **Tallentire** Cumb
26 E3 **Talley** Carmth
42 F8 **Tallington** Lincs
109 K3 **Talmine** Highld
25 N4 **Talog** Carmth
37 J9 **Talsarn** Cerdgn
47 K4 **Talsarnau** Gwynd
3 K3 **Talskiddy** Cnwll
54 G6 **Talwrn** IoA
37 K3 **Tal-y-bont** Cerdgn
55 L7 **Tal-y-Bont** Conwy
47 J7 **Tal-y-bont** Gwynd
54 H7 **Tal-y-bont** Gwynd
27 N4 **Talybont-on-Usk** Powys
55 L7 **Tal-y-Cafn** Conwy
28 E6 **Tal-y-coed** Mons
54 G10 **Talysarn** Gwynd
5 K7 **Tamerton Foliot** C Plym
40 G6 **Tamworth** Staffs
40 G7 **Tamworth Services** Warwks
21 M12 **Tandridge** Surrey
73 L9 **Tanfield** Dur
73 L9 **Tanfield Lea** Dur
19 K9 **Tangley** Hants
10 E8 **Tangmere** W Susx
111 a7 **Tangusdale** W Isls
111 h2 **Tankerness** Ork
51 J2 **Tankersley** Barns
23 L9 **Tankerton** Kent
110 G6 **Tannach** Highld
95 N5 **Tannachie** Abers
93 N4 **Tannadice** Angus
40 E11 **Tanner's Green** Worcs
35 L4 **Tannington** Suffk
85 L10 **Tannochside** N Lans
51 J8 **Tansley** Derbys
42 F11 **Tansor** Nhants
73 L9 **Tantobie** Dur
40 E12 **Tanworth in Arden** Warwks
36 E10 **Tan-y-groes** Cerdgn
111 b3 **Taobh Tuath** W Isls
20 E7 **Taplow** Bucks
75 J3 **Tarbert** Ag & B
83 N8 **Tarbert** Ag & B
111 c3 **Tarbert** W Isls
84 F3 **Tarbet** Ag & B
97 L10 **Tarbet** Highld
108 D6 **Tarbet** Highld
76 G6 **Tarbolton** S Ayrs
86 B10 **Tarbrax** S Lans

6 B9 Torquay Crematorium Torbay
87 J11 Torquhan Border
104 H11 Torran Highld
85 K8 Torrance E Duns
76 F3 Torranyard N Ayrs
105 N10 Torridon Highld
105 M10 Torridon House Highld
96 G5 Torrin Highld
75 M5 Torrisdale Ag & B
109 M4 Torrisdale Highld
110 A11 Torrish Highld
63 J9 Torrisholme Lancs
107 K2 Torrobull Highld
95 Q2 Torry C Aber
86 B5 Torryburn Fife
6 a2 Torteval Guern
78 G12 Torthorwald D & G
10 G8 Tortington W Susx
39 Q7 Torton Worcs
29 J9 Tortworth S Glos
96 F2 Torvaig Highld
62 F4 Torver Cumb
86 F5 Torwood Falk
79 P2 Torwoodlee Border
51 P4 Torworth Notts
97 J3 Toscaig Highld
33 J4 Toseland Cambs
63 P10 Tosside Lancs
34 F4 Tostock Suffk
104 B11 Totaig Highld
104 F11 Tote Highld
104 G9 Tote Highld
9 K9 Totland IoW
50 H5 Totley Sheff
5 Q7 Totnes Devon
41 L1 Toton Notts
88 E5 Totronald Ag & B
104 E8 Totscore Highld
21 M5 Tottenham Gt Lon
43 Q7 Tottenhill Norfk
21 K5 Totteridge Gt Lon
32 E11 Totternhoe C Beds
57 P6 Tottington Bury
9 L5 Totton Hants
16 G9 Toulton Somset
107 P6 Toulvaddie Highld
22 F11 Tovil Kent
84 C8 Toward Ag & B
84 B9 Toward Quay Ag & B
31 P4 Towcester Nhants
2 D7 Towednack Cnwll
20 B3 Towersey Oxon
101 N11 Towie Abers
73 K11 Tow Law Dur
41 L10 Town End Cambs
84 G7 Townend W Duns
50 F1 Townhead Barns
78 G10 Townhead D & G
70 C3 Townhead of Greenlaw D & G
86 D4 Townhill Fife
11 N6 Town Littleworth E Susx
19 P8 Towns End Hants
2 E8 Townshend Cnwll
44 C11 Town Street Suffk
80 H8 Town Yetholm Border
59 N3 Towthorpe C York
59 L6 Towton N York
55 P6 Towyn Conwy
56 G10 Toxteth Lpool
53 L10 Toynton All Saints Lincs
21 P12 Toy's Hill Kent
76 G7 Trabboch E Ayrs
76 H7 Trabbochburn E Ayrs
100 D4 Tradespark Highld
27 K3 Trallong Powys
51 J9 Tramway Museum Derbys
86 H7 Tranent E Loth
56 G10 Tranmere Wirral
109 Q5 Trantelbeg Highld
109 Q5 Trantlemore Highld
26 E5 Trapp Carmth
87 L7 Traprain E Loth
79 M3 Traquair Border
58 B6 Trawden Lancs
47 L4 Trawsfynydd Gwynd
27 L9 Trealaw Rhondd
56 H3 Treales Lancs
54 C6 Trearddur Bay IoA
104 E10 Treaslane Highld
4 B5 Trebetherick Cnwll
16 D8 Treborough Somset
4 H5 Trebullett Cnwll
4 H5 Treburley Cnwll
27 J3 Trecastle Powys
24 G3 Trecwn Pembks
27 L7 Trecynon Rhondd
27 N7 Tredegar Blae G
29 M3 Tredington Gloucs
30 H5 Tredington Warwks
28 D9 Tredunnock Mons
2 B10 Treen Cnwll
51 K4 Treeton Rothm
24 F2 Trefasser Pembks
27 N3 Trefecca Powys
37 Q3 Trefeglwys Powys
24 G4 Treffgarne Pembks
24 F4 Treffgarne Owen Pembks
27 M10 Trefforest Rhondd
37 J8 Trefilan Cerdgn
24 E3 Trefin Pembks
48 B2 Trefnant Denbgs
48 F9 Trefonen Shrops
46 F3 Trefor Gwynd
55 L8 Trefriw Conwy
4 G4 Tregadillett Cnwll
28 E6 Tregare Mons
37 L8 Tregaron Cerdgn
54 H7 Tregarth Gwynd
4 F3 Tregeare Cnwll
48 D8 Tregeiriog Wrexhm
54 E3 Tregele IoA
24 E3 Treglemais Pembks
3 L3 Tregonetha Cnwll
3 K6 Tregony Cnwll
3 M5 Tregorrick Cnwll
27 P2 Tregoyd Powys
36 G10 Tre-groes Cerdgn
38 C3 Tregynon Powys
25 P5 Tre-gynwr Carmth
27 L10 Trehafod Rhondd
5 J8 Trehan Cnwll
27 M9 Treharris Myr Td
27 K8 Treherbert Rhondd
4 H5 Trekenner Cnwll
4 C3 Treknow Cnwll
56 C11 Trelawnyd Flints
25 M3 Trelech Carmth
24 D3 Treleddyd-fawr Pembks
27 M9 Trelewis Myr Td
4 B4 Trelights Cnwll
4 C5 Trelill Cnwll
3 J7 Trelissick Garden Cnwll
28 F7 Trellech Mons
56 D11 Trelogan Flints
47 J4 Tremadog Gwynd
4 E3 Tremail Cnwll
36 D10 Tremain Cerdgn
4 F3 Tremaine Cnwll
4 G6 Tremar Cnwll
5 J8 Trematon Cnwll
48 C2 Tremeirchion Denbgs
3 J3 Trenance Cnwll
3 L2 Trenance Cnwll
49 M11 Trench Wrekin
2 G9 Trenear Cnwll
4 F3 Treneglos Cnwll
17 N11 Trent Dorset
49 Q7 Trentham C Stke
15 L3 Trentishoe Devon
27 K12 Treoes V Glam
27 K8 Treorchy Rhondd
3 M1 Trequite Cnwll
27 L12 Trerhyngyll V Glam
4 H8 Trerulefoot Cnwll
36 E9 Tresaith Cerdgn
2 b2 Tresco IoS
2 b2 Tresco Heliport IoS
2 E9 Trescowe Cnwll
2 H4 Tresean Cnwll
29 L9 Tresham Gloucs
88 G7 Treshnish Isles Ag & B
3 K6 Tresillian Cnwll
14 D11 Treskinnick Cross Cnwll
4 F3 Tresmeer Cnwll
4 E2 Tresparrett Cnwll
92 C4 Tressait P & K
111 k4 Tresta Shet
111 m2 Tresta Shet
52 A7 Treswell Notts
2 F7 Treswithian Downs Crematorium Cnwll
37 L3 Tre Taliesin Cerdgn
4 D3 Trethevey Cnwll
2 B10 Trethewey Cnwll
3 M5 Trethurgy Cnwll
28 F4 Tretire Herefs
27 P5 Tretower Powys
48 F4 Treuddyn Flints
4 D3 Trevalga Cnwll
48 H4 Trevalyn Wrexhm
3 J3 Trevarrian Cnwll
2 H4 Treveal Cnwll
4 D4 Treveighan Cnwll
2 H5 Trevellas Downs Cnwll
4 F7 Trevelmond Cnwll
2 H9 Treverva Cnwll
2 B10 Trevescan Cnwll
3 L5 Treviscoe Cnwll
3 K1 Trevone Cnwll
48 F7 Trevor Wrexhm
4 D4 Trewalder Cnwll
4 D3 Trewarmett Cnwll
4 F4 Trewen Cnwll
4 F4 Trewint Cnwll
3 K8 Trewithian Cnwll
3 L5 Trewoon Cnwll
10 D6 Treyford W Susx
65 P1 Trimdon Dur
65 P1 Trimdon Colliery Dur
65 P1 Trimdon Grange Dur
45 L3 Trimingham Norfk
35 L8 Trimley St Martin Suffk
35 L9 Trimley St Mary Suffk
26 B7 Trimsaran Carmth
15 J4 Trimstone Devon
91 Q4 Trinafour P & K
20 E2 Tring Herts
95 K9 Trinity Angus
7 b1 Trinity Jersey
92 E11 Trinity Gask P & K
16 F8 Triscombe Somset
90 E2 Trislaig Highld
3 J6 Trispen Cnwll
73 L3 Tritlington Nthumb
92 E7 Trochry P & K
36 E10 Troedyraur Cerdgn
27 M8 Troedyrhiw Myr Td
2 F8 Troon Cnwll
76 F5 Troon S Ayrs
59 J6 Tropical World Roundhay Park Leeds
84 H2 Trossachs Stirlg
84 H2 Trossachs Pier Stirlg
34 E3 Troston Suffk
30 B3 Trotshill Worcs
22 D10 Trottiscliffe Kent
10 D5 Trotton W Susx
62 H2 Troutbeck Cumb
62 H3 Troutbeck Bridge Cumb
51 K5 Troway Derbys
18 C8 Trowbridge Wilts
51 L11 Trowell Notts
51 L11 Trowell Services Notts
45 L8 Trowse Newton Norfk
17 Q7 Trudoxhill Somset
16 G10 Trull Somset
104 C9 Trumpan Highld
28 H2 Trumpet Herefs
33 M6 Trumpington Cambs
45 L3 Trunch Norfk
3 J6 Truro Cnwll
3 J6 Truro Cathedral Cnwll
6 B6 Trusham Devon
40 G1 Trusley Derbys
53 N6 Trusthorpe Lincs
39 Q4 Trysull Staffs
19 M2 Tubney Oxon
5 Q8 Tuckenhay Devon
39 P5 Tuckhill Shrops
2 F7 Tuckingmill Cnwll
8 D2 Tuckingmill Wilts
8 G8 Tuckton Bmouth
34 C3 Tuddenham Suffk
35 K7 Tuddenham Suffk
12 C2 Tudeley Kent
65 M1 Tudhoe Dur
46 D4 Tudweiliog Gwynd
29 L6 Tuffley Gloucs
19 M10 Tufton Hants
24 H3 Tufton Pembks
41 Q7 Tugby Leics
39 K5 Tugford Shrops
81 P8 Tughall Nthumb
85 P4 Tullibody Clacks
99 J4 Tullich Highld
107 P7 Tullich Highld
92 E5 Tulliemet P & K
102 G8 Tulloch Abers
83 P4 Tullochgorm Ag & B
98 E11 Tulloch Station Highld
92 H5 Tullymurdoch P & K
102 D10 Tullynessle Abers
21 L8 Tulse Hill Gt Lon
26 D6 Tumble Carmth
53 J10 Tumby Lincs
53 J11 Tumby Woodside Lincs
92 B4 Tummel Bridge P & K
12 C3 Tunbridge Wells Kent
79 J11 Tundergarth D & G
17 Q4 Tunley BaNES
49 Q5 Tunstall C Stke
61 M7 Tunstall E R Yk
22 H10 Tunstall Kent
63 L7 Tunstall Lancs
65 L8 Tunstall N York
45 N8 Tunstall Norfk
49 P9 Tunstall Staffs
35 M6 Tunstall Suffk
73 P9 Tunstall Sundld
50 E6 Tunstead Derbys
45 L6 Tunstead Norfk
50 D5 Tunstead Milton Derbys
20 B10 Turgis Green Hants
30 E9 Turkdean Gloucs
41 Q8 Tur Langton Leics
18 B8 Turleigh Wilts
28 D2 Turnastone Herefs
76 D9 Turnberry S Ayrs
50 H10 Turnditch Derbys
11 M3 Turner's Hill W Susx
86 D7 Turnhouse C Edin
8 B6 Turnworth Dorset
102 F5 Turriff Abers
57 N6 Turton Bottoms Bl w D
43 K10 Turves Cambs
32 D6 Turvey Bed
20 C5 Turville Bucks
31 N6 Turweston Bucks
79 L5 Tushielaw Inn Border
40 G2 Tutbury Staffs
28 G9 Tutshill Gloucs
45 K5 Tuttington Norfk
51 Q6 Tuxford Notts
111 g2 Twatt Ork
111 k4 Twatt Shet
85 L7 Twechar E Duns
80 C7 Tweedbank Border
81 L4 Tweedmouth Nthumb
78 H4 Tweedsmuir Border
2 H7 Twelveheads Cnwll
49 P2 Twemlow Green Ches E
42 G6 Twenty Lincs
17 Q4 Twerton BaNES
21 J8 Twickenham Gt Lon
29 L4 Twigworth Gloucs
11 K6 Twineham W Susx
34 E9 Twinstead Essex
15 N6 Twitchen Devon
50 H8 Two Dales Derbys
40 G7 Two Gates Staffs
41 J6 Twycross Leics
40 H6 Twycross Zoo Leics
31 P8 Twyford Bucks
9 N3 Twyford Hants
41 Q5 Twyford Leics
44 G5 Twyford Norfk
20 C8 Twyford Wokham
69 P8 Twynholm D & G
29 M2 Twyning Green Gloucs
26 G4 Twynllanan Carmth
32 D2 Twywell Nhants
28 D2 Tyberton Herefs
26 E6 Tycroes Carmth
48 C10 Tycrwyn Powys
43 M6 Tydd Gote Lincs
43 L6 Tydd St Giles Cambs
43 M6 Tydd St Mary Lincs
33 P9 Tye Green Essex
57 M8 Tyldesley Wigan
23 L10 Tyler Hill Kent
27 L9 Tylorstown Rhondd
48 B6 Ty-nant Conwy
91 J9 Tyndrum Stirlg
48 E7 Ty'n-dwr Denbgs
73 P7 Tynemouth N Tyne
73 N7 Tynemouth Crematorium N Tyne
87 L6 Tyninghame E Loth
77 N11 Tynron D & G
17 M2 Tyntesfield N Som
37 L6 Tynygraig Cerdgn
55 L7 Ty'n-y-Groes Conwy
27 M10 Tyn-y-nant Rhondd
32 C7 Tyringham M Keyn
27 J11 Tythegston Brdgnd
50 B6 Tytherington Ches E
29 J10 Tytherington S Glos
18 D11 Tytherington Wilts
7 J3 Tytherleigh Devon
18 D6 Tytherton Lucas Wilts
3 N5 Tywardreath Cnwll
47 J10 Tywyn Gwynd

U

35 M3 Ubbeston Green Suffk
17 M5 Ubley BaNES
11 P6 Uckfield E Susx
29 M2 Uckinghall Worcs
29 M4 Uckington Gloucs
85 L10 Uddingston S Lans
78 E3 Uddington S Lans
12 G6 Udimore E Susx
103 J9 Udny Green Abers
103 J9 Udny Station Abers
16 E12 Uffculme Devon
42 F8 Uffington Lincs
19 K3 Uffington Oxon
49 K11 Uffington Shrops
42 F8 Ufford C Pete
35 L6 Ufford Suffk
31 J2 Ufton Warwks
19 Q7 Ufton Nervet W Berk
75 L6 Ugadale Ag & B
5 N8 Ugborough Devon
35 P2 Uggeshall Suffk
67 J6 Ugglebarnby N York
50 G3 Ughill Sheff
33 N10 Ugley Essex
33 N10 Ugley Green Essex
66 H5 Ugthorpe N York
111 b6 Uibhist A Deas W Isls
111 a4 Uibhist A Tuath W Isls
88 E5 Uig Ag & B
104 B10 Uig Highld
104 E9 Uig Highld
111 c2 Uig W Isls
104 F12 Uigshader Highld
89 J11 Uisken Ag & B
110 G7 Ulbster Highld
53 L8 Ulceby Lincs
61 J10 Ulceby N Linc
61 J10 Ulceby Skitter N Linc
12 G1 Ulcombe Kent
71 L7 Uldale Cumb
29 K8 Uley Gloucs
73 M3 Ulgham Nthumb
106 B4 Ullapool Highld
30 E1 Ullenhall Warwks
59 M6 Ulleskelf N York
41 L9 Ullesthorpe Leics
51 L4 Ulley Rothm
39 L11 Ullingswick Herefs
96 C3 Ullinish Lodge Hotel Highld
70 H10 Ullock Cumb
71 N10 Ullswater Cumb
62 E4 Ulpha Cumb
61 K3 Ulrome E R Yk
111 k3 Ulsta Shet
89 J8 Ulva Ag & B
62 F6 Ulverston Cumb
8 F10 Ulwell Dorset
77 N9 Ulzieside D & G
15 K7 Umberleigh Devon
108 E8 Unapool Highld
63 J4 Underbarrow Cumb
79 P11 Under Burnmouth Border
58 F7 Undercliffe C Brad
49 J11 Underdale Shrops
22 B11 Under River Kent
51 L10 Underwood Notts
28 E10 Undy Mons
56 c5 Union Mills IoM
111 m2 Unst Shet
51 J5 Unstone Derbys
18 G9 Upavon Wilts
22 G9 Upchurch Kent
15 N6 Upcott Devon
6 C3 Up Exe Devon
45 J6 Upgate Norfk
7 M3 Uphall Dorset
86 C7 Uphall W Loth
15 Q9 Upham Devon
9 N4 Upham Hants
38 H9 Uphampton Herefs
39 Q8 Uphampton Worcs
17 J5 Uphill N Som
57 K7 Up Holland Lancs
84 G11 Uplawmoor E Rens
29 K4 Upleadon Gloucs
66 E4 Upleatham R & Cl
7 M4 Uploders Dorset
16 D11 Uplowman Devon
7 J4 Uplyme Devon
10 C7 Up Marden W Susx
22 C6 Upminster Gt Lon
17 N11 Up Mudford Somset
20 B11 Up Nately Hants
6 G2 Upottery Devon
39 J5 Upper Affcot Shrops
107 K5 Upper Ardchronie Highld
39 N6 Upper Arley Worcs
19 P5 Upper Basildon W Berk
11 K7 Upper Beeding W Susx
42 E11 Upper Benefield Nhants
30 C2 Upper Bentley Worcs
109 Q4 Upper Bighouse Highld
31 L4 Upper Boddington Nhants
30 H6 Upper Brailes Warwks
97 J5 Upper Breakish Highld
39 P10 Upper Broadheath Worcs
41 P3 Upper Broughton Notts
19 P7 Upper Bucklebury W Berk
8 H4 Upper Burgate Hants
71 N5 Upperby Cumb
32 G7 Upper Caldecote C Beds
27 L1 Upper Chapel Powys
8 E2 Upper Chicksgrove Wilts
19 K9 Upper Chute Wilts
21 M6 Upper Clapton Gt Lon
19 L11 Upper Clatford Hants
39 K2 Upper Cound Shrops
58 G11 Upper Cumberworth Kirk
101 M3 Upper Dallachy Moray
23 Q11 Upper Deal Kent
32 F4 Upper Dean Bed
58 G11 Upper Denby Kirk
12 B7 Upper Dicker E Susx
110 B3 Upper Dounreay Highld
35 K9 Upper Dovercourt Essex
85 L2 Upper Drumbane Stirlg
59 K2 Upper Dunsforth N York
10 F2 Upper Eashing Surrey
107 M9 Upper Eathie Highld
39 M12 Upper Egleton Herefs
50 D8 Upper Elkstone Staffs
50 E11 Upper Ellastone Staffs
10 B3 Upper Farringdon Hants
29 K6 Upper Framilode Gloucs
10 C2 Upper Froyle Hants
104 D11 Upperglen Highld
17 L7 Upper Godney Somset
32 G9 Upper Gravenhurst C Beds
19 L7 Upper Green W Berk
28 G4 Upper Grove Common Herefs
10 D1 Upper Hale Surrey
20 H9 Upper Halliford Surrey
42 C8 Upper Hambleton Rutlnd
23 L10 Upper Harbledown Kent
11 P3 Upper Hartfield E Susx
29 M5 Upper Hatherley Gloucs
58 F9 Upper Heaton Kirk
59 P3 Upper Helmsley N York
38 F10 Upper Hergest Herefs
31 P3 Upper Heyford Nhants
31 L8 Upper Heyford Oxon
39 J10 Upper Hill Herefs
58 G9 Upper Hopton Kirk
50 D8 Upper Hulme Staffs
18 H2 Upper Inglesham Swindn
26 D9 Upper Killay Swans
90 G10 Upper Kinchrackine Ag & B
19 K5 Upper Lambourn W Berk
40 C6 Upper Landywood Staffs
17 L4 Upper Langford N Som
51 L6 Upper Langwith Derbys
87 J2 Upper Largo Fife
50 D12 Upper Leigh Staffs
95 L3 Upper Lochton Abers
40 D5 Upper Longdon Staffs
32 G9 Upper & Lower Stondon C Beds
110 F8 Upper Lybster Highld
28 H6 Upper Lydbrook Gloucs
38 H8 Upper Lye Herefs
58 C11 Uppermill Oldham
39 P7 Upper Milton Worcs
18 E3 Upper Minety Wilts
101 L5 Upper Mulben Moray
39 L4 Upper Netchwood Shrops
40 D1 Upper Nobut Staffs
10 F6 Upper Norwood W Susx
59 M4 Upper Poppleton C York
9 K3 Upper Ratley Hants
30 G9 Upper Rissington Gloucs
39 L8 Upper Rochford Worcs
69 N6 Upper Ruscoe D & G
39 M8 Upper Sapey Herefs
18 D5 Upper Seagry Wilts
32 E7 Upper Shelton C Beds
45 J2 Upper Sheringham Norfk
84 D9 Upper Skelmorlie N Ayrs
30 F9 Upper Slaughter Gloucs
28 H6 Upper Soudley Gloucs
13 N3 Upper Standen Kent
45 L9 Upper Stoke Norfk
31 N3 Upper Stowe Nhants
8 H4 Upper Street Hants
45 M6 Upper Street Norfk
45 M6 Upper Street Norfk
34 C6 Upper Street Suffk
34 H6 Upper Street Suffk
32 F10 Upper Sundon C Beds
30 F8 Upper Swell Gloucs
45 K10 Upper Tasburgh Norfk
50 D11 Upper Tean Staffs
58 F11 Upperthong Kirk
10 F5 Upperton W Susx
39 L11 Upper Town Herefs
110 G1 Uppertown Highld
17 M3 Upper Town N Som
34 F4 Upper Town Suffk
26 D6 Upper Tumble Carmth
31 J5 Upper Tysoe Warwks
93 P8 Upper Victoria Angus
31 L5 Upper Wardington Oxon
29 K1 Upper Welland Worcs
11 N7 Upper Wellingham E Susx
35 K2 Upper Weybread Suffk
19 Q11 Upper Wield Hants
31 Q10 Upper Winchendon Bucks
18 G12 Upper Woodford Wilts
18 B6 Upper Wraxall Wilts
42 C9 Uppingham Rutlnd
49 L12 Uppington Shrops
66 C9 Upsall N York
81 J5 Upsettlington Border
21 N4 Upshire Essex
9 L2 Up Somborne Hants
23 N10 Upstreet Kent
31 Q10 Upton Bucks
42 G9 Upton C Pete
32 H2 Upton Cambs
48 H2 Upton Ches W
4 G6 Upton Cnwll
5 N10 Upton Devon
6 E3 Upton Devon
7 Q6 Upton Dorset
8 E8 Upton Dorset
57 J10 Upton Halton
9 L4 Upton Hants
19 L9 Upton Hants
41 J7 Upton Leics
52 C6 Upton Lincs
45 N7 Upton Norfk
51 Q5 Upton Notts
51 Q9 Upton Notts
19 N4 Upton Oxon
20 F7 Upton Slough
16 D9 Upton Somset
17 L10 Upton Somset
59 L10 Upton Wakefd
56 F10 Upton Wirral
28 H4 Upton Bishop Herefs
17 Q3 Upton Cheyney S Glos
39 M4 Upton Cressett Shrops
10 B1 Upton Grey Hants
15 P10 Upton Hellions Devon
18 D11 Upton Lovell Wilts
49 K11 Upton Magna Shrops
17 Q8 Upton Noble Somset
6 C3 Upton Pyne Devon
29 M6 Upton St Leonards Gloucs
18 C10 Upton Scudamore Wilts
30 C4 Upton Snodsbury Worcs
29 L1 Upton upon Severn Worcs
30 B1 Upton Warren Worcs
10 F7 Upwaltham W Susx
43 N9 Upwell Norfk
43 J12 Upwood Cambs
18 F8 Urchfont Wilts
57 P9 Urmston Traffd
101 K3 Urquhart Moray
66 D7 Urra N York
106 H10 Urray Highld
95 M10 Usan Angus
73 M11 Ushaw Moor Dur
28 D8 Usk Mons
52 F5 Usselby Lincs
73 N8 Usworth Sundld
49 K3 Utkinton Ches W
58 D5 Utley C Brad
15 P11 Uton Devon
53 K5 Utterby Lincs

40 E2 Uttoxeter Staffs
20 G6 Uxbridge Gt Lon
111 m2 Uyeasound Shet
24 G6 Uzmaston Pembks

V

6 c1 Vale Guern
16 F3 Vale of Glamorgan Crematorium V Glam
37 L5 Vale of Rheidol Railway Cerdgn
54 D6 Valley IoA
104 G9 Valtos Highld
111 c2 Valtos W Isls
22 E6 Vange Essex
111 k2 Vatsetter Shet
96 C2 Vatten Highld
27 L6 Vaynor Myr Td
111 k4 Veensgarth Shet
27 P2 Velindre Powys
14 G9 Venngreen Devon
6 E5 Venn Ottery Devon
9 P11 Ventnor IoW
5 M8 Venton Devon
19 K9 Vernham Dean Hants
19 L8 Vernham Street Hants
8 G5 Verwood Dorset
3 K7 Veryan Cnwll
62 E8 Vickerstown Cumb
3 L4 Victoria Cnwll
111 k3 Vidlin Shet
101 K3 Viewfield Moray
85 M10 Viewpark N Lans
22 D10 Vigo Kent
6 c2 Village de Putron Guern
12 C6 Vines Cross E Susx
22 F11 Vinters Park Crematorium Kent
20 G9 Virginia Water Surrey
4 H2 Virginstow Devon
17 Q6 Vobster Somset
111 k3 Voe Shet
28 D2 Vowchurch Herefs

W

62 C4 Waberthwaite Cumb
65 K3 Wackerfield Dur
45 K10 Wacton Norfk
30 B5 Wadborough Worcs
31 Q10 Waddesdon Bucks
6 B10 Waddeton Devon
52 E4 Waddingham Lincs
63 N12 Waddington Lancs
52 D9 Waddington Lincs
3 L2 Wadebridge Cnwll
7 J1 Wadeford Somset
42 E12 Wadenhoe Nhants
33 K12 Wadesmill Herts
12 D4 Wadhurst E Susx
50 H6 Wadshelf Derbys
51 M2 Wadworth Donc
53 N10 Wainfleet All Saints Lincs
53 M10 Wainfleet St Mary Lincs
4 E2 Wainhouse Corner Cnwll
22 E8 Wainscott Medway
58 D8 Wainstalls Calder
64 D6 Waitby Cumb
53 J4 Waithe Lincs
59 J9 Wakefield Wakefd
58 H10 Wakefield Crematorium Wakefd
42 D9 Wakerley Nhants
34 E10 Wakes Colne Essex
35 P2 Walberswick Suffk
10 F8 Walberton W Susx
70 C2 Walbutt D & G
17 M6 Walcombe Somset
42 F3 Walcot Lincs
49 L11 Walcot Shrops
18 H4 Walcot Swindn
41 M10 Walcote Leics
35 J1 Walcot Green Norfk
52 G11 Walcott Lincs
45 M4 Walcott Norfk
59 M10 Walden Stubbs N York
22 F10 Walderslade Medway
10 C7 Walderton W Susx
7 L4 Walditch Dorset
73 M10 Waldridge Dur
35 L7 Waldringfield Suffk
12 B6 Waldron E Susx
51 L4 Wales Rothm
17 N10 Wales Somset
52 G5 Walesby Lincs
51 P6 Walesby Notts
28 G5 Walford Herefs
38 H7 Walford Herefs
49 J10 Walford Heath Shrops
49 M6 Walgherton Ches E
32 B3 Walgrave Nhants
57 N8 Walkden Salfd
73 M7 Walker N u Ty
79 M2 Walkerburn Border
51 Q3 Walkeringham Notts
52 B5 Walkerith Lincs
33 J10 Walkern Herts
86 F3 Walkerton Fife
8 H8 Walkford Dorset
5 L6 Walkhampton Devon
60 G6 Walkington E R Yk
51 J3 Walkley Sheff
57 Q3 Walk Mill Lancs
30 D2 Walkwood Worcs
72 G7 Wall Nthumb
40 E6 Wall Staffs
76 E10 Wallacetown S Ayrs
76 F6 Wallacetown S Ayrs
11 N7 Wallands Park E Susx
56 F9 Wallasey Wirral
19 P3 Wallingford Oxon
21 L9 Wallington Gt Lon
9 P6 Wallington Hants
33 J9 Wallington Herts
8 F8 Wallisdown Poole
111 j4 Walls Shet
73 N7 Wallsend N Tyne
86 H7 Wallyford E Loth
23 Q12 Walmer Kent
57 J4 Walmer Bridge Lancs
40 F8 Walmley Birm
35 M2 Walpole Suffk
43 N6 Walpole Cross Keys Norfk
43 N7 Walpole Highway Norfk
43 N6 Walpole St Andrew Norfk
43 N6 Walpole St Peter Norfk
40 D7 Walsall Wsall
58 C9 Walsden Calder
41 J10 Walsgrave on Sowe Covtry
34 G3 Walsham le Willows Suffk
59 K4 Walshford N York
43 M7 Walsoken Norfk
86 C12 Walston S Lans
32 H10 Walsworth Herts
20 D4 Walter's Ash Bucks
13 L1 Waltham Kent
53 J3 Waltham NE Lin
21 M4 Waltham Abbey Essex
9 P4 Waltham Chase Hants
21 M4 Waltham Cross Herts
42 B5 Waltham on the Wolds Leics
20 D7 Waltham St Lawrence W & M
21 M5 Walthamstow Gt Lon
71 Q3 Walton Cumb
51 J7 Walton Derbys
59 K5 Walton Leeds
41 N9 Walton Leics
32 C9 Walton M Keyn
38 F9 Walton Powys
17 L8 Walton Somset
35 L9 Walton Suffk
10 D8 Walton W Susx
59 J10 Walton Wakefd
49 L10 Walton Wrekin
29 M3 Walton Cardiff Gloucs
24 H4 Walton East Pembks
17 K2 Walton-in-Gordano N Som
57 L10 Walton Lea Crematorium Warrtn
57 K4 Walton-le-Dale Lancs
20 H9 Walton-on-Thames Surrey
40 C4 Walton-on-the-Hill Staffs
21 K11 Walton on the Hill Surrey
35 L11 Walton on the Naze Essex
41 N4 Walton on the Wolds Leics
40 G4 Walton-on-Trent Derbys
17 K2 Walton Park N Som
24 F6 Walton West Pembks
58 C4 Waltonwrays Crematorium N York
65 M4 Walworth Darltn
21 M7 Walworth Gt Lon
24 F6 Walwyn's Castle Pembks
6 H2 Wambrook Somset
10 E1 Wanborough Surrey
18 H4 Wanborough Swindn
21 K8 Wandsworth Gt Lon
35 P2 Wangford Suffk
41 N5 Wanlip Leics
78 E6 Wanlockhead D & G
12 C8 Wannock E Susx
42 F9 Wansford C Pete
60 H3 Wansford E R Yk
12 F2 Wanshurst Green Kent
21 N6 Wanstead Gt Lon
17 Q7 Wanstrow Somset
29 J8 Wanswell Gloucs
19 L3 Wantage Oxon
41 J12 Wappenbury Warwks
31 N5 Wappenham Nhants
12 C6 Warbleton E Susx
19 P3 Warborough Oxon
33 K2 Warboys Cambs
56 G2 Warbreck Bpool
4 F3 Warbstow Cnwll
57 M10 Warburton Traffd
64 D5 Warcop Cumb
72 G7 Warden Nthumb
31 L5 Wardington Oxon
49 L4 Wardle Ches E
58 B10 Wardle Rochdl
73 N8 Wardley Gatesd
42 B9 Wardley Rutlnd
50 F6 Wardlow Derbys
33 M1 Wardy Hill Cambs
21 M1 Ware Herts
8 D9 Wareham Dorset
13 J4 Warehorne Kent
81 N8 Warenford Nthumb
21 M1 Wareside Herts
33 J6 Waresley Cambs
20 E8 Warfield Br For
6 B11 Warfleet Devon
20 C7 Wargrave Wokham
44 F2 Warham All Saints Norfk
44 F2 Warham St Mary Norfk
72 F5 Wark Nthumb
80 H6 Wark Nthumb
15 L7 Warkleigh Devon
32 C2 Warkton Nhants
31 L6 Warkworth Nhants
81 P11 Warkworth Nthumb
65 N8 Warlaby N York
4 E6 Warleggan Cnwll
58 D8 Warley Town Calder
21 M10 Warlingham Surrey
59 J9 Warmfield Wakefd
49 N4 Warmingham Ches E
42 F11 Warmington Nhants
31 K5 Warmington Warwks
18 C10 Warminster Wilts
17 P2 Warmley S Glos
51 M1 Warmsworth Donc
7 Q5 Warmwell Dorset
9 Q3 Warnford Hants
11 J4 Warnham W Susx
10 G8 Warningcamp W Susx
11 K5 Warninglid W Susx
50 B6 Warren Ches E
24 G8 Warren Pembks
78 F2 Warrenhill S Lans
20 D7 Warren Row W & M
22 H11 Warren Street Kent
32 C6 Warrington M Keyn
57 L10 Warrington Warrtn
86 F7 Warriston C Edin
86 F7 Warriston Crematorium C Edin
9 N6 Warsash Hants
50 E8 Warslow Staffs
60 E4 Warter E R Yk
65 L10 Warthermaske N York
59 P3 Warthill N York
12 D8 Wartling E Susx
41 P3 Wartnaby Leics
56 H3 Warton Lancs
63 J7 Warton Lancs
40 H6 Warton Warwks
30 H2 Warwick Warwks
71 P4 Warwick Bridge Cumb
30 H2 Warwick Castle Warwks
31 J3 Warwick Services Warwks
111 h1 Wasbister Ork
62 E1 Wasdale Head Cumb
3 M2 Washaway Cnwll
5 Q8 Washbourne Devon
35 J8 Washbrook Suffk
16 C11 Washfield Devon
16 E7 Washford Somset
15 N9 Washford Pyne Devon
52 E8 Washingborough Lincs
73 N9 Washington Sundld
10 H7 Washington W Susx
73 M9 Washington Services Gatesd
30 H3 Wasperton Warwks
66 D10 Wass N York
16 E7 Watchet Somset
19 J3 Watchfield Oxon
63 K3 Watchgate Cumb
5 P4 Water Devon
33 M4 Waterbeach Cambs
10 E8 Waterbeach W Susx
79 L12 Waterbeck D & G
60 D6 Water End E R Yk
50 E9 Waterfall Staffs
85 J11 Waterfoot E Rens
21 L1 Waterford Herts
86 F11 Waterheads Border
50 E10 Waterhouses Staffs
22 E11 Wateringbury Kent
97 J5 Waterloo Highld
85 N11 Waterloo N Lans
92 F8 Waterloo P & K
24 G7 Waterloo Pembks
56 G8 Waterloo Sefton
10 B7 Waterlooville Hants
71 P10 Watermillock Cumb
42 G10 Water Newton Cambs
40 F8 Water Orton Warwks
31 N11 Waterperry Oxon
16 E10 Waterrow Somset
10 G6 Watersfield W Susx
57 N4 Waterside Bl w D
76 G9 Waterside E Ayrs
76 H3 Waterside E Ayrs
85 L8 Waterside E Duns
104 A11 Waterstein Highld
31 N11 Waterstock Oxon
24 G7 Waterston Pembks
31 P7 Water Stratford Bucks
49 L10 Waters Upton Wrekin
20 H4 Watford Herts
31 N1 Watford Nhants
31 N1 Watford Gap Services Nhants
58 F1 Wath N York
65 N11 Wath N York
51 K1 Wath upon Dearne Rothm
43 P7 Watlington Norfk
20 B5 Watlington Oxon
110 F5 Watten Highld
34 G2 Wattisfield Suffk
34 G6 Wattisham Suffk
7 L4 Watton Dorset
60 H4 Watton E R Yk
44 F9 Watton Norfk
33 K11 Watton-at-Stone Herts
85 N8 Wattston N Lans
27 P9 Wattsville Caerph
95 K4 Waulkmill Abers
26 E9 Waunarlwydd Swans
37 K4 Waunfawr Cerdgn
54 G9 Waunfawr Gwynd
32 C8 Wavendon M Keyn
71 K6 Waverbridge Cumb
49 J3 Waverton Ches W
71 K6 Waverton Cumb
61 J6 Wawne E R Yk
45 P5 Waxham Norfk
7 K2 Wayford Somset
7 L4 Waytown Dorset
15 Q9 Way Village Devon
16 F7 Weacombe Somset
19 K1 Weald Oxon
21 J5 Wealdstone Gt Lon
58 H5 Weardley Leeds
17 K5 Weare Somset
14 H7 Weare Giffard Devon
72 F11 Wearhead Dur
17 K9 Wearne Somset
65 M2 Wear Valley Crematorium Dur
44 E6 Weasenham All Saints Norfk
44 E5 Weasenham St Peter Norfk
57 P8 Weaste Salfd
49 L1 Weaverham Ches W
67 L12 Weaverthorpe N York
30 D2 Webheath Worcs
102 H8 Wedderlairs Abers
41 J8 Weddington Warwks
18 F8 Wedhampton Wilts
17 L6 Wedmore Somset
40 C8 Wednesbury Sandw
40 C7 Wednesfield Wolves
32 B12 Weedon Bucks
31 N3 Weedon Nhants
31 N5 Weedon Lois Nhants
40 F6 Weeford Staffs
9 M2 Weeke Hants
32 C1 Weekley Nhants
14 E11 Week St Mary Cnwll
60 H6 Weel E R Yk
35 J11 Weeley Essex
35 J11 Weeley Crematorium Essex
35 J11 Weeley Heath Essex
92 C6 Weem P & K
30 D3 Weethley Warwks
44 C11 Weeting Norfk
61 N9 Weeton E R Yk
56 H2 Weeton Lancs
58 H5 Weeton N York
58 H6 Weetwood Leeds
57 Q4 Weir Lancs
5 J7 Weir Quay Devon
111 k4 Weisdale Shet
44 H7 Welborne Norfk
52 D11 Welbourn Lincs
60 C1 Welburn N York
65 P7 Welbury N York
42 D3 Welby Lincs
14 E8 Welcombe Devon
41 N10 Welford Nhants
19 L6 Welford W Berk
30 F4 Welford-on-Avon Warwks
41 Q8 Welham Leics
51 Q5 Welham Notts
21 K3 Welham Green Herts
10 C2 Well Hants
53 M8 Well Lincs
65 M10 Well N York
29 L2 Welland Worcs
93 N8 Wellbank Angus
30 H3 Wellesbourne Warwks
32 H10 Well Head Herts
21 P8 Welling Gt Lon
32 C3 Wellingborough Nhants
44 E6 Wellingham Norfk
52 E11 Wellingore Lincs
62 C2 Wellington Cumb
39 J11 Wellington Herefs
16 F11 Wellington Somset
49 M12 Wellington Wrekin
29 J1 Wellington Heath Herefs
17 Q5 Wellow BaNES
9 L9 Wellow IoW
51 P7 Wellow Notts
17 M7 Wells Somset
44 F2 Wells-next-the-sea Norfk
33 Q11 Wellstye Green Essex
92 E10 Welltree P & K
86 C5 Wellwood Fife
43 N10 Welney Norfk
48 H8 Welshampton Shrops
48 G8 Welsh Frankton Shrops
28 F5 Welsh Newton Herefs
38 E1 Welshpool Powys
16 D2 Welsh St Donats V Glam
71 M6 Welton Cumb
60 G8 Welton E R Yk
52 E7 Welton Lincs
31 N2 Welton Nhants
53 M9 Welton le Marsh Lincs
53 J6 Welton le Wold Lincs
61 N9 Welwick E R Yk
32 H12 Welwyn Herts
21 K2 Welwyn Garden City Herts
49 K9 Wem Shrops
16 H8 Wembdon Somset
21 J6 Wembley Gt Lon
5 L9 Wembury Devon
15 L9 Wembworthy Devon
84 D8 Wemyss Bay Inver
33 N9 Wendens Ambo Essex
31 M9 Wendlebury Oxon
44 F7 Wendling Norfk
20 D2 Wendover Bucks
2 G9 Wendron Cnwll
33 K7 Wendy Cambs
35 N2 Wenhaston Suffk
33 J2 Wennington Cambs
22 B7 Wennington Gt Lon
63 L8 Wennington Lancs
50 H8 Wensley Derbys
65 J9 Wensley N York
59 L10 Wentbridge Wakefd
38 H4 Wentnor Shrops
33 M2 Wentworth Cambs
51 J2 Wentworth Rothm
16 F2 Wenvoe V Glam
38 H10 Weobley Herefs
10 G8 Wepham W Susx
44 B9 Wereham Norfk
42 G9 Werrington C Pete
4 H3 Werrington Cnwll
48 H2 Wervin Ches W
56 H3 Wesham Lancs
9 N4 Wessex Vale Crematorium Hants
51 J8 Wessington Derbys
44 C7 West Acre Norfk
5 P10 West Alvington Devon
15 P6 West Anstey Devon
53 J8 West Ashby Lincs
10 D8 West Ashling W Susx
18 C9 West Ashton Wilts
65 L3 West Auckland Dur
67 L9 West Ayton N York
16 G9 West Bagborough Somset
57 K11 West Bank Halton
52 G7 West Barkwith Lincs
66 H5 West Barnby N York
87 M6 West Barns E Loth
44 E4 West Barsham Norfk
7 L5 West Bay Dorset
45 J3 West Beckham Norfk
20 H8 West Bedfont Surrey
23 M10 Westbere Kent
34 F10 West Bergholt Essex
19 P7 West Berkshire Crematorium W Berk
7 M5 West Bexington Dorset
44 B7 West Bilney Norfk
11 L8 West Blatchington Br & H
73 P8 West Boldon S Tyne
42 C2 Westborough Lincs
8 F8 Westbourne Bmouth
10 C8 Westbourne W Susx
58 F7 West Bowling C Brad
44 F8 West Bradenham Norfk
63 N12 West Bradford Lancs
17 M8 West Bradley Somset
58 H10 West Bretton Wakefd
51 N12 West Bridgford Notts
40 D8 West Bromwich Sandw
40 D8 West Bromwich Crematorium Sandw
23 Q8 Westbrook Kent
19 M6 Westbrook W Berk
15 L6 West Buckland Devon
16 G11 West Buckland Somset
64 H9 West Burton N York
31 N7 Westbury Bucks
38 G1 Westbury Shrops
18 C9 Westbury Wilts
18 C10 Westbury Leigh Wilts
29 J6 Westbury on Severn Gloucs
28 G12 Westbury-on-Trym Bristl
17 M6 Westbury-sub-Mendip Somset
52 B3 West Butterwick N Linc
56 H3 Westby Lancs
20 G10 West Byfleet Surrey
68 F11 West Cairngaan D & G
45 Q7 West Caister Norfk
86 B9 West Calder W Loth
17 N10 West Camel Somset
8 B10 West Chaldon Dorset
19 L3 West Challow Oxon
5 P10 West Charleton Devon
10 H6 West Chiltington W Susx
17 L12 West Chinnock Somset
20 G11 West Clandon Surrey
13 Q2 West Cliffe Kent
22 G6 Westcliff-on-Sea Sthend
17 M12 West Coker Somset
17 P8 Westcombe Somset
17 N7 West Compton Somset
7 N4 West Compton Abbas Dorset
30 G9 Westcote Gloucs
31 K8 Westcote Barton Oxon
31 Q10 Westcott Bucks
6 D2 Westcott Devon
11 J1 Westcott Surrey
59 P6 West Cottingwith N York
19 J8 Westcourt Wilts
59 P9 West Cowick E R Yk
26 E10 West Cross Swans
71 M6 West Curthwaite Cumb
11 Q9 Westdean E Susx
10 D7 West Dean W Susx
9 J3 West Dean Wilts
42 G8 West Deeping Lincs
56 H9 West Derby Lpool
43 Q9 West Dereham Norfk
15 J4 West Down Devon
4 C4 Westdowns Cnwll
20 G7 West Drayton Gt Lon
51 P6 West Drayton Notts
110 E2 West Dunnet Highld
60 H8 West Ella E R Yk
32 E6 West End Bed
9 M5 West End Hants
17 L3 West End N Som
45 Q7 West End Norfk
20 F10 West End Surrey
8 E3 West End Wilts
19 Q8 West End Green Hants
110 D5 Westerdale Highld
66 F6 Westerdale N York
35 K7 Westerfield Suffk
10 F8 Westergate W Susx
21 N11 Westerham Kent
73 L7 Westerhope N u Ty
6 B9 Westerland Devon
29 J11 Westerleigh S Glos
29 J12 Westerleigh Crematorium S Glos
86 B7 Wester Ochiltree W Loth
87 K2 Wester Pitkierie Fife
105 P6 Wester Ross Highld
93 R5 Westerton of Rossie Angus
111 j4 Westerwick Shet
22 E11 West Farleigh Kent
31 M4 West Farndon Nhants
48 G9 West Felton Shrops
17 P5 Westfield BaNES
70 G9 Westfield Cumb
12 F7 Westfield E Susx
110 C3 Westfield Highld
85 M8 Westfield N Lans
44 G8 Westfield Norfk
85 Q8 Westfield W Loth
92 H6 Westfields of Rattray P & K
72 G12 Westgate Dur
60 D11 Westgate N Linc
23 P8 Westgate on Sea Kent
19 J8 West Grafton Wilts
20 C11 West Green Hants
8 H3 West Grimstead Wilts
11 J5 West Grinstead W Susx
59 M8 West Haddlesey N York
41 N12 West Haddon Nhants
19 N3 West Hagbourne Oxon
40 B10 West Hagley Worcs
35 N1 Westhall Suffk
51 K11 West Hallam Derbys
60 F9 West Halton N Linc
7 P7 Westham Dorset
12 D8 Westham E Susx
21 N6 West Ham Gt Lon
17 K6 Westham Somset
10 E8 Westhampnett W Susx
51 K5 West Handley Derbys
19 L3 West Hanney Oxon
22 E4 West Hanningfield Essex
8 G2 West Harnham Wilts
17 M5 West Harptree BaNES
10 C6 West Harting W Susx
16 H11 West Hatch Somset
8 D2 West Hatch Wilts
93 P8 West Haven Angus
17 L7 Westhay Somset
40 D11 West Heath Birm
110 B11 West Helmsdale Highld
19 M3 West Hendred Oxon
20 H3 West Hertfordshire Crematorium Herts
67 K11 West Heslerton N York
17 K4 West Hewish N Som
39 L12 Westhide Herefs
95 N1 Westhill Abers
6 E4 West Hill Devon
11 M4 West Hoathly W Susx
8 C9 West Holme Dorset
39 J11 Westhope Herefs
39 J5 Westhope Shrops
22 D6 West Horndon Essex
42 H4 Westhorpe Lincs
34 H3 Westhorpe Suffk
17 N6 West Horrington Somset
20 H11 West Horsley Surrey
13 N3 West Hougham Kent
57 M7 Westhoughton Bolton
63 M7 Westhouse N York
51 K8 Westhouses Derbys
8 F8 West Howe Bmouth
21 J11 Westhumble Surrey
92 G10 West Huntingtower P & K
17 J7 West Huntspill Somset